THE EDUCATION OF LEV NAVROZOV

Harper's
MAGAZINE PRESS

Lev Navrozov

THE
EDUCATION OF
LEV NAVROZOV

A Life in the Closed World Once Called Russia

HARPER'S MAGAZINE PRESS
Published in association with Harper & Row
New York

"Harper's" is the registered trademark of Harper & Row, Publishers, Inc.

THE EDUCATION OF LEV NAVROZOV. Copyright © 1975 by Lev Navrozov. All rights reserved. Printed in the United States of America. No part of this book may be used or reproduced in any manner whatsoever without written permission except in the case of brief quotations embodied in critical articles and reviews. For information address Harper & Row, Publishers, Inc., 10 East 53rd Street, New York, N.Y. 10022. Published simultaneously in Canada by Fitzhenry & Whiteside Limited, Toronto.

FIRST EDITION

Designed by C. Linda Dingler

Library of Congress Cataloging in Publication Data
Navrozov, Lev
  The education of Lev Navrozov.
  Bibliography: p.
  Includes index.
  1. Navrozov, Lev. I. Title.
H59.N38A33 1975   300'.92'4 [B]   73–6314
ISBN 0–06–126415–6

75 76 77 78 79 10 9 8 7 6 5 4 3 2 1

Contents

Acknowledgments

When I arrived with my manuscripts in the United States, these editors and authors read the present first book of my cycle and gave me generous encouragement: Larry Freundlich, Nelson Aldrich, Robert Massie, and Suzanne Massie. These Americans (and in particular my editor, Larry Freundlich, who boldly undertook literary and financial responsibility for an author unknown outside his Russian underground milieu) personify for me the generous goodwill of the United States, and it is to many Americans I have met on my arrival and to these hospitable shores that my acknowledgments are also due.

The individuals and institutions of Israel and the United States who had helped us to get out of the territory once called Russia and settle in the United States are too numerous to list, but one family I must mention: Daniel Rose, whom we had the good luck to meet when he was in Moscow as an American tourist, his wife Joanna, and her parents, Philip and Lillian Semel.

My son Andrey, Jadviga Urbanowicz and Sara J. Black helped me to retrace the sources in the West. And I owe a great debt to my wife and my mother who have borne with me, one of those men who are immersed all their life in their egomaniac "search of the absolute" at the expense of their devoted family. Nor did the eternal need to conceal my manuscripts, to retype them clandestinely, and burn the draft copies make this "search of the absolute" any easier for my wife.

The Rocking Nest

1

"The West, the West," my guest chimes, looking indolently on. "I *was* in the West."

He likes our country house, and he is sitting leisurely, arm winglike over chair back, *shedding words.*

> Oh, let us shed words
> As our garden sheds its amber.

"I was in the West. I talked with Ezra Pound just as I am talking with you—I dined with Sartre. Nothing special. You exaggerate, really."

What he also likes is our almost extraterritorial seclusion. There, outside, beyond that fence that runs all around our estate, he is a *writer*, which is not what was once meant by the word here or is meant now in the West. It means that he is an official, or better say a *ranker*, attached to the department of *literature* in a definite rank: he is a *member of the board of the union of writers*. Everyone is attached to some department, because if he is not, he is a *parasite*, that is, a criminal, to be exiled to some remote area to work there as a serf peasant. I am not attached to any department, a circumstance I recall sometimes with the numbness of a criminal too long and too safely immersed in his crime, and sometimes with my father's Russian slothful despair which has been provoking my mother's high-pitched lament, addressed once to my father and now to myself: "But why didn't

you do it long ago? You are a psychopath, a real psychopath."
As a *translator of literature* (how metallic is the name of my *profession*) I could have become a *member of the union of writers* many years ago. But I did not. Horribly enough, I have not become even a *trade union member* at any departments for which I free-lance. Am I a *parasite?* Not far from my country house is the country house (with less acreage) of a *member of the politburo* or a *candidate member of the politburo* (I have never been interested which exactly). Surely *parasites* live in huts, not in country houses with more acreage than that of *members* (or even *candidate members*) of the *politburo?*

I am a psychopath, a real psychopath, or at any rate a statistical exception—a Poisson's rare event, eluding the departmental mesh. No department can understand that I *could* become a member of some department (with all the advantages accruing) but would not. Each department assumes that I belong to another department, perhaps so very high that no one knows my rank.

I am the only strictly private person in the country, as my guest calls me, living on a kind of extraterritorial estate, and he likes to come and forget his rank for a while and simply be a temporary dweller of this island outside of time and space.

"And what is there?" he once asked, pointing at something looming between the trees beyond the invisible fence.

"Oh, there?" I peered. "Serfdom."

Foreign correspondents stayed the night at my country house after a New Year's party, and nothing happened. My son never joined any *children's organization,* nor did he ever go to school.

"See?" my guest exults. "You are freer than you would have been in America."

"Yes. Except that I can't spare, say, one hundred billion dollars a year to defend my freedom. I merely exist in a crevice between departments. This, by the way, is why I get all the books from abroad and you don't. The department of literature that watches over you will not watch over me, because I am not its responsibility."

Our timeless serenity is actually only a few miles from an airport where foreign statesmen land, some score miles from Moscow. But as one rides from the airport, it is all forests, and we are lost in them. We are pleasantly invisible.

I like him for his genuine—that is, self-analytic—sincerity. It is so rare. He brings his newly published book. He knows I will not say a word about it, and he is grateful, but he can't resist opening and admiring the page bearing his picture. Holding the open book in his outstretched hand, raised so that he has to look up to gaze at the portrait of an elderly man, obviously having a bad liver, he finally recites in a languishing whisper the famous line a Russian poetess once addressed to her aristocratic seducer: "How handsome you are, O devil."

Then he asks me apprehensively if I expect anyone today.

"People are monsters," he explains. "*Mon-sters.*" As a shy afterthought he adds: "I am a monster, too, of course, but at least I can abide myself."

Today he is out of luck. Very carefully I break the news. Yes, it will be *that* man's wife. But she will only drop in on her way somewhere—much too important to stay long.

My guest's rank in *literature* is not the highest, and he shuns people either below his rank (because they may try to humiliate him if only to take revenge for their lowliness) or of the same rank (because they may be even more insolent, entitled as they are to regard themselves as his equal). But *that* man is younger than he—once his rank in *literature* was properly lower, and now it is higher!

"I know that the man is a kind of tumor inside my brain," he says in one of those flashes of lucidity for which I like him so much. "I am like a clerk in the department of railroads who can talk only about another clerk promoted ahead of him. 'Injustice,' he cries out like Prometheus to the blind heavens. But he forgets that neither his listeners nor the blind heavens may belong to the department of railroads, and the immensity of injustice is lost upon them."

Unlike Prometheus in Aeschylus, my guest can enact his fate only in mute oppressive gloom throughout *that* man's wife's visit.

"I know this is stupid," he says. "I picture myself very elegant and ironic. With a carnation in my lapel. Saying something really devastating about her husband, but in such a subtle, witty way that everyone is charmed. But it doesn't work."

Her husband. Well, on the one hand, he is a famous writer. Almost like Gogol, Chekhov, or Steinbeck. On the other hand, he is a serf of a high rank, much higher, indeed, than my guest's, and as such he is allowed to go abroad quite often, while my guest went out once or twice in his life: this is what he means when he says that he *was* in the West.

In the early eighteenth century in Russia, under the tsar or rather serf owner Peter I, there were as yet no noblemen in the later-day sense. Noblemen too were serfs, only they were ranked. These ranked serfs were attached to various departments. Literally, the words *serfdom* and *serf* in the Russian language mean the *right of attachment* and the *attached*.

Her husband is attached to the department of literature.

Private, that is, small-scale serf owners in Russia before 1861 owned serf musicians, serf engineers, or serf actors who did not differ outwardly from musicians, engineers, or actors in the West. Some serf owners even had serf astronomers, serf composers and serf theologians. But serf writers—what are they for?

The answer involves a certain linguistic difficulty. Even the English language (not to mention Russian) carries residual servile psychology. Is this surprising? Here is one of the numberless plaints that what the government had done was to transform "every man not merely into an inquisitor, but into a judge, a spy, an informer—to set father against father, brother against brother." Russia after 1917? No, England shortly before, historically: the fathers of those Englishmen who lived in 1917 could well remember the time.

"You Russians have never known freedom," a Britisher who had been in Britain a spy for the owners of Russia explained to me with Byronesque languor. Like a tone-deaf music-hating German explaining that only Germans can really create and understand music, for did not music flourish in Germany as nowhere else?

Actually, all mankind lived in the underworld of history for millennia, and even the English-speaking countries have emerged from the dark millennia of unfreedom "right now" by the scale of history (and have survived so far owing perhaps just to the British Channel and the Atlantic Ocean). It is not, therefore, surprising at all that servile psychology is still built even into the English language. Those who seize only a bank transport are in this language called private persons and hence bandits (especially if they come from the poor, did not go to college, and want money just to live better). But those who seize one-sixth of the inhabited globe with everything and everyone therein are called a *state*. Similarly, small serf owners are called private persons and hence serf owners, while *very* big serf owners can only be called a *state,* and their serfs *subjects* (or *citizens*).

About twenty-four centuries ago an Athenian said:

If you are caught committing any of these crimes on a small scale, you are punished and disgraced; they call it sacrilege, kidnapping, burglary, theft and brigandage. But if, besides taking their property, you turn all your countrymen into slaves, you will hear no more of those ugly names; your countrymen themselves will call you the happiest of men and bless your name . . .

He might have added: "and for the next twenty-four centuries even the languages of the freest countries will be so constructed as to call sufficiently big serf owners a *state,* and their serfs *citizens.*"

In the big serf ownership that post-1917 Russia is, the *state* does not exist even in the sense of Hobbes (characteristically, the Russian word translated into English as "state" actually means "lordship," "masterdom," and the word translated as "power" derives from the verb "to possess," "to own"). In the autocratic State of Hobbes the subject had

the liberty to buy, and sell, and otherwise contact with one another; to choose their own abode, their own diet, their own trade of life, and institute their children as they themselves think fit; and the like.

None of these seven liberties of Hobbesian Absolutism, nor "the like," exist today in the serf ownership once called Russia.

There is an obvious benefit for a serf ownership to play on the residual servile psychology and ignorance of the populace of democracies and simulate a *state* (or even the *world's only genuine democracy*). In this way the serf owners are "recognized" by democracies still playing an important role in the world, and their serf ownership is thus "legalized" as a *state*. But, of course, only big serf ownerships can afford this *state* simulation, and the bigger they are the bigger and better *state* simulation they can afford, and the more serfs they can attach to activities like literature (what *state* can there be without literature?) and not only to theater or music, as small, *private* serf owners did in Russia before 1861.

What should this *literature* be like? On the one hand, it would be the best if it consisted of one sentence: "Be infinitely devoted to your beloved owners," repeated as many times as is necessary to fill in each book of a required thickness. All the serfs in the serf ownership would read the sentence over and over again and would be infinitely devoted to their beloved owners.

But then those nosy intellectuals in the West would say: What sort of literature is that? The outside world remembers the Russia of the first half of the nineteenth century essentially owing to one man: Gogol. From the point of view of foreign prestige the department of literature should produce literature, not *literature*. But the trouble is that Gogol was not a serf: he was not attached. He did not write over and over again: "Be infinitely devoted to your beloved owners." In fact at school we were told: "Gogol exposed mercilessly the entire regime of Nicholas I." Having done which, he would go back and forth between Italy and Russia, never molested or impeded.

The department of literature does not prescribe any uniform. A *writer* is to be dressed like Gogol or Chekhov or Steinbeck. This *is* his uniform. He should look like a writer. Many serfs look in fact as though they were in old Russia or in the West, in freedom. Partly the *writer*'s rank is explicit (*member of the secretariat of the union of writers*), but partly it is implicit yet decisive, just as it would have been at the eighteenth-century Russian court.

That man. That writer-*writer*. Her husband. Why can he be a *writer* and I cannot? I would become sick if I were to put on *real* tweeds and loll in a chair somewhere in Paris or New York. Like those two serf boys of the pre-1861 times playing at gentlemen in the drawing room when their owners were visiting somewhere. Smoking *real* cigars, too. The boys so believed they were gentlemen that when their owners came they attacked them as intruders in the agony of disillusionment, and one boy cut his throat with a razor.

He is better than I am. He is kind, tactful, generous, a better man really, and once he helped me without any prospect that I would ever be important enough to reciprocate. Whenever he meets me he quotes something from a short manuscript I gave him to read several years ago, and he says what only very considerate successful men say to failures.

How can he enjoy being a serf *writer*?

It is, perhaps, simply that he comes from a poor family, yes, perhaps of a long line of pre-1861 serfs. I am more finicky—more squeamish. I cannot eat if someone has spat into my plate. Is this connected with my getting carsick so easily? I cannot go to Paris or New York and play at being a writer. In him, the generations of hungry, miserable, humiliated people clamor for what a high serf rank may give him—they devour it all wolfishly even if serfdom has spat into his plate.

I first met him several years ago when the times were the most lenient in the last thirty or forty years, and he was very much like any writer who had succeeded in any other country. In old Russia. In the West.

He was a success. Almost as in any other country. And I was a failure. Almost as in any other country. Of course, I could blame the society, but what failure doesn't? At that time I still lived in what would have struck him now as monstrous super-slums compared with his new apartment with its vestibule of marble. I did not want to work for money more than two or three days a month, and under my suitcoat I wore my late uncle's lilac shirt which he had bought in England in the twenties. The shirt had a huge stain, like a strange, dark, vast continent on a map, so good for navigation, with many coves. The continent was also lilac, only a darker hue, but a *commission store* would not accept the shirt for resale (though the stain was invisible under a suit, especially with a tie), and so I got it as a gift, but I had lost one of my copper cuff links and discreetly kept the parting cuff together. He was a success, almost as in any other country, and success is success. He traveled abroad and had all the latest books and magazines and records, and he said: "Salazar in his diary. . . ," and Salazar's diary was just out.

In a closed serf territory, even those who once belonged to the country's creative genius finally begin to write and say something musty—something smelling of old bookcases. That terrible, all-pervading musty smell. And here he said: "Salazar in his diary . . . ," and Salazar's diary was just out.

I met him and his wife perhaps exactly as a failure meets a success anywhere. He had wanted to or agreed to meet me, and that was important if I wanted to publish, and I did want. It was the best time in the last and perhaps the next thirty or forty years, but a failure forgets what he wants when he meets a success.

I do not know what started me off. Perhaps it was his words: "Salazar in his diary. . . ."

Or perhaps it was his wife's stockings. As I kissed her hand (I behaved like a derelict Russian gentleman), I looked at them, as from a bridge at a cityscape below, the stockings (God knows from what exclusive shop in what Western capital) were finely webbed in black like a cityscape of a French artist whose name I forgot.

I was not a nobody, a funny beggar, just a maniac most likely, holding together the cuff of his late uncle's shirt. I was free, young, happy. I forgot about the cuff, and when I noticed it, I would not understand how I could be so conscious about the missing cuff link, and I almost flaunted the parting cuff. It even gave a new turn to my euphoria: it was a note in a keyed time, both spontaneous and contrived, for everything was unexpected and everything known in advance.

He listened, and said with genuine regret: "How you are wasting yourself. God, how you are wasting yourself."

In hindsight I knew that this had been a good pretext for me to say something like: "But who will publish me?" with a broad hint that I knew he had pull, and that if he helped me . . . But instead I did what a failure usually does. I said: "Wasting?"

The word was simply another note in the euphoria. "Wasting? Do you mean that what I am saying to you two is wasted? And if it is *published*—duplicated on an industrial scale for millions of strangers to buy—it will not be wasted?"

As a failure often does, I was making up prodigiously for years of humiliation—I was drinking in my transient glory, I wanted nothing else. I was waving my parting cuff, it was now my first violin, I was speaking with eternity.

To say something like: "But who will publish me?" was inconceivable.

2

"What do you want to go away to the West for?" his wife asks me, childlike—as though it is only a matter of my wishes. She has caught the drift of our conversation or rather my wife told her.

I would answer if she listened. But she won't. Either because I am not important enough or she doesn't understand and gets bored. I would tell her that the *collective* which I had avoided so far will catch up with me at death. Her husband belongs to a very high rank, but for the rest of us there are two kinds of perfectly identical pinewood coffins. The screaming red kind and the imitation oak kind. They are identical everywhere and are sold in identical shops. I would not tell her this because I would sound like a peevish miserable old man, complaining of scarcities and shortages to a high society lady.

In the cities which foreigners are permitted to visit, identical (white) flowers can also be bought for the occasions of birth, marriage, or death in identical shops with identical signs FLOWERS (green background, white letters). They smell of collective oblivion, of paraffin—or just of the hothouse where they are mass-produced?

Yesterday, yes, it was just yesterday that the little girl, I mean our neighbors' friend's daughter, rang us up in the evening, and we had decided we did not care to see these people. She (I mean the little girl's mother) seems to be coated all over, as with paraffin injected into anatomical exhibits to make them more lifelike, the paraffin wax melts in her features, one recalls hemp for some reason (her hair?), and she wiggles (our ladies say with indignation), but who will care to look if she does? But the other one, her friend, is all in black, large, heavily Russian, yet anyway they all get drunk every day, swap men, we cannot receive them, and our ladies say they are not stage directors at all, but the wiggler is a theater tailor or something and the Russian heavy is dress model. Recently the wiggler and the model rushed off to baptize the model's child in the local church. We saw that church, too. It was a luminously sunless day. There was no one outside the church, and a neat coffin lid, the bright red, not the imitation oak kind—an unbearably clear vision—leaned neatly against the whitish wall. The dapper red coffin lid seemed to have come on its own—to live its own natty life in a well-lit empty universe. And this was the church they took their child to, but the church was closed—they missed the baptism as one misses scarce goods rarely on sale, and went back—to get drunk most likely. But certainly we could not receive them, and the little girl's call was a cheap trick, of course, but I said they could come.

There had been a crowding of events all day, no events really, but everything seemed an event, and now it was the worst crowding of events, because as I spoke in the thickening dusk of the hall I was sorry for them, I was all adrift—I was in the mood to lavish tearfully whatever I am or whatever I have on anyone, and my wife also has fits of generosity—she would suddenly buy someone a present so expensive that it would frighten the beneficiary, yet her fits of generosity seem to me sudden, strange, nor do they always coincide with mine, and I prayed those people would not come, and I prayed that should they come my wife would also be in her sudden, strange fit of generosity, but I could not explain anything in that mood.

Then she said the wind was so strong that it would overturn the mattress. Or perhaps she was afraid it might rain. A mattress was being aired standing upright on our second-floor terrace, and another one down in the garden.

But that mattress on the second-floor terrace was already an event too.

I know this does not mean much. In fact, it does not mean much even to me. I cannot recapture the state, because it was yesterday. We die at night, to be reincarnated, and only a registrar's or antiquarian's knowledge of yesterday remains.

Of course, there was that electric light on the terrace, still anemic, yet making the outside black, and everyone knows this is disturbing (with a wind, and restless birch trees). But there was something else besides.

Everything was an event, and events fleeted. It was not so disturbing as—fleeting. I rushed on to save the mattress from whatever endangered it, scraped my finger, but it turned out it was not that mattress, it was the other one down below.

But I first put iodine on the abraded skin. I took my time dabbing at it, and blowing too, relishing the sensation because it was so real.

"What do you want to go away to the West for?"

She will not listen to more than ten words on end. Her husband has a *very* high rank in *literature*. She believes that his rank and his talent correlate. She thinks that many others are, indeed, yokels who have been promoted so high in *literature* because they serve *them,* while her husband has been promoted for his talent only. When he is demoted a little, that proves to her that he would not sacrifice his talent for *their* favors, and when he is promoted still higher, that shows her that even *they* have to reckon with his talent.

Still, imperceptible as his demotions are to an untrained eye (no invitation to the Kremlin New Year's party), they depress her terribly, perhaps because as a Russian woman, wise rather than intelligent, she senses how easily they may suddenly roll all the way down. Talent or no talent.

She was drinking much on one such occasion, and when somebody cautioned: "You are getting drunk," she said to me: "It's good, I'll get drunk and untie on you."

To untie on someone means to transcend, to forget the self, dissolve in another and hence in bliss. Perhaps she meant in heaven where there are no ranks.

Then she began to brood. "Tell me, why don't they put us all into *one* prison camp?"

This seemed to her unbearable. "I know they will divide us," she said, now weeping in all earnest. "We'll all be in different camps. But what harm would it do them if we were all together?"

She is generous, kind, impulsive, thoughtless, we all love her. Except for my guest, of course. Her face was bloated, like a huge child's, only all going to pieces, and we began soothing her by reminding her that she wanted to leave everything and go to a small town to work as a nurse. She had even had a nurse's dress and cap designed for her, which is quite important, for once she wrote from London: "I haven't found a single decent rag to buy here."

But her husband has since been promoted again, the windows are a liturgy of sunshine, and it is in this mood that she asks me why I want to go to the West. I know I cannot count on her attention for more than ten words, and I answer her quickly:

"I want to be buried in a metal casket."

The answer is a huge success: she laughs briefly.

"In Mexico," she launches in a strong flowing contralto on a *really* interesting story, "they didn't book a hotel for us."

"Why?" asks my wife in a voice which is both piping, almost reedy, and low-keyed like Indian singing in two registers.

"The devil knows. There was some mix-up. And we took a room in a hotel opposite the undertaker's. And they carried metal caskets all the time."

She is laughing loudly the Russian merchant way, with some struggle for breath, trying to bunch up her lips, her face all in a mess with laughter.

"We were so sick of them."

3

But yesterday. Ah, yes, iodine. Dabbing my finger because the sensation was so real—it returned me to reality from that fleeting, that crowding of events.

Then I rushed downstairs and outside for the sake of rushing about and being concerned with something real like the saving of a mattress.

The outside which had looked so black was really a rustling loneliness, somehow soothing. After such a wind my son would find wind-fallen nests in the morning.

I was now so calm or so transparently lonely that I could meditate like that, something you were supposed to do on your estate in those old times—to pace an alley and meditate.

What year is it now? Well, if asked like that, I will not think: 1956, because I know this is not true, but I will think that the year is 1956 and some time more. But certainly not, say, *nineteen sixty-eight*—no, by no means, this is quite unbelievable. Strange, dark, frightening numbers: *sixty-eight.*

Czechoslovakia, twelve years after *Hungary.* The time in Russia is clocked by her western periphery. Much more now than in the last century when it was said: "Two years after the first Polish uprising."

In 1956. *Hungary.* The *fascist putsch*, they called it. The huge blue mailbox outside the central post office, not far from our house, the safest mailbox because the number of letters dropped there is the largest, and hence the chance that the mailbox will give them some clue is the lowest. It is so silly: one of the thousands of clerks of their *secretariat* will just pass my letter to the *relevant section* of the *relevant division* of the *relevant department* of the *organs of state security*. A letter nowhere. Its only use will be to track me down.

Did I already secretly believe that the possession-power had become more lenient? Or was it merely the eternal thoughtlessness, ever forgetful and hoping, the youthful joy of life, still intoxicating my brain and making it oblivious to self-destruction? Or perhaps I am what is called the suicidal type—like Aunt Olya?

To perish now owing to this letter? All life to cherish the flicker in the deepest soul-catacomb loneliness, and then suddenly let them triumph because of some trifle, coincidence, slip, and perish like all the others before me. True, I bought the paper, ink, and pen each at a different store. I also used a pair of gloves. But who knows? A deceptive feeling of self-survival —a feeling intrinsic to life—suggests to every criminal that all precautions have been taken.

Anyway, here I am in my memory, a tiny figure hurrying along with the face of my *passport* photograph at that time, a perfectly normal, reliable face—on the *nationality* line my *passport* says in a calligraphic hand: *Russian*. Which means my father's ancestors were perhaps Tartar or even Chinese (there were quite a few Chinese in Moscow before the thirties) and adopted Christianity long ago enough for anyone to know his ancestry. You may put my passport face on the poster: these *en face* photographs do not even show that my nose is Jewish like my mother's, or rather the Jewish nose is probably Hittite, but such ethnic subtleties are too fine for them. My passport photograph face is the kind of face many Western intellectuals have been admiring as an expression of the health, purposeful vigor, and confidence of the new man, as opposed to Western morbid alienation, decadence, and everything else.

In hindsight I think that dangerous as that letter was or seemed to me, it saved me perhaps.

I dropped it into the mailbox, but my thoughts were running on, I came home, wrote more, and kept on studying and writing every day, often twelve hours a day. In the sixties it might have seemed that one could and should have voiced his dissidence publicly. Those who would have done so are now perishing. I would not be provoked, because all my spiritual power went into my new pastime or insanity. In case of a search they would have taken my writings away, and everyone would naturally have assumed that I had got away scot-free. His manuscripts were taken away in a search! And he is displeased, too. People die in prison because few can really survive it, and he is worried about some manuscripts of his.

I was like a woman with child, guarding a life the infinite value of which no one would perhaps ever appreciate but myself. To others these were mere manuscripts, quite possibly a maniac's scribblings. I would not argue. No mother would, to explain how infinitely valuable her child is. I just guarded, with obtuse, silent, and cunning stubbornness.

A pursuit like mine became possible only after 1953 as it gradually transpired that one could study and write in the privacy of one's home and be safe as long as one did not try to voice any dissidence publicly. Before 1953 it had been impossible—not because one did not want to take the risk, but because sustained intellectual activity is incompatible with constant danger. One can conspire, kill, explode, knowing that he must kill himself rather than let himself be caught alive. But one cannot engage in sustained intellectual activity, knowing every second that he may be caught the next or will have to kill himself.

I wonder: what if I had not been able to study and write in the privacy of my home because the pre-1953 plague would have continued? Into whom would I have been transformed? Into what would I have put the life of those years? What would have been vital enough in my compressed life to die for?

The pre-1917 generation surviving into the thirties was as defenseless as an old strain of microbes against a new antibiotic. But the new strain born after 1917 developed immunity, a defense mechanism, including—well, call it paranoia—except that it is more necessary for survival in such an environment than the blinking of the human eye. The life-and-death struggle of ever more paranoiac paranoias. Great Stalin's paranoia trying to penetrate through an ever more paranoiac immunity of lethal human life around him. He defended himself by all means he knew against lethal human life, which defended itself against him by all means *it* knows, and it knows a lot.

But suddenly, in 1953, great Stalin was said to have died, or at least he seemed to have vanished no one knows exactly when and how, and in several years it became clear that one could safely write in the privacy of one's room. Into this, my life went.

In that study of mine I wanted some base year in the twentieth century to refer all data to, and I chose 1956, and I know that the year now is not 1956, but it seems to me that it is *almost* 1956, and it will stay that way always.

4

After the successful writer-*writer*'s wife's brief visit my guest tries to regain the word-shedding mood.

> Oh, let us shed words
> As our garden sheds its amber.

"People are always discontent. Straining elsewhere. Waiting. There and then they will begin to live in good earnest. What a time that was in Russia to live in—well, in, say, 1912."

We invoke the names: Stravinsky, Blok, Shalyapin, Rachmaninoff, Stanislavsky, Kandinsky, Pasternak.

"My God!" he moans. "Freedom. *Pravda* appeared legally from 1912. *Pravda*! A newspaper published by a group calling openly for the overthrow of the regime could be bought on a newsstand for two kopecks. No, they would not *live*. 'We are born of Russia's age of horror.' Age of horror. Well, instead they got the age of joy. With Lubyankas all over the country to cheer them up. There is nothing like an efficient network of torture chambers for good cheer."

I want to explain to him that the free expression of discontent had nothing to do with the collapse of the regime, but he will not listen. So I falter and stop.

"Never mind," he says. "Let us live. Everyone is unhappy. Before 1953 everyone was happy. Then it became safe to be unhappy, and everyone became unhappy. I *am* happy. I now have all the freedoms I need: the freedom of thought and the freedom of ecstasy. As long as I think and feel without succumbing to the vanity of publishing it I am safe. Or at least I have been, here in Moscow, anno domini—"

"These are not quite freedoms. Rather leniencies. But I agree. The ecstasy of writing without the need of jumping up at every rustle. What a divine freedom. A stack of paper. . . ."

Indeed, paper has always been on sale—before as well as after 1953. Typographic print or multiplying equipment are guarded like top secret weapons. But paper has always been on sale! Yet those in possession-power could make criminal the very act of writing privately. All paper could be issued, just as money, blanks, or documents, to *schools,* the *union of writers, research institutions*, and other such *state* users, which would be obliged to return the written paper for censorship and storage in supervised files.

Yet here you are: go and buy paper, and in the cities which foreigners visit even shortages of paper are quite rare. True, typing is vaguely dangerous. *They* have a typeface print of every office typewriter in the country, so that no one could steal in (at night, for example) and use it in the hope of not being tracked down to a private typewriter. But why should one type anything? Vanity again? Just use a pen, better an old pen and inkpot, some silver antique, and pen it, write it (aren't you a writer?), splattering ink from time to time in fanciful blots or nervous sparks over the soft, silent, cosy paper between the scrawls you can pattern over the white rectangle at your pleasure.

"What a divine freedom!" I repeat. "To be able to write quietly at home on your own, privately bought paper. No fear of search and death provided you are content just to write—well, for yourself or for posterity. A stack of paper. . . ."

"I *am* happy."

"Also, we have had thus far the freedom of conversation in the privacy of our homes," I go on cataloging the leniencies.

"Well," he says vaguely, to imply that in the privacy of *my* home there is no such leniency because for all my unattached state, my home is certainly bugged, in his opinion, since I receive foreigners. "We should really go out. For a walk. Man must live for his complexion."

Perhaps these leniencies we have been enjoying in Moscow are something like the *live fish store* in Moscow in 1935: outside there was famine, but a Muscovite could buy *live* fish of many varieties (brought from Astrakhan in special cars), to the delight or amazement of foreigners. Even in Leningrad (as St. Petersburg was renamed in 1924: imagine New York some day renamed Bonosky-City—or perhaps New Leningrad?), which is also a foreign-visiting city, but of the second-best rank, a young man who wrote with his finger on a freshly fallen snow in 1968: "Get out of Czechoslovakia" was *sentenced* to five years, and that was perhaps the end of him. In Moscow that would have been impossible in 1968. After all, there was no proof of his crime, since the snow had melted, and no proper obliquely lighted photograph had been taken. The foreign correspondents in Moscow would have got wind of the *trial* and written humorous stories in their newspapers about freshly fallen snow as new mass media. So there is a big stepdown even from Moscow to that Lenin-City, formerly St. Petersburg. And what is happening in the country at large where no foreigners have been allowed to tread?

The privileged leniency, politeness, refinement Moscow has been enjoying may change overnight, and vigilance may always take a new form. Did not the population rejoice in 1933 that the *right to arrest* had been removed from ordinary *members of the party* who had been armed for the purpose ever since 1918?

In 1933 an inhabitant who did not know the past could believe that the possession-power which owned him was good *inside, in its heart of hearts, in its essence*. He could believe that there was a certain limit to evil in man. Or at least in twentieth-century man. Or at least in the people who owned *him*. The "secret letter" of 1956, "read to all working people," gave a glimpse into the *inside*—into the infernal unknown. "Oh, so that's what you really are. There is no limit to evil in man. The hell on earth did exist. And how can I know it does not exist right now? Has not emerged just this morning? Is not hidden still deeper inside, even more secretly than before 1953?" Now the fear of hell on earth is not weaker: in a sense it is stronger than before 1956. The *secret letters* were not only revelations made in the struggle for succession: they were also messages of infernal terror, if totally unintended.

"They have bought Japanese electronic equipment—you know, of course," my guest says.

That Japanese equipment has recently been a frequent topic, with elaborate descriptions of devices that allegedly monitor a conversation in a room from outside by recording a beam reflected off the vibrating window glass. That is, if the room has not yet been bugged from the inside.

"All right," I say. "But listening to our tapes they must be moved, really, if they have any intelligence at all." Involuntarily, I speak more loudly and distinctly, as though to make a good tape recording. "At least we will, whether under Nicholas the Third, Shih Huang Ti, or Sashka the Skew-Eyed, always think that in the sixties there existed in Moscow the freedom just to live, to think, to write in the privacy of one's home, while there was no such leniency before 1953."

This reassures and inspires him.

"O God," he says, his big hand thumping his chest, and I recall that his father was a fervent Orthodox Church believer in his youth, and the gesture was perhaps quite natural. The Russian "O God" has three syllables, the Slavic vocative case. He blows out the first syllable with such subtle naturalness that it seems he has been brought up in his father's faith since childhood, his big light eyes gazing heavenward or toward the imaginary microphone. "O God, thank Thee for having enlightened them so that they do not unleash the plague upon us and still let us live in the privacy of our homes. What am I compared with their omnipotence?"

He subdues his voice to a whisper—partly as a conversational tragic technique, partly to avoid at least some of the new Japanese equipment.

"They have squelched Czechoslovakia. As my boot might—a ladybug. Nothing new, of course. People simply have no memory. Georgia was reconquered in 1921 in exactly the same way. 'The working people of Georgia have applied for help.' See? In forty-seven years they had not even thought up a new cliché. Nothing new has happened since 1921. Everything was clear by 1921. And yet we thought: Czechoslovakia—the oldest university in

Central Europe, the democracies will at least forego their trade with the invaders as a sign of protest. Forego their trade! We forgot that your pet British signed a very cordial trade agreement with dear Soviet Russia in 1921! Right when the suppression of the Kronstadt uprising and the conquest of Georgia were both full on. Forego their trade! And what am I compared with that squelched ladybug of Czechoslovakia? A *microbe*."

"O God," he intones again. "They let me, a *microbe,* live free from the fear that I may perish just at the whim of some junior Lubyanka clerk. And the freedom from that fear means the freedom of ecstasy and thought. Have I deserved so much? Would *I* have been so lenient to *them*, had *they* been— No, not even crawling infinitesimally at my omnipotent shoes. But existing invisibly inside a test tube in my cold—scientific hand."

5

Throughout the sixties he has been worried that some of those who dared to express their dissidence openly after the mid-fifties will finally draw him into some act of displeasing those in possession-power: he will be asked to sign a plea for the release of someone imprisoned for open dissidence, and the signing will make him an open dissident himself, also to be finally imprisoned. If he had refused flatly to sign anything several years ago, he might have come to be regarded as a coward, lick-spittle, go-getter by a certain independent public opinion which began to emerge.

He tried to joke them off. "Look, right now I cannot challenge a nuclear power to an all-out fight because my liver is out of order." Another *mot* of his: "Nietzsche said, 'To be a hero one must have a heroic stomach.' Does anyone know of a stomach so heroic as to brave *our* prisons?" Or: "The regime at least still leaves me alone in my house. If you boys could defend me against the tyranny of my family." To me he complains: "These microbes believe that the microbiologist lets them be because they are too brave and noble and dedicated to be killed. They think they are fighting him by trying to displease him. Finally, it will end up as in the thirties."

"Well, what do you want? The possession-power cannot sign a contract with all its human property down to the last man: 'We grant you herewith the freedom to live in the privacy of your homes, at least in the cities visited by foreigners, and you undertake, for your part, never to spread publicly what you create or think, not to mention crimes like assembly or association. If any of you violate this contract we will, for our part, empower our secret network personnel to act entirely at its own discretion even in Moscow, just as they did between 1918 and 1953."

"No. No such *contrat social* is possible, I suppose."

"No. Before 1953 anyone suspected of less than infinite devotion would disappear. There was no martyrdom. He would vanish into the infernal unknown, and that's all. He might reappear. But as a different person inside apparently the same physical frame, perhaps, as a repenting ogre who has been poisoning children, preferably orphans, to spite the paradise on earth all around him. What sort of martyrdom can there be if there is no continuity of person before and after the disappearance? Now there is a chance of martyrdom. At least in the cities which foreigners can visit. If *sentenced* to several years of *imprisonment,* and not to *psychiatric treatment,* a martyr may at least hope that he will die his own self, a hopeless cripple suffering from some disgusting chronic disease, yet still perhaps his own self. See? Just as someone crucified in a Roman province two thousand years ago died his own self. As long as there is a chance for martyrdom there will be martyrs. But I am not sure there is that chance any longer even in the cities which foreigners visit."

"I only know that those fellows you meet will draw you in," he mutters gloomily.

"Crucified. The right to martyrdom. To a martyr the *investigator* has just said that they might *arrest* his daughter on suspicion as an accomplice and *imprison* her during the *investigation* by sheer mistake with thieves who will put her under a streetcar— that is, they will rape her to death. Suppose a foreign correspondent will know. So what? A sheer mistake. Mistakes happen even in the best of prisons. Crucified? It was nothing, a Roman colony, you know—a relatively high level of humanity. They hammer nails into your wrists, it is really nothing, comparatively."

"Insane, insane even to hear this." His face is terrible like a huge sick swollen liver. He has a son and a daughter. I am sorry I said what I said.

"The martyr was unprepared," I explain by way of apology. "He thought: martyrdom. I would be crucified. He could not understand that this is no Roman colony of two thousand years ago."

"You may yet get involved, too," he repeats. "Those fellows you meet . . ."

"No. I kept quiet before 1953, didn't I? If I had voiced my dissidence now, what would this mean? Simply that I didn't do it before 1953 because I knew the danger was too enormous—too inhuman to bear—and I did it now because I believed that the danger was not so great. I would have contributed to the inverse moral scale: the worse the regime, the fewer the protesters, and vice versa."

The idea appeals to him immensely, but I immediately disappoint him.

"Yet suppose no one would have been a martyr in the sixties when there was a chance for martyrdom, or at least martyrs thought there was? This is also terrible. All are serfs behaving as though infinitely devoted to their owners in order to preserve their lenience, quite accidental and temporary anyway."

"I only know that I must keep away from all this," he mutters, wondering perhaps whether he has been too careless of late.

"We are only microbes—why should we displease those who let us live though they may kill us as easily? But it can all be turned the other way around. Having found that their property consists of perfectly safe, mute, invisible microbes like you or me, those in possession-power will not be deterred even by the tiny displeasure that microbes may cause them. To those in possession-power these martyrs speak for us: 'Look,' they say, 'here is what we are, and for each of us who accepts martyrdom for making it known, there are, obviously, unidentifiable numbers of microbes who may come out into the open much more dangerously for you.'"

"Those fellows you meet," he concludes, "will draw you in before you know it."

"Life will live—and moan and scream and scream until it can, and when there is no more martyrdom again, it will all hide back. Into everyone's own self. An infinite country, with infinite lines of defense where life can still fight even in the minority of one against all mankind—and win."

"They will draw you in before you know it. Yes: before you know it."

6

"How wondrous Thy works are, O God," he comments on his city dweller's deep breath of air as we go out into the evening made bluish by the remote fires of autumn leaves.

We walk up and down the alley, and now he feels quite free from the microphone, especially if he speaks in a low voice, in a soft evening whisper almost.

"You mean you would drop everything here if—I know this is unreal, but just imagine."

On his face is the kind of smile which accompanies unreal but exciting conjectures.

"Yes."

He instantly believes, perhaps because of my smile.

"You would just leave all this?"

"Look: if I have a chance and don't go, what will I be? A quietly aging serf? A young serf may be a frolicking beast at least enjoying himself, but a quietly aging serf . . ."

"Shsh. You are shouting. Someone's passing. It's all very well for you because you are the country's only strictly private person, but I serve. Department. Chiefs. Rivalries. Let's go up the alley and sit down again. It's all about nothing. There will never be a chance. It's all nonsense. We just upset ourselves. It's poison. Another dream about *there*, contaminating our life."

We sit down on a bench, and he tries to recapture the word-shedding mood.

"I *am* happy. The rest is all poison." He looks at the sky, putting his face under the last manna of light. "The mystery of life. This is all that is worth living for."

"Look at those treetops. In the morning my son finds fallen nests when there is such a wind as yesterday's. Earlier in summer the fledglings in the nests up there were not aware of living so precariously over an abyss. . . ."

"So many people are innocent, historically. They are happy. They live. Tell them you live in the Golden Horde. They will not even understand. Serfdom? I am a serf. To go away? To drop the warm stove bed I have been making all my life. You say I have a serf rank. How many people here do you think have a serf rank like mine or higher?"

"Well—quite likely, only one percent of one percent."

"Ha! You see?" He settles for a more leisurely posture. "I am Prometheus, as you know. And for me the universe divides into two unequal parts." He pauses. "One part looms very large: it is my liver. The other is the rest of the universe. But you will not understand because your liver is healthy."

"How can I? One who feels healthy will hardly understand the self who was sick just an hour ago."

"Literature for me is, essentially, what it would have been for Prometheus: a way of keeping my liver in order. With you it is different, of course."

"I have no excuse like yours. So with me it's just vanity. Please imagine my vanity as your liver if you can."

"Very well. That larger part of the universe, my liver, is so infinitely larger because the smaller part of the universe depends on it. What is this smaller part, including my wife and children, if it cannot live without my liver? We haven't a kopeck against a rainy day. As soon as my liver is no more. . . . By serf rank I belong to the upper one percent of one percent. This means that the best one percent of one percent of the country's physicians will treat my liver."

"But perhaps in the West you—"

"Ah, come on," he says harshly like a hard practical man to the daydreamer during an emergency. "Some manuscripts of Remizov—man alive, of *Remizov*—have not yet been published. Some friend—an old taxi driver in Paris—keeps them, and when he dies, thank God if someone buys them. Because Remizov is an émigré. He represents his own self, and that's all. Now, if an imitator of an imitator of Remizov here writes something . . . well, with some message like. . . ."

"Freedom is not to be sneezed at," I prompt.

His laughter seems to strain out in small tight flat streams.

"Yes: freedom is not to be sneezed at. And he will be received in state in the West. Because he represents, whether he conforms or rebels, great Stalin's nuclear superempire. He is another Stalin's daughter. We are all Stalin's daughters. To stay in the West? What will I be there? Remizov was a nobody there. Now, me they receive in state. I talk with Ezra Pound—I dine with Sartre."

For a while he sits at peace with a thickening evening, his head rising up against a still limped skylight. Then he decides to attend to my case too.

"But you—you personally—what else do you need? A little bit more freedom to publish. I understand, yes. As noblemen had under Nicholas I. Writers do not really need more freedom than that. If they have more, they are tempted to turn political—political propaganda then begins to pay in every sense. A little bit more freedom, yes, but what else? You live in an abbey of Thélème, look around, what else can you want? You will never have this in the West. Not even you. No, sir." He lowers his voice to a level of departmental discretion. "Is that country house we pass—I mean round the corner—"

"Yes."

"My God. Not to meniton the smaller fry all around. Think of the hell he has been through to get it, while for you it was just another intellectual pastime. In a country where every garbage man living in barracks is attached to some department, you are a private person living in an abbey of Thélème. You have outsmarted our possession-power, you have."

"It is so pleasant to be smart. Yet all this happened by chance. Really. When I was twenty the English-speaking civilization suddenly became for me something like the grass that a sick dog looks for in order to cure itself. My new craze was regarded by practical people as totally useless and even harmful to my future serf engineer's career. But no one is more impractical sometimes than practical people because too many people are practical, and when too many practical people concur to do something practical they are paid rottenly. Certainly so in this country, where one is paid well only if one is unique, if one is a one-man trade union which has cornered the labor market. I was absurdly impractical and hence unique. Here I am explaining how smart I am, actually. Man is so vain that even when he wins one ruble or a ballpoint pen in a lottery he attributes this to his special virtues and thinks up a success story. But really, a sheer trifling accident helped me."

"What trifling accident?"

"Suppose we go in. We'll sit in that anteroom—you know, directly in front of my study. Besides, all this is history, and no one is interested too much in history, not even our *organs of state security*."

7

"The trifling accident was that great Stalin had been preparing to acquire the rest of the world."

"Yes, I remember—it was in the air."

"Not just in the air. Do you remember that Spanish was to be taught in schools, and hundreds of Spanish teachers in Moscow alone were in training openly in the early fifties? What was the purpose of teaching Spanish on an almost countrywide scale? To translate Lope de Vega once again? In China the possession-power had to be left to the natives, instead of Chinese-speaking passport-Russians, with their families here as hostages. In South America the mistake was not to be repeated."

"To think that I knew it. Of course. I never wondered somehow. All the country suddenly studying Spanish."

"So preparations were made to acquire the rest of the world, and practically it was only the English-speaking countries that were then in the way. Naturally, all the former citizens of these countries who had come here began to be exterminated. How else? Suppose there was one spy among them? Surely it was worth great Stalin's while to destroy all who had come from the English-speaking countries in order to destroy one spy? But there was one obstacle. Any number of reliable passport-Russians could be drilled in English on a mass scale to be *our* spies, not to mention prospective overseers of all ranks in the United States, and so on. But something else was also needed—British-

American writers, scholars, intellectuals, made out of those passport-Russians who had never been abroad and had no relatives abroad. Who had never been on the enemy-occupied territory during the war. Who in short could not contain a single enemy spy, for they had never been in contact or communication with any foreigner, had never been exposed to any ideas except *our soviet ideas of infinite devotion* to great Stalin, and could have no personal grudge against the regime. Having made enough British-American writers, scholars, and intellectuals out of this sterilely pure infinite devotion, great Stalin would be able to exterminate all the real Englishmen, Americans, Australians, and all the others, down to the very last man who might be just that spy on account of whom the whole *operation* began to be carried out in 1949."

"I see. So the order was: grow homunculi."

"Exactly. The order was unreal. In 1943 it became clear that it was possible to build a rocket that would hit New York in case America dared to hit Moscow in order to retaliate for the invasion of Europe 'down to the English Channel.' But the homunculus order was impossible in principle. The Russian word *jizn* is *life* in English. Actually either word is its own cosmos. *Jizn* begins from a plaintive *j*, the same as the start of the word *stomach*—or the old word *bread*. This *j* is something raw like the black sour bread in the village, and burning, smarting, scalding, vital, dark, intense, and then *j*, via pity and plaint, bursts into the ending *izn* like a fount, but in this fount the *z-z-z* is a fierce spray (like milk hitting a pail) and the palatalized *n* is a soft nothing, the sound a baby makes when it strains happily to say something but knows no words as yet. We are aware of this because we had a childhood here, and as writers we have preserved our knowledge and perhaps developed it as we have been living that life—that *jizn*. How can an outsider understand it? How can a Russian understand the cosmos of the English word *life*? Or any other word? Or how the cosmos of one word weds that of another? The order was impossible, see? But who would have thwarted the order of great Stalin? After all, great Stalin did not just once create the world—he was creating it like a living ubiquitous omniscient wrathful deity, and whoever could doubt that such homunculi could also be created if *he* ordered so? Make such homunculi. '*His personal order*,' they whispered. Any resources, of course. I was after the grass that could alone cure me, and that was the English-speaking civilization. To study it unmolested, I had to be attached to an *establishment of higher education* where its language is studied. And here a certain *special faculty* was about to open. The intention of myself and that of a certain entity called great Stalin coincided accurately to within a month. Great Stalin wanted me to begin immediately to study, to know, to feel the English-speaking civilization as might an American or British writer-intellectual who was born there. In order to acquire and kill the English-speaking civilization. I wanted to study, to know, to understand it in order to defend, to cure, to save life within me from him, that is from death."

"But suppose he would start the war when—"

"Look. Later I met his English *referent*. A homunculus. Churchill describes him. Sir Winston doesn't mention the fact, however, that the man was an atrociously crude homunculus, compared with genuine Sir Winston. Suppose great Stalin got wind of the fact. What? A rotten homunculus, a bad imitation, an obvious waster of production? What would the trembling high-ranking serfs have had to do?"

"I cannot stand it," he says claustrophobically. "Wait a second. Let me take a breath. You mean they would've had to put you—"

"I was the only decent homunculus. Of course, I was not real either. I will never understand the word *life* in English as I understand it in Russian. But of all the homunculi I was the only completely lifelike."

"But what—how could you—" Then he says weakly: "He was paranoiacally suspicious."

"For every paranoia there is a superparanoia. A microbe may kill a man no matter how paranoiacally hygienic he is. But all this: might have. Actually, I just followed my impulse like a sick dog looking for the cure-grass. I don't know what would have happened *if*."

We sit in the dusk, and he complains of insomnia which my tale will produce. Still, he wants more.

"But what about the other homunculi? You say the growth of homunculi was ordered on a vast scale."

"The other homunculi did not fulfill the order. But something or somebody called *our-dear-comrade-stalin* was announced to be dead before the first graduation was made. So no one suffered. Except morally, of course. Ai-ya-yai, to fail to fulfill his *personal order*."

"What happened? Were you more able?"

"Able? I was the least able. An American journalist told me that when he studied Russian in the American armed forces there was an ability test. Some scientists had composed one artificial language, and on the strength of the test the subject's ability for each particular language was determined. I would have got the lowest mark. I have no memory of that kind at all. In general, this kind of *science* is really unopposed here, but ironically, there was no ability test in my case because ability tests were swept away in the thirties as giving undue preference to the intelligentsia at the expense of the working masses. Even without those ability tests, I flunked the ordinary entrance exams. I had no ability at all. But I was admitted without any ability at all because they were in a feverish hurry (*his personal order*) and it is only my passport-Russianness and all the other signs of my sterilely pure infinite devotion to great Stalin that were important."

"But how—"

"Life touches a dunce, and he remembers several million notes of music in definite succession. With different characteristics like loudness, speed, or timbre. Call in those scientists and let them test his ability by asking him to memorize several million telephone numbers. Or still worse, several million notes of some test music of their own invention. With telephone numbers he will perhaps manage two or three. Though I cannot remember a single digit of our telephone number which we have had for three years. As for their scientific test music, the very first bar of it will simply produce in him a cerebral chaos, rating him as a moron. As a moron I squirmed in somehow. But life touched me."

"You mean God touched you—God."

"You may call it life, or God, or schizophrenia with strong dissimulation defying psychiatric detection. Anyway, the others were failing to fulfill the order, as anyone would fail, trying to memorize several million notes like telephone numbers and then link them up into music by memorizing other telephone numbers. My memory was soon thought to be superhuman. They didn't know I cannot memorize one telephone number in three years."

I see him off to the gate. I feel spent, and what a lonely wooden sound, that banging of the gate.

As I go back, I imagine him as a sea plant, one end of it attached, the other waving in a current. A Tartar (is it his shirt?) sitting on the ground in a marketplace before some junk no one buys and shouting something no one wants to listen to. Or has he no legs? One of those war invalids? Or have his legs been dug into the earth? The Golden Horde. A wind: the treetops are circling.

The fledglings in the nest up there earlier in summer were not aware of living so precariously over an abyss, and that circling of the treetops seemed to them to exist solely to rock them to sleep or just for fun.

8

I could not yet read thick, grown-up books, and they read to me a book about how unhappy Charles Dickens was as a child and how he grew up and passers-by in London would say whenever they saw him: "That's the famous writer Charles Dickens, don't you know?"

Well they might. No one could ever write a better book. No soul would hold it, there would not be enough tears.

However, I soon found that the book had actually been written by a certain Charskaya. Later in life I learned that her name had been used in the expression: the *gutter-press cheap sentimental novels of Charskaya*, ever since the beginning of the century, and when, in the middle of the century, there was no Russian literature left to speak of, every few years someone would still intone: the *gutter-press cheap sentimental novels of Charskaya*.

Anyway, the discovery was confusing. I had assumed that only Dickens could write so well about Dickens. He was an ugly duckling, and then he became a swan.

This is what happened in the Andersen tale I had been reading and rereading without grown-up aid. I did not know that a couple of years before the tale had still been called a *typical leaflet of petit-bourgeois propaganda*. If it were, I certainly fell for it, with beautiful pictures, and I understood that Andersen had told a parable, and Dickens the real story. Dickens wrote about how he had been an ugly duckling, so that all read his book and were crying because they had been so unfair, and loved him ever after, and what else was worth writing about?

It was decided that on no account should the book be read to me again because it made me cry, and I would swear that I would not cry this time, I would swear on my honor, coax, and pester everyone until the reading started again, and I would be safe until that sentence: "The milkmaid knocked loudly on the door and shouted that she would give no more milk."

"And butter? Was there butter?" I had asked dismayed at the very first reading.

I did not remember having ever been unhappy, nor could I imagine that anyone else might be ever. True, our neighbor girl Nina, two years my senior, had something wrong with her legs; she walked with crutches. Yet that was no misfortune, but an advantage. Here she was walking with crutches expertly and as much as she liked while I had to borrow them from her—and only for a very short time—just to *learn* how to crutch-walk. And before I got my teeth into it—just as I had made several pathetically laymanish hobblings—I had to return the crutches, often simply at her regal whim. Besides, the crutches gave her a kind of omnipotence. "I'd lam him one with a crutch," she would say with an air of awesome finality.

When I heard for the first time that sentence about there being no milk for little Dickens, I felt what someone feels when he realizes suddenly that his view of the world has been a terrible delusion, but nobody pays any attention because nobody has shared the illusion. "Well," they seem to shrug, "if you had such a silly illusion, who is to blame?"

"And butter?" I floundered, feeling that my face had somehow flattened into a pancake, and was all taut, awry, and ugly, with one edge of it seared as by a scalding wind. "Was there butter?"

Polya, our *domworker,* meaning domestic worker because there were no maids anymore, spoke in a voiceless voice. As there is flameless fire so there is a voiceless voice. Plaintive songs are called *sufferings* in some areas of Russia. It was that kind of voice except that Polya spoke *her* sufferings almost inaudibly, as though she had no strength left, and whenever she tried to speak up, something wheezed softly in her throat back to a voiceless suffering. Do you care to visualize our Polya? It is so simple. When I saw *Mona Lisa* I could not help believing it was our Polya, and I cannot shake off the impression more than thirty years later. Our Polya was like Mona Lisa if that Mona Lisa had been put through the life of the Russian village, including *de-kulakization*, had become thin, haggard, furtive, and had lost forever that Mona Lisa's *kulak* smile. Sometimes Polya smiled, too, but her smile was almost painful, as though smiling were a mortal sin in which she would guiltily indulge, and evoked a reddish candlelight on a burial vault of clay deep underground.

"If there was not even milk," she said voicelessly, "what butter could there be?" She also lisped a little and even winked her eyelids whenever she said something so well reasoned out. Yet then her eyes would again be dark, suffering, and frightened unless she sinned by smiling.

"But if there was no butter," I pressed on, suddenly seeing an obvious weak point in the other side's argument, "how could he eat bread and butter?"

"He couldn't eat bread and butter. And here, see, you have it," my mother rejoined happily. (She was rummaging in her wardrobe: in my memory there is still the faded arpeggio of the mirrored door being opened.)

As *that* sentence in the book would approach, I tensed up, I was sure I would brave it this time, but this is like a light skiff casting off, here we are, surely I am not crying, why, I am, full on, and since it was full on, I could cry as much as I liked, it didn't matter now, because after this page I would be safe almost up to the end, up to when Dickens walked with his cane about London and everyone would say: "That's the famous writer Charles Dickens, don't you know?" But here I could cry my fill because it was the end, and who would think of the next reading?

There were no Sundays at that time because Sunday in Russian means Resurrection. So there were days off instead (only our neighbor Anastasia would announce cryptically: "Resurrection! Today is Resurrection!"). And on a day off mother took me as usual for a walk, a great event because all the other days she was away at her work, working as a doctor. A doctor was more important than a medical nurse, and medical nurses had once been called sisters of charity. I had postcards with allegoric pictures and captions under them like *tranquillity, rivalry,* and so on, and one postcard pictured a very sad lady and children, and the inscription was: *charity,* and so I knew what charity meant because she *doved* one of the children. To *dove* means to take compassionate care of, but really it applies to children who are *doved,* that is, the child's head is pressed to the loving adult's chest and sheltered in the clasping arms, perhaps with some endearments cooed.

We walked through a quiet cobble-paved street; the cobbles were like huge grains of buckwheat porridge (what porridge do *you* like?) only of different hues—grayish, pinkish, greenish— while in our street the cobbles were even black bars.

Within the next few years all that was asphalted over because asphalt was thought to be part of perfection. Gone with the cobblestones were imperfections like beggars, tea drinking on whispering summer evenings outside dovecotelike houses with windows mirroring a pinkish sky behind mazy fences, Chinese laundrymen and their laundries, the forty times forty of Moscow churches, women who sang too much in cellars, the outer ring of boulevards with trees and fountains, orphans who had become waifs, lanes running in shelves with stone steps from shelf to shelf, people who looked suspicious.

But on that day off, Moscow around us was still largely cobble-paved—not yet as perfect as asphalt.

Making the most of the day-off walk, I would sprint ahead, to stop and wait for mother to walk up, and as I stopped in this way and turned my head I saw near the level of my eyes. . . .

It is difficult for me to understand myself at that time, and sometimes I make a kind of mental trick and I think I understand, but then it escapes me again.

In a broad, merciless, somewhat bluish daylight I saw cold-reddened, cold-chapped, trembling hands, supplicating, yet unable to supplicate because they were trembling-trembling-trembling.

Cold is something every Russian child knows no matter how sheltered. It was early spring, I was wearing my coat called a spring coat, I have a memory of icicles, and I knew that if I had lost my mittens (which I often did) my hands would be cold even if I thrust them into my pockets.

Then my eyes went up to his face. It was big (and seemed

bigger to me as a child), bloated, cold-chapped, and also trembling.

But it was something else that frightened me for life.

His face was perfectly impassive. For thirty-odd years I had thought it was just an accidental impression until I read not so long ago: *paralysis agitans*, also called Parkinson's disease, shaking palsy—marked by masklike facial expression. But how could I know it then? To me his face said: "I don't ask you for anything, don't mind me, go on, go on, leave me like that, and be happy, while I will be trembling-trembling-trembling."

I stood waiting for my mother because my mother was something more than even a sister of charity, and now surely it was the chance of her life.

However, she came over on the other side of me, her face averted.

"Let's go," she said.

"Look," I said because I was sure she was not seeing.

"He is sick," she said, pulling me away. "This is a disease."

I let her drag me a few steps away.

"Sick?" I gasped, and the sky over the not yet quite perfect Moscow burst into fiery red and white tears. "If he is *sick*, why don't you *treat* him?"

Passers-by began to halt with their usual unsolicited and irrelevant educational wisdom.

She did not try to deceive me. She tried to explain, and according to her explanation, we had better go home to do something about it—to phone Professor Kroll, for example.

So she was dragging me home, and I had realized that Kroll or no Kroll, I was to break through her indifference and make her see all this as I saw it. I tried to keep myself under control and reason with her.

"I implore you to cure him," I repeated, hot, desperate, dry-eyed, counting very much on the word "implore," which could not fail to move her. They had promised to buy me a pair of crutches so that I could have my fill of crutch walking, and also gold teeth which were said to be bought from a dentist rather than grown naturally, and I broadly hinted that if she cured *him* with or without Kroll's help, no crutches or gold teeth would be expected. I knew that money was hard to come by, a pair of crutches cost a small fortune, and as for gold teeth, there is nothing more expensive than gold. For seventeen kopecks in *gold* you can buy two pounds of tomatoes. By relieving her from the obligation so onerous, I wanted to stimulate her because I felt that my spiritual pressure was inadequate.

When we came home I recalled everything again, but my tears did not seem to shake her out of her indifference, and so I laughed and saw that I had succeeded much better. I have a poor heredity, you know. Aunt Olya, Mother's sister, shot herself when she was young for no apparent reason at all. And whenever Father began to drink, he could not stop it, and drank more and more, like someone falling a steep river bank. So my laughing frightened Mother, and I laughed more. I was using my poor heredity, and as I laughed, I also cried because I could not only laugh.

9

I have said that when I stood in that cobble-paved street, waiting for my mother, she came over on the other side of me, her face averted.

I said "averted" because I don't remember her expression. Perhaps there was, momentarily, despair in her face, and then just a hard crust over helplessness, for she was to save her son.

She could not very well say to me: "I shouldn't have given birth to you. In the summer of 1928, a few months before you were born, something happened, and life has since been swaying back into the abyss. Just as before 1922."

Nor could I say then though I might at various times later: "Perhaps you'd better have married that Japanese gentleman. Remember you told me?"

"Ha-ha-ha, yes," she laughs in my imagination. "When he proposed he asked if I didn't accept because I thought we'd have to live in Japan? We could live anywhere I liked, he said. Except, of course, Russia, impossible to settle in, and we laughed at his horror of Russia. He was a comic figure from a comic country. Everything un-Russian was comic—or philistine."

Like many adolescents, I could not argue. I would flare up, and sputter out something incoherent, shouting and stammering. But in my imagination I say grandly: "You simply did not understand other countries. Unfortunately, Russian literature which showed Russians so human, different, alive, often showed foreigners just as vaudeville types."

"They *are* philistines. Philistines. A German girl, with her fiancé's blessing, spends the first night with someone rich who buys her a dowry—furniture, curtains."

She does not care to understand what I say. Not even in my imagination. She just recalls: "You know, when my father—your grandfather—died I locked myself in my room. And read all those Dostoyevsky novels day and night. To forget. Not to see anything around. I read myself unconscious."

"And the life of Vitebsk seemed to you so drab and petty and freakish after all those Russian soul-infinities of St. Petersburg and Moscow. I saw the Vitebsk photographs. Why is it that it is only in retrospect that life looks like life, and when you are within it, you can notice it no more than you can a cloud when you are within that cloud? Those Vitebsk photographs, all pasted on cardboard, with the photographer's monogram in a corner, are so nice, of an old tobacco color, and there is a smell—they smell like a torn kid glove I found in your dressing table."

"Yes," she says. "We had our city photographer. And our city artist. His name was Pen."

Whenever Chagall is mentioned, one of my aunts says: "Ah, it's that boy who studied under Pen? Pen was a very good artist." Then we yell about Chagall, we shout the names of strange lands and cities, of magnificent operas and clinics, and the names seem so iridescent in Aunt Vera's apartment with a corridor all hung up with old junk of all sizes, including misshapen troughs, of course.

When we stood the other day in the corridor, preparing to go, already in our fur coats, one of their neighbors, an adolescent, passed by. Because they do not speak to their neighbors at all, or these neighbors in particular, the boy passed by silently, ghostlike, between our fur coats. A ghost? A Cruikshank illustration of Dickens? A pale gawky boy in a rather soiled nightshirt tucked into his trousers, a huge V-cut at his collar showing his greenish flesh. He appeared and passed between us as though *we* were ghosts, invisible to him, in spite of our fur coats.

That aunt of mine who lives there—Vera, not the one who says: "Yes, Pen was a very good artist"—gave me in my youth a book of a unique poet who deleted more and more verse in his later editions because he believed that no poet can hold the reader's attention for more than twelve lines or so. But Aunt Vera wrote in all the deleted lines in her reverent neat pearly handwriting, and that handwriting, just like the yellowed paper and the elongated type, became part of the poet's uniqueness. As I looked at that dimly lit cavelike corridor with all the junk on the walls, and recalled that to cap all the miseries something was wrong with Aunt Vera's kidneys, I also recalled in her neat pearl-like maiden handwriting:

> So eternity cometh at last
> To confine us in silence for good.

"Chagall," we shouted. We gesticulated wildly to show the splendors of strange fantastic lands, we yelled—we shut our eyes as though dazed, and then not Aunt Vera, but the other aunt, said: "Yes, Pen was a very good artist."

"On some of those Vitebsk photographs," I say to my mother in my imagination, "you wear big white hats like swans, and there is one where you sit at a very long table, ostensibly having tea, because there is a tea set of many dainty pieces, but you all wear sedate black pillbox hats, and the men are bourgeois, with pince-nez and all. That torn kid glove I found in your dressing table. You wore kid gloves at balls in Vitebsk—"

"All the same we yearned for Petersburg or Moscow. But Jews could not live there permanently. Unless they were of the first merchant guild. But your grandfather was of the second."

"Or unless Jews had higher education. Or had enrolled at a college."

"Oh, yes. When I matriculated I lived in Petersburg."

"Or unless," I press on, "Jews worked at a drugstore, or assisted in any other way in medicine or pharmacy. Or unless they plied some trade or craft, including distillery. Or unless they had been in military service. Or unless they adopted Christianity and ceased to be Jews, and I'd like to see how a passport-Jew could ever cease to be a passport-Jew today, and how anyone could, passport-Jew or passport-Russian or passport-anything, leave Vitebsk for residence in Moscow of his own free will!"

"When your grandmother was sick and we wanted to place her in a private hospital in Petersburg, the Morozovs arranged for the permission—Morozov was so good to us. He received us in his office at the Winter Palace. He was wearing a blue ribbon over his shoulder. You know how they were worn, aslant— across his chest. Because we could not live in Petersburg or Moscow we dreamed all the more of them. When the tsar was overthrown . . ."

"Overthrown?" I shout—no, not in this imaginary conversation, but in my real youth. "God, you deserve the famine, typhus —and terror too. Overthrown? The tsar abdicated. Who overthrew him? Uncle Anas? All the heroes like Uncle Anas ran off Znamenskaya Square when they imagined that someone had fired a shot at them. They overthrew him!"

"Oh, you don't know. Some of those tsarist officials were nauseating, yes—nauseating. And *pogroms*. We never saw them, but we read about them a lot, and the tsar . . ."

The word *pogroms* wrought havoc in my adolescent mind. I knew that Russia before 1917 was a semiconstitutional monarchy, in which civic evolution took place, as in Denmark, Sweden or Japan. The jury trial, the freedom of the press practically unlimited and extended even to the newspaper *Pravda* in 1912, thousands of independent organizations, including political parties, trade unions or national-minority groups (even much earlier, 1,572 Zionist organizations were officially functioning all over the country, for example), not to mention the Duma (parliament) in which at least all political opinions were expressed and officially published: such were some of the results of this civic evolution which I could easily glean even from the myths of propaganda as it described the mythical *heroic struggle* of mythical *revolutionary heroes* like great Lenin who duly razed (in perfect safety) all these results to the ground. There was no reason to doubt that if not for this *revolutionary heroism* the semiconstitutional monarchy of Russia would have become a full-fledged constitutional monarchy as it is in, say, Denmark today.

When I explained this, the retort was: *pogroms*. It was the same as the retort: Negro lynchings, to prove that civic progress in the United States or in general is evil. Pogroms or Negro lynchings are blamed on civic progress which is the only known remedy against these evils, and not on those who were re-

44

sponsible for these evils and out to destroy the only known remedy. In case of Russia before 1917 the mental trick is especially convenient since both civic evolution and medieval bigotry can be conveniently lumped together into a single composite myth: the *tsarist regime.* It is the same as if in the history of America one were to fuse into a certain single "presidential regime" those who, say, owned or lynched Negroes and those who emancipated them or promoted their civil defense.

Of course, civic evolution and total or perfect serf ownership has each its own pleasant and unpleasant aspects, and it is a matter of taste which to choose.

Certain forces which once existed or still exist in every democracy of today were responsible for the arrest and trial of Mendel Beilis in Russia in 1911 (or Captain Dreyfus in France somewhat earlier). Were the police, the Protection Department (an investigative branch), or the tsar involved? This is irrelevant: if they had been, it is even more remarkable that the jury in Russia returned a verdict of not guilty, and no forces in the country could do anything about it.

Between 1918 and 1949 the network of propaganda kept expressing its *infinite indignation* over the Beilis case of 1911: those reactionary forces had put the poor Beilis on trial—only in the tsarist regime could there be a case like that. And the network of propaganda is right: in a perfect serf ownership there are neither reactionary nor progressive forces that would have any civic, legal or political authority, and there can be no case like that. Nor can there be any *private pogroms,* that is pogroms made by independent forces and therefore taking the scale of a town or settlement, and never the scale of Moscow or Petersburg. Just as in a perfect serf ownership there can never be protest marches, social movements, rallies, riots, clashes with police, strikes or any other good or bad activity of any independent spontaneous big groups in evidence in, say, the United States at this writing or in Russia before 1917.

There may be only one tiny unpleasantness in a perfect serf ownership. In the spring of 1948 great Stalin upheld the newborn State of Israel. That evoked a fresh outburst of belief among many statesmen, scholars and intellectuals residing cozily in democracies that say what you like but a serf ownership is, essentially, very good, especially if compared with the *tsarist regime*. Indeed, great Stalin *himself* was said to have suggested to the Israeli Ambassador Golda Meir drawing up the lists of those Jews in Russia who wished to go to defend Israel. Anyway, the lists were drawn with zest. A Soviet Jewish Volunteer Army, so to speak. See? Nothing is more perfect than a really perfect serf ownership. But anyone can change his mind, right? Great Stalin changed his mind—as suddenly. And duly handed over the lists of volunteers to his *organs of state security*. And all the volunteers *disappeared*. And Jews who had never intended to volunteer began to *disappear* too. Nothing as horrible as a pogrom in old Russia when a platoon of soldiers got drunk, rioted, and swooped on Jewish shops somewhere in Kishinev. Simply nice, neat, discreet *disappearance*. True, finally some circles abroad got uneasy. A fairly famous *friend of the soviet union*, indeed, even complained during his vastly enjoyable tour of the country that *reactionary propaganda* had the nerve to lie that so and so had disappeared. "Ha-ha-ha! He *is* a victim, indeed! A victim of reactionary propaganda! He's not in Moscow, I think. But he is coming Friday. You'll see him." And he *saw*. Everything was perfect. Except that the victim of reactionary propaganda put his hand on the table and quickly removed it. Too quickly. Or not quickly enough. Anyway, the *friend of the soviet union* noticed that the hand of the victim of reactionary propaganda had no fingernails, and worse, the *friend of the soviet union* showed that he had noticed. Well? The *friend of the soviet union* promptly perished in a car accident. Oh, a pure accident. Quite esteemed Western experts and even his wife still believe it was a pure accident. They analyze it so expertly. If at a distance. Who can compare all this with a platoon of rioting drunken soldiers looting shops?

A three-volume *History of the Jewish People*, published in Israel in 1969, describes in this way the "most horrible pogrom" in pre-1917 Russia (the pogrom was caused, in the authors' opinion, by Krushevan's newspaper *Bessarabets* in Kishinev):

The vehement propaganda soon had effect, and the most horrible pogrom occurred in Kishinev in April 1903. According to official data, more than 50 persons were killed and about 500 injured; hundreds of homes and shops were looted and destroyed. The wanton outrage shook the public opinion of the entire world as well as of the progressive circles of Russia.

There is one detail. If all the murderers, looters, rioters, lynchers and so on in the United States were counted up between 1861 and 1917, the numbers might seem staggering. But there is one point: they were considered criminals, not the holy vehicles of the divine will of the sacred *state*. I remember my surprise in childhood when I stumbled, browsing in Father's bookshelves, on David Aizman's story *The Heart of Being*. The entire plot hinged on the fact that a participant in a pogrom was in hiding as a fugitive from justice and was as afraid to be identified as any other murderer would. The Jewish writer David Aizman simply took this for granted in the *tsarist regime*.

Anyway, "more than 50 persons" killed in a riot of drunken soldiers "shook the public opinion of the entire world as well as of the progressive circles of Russia." And in 1948 Jews simply began to disappear all over the country—perhaps 5,000, and not 50, disappeared one fine day, not different from any other fine day—and while some paranoiac, hysterical, or altogether fascist characters could claim that they were tortured and/or exterminated by *heroic labor* (hunger and frost), most media abroad, manned as they were mostly either by *friends of the soviet union* or those who refuse to imagine that there may exist a civilization different from their own, could retort that there was no hard evidence for the disappearance of any Jews, and certainly not for anything bad happening to them after their disappearance.

However, the pleasant mystery did not suit great Stalin: he decided to torture some of those who had disappeared without hard evidence into the confession of their heinous if imaginary Jewish crimes, have them hanged on Red Square after a flamboyant *trial*, and organize—no, not one of those funny microscopic provincial pogroms when a platoon of drunken soldiers swooped on some Jewish shops, but a well-organized, perfectly centralized, country-wide pogrom after which *all* surviving Jews except those pronounced personally to be aryan would be carried to the death-by-labor camps.

The network of propaganda was quite right when it proclaimed before 1949 that the Beilis case would be unthinkable on the territory of Russia after 1917. Indeed: in a total serf ownership all the population down to the last man would express their infinite love for Jews (or *communists,* or Blacks, or men wearing broad trousers, or North Americans) and within an hour participate in the country-wide extermination of any of these, depending on the current pseudo-tsar-god's current will or whim.

But in my adolescence I could not present a cogent argument. I simply felt that the retorts like pogroms or Negro lynchings to condemn civic evolution in Russia or in the United States were worse than false: they condemned civic evolution for the evils against which it is the only remedy known.

"The tsar! What about the cholera riots in which the mobs massacred doctors *for spreading the cholera*? Did the tsar want to get rid of doctors or did he believe that doctors spread diseases? When a mob massacred all who were more prosperous or educated, this is called a *class-conscious revolution,* and when the same mob turned on Jewish shops and homes only, this is called a pogrom organized by the tsar on purpose—to suppress that *class-conscious revolution,* of course. That Sunday march of one-hundred-forty-thousand people in 1905 on the Winter Palace, his residence. Did the tsar gather one-hundred-forty-thousand people and instigate them to march on his residence? So that he would have either to have fire opened to stop them or be trampled to death in his own residence? I wonder: did the tsar finally organize in 1917 that country-wide massacre in which he and his children and even his family doctor were shot?"

"But we believed—"

"You believed! You all believed that Rasputin whored around with all the court, not to mention the worst court whore Vyrubova, but then after the tsar's abdication and everything, a medical commission established that the whore was a virgin. Didn't you like to tell me that Krushevan story?"

Once a young Jew approached Krushevan, the editor of *Bessarabets*, right on the main street of St. Petersburg and struck him with a knife. The Jew was sentenced to five years but granted amnesty by the tsar before his term expired.

"I don't know about the tsar," mother concedes, "but *they* were nauseating—nauseating."

"But who—*they*? Are jurymen *they*? Don't you like to tell me how the jury acquitted Beilis?"

Mother likes, indeed, to tell how Beilis was on trial, and how all decent people (including Christian church dignitaries) protested, and the council for the defense was met everywhere with applause, and Beilis was acquitted.

"See?" I say to her. "The jury trial! And *they* could not overrule its verdict!"

"Oh, you don't know, some of them were nauseating—nauseating."

Mother has two words when recalling someone in her life: *charming* and *nauseating*.

"Some of them were nauseating. Nauseating, see? Nauseating. When I went to Petersburg to place my mother in a private hospital . . . I was to see Petersburg, the Nieva and everything."

Mother's expression changes from nausea to youthful charm.

"With me—I mean in the compartment—were two officers. From *War and Peace* or whatever we had read. Back in Vitebsk Sasha had liked me, all Vitebsk knew it. They were of an old aristocratic stock, they were all charming—charming—and he liked me, and perhaps the officers liked me, but their idea of courtship was to tell each other jokes about Jews. Perhaps they thought I would appreciate them, but they forgot that I had no right to live in Petersburg."

"What did you do?"

"I rose and said: 'You scoundrels—' Yes, that is what I said: 'You scoundrels—' Yes, I said: 'You scoundrels—!' And I burst into tears, of course. Ha-ha-ha!"

"What did they do?"

"Oh. They were so embarrassed. They slipped out, and never returned. And when the tsar—well, abdicated, all we knew was that now we would all move right away to Petersburg or Moscow. And when I came, your father, and his friends, but your father especially, were just the Russians as I had imagined them."

"I understand. I wouldn't tell you, but since our conversation is imaginary I might as well. I browsed in the old letters and read half a page which was not really a letter but notes you exchanged with Father because you could not speak—most likely at some literary readings Father was to attend. At that time my feeling was just amazement, though I was not much interested and stopped reading. But as I recalled it later I thought that I had never read anything like that. I stopped reading also because it was unpleasant to think that such a great, unique soul-passion was connected with you. Every generation thinks itself human, and their immediate predecessors only ridiculous or irritating grotesques. And here I discovered that my loves were perhaps small, paltry—all their artistic yearnings to the contrary —compared with that artless vastness, with those wild hasty running-down lines, never intended for an outsider, and to think that it was connected with you, so haggard, unfeminine, having nothing left in you except that falsetto exultation at my survival over the abyss."

"Have I changed that much?"

"Remember your photograph on your gold-medal gymnasium-leaving certificate? It belongs to that world of kid gloves and long tea tables and cars still looking like carriages, of the world of ladies and gentlemen, of good manners, of personal integrity. Is it true that when Grandfather died he made you all swear that you would first pay all the debts no matter whether this would or would not leave you with a single kopeck?"

"Oh, yes. Of course."

"Here you are. Sounds like an old novel about the merchant's honesty. On that school-leaving certificate you have an open all-loving face, you have the laughing lips of a *baryshnya*— a young Russian lady—going to Petersburg. Now you belong to this world of scrambles for survival raging since 1918 under misshapen troughs hanging on the walls in communal-apartment corridors."

The time up to 1921 was even officially called *razrukha,* which means: breakdown of everything, disintegration into chaos, rack and ruin all over. In 1921 *capitalism,* that worst evil on earth for the elimination of which almost anything had to be endured, was invited to save the country, and the worst evil on earth did save it, and within six years, between 1921 and 1927, the worker's real average wages increased ten times, a level never since attained over the country at large. Whereupon the *capitalists* who saved the country were duly exterminated, for is not *capitalism* the worst evil on earth? Some *communists* learned from all this nothing except several new clichés, but my mother learned something.

Before 1917 her elder brother graduated from the Sorbonne and became a well-known psychiatrist, later the publisher-editor of a magazine entitled *Genius and Insanity*. Mother also decided to be a psychiatrist. That was part of the iridescent world of St. Petersburg and Moscow. Psychiatry. Dostoyevsky. Genius. Insanity. But she managed only to take a degree in general medicine and was mobilized in 1919. She became a neurologist because neurology was and is in great demand, while psychiatry became unimportant. If Freud's neurotics had faced the alternative: stop being neurotic and never be late for your work for more than twenty minutes, or go to your death in a prison camp, they would have been cured in the sense that they would have behaved like all the others and would have done what was ordered. The purpose of my mother's huge *disablement expertise institute*, at the center of the countrywide network of *disablement expertise commissions,* has been to detect hysteria and all the neuroses which Freud and others have been treating in order to deprive the neurotic (that is, *malingerer*) of the right to have an easier job by virtue of his alleged disease.

From the breakdown of everything which started in 1918 and grew worse until the worst evil on earth saved the country, Mother learned that doctors would be the last to starve and freeze—except for the possessors of the country themselves, who would starve and freeze in inverse ratio to rank. But no matter how much food and fuel and floor space the owners of the country have for themselves according to rank, they may also fall ill all the same and need doctors. All men of learning or imagination—musicians, engineers, actors, astronomers, composers, writers—would die of hunger or cold before doctors.

When life swayed back into the abyss in 1928, mother knew that she had to cling to what was called vaguely: *service,* an old Russian word ("Mother is out—she's gone to service, she is at service now, who's calling, please?"). A doctor attached, a doctor who *serves*, whether as the highest-ranking doctor treating the pseudo-tsar-god himself, or as a detector of hysteria in Moscow, or as a sorter of death slaves in a remote death camp, will not perish so easily, and the doctor can always share the food or fuel with the family—there is no rule forbidding to do so, none at all. The doctor may give *all* milk she receives to her child, something little Dickens did not have when his father went bankrupt—or so Charskaya described it at least.

There will always be the sick, no matter what hells or paradises the owners of the country may invent, and some meals will always be distributed among the sick, and how can you do the doctor out of them, eh? He has to *taste* these meals to start with, because who else will be responsible if the sick of whatever rank die after these meals? While tasting, the doctor may put away some food tasted into a glass jar (with an ingratiating little smile: "This is for my son"). And don't you start quarreling with the doctor on account of that, because the doctor will not sign the meal statement, and where will you then be? Don't you start quarreling with my mother on account of me, because there is concentrated Jewish willpower within her made out of Jewish neuroses, and that willpower will destroy you because your death is my life.

The time between 1921 and 1928 is still officially styled a *retreat*. If we call the regime in Italy between 1922 and 1926 simply *fascism,* the same between 1926 and 1937 *bad fascism,* and the same between 1937 and 1943 *very bad fascism,* then the name *bad fascism* or *very bad fascism* can perhaps be applied to the best of these blessed years in Russia between 1923, when *partially admitted capitalism* really got under way, and 1928, when it began to be crushed in all earnest, though some Italians may claim that, say, Jews were persecuted in Italy under *very bad fascism* in the sense that they were no longer admitted to the Fascist party, while the victimized groups in Russia continued to disappear in the torture-death stations, and this is not quite the same.

Those victimized groups were out of luck, while for the rest of the population *bad* or *very bad fascism* was a now nostalgic and never recaptured blissful time of plenty and freedom, owing to which I was born.

10

"In 1928, the year you were born in, life was still so different, so exciting," Mother sings songs about the last glimmer of *bad* or *very bad fascism*. "There were still private shops—you could buy anything. There were so many different trends in art. One literary group was called *Nothings*. Yes, *Nothings*."

"I know. One group said that writers or intellectuals should have no political rights like voting, but at the same time be released from all political obligations as well. To be idiots in the original sense of the word. Not a stupid idea."

"Liza lived with us at that time, and she said: 'Girls, I am dying for lamprey. With lemon juice.' 'Well,' we said, 'a rich man is due to come right now. He may buy it for all of us.' 'Who is that?' she said all agog, and she was beautiful, Liza, she was really beautiful. 'Misha Koltsov,' we said. Koltsov. He was in Spain with. . . . What's his name?"

"Hemingway."

"Koltsov was later shot." Mother looks into a blank distance.

"I know. He extolled the shooting of others quite enough to become one day just one of them. But don't dissipate the mood. Let's go back to that cozy feeling in 1928, when you sat with Liza, and our street was still cobblestoned, of course, and there was a church opposite, there, to the left, and the ancient Red Gate behind. So you sat with Liza, waiting for Koltsov."

"He bought us the lamprey and lemons. I don't know why we

enjoyed them so. . . . He married Liza afterward, but we soon stopped seeing them, because they became so important. Once they invited us, and all were dressed up, but your father paid no attention to what he wore. None at all. We lived out in the country in summer, and I was to come in the evening, but in the morning, while your father slept, his suit was stolen through an open window. He draped a bedsheet around himself and went to Moscow and walked like that through Moscow, but he looked so unperturbed that passers-by assumed he was from India or something. That time at the Koltsovs' he turned up—in high-boots. I would not, of course, have let him, if I'd seen. But we didn't come together, and he came from somewhere—in high-boots. They never invited us again. Never."

For a while Mother keeps the forbidding expression of the Koltsovs' never inviting Father in highboots.

"But this was later, and that was a good year when you were to be born, I mean the beginning. But in the summer of that year—you were to be born next autumn—in the summer of that year something happened."

"What was it?"

"I don't remember. Perhaps it was that Bukharin said, yes, he said: 'I am trembling from head to foot.' He said it privately, but it spread. 'I am trembling from head to foot.' He alone knew something about good literature. With Trotsky also gone, there was now no one to intercede. But something else happened. I don't remember."

"The rations? The rations began to be introduced in 1928 again."

"Not in Moscow. In Moscow they appeared after you were born. It was something else."

"The Shakhty trial? Remember there was a book entitled *Human Pests*? It was perhaps the first time that the word *pests* translated abroad as 'wreckers' really went into wide circulation. Between 1918 and 1928 the word 'insect' had been used. Great Lenin had set it afloat. But it was certainly imperfect: 'insects.' Not just insects, but pests: there are human pests—as there are agricultural pests, and there is human pest control, human entomology. It was also on the cover of that book that I saw for the first time the photograph of a pest. A pest, a harmful insect under study, an engineer from Shakhty, and his horrible shaven head might very well be that of some insect enlarged as in a book of science. Only his hand covering his eyes was human. At that time a pest could still cover its eyes, a strange freedom that still existed—the freedom of a pest to cover its eyes as though to block out the human dream from which the pest cannot wake."

When the pest trial opened, *Pravda* stated that there had been no *human* pests before. But what a chance for scientific study there was now!

A good collection of this new species is now in this white-columned hall. It must be studied as the plantbug is studied.

Yet on the thirty-second day of the pest study, when one of the pests began to explain in a human voice how harmful it, a pest, was, there was a human scream. Impossible, absurd, and simply untrue as the event was (a pest screaming in a human voice!), *Pravda* had to describe it because there were foreign correspondents in the hall—it is also for the benefit of *all progressive mankind* that the whole pest show was held—and some of these foreign correspondents would anyway have claimed that a pest screamed in a human voice just because another pest was exterminated for the benefit of the *most progressive society on earth*.

Hysterics in One of the Boxes

At that moment a hysterical scream comes from the boxes where the wives of the defendants are: "This is not true! Kolya, why are you saying this? Don't believe him, this is a lie!"

Skorutto covers his eyes with his hand and sinks onto the chair. The president of the court announces a ten-minute intermission to enable the defendant to calm down.

After the ten-minute intermission, not only the pest did not calm down, but on the contrary he began to retract his written confession of the day before, and again *Pravda* had to report—because of those foreign correspondents—what the pest said in a human voice:

"I have just said that I handed in the statement yesterday . . . But I cannot confess, I just cannot . . . Please understand the nightmare I have been through. . . . For seven years I worked for the Soviet power with infinite honesty. . . ."

The pest said he wrote his confession "in an incredible psychic state." "But it" (his confession) "is a lie, an insane lie."

"But it is a lie, an insane lie," exclaims Skorutto. "I never lied to the Soviet power, for seven years I worked. . . ."

The president of the court asks the defendant to calm down: the court inquiry will help to find the truth.

Besides, that pest Skorutto said that the *other* confessions were also carefully thought out, consistent, as-plausible-as-possible lies!

I *had to* write just what would sound *credible,* but, of course, it is all a lie, it is all a fable, it is all my invention, just as Matov, Bratanovsky, and the others lied and invented."

Skorutto persisted in this comedy of denial for four hours of the morning session.

In the intermission between the morning and evening sessions the *court* took a brilliant legal measure.

"In the intermission," announces comrade Krylenko, "an urgent investigation was made for prosecution concerning one circumstance in the first, 'false' confession of the defendant Skorutto, viz., that he furnished his apartment with the 1,000 rubles he had received from Rabinovich in 1925. The investigation—the interrogation of the superintendent of the house, the janitor, etc.—has confirmed all the deposition of Skorutto in that part thereof."

The only trouble is that the superintendent or the janitor might have testified in all truth or quite falsely that the pest Skorutto did furnish his apartment because they might have seen the furniture brought up, but they could not know that it had been bought precisely with 1,000 rubles, and precisely with *the* 1,000 rubles the pest Skorutto had received precisely from a Rabinovich precisely in 1925.

But this brilliant investigation which "confirmed all the deposition of Skorutto in that part thereof" was superfluous. After the intermission the pest Skorutto realized again what a harmful pest he was.

"Forgive me," continues Skorutto dramatically, "but I have been in hell. I cannot stand it any longer. I confess everything."

"Wholly and totally?" asks the president of the court.

"Yes," confirms Skorutto again. "All that I wrote in my first statement is true."

"The Shakhty trial?" I ask my mother. "Was it the Shakhty trial?"

"Yes, Shakhty. Those engineers. Perhaps. It dragged well into the summer. We could not stand reading about it anymore. But there was also something else. I don't remember. The centenary of Tolstoy was a good sign because it was against those proletarian writers. How they raved. They wanted no writers except themselves, and Trotsky, yes, it was still Trotsky, or perhaps it was already Bukharin, said to them—oh, good for him—he said to them: 'But look, you are simply jealous. You are underpinning your professional jealousy with a Marxist basis. There are many talented writers among the fellow travelers, and whom do you have? Lelevich?"

Mother repeats this several times. Trotsky-Bukharin's words still seem to her witty, brilliant, significant, as would the words of any top ranker regarded as intercessor. My remark that it was Bukharin (Trotsky was already about to go on his trip abroad and to death) who insisted that the Shakhty pests should be *sentenced* to death—as against the more lenient attitude of great Stalin—does not impress my mother very much.

In a gang of thieves, as we learned when we were in the Urals, there is always an *intercessor*. If a layman falls among them, all of them terrorize, persecute and humiliate him until one of them, an *intercessor*, suddenly shows sympathy—and seems to the layman by contrast the highest incarnation of humanity—usually to the advantage of the gang as a whole. Yet *intercession* is not a purely assigned role: rather a kind of sympathy may actually spark in one of the members of the gang, though, of course, an actor who plays sympathy on the stage also proceeds from a certain spark of *real* sympathy in his psyche.

"Yes, we thought that the Tolstoy anniversary was the only good sign. Bukharin said: 'I am trembling from head to foot.' And there was a congress of proletarian writers. Do you know how many there were of them? More than four thousand! We thought that now they would devour everyone. But no! Nobody noticed the congress, while the centenary of Count Lev Tolstoy was celebrated—oh, with such pomp! It was announced that his works would be published in ninety-two volumes! With all rough copies and variants. There was the commemoration conference at the Bolshoi Theater, and all that. Yes, we thought it was the only good sign, and we named you Lev therefore, though your father thought it cheap, and wanted to name you Ivan. Ha-ha-ha! Horrible—Ivan. Do you remember the Urals?"

"I remember snow so impossibly far away—on the other side of the universe. It was a river valley."

"When the famine started, and there was rationing all over again, just as seven years before—only then we had been quite young, and now there was you—we went to the Urals. Your father got a mission there, to conduct literary courses among thieves. Thieves were everywhere then. It was hoped at that time that they could be reformed, in colonies which were named communes, and thieves are fond of art—some of them wrote poetry."

"It was a river valley, I don't remember it in summer except that in a recurrent dream I was tumbling down its steep banks, and at the water's edge I clutched at some bag."

"The women were grave hysterics. They always acted something they were not, and wept and thought up wild fantasies about themselves. How they were bastards of the nobility and what amazing men courted them and all that. Thieves never steal anything from what they call *artistes*, never, and at first it was all exciting, but then your father was bored, and the famine struck even the rich Urals too, while in Moscow we could at least get better rations, and we went back to Moscow, but here it was going from bad to worse. Those proletarian writers had been closed—disbanded. But joy was premature—all writers' cooperative publishing houses and their magazines were soon closed too. And the *Dipper* and *Circle* and *Today*. Just like all private shops. Remember the German cobbler in the corner house? He had two daughters—girls of your age. So fair-haired that you got frightened. Remember? When we came he was still there for a while. But then everything was the *state*."

The *state*. Masterdom. What a word in Russian: the adjective has fifteen letters—the very word is leviathan, its armorlike scales dully glimmering as it uncoils its five crustaceous syllables.

"Yes, everything was now the *state,*" Mother says again. "Writers were helpless, and your father was terrible. He could charm any person if he did not want anything from him, but if he knew he must ask for some favor he became tongue-tied, awkward, pitiful, and he would forget to ask or would say afterward that there was no convenient moment. He would smile, that sort of smile, and I had not the heart to reproach him. He had no will for anything practical. He was a psychopath. A real psychopath."

"That dream: I clutched at some bag right at the water's edge. But it slipped off with me, of course, and under water I went, down, down, and I was in agony until I touched the river floor."

"Then his drinking bouts began. True, when we met, I knew he drank. But I didn't know what it was like. No men in our family or among our friends had drunk heavily in Vitebsk."

"I see. His drinking was to you part of his soul, right? Whenever I met later a heavy drinker who was quite an ordinary person, I would be stunned—I assumed that every drunkard was a big-hearted, soulful genius in search of the infinite."

"But there was you. There was no turning back. I had to work like a horse."

"Yes. A raisin-lipped Russian-crazy *baryshnya,* you became a haggard drudge, a shrill Jewish concentration of willpower, saving her son from the Russian chaos of which my father was a part. But that dream: down, down I go in agony until I touch the river floor, a light jolt, sweet and reassuring, because this is the end, and there is nothing to struggle and be sorry for."

11

One of the doors of the nest my mother had made opened on a balcony so delightfully high (the fifth floor is still quite a treetop for Moscow) that I could run out and see the whole world from end to end.

When something happens in that world—*kirovs funeral,* they shout wildly, for example—here you are: that *kirovs funeral* is going to pass right below our balcony because it has to go from the terminals in that bluish haze over there on the left, beyond even the corrugated-iron fence we reach with Polya when we take a walk.

I am very old: I am six and one week and several days, but I get somewhat confused when I begin to count the days. Before my sixth birthday I also thought of my age, and of death— not of my own, of course, because that seemed to me unimportant, but of my parents'. Yet at least my sixth birthday itself was timelessly happy. That was my last birthday which was entirely happy—as happy as when one does not remember himself from happiness, as Polya says. There were very many guests, children and grownups, and they all gave me the presents because they loved me: this is how the world is arranged—to love me. This is its goal, its raison d'être, so that everyone who came gave a present to me—they were all so glad I was born. In Russia it is said: "I congratulate you on your birthday" (not: "Many happy returns of the day"). They congratulated me on my having been born. Everyone said: "I congratulate you on your birthday" and gave me a present. The guest could enjoy that present too, but out of love of me the guest would part with the present and give it to me—just because he was so happy I was born. No guest could overcome his self-denying joy at my having been born six years before, and since they kept coming it was a sustained adoration whose waves were carrying a timeless oblivion which an outsider would perceive as inane shouts, unprovoked laughter, and meaningless running about.

In retrospect I recalled the week-old event with a touch of old-age skepticism—reflective coldness. I was glad that at least there was an exciting occasion: that *kirovs funeral.*

Anyway, everyone shouted: *kirovs funeral, kirovs funeral.* The combination of the two words promised a unique spectacle for the populace—never miss the coronation of Nicholas II or the tricentenary of the House of the Romanovs, or the funeral of Kirov, and that *kirovs funeral* was to pass by just below, like a train I could see through a chink in that corrugated iron fence which we reached with Polya. Of all the splendors of life a train passing right under the street which was actually a bridge and watched through a chink in that fence was the sparkiest and smokiest.

That fence was part of the mystery. A very strange fence—corrugated. A stick passed over it produced a clatter, and Polya would appeal in voiceless sorrow to my age of reason: "How long will you make mischief? You are not little anymore."

Perhaps the *kirovs funeral* would fill the whole street with the greatest clouds of steam and smoke imaginable and would send the reddest sparks through the whole world?

I keep running from the balcony into the room to announce the latest and ask whenever that Kirov's funeral will pass at last.

Father sober. There are two fathers, sober and drunk, but there is actually no drunk father, because when he is father sober, father drunk does not exist, we believe he does not exist, there is no such person, let us not even think there is.

Father sober. He is so intelligent when he is sober that Mother and I and all writers and poets in suits with darned holes think that father sober is the most intelligent man on earth, except Shakespeare, of course, because Shakespeare stands in the right top corner of our bookcase in huge volumes with black real-leather corners and backs on which is inscribed in gold: Shakespeare. See how old I am? I am past that age when Charskaya was so unique because I liked her, and now what others think is more important to me.

Father sober. And you know that he is sober because then he has such an intelligent face, though it may be different depending on his smile. And when he is father drunk, he often makes his face very stupid for fun and also for everyone to pity him. I ask father drunk: "Pa, who is a greater writer—you or Shakespeare?" I ask him for fun, because Shakespeare is greater, of course, or who would have published him in those splendid books with real-leather corners and backs and everything? And Father screws up his eyes to make the stupidest face and says: "I." I writhe with laughter. "But you say so because you have been drinking." "I am sober as the Lord," he says with the stupidest expression again.

Father sober is sitting on the divan on which he sleeps at night, and on which our guests sit when we have guests, and we romp if there are no guests.

Everything is so nice. Father sober. This is a great happiness in itself. You cannot imagine what a happiness this is. And then there will be that *kirovs funeral*. It will be almost as exciting as my birthday. It will be a kind of birthday, but like a huge train which will fill the whole universe with smoke and sparks.

"When—when will that *kirovs funeral* pass?"

12

Today I view the event more soberly. That Kirov was a top ranker, and on December 2, 1934, *Pravda* announced that he had been shot to death at 4:30 P.M. the day before. "The person who fired the shot has been apprehended. His identity is being established."

The *Pravda* issue gave much of its space to the wrath of all working people: " . . . the assassin sent by the enemies of the working class . . . ," "The villainous hand of the enemy . . . ," "To the treacherous shot of the enemy . . . ," and so on.

It is not surprising that all working people began pouring out their wrath on someone whose identity had not yet been established, and on the enemies who had sent him (how could anyone know anything about that if he had not been identified?). For half a century all working people have been pouring out in this way their love or wrath on anyone or anything at a moment's notice. Something else is interesting: it was clear to every reader of *Pravda* (if he cared to know) that someone at the top had known that the event would take place. In a more or less free modern country it is difficult to suppress news. In a society like post-1917 Russia even the news of an all-out war, the Nazi lightning-speed invasion in 1941, was kept secret for about eight hours, and for six hours the radio stations were reporting the peaceful idyll of the paradise on earth while the *soviet* armed forces were minced up, cities bombed, and territory quickly lost. News can be kept secret as long as it is necessary for those in possession-power to digest it and decide how it should be conveyed to the common population if it has to be at all. A minor yet unpleasant trifle like the killing of a top ranker certainly need not be reported except as an obituary a few days later, announcing that his death had just occurred "after a short but grave illness." Instead, not only the news that Kirov was shot at 4:30 P.M. was flashed sprightly on the dot as in the best of democracies, but the forthcoming issue of *Pravda* carried perfectly coordinated reports on *meetings of working people* who had already gathered last night and expressed, one and all, their absolute certainty as to who the unidentified person was morally, psychologically, and politically, who had sent, backed, paid him, what was the purpose of the whole evil design, and how that purpose must be foiled.

A meeting is in progress at the textile factory Worker. The horrible news about the unprecedented villainy at Smolny has evoked among the workers a mixed feeling of sorrow and vengeance. We can hear sobs and shouts: "No mercy for the villain."

The man had not even been identified, according to *Pravda*. But *all working people* already knew everything, including the need to show no mercy and expose more enemies.

Three demands sound again and again in the textile workers' speeches and resolutions:
The *first*: ruthless retribution to be meted out to the villain. The *second*: more alertness and vigilance to expose the enemies of the working class. The *third*: greater economic and military might of our country.

It is only a day later, on December 3, that *Pravda* announced that the man who fired the shot had been identified: Leonid Vasilyevich Nikolayev, born 1904, a former official of the *workers' and peasants' inspection*, and hence a *communist* by implication. That was all the information available for about three weeks, and for about three weeks the absolute certainty of *all working people* of former Russia as well as of *all progressive mankind* as to the meaning of the assassination of a top-ranking *communist* by a medium-ranking *communist* remained as absolute as on the first night. Right on

December 3 the *Pravda* readers learned that "more than three hundred representatives of the literary and theater world of Moscow" had declared in their letter that "in response to the attack of the enemy" (that is, *communists* like Nikolayev?) they would "rally even more closely around"—whom? Certainly not around *communists?* Around whoever was in possession-power. The serf *writer* Sobolev, thriving today as he did then, contributed a personal article writing which he must have become aware of the fact that nothing was known about the event except that the thirty-year-old Nikolayev was evidently a *communist:*

I do not know as yet who and what the killer was, but I do know one thing: whoever he might be, he is backed in some way or other by the moribund class in its last violent death struggle.

The end of his piece expresses no less absolute certainty:

We part with you, comrade Kirov. Thank you for your Bolshevik life. As for your death, the entire old world will be called to account: we will destroy it, and the time is in the offing.

In France, André Malraux was elected to the presidium of a "gigantic meeting," as *Pravda* reported enthusiastically.

The walls are covered by huge posters: They Have Killed Kirov— Let Us Be Vigilant! and We Demand the Expulsion of the White Guards from France!

Finally, in about three weeks, *Pravda* announced the very first and the very last, the absolute, eternal and never-to-be-doubted result of the *investigation* which confirmed all that absolute certainty which *communists* (and *all progressive mankind* in general) had been expressing all over the world ever since the fatal shot rang out, and almost, indeed, before it did: Nikolayev was a *communist,* and the *enemies* who had been behind him were (naturally) also *communists.* Such as Zinoviev or Kamenev, for example, not to mention the smaller fry, too small to mention. How correct all the *communists* and even ordinary *working people* had been throughout those three weeks. "The death of Kirov will cost the enemies dearly!" How true. It did cost *communists* dearly. In Moscow, Vladivostok, or Paris they had known the truth before the *investigation.*

During the *investigation* Nikolayev first "tried to represent his crime as an 'act of personal despair.'" He changed his mind, of course.

But it is noteworthy that the *German press took up exactly the same position* as it reiterated: "Nikolayev acted for personal motives."

Do you understand *Pravda*'s emphasis? The Communist Nikolayev was connected with Nazi Germany too! And with the White Guard émigrés in Belgrade, of course, as is clear from a similar "coincidence": *Pravda* takes the word in quotes, for who will believe it is a coincidence?

Such is the situation with the international connections of the terrorists, fulfilling an assignment of the worst enemies of the Soviet Union, preparing war against it.

But all that worldwide Communist-Nazi–White-Guard conspiracy apart, what was it all about, really?

It was just that great Stalin had decided to get rid of his *junior comrades*. A common case in history: the chieftain wants his retainers to be serfs infinitely devoted to him, while they aspire to be *gesiths* or *comites*, as the Anglo-Saxons called them in the eighth century, which means *comrades* (the corresponding ancient Slav name of a chieftain's retainer means "friend" even today). Their aspiration may come from the fact that a *gesithcund* (a *party*) may have seized a country quite recently and the *gesithcundmen* (*members of the party*) can still remember a time when they were the chieftain's comrades, almost equals, and in fact, their *senior comrade* did act then as the "kindest and gentlest of men, the most considerate to his people," to quote *Beowulf*. The common procedure in this common case is that the kindest and gentlest comrade who came on top kills off his old comrades and promotes instead common serfs from lower strata who will remember that they are only low serfs who owe their elevation to him alone and depend for their life and death entirely on his benevolence. The old comrades for their part may counter his possessiveness the way they did in the England of Magna Carta. However, the trouble was that with inevitable statistical exceptions, *communists* do not know history: they are barbarians who imagine that their crude struggles, ending usually in their own death by torture, are something brand new.

Since 1917 the belief has, naturally, been growing that, say, Ulyanov-Lenin, Bukharin, or Lunacharsky are not only the kindest and gentlest of men (or of Beowulfs?) but are also the greatest of intellectuals.

I am addressing the population of the United States: "Do any of you people know the name of the greatest of thinkers, Comrade Bonosky?" No. Comrade Bonosky is in exactly the same position in the United States as Comrade Ulyanov-Lenin (or Bukharin, Trotsky, Lunacharsky or nearly all other *comrades*) were in Russia before 1917. Comrade Bonosky and Comrade Ulyanov-Lenin wrote for publications which were read by one or two per cent of one per cent of the population and had to be subsidized anyway. In fact, Comrade Ulyanov-Lenin was worse off intellectually than Comrade Bonosky. I hope that at least publications like *The Worker* publish whatever Comrade Bonosky writes. While Ulyanov-Lenin's comrades rejected totally some of his contributions even in their own press. If Ulyanov-Lenin, or Trotsky, or Bukharin, or Lunacharsky could have been a first-rate provincial journalist in Russia like Doroshevich in Odessa (whom Trotsky imitated) he would not perhaps have graced the *party* with his membership. Inversely, should Comrade Bonosky seize with his *gesithcund* the United States, thousands of scholars in hopefully surviving democracies (not to mention the immediately enserfed scholars in the United States) would find the greatest of intellects in every sentence of his. The very name of, say, a newspaper like the New York *Times* would be remembered because once it rejected great Bonosky's 700-word effort. The legend on the glass case, enshrining the effort *in the original* at the Bonosky Museum—right opposite the Bonosky Monument, you know, Bonosky Plaza in Bonosky-City (former New York)—would mention the ill-starred newspaper, and this is only how its name would be known.

Alas, beneath the veneer of *education*, great Lenin or even greater Bonosky remain barbarians, willingly or accidentally ignorant of the social history of mankind and leading themselves and others, should history give them a chance, to Beowulfian self-deification and Beowulfian self-destruction.

Anyway, the kindest and gentlest of Beowulfs, the *senior comrade* Stalin, decided to get rid of his *junior comrades.*

In 1931 a *communist* named Ryutin wrote an underground letter in which he called his *senior comrade* Stalin a Grand Agent-Provocateur. There is no hard evidence to confirm the fact, or rather the hard evidence if any lies in the top secret archives. But then nearly all of the post-1917 history of Russia is in these archives, and therefore I will mention sometimes just rumors, with express stipulation that they are just rumors. Anyway, cases like the Ryutin case or Ryutin rumor were quite likely and indeed inevitable. Naturally, great Stalin demanded that *communists* could be shot in such cases just like anyone else. Until then they could only be *imprisoned.* The distinction was rather technical because anyone could be safely put to death during the *investigation* before the *sentence,* but the *senior comrade* naturally felt that as long as his *junior comrades* had such a privilege even in principle compared with common serfs, they had a certain degree of freedom for themselves, were not *infinitely* devoted to him, could even depose him perhaps, if they rallied all together. Anyway, the *senior comrade* reportedly wanted Ryutin to be *officially* murdered, but the *politburo* reportedly opposed the measure in its desperate courage of mortal fear, for that much they understood: their turn could easily be the next. True, who could say to what extent they opposed him? Perhaps he had naturally wanted them to yell, one and all: "Let us shoot that villain Ryutin, or better still, let us put him to death in the most horrible way!" But instead they just mumbled consent. So they opposed to a certain extent. With the Shakhty engineers it had been the other way around: most of the *politburo* members, including Bukharin, insisted on their *official* extermination because those were simply pests, not *communists.* But in the case of the *communist* Ryutin the top rankers clung to *their* last nominal privilege not to be exterminated as common serfs. It would have been silly for great Stalin to insist on the *official* extermination of Ryutin. What was the use for great Stalin to exterminate that tiny insect Ryutin if his top rankers opposed him? Did not great Stalin know what they had been saying about him in the privacy of their homes or even offices? Eavesdropping had been practiced since 1918, for there had always been enemies all around and inside and everywhere.

The pseudo-tsar-god was displeased. So Ryutin was not bad enough to be openly, *officially* shot! But suppose a *communist*—say, a certain Nikolayev—kills not just some low-ranking *communist* but a top ranker himself? Adulated by *all working people* according to his rank and hence mourned according to the same rank? Will anyone *then* say that the assassin (and all the enemies backing him) can be merely imprisoned?

(The Rohm massacre in Germany had happened in the summer of 1934. So there were people who had the guts to go ahead and do it. The pseudo-tsar-god had named himself Stalin, which comes from the word "steel" in Russian, and that perhaps also confirms that he was a timid, insecure, scared man, and always needed encouragement.)

In other words, a *communist* had to kill a top ranker, and it would not be bad at all if that top ranker were the top ranker Kirov, the *party secretary* at Leningrad, Lenin-City. That Kirov had been very much against the shooting of Ryutin. And Lenin-City had in general always tended to become a kind of feudal principality as opposed to the *center of centers,* Moscow. The top ranker to be killed by a *communist* must be *our dear comrade* Kirov, and great Stalin had only to wait for a good natural chance.

In a relatively prosperous year, 1928, *Pravda* exposed a very low-ranking chief because a campaign was on to expose such chiefs. The chief's role in the hierarchy of possession-power was to certify, in the capacity of a medical orderly, the fitness of those who wanted to work in the asbestos mines of the Uralasbest State Trust. But since it is often practically impossible for a commoner in a serf society to fight against the abuses of local chiefs, the chief deprived young girls of the high privilege of working in asbestos mines (where anti-silicosis measures were unheard-of) unless they *cohabited* with him. And some of them had no choice, according to *Pravda*. That is, it was the choice of dying of hunger immediately or *cohabiting* with the local medical Beowulf and dying of asbestos silicosis in several years. Elsewhere, in the city Shatsk, Ryazan Gubernia, *Pravda* reported a few days later, one tiny chief compelled the local young girls in a similar way, while another tiny chief simply raped a young girl on a train, but both were covered up by the other tiny chiefs.

The trouble is that a *communist* like Nikolayev or a top ranker like Kirov are always surrounded by secretaries, subordinates, chauffeurs and others who gossip. With the chief of the *organs of state security* Beria it was different: the whole country was his harem, but those who knew also knew that they would disappear into torture-death if they ever opened their lips, and even the post-1953 *secret letter* about Beria is still unknown in the West (which shows once again that societies like post-1917 Russia have been impenetrable to Western intelligence). But as a tiny chief would put it: "Comrade Kirov had no possibilities of Comrade Beria." So the rumor had it that Kirov . . . Here the author's pen begins to tremble. How can he dare to apply to the top ranker Kirov the same words that *Pravda* applied to some tiny local chief, some medical orderly at a mine in the Urals? With respect to great Stalin, Kirov was a tiny local serf, or rather, that is what great Stalin wanted him to be. But with respect to those below him, *he* was the local deity, elevated above the tiny wretched medical orderly in the Urals almost to the heaven of possession-power. Therefore, perhaps, Nikolayev's wife was on the contrary happy at the sheer thought that the deity, so possessive and powerful, would condescend even to cast a casual glance at her. But as the rumor had it, Nikolayev did not think so.

Bukharin called great Stalin lazy. But what was the hurry? Let a natural chance come naturally. Let us watch it. Let us cultivate it if nature is not perfect. When a top-ranking comrade is after women, there will always be a lower-ranking comrade who will be offended. A commoner will not perhaps be offended because he is too low. But a *member of the party* of a medium rank is quite likely to have that kind of pride. "*My* wife? Is this ancient Persia or what?" Especially a young man.

According to another apocryph, current among veteran *party members* and hence strictly asexual, Nikolayev was a *member of the party* from early youth, but then found that reality had diverged from the idea. Anyway, he was an official of *workers' and peasants' inspection,* and he was *obliged to* critize the local abuses in his official capacity. This *inspection* actually represents the *center* watching the local abuses, especially those directed against the *center*. The version does not contradict our family legend: surely Kirov's seizure of the *inspector*'s wife was a local abuse the *inspector* was to fight? But the local deity Kirov was too omnipotent for any *inspection* whatsoever and retaliated. And does a medium ranker, even if an *inspector,* stand a dog's chance against such a local deity like Kirov?

Whether the grotesquely unequal struggle had been caused by a wife, or Nikolayev's honesty in his duty of inspection, or both, the case was bound to come under the eye of the *organs of state security.* H'm. So Kirov was hated by a medium ranker named Nikolayev.

A *friend* appeared in Nikolayev's life, and friends are so welcome in such a desperate, indeed hopeless, if not suicidal, struggle against local deities. The *friend* was a phony. But *communism* is so theatrical, contradictory, and deceptive that it is hard for a communist to detect phoniness in a *friend*. Great Lenin never detected phoniness in Russian police agents at his side before 1917. Nor did Trotsky see anything phony in his assassin's belief in *real communism*, that is, the same post-1917 regime, but with the *hero* Trotsky instead of the *villain* Stalin. Nikolayev's *friend* encouraged him to *fight* that Kirov and reported the progress. *Friends* are so bold, inspiring, efficient. You almost faint from fear, you have no strength anymore, you change your mind, but a steady, strong, helpful *friend* is always at your side. Good for you Nikolayev! You *are* a hero. I know that you keep a diary, but me you can trust. Perhaps posterity will see how right you are about Kirov as personifying *party bureaucracy.* And a *friend* may suggest an organization. Awfully secret, of course. And Nikolayev must be its leader, while the *friend* will be his first proselyte, disciple, subordinate. And a *friend* may also hint that he has big pull up there. So that the liquidation of that Kirov will be *really* approved of, and the *friend* will not lie at all in this respect. Why, the friend can prove his big pull up there. See that bodyguard Borisov of Kirov? Tommorow at 4:00 P.M. he won't be there. Want a bet? That Kirov personifies the evil, *party bureaucracy*, or whatever, and there are some up there who secretly sympathize with you, Nikolayev. So your heroism will, indeed, be safe and glorious as heroism should be. They will intercede. On the other hand, if you change your mind or fail, those mighty intercessors up there will give you up in disgust. And surely you have gone too far or far enough. . . . And the *organs of state security* know, of course. And you have challenged the local deity Kirov, who has infinitely bigger pull at the *organs of state security* than you ever had even before your feud. Suppose he learns that you were going to kill him? And yet you *fail* to kill him. Who will then intercede for you?

In short, that Nikolayev had now only to be *operated* through his *friend*. And *after* the event, what would he be able to blab before duly shot? That a certain friend of his had told him that certain people up there would intercede? That would be a lot of fun! His *friend* meant Kamenev and Zinoviev, no doubt!

Of course, great Stalin could have asked some ordinary agent of the *organs of state security* to do the job. But to begin with, that would have been a secret conspiracy against Kirov and hence all *members of the politburo*. And what if the agent would not run the risk and would decide to sell great Stalin to the *politburo* because he felt that they all, rallied together, were still stronger than great Stalin? While that piece of nature Nikolayev was perfectly safe: a hater of Kirov (to hate such a man!), a hater of (the) *party bureaucracy* (aha, of the *party*!), a *communist* babbling about some intercessors up there (aha, that *communist* is not alone—it is a conspiracy running up to some top rankers!).

Do not construct telltale artifices, but, whenever possible, do cultivate nature, take your time, and play only safe, as every party secretary of every rank will tell you confidentially.

Meanwhile, there was a lot of other work to do. A pseudo-tsar-god who wants to attack a certain country outside or a certain population group inside must conciliate the other countries or population groups.

In 1932 *Pravda* published a *decision on legality*. There had been *some violations of legality* (for example, more civilians had been *liquidated* than later in Nazi Germany). Trifling as these *violations of legality* had been (*all progressive mankind* had barely noticed them), even they would be eradicated completely. A new era would begin, an era of inconceivably perfect law, order, and safety. The *decision* instructed all the local chiefs all over the country:

1. To check the incoming complaints against violations of revolutionary legality on the part of the relevant officials and to ensure henceforth the speediest inspection of cases involving such violations. . . .

The *secret instruction* of May 8, 1933, to all the local chiefs stated that henceforth *arrests* could be made only by the *organs of state security* or by ordinary police. Before, every *member of the party* as local chief had been able to *arrest* any commoner and was armed for the purpose. I remember that when I first read what Ulyanov-Lenin had said to the tenth *congress of the party*: a "good communist is at the same time an agent of the cheka" (that is, the *extraordinary commissions*, as the *organs of state security* were called between 1918 and 1922) and as an "agent of the cheka" he must "drag" any suspect to the *organs of state security*, I thought that the word "drag" was just a figure of speech. But no, it had been the literal truth since 1918 and up to May 8, 1933, and great Lenin never parted with his revolver.

Many other leniencies were mentioned in the *secret instruction*, such as:

The regional medical expertise commissions will be empowered to substitute forced labor, instead of the dispatching to camps and settlements, for the disabled, invalids, old men, mothers with babies, and pregnant women, regardless of the term they have been sentenced to.

Before May 8, 1933, they were practically exterminated by any *sentence*: if the toughest male found it quite a strain and problem to survive for a single day, what was the chance of an invalid, old man, baby, pregnant woman? Now they were to serve the term only in forced labor: that is, staying at home at night and doing hard or noxious work by day on prison fare.

Meantime the suitable lower-ranking comrade offended by the top-ranking local Beowulf Kirov was ready, as he could well be expected to be. At 4:30 P.M. on December 1, the *communist* Nikolayev came up from behind *our dear comrade* Kirov, just as *our dear comrade* Kirov was entering his office, and fired the pistol into the back of his head, or this is at least how it happened according to *Pravda*, and *if* the account is true, **the** gesture of

Nikolayev was so professional, indeed, that perhaps Nikolayev had been tipped as to how to proceed—also gratuitously: why not help a good man to take revenge for his wife? Nature needs a bit of cultivation sometimes.

On the other hand, *Pravda* could very well invent all this efficiency. It was said that Nikolayev almost bumbled into Kirov, fired, and fainted: there was no *friend* at his side any longer to hold him up, and he collapsed. Nor had his *friend* been quite accurate: those up there perhaps approved, yet met the news with infinite, if phony, horror, and had him and that bodyguard Borisov and all the others shot, quite *officially*.

Anyway, here I am waiting for the gorgeous *kirovs funeral*, and keep running to the balcony and back. Father sober sits on our versatile divan. He is smiling his hesitant smile. When he thinks, there is in his eyes a funnellike hole through which everything disappears in a vortex. Then he emerges, with that smile of his, and his eyes shine blackly and sometimes flip merrily like the upper tip of a spinning top.

"At least one man has avenged himself," he says. "Perhaps the whole meaning of history is at least for one man to avenge himself."

"You've gone mad," says my mother, dismayed and fluttering about.

"Now there will be a real Jewish pogrom at the top."

"What nonsense. What nonsense. What nonsense," Mother repeats in different keys but in diminuendo. The she reflects in a calm flat voice:

"Neither Kirov nor Nikolayev is Jewish."

But there is a funnellike hole in Father's eyes again.

"Stalin and Hitler will meet."

He says this first with an embarrassed smile, but gaining confidence as he goes: "They will meet and shake hands."

He even nods his head as during a vigorous handshaking.

I am displeased with their insufficiently festive mood, I want them to enjoy the occasion more intensely, and therefore I try to infect them with my excitement.

"It's e-nor-mous! It's thousands of people, *thousands*! All the street till the Lermontov Garden on my right hand—"

"On your left hand," Mother interjects and is immediately sorry because a trifle may deflate my mood as easily as another trifle has built it up. "I mean on the right hand, on Butchers' Street, there are many people, too," she ingratiates to mend the situation.

"Yes, Butchers' is all *black* with people. I am so terribly glad. But when will the *kirovs funeral* pass?"

I do not remember any *kirovs funeral* passing. The corpse of Kirov or at least some corpse existed because great Stalin kissed it as he said the last goodbye to his dear comrade. Perhaps the funeral did pass, but was so insignificant compared with a train passing under the bridge that I forgot it. Yet even if that was an invisible funeral, our street was henceforth to be called not Butchers', but Kirov Thoroughfare.

13

The other door of the nest my mother had made opened on a kind of nomadic camp which had once been a five-room apartment in a six-storied house built in 1914 (pseudo-Moresque style) by a Dutchman named Bloom who had adopted Russian Orthodox Christianity and hence became Russian. It was this five-room apartment that Bloom himself had occupied, while his son lived in St. Petersburg, and his wife mostly in Denmark.

In 1918 Bloom fled because all people who had an income of 500 rubles (about $250) a month or higher, owners of urban realty, shares, or savings worth more than 1,000 rubles (about $500), as well as employees of banks, stockholding companies, or state offices had been announced in December 1917 to be pariahs who ultimately faced death in pogroms or the network of extermination stations, called *extraordinary commissions*.

The pariahs dropped their property as they fled (and Bloom even left gold, jewelry and securities in the safe), and now it could also be divided among the rest of the population.

The Trotskys got a better residence in the Kremlin than the Radeks. Comrade Madame Radek was naturally furious. Her husband was to make *ein Streich* in Germany, whereupon all the world would become *ours*, because Germany was believed to be the key to Europe, and hence to the hemisphere, and hence to the world, and no one would then need Trotsky and his *militarism*, and yet the Trotskys had been given a better residence.

True, Ulyanov-Lenin's Kremlin residence was simply shabby: it had belonged to the Prosecutor of the High Court, with its largest room now assigned for all those top conferences. But how else? Foreigners would visit him: they must see him as a saint, and the Kremlin apartment of the *tsarist* Prosecutor of the High Court is about the limit for a saint. Besides, he had no taste anyway, for what was he? A grubby provincial, compared with Comrade Madame Radek. His country residence (in Hills) had belonged to the Governor of Moscow. The smallest room in this villa had three large plate-glass windows and three cheval glasses. Of course, the balconies and everything. Now what did this grubby provincial do? "Light the fire," he said. There were two fireplaces in the adjoining room. This done, the villa nearly caught fire. He did not know that quite a few fireplaces in *really* nice villas *must* be decorative. Give him not only the tsar's Rolls-Royce but all the tsar's palaces as well, and they all would be simply wasted.

However, the cultivation of Ulyanov-Lenin was not at all something as hopeless as it seemed to Comrade Madame Radek. Ulyanov-Lenin's wife, describing the summer residence in Hills, said that it was "richly furnished and standing in an excellent park." After a touching description of the two of them being un-used to "these rich chambers" (well, Ulyanov-Lenin had not been the Governor of Moscow), she finally sounds reassuring: her Ilyich got used very quickly to these rich chambers:

Hills afterward became Ilyich's regular summer haunt. By that time the place had been properly "mastered" for the purpose of relaxation and work. Ilyich took a liking to the balconies and the big windows.

However, there is one more reason why Ulyanov-Lenin lived more *modestly* than Trotsky, Radek, Zinoviev, and the other top rankers of his. Until and unless the chieftain turns his former *comrades* into serfs depending on his (perhaps inadvertently) raised brow for their life and death, he *has* to be more *modest* than each of them, for if they all rally against him, he may lose overnight his possession-power, including whatever rich chambers he has.

As for Comrade Madame Radek and Comrade Madame Trotsky, their rivalry was natural, because after all the Kremlin was a medieval fortress, not a set of Crimean palaces which one could pick and choose. Just as in the Middle Ages, the owners of the country lived again in a fortress. At school we were taught that such fortresses lost importance with the advent of cannon. *If* an enemy has cannon. Actually, say, the Berlin Wall is quite effective because the population of East Germany has no cannon. The wall all around the Kremlin is many times higher and thicker than the Berlin Wall. The new residents of the Kremlin could henceforth do any harm to the population, while the population could do nothing to them as long as it was atomized into separate individuals forbidden to form any independent group or possess even a hunting knife. So in view of this absolute safety, the residents had to put up with certain limitations on their developed or quickly developing liking of balconies and big plate-glass windows.

But when the loot began to be divided among all the other working people, it was found that there were not enough even decent Kremlin residences or Moscow Governor's villas to go around, and the other working people, like my mother, got whatever remained, in particular, the drawing room of Bloom's apartment on the fifth floor of his house in pseudo-Moresque.

By now our Vitebsk second-guild business, created by generations of Jewish industry and intelligence, had been lost, but instead Mother could get a former drawing room in a former apartment in a city where great Russian writers and poets *walked in the street*, and if you could meet a great Russian writer or poet somewhere in St. Petersburg or Moscow, would you think of some silly trade in some silly woolens in some silly Vitebsk?

> So eternity cometh at last
> To confine us in silence for good

You meet *him* in the street. Like on that photograph with an Apocalyptic sunset in the background, and although three generations know that it is not a sunset but a tablecloth on a table in the background, it still looks like an Apocalyptic sunset. So many people would like to appear backgrounded by an Apocalyptic sunset, but it looks, on the contrary, like a tablecloth. To meet *him*.

> So eternity cometh at last
> To confine us in silence for good

However, my mother was not alone in wishing to live in the capital. Many wanted just the same.

Rents were, especially after the end of the *retreat*, simply named by those in possession-power: they were the new country-scale landlord. It has since been said that the new superlandlord fixes very low rents while "the working people in the capitalist countries are forced to spend 20 to 30 percent of their earnings as rent which is steadily rising." It is true that the new country-scale landlord could well fix very low rents or no rents at all, because after the end of the *retreat*, the superlandlord was also the overall monopoly fixing the prices of all goods and services as well as all wages, and what the owners of the country lost in rents, they could take out in prices and wages twofold, five-fold, or tenfold. So without any loss whatsoever the superland-lord could even abolish rents in order to impress mankind. But mankind seems to have been quite impressed as it is.

In 1928 *Pravda* proudly announced that the "rent of a worker or office employee must not exceed 1.32 rubles per square meter," and since then foreigners have been writing about how fantastically low this rent is in terms of dollars or a percentage of wages. If calculated for Bloom's apartment, this fantastically low rent would exceed about seven times the lowest wages, given by the same *Pravda* article, and would equal the highest. The whole trick was that the *living space* which, say, a doctor had been able to rent at his bourgeois will to reside in bourgeois solitude before 1917, could now be granted as a rare privilege to twenty or thirty or forty happy doctors, engineers or scientists, and so the *rent* thus divided would be quite low for each attached *tenant* (while foreigners would see what they would be allowed to see).

There was one consequence of this *socialism* or superland-lordism. In free-market societies rents react spontaneously to any advantage or disadvantage of any dwelling under the sun. Should all the population desire to live in the capital, the rents in the capital would go up. Here the superlandlord could not and need not notice all such supply-demand fluctuations. Yet the *retreat* was over in 1928, the society began to be rewarded, supplied, and inspected from the *center*, and hence the farther off the *center*, the more pauperized, lawless, and savage life became. So everyone would like to live as near the *center* as possible. But the superlandlord's rents in, say, the best-supplied, safest, re-splendent exhibition for foreigners, Moscow, did not differ essentially from those in some famine-stricken godforsaken hole in the grip of local *private* bandits and local *state* chiefs, those *heroic idealists* in the provinces who usually could not read or write. The result was a countrywide stampede toward at least the local centers, if one could not reach the center of centers, Moscow.

The stampede filled in Moscow everything that had a roof—churches, warehouses, bathrooms—for rents were low, very low indeed. Happy working people would have filled all the streets, too, owing to low rents, but to begin with, they would have frozen to death.

The stampede was, in a way, desirable for the possession-power, because the highest concentration of manpower possible on the available floor space (or as it came to be called, *living* space) meant the cheapest housing of manpower that could be used at the *center*. But there had to be some cities which foreigners could visit, and what would they say back home if they happened to peep inside some living space? Besides, it would be possible to concentrate in Moscow all the offices that would register, inspect, control, say, the growth of every ear of rye, but the actual growing of it would be impossible in Moscow, for who would engage in an occupation so low, not to mention the asphalt so perfect all around?

Frantically, orders began to be barked in the early thirties to bar the stampede until it became as impossible for one born in, say, Minsk to become a Muscovite as it had once been impossible for a kitchen maid's son to become a count of his own will alone. A born Muscovite was henceforth to be a Muscovite unless *sent out* (the word "exiled" means "sent out") by those in possession-power, while if someone born in, and hence *signed in*, that is, attached to, Minsk stayed the night in Moscow of his own will, he was liable to be seized and tried for his crime, though today the criminal period begins after seventy-two hours of his stay.

The population split into territorial castes, in addition to departmental castes, both forming a highly complex territorial-departmental caste serfdom. The word "caste" is freely applied to India today (not unsimilarly, everyone on earth learns of English *medieval customs* today, and some Americans were against aid to Britain during her duel with Nazi Germany because surely a *republic* must not aid a *monarchy, empire, aristocracy*). Never has the word "caste" been applied by the network of propaganda to post-1917 Russia. And hence very few outside intellectuals, officials, experts on Russia have ever used it. For when a social reality emerges—live, raw, vigorous—it remains for a long time unnamed, unperceived, and often, indeed, hidden (especially in the twentieth century, generally assumed to be *advancing* spontaneously through certain overall global *progress*). On the other hand, quaint relics, often of dwindling, transformed, or purely museum social significance compared with their erstwhile essence, are mentioned incessantly because schoolchildren all over the world know their names. A caste society originated in Russia in 1918, and consolidated in the early thirties, not as a quaint historical relic, nor as a misunderstanding to be set aright by some adult children from the *league of nations* or other such *international organizations*, but as a vigorous, ruthless, cardinal reality to exist henceforth perhaps for millennia all over the world when the very names like *league of nations* have long been forgotten.

Since then one has been able to migrate of his own will only *down* the territorial castes. In principle an urban living space can be got of one's own will only by one's *exchange* of his present living space for a living space desired elsewhere, a tremendously hard and complex process which often lasts years and is subject to a host of rules. But even if someone from Minsk had managed to meet all these rules and to tempt some Muscovite to give him some nook or corner in Moscow *in exchange* for the best living space in Minsk, he would never be attached—*signed in*—for residence in Moscow: only an *equivalent-living-space* exchange is permitted in general, and the *exchange* for a *living space* in a higher caste is forbidden in principle.

It is possible in principle to move of your own will only from Moscow to Minsk, from Minsk to Vitebsk, from Vitebsk to a construction site, from there to a slow-death camp, and from there to a quicker-death arrangement.

But not in the opposite direction, not up the castes. If you are born a *peasant* you will die a *peasant*—or in a still lower caste. Of course, in history there have always been ways of wiggling into a higher caste. A young girl in a higher caste may bestow her favors on you, for example (as it happened in India in the *real* caste system several thousand years ago when a commoner could rise to a higher caste "either by his wisdom or prowess or favors of those above"). However, the parents of the higher-caste lady on the same living space may not agree to have you *signed in*, suspecting that you are a low-born adventurer who loves and respects their daughter for her territorial caste, and not for her charm and beauty. In the thirties you could become a *domworker* and live in the living space of the family you served. But finally that had to be banned completely because all the country outside Moscow could thus become domworkers to domwork their way into the higher estates. Only the Muscovites do not need to become their own domworkers, because their territorial caste has been the highest except for some secret areas where, say, weapons are made, *closed health resorts*, and so on.

My mother seized the drawing room of Bloom's apartment soon after Moscow became the capital in 1918, and my father was a Muscovite, and so by either parent I was to belong to the country's highest territorial caste. I was perhaps luckier than if I had been born a count—that Count Lev Tolstoy, for example —exactly a century before.

14

In my youth I mentally reconstructed by eyewitnesses' reports Bloom's house as it had looked before 1917, and if I came home with my friends I would begin to improvise right in the street.

"A cab is drawing up—Mrs. Bloom comes from Denmark for Christmas."

Denmark and *Christmas.* Strange, almost forgotten, words, except for the vague belief that *Denmark* and *Christmas* exist— somewhere. True, our neighbor Anastasia said *Christmas,* but the word was associated with her raw poverty, it was something quite different from the world of Hans Christian Andersen.

"Mrs. Bloom comes from Denmark for Christmas," I say launching on the imaginary life in which one person occupied a *whole* apartment. Mrs. Bloom lives in Denmark like Solveig (though Solveig lived in Norway, strictly speaking, but Norway sounds equally unreal). She also occupies a *whole* apartment, perhaps. To re-create a mode of life so remote, strange, and beautiful, I accompany my tour with the song of Solveig: "A winter will pass, and a spring will go," in German with a *real* accent I have picked up. I can say: *die Schwalbe* or *der Winter* so much in German as to evoke the swallow of the Germanic wistful epic and Brueghel's winter. "A winter will pass, and a spring will go."

Der Winter mag scheiden, der Frühling vergehn.

"This is where the cab stops at the curb, and the cabman unfastens the bearskin and helps Mrs. Bloom out."

Der Winter mag scheiden, der Frühling vergehn.

"The porter opens the heavy dark oaken door—no, not the ocher-pained makeshift. There was a real door. In my childhood. I remember."

As I enter with my friends I make a welcoming gesture. I ignore the broken, dirty, or slushy steps.

"Here is a carpet, of course. Come up to the wall: it's marble under all this dirt."

I conjure up more ghosts as we enter the apartment itself.

"Look first at the walls. White atlas all over. Well, *now* it's the paint of a special color, I call it *socialistique*. Never mind, we have no enemies among our neighbors, so they won't inform on us. The socialistique is peeling off because the roof leaks over the corridor as well. And the floor wobbles a bit too as a result. But otherwise we have a very good corridor. The neighbors at my aunt's hang everything on the walls. A huge wicker box. Any junk that may crash in on you. Our walls are practically empty, especially on the left over there, because the Grekhovs have no junk—no nothing—they have only a huge iron-bound village coffer, but one can only hang it up on railroad rails.

"The atlas on the walls is white, the carpet blue and white, here are leather chairs—where now is that junk in the niche."

Der Winter mag scheiden, der Frühling vergehn.

15

While the owner of the house fled abroad, his son Nikolay Nikolayevich came from St. Petersburg and stayed.

Nikolay Nikolayevich was inclined to suicide. I do not say he had a suicidal mania, because he might have thought that it was trying to live that was a mania. Denmark at peace would have killed him at once, while war, terror, famine, and so on are said to stimulate in those inclined to suicide the mania to live. The worse it was for Russia the better it was for Nikolay Nikolayevich (but between 1922 and 1928 Russia must have proved to be not bad enough for him, because he poisoned himself before I was born).

The nomadic wave drove him into one corner room, though the room had beautiful tall narrow windows which looked from the outside like organ keys. Inside, the sky was unobstructed by the house opposite. Later I was in the room once, and I thought: How can anyone be unhappy if he lives in such a room and sees these windows whenever he likes? Swallows were tracing the sky invisibly, and if a swallow is a dead soul, then the dead souls of Nikolay Nikolayevich were screaming thinly over invisible tracings of their own in their mania to live or to die.

Every grabber of a former bedroom or a former study or any other piece of *living space* (for there were no bedrooms or studies or anything like that any longer, but just living space) was likely to live and to die on the living space thus seized: that was usually his only treasure, his manor, or his eternal serf abode attached to him forever and bequeathed to his children. Though now I have here, on this estate, three houses, I am attached to the same living space under a leaking roof, Bloom's former drawing room, the eternal abode to which I was born. For I have not risen in rank: I am simply a very rich commoner of the territorial caste in which I was born. On the other hand, if I had been born in a lower caste, such as Minsk (not to mention Vitebsk) and my eternal abode had been there, I would not have been entitled to live in *any* house near Moscow no matter how rich I might be.

But while often unable even to *exchange* their eternal abode for an *equivalent* space, its inmates may lose it so easily on so many occasions. If one of them dies, there may be an excess of living space, because there is a quota per inmate, and a family in our neighborhood once concealed the fact that one of them died and kept the corpse as though the tenant were still alive and hence entitled to its share of the living space. Living space has influenced all social relations, and there have been marriages of living space, living-space crimes, and struggles for inches of living space more fierce perhaps than for multi-billion fortunes, chains of casinos, or colonies promising gold, ivory and spices.

Those who grabbed a living space which was a library, right after the legitimate tenants or owners had fled, seized all the property therein, which was henceforth theirs. The Grekhovs got nothing: they rolled in only in the early thirties, and those who had surged into Bloom's library when Nikolay Nikolayevich overcame his mania to live had stripped off a unique tekhin carpet, carried all the books away somewhere, and vandalized everything else, so that the Grekhovs had nothing except those iconlike windows and their own huge village coffer which they kept in the corridor to sit on and sing during holidays.

Grekhov was a smith: the *soviet state emblem*, duly designed by the tsar's designer for his new clients, is a hammer and a sickle, and the hammer was Grekhov's tool. But was Grekhov a proletarian? Highly skilled workers are not proletarians, but the *bourgeois top crust of the working class*. Anyway, one cannot be choosy because he was the only claimant to proletarian pedigree in Bloom's former apartment or perhaps in his whole house. All the others belonged to the middle class, just as before 1918, except that it was all from the provinces: my father was the only old Muscovite.

After the autumn of 1917 some population groups were proclaimed aryan while others non-aryan—with the rest intermediate between them and mostly striving desperately to belong to the aryans rather than the pariahs. The castes kept changing, of course, with aryans yanked down and pariahs elevated, so that in the aryan-pariah patterns of, say, 1918 and, say, 1953, the aryan-pariah poles are quite neatly reversed.

It is only immediately after the autumn of 1917 that low-skilled workers were the most aryan. True, there were not enough Kremlin residences, villas or even partitioned communal-apartment cubicles *at the center* to distribute among them, but initially they could insult, rob, maim or murder with complete impunity any nonaryan unless he was one of those who had been granted individual aryan immunity (as nonaryans useful to those in possession-power).

But already in the early twenties, when a proletarian said to someone who looked like a gentleman: "You, not-yet-knifed bourjuy" (the implication was that some *bourjuys* had not yet been knifed), the standard retort was: "Not so loud: it's not nineteen-eighteen now." The situation of 1918 resembled that of 1953 in this respect as well except that instead of a "non-proletarian element" (very polite and official—as a term in deportation-extermination, for example), "bourgeois" (barely polite—menacing), "bourjuy" (colloquial—in pogroms, for example), and "bourjuin" (vicious) in 1918, there were in 1953 "cosmopolitan" (very polite and official), Jew (barely polite), "jid" (colloquial) and "jidovin" (vicious). However, after the uprising of workers and sailors in Kronstadt in 1921, the aryan-ism of workers began to go down.

Yet in 1928 *Pravda* still wrote:

Those not admitted to institutions of higher learning on the strength of their own documents are trying frantically to get certificates stating the "worker's position" of their fathers ("since 1924 my father has been considered a worker. . . .") in order to pass somehow for the "first category" at least retroactively.

The *Pravda* article also noted that there were still vacancies at the higher schools of Moscow for "natmins." Natmins meant national minorities and, in the present case, mostly Jews, because Kazakhs or Uzbeks were not likely to rush to Moscow in great numbers for higher education. While thousands of ethnic Russians in Moscow had not been admitted for all their zeal to prove they were aryan, there were still vacancies for more Jews, for they were aryan by definition, no matter whether *proletarian* or not.

To obtain the enrollment situation of today it is only necessary to transverse ethnic Jews and ethnic Russians.

In 1928 *Pravda* poked robust fun at those ethnic Russians who had been barred from higher education on account of their pariah origin and tried to impersonate aryans:

However, the "clients" keep coming. Of course, all of them are "workers" and "peasants": this is at least what follows from their applications.

Pay attention to *Pravda*'s magnificent humor: today "Russians" and "Ukrainians" instead of "workers" and "peasants" would bring off the same humorous effect provided the reader knows that the pariahs trying to wiggle in as "Russians" and "Ukrainians" are Jews somewhere in Kiev. *Pravda* did not confine itself to robust humor, though, and insisted that the pariahs had been barred quite correctly.

But it is a rare application that is certified by documents on the applicant's social position, and therefore the class physiognomy of all these masses left outside the higher schools cannot now be established.

Since the Grekhovs were *proletarian* they could have gotten education for their children despite being Russian. But that was the whole trouble: the children of Russian outstanding thinkers, clergymen or tradesmen were not admitted since they were pariahs, while the children of the *proletarian* Grekhovs would have been admitted, but they could not or would not finish even primary school.

By 1928, the Grekhovs had realized that their (quite transitional) aryan origin and essence, their currently blue proletarian blood (only slightly tainted by high skill at that time because the Grekhovs had come from a village shortly before), their ex-

clusive hammer-and-sickleness gave them hardly anything beyond the possibility of becoming hammer-and-sickle snobs, bigots
and scoundrels while sinking after 1928 into a new abyss of
poverty when their wages dipped back to about one-tenth of the
level of 1928, that is, back to 1921.

True, the Grekhovs were honored in a rare way somewhat
later, in 1935. The pseudo-tsar-god named Stalin decided to
crown, though not with any ordinary crown of an ordinary tsar.
He was not just a tsar. He was a super-tsar, a tsar-god, or at
least a pseudo-tsar-god. The oldest extant crown in Europe (dating from the 7th century) weighed less than a pound and contained less than two hundred gems. His supercrown was to weigh
six tons and contain ten thousand gems. Naturally, he could not
wear it on his head, and it was installed on the four Kremlin wall
towers—*over* the pseudo-tsar-god's head, so to speak—in the
form of four fifteen-feet-wide stars, gilded and inlaid with gems:
the "country's best jewelers have cut and finished them," *Pravda*
exalted.

Of course, if arcs of gold had risen from these stars and criss-
crossed somewhere at a high point over the center of the Kremlin,
that would have been a completed crown several miles wide and
as high. But this was unfeasible, and only a poor ephemeral
semblance was realized later by means of the beams of military
searchlights. Still, there was enough food for triumph. When the
tsarist double-headed eagles were removed off those Kremlin
towers in the process, it turned out that they were made—of
ordinary cheap roofing iron! They were put even on show so
that the population could see for themselves how poor, drab, and
insignificant the tsarist empire was. But where did the Grekhovs
come in? The inlaid gems designated, against a background of
gold, a hammer (and a sickle), the hammer on the star over the
St. Nicholas tower being seven feet long! Certainly a great occasion for the smith Grekhov to rejoice. Instead the Grekhovs
were just gloomy, and strangely enough, they were right: a
genius of all fields of human endeavor, great Stalin did not yet
know that gems sparkle only at a short distance—on the finger
of some beauty at a ball, for example, or on an ordinary crown
during an ordinary royal ceremony. But when those gemmed stars
were installed, they refused to sparkle when they were viewed

from below, so far away. Fish scales could have been glued to the stars with exactly the same effect. Naturally, the gemmed stars (and not they alone) were removed and thrown out, and stars of red glass with electric lamps inside were put up instead, *without* either a hammer or a sickle. Merely five-pronged stars signifying the five inhabited continents (both Americas being one continent, we were taught at school).

The Grekhovs could not help seeing that the blue blood proclaimed to be in their veins was thinning out with every year, and they got nothing except a smith's wages of about one-tenth of the level of 1914. They decided to make a real *great october socialist revolution* for their own family only. To this end Anastasia went to work as a janitor in our house after Bloom's janitor had disappeared. Though janitors had been considered very unproletarian before 1917 because they had often reported *bolshevik* activity to police agents, now they were considered certainly more aryan than smiths: they were in a way the lowest-rank chiefs, their brooms like fasces with an ax evidently turned so as to be invisible, but even more dangerous as a result. Besides, Anastasia was a village rowdy, with a vast sense of the sardonic. When a chief concerned with house superintendence would say that another chief said that her plywood cubicle behind the elevator where brooms and shovels had been kept under the tsar was good enough for her family, she would moo: "Uh-huh."

With her elbow akimbo, fist on hip, the other hand grandly on the broom: "May *he* live on *my* living space!" she would bellow as a village smith's wife should, for are not the bellows as proletarian as the hammer? "He would croak in no time!" she would go it hammer and bellows. Then she added in sweet beatitude like a pagan goddess turning to humility after justice has been done: "That would be good."

The janitor knows when living space is vacated, and as soon as the former Bloom's library was empty, after much nomadic vandalism, the Grekhovs moved for the assault (under the sign of a hammer and a broom, or rather a broom and a hammer), the former Bloom's library fell, and a new era began for the Grekhovs. Anastasia immediately dropped her broom-fasces career in order to live for her full pleasure, for she was now a fine lady, with a living space like that.

The Pushkins who moved into Bloom's dining room did not get a thing inside either because their predecessors had also squandered everything except a buffet of carved oak which they gave to us in exchange for something.

We had moved (into Bloom's drawing room) earlier than anyone else, and whatever little remained of Bloom's furniture was finally assembled in our room and was cherished like priceless family relics.

All our property had thus also been gained through robbery aggravated by large-scale murder, and while having taken no part in the crime as such, we accepted our share of the loot. But unlike many others who wasted their share because they did not even understand its value, we would say in awe: *Alexandrine*, and mother would shriek all her life whenever anyone touched the Alexandrine too rudely or tried to put something hot right on the table or dust it with a wet cloth.

Nikolay Nikolayevich must have felt Mother's awe because he gave Mother an Alexandrine three-mirror dressing table. Mother described, always in the same words, how "one fine day" he ("tall, pale, and very handsome, very—oh, he was a *charming* man, charming") arose before her and said: "I want you to take my dressing table. My mother's. Please. I don't need it, believe me." Mother would repeat, to reproduce the exact tone: "Please. I don't need it, believe me," and would press her hand to her heart.

She also said that in his room there had been a grand piano, but he needed it because he played over and over again a Chopin prelude and something else, she forgot which.

"No one wanted to teach him music. He was told that he was tone-deaf, hopeless. But here"—Mother paused to emphasize the irrationality of human passions—"but here—he loved music. His father all but begged on his knees even Rachmaninoff himself to teach his son—and paid enormous sums, enormous. He learned to play one piece. Ha-ha-ha! Chopin prelude. He was always playing it."

16

For me at the age of six or so, the former drawing room in Bloom's apartment was a spacious and beautiful home because my parents had made it and were with me. While the Pushkins could not raise flowers because there was no sun on their side, since their windows faced a dull or just respectable backyard, molten rectangles of it warmed our parquet floor (which our Polya regularly waxed) and set aflame Bloom's Alexandrine mahogany so that its depths went still deeper below the dendritic fire. In the right-hand corner was Father's writing table, also Alexandrine mahogany, with shelves on both sides. There Father would write and sometimes laugh at something he wrote about. Across the room ran a curtain, and behind it stood my bed and Polya's. A spacious beautiful home, a nest, a family manor.

If I longed for company I could go into the corridor which, owing to the Grekhovs' destitution, was empty and hence a very good playground.

The Pushkins had received from their native Ufa some belongings of theirs in a crate so huge that when stood on end it was taller than I was, and we would put it down, making a long table, at which we would either play at grain-proc or just paint.

Pushkin, Nina's father whom we all called Uncle Seryozha, worked at a department called grain-proc. He made stationery for them. Grain-proc is the abbreviation for grain-procurement. Somewhere there lived strange miserable outcasts called *peasants*.

When grain was taken away from them entirely free, it was called *procurement,* grain-procurement, or grain-proc for short. "Is this the grain-proc?" Uncle Seryozha would ask over the phone in an unusually stentorian voice showing his attachment to an important department.

So much grain was grain-proc'ed from those peasants that they would die of hunger, but few Muscovites knew because it was a top military secret, and of those few who knew, few were interested. Since those *peasants* were attached to their own territory, they were of no more concern to Muscovites than the native population of a strange remote country to carefree, holiday-making, prosperous tourists. The grain-proc found it cheaper if Uncle Seryozha wrote stationery for them by hand which they then had duplicated. He had a handwriting as neat as type, a matter of our wonderment. In his typelike hand he would make all kinds of blanks, with inscriptions such as: *procured, total.* Many blanks would be canceled as outdated as soon as they were run off, and Uncle Seryozha would bring home whole batches of them.

We played at grain-proc by very busily filling out all kinds of *real* blanks and passing them to each other with airs of great concern.

But happily for us we could drop grain-proc as soon as it palled. Then I would ask Nina timidly if I could have some practice in crutch walking, but Nina, the regal crutch owner, would say sternly: "Have we decided to paint or haven't we?"

17

The yellow-lit corridor of my eternal abode was present even in my dreams throughout my life.

In some *pre-school children's collective* I saw a postcard. An adult was showing it, but there was a knot of children, and as in every *collective* I was with those who could not get to the *center* —to the source of supply of some scarcity—and only heard: Nesterov, flyer Nesterov in a crash, and we shouted in despair that we could not see it, that we could not get in, until the adult held up the postcard. Nesterov crashed at the dawn of aviation as he attempted to loop the loop—could it be a snapshot? He was lying flat on his back, unable to extricate his hands pinned backward to the wings, or so I imagined it. In one of my dreams I saw Nina like the flyer falling, her arms pinned to her crutches, down, down, down, because our corridor would turn to a crate-like well, and down she was falling with her crutches, and then I dreamed about the dragonflies I had put into a jar and they struggled and broke their wings, and then it got mixed with the explorer Amundsen who had perished in a plane all alone somewhere over a pole, and still later as a young man I had a recurrent dream of war with a civilization which we called in our youth the West as incarnation of certain nobility, old-fashioned and therefore pathetic and therefore doomed and therefore beautiful, with its belief that one life, a life, matters, and indeed is even more worth defending if it is the life of a child, or a woman, or a defenseless lonely man. Naturally, the West could not in my dream defend itself against *our* ground forces, and relied on aviation. But something went wrong, and in despair —in the last lonely despair, like that of the explorer Amundsen —planes of the West crashed in the streets of Moscow uselessly. They wanted to hit *government* cars, but they missed them and crashed, so that when I looked down some side street they were like the broken dragonflies in my jar, and as a plane crashed near me, it was Nesterov all over again, only it was not Nesterov but Nickolay Nikolayevich with the very aristocratic face of an artist I had studied with, and also my uncle Valentin.

Uncle Valentin looked rather like actors who play effete White Guards. Only handsome actors usually play them, but there is often something unpleasant about their faces, while there was nothing unpleasant about Uncle Valentin's face, and the more he drank the more pale, sublime, and handsome his face became. As though it burned in alcohol.

> All people know, all people know:
> Life is no gain,
> And put a pistol to the temple
> Again and again.

Uncle Valentin would not say this, of course, but instead he said to my father in a low calm voice: "Andrey, I cannot drink any more."

But then I knew the pilot was not Uncle Valentin, but the only Britisher whom I had spoken with so far and who was the handsomest man I had ever seen, though he was half-Lettish, as often happens with purest incarnations of national beauty. Blood was streaming down his perfectly immobile Apollonian face, he was helpless, with his arms pinned backwards to the wings. A leather-coated man got out of the car which the plane had just missed (my father had worn such a coat in the Urals when he taught literature to the thieves), and we were approaching the flyer from two opposite sides.

Now I recognized the leather-coated man.

The ship *Cheluskin* had started off on a voyage along the *great northern route,* and it was a great worldwide triumph because never had a passenger ship successfully plied that route.

Then the ship was, predictably enough, crushed by ice floes, and it was an even greater worldwide triumph because never had the passengers of a ship shown such *boundless heroism* as these *soviet* passengers who escaped, with hardly any losses to speak of, onto an ice floe where they lived as happily as anywhere else under their own, dear possession-power. The worldwide triumph was so great that it became yet another festival in Moscow, and almost life-size mockup *Cheluskins* were built in the parks. At night they were all illuminated by lines of electric bulbs, but youngsters unscrewed them because a bulb cost a lot of money. As I walked with Polya in our nearest park, we passed a mockup *Cheluskin* way off on the grass and saw a boy jumping on another's shoulder and unscrewing a bulb. But there were two men inside the ship waiting. They suddenly appeared as from a trap, as from behind a theater stage wing, as from a door in a dream. One of them wore a leather coat. I only remember the low whine of the boy who saw them first.

In my dream I heard the leather-coated man saying to the airman in a quiet, matter-of-fact voice: "You will be shot." And when the flyer's face was very near I saw that he was not Apollonically calm but actually sobbing in a terrible, noiseless way. I kept firing a standard officer revolver TT-38 at the man in a leather coat, and knew I was missing and knew he was missing or perhaps I was already dead.

18

"Oh, you will go to a children's garden!" my mother announced in a happy sopranino register. The German word *kindergarten*—which actually means no more than a "place for raising children," just as an "oyster garden" means in English no more than a "place for raising oysters"—had been translated into Russian as *children's garden*.

"Would you like to go to a *children's garden?*"

I could be persuaded to do anything with the promise of some flowers—to be illegally plucked in a park, or procured in some other way. I didn't know that flowers could simply be bought, and perhaps they couldn't be at that time, or perhaps even my generous parents could not afford such extravagance. Later I was told that flowers are beautiful in order to attract bees, an explanation which reminds me of Paracelsus' recipe, in his *De Generatione Rerum Naturae*, for raising a homunculus as easily as one can raise an oyster. There is a time to know everything down to the raising of a homunculus. There is a time not to know even why flowers are beautiful, and that was the time I was in, and therefore a flower was to me like knowing nothing and then—a flower.

I was sure that a children's garden is, by definition, a garden where children are allowed to pluck flowers, and these flowers are children's, that is, while large field ox-eyes are adult flowers, garden daisies are children's ox-eyes.

When we arrived I did not ask: "But where is the children's

garden?" A stark reality already filled everything: "This is it. That cold hard blue wall. There is no children's garden. It is just a pretty name. This is what they call it. My God, what a trap. And my mother and father are away. I have bartered them for a pretty name which just does not mean anything. They call that cold hard blue wall a *children's garden*. A sinister sense of humor they must have."

I should have noticed that the blue of the wall was oil paint. Only a very rich *children's collective* could afford oil paint. But such class distinctions were of no interest to me: the blue of the wall was as cold and hard as could be—it glistened, it was relentless, boring, perhaps causing headache.

Our bedclothes had not arrived with us, and so each of us was issued two sheets of glossy colored desk paper, one to sleep on and the other to cover with.

My mother would always take off my bed sheets and shake them out before sleep because otherwise there might be *crumbs* which might spoil the whole transcendent bliss of curling up and going to sleep. Once she was on duty at her *service*, and Father said: "What crumbs? I'll sweep them with my hand." I was shocked but I somehow hoped he could do it that way as well as Mother did by the more complicated process of shaking out. It didn't work, of course, it was absurd to suppose that crumbs could be removed by a procedure so simplistic, and I felt how inadequate Father was without her.

True, he was indispensable in his own way. When I was washing my face with a despondent motherless heart in our communal kitchen before going to bed, he splashed some water on me. I retaliated, and finally we were racing all over the communal kitchen, seizing whatever water our neighbors had stored in dippers, pans, and other utensils because there was no running water sometimes, and toppling them on each other. Mother would have wailed and screamed, of course. But now we enjoyed our reckless if sad motherless freedom, because the neighbors crawled out uncertainly and simply watched in awe as Father half-stopped the faucet with his finger to keep me off with an umbrella-like spout, and the water flooded inch-deep our floor, and I dipped water from a pail and hit Father with limpid protean missiles.

However, when the excitement was gone and I had to go to

bed, a loneliness crept over my heart again—and whoever heard of sleeping without your bed sheets properly shaken out?

Now there were no bed sheets at all. We slept on rustling desk paper, but everyone who enters a greater degree of unfreedom in an infinite series of degrees of unfreedom must realize at once that he is in a new life, and no comparison with his former life is possible.

If the morning weather was unfit for a walk, we would scissor out the cherries printed on one side of a picture book and paste them on the other. It didn't matter what we did. It was all exercise. They told us and we did it.

The next morning *she* would examine our books.

She also read us a story about a toad, and when she read about the toad putting out her tongue to catch a midge, she put out her tongue. Freezing, we were looking at her tongue, two rows of endless knobs, a furrow in the middle running into a horrible abyss.

Now we knew: *she* was the toad.

We stood in line, each of us pressing his book to his body and whispering the last prayer for the cherries not to come off. But the starch paste was not made anew every day. Some water was added instead. This is why the cherries would not stick.

The huge toad many times larger than ourselves, human midges, checked the cherries; she wanted us to learn how to paste well because that would stand us in good stead in *life*.

Was she to blame that she was a toad? Perhaps she was, essentially—well, Deanna Durbin, that American movie star who haunted many Russians even when few American movie critics remembered the name, that Deanna Durbin whom one of my uncles, a straw-haired blue-eyed village teacher, saw in a movie. He said that there were no such movie actresses in our country, was denounced, but was sentenced to only five years, though he had also played chess with a *trotskyite*. Perhaps she was Deanna Durbin, only metamorphosed into a toad by evil witchcraft as happens so often in fairy tales. The trouble is that movie stars will not work as kindergarten personnel unless they have been metamorphosed by evil witchcraft.

But even if they do, how can one be sure that a six-year-old will like a certain movie star? Perhaps because I was a weakling, I liked generous shoulders which are called in Russian tsarish, so that a Russian genius of joy in verse did not miss the chance to say: the tsardom of your shoulders. The tsardom of your shoulders, the spreading tree of your blood vessels—your portal vein welling powerfully under your whiteness, and, of course, your plaits, each ending in a bunch of tassels of hair of all kinds, some almost prickly, others ticklish, and still others—oh, so soft.

Anyway, Deanna Durbin, metamorphosed into a huge toad, was taking my picture book.

Considering the event scientifically, the cherries held on owing to friction, provided she took the book slowly enough and at a moderate angle. But the more sharply she pulled and the steeper the angle the more cherries poured down. And the more stupendous her sarcasm was.

"E-e-e-h," she would say, imitating the disastrous downpour of cherries, "it never rains but it pours."

This seemed to us the highest peak of sarcastic descriptiveness. We didn't know that "it never rains but it pours" is a set expression hundreds of years old. We thought she invented it on the spot, so enormously witty, scathing, devastating, and if we could have treated all this calmly, as observant outsiders, we would probably have said: "What a pity that such a gigantic mind is wasted on insignificant midges."

Not everyone felt like me, though. There must have been children unloved or unloving or parentless—orphaned by nature, circumstances, their own parents, or themselves.

Once I lost my galoshes and stood alone crying. Not because I was sorry for my galoshes. All my life I have been losing things, but never was sorry—perhaps because my father was never sorry. As a matter of fact, in collective captivities I dropped many things deliberately, I do not know why. Perhaps I felt that I lived in a society where man had better not be encumbered by any property. I was crying because someone in charge was quite agitated by the loss and said something unkind to me. Not even rude. Just unkind.

One of the boys saw me and said with sympathy: "Afraid they'll send you home?"

I do not remember any remark in my life that showed me in a more sudden flash how different human beings and their lives are.

But there were others: lost souls like myself.

Nothing mattered for us any longer, whether children's daisies or a huge toad.

As in every *children's collective* of this kind, the children established in microcosm an infantile or prehistoric political order as primitive as that established in Russia in the autumn of 1917, but we, lost souls, were not interested in the supremacy of a boy who became the chieftain because he was overage and wore huge caulked shoes.

We, lost souls, would wander or rather float to each other, very close, eye to eye, as adults hardly ever do, and eye to eye it was because one does not see two eyes in this way but only one eye. We said nothing, there was nothing to be said, we were gazing into each other, anguish into anguish. The anguish was of the color of old family photographs, and finest tobacco filaments were trembling within.

I say anguish because I can find no better word for the Russian word *toská*, which combines a vague yet acute yearning with drilling boredom, emptiness, tearful loneliness, and nostalgia—the yearning for a yearning, as someone defined the word in a West European language.

Sometimes I would try to hearten the other anguish because it was my anguish, but only *there,* and the other anguish would try to hearten mine.

The worst began with the coming of the first quavering *shaggies* in the sky.

We were looking up: here they were—the *shaggies*. The universe was busy producing *toská*.

We floated to each other. We gazed into each other. And into the sky.

"Here it begins."

Something stretched us like evening shadows. *Toská*—oh, what a *toská*.

"But we'll have supper yet," the other anguish heartened up. "We'll still get the little darling hot meat."

When not eye to eye, the other anguish was a boy of my age looking like a piglet, but with huge iconlike eyes, and the icon-eyed piglet jumped on one leg, head tilted, and repeated: "We'll still get the little darling hot meat."

"The food is very good there. Very good," our parents must have said. "Have you heard how much it costs for one child? I mean the whole upkeep? Vysotskaya told us. Seven times as much as in an ordinary kindergarten not far from them. My dear, we pay a fraction of the cost. They have one service personnel unit for every two children, can you imagine? And the food is very good, very good."

Our *kindergarten* differed from most *kindergartens* for common Muscovites (not to mention any lower territorial estates) perhaps much more than Eton differed from parish orphanages in the day of Dickens. If we had been hungry it would have been still worse. Food substitutes for love—to some extent. It cheers, consoles, makes one even somewhat drunk. "The situation is not so disastrous," an orphan may say after a hearty meal. "Mother and Father may yet reappear. Anything may happen."

"The food is very good there," our parents said. "Very good."

The very good food we took as their flesh and blood. To be able to face the nothingness called night.

Lost souls, we kept sending postcards to our parents, and I wrote only two words: "Boredom, *toská*," but our parents were so far away, as if on a distant star, that they could not decode our human language. "The food is very good there," they said. "Very good, very good."

Why am I alone in a forest? I must have fallen behind because the clay is slippery after yesterday's rain, it is going to rain again, and the universe must already be oozing its *toská*, but the aspen trees are holding it back and the sky between them is still luminous. I know that grownups wring their hands in despair. I want to wring my hands in despair. The aspen trees are like eyelashes. I am gazing into the luminous anguish and keep gazing until I am no more, and Mother never stood by the steamboat railing, the sun was never dazzling her eyes, my bare feet never trod the worn boards of the bridge, and Father never walked somewhere near, there was never anything, the sky is not alive, this is just a rain, the rain is not alive, the aspen trees are not alive, the clay is not alive. And the aspen trees moved and whispered aloud, all at once, and one of them shrugged and gave me a bleary white look: can't you see that everything is dead?

I was the messenger of a new salvation among the lost souls. We are all dead, I heartened them; there is nothing alive, I whispered into the anguish eye to eye.

"Ma is not alive?" the anguish almost smiled at the absurdity of the new faith.

The eye was different from the sky between the aspen trees, the eye was alive like Ma, there was some warm flickering light in it, and the eyelashes went rat-tat.

"Yes, Ma is alive." Our lights grew warmer together, we had one eye, we were one anguish, one warmth, one life.

"Ma is not alive!" The absurdity of it almost moved us to mirth: tiny sparks even ran in finest filaments.

We parted or rather floated apart, our anguish divided into two, and each anguish became a wandering soul again, and so I kept wandering until I met someone huge, in white overalls, washing the floor, and when she looked up I saw her mouth was of the color of brick in the sun.

I watched her washing the floor. I had to do what lessened the anguish, and watching her lessened the anguish, perhaps because she washed the floor in rhythm.

"Do you have a mother?" she asked in keeping with the floor-washing rhythm.

I trembled. How did she know? Oh, what luck I'd met her.

"Yes," I said, my eyes shut. Ma stood by the steamboat railing. The sun was dazzling her.

I was waiting for a new miracle.

"And a father?"

"Yes!" I said. The surface of some boards of the bridge had been turned by weather into almost a carpet of dry fiber. I could not see Father, because I studied the boards as I stepped on them, but he was near.

"That's good," she concluded. I was so glad I had found her. That's good. The heart aching had nearly passed. That's good.

"And a grandfather and grandmother?"

Now I wanted to repay her for her omniscient love for me. I knew that what I was going to say would be terribly funny just as an actor knows: here is when a laugh comes. That would be my pay for her omniscient love for me, because nothing can be had for nothing, and perhaps my pay would be enough for some more of her omniscient love for me in the future.

I looked at the ceiling, letting my eyes roam absent-mindedly. "A grandmother and grandfather?"

The trick was to play complete indifference—almost suppressing a yawn.

"I really don't know where they are. They must've croaked."

I had been expecting her to smile, I had been prepared to exert all the creative powers of my soul to make her smile, but instead she put her forehead on her hands on top of the stick of her floor brush to laugh to her heart's content. She raised her crimsoned face and wiped away tears, her lips soaked like bricks after a rain.

Now whenever she saw me she would first call up whomever she could from among the *technical personnel,* as cleaning women came to be called. She did not know I was acting, and I knew that this was art: that she should not know.

"How can you say this about your grandfather and grandmother?" she would ask after her bout of mirth was over, her face wearing the expression the spectators under Alexey the Quietest had probably had as they strode to a bathhouse because a bathhouse after a theater was obligatory to wash away the theatrical sin.

What frightened me was that each time she said this sooner than before: her bathhouse piety set in earlier each time, and I was thinking of that performance when she would not laugh at all but would immediately pity my grandfather or grandmother.

How difficult happiness is. How impossible to produce collectively even for such insignificant midges. How difficult it is to raise homunculi or children or even perhaps oysters. Here were the Toad and the Daw wanting us to drink after a walk, not just boiled water, but wonderful cranberry water: we come back from a walk, and here you are—wonderful cranberry water.

It was certainly an additional effort for them. No law or rule of man-inflicted orphanhood made it binding on them to give us cranberry water instead of just boiled water. Cranberry water was their gratuitous contribution to our happiness, and if five or ten midges become thirsty after a walk, three jars of cranberry water are more than enough.

But stupidly, some of us would get thirsty as soon as we left for a walk, or perhaps we imagined we were thirsty, because we remembered the cranberry water shortage the day before, and we told others we were thirsty, which made them also thirsty, and finally our walk was a cry for the wonderful cranberry water, since we were not allowed to drink raw water, and there was no boiled water either because the wonderful cranberry water had been prepared instead.

Naturally, we could not come back earlier than we should, and we kept inflaming each other by tales of thirst and thirst quenching, we would suck in air to cool the tongue—oh, would we *ever* get back?

An adult may alienate his sensation of thirst from his personality at least for a couple of hours. But at that age each of us was nothing but a feeling of thirst, and we did not know how long a couple of hours lasts and how it differs from a century or eternity.

At last. The three jars. A small glass in everyone's hand.

A queue. All are rushing in. All except Lutik, of course.

Lutik is past everything. He is past even thirst. He will walk by the wall, back and forth, back and forth.

Some seem to force themselves to drink. But who can be sure they are not thirsty and are drinking simply because water, that is wonderful cranberry water—has become such a crazily coveted scarcity? Perhaps they are simply sensible, believing that once you've got your little glass of precious moisture, consume it rationally, swallowing it carefully and at the longest intervals possible.

As for the order of the line, neither the Toad nor the Daw could establish it, and according to the infantile order, the chieftain may get everything and a tribesman nothing, and therefore the boy who was the chieftain had drunk three glasses under the protection of his huge caulked shoes while others who had not yet drunk even their first glass, were screaming to say that it was not fair, but they did not know the word "fair" and their plea was indistinct like the screaming of birds, and the supplicating glasses circled frantically near the mountainlike Toad or craglike Daw, while others sat way off, weeping, and still others believed: be content with what little you have and you will be happy, and having got finally their first glass they savored it like a kiss, without the vain thought of a second glass, and only Lutik kept pacing as always by the wall, back and forth, back and forth, and out of respect for his fierce pride he was asked individually whether he was thirsty. He halted: "No." And again back and forth, back and forth.

This is how this life is: there must be thirst, and we should struggle for each little glass of wonderful cranberry water, but worse than that, there must be *toská*, oh, what a *toská*!

Just as no one knows why suddenly the sun.

The day had been all bleakness, and toward evening the midges danced madly: sun, sun.

As I am writing this I do not want to know what Paracelsus knew, I want to know nothing, and then suddenly—the sun. Madly dancing midges know nothing about the sun, and as I am writing this I want to know nothing but simply: sun, sun.

Where did she come from? How had her smile appeared, and her off-the-shoulder sarafan of the color of an evening sun when it is like honey, and above the sarafan the generous tsardom of summer, or perhaps it was all her smile but I never looked so as not to go blind.

"Oh, my poor little sparrows," she said. We were wearing brown smocks. In gray smocks we would have looked like patients or convicts, but in brown smocks I hope we looked like sparrows.

Alexandra Pavlovna, Tsarina Alexandra, what a beautiful name, a tall palace gate, may I just press my forehead against the wrought-iron scrolls? And Pavlovna is a round handrail of smooth warm wood. I'll just put my hand on it, I'll enter thy tsardom, the sun is for all, even for the tiniest midge.

19

I do not know whether Alexandra Pavlovna's tsarish shoulders were part of nature, but anyway, in my collective summers I can recall no other nature. If I try, as one tries to recall the telephone number of a person he does not really want to call up, I recall that in some later collective summers there was a sky—there were masts painted white and blue, backgrounded by a sky, but the sky seemed to be a photograph, perhaps a good three-dimensional color photograph or even a mockup with electric lighting, but not a live sky.

As one who grew up in a society in which the only allowed and obligatory religion did not preach God, fortunately—for me and for God—I never associated the sky with the word God in childhood or adolescence, but whether the sky was alive or not was crucial for my mood. Mother, who believed that God was something an old peasant woman imagined because she had not presented a doctorate in neurology, collected in her youth books on French art and recalled that when Corot died he said: "I think I see a perfectly rose sky." This did not contradict in her mind her doctorate in neurology. "Look—look," she would say. "No—not there, but there, above those trees."

It is from this family worship of the sky that there stemmed in my adolescence a more esoteric, lonelier, sadder sky-sensitivity even more essential for my happiness. If the sky was not alive, then everything was made from more or less realistic materials with a satisfactory verisimilitude, so that when one sees the sky one thinks, bored, empty, with a kind of transfixing sobriety: "This is the sky," and then if one is an adult, one grabs at vodka, cocaine, or something, but if one is a child, one just suffers on because one takes for granted the transfixing sobriety of life.

Skyless—dead, never lived, were my collective summers, and if those who had invented them had simultaneously invented immortality (for full measure), I would have asked them to take away their dead immortality and just leave me my two lives—two summers, or rather one summer was just a summer month and the other a full summer, but it doesn't matter because both were lifelong.

After some hard bargaining with my parents I agreed that I would suffer through the rest of the next summer in the *kindergarten* if I spent one summer month with them.

Quite often parents try (sometimes quite desperately) to put their children into *nurseries, kindergartens, boarding schools* of all kinds, including *military schools,* or simply orphanages called *children's homes,* because they have no money to keep them: except for the highest privileged ranks, the possession-power has been squeezing its human property dry since 1928, spending a tiny fraction of the money thus squeezed on collective *social benefits* which are *free of charge* or at *a big discount.* All *social benefits* were proclaimed as of 1964 to cost monthly per toiler about 30 rubles (the sum which bought in 1964 half of one Italian $1.40 "bologna raincoat"). While making this exultant, ubiquitous (and certainly not understated) declaration, the network of propaganda also proclaimed that these *benefits* increased the *average wages* by thirty-five percent. Not an inordinate exaggeration, perhaps: since the monthly pay of a common rank-and-file doctor, engineer or scientist in Moscow bought two $1.40 raincoats, the *social benefits* all costing half of a $1.40 raincoat could well increase the *average wages* in cash by thirty-five percent.

In the mid-sixties the network of propaganda thought it useful to publish some common monstrous delusions of the population in order to crush them by its entire vast collective intellect. One such monstrous delusion was published as follows:

However, once I heard this opinion from my friend. He alleged that the free-benefit funds are created by deductions from our pay, and thus, if we do use something free of charge, this is simply because we have paid for it. "Is this expedient?" the comrade asked. "Is it not better to make no deductions at all and let everyone spend his money according to his needs and tastes?"

What a monstrous heresy. When majorities in many West European countries want free-of-charge benefits (at the expense of those who are richer than they?), in Russia the revulsion for such benefits is so strong that the network of propaganda had to divulge it to be able to deal with the monstrous heresy in its columns.

Poor monstrously deluded comrade. The trouble is that the same issue of *Izvestia* proudly announced that the *average cost* of one day's stay in hospital was currently five to six rubles. Even according to the *official rate of exchange*, favoring the ruble as much as those in possession-power wish, the sum equalled less than $7, but this is plenty, because as of that date a doctor for commoners earned in a month a sum which bought two $1.40 "bologna raincoats"! Only collective *free-of-charge bene-fits (of socialism)* can cost those in possession-power so little, and yet allow them an easy, invisible, and infinite variation of the *average cost* (say, $7 as *average cost* of one day's stay in hospital) so that one rank or caste attached to certain hospitals could have *free* the world's best (and the world's most expensive) medical treatment, and another, attached to other *hospitals*, would be doomed to *free* extinction, while the average cost would remain very low despite inefficiency, embezzlement and lethargy growing usually apace with the distance from the *center* of supply, instruction and inspection, and from the apex of rank in each *peripheral* territory.

In *Treasures of Art*, a huge folio we proudly owned, there was Giorgione's *Judgment of Solomon*. Originally Mother had to explain its meaning: when the motherhood of a child was disputed between two women a little less than three thousand years ago, the wise Solomon said: "Let us cut the disputed child into two." One of the women cried: "Oh no—rather give it to her!" Thus the wise Solomon knew that she was the mother.

Every year millions of mothers rather give their children to *them* from babyhood—mostly because they are the mothers.

Her child will not be hers but *theirs*, it will lose its family identity—its resemblance to its parents, its home, its origin, and for
about half of the population—its mother tongue, yet it will live
and perhaps get into a higher estate by territory or department—
it will live, and is not this what the mother wanted a little less
than three thousand years ago? Besides, *both* parents have to work
to survive, and finally, unless their child is in a *kindergarten* they
cannot use *social benefits* like a *house of rest* during their vacation because no children are admitted to a *house of rest*: there
are no family rooms, but only bedrooms for adult men and those
for adult women: a proper collective.

All *social benefits* are ranked in cost according to numberless
castes by territory and department and numberless classes within
each caste, and when the *kindergarten* is of a very high rank, as
the one in which I was, there is an additional temptation: "The
food is very good there, very good."

The American Quaker Alexander Wicksteed wrote that as a
"very sane doctor with wide experience" had told him, "at a conservative estimate 80 percent of the population of Moscow were
seriously tuberculous." This did not prevent Dr. Wicksteed from
being a *friend of the soviet union*. Evidently, all that is important
is that *you* and *your* family should not be seriously tuberculous.
Besides, when one has said since 1919 that he is a *friend of the
soviet union, the soviet people* or *the russian people*, one has
meant that he is a friend of the upper caste, of the collective
serf owners, and surely they are not tuberculous.

I was found to be tubercular, too, and good food was very
important—good food and fresh air—and my mother thought
it would be better for me to be *theirs* and healthy than *hers* and
soon dying of consumption.

I was simply told that there was no money, an adequate explanation which I knew so well. It was up to me to enter into a deal:
I was to sell myself for two months of collective captivity named
the *kindergarten* in order to buy one summer month with my
mother and father.

Long before, when I had been very little if seen from the vantage point of my six-year-oldness, I had lived with my mother out
in the country. I did not remember very much except that once
she had promised to take me in a boat across a river.

We went to the river. And *saw* it. I had never seen a river before. Could we really get into something Mother called a *boat* and *glide* over the delight she called a river ("Don't be afraid: it's water just as from a tap or in a pool")? We would not only look at that delight, but we would glide over it, an impossible translation of an exquisite and daring dream into reality.

And the other bank was all ox-eye daisies.

No, I did not go into the two-months-of-agony-for-one-month-of-bliss deal blindly.

"Will there be a river?" I asked, wishing to sell my self-incarceration for a sterling value.

"Yes," sang Mother. "And you will bathe in it."

In Russian, to *take a bath* (in a bathroom) and *bathe* (in a river) have entirely dissimilar roots. I had never taken a bath in a bathroom either, because the bathroom was for the entire nomadic camp, and so we never used it for baths. I simply stood in it and was *washed* with water heated on a gas range in the kitchen and brought over in pails, dippers, and saucepans. All that was quite enjoyable and vastly entertaining, but it had nothing to do with bathing in the sense: bathing in a river.

Bathing in a river. Not just gliding over that delight. Vaguely, remotely I could imagine that: *bathing in a river*.

"All right," I said, subdued by the obviously enormous price.

We were to spend the month in a former estate called Odoyevo. The estate, just as our city abode, had been gained by armed robbery, and I have since read so many variations on how the owners were robbed and slaughtered or banished that today it is for me like a haunted castle for a believer in ghosts. But I did not know then what had happened before I was born, and I simply saw a white stone house with a flagstoned-floor terrace. There were swallows' nests at the eaves.

Had the Odoyevo estate been converted into a *house of rest?* And if it had been, how could I go there with my mother and father? But thanks to some lucky star, the *house of rest* for writers was not a *house of rest* at all: it was a *house of creativity*, and that made all the difference in the world, because in the *house of creativity* a writer could get a *separate* room and hence take his child along with him and the child's mother, too. I mean my mother, see? Oh, what had I done to deserve such unheard-of luck?

20

Unheard-of luck it was, because I was not born under Sagittarius, the archer—I was born under the *organization of the country's first machine and tractor station on the shevchenko state farm, odessa region.* Or if you want another star of the same constellation: *the commissioning of moscow elektrozavod, the firstborn of soviet electric machine building.* This is the cliché *Pravda* used then, in 1928: the *firstborn of soviet electric machine building,* and as I leaf now through the latest *textbook of history* the cliché is the same as though a huge machine had since been writing all this for another huge machine to read it, or perhaps all this had been taken from the memory store of some age-old and ageless universe-machine because the pages almost crumble at a touch as from old age (though actually it is just too much sawdust in the paper).

The *district maternity ward* where I was born was in Sokolniki, way beyond that terminal from which the *kirovs funeral* was to come, near that park in which two boys tried to steal an electric bulb from the Cheluskin mockup, and Father flagged down a cabbie to take Mother and me home. Not all at once was all private activity for private people wiped out: it was only by the mid-thirties that private entrepreneurs known as cabbies were swept out, along with Das Kapital of their horses and buggies, and since a decade or two was to pass before taxis could be supplied in quantities even to Moscow to give it a supermodern air, little individual private traffic was possible even in Moscow. But in the autumn of 1928 Father just flagged down a cabbie like that, and off we rolled, which I can imagine so well because four years later we still could take a cabbie, though with more difficulty. I sat in the open back seat on black leather, shielded by a huge half-umbrella-like canopy. And here we rolled smoothly, lightly, across Moscow over the cobbled streets. Here we went and here we came.

But the elevator to the fifth floor did not work.

For about ten years after the autumn of 1917, the janitor whom Bloom had once employed looked after the elevator on his own, for nothing, perhaps in the vague hope that the Blooms would come back (to join the suicidal Nikolay Nikolayevich) and would pay him again the insanely extravagant seventy-five rubles a month, plus leather coat, holiday bonuses, and all that. The janitor could not believe in the stability of the unreal society, and for about ten years he had been on a one-man strike against the new regime—only not by a work stoppage: on the contrary, he worked free in order to keep his part of the old regime going even if everything else had collapsed. "But just before your birth," Mother exclaimed excitedly to show the unpredictable intertwining of destinies, "they evicted him or something—as a nonproletarian element."

That gave Anastasia Grekhov the broom-fasces chance of her life, but the elevator stopped. When Ulyanov-Lenin still lived in Smolny of Petrograd-Petersburg, he wanted to start the elevator there. But no stupendous exertion of his dialectical intellect could start it. Evidently to create a new society and a new man is much easier than to start an elevator. Then he said that those responsible would be shot unless the elevator worked. And *that* elevator worked. I read the story in my youth as part of edifying reading about great Lenin, but I have been unable to retrace the source since then. The gentle reader may therefore dismiss this story and simply assume that great Lenin did not live in *our* house, and so the elevator would stand still for months, and then would be under repair for months, and then would *work* (oh!) *for hours* to withdraw again into a dark, secret, metallic stasis, like a stubborn introvert, keeping its own counsel.

In the *maternity ward* my mother wept because her bed was near a radiator and she could not stand the heat, but there was no room to move away the bed, and in a *collective* the individual whims must, indeed, be ignored. Anyway, my mother was too weak even to stand, let alone climb five flights. But perhaps women know when they choose husbands in epochs like this. Mother could not even hold me, and Father carried me up while Mother waited sitting on a bench in a niche. There were two beautiful dark oak-lined niches with built-in dark-oak benches on both sides of the entrance door (pseudo-Moresque—the basilica motif?), and she said to my father: "You've been so long." "I unwrapped him to see whom he takes after," Father said and carried her up the five flights.

21

It was into this machine-universe that I was born, where humans were to be expendable machines while elevators humanly unpredictable, and the entire machine-universe with its machine-like humans, humanlike machines, and dead skies was being created, actuated, and operated by the humanlike pseudo-tsar-god.

In the Greek Orthodox Church there was an icon called the Apotheosis. When Pokrovsky, as of 1917 the only *bolshevik* who was a professional historian of Russia, debunked at the beginning of the century the myth of Peter I created by nineteenth-century official history, he reproduced in his *History of Russia* another Apotheosis: that of Peter I. The implication was clear: that ruthless big serf owner, that warlord whose deathbed wish was to drum a military drum, that ignoramus who made three mistakes when writing the word "shoot," and who could not multiply numbers with zeroes—that reincarnation of the worst in Russia was represented in place of Jesus Christ: he was deified!

Thus Pokrovsky delivered (as he imagined) a *revolutionary-progressive-scientific*, etc., blow to both: the state and the church. The reader was to conclude by sheer association that if the Russian *state* and *church* of the early eighteenth century were so monstrous, its twentieth-century namesakes were and would be as bad, for weren't they called by the same names?

In 1918, on the first anniversary of the *great october socialist revolution,* that is the seizure (or conquest from within) of Russia by Ulyanov-Lenin and his (*junior*) *comrades,* there appeared in a mass edition a poster (you may call it a picture or an icon): the apotheosis—with Ulyanov-Lenin in the large oval instead of Christ (or Peter I) and his twelve top rankers in the small ovals instead of the apostles. Since too few miracles had been wrought so far, the designer, the same who had served for Tsar Nicholas I and was commissioned to design the hammer and sickle emblem, designed all around the ovals some general symbols of power and glory in anticipation of more specific *unprecedented triumphs of socialism.* And in one of the ovals there was—you will never guess who. The historian Pokrovsky!

Gods are as perfect as they wish, and have all the attributes of perfection they want. Ulyanov-Lenin and his men, down to the tiniest *chief,* desired to possess as part of their perfection all the attributes which are expressed by words like modesty, self-effacement, self-sacrifice, altruism, selflessness, self-negation, kindness, and so forth, and which I for the sake of brevity will denote by one term: self-sacrifice.

How can it be otherwise? Ulyanov-Lenin called his possession-power *dictatorship,* which he defined way back in 1906, and in 1920 he repeated his definition:

The scientific concept of dictatorship means nothing else but completely unlimited power, restrained by no laws or rules whatsoever, and relying directly on violence.

Where is the guarantee that those who have obtained this kind of power over the population of a country will not henceforth use it for their own benefit, and when they are dead and buried in pyramid-like mausoleums of Labrador marble, their successors will not continue to use it for their own benefit, and so forth for ever? The only guarantee is the attribute of self-sacrifice. Those wielding *dictatorship* actually own the population and can do it any harm with impunity, but given their attribute of self-sacrifice, why should they? On the contrary, they will always be ready to sacrifice themselves for their beloved population. Thus, some parents would rather starve themselves to death, giving their last food to their children. Or some animal lover would sacrifice himself for the sake of the pets he owns, though he can have them destroyed with impunity.

Naturally the *party* is often called *our mother*, while pseudo-tsar-god II named Stalin was prior to 1956 *our father* (*teacher and friend*), and *grandfather Lenin* is a cliché in *children's literature*. When these parents and grandparents pay in Moscow a rank-and-file doctor, engineer or scientist a *monthly salary* buying two Italian $1.40 raincoats (as of 1964) this is a miracle of parental self-sacrifice by itself. To think that in some countries there is *no socialism*, and the wicked *private* employers loot their employees, or the wicked authorities pay them those wretched unemployment benefits when they are unemployed. But the miracle of self-sacrifice of the *mother party*, our *father* great Stalin and our *grandfather* great Lenin does not end there. To that miracle of monthly pay to a doctor, engineer or scientist, buying two Italian $1.40 raincoats, they add *social benefits* (which cost them on the average in 1964 half of one $1.40 raincoat). Needless to say, they bestow these *benefits of socialism* not as a doctor's, engineer's, or a scientist's own money extracted from him against his heretical will, but as gifts bestowed on their beloved children: they, the parents and grandparents, have made this money—created these gifts, owing to their parental wisdom they call *socialism*, and owing to their attribute of self-sacrifice, they lavish these gifts on their beloved children. But why so many—and not more? Because the parents and grandparents know which is good for their children and which can only spoil them, and they know what they can afford.

A similar argument can be made for an animal lover and the animals he owns, given the animal lover's attribute of self-sacrifice.

Naturally, the owners' self-sacrifice and hence benefits lavished on their beloved human property make an especially poignant contrast with the tragedy of those countries in which there is no *socialism*, and the orphaned children aged eighteen to sixty have to earn money (the hard way, of course) and buy benefits (yes, exactly the same and even worse!) at exorbitant prices, while here they get them free, at the expense of their loving owners' wisdom and self-sacrifice they call *socialism*.

There may be, indeed, one person in a thousand, a hundred

thousand, or a million people who always lives entirely for the sake of perfect strangers. I have been privileged enough to have met people like that or almost like that. It is only not clear why their percentage must be higher among, say, those who call themselves *communists* than in any other randomly sampled group. According to *Pravda*, already in the autumn of 1919 there were *party* "organizations which were not afraid to throw out approximately *one-third* of their members and candidates. About *one-third* of them were purged in the general purge of 1921 as well." Who were those thrown out and purged? On the eve of the purge of 1921 *Pravda* stated:

Crawling into the Party for the sake of career, privileged rations, and high patronage have been shrewd climbers, well-groomed girls with curled locks, "jolly fellers," and departmental yes-men. All of them should be swept by a ruthless brush out of the clean Communist home.

As Ulyanov-Lenin said: "Stuck to us somewhere are careerists and adventurers who have named themselves Communists. . . ." But how can one be sure that careerists and adventurers were purged, and not on the contrary retained, in each purge? What *communist* is not a careerist if his *joining the party* ensures a good career for him in case of the *party*'s success (such as *head-of-government* rank for Ulyanov-Lenin, whom neither relative, nor absolute majority of the population ever elected directly or indirectly to the post)? Or perhaps, this is not a career, but an adventure? How can "shrewd climbers," mentioned by *Pravda*, be detected in a purge if they are shrewd enough? The "well-groomed girls with curled locks" can, of course, be purged, with the result that next time such girls will look untidy and wear their hair plain—at least in public. Those "jolly fellers"—how can they be identified? And certainly many superiors will try to keep more "departmental yes-men" and on the contrary to purge more no-men. As Ulyanov-Lenin complained: the "predominant fact in most local checkup commissions" was the "settling of personal and local scores in districts during the purge of the Party." Shame on them! Instead of really detecting, say, a *jolly feller*, behind the appearance of a *communist*, they just settled their personal and local scores. They only *pretended* to have believed that their personal or local enemy was a *jolly feller* in order to purge him! Whereas actually he might have been a *real communist*, and not a *jolly feller* at all. So who have been purging whom since 1919 every few years: have *real communists* been purging careerists and/or adventurers and/or jolly fellers, or the other way around?

Nevertheless, even more miraculously, the attribute of self-sacrifice grows (like all privileges) automatically with rank. Inversely, as the rank decreases all the attributes of perfection decrease accordingly so that the lowest chief may, in *soviet literature*, be only an awfully good man, an altruist, a hero in a pinch, yet with human egoistic weaknesses sometimes, which he is to overcome or cease to be even the lowest representative of the pyramid of perfection.

By virtue of his rank, Ulyanov-Lenin was the highest incarnation of self-sacrifice.

On October 8, 1922, *Pravda* called him the *leader of the globe*: the Russian word translated as *leader* means *chief* (of a tribe, for example) and is applied to Moses. He was the new Moses of mankind—mankind was his tribe, so to speak, and he was its chief. Yet his perfection, and in particular self-sacrifice, was so unimaginable that he *received pay*—yes, just like a clerk or a smith! In fact, a *salary of 500 rubles*. But the full enactment of the miracle of self-sacrifice was still ahead.

He ordered that the salary of a certain Gukovsky be raised to 2,000 rubles a month. That contradicted great Lenin's own *law* according to which no one was to get more than 500 rubles, but great Lenin's infinite concern for a certain humble ordinary man, Gukovsky, was above even his own *laws*. Then it was decided to give the Moses of mankind also a *raise of 300 rubles*.

What hell broke loose! Those directly responsible were *strictly reprimanded* by great Lenin in an elaborate memorandum, which has since been reproduced in his *works* and all over the world, and perhaps as long as more or less free societies last, there will always be there tender-hearted biographers of great Lenin marveling at this miracle of self-sacrifice.

Actually, every pseudo-tsar-god passes through three phases in his relationship to his comrades. When he collects his *party* (*gesithsund*) he must show to them that he is the "kindest and gentlest of men," as *Beowulf* has it, a selfless (indeed almost fleshless) comrade of theirs, living only for the sake of *their* well-being (including even the minutest detail of their health) and for their victory (that is, the conquest of a certain country with a prospect for more). The harder this previctory life and the lower the chances of victory in their estimation, the more he has to humble himself with respect to them.

The second phase begins (as possession-power has been seized) when whatever he says goes unless they all rally against him, though they can still argue against him with impunity especially at *closed party meetings.*

In the third phase his *comrades* must have *boundless faith* in him, or perish: they must be his serfs albeit ranked.

Between the autumn of 1917 and the autumn of 1922 Ulyanov-Lenin moved from the second to the third phase. However, self-sacrifice, humbleness, kindness to his comrades, which is a must in the first stage and partly in the second, may become in the third a deliberate court convention elevating the pseudo-tsar-god above his serf subordinates. Great Stalin's top serfs turned up in public wearing decorations studded with diamonds, while *he* appeared to his mankind, at least up to 1941, as a pauper who always wore apparently the same cotton tunic.

The *socialist* Angelica Balabanoff described her audience with great Lenin's subordinate Zinoviev in this way:

Zinoviev received us in that particular carriage which the Tsar had used for audiences with his representatives and staff members when he had travelled about the country. Now Zinoviev had taken all the airs and manners of a Tsar.

His subordinate Zinoviev was a tsar. Apart from everything else, surely great Lenin could not descend to the level of a subordinate of his. But who is higher than a tsar? Only God. He, great Lenin, must appear to his mankind as a pauper: for does he not figure in the Apotheosis instead of Jesus Christ? Let all the world know that he lives on 500 rubles like a minor clerk while a certain Gukovsky receives 2,000 rubles, owing to his, great Lenin's concern, kindness, self-sacrifice, which is above even his own *laws.*

Finally, for what purpose on earth, except showing mankind

his divine self-sacrifice, did great Lenin need that *salary* of 500 rubles and that *raise* of 300 rubles? Very movingly his wife describes the time in the autumn of 1917 when all the money was still in the State Bank, which did not want to recognize dear Vladimir Ilyich Lenin as the owner of all the money in the country: dear Vladimir Ilyich simply wrote on a piece of paper a *law* whereby the "State Bank was ordered to waive all rules and formalities and hand over" to a Gorbunov (a capital fellow, that Gorbunov) 10 million rubles. Gorbunov and his pals compelled the teller to pay out the sum, and told the rest of the story in this way:

We had difficulty with the bags for taking the money away in. We had not brought anything with us. At last one of the messengers lent us a couple of old sacks. We stuffed them full to the top with money, swung them on our shoulders, and hauled them out to the motorcar. We rode back to Smolny, beaming. At Smolny we shouldered the bags again and lugged them into the private office of Vladimir Ilyich. Ilyich was not there. While waiting for him to come, I sat down on the sacks with a revolver in my hand, "mounting guard." I handed the money over to Vladimir Ilyich with great solemnity. He received it as a matter of course, but actually he was very pleased.

However, having expropriated all the money, great Lenin began to have much more money printed, soon it cost one million rubles to have one's shoes blacked, and so his *salary* of 500 rubles and his *raise* of 300 rubles, over which the latest American biographer of great Lenin still sheds his scholarly tears, were just waste paper. Money had no value, while the value of values was food. Food bought everything on sale as once gold did. But hardly anything bought food—except some other food.

Food determined wealth and status, and it was then that the country split into thirty-four food castes, and though the author should have started scanning the vast food hierarchy from the highest, the first, food caste represented by great Lenin himself as, actually, the only important, he rather disrespectfully starts with the thirty-fourth caste—from the pariahs who received no food at all. The reader should not imagine that the author will describe the starving out of existence of those despicable pariahs called bourgeois (barely politely), bourjuys (colloquially) or bourjuins (viciously). The author wearily realizes that perhaps too many of his readers assume that certain groups of pariahs have to be exterminated if the most equal (just and altruistic) society in human history is to be established, and what is better for the purpose than giving them no food and thus saving food for the higher castes? However, there also originated quite involuntary concentrations of natural pariahs who would die of hunger by the million even without any intention of those in possession-power and indeed to no lofty purpose of theirs at all.

Though the signs of the unprecedented famine were all clear early in 1920, it was only in the summer of 1921 that great Lenin stated: "Several gubernias of Russia are hit by famine which is evidently only a little less severe than the disaster of 1891."

The famine of 1891 is outlined in the book *Young Lenin* because great Lenin has immortalized that famine: the book describes how great Lenin fought against the relief to the famine-stricken population. I will return to his *struggle* later, but meanwhile I will merely note that the book mentions only 964,627 famine-stricken people in 1891—no other figure is given, while in 1921 *Pravda* mentions the figure of twenty-five million in the Volga region. "Evidently, only a little less severe" said great Lenin. No cause for excessive worry.

In 1891 great Lenin was not sorry for those who died owing to his *struggle* against relief work because he did not own these people. After 1917 the populace was his property. Naturally, he valued his property, and he would not have destroyed willingly even one-tenth of it if not for the following consideration. From now on, famines reflected badly on *his* regime and thus undermined it. Therefore, it was necessary to conceal or understate them as long as possible, and now, with a supermonopoly on all information, this could be done easily. It is better to lose one-tenth, or, indeed, nine-tenths of your serfs, to death, than to lose the possession-power, that is, to lose *all* of your serfs who will be taken away from you. Besides, as long as you still own any serfs at all, they will bear more serfs and will finally make up for the loss.

Pravda began to sound the alarm to get relief from abroad only when it was realized that practically all the populace, except perhaps the Kremlin dwellers, was in danger, and if all the serfs except the Kremlin dwellers died who would feed, say, the pets Bukharin kept in the Kremlin?

Ulyanov-Lenin was right when he attributed the famine to the *civil war*. The Constituent Assembly opened in January 1918. Yet hard as they tried, he and his *party* were unable to garner more than a quarter of the votes despite their unfulfilled and unfulfillable promise to bring peace to Russia without concluding a separate treaty with Germany, to stop the wartime food shortages, or to raise all the wages as high as the wage-earners wanted. At school I wondered: why did the network of propaganda inculcate into our minds that great Lenin and his *party* garnered a quarter of the votes in the Constituent Assembly? Surely one quarter was not even a relative majority. Later I knew: the voting had been held *after* the *party* seized possession-power. No more had to be said. That meant that never has the *party* ever had a free electoral support of even one quarter of the population. But what was the actual support after it had failed in 1918 to keep all those fantastic promises of 1917? One percent of the population? The Kronstadt uprising of sailors, soldiers and workers in 1921 indicates much less than that. With such a tiny minority great Lenin wanted to establish *dictatorship* (see his definition), that is, own the population without any reservations, yet those scoundrels (more than 99 percent of the population) resisted! This three-year-long resistance to his conquest of the country and the ownership of its population Ulyanov-Lenin named *civil war*, and surely it was one of the causes of the famine. But *Pravda* gave another cause as well: Ulyanov-Lenin's method of taking away all the *food surpluses* from each farmer on the theory that everyone must be an infinite altruist (like great Lenin) and give away to others whatever others *assess* to be quite *superfluous* for him. The method was called the *food assessment*, and *Pravda* bemoaned its harm—after it had been abolished in favor of *partial admission of capitalism* in March 1921:

The food assessment killed in the farmers all the desire to restore their farms. The food workers, ignoring the farmers' psychology and way of life, simply came and took away food surpluses, and not food surpluses only, on account of future blessings of which we had the vaguest idea. The policy killed in us, farmers, all the initiative and desire to increase the sown area and improve the tillage of our fields.

On January 28, 1922, *Pravda* described some of the results of the method in an article entitled "Cannibals":

Mukhin, a villager of the Buzuluk Uyezd, Efimov Volost, stated to the investigator:
"My family is of five people. There's been no bread since Easter. At first we ate tree bark, horse meat, dogs and cats, and also picked bones and ground them. There's a lot of corpses in our village. They are lying about in the streets or are put into the village barn. In the evening I stole into the barn, took the corpse of a boy of seven, brought it home on a sledge, cut it up with an ax, and cooked it. We ate up the whole corpse within a day. Only the bones remained.
"Many eat human flesh in our village, but conceal it."

After a little less than two years of the famine, caused in particular by Ulyanov-Lenin's *food assessment*, *Pravda* referred in August 1921, to the "national disaster about which much has already been said, but no one has undertaken urgent and effective measures of struggle on the scene." Urgent and effective measures! But surely great Lenin had more important measures to attend to.

On October 1, 1920, great Lenin began to pose for Claire Sheridan, a sculptor, a ravishing British lady, a cousin of Sir Winston Churchill. He clambered onto a special high carousel and was revolved during a sitting so that the ravishing lady sculptor could immortalize in sculpture all sides of the greatest impersonation of self-effacement in human history. But she thought that the revolving was not enough. She knelt before the carousel to look at the deity of self-sacrifice from below, too, and asked coyly: "Are you accustomed to this attitude in women?" as she described it in her *Mayfair to Moscow*.

The immortalization of great Lenin's modesty in sculpture, painting, movies, and photography went full ahead. Surely it was more important than some famine which was, besides, *evidently* only a little less severe than the disaster of 1891? But to quote the same article of *Pravda* again:

Here is another document. It is an excerpt from the testimony of Chugunova, a village woman of the same volost:
"I am a widow. I have four children: Anna, 15, Anastasiya, 13, Darya, 10, and Pelageya, 7. The latter was very sick. In December, I don't remember the exact date, I had no food, and the eldest girl

prompted me to kill the smallest who was sick. I made up my mind and killed her at night when she was asleep. She was sleepy and weak, and she did not resist and didn't cry either.

"My eldest girl, Anna, began to prepare the corpse, that is, remove the entrails and cut it into pieces."

The article carries famine reports from all over the country—Kharkov in the south, Archangel in the north, and Tambov in mid-Russia—and recalls that under Boris Godunov three women killed a carter and ate him up. So it was not as in 1891, only a "little less severe," as great Lenin put it, but as under Boris Godunov (in 1602), only perhaps "much more severe." That summer of 1921, *Pravda* reported that in the Volga region "famine engulfs about 25 million of the population." But Kharkov, Archangel, and Tambov are no more in the Volga region than, say, Boston, San Francisco, and Cleveland are in Kansas.

How trivial all this is compared with the immortalization of self-sacrifice of great Lenin. At least twenty-eight documentaries were made to immortalize his self-sacrifice in every situation (including his playing with a kitten, of course). Yet no camera could really do credit to each minutest detail of the unique greatness of his self-sacrifice. The *socialist* Angelica Balabanoff claims that she said to Lenin defiantly (for she was a rebel, and one of her books was duly titled *My Life as a Rebel*): "I am one of the very few in Moscow today who do not have your portrait." Miss Balabanoff soon left Russia, and that was not the worst solution for her defiance. There were portraits of great Lenin literally everywhere, but was this enough considering the greatness of his modesty? In its review of memoirs of sculptors, artists, cameramen, and photographers who *incarnated the image* of great Lenin, *Pravda* wrote:

There is another trait of his: condescending as Lenin was in his evaluations or art, referring with a kind smile to Lunacharsky in such cases, he could yet speak clearly and bluntly when he did not like something. Thus he concluded that Malyavin's portraits of him did not catch a likeness, nor did he approve of Brodsky's studies.

As a *proletarian poet* Poletayev wrote about great Lenin:

No pen, no chisel, no brush
Has the power to encompass

> The vastness throbbing in this hand,
> The vastness seething in this head.

Great Lenin seemed to agree: he was satisfied with neither the splashy Malyavin, nor with the meticulous Brodsky—no brush, no pen, no chisel had, indeed, the power, and Angelica Balabanoff recalls with due piety:

Another time, on one of my visits to Lenin, I was greatly surprised to find a third person. "Don't worry," Lenin said, "you may speak freely in his presence. He is a trusted comrade, a sculptor. Just think, it is the eighteenth time he has come to model my head."

Eighteen sittings for one particular sculptor to model just the head alone (or perhaps just one side of the nape of the neck?). Who would be able to concentrate on urgent and effective measures of struggle against the famine? But on the other hand, how could, say, the left side of the nape of his neck be allowed to be modeled improperly?

"Oh, how modest you are, deity of self-sacrifice, how self-effacing, self-negating—living only for our happiness," numberless millions would be repeating all over the world, and here the left side of the nape of his neck had not been modeled authentically enough because there had been only seventeen sittings for this particular sculptor.

Besides, the real criminals responsible for the famine of 1919 to 1923 were soon discovered.

As of August 1921 American philanthropists fed 10,491,257 people simultaneously from field kitchens they had organized. How many people did they save? If five people have only four months' food, all of them may die: give them one month's food for one man and all of them may pull through. But who was to blame for the famine? *Pravda* answered on August 12, 1921:

Perishing under the blows of blind elements is part of the Russian people, part of mankind. But what is mankind, what are the starving, to the world bourgeoisie with its profits, with its appetites, with its insane luxury?

See? The world bourgeoisie was to blame, especially those American rich. At school we were taught that the American Relief Administration consisted of spies who had sneaked into our youthful and beautiful country to rob us of our wealth, happiness, and freedom, and indeed the sneaky criminals fed 40,944 metric tons of American food, for example to Simbirsk, great Lenin's birthplace, not to mention medical aid, medical equipment, medicines, and all that, and those 80,000 Russians who helped them in their nationwide crime which embraced even the children of Moscow began to disappear when the Americans were still in Russia.

22

Hard as I tried to enliven the boring famine of the drab thirty-fourth caste with glimpses into the royal-divine activity of great Lenin, the reader must be tired of associating with a caste so abysmally low, and the author will presently take him above the thirty-fourth caste.

One of the fantastic promises that gave Ulyanov-Lenin the temporary minimal support he needed to raze to the ground all civic development of Russia since 1861 (and all independence which had existed in any European society no matter how un-free) was his fantastic promise to end the wartime shortages of food. On October 20, 1917, several days before the openly announced seizure of possession-power, *Pravda* reported that a pound of rye bread would now cost (owing to those bourgeois in power!) 0.22 rubles and the best wheat bread 0.32 rubles. The average wages at the Putilov works were 10.02 rubles a day. And not only were the prices so exorbitant (few people in Russia knew then what really exorbitant prices are), but there were also irregularities in the supply of bread to Petersburg because of the war: 3,546 more carloads of meat and 390 more carloads of butter were bought in 1917 than in 1916, but 823 less carloads of grain. Thus one had to stand in line sometimes to get "some wretched pound of bread," as *Pravda* wrote.

When Ulyanov-Lenin openly took over in several days, there was soon not enough bread to give even a *quarter* of a pound a day to each inhabitant, and as for meat or butter, few inhabitants could now believe that such ever existed. The amount of food the Putilov worker had been able to buy for his real average wages before the takeover now seemed incredible. Then all the commoners were divided into common castes. The highest caste of commoners (blue-collar workers at the time) received a quarter of a pound of bread a day (in October, 1918, for example). They could be proud that while they would die of hunger in several years (with the addition of half a pound of frozen potatoes a day, and some horse meat or fish glue), they were the aryans among the pariahs—they were in the top caste of the common castes, and those below them and less aryan or more pariah were to die of hunger much more quickly than they. But who were the lower pariah castes? In particular:

People of the professions (lawyers, privately practicing physicians, litterateurs, etc.) and all the other citizens who do not fit the first two categories.

So not only the "people of the professions," but all who were not the highest two castes of commoners, were thereby the third or fourth caste.

According to *Pravda* of October 10, 1918, these pariahs were to get no bread at all: only one-eighth of a pound of (frozen) potatoes a day (one tiny frozen potato or just several frozen peelings?). Indeed, *Pravda* printed the following announcement which reduced some still lower pariahs to the lowest food caste: those sentenced to death.

The People's Commissariat of Social Security confirms thereby the need of depriving of rations all the kulak and bourgeois elements of villages and cities; the extras thus obtained should be used to increase the rationed supply of the urban and rural poor.

Instead of being depressed about getting one-quarter of a pound of bread a day, a smith was to be gleeful that a tiny frozen potato or several potato peelings would be snatched from the mouth of some pariah, in order to sustain his, aryan's, life.

But let us skip all intermediate castes (in one of which my mother was a doctor *in state service*) and rise to the top of the hierarchy, especially since all the intermediate castes in a caste society are usually just a thin neck connecting a huge low base of commoners and a tiny top of aryan wealth and glory, that is, food. Each caste was attached to its own food caste stores already in 1918. The word "store" was properly discarded as old-fashioned. Indeed, there could be no trade in the old sense any longer. The millennia of trade were over. These food caste "stores" were aptly named *closed distributors*. No trade: only *closed distribution*. The *closed distributor* of the *organs of state security*, for example, gave a notice in *Pravda* indicating what numbers on the cards of its members entitled them to admission on what days. This made it possible to give a different range of food for each rank each day: twelve days for twelve ranks within basically one institution. Surely caviar need not be issued to those who merely did a perfectly *legal*, that is, not secret, standard, mechanical job like shooting: they would be overwhelmed if they got some ordinary meat or butter.

There were individuals unique either because they were indispensable in the production of weapons and the production of the *means of production* (of weapons) or because they were world-famous and were therefore important either for propaganda or for foreign currency. *Pravda* reported in 1922 that allocated for additional *supply* to these unique individuals in the current year

are one million rubles of gold and academic rations the number of which, along with family ones, constitutes 16,000 and the value of which in current market prices exceeds 700,000 gold rubles a month.

But surely one genius in some field should not consume as much meat or butter as another genius in some other field? The value of each genius to his owners differs, and hence even this tiny superelite was divided into six castes (V, IV, III, II, I and 0), and each enserfed genius was promoted or demoted from caste to caste depending on his current value to its owners.

Finally, we arrive at the *very* top of the caste hierarchy of food, the value of all values. As Ulyanov-Lenin and his closest *comrades* announced the advent of the greatest equality in human history, the highest-caste *restaurant*, if a word so old-fashioned can be used in the context, was organized at Smolny where the *comrades* lived and gave orders (or *laws*) from. At first Ulyanov-Lenin was served by a certain orderly Zheltishev. But can a crude Russian orderly be a good waiter? Fortunately, a trustworthy Finnish lady was made general manager, and according to Ulyanov-Lenin's wife, she put Zheltishev, and the cleaners, and the waitresses through their paces. "Soon she had everything in the house shipshape, the way Ilyich liked," writes the enchanted wife. "We lived in Smolny up to March 1918, when we moved to Moscow." So everything was made shipshape in the highest-caste restaurant and everyone put through his or her paces simultaneously with the advent of the greatest freedom, equality and brotherhood on earth and well before the resulting biggest famine in the history of Russia.

At this point it is worth while getting better acquainted with Angelica Balabanoff, an Italian of Russian extraction, who was at one time a friend of Mussolini (the *fascist*) and who explains her own motives for becoming a *socialist* by quoting one of Turgenev's "Poems in Prose" which ends with one word of definition: "Saint!" And Miss Balabanoff gives many moving examples of her saintliness. During her life in Russia under great Lenin she would refuse to get herself a pair of glasses as too much of a luxury. Instead, she borrowed a pince-nez from an American comrade who happened to have two of them. Predictably, great Lenin learned about this act of self-sacrifice, and there ensued a harrowing scene of one saint admonishing the other for too much self-sacrifice to the detriment of her health. But no, Miss Balabanoff would not get herself a pair of glasses.

When I thought of the women who worked all day in cold factories, returning to unheated rooms and a piece of black bread, it was difficult for me to enjoy my own food.

The trouble with twentieth-century saints, of whom there will soon, perhaps, be hundreds of millions, is that they forget what they wrote in the previous sentence, and so after the full stop above, the saint Angelica writes:

And when, seated in the motorcar of the ex-Tsar, I watched these women walk from work at the end of the day because the streetcars were so overcrowded and ran so irregularly . . .

Of course, considering those poor women, a pair of glasses would be a mortal sin. But not the "motorcar of the ex-Tsar," from which it is so comfortable to watch them (even through a pince-nez) dragging themselves home "to unheated rooms and a piece of black bread."

A saint that Miss Balabanoff was, she could well understand great Lenin and vouch that "no one has ever doubted Lenin's own complete unselfishness and negation." Indeed, very few scholars or thinkers have ever done so—partly perhaps because many of them have regarded *themselves* as saints.

For there was unanimity about the honesty of Lenin's intentions and his utter unselfishness. When his enemies called him a fanatic, an enemy of freedom, they had to grant him unselfish motives.

When the saint Angelica came from Sweden to Russia she brought Swedish cheese to great Lenin as a gift from the Swedish *comrades*. True, she quotes great Lenin's letter to her in Stockholm which ends:

But I beg you, don't economize. Spend millions, many, many millions.

Not that she always agreed with great Lenin as to how all these many, many millions should be poured on many, many saints all over the world, including Sweden or Denmark.

With one of those contributions (I do not remember whether it was in jewelry or cash) I received, through a Bolshevik delegate, the suggestion that a Communist daily paper be established in Copenhagen. I was amazed at what seemed such a lack of revolutionary common sense.

So it was not the shower of many, many millions on saints all over the world (during the worst famine in the history of Russia) that amazed the saint Balabanoff, but a lack of (revolutionary) common sense as to the incidence or distribution of the shower.

Everyone knew that there was only a handful of Communists in the entire city of Copenhagen. What would the Danish workers, to say nothing of the government, think if a Communist daily, representing a huge financial investment, should suddenly spring up from nowhere?

Anyway, to a tainted mind like mine, the Swedish *communists*, on whom many, many millions of hard cash were poured to help them to seize their country, repaid a tiny fraction of these many, many millions in the form of a consignment of cheese to great Lenin. Most of them sent no such gifts to great Trotsky *after* he had lost his share of possession of Russia, and on the contrary laughed and jeered and applauded when an alpenstock crashed into the skull of great—no, not great Lenin, but great Trotsky, as it happened by chance. To the pure mind of Miss Balabanoff the sending of the cheese was a sign of infinite selfless love of saints for great Lenin (and great Trotsky?) transmitted via the saint Balabanoff, and since great Lenin was not a rank-and-file saint, but the generalissimo of saintliness, the saint of saints, the deity of self-sacrifice, he wrought yet another miracle of self-sacrifice:

I remember he was not easily persuaded to accept the cheese the comrades from Stockholm had sent him. "Give it to the children in Moscow," he said, and he accepted it only after my assurance that half of it had already been distributed to them and that I had brought him only the part that was meant for him.

Half and half. A real deity of self-sacrifice, great Lenin was. A superhuman sense of perfect social justice. Half of the cheese to him and half to the 50 million children of Russia. Or only of Moscow? Were the other children left without their fair share of that Swedish cheese?

An embarrassing question that haunted me from childhood is: Why did great Lenin need his equal share of that cheese if the highest-caste restaurant-in-residence had long been "ship-shape, the way Ilyich liked"? Where would he stow away his equal share of that cheese? In the Kremlin? At the Hills villa? Was food like medieval gold that a miser would hoard just to admire it? Was it an excruciating joy just to keep at the side all that cheese when, say, twenty-five million were dying of hunger in the Volga region? At tea, great Lenin amazed the saint Angelica by his humility even more.

They have brought me the sugar from the Ukraine, the bread from Central Russia, the meat . . .

And the caviar from Azerbaijan, of course. In July 1920 six freight cars of caviar came from Azerbaijan. The note of great Lenin's *secretary* concerning this occurrence (perfectly routine, as is clear from the note) is a superb example of precise behavior in the *new* society whose caste system was perhaps the most disparate and elaborate history had ever known, yet whose *new* intolerant, repressive, inquisitional religion forced everyone to pretend that Ulyanov-Lenin, the actual owner of all value of values in the country, the recipient of six cars of caviar during the worst famine in the country's history, the top ranker who had been fed at the shipshape highest-caste restaurant-in-residence, kept *fainting from hunger* (as has been shown to us in movies since childhood). According to the religion which forced everyone to pretend that the saint of saints Ulyanov-Lenin was starving like dozens of millions were, the *secretary* was to gasp in horror at the sight of the impudent scoundrels who had brought the caviar "to Lenin" and have them apprehended for such a monstrous, brazen, cynical bribe as no Gogol could imagine. On the other hand, according to the social reality of the caste system, she was to tell the owner of the country that *his* high-caste serfs had brought him *his* caviar, because these high-caste serfs wanted to keep their high caste, while the starving of dozens of millions of low-caste serfs did not matter for them, of course. "Will it be your divine pleasure, O Tsar of Tsars and God of Gods, to keep your caviar for the Kremlin table?" The note of the *secretary* to great Lenin is a masterpiece combining both attitudes, without any commitment to either: it leaves entirely up to great Lenin to have the caviar-donators shot for their fantastically insolent bribe whose value could hardly be expressed in any money of Russia at the time (compare great Lenin's worldwide row over the *raise* of 300 rubles). Or to treat the donated train of caviar as a routine occurrence (which great Lenin did) and to accept or readdress it in a perfectly matter-of-fact manner.

Waiting in the reception room are two comrades who have brought from Azerbaijan under Narimanov's mandate 6 cars of caviar at your disposal. They are waiting for your instructions.

"At your disposal." An expression having two meanings. One meaning: "This is for you." This meaning was quite acceptable because since childhood we have been told that "workers and peasants showed a moving concern for Ilyich and sent him food though they suffered from hunger themselves." In other words, six cars of caviar could simply mean a moving if somewhat raw expression of infinite love. Raw? But this is what the *workers and peasants* (that is, *party* rankers) are. Raw, simple, straight in their infinite love, knowing of no bourgeois, and especially Western-bourgeois, airs and graces. An inhabitant of Russia giving a bribe even to the lowest chief must explain how simple, guileless and hence perhaps somewhat raw his love is. But the secretary's "at your disposal" left open tactfully the other meaning. The Commissariat of Food and other local or central *state* agencies could be trusted with the distribution or storage of mazut, armored cars, or even rye flour, but certainly not caviar! And so the six cars of caviar, a product that was highly perishable in summer before the age of refrigeration, were hauled all over the country in mid-summer—all over the country struck by a famine the like of which Russia had never known, and handed personally to great Lenin—put squarely "at his disposal," for surely great Lenin would know better how to proceed than some Commissariat of Food. For example, great Lenin could use the same principle of perfect equality in the distribution of caviar as he had used for cheese: these six cars to the 50 million children, the next or previous six cars to great Lenin. Though caviar has been sent since then to high rankers as top secret parcels (*kremlin rations*), some half a century later this is as much of a military top secret as fifty years ago. For the extent of saintliness, growing with rank, must correspond to the extent of secrecy and simulation, growing with the same.

Great Lenin was a live transfer point of infinite love, that is, of infinite food. And if the value of values was so infinitely his, lesser values, like ordinary, inedible love, were his all the more so: those who sent six carloads of caviar during such a famine— would they not avalanche great Lenin with their verbal, inedible, infinite love? Of course, he resisted love as violently as he did a *raise of* 300 rubles or even (half of) the cheese from Swedish *comrades*. Before 1922 he had to resist love because this is a must in the second stage of the *senior-comrade-junior-com-rade* relationship. But by the autumn of 1922, infinite adulation broke down all his resistance completely, as might well have been expected after the *organs of state security* had become *officially* entitled to *imprison communists* as well. Before, only commoners could be *imprisoned* and shot *officially*.

The *Pravda* supplement on the occasion of the fifth anniversary of the *great october revolution* created the impression that the country, called Russia five years before, now consisted of two beings: one (all-important) was great Lenin, and the other (almost imperceptible) the entire population minus great Lenin. The outside world also existed only in connection with great Lenin. And his appearance next month before *communists* of fifty-odd countries, *Pravda* described in this way:

Applause. Stormy, joyous applause because the waiting seemed too long. Everyone wants to take in the minutest trait of our own Ilyich.

To make sure that he is as strong as ever. Hundreds of eyes are glued to Ilyich, and the applause will never end. Meanwhile, he is waiting in his usual manner, looking at his watch from time to time.

"Internationale." The entire hall is singing. For applause—ovation is somehow too little to express infinite love for the leader and boundless faith in him.

To think that less than two years ago a fairly high but not even top-ranking *communist*, Larin, had called great Lenin a demagogue in *Pravda*! That was a different era: the second stage, when Ulyanov-Lenin was still only the top *comrade* among his *comrades*. The third stage had started: he was now pseudo-tsar-god I, and his former *comrades* had to have *boundless faith* in (not only *infinite love* for) the Moses of mankind, or to recall that *communists* too could henceforth be *arrested* quite *officially*.

23

Before 1917 Ulyanov-Lenin and his *comrades* wanted to believe that the world in which they lived was all absolute evil. Great Gorky went to the United States and proved ("The City of the Yellow Devil") that life in America was even worse than in Russia, while great Lenin proved in his articles that life in Russia was even worse than in America. Everywhere this world of absolute evil was bound to be only still more evil (unless "razed to the ground," as the "Internationale" says in Russian translation). The only absolute good in this absolute evil was Ulyanov-Lenin himself and his *comrades* in the order of their allegiance or proximity to him. In particular, while the world of absolute evil was greedy, mercenary, and corrupt, he was the selfless founder of a brotherhood of saints ready to sacrifice themselves for the happy future of mankind. The question was: How could they *struggle* against the world of absolute evil? No organized brotherhood could survive for long if it struggled against the regime in Germany between 1937 and 1945, or in Russia between 1937 and 1953, or even in Russia between 1825 and 1853. The answer was: Because Ulyanov-Lenin and his comrades were not only saints, but also heroes. As the *greatest poet of the revolution* put it:

> Molten tin and lead
> > were poured
> > > into our mouths,

"Disavow!"
But
           only three words
               came
                  from our burning throats:
"Long
        Live
           Communism!"

See? The world of absolute evil poured molten tin and lead into their mouths, but they would proclaim their faith all the same, and since the world of absolute evil is infinitely ruthless yet cowardly (for cowardice is its attribute, just as infinite heroism is theirs), the world of absolute evil was unnerved, cowed, terrorized by their *infinite* heroism and finally defeated in 1917 in Russia, as it will be defeated everywhere.

But was Russia before 1917 such a world of absolute evil that only their superhuman heroism could brave it?

Ulyanov-Lenin created an organization whose avowed aim was to overthrow by violence any existing regime (whether semi-constitutional monarchy as in Russia before the spring of 1917, or democracy as in Russia in the summer of 1917, or democracy as in the United States). The membership of his organization did not essentially exceed that of the *communist party* in the United States today, and anyway it turned out later that the organization played no role whatsoever in the collapse of the monarchy in the spring of 1917 (after the event Ulyanov-Lenin commented on the stale news of this event in the Zurich newspapers: "If the Germans do not lie, then it's true"). But at that time the irrelevance of such an organization was by no means clear even in the English-speaking countries (not to mention Russia) especially since as part of *violence in the overthrow of the existing regime* Ulyanov-Lenin urged, in his special circular, to store acid in order to splash it onto the policemen as a result of which they would go blind. The other means recommended in his circular were fire arms, bombs, knives, brass knuckles, kerosene-soaked rags for starting fires "and so on and so forth." For its part the regime imprisoned Ulyanov-Lenin. The prison was naturally described as a dungeon or a torture chamber, but "what dungeons or torture chambers can break the will of a Communist?" In the world of absolute evil there are only absolutes: as *Pravda* summed up the pre-1917 regime in Russia right after its collapse:

The autocracy of ex-Nicholas the Bloodthirsty was built on the bones and blood of millions of destroyed lives; the blood of the people washed away the throne of the accursed heinous enemy of mankind. . . .

According to Ulyanov-Lenin's wife, it was there, in the dungeon of Nicholas the Bloodthirsty (who destroyed millions of lives so easily) that great Lenin

prepared *The Development of Capitalism in Russia.* He ordered all the necessary material and statistical handbooks in his legal letters.

Altogether he spent in the dungeons of Nicholas the Bloodthirsty about a year (that is, about as long as a Muscovite, *suspected* of the passing-on of uncensored manuscripts, may *officially* spend incommunicado as a preliminary checkup, *investigation,* even in these lenient sixties in Moscow).

Besides *The Development of Capitalism in Russia,* Vladimir Ilyich wrote leaflets and illegal pamphlets, and a draft programme for the First Congress (which did not take place until 1898, although it was planned for an earlier date), and gave his views on questions under discussion in the organization.

This amazing industry was due to a special diet prescribed by a Swiss doctor to improve Ulyanov-Lenin's health. As his wife noted:

My mother told me that he had even put on weight in prison and was as cheerful as ever.

But where is the world of absolute evil pouring molten tin and lead into great Lenin's throat proclaiming nevertheless his faith? To his sister Ulyanov-Lenin wrote:

I have here everything I need and indeed more than I need. My health is quite satisfactory. I drink my brand of mineral water: I order it and have it brought on the same day from the druggist's.

So it was not exactly molten tin and lead. It was *his* brand of mineral water. It would, indeed, be outrageous if *his* brand of mineral water could not be ordered in a tsarist dungeon anno domini 1896. He was working frantically for the overthrow of the regime by means of splashing acid onto its defendants, and the regime? Would they not give him promptly *his* brand of mineral water as ordered! Since 1918, and except for the time of 1923 to 1928, no common person *at liberty* has been able to order *any* brand of mineral water anywhere outside the cities and resorts which foreigners visit.

Great Lenin's letter indicates that he was one of those men who watch their digestion with intensity somehow depressing for those around him. Therefore, the author takes the liberty to conjecture that Ulyanov-Lenin would not have taken the risk of fighting against the regime with specially stored acid or whatever his *party* could lay hands on, if he had not known that in the dungeon of Nicholas the Bloodthirsty, his, Ulyanov-Lenin's, brand of mineral water could be ordered and promptly served.

Apart from about a year in *tsarist prison,* Ulyanov-Lenin spent three years in *tsarist exile:*

Life was surprisingly cheap in Shushenskoye. Vladimir Ilyich's monthly allowance of eight rubles procured him clean lodgings, and meals, and paid for laundry and mending—and even that was considered dear. True, the dinner and supper were simple enough meals. One week a sheep would be slaughtered, and Vladimir Ilyich would be fed with it day in and day out until it was all gone. Then they would buy meat for a week, and the servant girl would chop it up for cutlets out in the yard in a trough used for preparing the cattle feed. These cutlets were fed to Vladimir Ilyich for a whole week. But there was milk and cream enough for both Vladimir Ilyich and his dog, a fine Gordon setter named Zhenka, whom he taught to retrieve, and point, and do all other kinds of canine tricks.

Of course, the hiring of a really good servant was the problem in *exile* as well as throughout the pre-1917 life of the childless couple, and the subject crops up all along the memoirs (especially since the same problem haunted the Zinovievs and perhaps all the other *senior comrades*). Oh, for those blisses of the *exile.* Fishing in summer. Hunting in winter. And hunting in spring and autumn again.

Or we would stand on the fringe of the woods, listening to the babble of a brook and the mating call of the wood-grouse. Vladimir

Ilyich would ask me to hold Zhenka while he went into the woods. I would stand there holding the dog, who trembled with excitement, while I felt this tempestuous awakening of nature tingling in all my veins. Vladimir Ilyich was a passionate hunter, but apt to get too excited over it. In the autumn we went far out into the forest cuttings. Vladimir Ilyich would say: "You know, if I come across a hare I won't shoot it, because I didn't bring my bags. It will be awkward to carry." Yet as soon as a hare came bounding out he would let go at it.

After such an ordeal, a *bolshevik* (or another overthrower of the regime by violence) had a choice: to go abroad and overthrow the regime from there or slip into Russia from time to time if he relished some danger. There was a *bolshevik* named Kamo (which is a distorted "Whom" in Russian) because he kept asking: "Whom should I kill now?" The worst that could happen to him inside Russia if he were not careful while murdering was the death penalty, and since statistically there are always "small numbers"—exceptions—in a large population, there were statistical exceptions whom the death penalty did not deter (but torture quickly crushed all heroic terrorism against Ulyanov-Lenin and his *party*). However, Comrade Whom survived very well into 1917 (and was killed in the twenties, perhaps by his *comrade* named Stalin, who did not like the bank-robbery-with-murder stories of Comrade Whom involving his comrade Stalin). But to expose himself to danger was Comrade Whom's personal choice. Comrade Whom could very well have lived safely abroad. He would not. Ulyanov-Lenin did, and it is him that we would follow. To cross the border for residence abroad and shuttle back and forth was easier than it is now to move from Leningrad for residence in Moscow, never to mention a more disparate caste.

On our arrival there we were met by Comrade Bagocki, a Polish political emigrant, who immediately took us under his wing and helped us with all our domestic affairs and secret work. He taught us how to use the *polupaski* (special passes issued to the local inhabitants to enable them to cross and recross the frontier). These *polupaski* cost very little, and the important thing was that they greatly facilitated the work of our illegal comrades who traveled back and forth with them. We sent many comrades across with these *polupaski*.

Life in Europe is very pleasant, especially if you travel. Take Paris for example.

We rented an apartment right on the edge of the town in the Rue Bonier, a street running off the Avenue d'Orléans not far from the Parc Montsouris. It was a large airy flat, which even had mirrors over the fireplaces—a fixture in all the new houses. There was my mother's room, Maria Ilyinichna's (she had arrived in Paris by this time), our own room, and a living room.

Ulyanov-Lenin found that Paris was "very tiring," as he said in a letter.

But for a short visit or a joy ride there is no better or jollier city. It did me good.

Yes: every European city or resort is good if you know how to enjoy it. In London, meals in restaurants are inedible, and you'd better cook at home.

Besides, we were living at the organization's expense, and that meant we had to economize every penny.

Having forgotten this commendable afterthought, the wife of Ulyanov-Lenin writes on the same page:

Vladimir Ilyich took a month off to go to Brittany to see his mother and sister Anna, and spend a few weeks with them by the seaside. He loved the sea with its incessant movement and vast spaces, and could relax properly there.

The relaxing seaside of Brittany, the invigorating mountains of Switzerland, the intoxicating "Hofbrau of Munich which was famous for its beer," the exciting *party congress* of London, the entertaining opéra comique of Vienna—but there is no better or jollier city than Paris for a short visit or a joy ride. To think that a certain Ulyanov could, instead, be sticking it out all his life at some stuffy office in a dreary provincial town! And the moral?

The moral is that, unless any independent activity and independent association are penalized as they were in Russia between 1937 and 1953, or even as in Germany between 1937 and 1945, or even as in Russia again between 1825 and 1853, there is bound to be a certain number of people like Ulyanov-Lenin devoting their time to the *struggle* aimed at overthrowing the *existing regime* (no matter what it is) and making them the owners of the country. Just as in every country at least as free as Russia of 1861 to 1917, there is a certain number of gamblers or bank robbers. The number of aspirants to the possession of a country is the larger the longer *private* serfdom and/or other unfreedoms linger in the country, the higher the chances of the aspirants' success seem to be, and the more pleasant the aspirants' *heroic struggle* is (including, for example, a top ranker's trips to sea resorts at the *organization*'s expense). Incidentally, the aspirants' *heroic struggle* is quite irrelevant, except that it keeps the *organization* ready: their *victory* is a win in a game of chance, and they only must hang around somewhere (say, at some beerhouse in Munich) to be ready to pocket the win, or, to use their favorite word, to *seize* it.

24

Russia and Europe not being the world of absolute evil, was Ulyanov-Lenin the incarnation of absolute good? And in particular, the altruism of a future brotherhood, commune, collective, knowing no money or property, making no difference between mine or yours, sacrificing one's own self for the sake of poor others? To Gorky at Capri, Italy, Ulyanov-Lenin wrote in 1912:

Dear Al. M.! Haven't heard from you for quite a time. How's everything? How's your health?

I have received today No. 187 of *Pravda* with a subscription announcement for 1913. The business state of the newspaper is difficult: after the summer circulation decline the recovery is *very* slow, and the deficit remains. The pay to two permanent contributors has even to be suspended temporarily, making our position arch-difficult.

So the arch-difficulty was that too few people wanted to buy *Pravda*. After the successful seizure of Russia in 1917 a large number of people even in some countries of Western Europe began to believe that the chances of the seizure of their countries were fairly high. But before 1917 the number of such believers in Russia was very small, and besides, in summer many of them would go to the country or abroad. Surely the future happiness of mankind should not interfere with the present-day summer vacations. The pay to two permanent contributors had to be postponed as a result. You do not expect, do you, that, say, Ulyanov-Lenin will volunteer to contribute to a newspaper to establish a moneyless brotherhood when *his* pay is postponed? You do not mean, do you, that *he* will have to postpone a wonderful trip to the seaside of Brittany or to (God forbid!) the jolliest Paris?

Gorky himself donated money and collected money among his rich friends like the big factory owner Morozov, and great Lenin's letter to him is brotherly kindness at his best. While great Lenin's letter to Pokrovsky, that same historian Pokrovsky who was later deified as one of Ulyanov-Lenin's apostles, is in a different key.

December 21, 1916
My esteemed M.N.! I have received your postcard of Dec. 14, 1916. If you have been informed that the publisher owes me "apart from 500 rubles, 300 rubles," I must say that I consider that he owes me *more*, for he has received (1) my article about an agrarian problem, part 1, and (2) my wife's pamphlet on an educational subject. And I assume that once a manuscript has been delivered it must be paid for.

Though at that stage Ulyanov-Lenin had to be as kind, solicitous, self-effacing toward his *comrades* as he possibly could (and as he was in his letter to Gorky), here he forgot his infinite comradely kindness toward someone whom he calls the publisher. Not to pay him for his and his wife's manuscripts! An uncanny coincidence: the two figures (500 and 300) are the same as those on account of which he kicked up such a row a couple of years later as he spurned the *raise* of 300 rubles to his *salary* of 500 rubles. But that was just paper, which he could obtain or have printed in any quantity, and now it was *real* money, *his* money.

The sad truth is that *after* Ulyanov-Lenin grabbed the country, one sixth of the inhabited globe, in a game of chance, many scholars all over the world began to analyze each drab cliché of his as a priceless gem of versatile (and in particular prophetic) genius. But at that time each comrade realized (quite justly) that he also could write no less quickly. So Ulyanov-Lenin had pleaded with Pokrovsky to persuade Gorky to publish him even with big deletions and changes, and he himself inflicted on Gorky his wife's piece which was accompanied by his letter asking if Gorky would be interested and had time for reading it. Gorky did not publish it. But Ulyanov-Lenin said he had *delivered* it—and hence it should be paid for.

But who was that unbrotherly character whom he called the publisher? Gorky. In the former letter Ulyanov-Lenin wheedled money from his brother Gorky, and the tone was brotherly kindness at his best. In this letter he wanted to force his brother Pokrovsky to get money out of his brother Gorky, and the tone was icy arrogance, irritation, and hatred for a certain anonymous "publisher" (he did not wish even to mention him by name).

What was the *main* trouble of the brothers of a future moneyless brotherhood?

There is no money, there is no money!! This is the *main* trouble!

The emphasis is Ulyanov-Lenin's: this is the *main* trouble. Once a *bolshevik* was even assigned to marry a rich heiress, and the operation reportedly netted 280,000 rubles, which is a good half a million dollars of today. Soon thereafter a bank transport was robbed, but banknotes were so large that they had to be exchanged all over the world. And yet there was no money, ever, and money was always the *main* trouble for great Lenin, according to his wife.

He wrote to *Granat*, to Gorky, and to relatives about it, and once he even proposed to Mark Yelizarov, his sister Anna's husband, a fantastic scheme for publishing a "pedagogical encyclopedia" on which I was to work.

One can anticipate another row in the selling of his wife's work by the fiat of delivery, but there was a danger:

Ilyich waxed so enthusiastic about this fantastic plan of his that he wrote about care being taken that no one should steal his idea.

An amazingly keen proprietary instinct: he was afraid that someone would *steal* a potentially remunerative idea which even his wife called fantastic.

A more reliable source after 1914 was the Kaiser Government of Germany. The awe and horror wrapping the subject has always amused me. According to the hypocrisies that have prevailed even in the West for so many centuries, it was rather heroic, good, and noble for a certain Ulyanov-Lenin to seize one-sixth of the inhabited globe, with a prospect for acquiring all of it. But it was necessary for great Lenin to conceal the fact that he received unbeautiful money for this purpose from the Kaiser ("Fie! How unbeautiful—a German agent!") though the total sum, equal perhaps to some paltry half a billion dollars of today, constituted a ridiculous—microscopic—fraction of the financial value of the one-sixth of the inhabited globe, apart from its value that cannot be expressed by any money, for man's possession of man is beyond all money. It is the same as ignoring a huge bank robbery with many victims but being shocked by the bank robber's having failed to pay his streetcar fare while going to the bank.

Even in the comparatively more humane European history, the concepts of heroism, goodness, and nobility derive largely from *knights*, that is, the romanticized *just* warlords, *kind* strongmen, *saintly* gangsters, who fought, killed, and grabbed whatever they could. *Knights, revolutionaries, corsairs, musketeers, cowboys, guerrillas.* Ulyanov-Lenin's getting money from the Kaiser spoils the exciting play at great Lenin and his *revolutionaries*: the wildly romantic play begins to look as a cool business transaction of the German General Staff which knocked Russia out of the war (and got her territory on which one-third of her population lived) at a very cheap price indeed.

Before the mid-fifties even some of those Western scholars whom *Pravda* calls the *most rabid anticommunists* were distressed that the Provisional Government issued in the summer of 1917 such a crude canard: to claim that a certain German agent Parvus passed via Ulyanov-Lenin's *comrade* Ganetsky alias Fürstenberg the Kaiser Government's money to Ulyanov-Lenin! When the German archives had become available in the West after the Second World War, some Western scholars relented somewhat. Parvus alias Helphand does figure as a paid agent in the archives of the German Foreign Office. "According to Dr. Helphand," the German Ambassador in Copenhagen reported on 21 December 1915, "about 20 million rubles would be required to get the Russian revolution completely started." Parvus did receive directly from the German Treasury little nothings—like one million rubles (much more than a million dollars of today) at the end of 1915. "The sum of one million rubles," the German Ambassador in Copenhagen reported on January 23, 1916, "has already reached Petrograd." The Berlin Hauptarchiv does contain an agreement by which the declared capital of Comrade Ganetsky-Fürstenberg's company was provided by two German agents, Parvus and Sklarz, each contributing half.

It is a sad comment that it took the German archives and half a century for some Western scholars like Professor Futrell of Oxford, England, to grope vaguely in the sixties for something that was so clear in 1917.

Great Lenin declared publicly, in print, when the Provisional Government had published its *crude canard* in the summer of 1917:

Ganetsky was employed by Parvus as a tradesman or he traded with him.

Great Lenin was quite right: his subordinate Ganetsky, who *officially* became in the autumn of 1917 a high ranker (and remained such until 1937, then went the way of all Old Bolshevik flesh, but is now *rehabilitated*) was only employed by Parvus or traded with him. Just how much money Parvus paid out to his employee or partner as a salary or stock capital or credit or loan or profit—whether one million or fifty million or five hundred million rubles—was certainly their private business.

The *central committee of the party* decided in the autumn of 1917 to dismiss Ganetsky—to get rid of him, because he was a Kaiser agent's agent, for to be an employee or/and partner of a Kaiser agent *means* to be his agent, something that no one in 1917 could fail to understand.

Since Ganetsky (just like Trotsky or Radek) was Ulyanov-Lenin's man, and his *comrades* of the *central committee* need not even know him, Ulyanov-Lenin rushed a letter to the *central committee* to prove that an employee of a Kaiser agent during a war with Kaiser Germany is not his *agent*, but his *employee*.

Ganetsky earned his daily bread as an *employee* in the trade firm whose stockholder was Parvus. This is what Ganetsky told me. This has not been disproved.

See? This has not been disproved. It Ganetsky had simply taken money from Parvus, then he would have been his *agent*. But it has not been disproved that Ganetsky was his *employee*. Or he

"traded with him," great Lenin said. "Come here, my honest employee or partner, Ganetsky," the Kaiser's agent Parvus can be
imagined saying. "For today's honest labors of yours in my
trade firm for my benefit and satisfaction, here's for you, my dear
employee or partner, some little nothing of one million rubles,
or do you prefer it as capital for *your* company which will buy
goods here and sell them in Russia? Come on, old man, don't
be too modest. You are worth every kopeck or pfennig of your
salary. Or shall we call it a bonus? Or a fair share of our profit?
I have met your dear senior comrade Ulyanov-Lenin not so long
ago, but soon after our meeting he began to denounce me publicly
for my pro-Kaiser stand, though I have never tried to conceal it,
not even before our meeting. But certainly *your* money, the
money that *you* have *earned* from me, or *your* honest company's
profit or gross sales, you can safely transfer to your dear senior
comrade."

In *Pravda*, great Lenin bravely attacked in the summer of 1917
the *crude canard* of the Provisional Government:

No money whatsoever has been received by the Bolsheviks either
from Ganetsky or Kozlovsky. All this is a lie, the crudest lie out of
whole cloth.

Indeed, Ganetsky and Kozlovsky were simply members of some
alien or hostile party; by sheer chance great Lenin had barely
seen one of the two ages ago:

Let us add that Ganetsky and Kozlovsky are not Bolsheviks, but
members of the Polish Social-Democratic Party, that Ganetsky is a
member of its Central Committee known to us by the London Congress (1903) from which the Polish delegates walked out, etc.

So Ganetsky was just one of those Polish renegades who
walked out on great Lenin in 1903.

It is only odd that several months later, when great Lenin
came to own the country, both total strangers, one of whom
had walked out on great Lenin in 1903, received *officially* such
high posts: Kozlovsky was, indeed, appointed to the top of
Ulyanov-Lenin's secret police. Was Ulyanov-Lenin fond of ap-
pointing total if somewhat hostile strangers to the top of his secret

police? Or fight with the *central committee of the party*, as in the case of Ganetsky, for their appointment to high posts?

April 12, 1917

Dear friends! So far there has been simply nothing: no letters, no parcels, no money from you.

But who are these dear friends? The letter says: "To comrades Ganetsky and Radek." In that order. To the dear comrade Ganetsky, Ulyanov-Lenin writes:

Dear comrade, letter No. 1 (of April 22–23) has been received today 21/4, old style.
The money (2,000) from Kozlovsky is here. The parcels have not yet arrived.

And a telegram to Ganetsky suggests that a thousand kronen was no problem for the dear friends:

Detail two or better three thousand kronen for our trip.

True, great Lenin said elsewhere that he had collected the money for the same trip to Russia from the comrades in Stockholm, and on his arrival in Petrograd-Petersburg he applied to the Council (Soviet) of Workers' and Soldiers' Deputies to get paid for the same trip of his at least for the third time:

Attached hereto are the receipts of payment for the trip of our group. I received 300 Swedish kronen from the Russian consul in Haparanda (the Tatyanin fund). I paid 472 rubles. This money which I have borrowed I would like to be reimbursed by the Committee of Aid to Exiles and Émigrés.

N. Lenin

Also, great Lenin's wife recalls that her mother's sister died at about the beginning of the war and left them her property, including 4,000 rubles.

We lived mainly on this money during the war, husbanding it so carefully that we still had some of it left on our return to Russia in 1917.

Still had some of it on our return to Russia in 1917! But in the autumn of 1916 Ulyanov-Lenin wrote to his brother in a future moneyless brotherhood Shlyapnikov:

As for myself personally, I need a source of income. Or I will just croak, honest to goodness!! Everything is devilishly expensive, and there is nothing to live on. Money must be extracted *by force* (Belenin will speak about money with Katin and Gorky himself, *unless it is inopportune*, of course) from the publisher of *Letopis* to whom I have sent two pamphlets (let him pay; *immediately* and as much as possible!).

The legacy was a nest egg, see? It is to husband it and "have some of it left on our return to Russia in 1917" that great Lenin had been canting and whining in his letter to his *brother* Shlyapnikov and had been grabbing money *immediately* and "as much as possible" everywhere from the wicked Kaiser creature Parvus (via a hostile stranger, a good honest employee-partner of Parvus, a dear friend Ganetsky) to the Soviet of Workers' and Soldiers' Deputies in honor of which he named his regime the *soviet power*, after his elimination of its independent membership, of course.

And how wise great Lenin was in respect to his own self. Young people may enjoy moneyless brotherhoods as a kind of picnic, youth adventure, or part of sowing of their wild oats. But when one is getting old like Ulyanov-Lenin (and picnicking young people are not interested in old people, are they?), and all his life has been a lost gamble, and the victory ahead is as chancy as ever, and no one needs him because, after all, he is just an old bore at the best, oh, how he wants his own, personal, private money.

No one needs him? But what about his *comrades*? Here he wrote to the editors of *Northern Pravda*:

Let me repeat again that I cannot work without seeing the newspapers. You have been asked thousands of times—and yet you haven't sent either *Workers' Pravda or . . .*

Following is a long list of *bolshevik* newspapers (incidentally, all legally published under the tsarist regime!), and none of these newspapers the *comrades* bother to send to Ulyanov-Lenin. But the end of the letter is even more bitter.

The pay, *earned long ago* and promised, has not arrived! This is beginning to look like mockery.

Oh, no. The *comrades* did not mock him. They simply did

not care. Later, when he possessed one-sixth of the inhabited globe, they would say that they had always valued even a remote chance to die for him, the greatest man in the history of mankind (and so on), but now they would not trouble to send him newspapers even if requested to do so thousands of times (not to mention his money, earned long ago and promised).

25

During the early seventeenth-century period of Russian history which was called the "Tumultuous Times" before 1917, a "People's Revolution" between 1917 and 1934, and a "Polish Invasion" thereafter, a certain Grishka the Ragged seized the Russian throne in the Kremlin and became known as pseudo-Dimitry I (since pseudo-Dimitry II popped up later). To those who wanted to follow him for the privileges he had promised, he explained that the son of Tsar Fedor I, named Dimitry, did not die as a little boy but was he, Grishka the Ragged. Similarly, for those people who could not read and write in the eighteenth century, the "tsar's banners" (which the associates of a certain Cossack named Pugach meaning the Terrifier had clandestinely fabricated) were the best explanation as to why their chieftain, the Terrifier, was entitled to replace Catherine II.

In 1914 the number of schoolchildren in Russia came close to 10 million, school education was scheduled to have become universal by 1922, and that kind of explanation would not do. All those school and college students could read and write. Many of them could in fact quickly write thick volumes provided someone would publish them and pay for the writing (in which sphere Ulyanov-Lenin met some difficulties with his publishing comrades). But not everyone who can read and write so quickly can think as quickly (or at all). Just as once there were many people who were called illiterates, so in this day of universal training in the reading and writing of *educated* phrases, there must inevitably be many people who are intellectual illiterates—who cannot think though they can read and write *educated* phrases very quickly or even type them amazingly well.

The "tsar's banners" for twentieth-century intellectual illiterates are not therefore mere clandestinely made pieces of cloth with appropriate symbols designed on them, as for eighteenth-century literal illiterates, but *educated* combinations of words of a certain set or cluster of words such as *revolutionary, proletarian, progressive, socialist,* and *democratic,* which they can read, hear, and reproduce in familiar patterns.

They need not and do not know what the words mean, except something very good or even sacred, in contrast to the *enemy* cluster of bad or evil words. For example, those who named themselves *bolsheviks* in 1903 and *communists* in 1918 intended to overthrow the *existing regime* in, say, the United States (indeed, originally North America and Western Europe came ahead of Russia in their schedule) and establish their absolute serf ownership (see Ulyanov-Lenin's definition of his *dictatorship*). In other words, they intended, planned, and were ready to destroy *any* civic, legal, or social arrangement outside *their* possession and establish absolute serf ownership as had existed millennia ago. So *communists* as of 1918 were some of the most drastic counter-revolutionaries in human history, the most rabid fighters for unprecedented reaction or regression, the worst enemies of progress as the concept has evolved in the last three centuries, and the potentially or actually most ruthless exploiters of blue-collar workers as well (as most blue-collar workers of the United States realize very well and most of those of Russia sensed already in 1918, but it was too late).

Open even Western encyclopedias, monographs, studies. These most drastic counterrevolutionaries in human history are generally called *revolutionaries.* Why?

First of all, quite a few Western scholars of today describe how Ulyanov-Lenin pined in the unfreedom of the *tsarist regime.* But Ulyanov-Lenin's desire to smash the existing regime became all the more intense when a democracy, which he himself called the world's freest, had been established in Russia. And Ulyanov-Lenin did raze to the ground this freest democracy, not the *tsarist regime*. This often falls on deaf ears: open the latest Western studies and usually you will read how great Lenin pined in the *tsarist regime* so that he simply had to overthrow it. It is like reiterating endlessly the story of a bank robbery, each time connecting it with the robbers' dire poverty and each time screening out the fact that the robbers had become rich eight months *before* the bank robbery.

Second, the word "revolutionaries" seemed to great Lenin and his men so good. One who contributes to some progress in mathematics (or medicine) is simply gifted and wise. But one who revolutionizes—makes a real revolution in—mathematics (or medicine) is a mind of genius. Thus, a *revolutionary* is a mind of genius, revolutionizing not just some mathematics (or medicine), but life in general, with a beautiful heroic, and saintly dash of a knight-musketeer-movie-cowboy.

The modern civic societies which came to be called "democracies" in the nineteenth century are strikingly new, revolutionary, highly experimental societies, as against the millennia of unfreedom in which mankind, even in these few fortunate countries, lived and perhaps will always live. Yet those out to destroy these revolutionary societies are called *revolutionaries*. "The passion to destroy is also a creative passion," said the Russian *revolutionary* Bakunin. To destroy is, indeed, very exciting, unless *you* are destroyed. In mathematics (or medicine) no one out to destroy all mathematics in order to return to counting on his fingers (or to the treatment of wounds by dust) is called a revolutionary. Mathematics (or medicine) are assumed to be too serious for that. Whereas the life of society, infinitely more complex than mathematics (or medicine), is often thought to be a perfectly suitable field in which every destroyer, even for the sake of avowed counterrevolutionary regress and reaction, is a revolutionary if he calls himself one. Especially since no matter how free he is, he can always demonstrate that he is a *slave* (of *capital*, for example) and the society is a lunatic asylum, a dungeon, a torture chamber. He can also behave in any society no matter how free as though he were persecuted for his convictions (and not for, say, the splashing of acid into someone else's eyes) and as though there were no other way to put an end to this *persecution,* and all the *slavery, torture, genocide*, and such, but to take to arms and overthrow the *existing regime.*

So they are *revolutionaries*. Similarly they pick up all the other words that seem to them good, noble, heroic, to apply to themselves in accordance with rank, and all the bad words to apply to their enemies in accordance with their supposed extent of resistance. They must not distinguish between different good words, and between different bad words. Each of the two sets of words is to fuse in their minds into a single string or cluster of absolute good and absolute evil respectively. The mental process is described for so-called primitive tribes and is known as coparticipative association.

Comparing the fashionable anthropologist of the sixties Lévi-Strauss and the once no less famous anthropologist of the twenties Lévy-Bruhl one can draw the following anthropological rule: the more rational or reasonable is the society or milieu in which an anthropologist lives, that is, the more secure and comfortable his life is, the more he is inclined to imagine that he is a primitive tribesman (*un sauvage*), or at least that the thinking of the outstanding thinkers of the last three centuries does not differ fundamentally from that of primitive tribes such as the Bororo in Brazil. Lévi-Strauss even calls his studies quite fashionably *myths,* and he feels as quite *un sauvage* when he listens to Wagner and Stravinsky. He only forgets that when he, surrounded by electronically run bank accounts, humane doctors, exquisite restaurants and the entire late-twentieth-century ambience of a civically developed, wealthy and sophisticated society, listens to Wagner or Stravinsky in an air-conditioned or at least pleasantly ventilated building, it is just another way of his aurical and visual enjoyment, and it is not at all the same as living in, and thinking the thoughts of, the *société sauvage* that Wagner or Stravinsky allegedly evokes.

Born into *un société sauvage*, the present author perceives the difference between reason, as incarnated in, say, the outstanding thinkers of the world at large in the last three centuries, and *pensée sauvage*, as represented by, say, the Bororo tribe. Unfortunately, not all formally educated or uneducated people of today match the outstanding thinkers of the last three centuries, and the frequent proximity of *their* thinking to *pensée sauvage* does not delight the present author, as it does Lévi-Strauss, but depresses and horrifies him.

In coparticipative thinking, members of a primitive tribe fuse entirely different phenomena into a single chain or cluster: parrots-tobacco-boar-fire, and so forth. All these phenomena coparticipate in each other, and *we* coparticipate in all of them, unless they are evil, and then the evil *they* coparticipate in all of them, and they coparticipate in each other. The manichean dualism is already obvious: what is *we* is all *we*, and what is not *we* is all *they*. Similarly, what is *we* is *revolutionary* is *proletarian* is *progressive* is *socialist* is *democratic* and so forth. It is useless to ask: "But look—by 'revolutionary' you connote mainly 'conducive to the overthrow of the *existing regime*,' don't you? Why should the 'overthrow of the *existing regime*' lead to 'progress' or to 'democracy,' and not to a social structure which existed in Russia or China two or twenty centuries ago? Why should 'progress' be necessarily connected with blue-collar workers? Why is 'socialist' (run by a government's officials?) necessarily 'progressive,' or 'revolutionary,' or 'proletarian,' or 'democratic'?"

Such questions are meaningless because all the good words (and all the bad words, respectively) are not to be even identified separately: they are to fuse into a single coparticipative cluster: *revolutionary-proletarian-progressive-socialist-democratic*, etc., growing in extent with rank and culminating in the chieftain. Behaviorally, the manichean, coparticipative, earthly religions now filling millions of volumes in all countries are of no importance: they are merely verbal "tsar's banners," provided one is motivated to follow the chieftain or at least verbally sympathize with him or his cluster in a safely distant country.

Of course, the chieftain himself and his *comrades* are sufficiently motivated: he is to be the supertsar, and they are to be the superaryan nobility and superclerical clergy. But the proper motivation of a broader section of the population is more difficult to attain. Many eighteenth-century Russian serfs could be well motivated to follow any chieftain because any change could seem to them for the better. But in twentieth-century democracies and even in a semiconstitutional monarchy like Russia before the outbreak of World War I the populace is not so game.

Therefore, before 1917 Ulyanov-Lenin and his *comrades* had to belong and belonged to those people who react painfully to every sign—or indeed, rumor, suspicion, possibility of suffering, cruelty, lack of freedom, and so on. So sensitive or hypersensitive

they were. Real Don Quixotes, Jesus Christs, Florence Nightingales. Except that they reacted only when the event, rumor,
suspicion, possibility, or whatever could reflect badly on any of
the regimes they wanted to overthrow all over the world or
when the alleged victims could contribute to the goal and/or
carry them to possession-power.

In 1890 Ulyanov-Lenin read Chekhov's story "Ward Six." In
some tiny Russian town 200 miles away from a railway a doctor
finds the townsmen dull philistines and makes friends with a
"mentally sick but interesting young man" in the psychiatric
ward. Taking advantage of that, his rival manages to confine the
doctor himself. Having read the story, Ulyanov-Lenin felt that
Russia (or the whole world?) was Ward Six.

When I finished reading the story yesterday, I was seized by terror,
I could not stay in my room any longer, I got up and went out. I had
the feeling that I was also locked up in Ward Six.

Note hypersensitivity: the story is a fictitious, hypothetical,
accidental case in a faraway town. In any society, doctors in some
godforsaken hole may confine their lonely colleague, having
neither relatives nor friends, and striking the local townsfolk as
looney. But Ulyanov-Lenin was seized by terror—could not stay
in his room any longer. Watch how his hypersensitivity is linked
with the overthrow of the regime: Russia (or the whole *capitalist
world*) is Ward Six, and he, Ulyanov, is also locked in. How
mankind is suffering, locked in. But never mind: he will smash
the worldwide psychiatric asylum in which mankind is locked.

As Ulyanov-Lenin was seized by terror when reading an
imaginary story about a provincial doctor, a real disaster unfolded
around him: Samara, where he lived, was the epicenter of a
famine. A statistician of a local council set the "number of the
hunger-stricken population as of October" at 964,627 persons.
The gentle reader perhaps remembers that in the famine of 1919
to 1923 *Pravda* once mentioned rather briskly *twenty-five million*
in the Volga region. The counting unit of fewer than a million
deaths simply ceased to exist after 1917. But before 1917 no one
had counted victims on a megascale: the figure of 964,627
hunger-stricken persons boggled the mind. The *bolshevik*
Belyakov later described with scorn all the hectic activity which

had started at the news. "The so-called society sounded the alarm, the press began to make a noise . . . Radicals, Liberals, members of local councils, officials, and even reactionary philistines began to fuss and ballyhoo . . . Lev Nikolayevich Tolstoy came to organize dining rooms and left his son Lev Lvovich as his representative."

The government allocated about 2 million rubles for what was called "public works." It was decided to build an elevator in Samara, a port on Samara River for the wintering and repair of ships and barges, a dam on Samara River at the station Kryaj, also an elevator in Buguruslan and a very big dam in the mouth of the Kinel.

When a special committee for relief to the hunger-stricken population was set up in Samara, some *revolutionaries* joined it. Not to aid the victims, but to "use their work for revolutionary propaganda among the starving population." It might seem that great Lenin could be satisfied: the drought and hence harvest failure could certainly be ascribed to the government (why did it not know how to control droughts in 1891?), and the starving population be called upon to overthrow the regime. But no, great Lenin was not satisfied at all.

Lenin did not believe in the success of such propaganda among the starving population. This consideration of his played a large role in his negative attitude to our committee. Arguing against our views, he demonstrated that our dining rooms would be a kind of "propaganda by deed" in favor of the reconciliation with the regime which had generated the famine—and in this respect he was right, of course.

Of course, he was right. The more people died the more great Lenin and his men would be able to show their compassion versus the cruelty of the regime which had *generated* the famine (and drought?).

By destroying farm households, the famine destroys the belief not only in the tsar, but also in God, and in due time will no doubt push the peasants onto the road of the revolution and facilitate its victory.

And the *revolution* was Ulyanov-Lenin's possession-power, because anyone who was against it was not *revolutionary-socialist-democratic-proletarian*, etc., but on the contrary, *counterrevolutionary-capitalist-autocratic-bourgeois*, etc. So it was necessary to wreck the relief work for the famine-stricken population, including the relief committee which presented, indeed, a manifold danger to great Lenin.

It was essential to assure the population that every *existing regime*, whether in Russia or the United States or anywhere else, could only get *ever worse*: there was no way out except to overthrow it in favor of great Lenin's possession-power. The famine emphasized the prediction, while its alleviation weakened it. But much worse, the committee's relief work exemplified the civic spontaneity of the population helping itself on its own, independently of the government. This civic spontaneity, as part of civic evolution which had been on since the 1860s, was the gravest danger of all, because one can *overthrow,* that is, topple, a governmental hierarchy, but one cannot topple the independent civic activity of the overwhelming majority of the population for the simple reason that it has neither top nor bottom to be toppled: it is an all-pervading, mobile, rotating, spontaneous tissue, and not a fixed, rigid, towerlike or pyramidlike structure which can be toppled if properly undermined.

But the trouble was that the relief committee continued to work and save the starving population! Great Lenin and his men rushed heroically forward to eliminate the danger.

With the arrival of Vladimir Ilyich, our actions became more definite. True, our forces were not large, and yet we did not miss a single meeting of the committee, where we came with the exclusive purpose of interfering with its work, launching on trenchant criticism and thus breaking the forces of the committee.

Note the modesty of the heroic *bolshevik*: "our forces were not large." Of course: that was only 1891, the very beginning. Great Lenin was barely twenty. To have such small forces in only one city and cause the death of so many people by starvation as early as 1891! Nor was it that simple. To carry on its aid to the hunger-stricken population, the committee began to "conceal the places of its meetings" from great Lenin and his men.

Yet Vladimir Ilyich, while having at that time a really small dedicated following of fifteen to twenty young, inexperienced, inadequately prepared men, acted as an experienced military commander and succeeded in disorganizing the committee which consisted of experienced skillful veteran officials, some of whom had high social status.

But how did great Lenin accomplish—at the age of twenty, too, and against all these odds—such a brilliant feat of causing so many deaths by starvation, if the committee concealed its meetings from great Lenin to save its relief work? *Inside* the committee great Lenin had his men

who almost invariably informed us accurately as to the time and place of the meeting of the committee. Vladimir Ilyich would enjoy this hugely, while in the committee our appearance at its almost secret meetings would cause depression and irritation.

It is interesting that the relief committee could not kick out great Lenin aged twenty and his men: he and his men called themselves *revolutionary-progressive-socialist-humanist*, etc., and how can one kick out men who call themselves all that? If they had called themselves young college-trained megascale agents provocateurs or nascent global gangsters, *then* the committee would have dared to ask them to leave its meetings.

Apart from having routed the relief committee by the end of November 1891, the twenty-year-old Ulyanov is also proudly credited with having produced *animation* among all political exiles who lived in Samara under police surveillance and in all circles of young people. By *animation* is meant the cessation of that pernicious interest of some political exiles in the relief to the victims of the famine.

Animation set in among those under surveillance of all trends as well as in the circles of young people. The famine was no longer presented as the problem of problems.

In the spirit of this *animation* great Lenin and his men threw a party to celebrate the New Year, the year of 1892. True, members of the wrecked relief committee organized their own New Year's party with collections for the hunger-stricken population. At it again! So they had not been yet completely routed. To hell with them: great Lenin and his men would finish them off later, and meanwhile, at *their* New Year's party, great Lenin and his men would show the real spirit of *animation* at the epicenter of the famine.

That was the first big evening party in which Vladimir Ilyich took part. There was a lot of noise and merrymaking.

We will skip all but the very end of the merrymaking, because it does not differ from the merrymaking of any *vulgar philistines* whom *new men* were supposed to replace.

As was the custom of that time, every evening party, every merrymaking, was to end with dancing. I don't remember who announced a "general, direct and open quadrille" without sex and age distinctions. The emcee was to see to it that there were not a single person not dancing. So Vladimir Ilyich also had to hop the quadrille for all his worth.

The evening party was an all-round success: at the epicenter of the famine they ate, drank, and made merry, and some people find such activities more pleasant than dying of hunger. They did not donate a kopeck to those who were dying of hunger, which was also an achievement, because Ulyanov-Lenin, who is known to have tried, quite unreasonably, to squeeze money even out of his *comrades,* could not be expected to give away *his* money to strangers. Yet while eating, drinking, and making merry like any callous, humorless, tight-fisted *vulgar philistines*, they *fought* thereby for their *heroic ideal*: the *happiness of mankind* (which happens to mean their possession of it). For the more merrily great Lenin and his men hopped the quadrille, the bigger was their contribution to *animation* in Samara.

But what about their compassion? My God! Their compassion was infinite—simply infinite. Great Lenin was seized by terror when he read that story about a confined provincial doctor. Can you imagine his feelings when he was right at the epicenter of a *real* disaster of such a scope?

Were his feelings sincere? Why not? He sincerely caused the death from hunger of as many people as he possibly could and at the same time almost went mad with sincere compassion for them (and with sincere wrathful hatred for the regime). Both attitudes were equally necessary. If there had been fewer deaths from hunger, he could not have expressed the same scope of compassion for these people: the effect of his compassion would have been weaker. And if he had not expressed his compassion for these people, what would have been the purpose of causing the death of as many of them as he possibly could? By expressing his compassion for these people and his wrathful hatred for the regime, he inculcated into every discontented mind that the regime had to be overthrown, and in the *new,* that is, *his* regime of infinite compassion, all the discontented would find in him their infinitely compassionate champion, and all their discontents would be heeded, relieved, resolved.

In most people such emotional states are more believably acted out if they are *sincere.* That is, if great Lenin had said to himself while bemoaning those dying of hunger: "I am a hypocrite: I have done all I could to cause the death of as many of them as possible," the intensity of his compassion and his wrath might have been much weaker. Therefore, it usually pays to be *sincere*: that is, to entertain no extraneous thoughts while abandoning oneself entirely to, say, the compassion for those whose death one has been causing with zest, skill and single-minded persistence.

What a vast scope for infinite compassion any society presents to a *heroic idealist* like that! First of all, in Ulyanov-Lenin's future society there were to be no courts, prisons, armies, or any other *means of state coercion.* How cruel it is to put *anyone* even on trial. But to keep *anyone* in prison! Or to *kill* (oh!) *anyone* in war! As a favorite song of Ulyanov-Lenin and his *comrades* began: "With tears the vast world is flooded." Exactly: courts, prisons, droughts, diseases, wars, loneliness, old age, bad luck, boredom, and everything else down to the rivalry of doctors in a tiny provincial town are all *generated* by the infernal regime.

The pen name Gorky means Bitter. Said this *greatest revolutionary humanist*: "My heart has been skinned alive." That is, no matter how hypersensitive one is, his heart still has a skin, separating him from someone else's suffering, while Gorky's heart was raw, bleeding, having no skin at all. True, between 1928 and 1936 Gorky demonstrated not only a perfectly impervious two-inch-thick armor all over his heart, but in fact the total disappearance of this supposed organ of compassion. For he was endangered himself, and so he had no compassion to spare for strangers. But before 1917 his heart had been flayed. He had, indeed, an eye only for the horrible—diseases, deformities, pathology—and while there is nothing bad about this for a creative artist, his gift proved to be a real godsend for Ulyanov-Lenin's *humanism.* Gorky recorded his skinned-heart visions of syphilitic prostitutes, abnormal criminals, sadistic eccentrics, defective children—or simply abominable psychopaths—and these creatures humiliated or maimed or killed each other in doss houses, slums, or in the open, under a sky which was always glowering, leaden, and hopeless. There is such a facet to life, no doubt, and it is only wholesome for society to know it, but the *humanist* trick was that the reader was to believe that there was and could be nothing else in life until the overthrow of the regime in the United States, Western Europe, and Russia, and this overthrow would transform the world into a paradise on earth in which there would soon evidently be no death either, given *revolutionary-socialist-scientific-progressive*, etc., medicine.

Pity all the discontent in any *existing regime*. Pity the Russians of 1912 because their regime is still only a semiconstitutional monarchy, and not, say, a democracy as in the United States of 1968. Pity the Americans of 1968 because what does such a well-developed democracy lead to? Only bad manners, pornography, drug addiction, and all that. Pity the Russians after the collapse of the monarchy in 1917: here they have full freedom, and what does it lead to? Only war, food shortages, inequality, and all that.

Pity the Americans again because what sort of democracy is that, with all those courts, prisons, and armed forces? Democracy in the United States! Don't make great Lenin or great Gorky laugh in spite of all their tears. Why, the greatest revolutionary humanist in the history of mankind Gorky could publish in the United States only as many copies of his books as were bought (those Americans in fact deeply wounded great Gorky by their inattention). Meanwhile the rich can publish any trash in any number of copies! Great Lenin's *genuine democracy* will not only ensure all those *formal* democratic freedoms as in the United States, but will also secure them *materially*: for example, it will not simply guarantee the *formal* freedom of the press, but will also provide Gorky with free paper, printing ink, and presses. Thus the greatest revolutionary humanist will have the genuine, and not only formal, freedom of telling mankind about the tears flooding the vast world. And about a lonely doctor in a tiny far-away provincial town whom callous philistines proclaimed insane.

26

True enough, as soon as Ulyanov-Lenin and his *comrades* were in possession of Russia, there were henceforth no tears (on their territory). Tears are individual. Tears must be visible. Those who cry must have the inviolability not to conceal their tears.

Now mere human pests (which were then called *harmful insects*) were ground in a network of all-closed mills. What tears?

The muffled grinding noise maybe. If you put your ear to a mill.

Owing to the pest exterminators' culpable negligence, Gorky overheard—yes, screams. As the greatest revolutionary humanist on whose donations and collections Ulyanov-Lenin himself had largely led that wonderful life in Europe, Gorky still had even as late as the summer of 1919 the privilege of reporting his experience to Ulyanov-Lenin in a private letter, to which Ulyanov-Lenin replied in a letter suggesting to Gorky at least five times that he, Gorky, was insane:

To A. M. Gorky
31 July 1919
... all your impressions are totally sick. ... Your nerves have obviously broken down. ... Just as your conversations, your letter is the sum total of sick impressions carrying you to sick conclusions. This is all a pure sick psyche. ... It is clear that you have worked yourself up into sickness. ...

If Gorky had been hearing screams, and no one else did (the enemies of all kinds had been simply lying that they did), was it not clear where Gorky's sick psyche had to be kept? Unless that sick psyche went abroad *for treatment,* the quietest way for everyone concerned.

With Gorky safely away in Italy (to a *fascist* country a *communist* writer had escaped in search of safety) *Pravda* could, on behalf of *all working people,* merely jeer at his humanism, sensitivity, compassion, which *Pravda* had valued so high *before* the autumn of 1917.

M. Gorky is, as we all know, compassionate—so compassionate that this is a real disaster. He likes to turn on his waterworks on any pretext. And the pretext is always hollow.

The example of Gorky indicates that in a network or industry of selective compassion for those who may help to overthrow the regime no matter what it is, there may be some who are not pure hard-as-nails professionals of compassion like great Lenin. Gorky was somehow involved in his pre-1917 compassion because he tried to continue it *after* the autumn of 1917. But when steel-eyed professionals of compassion take over, they simply exterminate pests like Gorky, or if they cannot do it because they want to look humane in democracies, they kick him out of the country "for psychiatric treatment" and jeer in their super-monopoly of all media at his "waterworks."

Much earlier, in 1918, Gorky's newspaper, with all the newsprint, printing ink, and presses which the *genuine democracy* was to supply to him free of charge, but which still, fortunately, could be bought privately for filthy lucre, was wiped out, as though it had never existed. Inside the country, everything Gorky wrote from 1917 to 1919 was tracked down and destroyed, while abroad representatives of *all progressive mankind* would buy it or borrow it from libraries and then lose it (can't a fellow lose a book?). The long article "Gorky" in the 1970 *Britannica* evinces no knowledge of Gorky's existence from 1917 to 1919: perhaps he ceased to exist just for a couple of years?

But of course, it was a unique exception that Gorky was allowed to publish for so long. Three days after the seizure of possession-power *Pravda* announced: "We have closed some newspapers calling themselves 'socialist.'" See? Just calling themselves.

Whoever struggles against the revolutionary workers' and peasants' government serves Rodzyanko-Kaledin.

Thus, within three days of great Lenin's open seizure of the country it was announced that the only permissible creed in the country would henceforth be absolutely manichean and co-participative: those who would voice *any* dissident view would be said to coparticipate thereby in Rodzyanko, Kaledin, *capitalism*, trial by jury, Trotsky and nearly all Old Bolsheviks, Gestapo, Christianity, the persecution of Jesus Christ, (private) slavery, those *soviet* generals and officers who fought on the side of Nazi Germany, Winston Churchill, all those who only call themselves Communists, democracy, Empress Catherine II, Zionism, the collapse of a bridge in Brazil, liberals, Dostoyevsky, Communist China, Liberals, a poor literary taste, Social Democrats, famines, non-representational painting, and whoever and whatever, real or imaginary, is not *we* at a current moment and hence is *they*, the *enemy*, coparticipating in each other, and indeed constituting one heinous evil conspiracy of one multi-headed, protean, daily changing, and yet eternal and universal monster responsible for all evil on earth now, ever before, and always.

General Statute of the Press

1. To be closed are only the organs of the press (1) calling for open resistance or disobedience to the workers' and peasants' government (2) stirring trouble by obviously slanderous distortion of facts and (3) calling for activity which is criminal, that is liable as crime.

So *only* these organs of the press were to be closed. What remained? A single serf supermonopoly of all media obeying a single command from the *center* with the instantaneous automatic unthinking precision of a serf regiment. I call it for brevity the network of propaganda. But it is not just propaganda in the modern sense of the word ("war propaganda"). This *propaganda* is also the compulsory, inquisitional, one-and-only religion, the only source of knowledge beyond immediate experiences, and the creator of imaginary life.

Who was to decide that some statement was an "obvious slanderous distortion of facts," that is, deviated from the *propaganda*?

Decision on the Revolutionary Tribunal of the Press

1. A revolutionary tribunal of the press is to be set up at the revolutionary tribunal. Subject to its jurisdiction are all the felonies and misdemeanors perpetrated against the people via the use of the press.

2. The felonies and misdemeanors via the use of the press include any communication of false or distorted information on social phenomena, for this is a violation of the rights and interests of the revolutionary people.

Early in 1918 *Pravda* reported a horrible crime perpetrated by—no, not a newspaper! Now a leaflet had also to be tracked down.

For the last several days certain scared individuals have clandestinely distributed leaflets the wild hysterical expressions of which were aimed against the Soviet power.

Pravda was certain that the scared distributors of leaflets (allegedly *social revolutionaries*) and "such deliberate crimes must meet with the most severe punishment."

But if *such deliberate crimes* in writing (as in those leaflets) must be severely punished, certainly they must be severely punished in oral delivery as well, as in the case *Pravda* reported for general edification:

Retribution to an Enemy of the People

Vyatka, July 4. For counter-Soviet agitation, the clergyman Berezovsky is sentenced to the deprivation of political rights and eight years of social labor.

Not to write, but just to say something which one was not authorized to say was now a crime. On May 1, 1918, in Nikolskaya Street, Moscow, a certain Kokuyev said, according to *Pravda*, that the "Soviet power has seized all churches and stripped all icon mountings."

Between 1917 and 1923, the *soviet power* did strip all icon mountings: soon after Kokuyev said this the measure became officially known as the Confiscation of Church Valuables. But how can a certain Kokuyev be allowed to say this?

A member of the Moscow Soviet Khotinsky arrested Kokuyev on the spot, and a statement against Kokuyev was drawn at the City Commissariat on the basis of Khotinsky's testimony.

So, *arrested* on May 1, Kokuyev had been in *prison* for about five months in expectation of the *trial*, and *prisons* were such that he might not have survived at all. It was his luck that he was to be made a public example of, described by *Pravda*, and *put on trial*, instead of perishing without a trace.

Within a month of his possession-power the Moses of the globe dashed off on a piece of paper another important *law*.

The trial by jury began to sprout in England about a thousand years ago. It took a millennium for the most advanced democracies of today to develop their present legal-civic fabric. In Russia this legal-civic fabric, including trial by jury, had been developing since the 1860s. With a flourish of his great pen great Lenin swept away a thousand years of European legal-civic development.

What did he substitute instead?

Great Lenin learned that a "perfectly healthy fir tree" had been cut in the park of the Hills health resort which had been organized near his villa named the Soviet Estate Hills. Comrade Lenin expressed no wish to see Comrade Vever, who had allegedly ordered, as manager of the health resort, the felling of a tree, or to learn whatever the suspect could say in his defense. To begin with, the tree was not, perhaps, as *perfectly healthy*, as great Lenin thought without having ever seen it?

For the permission of such a damage to Soviet property, I prescribe hereby to subject Comrade Vever, manager of the health resort under the auspices of the Soviet Estate Hills,

to imprisonment for a term of one month.

The sentence will be executed by the Podolsk Uyezd Executive Committee, and furthermore . . .

Furthermore, great Lenin meticulously stipulated how to proceed if the criminal Vever had perpetrated no crimes before and if "any damage to Soviet property" had been detected again.

I instruct Comrade Belenky to read this decision to Comrade Vever and his assistants and make them sign a statement to the effect that the aforesaid has been announced to them, and it has been communicated to them that the next similar violation will entail the punishment of all the employees, and not the manager alone.

This historic document has been published by the network of

propaganda because it shows how great Lenin loved and valued even a single (perfectly healthy) tree of *soviet* (that is, his) property and how gentle and kind he was: everyone understands that to *sentence* one suspect or even *all* employees of the resort to a month of prison when perfectly irrelevant hostages were *officially* shot by the thousand is an act of unique gentleness and kindness. At the same time this uniquely gentle and kind *sentence* gives us a glimpse into the legal-civic nature of the new regime.

Dr. Blank, the grandfather of great Lenin, was a *private*, that is, small-scale, serf owner. When he punished his serfs, he was the constitution, legislature, prosecutor, court, and council for defense. His grandson received a serf estate the size of former Russia, with a prospect of its extension to the size of the world. Ideally, he was to punish in person all his serfs and be in the process everyone and everything from the law-giver to the executioner. But, unlike his grandfather's, his serf estate was too big for that. In the vicinity he could *sentence* some Vever. But what about the serf estate beyond earshot, especially when it had been extended to Africa, both Americas or the Antarctic? Hence the network of *courts* as extensions of great Lenin's ubiquitous eyes and punishing hands, necessary simply because the mega-scale serf owner cannot punish all his serfs personally.

So, according to the *law* which great Lenin penned within a month of his possession of the country, the *new court*, or the *people's court*, was to consist of a "permanent judge and two rotating assessors invited for each session by special lists," that is, exactly as this *people's court* exists today and exactly as it existed in, say, barbarous Europe prior to the first origins of trial by jury about a thousand years ago in Britain.

Nor did great Lenin relent four years later, when there was a complete peace, when every organization or association other than the *party* had been pulverized, when even a single unarmed passer-by could not safely say to another passer-by a word deviating from the *party's* one and only creed. Quite the contrary. In *Pravda* he declared that "for the public demonstration of Menshevism our courts must shoot, or else they are not our courts but God knows what."

In other words, the *courts* must constitute the pseudo-tsar-god's single network of inquisitional tribunals establishing such subtle heresies as *menshevik marxism* in contrast to *bolshevik marxism* and punishing all the heretics by death. Why by mere death, and not by torture to death? Torture was mentioned *officially* quite sparingly, while shooting was a good, pleasant, romantic word: death by shooting meted out on any occasion to hostages or suspects was thought to be noble, righteous, beautiful. But this does not mean that in reality unbeautiful torture to death was less rife than beautiful shooting. Great Lenin's *dictatorship*, that is, possession-power or superautocracy, as, say, in ancient China at its worst, was to include a permanent and ubiquitous persecution of heresies by beautiful death (and hidden torture), and great Lenin's sensitivity as to what constituted a heresy far exceeded that of the Inquisition in the medieval West or of the Holy Synod under Peter I of Russia, though great Lenin expressed his super-Inquisitional zeal in the most *democratic-revolutionary-free-progressive*, etc., language which many scholars, intellectuals or diplomats all over the world have been repeating with *democratic-revolutionary-free-progressive*, etc., fervor.

In May 1922 great Lenin penned an *article of the criminal code*. According to the *article*, beautifully shot were to be those found by the *courts* to be *guilty* of "propaganda or agitation" which "act" (no, not the *defendant* acts, but his "propaganda and agitation" act) "in the direction" of a certain "part of the international bourgeoisie."

Every inhabitant except Ulyanov-Lenin could thus be *officially*, beautifully and hence openly shot on the spot (or unbeautifully and hence secretly tortured to death) unless he repeated word for word what great Lenin had said. Even if he skipped inadvertently one comma, this omission could be said to "act in the direction" of a certain "part of the international bourgeoisie," especially since any real or imaginary beings can be called "that part of the international bourgeoisie," anything can be ascribed to these manichean forces of evil, darkness and hell on earth, and certainly the omission of a comma can be said to "act in the direction" of these coparticipating diabolical creatures and hordes.

Today, all *newspaper texts*, except purely local descriptive items, are dictated by radio to all the *newspapers* in the country, down to every comma, for God have mercy if a single *newspaper* deviates from the only and one sacred text even by a single comma once in a century.

Yet great Lenin was not satisfied with his *article of the criminal code*. His all-embracing definition of a heresy to be officially punishable (in 1922, the most peaceful, lenient, benign year of his possession of the country) by beautiful shooting seemed to him too specific. He wanted something more ambiguous, ambivalent, all-penetrating. In his second version of the *article of the criminal code* he inserted the word "objectively": "propaganda and agitation objectively contributing." *Subjectively*, the suspect may have intended no heresy. He may not even have realized that, say, the omission of a comma in the one and only sacred text will "act in the direction of that part of the international bourgeoisie." But *objectively*, the omission will, and therefore he is to be beautifully shot no matter what was his *subjective* intent or understanding.

Yet the great super-Inquisitor was still dissatisfied and produced the third, the most superinquisitional version, known as Variant 2b.

Variant 2b. Propaganda or agitation objectively contributing, or capable of doing so, to that part of the international bourgeoisie which etc. as before to the end.

Capable of objectively contributing. That omitted comma does not contribute even *objectively* to the coparticipating forces of evil, darkness, and hell on earth. But it might. It may yet. It is capable of doing so.

However, strictly speaking, the *court* was only a supplementary arrangement. Grave *political crimes* like the murder of any local chief by a commoner were to be handled secretly by the *extraordinary commission,* the initial name of the *organs of state security* in 1918. The *court* was to handle publicly much more trifling matters like petty bribes, larcenies, or the murder of a commoner by a commoner. Its public operation was to edify commoners. A certain Draznin collected rags for the institution which printed so much money for Ulyanov-Lenin and therefore needed so many rags. Allegedly, he gave a bribe to the tune of about $2 by exchange rate of 1913, though he claimed he gave the money for rags. Draznin laughed at the *trial* because he could not believe it was serious, but the *sentence* was: to be shot, and *Pravda* gave a unique description of Draznin on hearing the *sentence*.

And surprisingly, the constant expression of impervious cunning and suppressed mockery flew off his face. The pale drooping head with suddenly large eyes became spiritually beautiful and youthful again. Everything superficial, commercially vulgar, repulsive, had disappeared before the terrible breathing of death.

Just watch how spiritually beautiful and even youthful that ragpicker Draznin became as though he was purified of all evil just by shooting. Imagine what spiritual beauty and youth were attained after a long process of torture to death, and not just shooting. Unfortunately, some wicked vestiges of the tsarist past might fail to understand in what a blissful paradise they had found themselves (why, even practically painless shooting recaptured such spiritual beauty and youth for its dwellers)— and in their blind ignorance they might try even to flee from the paradise on earth, harmful and indeed fatal as it was for the beauty and youth of their souls. Therefore, on the day the *new court* was introduced, another *law* (or it was called, just a *rule*, which makes no difference whatsoever) introduced *special permits*, in addition to foreign passports with photographs and all, for those leaving Russia.

All persons going abroad, men, women and children, are subject to thorough personal search; to be searched are also all the personal effects of the leavers.

The *special section of the guarding of the border* was to do a good job, for had not some of its chiefs shuttled so easily across the border under Nicholas the Bloodthirsty?

The border was sealed. Safely cut off from the outside world and completely at the mercy of their owners and overseers, the dwellers could now only express their joy at being inside the paradise on earth in which even ordinary shooting (not to mention torture) made them spiritually beautiful and youthful.

With the country having become a hermetically sealed reservoir or container, its owners could now control any inside-outside passage of every bit of information or unit of humanity so that all outgoing or ingoing information could be useful for the *propaganda.*

A unique poet named Alexander Blok applied in 1921 for the *permission to go abroad,* to Finland, on the plea of poor health. No twentieth-century poet had the spiritual impact of Alexander Blok in Russia (the analogue nearest in time would be George Gordon Byron in Europe about a hundred years earlier). It was his verse that my aunt Vera inscribed in her reverent pearly handwriting whenever he had deleted it in later editions, and it is on his photograph that the tablecloth seemed the Apocalyptic sunset to the Russians of three generations.

> So eternity cometh at last
> To confine us in silence for good

And so eternity did. The twentieth-century Lord Byron of Russia, the most creatively free, proud, orginal of poets, became a serf, and the serf owners began to study the question: would it be in their interests to let him out?

Pavlov was the only Russian winner in science of the newly established Nobel prize (decades were to pass before three more Nobel prizes in science were awarded to inhabitants of Russia—all in fields connected with weapons). The Nobel prize serf Pavlov also wanted to go abroad in 1920. But here the case was clear to Ulyanov-Lenin: no. That Pavlov cracked odd jokes. Once someone asked him: "Own up, sir: you go to church so zealously only to spite the Bolsheviks." Answered the savant: "That alone, if nothing else, makes church-going worthwhile." But what could one do with that Nobel prize serf whose desire to go abroad could not be concealed from the outside world? To exterminate the pest? But all those scientists outside would squeal. Do not let him go out, but give him, despite the famine or anything, whatever he would want for his research (and personal comfort) on the scale that no democracy would afford. Do it even though this research is of no value for the production of weapons and means of their production.

With letting out the serf Alexander Blok the situation was more favorable. He was the only unique author of Russia who had written right in 1918 something that could be interpreted as "approval of the regime" in the sense that plague, fire, nomadic invasion can be "approved." Actually, he had done this "approval" as part of his unlimited riotous individualistic creative freedom: since the intellectual elite of Russia regarded the "new regime" as the greatest disaster since the Mongol invasion of the thirteenth century, *he* had to say something sacrilegious with respect to their belief.

> There was a lethal sweetness
> In my lonely iconoclasm

This proud lethal contrariness of a still boundlessly free individualist in 1918 could well be used for *propaganda* in 1921.

To: Central Committee of the Russian Communist Party
Copy: Comrade Lenin
July 11, 1921

The poet Alexander Blok, who has behaved quite loyally to the Soviet power throughout these four years and who has written several works which have been registered abroad as obviously sympathetic to the October revolution, is now suffering from a grave nervous disorder. In the opinion of his physicians and friends, the only possibility to improve his health would be a temporary leave of absence for Finland. I, personally, and Comrade Gorky are requesting this. All the relevant documents are in the Special Department. We are requesting the Central Committee to influence Comrade Menzhinsky in a sense favorable for Blok.

People's Commissar for Enlightenment
A. Lunacharsky

Comrade Menzhinsky was the relevant high ranker, later the *chief of the organs of state security*. The attempts of Lunacharsky and Gorky to influence him by citing several diseases of Alexander Blok went on at least from May to August 1921, and in August the serf was granted the permission to go to Finland, but the serf's wife was not (to be kept as a hostage?), though this was unimportant because the proud, iconoclastic, insanely free George Gordon Byron of the twentieth-century Russia only three years before, and now the wretched sick broken serf, Alexander Blok was dead.

The trouble was that, a short time before, a poet named Balmont had written a cycle of poems entitled quite bluntly "Hammer and Sickle." Overwhelmed, the serf owners let him go abroad. Now, the serf ran away, and declared that he had written "Hammer and Sickle" just to trick his owners into permitting him to go abroad. An identical pattern recurred in the case of the author Kuznetsov in the late sixties, as though time had stood still since 1921.

In 1928 the *greatest revolutionary humanist* Gorky explains the death of Blok in his letter to the *greatest representative of western humanism* Romain Rolland. First Gorky describes in his letter how the serf Balmont ran away from his owners. He is sure that this was an unspeakably mean act on the part of the serf, and this act

had, unfortunately, very bad consequences for Blok and Sologub in their requests for exit abroad, despite the stubborn intercessions of Lunacharsky for Blok.

If Gorky or/and Rolland represent a certain average social intelligence of twentieth-century mankind, how servile it is—how steeped it is in the mentality of serfdom. It is not only that the serf Balmont is a scoundrel because he ran away from his owners. Blok, whose one page is perhaps of more value than all the volumes of Rolland, Gorky, Balmont and many, many like them, including perhaps, alas, even the proud George Gordon Byron, was rightly held responsible (and compelled to die) for what another serf, Balmont, had done. It is not serf ownership at all, but the bad serf Balmont who is to blame for the death in captivity of the good serf Blok. If the serf Balmont had behaved as a serf should and died in captivity, then *perhaps* the serf owners had believed that the good serf Blok would not run away as the bad serf Balmont did. No wonder the *greatest representative of western humanism* was reassured on the score.

And if the average mentality of mankind is so steeped in serfdom, or at least large-scale serfdom, it was amply clear by 1921 that the visits of freemen from outside into the sealed reservoir could also be turned on or off or regulated with great precision to the best advantage of *propaganda*. Needless to say, within the reservoir the flow of freemen can be also all controlled and channeled, so that the outside world did not know of, say, the famine of 1932/33 when it happened, and in fact all the population of former Russia except for some tiny exhibition island like Moscow may, say, die of hunger, and the outside world would know nothing because all *foreign correspondents* would be kept strictly on that island. In a closed reservoir within a sealed reservoir. One of them dared in 1932–33 to report the famine. His *visa* was *revoked*, and some others were induced by similar threats or scoop rewards to denounce his report as unfounded.

In a democracy, if there is a certain view of a certain reality, there is always the opposite view of the same. The method is simply to let in and out those who have a view of a certain reality useful for *propaganda*, and bar those who have the opposite view of the same.

If a statesman, scholar or journalist of a democracy is granted his *soviet entry visa* he does not, usually, turn it down because such a *visa* has been denied to someone else. He accepts his *visa*, goes into the closed reservoir, or rather into its special show section beyond which he is not allowed to go, and presents the *truth as he sees it*, on the basis of what he has been allowed to see. He regards himself as an honest man: does he not present the truth as he sees it? The fact that all those who see the truth differently, namely too harmfully for *propaganda*, are barred seems to him irrelevant. Later he may change his view, be barred, and fume about those who are let in and gladly go to present the truth as they see it.

In the same summer of 1921, the following letter from the same Lunacharsky lay on great Lenin's desk:

I have received from Dr. Pelletier, our comrade in Paris, working for Communist newspapers, a proposal to come for a visit to Russia to see our life. Having read her numerous articles which have been sent to me, I have come to the conclusion that she is a serious and thoughtful person, undoubtedly a very good Communist and a truly well-educated woman.

However, Chicherin, *people's commissar of foreign affairs*, learned and reported to great Lenin that Dr. Madeleine Pelletier was considered by a certain French comrade a *hysteric*. What did that mean?

Great Lenin had a good reason to assume that the *communists* of any other country were motivated just like those of Russia: they wanted to grab their country and become its superaryan nobility, and later perhaps, the superaryan nobility of the world. Therefore, they could well be expected to look at a tortured victim in post-1917 Russia and say that the happy paradise-dweller screams out of joy. But as any other large group, there were statistically inevitable exceptions: *communists* or *sympathizers* who really had exalted (imaginary) visions of post-1917 Russia and were motivated mainly by such visions. This does not mean that their motivation was very strong and would resist a strong countermotivation: but as long as it was fairly safe to be motivated by such visions, they dedicated to them their time, energy and even part of their money sometimes, without any other motive. They were Communists as all *communists* pretend to be or imagine they are. These were *hysterics*, to be detected through reliable *comrades* abroad and barred quite strictly first and foremost.

In his letter, Chicherin warns great Lenin as to what might happen when a *hysteric* comes in touch with "our unprepossessing reality," as Chicherin puts bluntly (from which it is clear that Chicherin and great Lenin were certainly not hysterics). No more *hysterical* than perhaps his grandfather, a *private* serf owner, great Lenin wrote his *decision* (or *law*) on Chicherin's letter:

Comrade Chicherin:
I agree with you. The recommendation of Lunach[arsky] is arch-unconvincing, in my opinion.

Lenin

Had *dictatorship*, that is, total possession of all populace, been thus established? No. Not quite. These were only some prerequisites.

27

The gentle reader must realize what *immense task* was facing Ulyanov-Lenin and his *comrades*.

There had never existed total serf ownership in any country of Europe as far as recorded history goes. There had always been groups allowed to engage in certain independent activity. The Mongol invaders of Russia in the thirteenth century did not touch the church, an autonomous body which propounded a belief independent of the goals of the Mongol subjugation. No matter how far Absolutism tried to push its Monopolies, there had never been the monopoly of all trade, domestic and foreign. There had always been independent crafts and arts.

Already in the eighteenth century noblemen in Russia became free to dispose of their time and property. The result was their free culture in the sense that Gogol, a nobleman of the first half of the nineteenth century, could satirize the life of Russia as much as he liked and yet live wherever he wished. A free aristocratic culture, with its spirit of originality, criticism, sensitivity. And in the 1860s civic freedoms spread throughout the population.

The difficulty for great Lenin was not just to smash all independent institutions, organizations, and activities—from those comparatively recent such as independent newspapers, local councils of self-government, political parties, trade unions or national-minority associations, and down to those existing throughout the history of Russia, including the time of the Mongol invasion of the thirteenth century.

Total enserfment is not just mechanical destruction in order to break down all organized resistance imaginable and convert each human unit into a separate isolated defenseless *soul* (as a serf was called before 1861). Great Lenin had to enserf every *soul* psychologically—he had to destroy inside every *soul* all the psychology of independence that had been accumulating throughout the history of Russia, and especially after 1861 when all *souls* were emancipated and became citizens.

Imagine the effort that would be necessary in the United States for, say, some grandson of a Southern slave owner to convert all the population of the United States into Negro slaves, and the country into one total Negro-slave-plantation-like economy. This is only a comparison: the tradition of independence has been more vigorous and prolonged in the United States, and therefore a more vigorous and prolonged resistance might well be expected. For example, what great Lenin called so wittily the *civil war* would last in the United States not three or four years, but, say, twice or three times as long. But the comparison helps to understand what *immense task* was facing great Lenin and his *comrades*.

A certain section of the population of every democracy does not want to be invaded by countries like post-1917 Russia or post-1949 China. At the same time this section wants to derive benefits from such countries and hence "be friends" with their serf owners. Hence the convenient if self-deceiving semantics. An attempt at seizure, say, of Britain from outside (by Germany, for example) has invariably been called a *war of aggression*, while the seizure of, say, Russia from within a *socialist revolution*, that is something legitimate, natural and well-justified or at least something for which the population of Russia itself is only to blame and hence completely justifying British *friendship* (and trade) with the conquerors of Russia already in 1921, still amidst the open uprisings against them.

Despite such morally reassuring and commercially beneficial double semantics, both a *war of aggression* and *socialist revolution* are only different names for a ruthless war of conquest to enserf a population, and since the population of Russia had developed quite a substantial social tissue and psychology of civic freedom, great Lenin's war of conquest had to be also a ruthless war of subjugation by death and torture.

It is said that in a war of conquest the conquerors are always a different nation. Not that I agree with this cozy dogma, quite reassuring for a certain section of the population of every democracy. However, it will be recalled that great Lenin noted in 1915 that in Russia ethnic Russians constituted only 70 million people (43 per cent), while other nations one hundred million people (67 per cent). Originally, it is these 67 per cent, and in particular Letts, Poles, Jews, Georgians, and Ukrainians, that great Lenin and his *comrades* used to conquer a minority, ethnic Russians, and crush every resistance among them by destroying everything Russian and exterminating the bulk of the Russian intellectual elite, including statesmen, social thinkers and outstanding ecclesiastics. When large groups of Russians had to be subjugated, Eastern Mongoloid nations or even Chinese were used. As soon as this conquest had advanced far enough, ethnic Russians began to be used more and more to conquer every other minority separately: ethnic Russians were a minority with respect to all the others put together, but with respect to any of them separately, they were a majority and they could conquer all smaller minorities one by one.

It is well known that originally the *organs of state security*, the central mechanism of the conquest, consisted of Poles, Letts, Jews—without a single ethnic Russian anywhere at the top. The usual retort is that their chief of chiefs, great Lenin, was, on the other hand, a *pure* Russian.

But what does this mean? His father's Kalmyk origin has, of course, been concealed since 1943 when all Kalmyks, down to the last baby or veteran *communist,* were seized as a single group or cluster of evil, carried away no one knew where, and dumped on bare ground. But in 1937 it was still all right for the network of propaganda even to document the fact. His mother was half German, which is revealed in the sixties again. Her other ethnic half is still concealed, but it is admitted that the name of her father (a *private* serf owner) was Blank, which is no more a Russian name than, say, Ivanov is an English name. As though it were more pleasant for an inhabitant of Russia to be conquered by an ethnic German-Kalmyk than by an ethnic Georgian (like Stalin who even spoke Russian with a heavy accent) or by a *pure* German like Hitler who was perhaps no more *pure* German than great Lenin *pure* Russian. If some ethnic German-Kalmyk had moved to conquer Petersburg or Moscow from the Ukraine, Poland, Germany, Georgia or Outer Mongolia, *that* would be called a war of conquest, but since the conquerors seized first Petersburg and Moscow to subjugate then all the periphery, the war of conquest was not a war of conquest. It is very funny when indignation is expressed that the conquest has been going on beyond Russia as her border was as of January 1923 and indeed, over all the oceans and into outer space. As though the border of Russia as of January 1923 was a certain sacred line at which the conquest was to stop. Kiev or Tiflis, yes: it was inside the sacred line. But Prague? Oh, never! The idea is simply insane. It is so convenient for, say, the British to believe that Russia (or China) rightly belongs to that force of conquest which has conquered it, but at a certain line outside Britain, this force of conquest must in all decency stop (as a reward for British moral support of the conquest of Georgia by this force in 1921?). Yet it is merely convenient to believe so (helps to think less and pay less taxes for defense with an easier heart), but that is all.

The war of conquest of Russia had actually begun secretly as soon as the monarchy collapsed in the early spring of 1917. A conquest for possession is, essentially, the spread of the force of conquest over the country in the form of a network. At its closed stage this network could be conveniently presented as a *party*, a spruce, pleasant, modern word, cozily suggesting twentieth-century democracy rather than the armed force of a ruthless warlord of a thousand years ago. In the autumn of 1917 the network came into the open: now the conquest could be duly followed by subjugation and enserfment.

In the autumn of 1917 there were more than 300,000 *members of the party*, and they were armed: Ulyanov-Lenin's wife very lovingly describes how he would not go without his revolver even to a session of the Constituent Assembly, though he would be surrounded by his *comrades* there. It will be recalled that Al Capone had only several hundred *comrades* and kept part of Chicago very well *liberated*: by interpolation it can be visualized what it was like—a force of several hundred thousand distributed all over the country. In a conquest from outside a military force faces a front line. In a conquest from within, there is no front line: the forces of conquest are everywhere—they are fish in water, to use Mao's phrase—and fish which are secret when necessary, yet having official base strongholds all over the country. Within six months after the open proclamation of possession-power on November 7, by the West European calendar, a specialized network of the general network of conquest branched out.

Originally, the network was named the Extraordinary Commission. It was then renamed every few years, one name more beautiful than the other. A certain dark-haired man, *officially* alleged to be a former Polish nobleman named Dzerjinsky, was put in charge of it. The rank-and-file personnel of the *party* was in general purged in 1919 or 1921, and up to one-third of *communists* were discovered to be careerists and/or adventurers, if not worse. So not even *official* illusions can be harbored about the rank-and-file personnel of this particular network. Three chiefs of the network were later shot as Borgiaesque monsters of depravity. But that *first* chief of the network! Its founder and creator! No one can perceive the sweetest saintliness of his image except perhaps those old men into whose minds it has been inculcated since babyhood. Great Lenin was a Don Quixote (Jesus Christ or Florence Nightingale) smiling kindly, especially when looking on children (or playing with his cat). But then he was the pseudo-tsar-god whose image was to infuse joy, for he was building a paradise on earth. Not so the chief of the network. He was directly involved in *liquidation*. Suppose he would smile or wink—and *wrong, innocent, infinitely devoted* inhabitants would be *liquidated* by a sheer flippancy of his? A smile or a wink of his image is simply inconceivable, and has never been reported either here or abroad (most Western scholars largely pick up the stereotypes of *propaganda*, which clogs their minds with its imagery just as a special superpowerful transmitter "blinds" enemy receivers in modern electronic warfare). His image is that of a deity of righteous (*revolutionary-proletarian-progressive*, etc.) wrath, ever lugubrious, "merciless even more towards himself and his subordinates than towards the enemies," "fanatically honest in his faith," "ascetic," "entirely fearless." Even the *most rabid anti-communists* have been usually calling him, somehow respectfully, a fanatic, a Torquemada, a Savonarola (except that how could we know what Torquemada or Savonarola was like, if so many Westerners who met Stalin personally would, if not for the *secret report* of 1956, still assure mankind that he was an amazingly sincere, humane, and altogether trustworthy man?).

A certain Berezin, a subordinate of the deity of righteous wrath, bragged all over the city (he had sprees at the chic restaurant Vienna) that he appropriated or distributed as gifts the cars, pianos, cigarette boxes, gold rings, and other items he had taken away from victims during searches. In short, the drinking unruly braggart had made an embarrassing nuisance of himself. At that time the *party* began to think (as it did several times later) that its extermination network was assuming so much that it might endanger the *party* itself, and on October 8, 1918, *Pravda* wrote:

We will confine ourselves here to the indication of just certain trends evinced by No. 2 of the magazine *Weekly of the Extraordinary Commission*.

Pravda noted the "absence of inner restraint in the personnel of the Extraordinary Commission."

Now, in the absence of inner restraint, one shudders somehow when one reads the following "explication" of the All-Russia Extraordinary Commission addressed to all "Gubernia Extraordinary Commissions" (p. 11). This is what it says:

"In its activity the All-Russia Extraordinary Commission is entirely independent as it carries out searches, arrests, shootings, and submits *afterwards* a report to the Council of People's Commissars and the All-Russia Central Executive Committee."

With respect to this "afterwards," properly emphasized, *Pravda* said with a kind of black humor (did it come from Bukharin, who always combined ruthlessness with a certain trembling fear that he might some day fall among the exterminated rather than the exterminators?):

With respect to searches and arrests, the report submitted "afterwards" may yet lead to the redress of the wrong caused by the absence of restraint. But with respect to shootings, this can hardly be said.

In short, it was decided in December 1918 to make a *public trial* out of Berezin, and so *Pravda* reported, quoting the verdict:

P. Berezin is found guilty on the first counts of the charge, viz: trade in wine, failure to deliver the requisitioned wine to the repository of the All-Russian Extraordinary Commission, the stealing of a cigarette box during a house search, a murder during an interrogation . . .

Naturally, "a murder during an interrogation" (unintended death of the *defendant* under torture?) comes after "the stealing of a cigarette box."

The discussion of the sixth count of the Berezin case—his involvement with the Protection Department—will take place on receipt from Petrograd of the materials pertaining to the additional investigation of this charge.

They had not received the additional materials on his involvement with the pre-1917 Protection Department. There were only its archival documents. Perhaps Berezin had tailed great Lenin or his comrade Dzerjinsky a year or two before? Had received after 1917 a big promotion which he could not even dream of before 1917, it went to his head, and he began to swashbuckle all over the city?

But what was the reaction of Dzerjinsky, that knight of vengeance on the cursed tsarist past, that purest crystal of faith, that fanatical ascetic, merciless toward himself and his subordinates even more than toward the enemies? Surely he pulled out his revolver then and there and discharged it into the despicable monster, his subordinate Berezin, who had plunged into filth all those purest ideals for the sake of which he, Dzerjinsky, had agreed to fulfill the most unpleasant assignment of the greatest revolution in human history? After that, surely he did not sob violently in horror, disgust, and despair, tossing away his revolver, only because he was made, like Savonarola or whoever, of the purest fire of the most fanatical faith. Instead, *Pravda* reported this testimony of his in the court:

The opinion of Comrade Dzerjinsky (the chairman of the All-Russian Extraordinary Commission) about Berezin was more vague. He also mentioned the inclination of Berezin to cheap tinsel displays, to gold chains and rings, and agreed with his evaluation as a quick-tempered, easily aroused man.

And this is all. So someone was charged, on the strength of archival documents, with having been a secret agent of the Protection Department, the evil of evils of the *tsarist regime*, which was the evil of evils by itself in the *communist* manichean religion of the time. Besides, that devil from the darkest region of hell was found guilty of the theft of a cigarette box during a house search (not to mention that trifle of a "murder during an interrogation"). And according to Dzerjinsky, he is merely a quick-tempered, easily aroused man. Why did that scoundrel under interrogation arouse the poor guy in the first place? Is the poor guy to have no nerves at all? Who has never had a fit of temper? As for all those gold chains and rings which he stole from his victims, here Comrade Dzerjinsky agrees: why should he make such displays of them and look like a medieval bandit hung all over with his war trophies? Comrade Dzerjinsky considers such displays cheap.

Berezin became an employee at the All-Russian Extraordinary Commission on the mission direction of the Vyborg District, and no matter what can be said about his work, the attitude toward him was that of trust.

So much so that *after* Berezin had been charged and put in prison,

Comrade Dzerjinsky, being aware of committing an illegal act, let Berezin out of prison and granted him freedom of movement.

But why? Dzerjinsky explained that Berezin had reported to him, his chief, that in prison he had overheard some imprisoned White Guards talking of a conspiracy to kill great Lenin. See? But the White Guards were *in* prison. Why did Dzerjinsky have to let Berezin *out of* prison? Evidently, to catch personally the other conspirators. He, Berezin (charged with having been a secret agent of the Protection Department and found guilty of stealing wine and jewelry) could catch those White Guards like no else would.

Since 1918, the farther from the *center*, the more liberties the local chiefs have been taking, with less fear of a *demonstra-*

tional trial such as happened in Moscow to Berezin. The only danger is that the *center*, such as *Pravda*, might get wind of some picturesque case and publish it to amuse the more enlightened metropolitan readers and edify the backward provinces.

A certain Comrade Deutch came to Russia from the United States in 1917 and joined the extermination network station in Saratov. *Pravda*, on December 11, 1918, makes fun of Comrade Deutch's simple provincial mores.

> An imposing figure. He prances on a white steed, with a sombrero he brought from America, and with three revolvers and a hand grenade at his belt. He puts God's fear into the bourgeois and is an unprecedented success among the young ladies of Saratov. He shoots people personally, firing two revolvers at once. "I have found how to kill two birds with two stones. . . ."

Transferred later "for excessive cruelty" from the extermination network to the leadership of the ordinary city police (where cruelty cannot be excessive?), Deutch ordered ten thousand sombreros and commanded that every man of his wear one. A huge city-scale Western. Except that real men were really shot (and real women were really raped, and real children were really orphaned), while the superstar prancing on his white steed was as safe as in a movie. If this happened ostentatiously, for a large city to admire, what happened, then, secretly, *inside* the stations all over the country?

On October 6, 1918, the *Weekly of the Extraordinary Commission*, a specialized publication for guidance of the network, carried an article entitled "Why Do You Sentimentalize?"

> Tell us why you did not subject that same Lockhart to the most sophisticated torture in order to obtain the information—such a bird must certainly have known addresses galore. Tell us why, instead of subjecting him to such torture, a mere description of which would make the counterrevolutionaries freeze with horror—tell us why, instead of this, you let him leave the Extraordinary Commission?

Lockhart was a British consul, but at that time, the collapse of the regime in Britain and elsewhere seemed inevitable and the authors of the *Weekly* article thought therefore that the foreign diplomatic corps could also be safely subjected to the "most sophisticated torture."

A dangerous scalawag was caught. Extract out of him what you can and dispatch him to the other world.

In the nineteenth-century West there was a belief (which has survived in democracies) that what is morally bad, inhuman, repugnant must somehow also be ultimately useless. Alas, torture is morally bad, *but* useful to those in possession-power at least in three ways.

The first use is inquisitional: to know what anyone *arrested*, that is, caught alive, knows (where he has hidden grain, gold, or jewelry, who are his friends, relatives, or members of his group, what were his actions, intentions, or purposes).

The second use is motivational. In 1906 Russian scholars "proved statistically" that the death penalty does not reduce the number of murder cases, and once the Duma even voted unanimously(!) for the aboltion of the death penalty, for who wants to earn the reputation of both heartless *and* unscientific man? In 1918 great Lenin introduced, apart from the "death penalty on a mass scale," the torture penalty. Both death *and* torture penalty reduced the number of those who attempted any respective *crime* (that is, any action great Lenin had banned under pain of these measures) practically to zero, or what is known in statistics as "small small numbers." For example, between 1861 and 1917 there were in Russia certain small numbers (let us say, 1 per 1,000,000 of the population) who kept assassinating high-ranking officials in order to force the regime to do what they wanted. After 1917 some of these people tried to do the same—and well they might, for the new regime was as cruel to them and to the common people as no one had even imagined possible in the old regime. After three cases, all this terrorism stopped, and some of the most fearless terrorists of Russia (and hence of the world), those who would be the bane of any democratic or semidemocratic regime, abjectly confessed and repented. They were ready to face the death penalty in Russia before 1917. Death may be deliverance to those being inclined to suicide. But what is the death penalty *compared* with the torture penalty (especially if torture includes the family)? Death is then the greatest happiness on earth which can be granted to an inmate of a torture-death station and to his family for his exemplary behavior, including confession and repentance.

The motivational use of torture-death makes it possible to control a serf at a distance by keeping his family as hostages (the motivational basis of a serf's *infinite devotion* in war, guerrilla war, or overall espionage abroad).

The third use of torture is obliterative. Only torture can obliterate reliably every trace of torture (or of murder, robbery, compulsion, and so on). Those who know will not divulge the *top state secret*, but on the contrary will assure everyone (including even themselves) that they are the freest (and happiest) people on earth, provided the same awaits them if they do not dissimulate properly, while the bodies of those tortured can be reliably destroyed, and the proof of their guilt will be their *confessions*.

Said Dzerjinsky and his subordinate Zaks in an interview to Gorky's not-yet-closed newspaper *New Life* on June 8, 1918, to describe the new spectacular system of justice which knew no error, doubt, or delay:

We try cases very quickly. In most cases the time between the capture of a criminal and the sentence is measured by 24 hours or several days, but this does not mean that our sentences are not justified. Of course, we may also make mistakes, but thus far there have been none, and our records prove this. In nearly all cases, the criminal, cornered by evidence, confesses his crime, and what argument has more weight than the confession of the accused himself?

So imagine yourself in charge of one of the stations of the network. Assume that you are not a sadist, or a sadomasochist, or a psychopath, or a rapist, or a robber, or any other criminal. Finally, suppose that you will remain a person of good will, intelligence, and sympathy even if there is no external motivation for you to be such (and this will be the riskiest supposition of yours). But you have to gather sufficient evidence to corner the defendant—to do within twenty-four hours (or several days) what it often takes the *bourgeois* court months or years to accomplish (with all those laboratory tests, testimony, expertise, and what not), and besides your defendant *must* confess, which he need not do in the *bourgeois* court at all!

Besides, Dzerjinsky assumed in his picture of his so far never erring justice that there was one *defendant* for each *interrogator* to deal with at least for one day, if not several days. But what if a hundred, or a thousand, or ten thousand *defendants* per *interrogator* are *arrested* within a day or several days?

In 1918 the *party* was not yet a perfect serf army in which everyone without a single exception obeys a single command with amazing precision and without a split second's doubt, delay or hesitation no matter what the command is. And so *Izvestia* carried the following dissident, not to say heretical, sacrilegious or criminal, item, entitled "The Graveyard of the Living."

On December 1 we peeped into the Tagan prison. I say "peeped into," for it is not enough to spend three hours there as we did in order to know everything that is happening.

The Tagan prison is in Moscow, not so far from the Kremlin.

The cells for those under interrogation: several cells are over-crowded by sick people in high fever. Everything is together: typhus and the Spanish flu. These half-dead have been lying for a week or longer; the sick are not sent to hospitals. The temperature in the cell is 5 to 7 degrees and drops to 3.

In all the other blocks and solitary cells is the same filth, are the same harrowed faces, hunger-crazy eyes, and stretched bony hands in the iron cages. The low moan of almost a thousand people, plead-ing for amnesty and complaining that they have been here for two or three months without interrogation, for more than a year without trial, makes it all unreal, a frightening oppressive nightmare.

See? So it is not likely that you will have a day or several days to corner one *defendant* with evidence so weighty that he will confess. Perhaps only several minutes or several seconds per *defendant* will be at your disposal. What can you do? Within several seconds you can only give an order to torture him (un-less he or she has already been broken by his *stay at a place of detention*) until he signs his *confession*, then shoot him or her if the *defendant* is still alive and get rid of the body somehow, while the *confession* will be the document the *center* can always inspect or show to whoever wants to see it.

But who might want to see such documents at the very top, in the office of Dzerjinsky himself? Similarly, one may ask: Why did Hitler, the *head of the state*, give no *written* order for the extermination by his *secret state police* of 6 million human pests—Jews, in his particular case? So far there has always been a certain risk or hazard that the democracies may not be defeated, and some people may yet be held responsible by those silly outdated laws which refuse to recognize that human pests exist just as agricultural pests do. There is also an odd chance that some comrade may use hard evidence as a tool in the struggle for possession-power. Against these odd chances everyone must leave as little hard evidence as he possibly can.

It will be recalled that the key documents of the life of former Russia between 1922 and 1953—post-1953 secret *reports* and *letters*—do not exist as hard evidence. One of these *reports* was passed clandestinely abroad about half a year after the secret oral delivery of the allegedly identical *report*, and was published there. But it can always be claimed that the publication is a forgery, and there is no hard evidence to disprove the claim.

"How could I know?" Dzerjinsky might say in a pinch. "Here are all the documents—the records and the confessions. Those criminals perpetrated heinous crimes, and they were shot. The death penalty, you know. Oh, I was always against it, but struggle is struggle. Many enemies. Heinous criminals. I meant well. Lived only for the happiness of suffering mankind. With tears the wide world is flooded. Perhaps I am a fanatic, but I am honest. A fervent believer, you know. Like those early or medieval Christians. Surely I could not be present at every interrogation all over the country? I trusted my comrades—I took them for real Communists, heroic idealists, like myself. If I had ever known that any of them killed anyone during an interrogation, you cannot even imagine my horror, wrath, and despair—I would have been more merciless to that filthy monster than even to myself, not to mention the enemies."

In the sixties, with all those German archival documents before him, Professor Futrell of Oxford doubts Ulyanov-Lenin's knowledge of his agent's having been on the take from the Kaiser's Government. "Anyway, apart from the telegrams and their possible interpretation, there is nothing that can be called hard evidence." Such as Ulyanov-Lenin's written order (preferably in triplicate) to his dear friend Ganetsky, authorizing him to take money during the war from the enemy government for the destruction of the democracy of Russia and the establishment of his, Ulyanov-Lenin's, possession-power. Exactly. No hard evidence.

28

Several thousand torture-murder stations absorbed humans suspected to be pests, tortured them for inquisitional, motivational, and obliterative purposes, and disposed of the bodies the best way each station could.

Instead of publishing maps indicating the *means of production* and other nonsense which ends ultimately in torture chambers for those in possession-power themselves, the latter would do well to publish, at least for their own secret contemplation, a map of means of torture under the sway of great Lenin. Of old means like red hot metal (Tsaritsyn), or burning candles (Simferopol), breaking of arms and legs (Tyumen), or slow crushing of the head with a belt mechanism known as "death crown" (Armavir). And of new means like broken glass (Simferopol again) or rubber (Pyatigorsk). Exotic reminiscences should be all marked such as scalping (Kharkov), rolling within barrels stuck with nails inside (Voronezh), sawing of bones (Kamyshyn), impalement (Poltava), boiling alive (Odessa), or crucifixion of priests and monks—as a practical joke, of course (Ekaterinoslavl).

But had the personnel so quickly really developed a skill sufficient to produce the most sophisticated torture which the specialized *Weekly* demanded for the British consul in 1918? At any rate Kiev ought to be marked on the map by a special symbol. Not because the torture personnel buried the *defendants* alive, then exhumed them and buried them again, and all that routine stuff, but because the personnel used the torture by rats, which Orwell described later in his *1984*, evidently drawing on the memoirs dating from the time that some influential Western scholars still call the *epoch of heroic idealism* in Russia.

But where is the hard evidence for all this? Hard evidence can only be discovered when outsiders are able to get inside a sealed society. To open it. As happened in Germany by 1945. As long as a sealed reservoir is sealed, and all entry of foreign matter (such as *foreign correspondents*) is hermetically controlled, there are only memoirs and memories of victims and witnesses. But anyone can, of course, contend that they are all liars, as has been contended by the *friends of the soviet union* since 1918 and often believed. True, it is difficult to believe that, say, the contributors to the book *Cheka: Materials on the Activity of Extraordinary Commissions* could be all liars. The contributors were Social Revolutionaries some of whom had spent their lives in the prisons of the pre-1917 regime for their terrorist activity against it and were all for its violent overthrow. Why had they not *lied* in the same manner about the pre-1917 regime which they hated so? Before 1917 they had described abuses in the prison life of the old regime: if some Ulyanov-Lenin had not received in prison *his* brand of mineral water, that would have been regarded as brutality, to be exposed, branded, publicized. But before 1917 not even an extremist villifier of the pre-1917 regime like Ulyanov-Lenin had ever mentioned or imagined a country-wide network of specialized torture-murder stations, each station using its own well-worked-out kinds of what constituted in the experience of its personnel the most sophisticated torture within the available costs, skills and equipment. Before 1917 the very idea that such a network may exist in modern times had never occurred even to the most imaginative, unbalanced, or mendacious haters of the pre-1917 regime. Yet after 1917 all witness reports or memoirs of Socialist Revolutionaries of different factions, including the most inveterate haters of the pre-1917 regime, began to describe something else than the hypothetical prison brutality of not giving to Ulyanov-Lenin *his* brand of mineral water:

. . . the Cheka-men got a denunciation that Dombrovskaya was hiding jewelry she had received from a relative, a certain general. That was a sufficient reason for torture. Preliminarily she was raped, and they did to her every outrage they could think of. The raping proceeded according to seniority. The Cheka-man Friedman was the first, the others followed suit. After that she was tortured to find where she was hiding the jewelry. First they kept cutting her naked body with a knife, and then crushed her fingers with pliers.

But of course, the *friends of the soviet union* have been well able to dismiss all memoirs, testimonies, rumors, or memories as presenting no hard evidence. Their only problem is that references in the *soviet press* like "the most sophisticated torture" in the specialized *Weekly* in 1918 exist and will exist unless the *friends of the soviet union* destroy all these sources in the libraries all over the world. Barring this alternative, all that the *friends of the soviet union* can do is to imagine some other kinds of the "most sophisticated torture" than those I have mentioned on the torture map according to memoirs and memories. And if they imagine something less sophisticated than that, the problem will reduce either to their lack of sophisticated knowledge in the field, or to their unwillingness to use this knowledge, to recall, to imagine what the most sophisticated torture must be in a vast country-wide network of top secret specialized institutions.

Still, perhaps some *friends of the soviet union* may care to visualize, at least half a century later, a humdrum weekday of an ordinary average institution of this kind during the *era of heroic idealism?* In 1923 a poet named Voloshin published (abroad) a book entitled *The Verse of Terror.* When I found the book, it was so brittle that even the cover crumbled at a touch: a few more years, and the book would have disintegrated into dust. One poem in the book, "The Terms," was a list of *terms* used in secret, unbeautiful torture, and another described the *official, beautiful* routine:

> They used to come to work in the evening.
> They read denunciations, reports, cases.
> Then they signed the sentences.
> They yawned. They drank wine.
> Vodka was issued to the soldiers.
> By candlelight they read out the names of men and women.
> They drove the men and women into a dark backyard,

Took off their shoes, clothes, underwear,
Tied these up in bundles and put onto carts.
Then they divided the rings and watches.
At night they drove the men and women barefoot
Over the ice-crusted land,
Under a north-east wind,
To the wasteland beyond the city limits.
They bayonetted the men and women to the edge of a ravine,
And lit up the targets by flashlights.
The machine-guns worked for half a minute.
They finished off with bayonets those who were still alive
Or just pushed the dying into the pit.
Quickly they threw some earth over.
Then they went home, singing a soulful Russian song.
And at dawn the wives, mothers, dogs
Stole to the same ravines.
Clawed away the earth. Gnawed, snarling, the bones.
Kissed the dear flesh.

As for the practical functioning of the torture-murder network, Dzerjinsky was really worried about the local disposal of waste products of the network, namely, corpses, in an unorganized, inefficient and uninspectable, way, very bad from every point of view, including hygiene. But it was soon found that not every pest had to be so disfigured or injured as to need immediate extermination. After all, a modern hospital does not use all its equipment and medicines on every patient. Similarly, many pests would crack up and collapse and go to pieces at the mere thought of the network. Other pests would recover and look quite ordinary after a while, and hence these semi-finished products could be collected alive from each station and carried in freight cars into special enclosures to be exterminated there by *heroic labor*. The special enclosures (initially named concentration camps, after the wartime camps for enemy aliens, until the word had become *fascist*) could finish off the human waste of the torture-murder network with maximum labor output at minimum cost.

In Nazi Germany a kind of euthanasia was used for human pests a couple of decades later. Fools! They wasted the labor of millions of pests, and besides their lethal gas is always mentioned as a symbol of inhumanity, while surely there is nothing bad about *heroic labor*?

Nicholas I did not believe that in his country there were serfs or slaves. There were the *attached* or *souls*, not serfs or slaves. He was deeply concerned with the plight of Negroes in the American Southern States. He did not want to introduce capital punishment as in that godless Western Europe. Capital punishment was proclaimed to have been abolished in Russia in the mid-eighteenth century, while in England a theft of property worth 40 shillings or more was punished by death. Could Nicholas I introduce capital punishment, that barbaric stigma of West European brutality, in his enlightened, kind, merciful Russia of the first half of the nineteenth century? Never! When a governor submitted an application which requested the death penalty for two smugglers, Nicholas I wrote his decision: "Those guilty should run a gauntlet of one thousand men twelve times. Thank God, the death penalty has never existed in our country, and it is not for me to introduce it." True, the evil-doers would die long before that wholesome gauntlet exercise was over but who except God was to blame for having made them so frail?

Those Nazis put human pests to death by gas. A real symbol of inhumanity to be cited in every periodical of the world. Thank God, in our country there has never been the death penalty—at least since 1917: simply human pests began in 1918 to be put into enclosures, after a proper legal treatment at a torture-murder station, and if they died long before their wholesome exercise of *heroic labor* was over, who but nature was to blame for their frailty?

They could, indeed, be processed even into mobile projects like the construction of a railroad. In the middle ran the *rail*way, while the waste product, that is, dead humanity, was dug in on both sides in two parallel trenchlike graves or *human*ways. The enclosed area moved ahead, loaded with ever new humanity, rails, and ties, and left behind one surface line of rails and two underground lines of corpses. The average life of enclosed humanity could be regulated so as to obtain the maximum output for each kopeck of upkeep. If the upkeep were too low the enclosed humanity would die too soon, and if it were too high, the process would be too expensive. Later it was established that the optimum average span of a human unit should be about eight years (and hence the common *sentence* of twenty-five years ensured a safe margin of extermination).

Nazi Germany had no vast expanses rich in natural wealth on which any number of human pests could profitably be labored to death in huge enclosures, but gas and gas chambers could be cheaply produced. The reverse was true of Russia in 1918 (and for many years to come). And the corpses of those who died naturally through their natural frailty could be simply dumped in those expanses where no foreigner could see them.

One of the young *bolsheviks* was Osinsky, whose brightness was inferior only to Bukharin, his former college chum. He was a son of a veterinary, and he combined his youthful love for wars from within with his father's science. His article in *Pravda* in 1918 was titled "The Proletariat-Run Furnace of Fire." The old Biblical Church–Slavonic expression "Furnace of Fire" was used. The proletariat would run the holocaust like a furnace. He, Osinsky, a bright middle-class darling, along with two children of high-ranking *tsarist* officials, Ulyanov-Lenin and Bukharin; a son of a landlord or a big *kulak*, Trotsky; and other children of middle-class parentage, personified now and forever the Russian and world *proletariat*, and in the proletariat-run holocaust-furnace they were to reduce to ashes the less aryan part of mankind, including all recalcitrant blue-collar workers. But who were the nonaryans? The bright middle-class darling Osinsky saw them clearly in his holocaust-furnace vision:

These are intellectuals and professional people, high-ranking and medium-ranking office employees, officers, kulaks, priests, etc. They figure mostly as "socialists"; only they postpone the introduction of Socialism onto the next centuries. It is these strata that present a real military danger.

In his war from within, the veterinarian's son followed the best in his father's science: all non-aryans must be registered, to begin with.

Those registered will be divided into three groups. The active and dangerous we will exterminate. The not active and not dangerous but valuable for the bourgeoisie (rich people, prominent personalities) we will lock in, and for the head of one of our leaders we will take ten heads of theirs.

The third group we will use for unskilled work, and those who cannot do it we will confine to concentration camps.

Somehow contradicting Dzerjinsky's self-appraisal of the new system of instantaneous yet unerring establishment of the defendant's guilt, his young Lettish helpmate Latsis boldly wrote:

Look for no evidence or proofs that the defendant acted against the Soviet power by deed or word. The first question you must ask him: to which class he belongs, what is his origin, upbringing, education, or occupation. It is these questions that must determine the destiny of the defendant.

When the *party* decided at the close of 1918 that its torture-murder network was endangering the *party*, the *party's* man criticized Latsis in *Pravda*:

I can imagine Karl Marx or Comrade Lenin in the hands of such an investigator.
   "Your name?"
   "Karl Marx."
   "Your origin?"
   "Bourgeois."
   "Your education?"
   "University."
   "Occupation?"
   "Lawyer, author."
What else do we need to know, to look for evidence of guilt, to see whether he opposes the soviet by force or by word? To be shot—and that is that.

Pravda indicated the most noble, romantic, beautiful end. More prosaically, it would be: "Karl Marx? An author? From a bourgeois family! Beat him with a nailed glove till he confesses, then off to a concentration camp as third group. Next!"

29

I realize that the serf world I was born into is no more interesting than, say, Egypt under one of the three Psamtiks or Babylonia under one of the two Nebuchadnezzars. But man is so vain that he thinks the world *he* was born into is interesting for some obscure reason. My only hope is that since some of my readers might yet become one day part of the world of which I write, it will be more interesting to them to read about how a certain former unordained priest (named great Stalin) ousted pseudo-tsar-god I (named great Lenin) than about how a certain harem eunuch (name unknown) ousted some Xerxes or Artaxerxes.

As the reader may recall, Ulyanov-Lenin naturally wanted his comrades to become ranked serfs, while the comrades wanted as naturally to be privileged free supernoblemen, high above the commoners who were doomed to mute serfdom.

In 1919 *Izvestia* published an item entitled "Can It Be a Medieval Torture Chamber?" The very title was outrageous: how could Ulyanov-Lenin and all the others protest their innocence, so befitting heroic idealists not of this earth, their highbrow ignorance of what was happening, if some comrades published such articles in the superofficial press? No, the comrades were anything but a monolithic military force obeying one and all the chieftain's command. Some comrades thought that torture was not yet efficient, extensive, and sophisticated enough, while others believed that torture was not part of *dictatorship* as defined way back in 1906: though "completely unlimited power restrained by no laws or rules whatsoever," *dictatorship* must yet draw a line at shooting, because torture is somehow unromantic. Whoever heard of a handsome movie actor, noble and glamorous like that Comrade Deutch from the United States in the streets of Saratov, pushing broken glass into the mouth of some hostages? Middle-class mega-scale criminals are not merely after some paltry money: they are, above all, after adulation, woven out of the stereotypes of bad movies and novels, and any amount of shooting can be done very beautifully according to these. But torture had not been sufficiently glamorized by 1919.

Early in 1921 *Pravda* carried an article which called great Lenin a "principled demagogue" ("There are two kinds of demagogues: unprincipled and principled," the article sneered.). Then four methods of his demagoguery were discussed quite vitriolically: deafening, blinding, self-denial, and camouflage. In less than two years the *Pravda* reader would have thought that he had gone mad if he had seen an article like that in *Pravda*.

In short, the erstwhile comrades had yet to become ranked serfs doing whatever they were ordered to do and glorifying the great leader (as they began to do by the autumn of 1922). To this end, a chancellory (or vizierate) was set up in 1918. It had thirty men in 1919, 150 in 1920, and 600 in 1921, not including the guards and communication personnel. Of course, it was not called by such an old-fashioned name as a vizierate: it was a growing serf bureaucracy the history of which from 1918 to 1922 would take a huge volume, with many intrigues, reshuffles, divisions, or mergers, each bringing with it a new name, even more *revolutionary-progressive-socialist*, etc. than the other. The vizierate was to kick out or at least demote all *members of the party* who did not want to become ranked serfs of Ulyanov-Lenin, or if their rank was too high, to kick out or at least demote "their men" who *elected* them at lower levels. Naturally, *members of the party* freshly made or promoted, as opposed to those kicked out or demoted, had no pedigree of comradeship, and they could well be relied on not to demonstrate in *Pravda* that Ulyanov-Lenin was a demagogue or expose torture in *Izvestia*. They were happy enough to become ranked serfs, which for them meant membership in a high caste.

The job had been done in rough outline by March 1922, and great Lenin was delighted with the head of the vizierate and accorded him the title of—Grand Vizier? Fie, how *reactionary-autocratic-tyrannical*, etc. Of course: General Secretary. There was a murmur from Trotsky's men against the grand vizier named Stalin, but early in 1922 great Lenin still stoutly defended *his* man Stalin:

A gigantic job. But to be able to handle the inspection, a man of authority should be at the top, or we will be steeped, immersed, in petty intrigue.

Great Lenin still trusted his grand vizier. For the latter behaved just as thousands of previous viziers had in history—or just as great Lenin himself behaved for that matter.

Great Lenin would humble himself to total self-effacement to secure the help of someone he needed. Great Lenin would exist solely to care for the health of, say, Trotsky, while a few months earlier he had publicly called him a little Judas (and Trotsky reciprocated in kind).

We all tend to be nicer to those whom we need and colder to those whom we do not. Only what may be at stake in the struggle for possession-power at the top level is the ownership of the globe versus death in a torture chamber. Naturally, the range of change is as vast: the sweetest self-effacement, if this helps your possession-power, and the calmest consignment of the *comrades-in-the-revolutionary* struggle to the torture chamber if that helps the same.

Late in 1922 Ulyanov-Lenin complained that his grand vizier was rude. Yes. Because he had no need for Ulyanov-Lenin any longer. In particular, because he had been promoting men and these men's men (and these men's men's men) who would glorify great Lenin (or anyone else) but who were actually, devoted personally to him, the grand vizier; for they knew that it was on him that their promotion and demotion depended. So he was rude to great Lenin. Not polite, eh? He would have great Lenin scalped if *that* were safe and helpful to any degree at all.

But early in 1922 the grand vizier Stalin had still thought that he needed Ulyanov-Lenin to keep him on in his grand vizierate for a while, and he charmed Ulyanov-Lenin just as he charmed nearly all Western statesmen and diplomats from 1941 to 1945 to the extent he needed each of them.

He charmed Ulyanov-Lenin and many top rankers by Ulyanov-

Lenin's technique of infinite self-sacrifice. He, the grand vizier, was so infinitely modest that to be forever just someone else's grand vizier keeping the *party* under the thumb for someone else's possession-power was the greatest happiness on earth for him, an insignificant, if devoted and diligent registrar.

Thousands of infinitely devoted grand viziers before him had duped their potentates exactly in the same way, but he had natural advantages. The top-ranking comrades thought that they were *great* public speakers: they would even like to indulge in the belief that the populace *labored and fought heroically* for their possession-power not because of the torture-murder network, but because their genius in public speaking inspired wild enthusiasm in the populace, leading to its *mass heroism*. But the grand vizier could not vie with them because his Russian was still bad even in 1953 after sixty-odd years of practice, and when agitated he became inarticulate. Besides, in the usage of a certain stratum in Russia the expression "intellectual person" (*inteligentnyi*) is used in the sense which Chekhov mocked in his sentence: "He considers himself an intellectual person because he uses a soap that makes everyone sneeze." To say that someone "is not even an intellectual person" is to imply that he can neither use his fork, nor recognize Beethoven's *Eroica*. Said (or rather shouted) Bukharin in 1928: "We are creating and will create such a civilization compared with which the capitalist civilization will be the same as a 'dog's waltz' compared with Beethoven's *Eroica*" (stormy prolonged applause). See what an intellectual person? *Eroica* and all that. He certainly used a very intellectual soap too. Trotsky, Bukharin, Lunacharsky, and by a stretch great Lenin and even Zinoviev were "intellectual persons" because they were of middle-class parentage, while the grand vizier was not! He could give himself away by any word or gesture. By definition he was forever to remain happily buried deep inside his chancery, well concealed from the wildly enthusiastic populace inspired by the flowers of intellect and soap fragrance of the "intellectual persons." As grand vizier he was the safest man. He was a blind man employed to guard an architect's designs. A eunuch instilling *party discipline* among his potentate's women. Nothing could be funnier than to imagine him as pseudo-tsar-god instead of Ulyanov-Lenin—or Bukharin or Trotsky or Zinoviev. He was a funny figure, and there is no more useful humility than that of a clown: thus he far out-Lenined great Lenin in comradely self-effacement.

When it was too late, great Lenin noticed that he had been duped by his grand vizier and began to write secretly a *letter to the congress* about the dismissal of his grand vizier. Why had not great Lenin noticed this earlier?

Because great Lenin, perhaps just as even greater, though still totally unknown Bonosky, was no less stupid, or no more intelligent—even in the most ordinary sense of the word, than any randomly taken winner of any randomly taken lottery. For his grab of Russia was a lottery win.

Essentially, it was a mutiny of soldiers who did not want to go to the front, draft evaders and deserters. He turned out to be at the head of the mutiny for these four reasons. First, he desperately wanted to own megaproperty—the country and perhaps later the world—and had been hanging around, waiting for his chance, since 1891. The urge to possess human or other property has nothing to do with intellect in any sense. Second, he was German on his mother's side and in his habits, as the network of propaganda admits again in the sixties. In 1914 he wrote in a letter that the "*least* evil would be now and immediately—the *defeat* of Tsarism in this war. For Tsarism is a hundred times worse than Kaiserism." In other words, Russia as she was in 1914 was a hundred times worse than Russia defeated and turned into the Kaiser's colony. Hardly any ethnic Russian would have agreed. Just as hardly any German would have agreed that conquered by the Russian tsar, Germany would as a Russian colony be a hundred times better than she was in 1914. Great Lenin acted therefore with confident zeal when he took money from the Kaiser. If the result had been only the German conquest of Russia, even that would have been a hundred times better—for great Lenin with his German ethnic and psychological background. But while he was German by his mother's origin, and one hundred times German by his privately expressed belief that the Kaiser's Russia would be a hundred times better, he was a *pure* Russian officially, which was also an important coincidence because a German or even a Jew as top leader of the antiwar mutiny would have been mobbed (there were German pogroms during the war). Third, while at the head of the mutiny to knock

Russia out of the war, he had to call realities by irrelevant fantastic names—for example, to call Russia's surrender to the Kaiser the "victory of the world proletariat." This ability is quite common, and does not involve intellect. Fourth, he had to look a gentleman, an "educated person," rather than a common criminal, a tough, or a blue-collar worker. This appearance was necessary to figure as a reputable leader of a reputable party while stirring up an antiwar mutiny with the Kaiser's money.

All these traits have nothing to do with intellect. They indicate once again that sometimes it takes less intelligence to grab a country than, say, to steal three rubles, and sometimes the grabbing of a country may indeed be purely accidental and involve no intelligence at all. These traits of Ulyanov-Lenin happened to fit by chance his *historical role* just as, say, those of Nikolayev happened to fit his (in the *assassination* of Kirov. *History* (that is, the mobs of soldiers in the case of Ulyanov-Lenin) selected both owing to their peculiar sets of traits, having nothing to do with intellect, and both naturally turned out to be vicims of *history*, though both imagined themselves to be its creators. The wretched end of Ulyanov-Lenin as a victim, duped quite easily by his vizier the way numberless potentates had been duped before by their viziers, had been a top secret in the network of propaganda until Khrushchev had some data published as another dose of exposé of (once great) Stalin and, hence, of Khrushchev's rivals.

When the majority of mankind, from the network of propaganda here to Sir Winston Churchill there, seemed to enjoy its mythical image of great Stalin, I did not argue, even when it was safe. Nor will I question the genius of not-yet-great Bonosky if he or any other grabber of megaproperty is a *success*. Similarly, it is perhaps a sheer waste of time to prick the success-bubble of great Lenin's *genius*. Yet one example may suffice.

On the very first page of his bulky study, the latest American biographer of Ulyanov-Lenin declares that great Lenin "might have become," in particular, a "chess champion." He would not, because of his preoccupation with the overthrow of the regime. From his genius in chess, his more universal genius in "strategy," "tactics," "analysis" and what not is inferred. Actually, at the peak of development of his genius in chess, Ulyanov-Lenin lost sometimes a game to his chief at a law office, Hardin, a lawyer in a provincial town, even when Hardin gave him a knight before the game as "odds" to a weaker player. In other words, if we assume that the lawyer Hardin played at the level of a Great Master (that is, a player of world renown), then his subordinate Ulyanov-Lenin played at the level of dozens or even hundreds of thousands of amateur chess players in Russia, some of them youngsters or children.

Ulyanov-Lenin's ability at a quite mature age to play chess at the level of a fairly ordinary youngster or child in Russia has thus been converted into great Lenin's universal analytic genius of which his genius of chess playing is only one dazzling manifestation.

Accordingly, success-worshippers have their own explanation of Ulyanov-Lenin's failure to notice in due time that he had been duped by his grand vizier. Great Lenin was under such an enormous strain of creating a new society (and a new man) that he simply had no time to think of such egocentric matters (self-sacrifice again). Only when he fell sick as a result of this superhuman, all-absorbing, all-consuming work did he attend to the danger. Before his sickness his gigantic industry (typical of all *communists*) had not left him a second of time to think of the torture chambers into which his whole *party* was to go ere long.

His schedule for the week just before his gigantic work broke down his health was as follows:

December 7. He came from his Kremlin apartment to his Kremlin office at 10:45 A.M. Attended the *meeting of the politburo*. Left for home at 2:20. Came back at 5:30 P.M. Spoke over the phone. Left at 6:15 for his (formerly the Moscow Governor's) villa in Hills.

December 8. Did not appear at all, but graced his secretaries with *two* telephone calls.

December 9. Ditto, but graced them with *one* telephone call.

December 10. The same gigantic (superhuman) effort as on December 9.

The stupendous labors of the next two days are worth describing verbatim, from the secretaries' journal:

December 11. Morning (record of N. S. Alliluyeva). No assignments. Vladimir Ilyich has not phoned. Check: in the evening the temperature in the office must be not less than 14 degrees.

It is not clear why the morning secretary should alert the evening secretary as to the checking of the optimum Réaumur temperature for Ulyanov-Lenin in the evening. Evidently, at least that had to be *done* during the long, long day.

December 11. Evening (record of Sh. M. Manucharyants). No assignments. Vladimir Ilyich has not called.

December 12. Morning (record of N. S. Alliluyeva). Vladimir Ilyich came at 11 to Moscow, appeared in the office at 11:45, stayed for a while, and went before 12. At 12 he expects Rykov, Kamenev, and Tsuryupa.

Rykov, Kamenev, and Tsuryupa stayed until 2. He left at 2.

There is no assignment for the evening.

Some content of this feverish supergiant work is also noteworthy.

Professor Rojkov (a historian) was once a *bolshevik*. As statistical exceptions, reputable historians could also be *bolsheviks*. As statistical exceptions, some *bolsheviks* also proved to be decent men and left *bolshevism* as Professor Rojkov did in 1907. Unfortunately, the names of those who refused to be mega-scale criminals are not even known: it does not pay to turn down the loot. In 1922 Professor Rojkov declared that he had abandoned *all political activity*. At that time this was enough to gain safety, because the purpose of those in possession-power was still to stop all organized political activity against them, and those who recanted publicly were rewarded with safety. Besides, before 1907 Rojkov was a top-ranking *bolshevik*, a *member of the central committee*, and at the top they knew him as one of their own. Finally, he was a historian with a long string of bulky volumes published by reputable bourgeois publishers, and there were very, very few such reputable intellectuals who were at the time at least "apolitical" rather than suicidally hostile to the "new regime." In short, Rojkov eminently qualified for safety in 1922, and all top rankers agreed. But not Ulyanov-Lenin, who found enough time (during one of his rare sojourns at the office on December 7?) to make the following herculean effort in his creation of a new society and a new man:

Comrade Zinoviev:
I do not suspect you a *teeny-weeny* bit of a bias for Rojkov. *Not* a *teeny-weeny* bit.

But judging the matter on its own merits, I am very much afraid: he will tell any lie he pleases, *even in the press*. He will tell a lie, and we will be tricked.

This is what I am afraid of.

Their motto: lie, leave the party, stay in Russia.

This is what we should ponder and *talk over*.

Great Lenin attended that *politburo meeting* on December 7 which started his superhumanly busy week already described. But the *politburo* waited until Ulyanov-Lenin left, and in his absence passed a decision: to permit the former *bolshevik's* residence in Moscow. Great Lenin proved to be more pettily vindictive than any member of the *politburo,* including Stalin, as well as more suspicious and more inclined to waste his rare sojourns at the office (or still rarer telephone calls there) on frightful nonsense from any point of view.

Great Lenin read the transcript of the *politburo meeting.* To let that microbe Rojkov exist in Moscow! Not while great Lenin is the *leader of the globe.* Five days later great Lenin had a stroke—fell ill under the strain of such superhuman labors. After the stroke he wrote another letter protesting the decision to permit Rojkov to live in Moscow. This time the *politburo*, caught at its boyish prank, complied (after all, a microbe is a microbe even if a former *bolshevik*), and the secretary Fotiyeva made this historic entry in the journal on December 14:

He was very pleased learning about the Politburo decision on Rojkov, laughed and said that it was very good news.

He ought to have danced too. Such breathtaking news. There is pleasure in collectively exterminating millions of pests, but there is also pleasure in throwing out just one tiny pest individually. Two days before another stroke, great Lenin wrote still another letter: to make sure that the former *bolshevik* Rojkov was watched properly in exile.

Such were some of the herculean labors of great Lenin, and it was only during his illness that he decided to write a letter about the dismissal of the grand vizier. But this letter was being written secretly, almost as we write our underground letters. Now, however, the grand vizier came into the open and would not allow great Lenin's wife to take dictation from her husband. The grand vizier knew better than Ulyanov-Lenin's wife what was bad for her husband's health. All those letters about Rojkov had not been detrimental to his health (how the grand vizier laughed at the way great Lenin used his time). But *that* letter was! The wife appealed to Zinoviev:

Lev Borisovich,
Because of a short letter which Vladimir Ilyich dictated to me by permission of the doctors, Stalin allowed himself yesterday an unusually rude outburst toward me.

Let us skip other moans and pleas and read just two more sentences:

What one can and what one cannot discuss with Ilyich, I know better than any doctor, because I know what makes him nervous and what does not—in any case I know better than Stalin. I appeal to you and to Grigory, as to close friends of V.I., and beg you to protect me against rude interference in my personal life, as well as against mean insults and threats.

As an apocryphal anecdote had it, the grand vizier later said to her: "Look, Krupskaya, I can always appoint another Lenin's widow." He could: that was the job of his chancery—promotion and demotion. And dismissed as Lenin's widow, she would be a nobody, and anything may happen to a nobody, just anything on earth.

Zinoviev and all the top-ranking comrades either supported the grand vizier in his health care for great Lenin or did not oppose him. Though they were already afraid of the grand vizier with his chancellory, but they were afraid even more of great Lenin and of Trotsky (and *his* men). The grand vizier had never shot humans, that is, *communists* (and as for pests, it didn't matter, of course, and moreover, Bukharin had a lead over the grand vizier up to 1928). But Trotsky had shot humans—*communists*. Presumably because he had not been even a *bolshevik* before 1917: he and his men were outsiders who became Ulyanov-Lenin's men. And since he was not even a *bolshevik* before 1917, for him it made no difference at all whether to destroy a human being (a *communist*) or a pest—a microbe (a commoner).

While Trotsky was a danger, great Lenin was a greater danger still, *if* he recovered. In March 1920 he had already announced (too soon!) that

the soviet socialist democracy is in no way inconsistent with the rule and dictatorship of one person; the will of a class is at times best carried out by a dictator who alone will accomplish more. . . .

Since Ulyanov-Lenin had been sacrificing himself all his life, he, obviously, wanted to make the final supreme sacrifice—to be that *one person*, that *dictator*, with his *comrades* as his serf underlings rather than sharers of possession-power.

But this is precisely what *they* did not like: they also wanted to sacrifice themselves, at least to the extent of sharing in the possession-power as junior partners. They did not want to be serfs, just like the rest of the population, albeit of high rank. They wanted to keep their noble privileges like the formal immunity from *arrest*, that is, from torture in the torture-murder network. From 1922 this privilege did not exist. How would Ulyanov-Lenin use its absence?

At the eleventh *congress of the party* in March–April 1922, Ulyanov-Lenin said, referring to Shlyapnikov, who still dared to have his own opinion, that machine guns should be used in such cases. Against *communists*? Even against top-ranking *communists* like Shlyapnikov? Ulyanov-Lenin understood that he had gone too far and decided to reassure the *congress*:

Poor Shlyapnikov! Lenin is going to train machine guns on him. What is really meant are party measures, and not machine guns at all. Machine guns are meant for those people who are now called Mensheviks, Social Revolutionaries. . . .

The *congress* was to be completely reassured. Only pests like *mensheviks* or *social revolutionaries*, and not humans, were to be machine-gunned. Shlyapnikov had simply misheard great Lenin. To machine-gun us, Communists! Ha-ha-ha! Shlyapnikov had imagined God knows what out of fear. But had he really? *Pravda* had printed Ulyanov-Lenin's speech, and every reader could easily check it from a back number. Here it was: the machine guns with the aid of which

it is necessary to mete out a severe, cruel, ruthless retribution for the smallest violation of the discipline, and this applies not only to some of our intra-Party matters, but also even more to these gentry like Mensheviks or all the gentlemen from the 2½ International.

So Shlyapnikov had heard it quite right. True, great Lenin did urge the machine-gunning of the *mensheviks* and other pests. But he first mentioned "our intra-Party matters," that is, *communists, us, humans*. Not that Ulyanov-Lenin would machine-gun *real* Communists. Oh, no. But the trouble was that all of them would prove to be *not* real Communists, see? And he would take on new *members of the party* instead. While his old comrades would be deviationists, opportunists, traitors. Each of them had already done something bad like that Rojkov whom Ulyanov-Lenin had persecuted with such gusto against everyone's will. Trotsky had simply been a little Judas before 1917. Zinoviev had *betrayed* the open seizure of possession-power in the autumn of 1917. And Bukharin had *scabbed* the separate peace with Germany. No, the *communists* did not like a severe, cruel, ruthless retribution to be meted out to *them*. Not even with machine guns, not to mention something much worse. It was an extraordinary escape, rescue, salvation, when the possessive, domineering, ruthless pseudo-tsar-god I fell ill right after he had come into his own. Now the others would confine him—immure him inside his own house. Then, the more upset he would be as a result, the more vigorously his disease would progress—and the better the chances of their survival and possession would be.

As for Trotsky, he did love Ulyanov-Lenin. When he needed him, of course. Before 1917 Trotsky did not need him, and hence hated him and called him a "slovenly shyster" or a "professional exploiter of every kind of backwardness in the Russian working-class movement" (and said that the "whole edifice of Leninism is now built on lying and falsification"). Then Trotsky needed him and loved him between 1917 and 1922. After his expulsion abroad, that is, into his death, Trotsky loved great Lenin more and more because the network of propaganda had been metamorphosing the "slovenly shyster" into a genius-messiah compared with whom Pericles, Moses, Christ, or Leonardo da Vinci were narrow-minded bungling half-wits—and why not be the closest disciple or apostle of such a being? How Trotsky loved that being! But in 1922 Ulyanov-Lenin fell sick, and how could Trotsky love him? Like everyone he was mortally afraid of great Lenin: he hated him now perhaps much more than he had hated him between 1903 and 1917—he hated him as every *comrade* usually does when his former *comrade* and now the new pseudo-tsar-god is converting him into his ranked serf. But in contrast to his hatred of 1903 to 1917, he now had to conceal it more and more—as every *comrade* usually has to, when his former *comrade* turns into his owner, at the third stage of *comradeship*. On the other hand, Trotsky was great Lenin's man, and with great Lenin's collapse he would be kicked out too. Yet if he helped the sick Ulyanov-Lenin against the will of all the top-ranking comrades, they would kick out Trotsky all the more quickly as soon as Ulyanov-Lenin got irreversibly ill or died. So Trotsky did not even defend Ulyanov-Lenin's point of view before his *comrades* on the so-called Georgian affair, despite Ulyanov-Lenin's direct appeal to him, Trotsky. He just watched great Lenin being cut off from the world by the *comrades* on the plea of their care for his, great Lenin's, health. No, Trotsky did not love the sick Ulyanov-Lenin at all. Perhaps, no more than all those *communists* of all countries loved Trotsky when *he* had lost possession-power (and was killed).

On February 11, 1923, the jolly doctor who called on Ulyanov-Lenin was especially jolly.

Two days before, the doctor had said that his patient Ulyanov-Lenin could see all the visitors he liked—it would do him a lot of good. Now, however, even though Ulyanov-Lenin's health was better, the doctor said that not only were visitors not permitted but that he was to receive no political information. For strictly medical reasons, of course.

Ulyanov-Lenin was not *that* stupid. Even after the doctor's visit his lips trembled. He understood.

As great Lenin, or rather not great Lenin anymore, but a pitiful lone serf, trapped, betrayed by everyone, struggling against forced confinement, finally *understood*, he asked the doctor what exactly was meant by political information.

"Well," said the doctor (as recorded by the *secretary* Fotiyeva), "you are interested in the consensus of Soviet employees, for example."

That the jolly doctor could only know from the *politburo*. So he was as jolly as that jolly Dr. Khobotov of Chekhov's "Ward Six." As the *secretary* Fotiyeva commented:

Besides, apparently, Vladimir Ilyich has formed the impression that it is not the doctors who give recommendations to the Central Committee, but it is the Central Committee that has given instructions to the doctors.

But how could it be otherwise? Great Lenin was cut off from the world, his wife was insulted, he was snubbed, and no one interceded. Not a soul. Now, who would intercede should some jolly doctor *disappear*? Or the *secretary* Fotiyeva herself, for that matter? She made entries in that journal as she was told to. Then it was safely locked away and reappeared in forty years. Because Khrushchev wanted it to. Her only record of the inmate-prisoner's opinion of *her* role is as follows:

On January 24 Vladimir Ilyich said: "First of all, about our secret matter: I know that you are deceiving me." To my reassurances, he answered: "I have my own opinion about this."

Chekhov was a unique writer who represented the peak of humanism in Russia. He could show how an imaginary provincial Russian felt when he was confined in a small remote town. No one could show that with respect to Ulyanov-Lenin, and no one was interested. Tricked out of his possession-power, he was innocuous, and therefore his *comrades* were building up his world glory as never before, for that world glory now radiated on them without yet presenting any danger. But his own human self was as uninteresting as the last serf in the last concentration camp or the last *special* psychiatric ward. He might get upset, which would be fatal after his previous strokes (Chekhov's character had had no previous strokes), or rave, curse, weep, or bash his head against the wall: that was *his* business, and no one would know about it, which was all that mattered. He was now like the common population, living or dying behind an impervious wall, and nothing—nothing would be heard outside.

Ulyanov-Lenin refused to take medicines or see the jolly doctor or any other doctor or nurse, or anyone except his wife or sister. No one objected. It didn't matter anymore. Paranoia? In the new world brotherhood of his selfless infinitely devoted comrades, it was only his wife or sister who might put up some resistance if ordered, say, to hit him with an alpine ice-ax.

Meanwhile the inmate-prisoner was glorified more and more, just as Kirov was later glorified in crescendo from the minute he was killed (if not even well in advance). Since he had received food in the first of the thirty-four castes, he was buried in the first caste too. To be buried in the thirty-fourth caste is to be thrown into a trench or pit, as a *hero of battle* or as an exterminated pest, with millions of others, nameless, unknown, often secret, though numbered, registered, reported to the top. As befitting his former first caste, the dead body of the inmate-prisoner, glorified as messiah of equality, was embalmed and enshrined like that of both Oriental pharaoh and Christian saint. If the first caste meant in terms of food six freight cars of caviar sent from God knows where all across the country hit by the worst famine in her history, then the first caste required in burial a pyramid-mausoleum of Labrador marble, presumably taken out of storage against the day villas would be built for the poor in the nascent paradise on earth.

The rest happened just as some Russian émigrés had predicted in 1922, much to the amusement of *Pravda*, which quoted them to show to what lengths of absurdity evil canards can go. First of all, Trotsky, one of Ulyanov-Lenin's men picked from among outsiders, who had shot human beings (that is, *communists*), was started on his way down and then abroad, that is to death, for the murder of someone abroad is the best way to avoid the charge of complicity. All *communists* were to cheer at the news of the murder: they all were to know, and they did know, that great Stalin had done it, and at the same time they did *not* know that great Stalin had done it, and indeed, an involuntary thought that he might have done it would have been a heinous crime.

Zinoviev and the grand vizier Stalin came on top: one city was named Zinovievsk, another Stalingrad, in 1925. But the grand vizier had promoted so many of his men and their men's men and their men's men's men that in 1926 he could come into the open against Zinoviev and *his* men. Zinoviev "considered himself an intellectual person," and naturally expected that the flowers of his intellect and the fragrance of his soap would overpower the grand vizier and all his men. But the grand vizier's men enjoyed Zinoviev's speech as they would a clown's act, jeering at him if they felt like it, interrupting him, or even mimicking him (this last being unreflected in the *proceedings*).

Naturally, Bukharin, along with all the others, participated with zeal in the ouster. Bukharin assumed that the flowers of *his* intellect were indispensable. He was not some Zinoviev, you know. Remember that one about a dog's waltz and Beethoven's *Eroica* he delivered in 1928? In 1929 he was pulled down on *his* way to the torture chamber.

Pseudo-tsar-god II named great Stalin had no more top-ranking rivals, and he assumed the appellation that *Pravda* had applied to Ulyanov-Lenin in 1922, shortly before his forcible confinement: *our leader, teacher, and friend.*

30

Communists outside of China or Southeast Asia, or those who simply believe that (the word?) *communism* is better than (the word?) *fascism* because the former word belongs to the cluster of good words and the latter to that of bad words in their manichean coparticipative imagination, have tended—especially since the *secret letter* of 1956—to regard pseudo-tsar-god II as the villain of the post-1917 piece of Russian history who grievously damaged or at least soiled great Lenin's nascent paradise on earth. This accords with ancient and medieval apocryphal mentalities in which a more recent big serf owner turns into an ogre, while a more distant one turns into a kind swain or wizard —a strict wizard perhaps, but the people will become unruly without strictness (I am shocked to find that already today some people explain in that eerie fairytale-teller's voice how good it was once upon a time under Stalin compared with the wretched now).

Accordingly, when all the occasions of wicked Stalin's deviation from great Lenin were unearthed between 1956 and 1964, wicked Stalin was found to have been an evil deviationist! No wonder he derailed great Lenin's lifework.

But the result of this painstaking research to unearth wicked Stalin's deviation is striking: in all cases of wicked Stalin's deviation up to the autumn of 1917 wicked Stalin showed himself much more inclined to tolerance, civic evolution, democracy than great Lenin.

"After the Revolution of 1905, Stalin assumed a conciliatory attitude towards attacks on the philosophy of Marxism. . . ." "Attacks" means criticisms, for any criticism can be and is called an "attack." And instead of calling the critics Judases, renegades, traitors and thousands of other such names great Lenin immediately applied to any critic in long manichean co-participative strings, wicked Stalin "assumed a conciliatory attitude." "Our Party is not a religious sect," he said in a letter in 1912. But of course, it is: great Lenin wrote a book in which he presented the one and only philosophy so that every *member of the party* knew the one and only truth or creed on earth—or else be denounced as a little Judas, for example.

After the collapse of the monarchy in the spring of 1917 wicked Stalin— It is so wicked that I just cannot bring myself to say it. He was practically for democracy! The *party* was to forget that it was a *party* aimed at the establishment of *dictatorship* (as great Lenin had defined it in 1906) and to transform into a party, just like other parties.

The very name *bolsheviks*, that is, *communists, Pravda* under wicked Stalin's co-editorship would not even mention—they all were simply "Social Democrats." But how would *Pravda* announce the arrival of great Lenin? The leader of whom? How to avoid the word: *bolsheviks*? The editor Stalin, and the editor Kamenev, both wicked, found a way out:

On April 3, word spread in Petrograd at noon that in the evening the leader of the revolutionary part of the Russian Social Democratic Workers' Party Comrade N. Lenin was to arrive by train, Finnish Railroad.

But even before, wicked Stalin and wicked Kamenev had deleted one-fifth of the first of two great Lenin's "Letters from Afar" (that is from Switzerland, to put it more precisely) and had refused to publish the second letter at all! Because the deleted part and the second letter called for the overthrow of the existing regime (this time not the semiconstitutional tsarist monarchy but a democracy which even great Lenin called the world's freest). If great Lenin had not fallen sick at the end of 1922, that alone could have cost wicked Stalin at least what it cost Rojkov. Joseph Djugashvili-Stalin, who later begat both Hitler (by threatening Germany with a conquest from within and outside) and Mao (by secret and open aid to his conquest from within) and who out-Hitlered Hitler and perhaps even out-Lenined Lenin, might have suffered for his inclination to democracy along with Kamenev and Zinoviev.

Wicked Stalin was, indeed, appointed to head the negotiating committee to unite with whom? The *mensheviks*! Those *mensheviks* who were later exterminated as the worst enemies! Great Lenin said on April 4, the next day of his arrival: "I hear there is a unification tendency in Russia. That is a betrayal of socialism." Indeed, about half of his comrades favored the *unification*, that is, were traitors. For if they had succeeded, then, say, Plekhanov or Tsereteli or Martov, and not great Lenin, would have been the leader. What socialism can there be if you are not the leader, chieftain, Moses? And the traitor of traitors who decided to betray great Lenin to democracy was wicked Stalin, who *headed* the committee.

It was very well for Djugashvili-Stalin to betray: those Georgians like Chkheidze or Tsereteli were chummy with him, a Georgian. How he had published letters of condolence and sympathy all over a *Pravda* page when the son of Chkheidze, that Menshevik, that renegade, that enemy, died! If Ulyanov-Lenin's *party* and Plekhanov's party merged, and democracy continued in the country, that Djugashvili would be the first mate of Chkheidze or Tsereteli because he would represent the Bolsheviks, and at the same time was the only top-ranking Bolshevik so chummy with those Georgian leaders of the Mensheviks! And Ulyanov-Lenin would be automatically pushed away and down as a quarrelsome, arrogant, self-centered bigot from the wild Volga provinces who once even insisted that everyone should embrace and profess only his interpretation of philosophy as the ultimate truth. Oh, that Georgian, traitor of traitors! To think that he would have realized that merger—that betrayal of betrayals—if Ulyanov-Lenin had not arrived from Switzerland in the nick of time!

Trotsky later (in 1927) described with gusto this near-miss treachery and even quoted with glee how wicked Stalin replied when someone said that in the proposed merged party there would be disagreements, and again wicked Stalin's reply was so monstrously wicked that I am afraid even to reproduce it. Said wicked Stalin: "There is no party life without disagreements"! One can understand Trotsky's glee: could anything more criminal, immoral and stupid be said?

Finally, when Ulyanov-Lenin and Trotsky decided in the autumn of 1917 to finish off democracy and complete openly their seizure of the country, Kamenev and Zinoviev spilled the news beforehand in an *enemy* newspaper by way of protest, and wicked Stalin argued against the expulsion of the two *traitors* from the *party* (no, it was not destined to be a party!), published Zinoviev's reply to great Lenin, and even officially offered to resign as editor in solidarity with the two *traitors* (owing to this incident he later came out the winner in the pseudo-tsar-god's succession lottery: Zinoviev and Kamenev supported him even when they feared the growing might of his chancellory; they thought that in 1925 he was the same man he had been in 1917; they forgot how *they* had changed).

As for the final open smash of democracy in Russia and the grab of possession-power, celebrated annually on November 7, with all representatives of all democracies, as the *great october socialist revolution*, wicked Stalin studiously avoided the participation in the megacrime.

The final open grab of whatever had not yet been grabbed secretly was made by Trotsky and his men (with a vast mob of deserters and soldiers who did not want to go to the front) in collusion with Ulyanov-Lenin personally, and practically without the *party*. If there had been no *party* at all before 1917 and none of its *revolutionary struggle*, *ideology* or anything else from 1903 to 1917, the country could be grabbed as easily by Ulyanov-Lenin, Trotsky and whoever would have joined them right on the spot in the grab and received his share of the loot in rank and wealth. Even *after* the open grab Ulyanov-Lenin said when he was afraid he would be outvoted in the *central executive committee*:

If the majority is yours, take the Central Executive Committee and go ahead, *while we will go to the sailors.*

Not to the *workers and peasants.* But to the *sailors.* Lenin and Trotsky would go to the sailors. The sailors who did not want to go to the front would carry Lenin and Trotsky to possession-power because Lenin and Trotsky would ensure safe desertion. As a result of desertion Germany seized about a third of the country (in terms of population) and could easily have seized the rest, but nothing venture (on a mega scale), nothing have (on a mega scale), right? And those sailors who were ready to bring the two megagamblers, Ulyanov-Lenin and Trotsky, to possession-power would have smashed not only all the democratic institutions, but also all the *bolshevik* or *communist party* with all its *ideas* as well, should that *party* have opposed great Lenin and great Trotsky in their megagamble for the country and perhaps the world.

The *party* therefore, simply waited. If the two megagamblers failed and were put on trial as megacriminals, the *party* would declare that it had nothing to do with the two madmen whom the *party* had intended to expel.

And wicked Stalin belonged to those who were especially unwilling to commit themselves to the megacrime of open destruction of democracy.

How can one account for this consistently treacherous deviationism of wicked Stalin?

When the monarchy collapsed in the spring of 1917 and Djugashvili-Stalin proved to be one of the respectable leaders of a respectable party in a democracy, he was satisfied. Perhaps because he was a son of a cobbler and a washing woman. Or perhaps because he was not an inveterate careerist but a careerist who says: "I have achieved enough. Let me now enjoy life." For *him,* his status as of the spring of 1917 amounted to a magnificent career. (Sorry: the word *career* belongs at this writing to the bad pole of words, along with the words: *fascist,* Zinoviev, surrealism, and such, and therefore in the *soviet* serf bureaucracies they say instead *growth,* a charming metaphor taken from botany: "The starting salary is small, but you have fine prospects for quick *growth,* a closed hospital, and a special pension"; a *communist* has nothing to do with *career*—only with *growth*—because *careerists* and/or *adventurers* are criminals and/or scoundrels to be purged.) By his own estimation Djugashvili-Stalin had achieved magnificent *growth* while Ulyanov-Lenin estimated wicked Stalin's satisfaction as betrayal. Which it was.

Parties named *social democratic* in Western Europe also pro-claimed originally all kinds of ignorant, sweeping, dangerous intentions which they, fortunately, have been steadily betraying. Some of them have *betrayed* them so completely that they differ from their opponents only by policies which are irrelevant to these original intentions. *Communist parties* also were, at their inception, concentrations of social ignorance. But it should be borne in mind that the word *communist* means nothing except a symbol, and similar or worse concentrations of social ignorance may assume any other names: *liberators, anticommunists, neo-communists*, and so on. On the other hand, a benign civic environment may gradually diminish the overall level of social ignorance of a certain *party*. In Russia the process had begun long before 1917 when there had appeared *liquidators*, that is, the *bolsheviks* who were for the *liquidation* of all illegal activity (that is, for the conversion of the *party* into a party) and against whom Ulyanov-Lenin fought, branding them the worst enemies. Following the collapse of the monarchy, the environment became still more benign, and the trend now touched even Djugashvili-Stalin, despite his erstwhile involvement in bank robberies on assignment from great Lenin.

For Ulyanov-Lenin, Stalin's behavior was a betrayal—perhaps because Ulyanov-Lenin was a son of an official of the fourth rank in the fourteen ranks of government officials. For him, a son of a fourth-rank official, a Hereditary Nobleman, to become just another "politician in opposition"! With a prospect to sink in some merged party below that cobbler's son Djugashvili whose name he once could not even recall.

No, Ulyanov-Lenin would not let those sissies deprive him of his victory at the end of his lifelong gamble. Unlike those sissies, he had the daring (of splashing acid with complete safety into somebody else's face). Many *bolsheviks*, including even that Georgian ex-bank robber (what was his name?), proved to be sissies just when the crucial coveted redeeming moment of his whole otherwise lost life came up. Fortunately, an outsider, Trotsky, and his men turned up. The "professional exploiter of every kind of backwardness in the Russian working-class movement" pressed to his bosom the "little Judas" and, indeed, declared that "since then, there has been no better Bolshevik" than the little Judas. Since then—since when? Since the little Judas agreed to help the professional exploiter of backwardness to destroy democracy and grab the country. Since that very moment the little Judas became not only a real Bolshevik, but the *best* Bolshevik. And between 1917 and 1922 the two best *bolsheviks* put Djugashvili-Stalin through a school which he entered as a man from the lower classes, satisfied by his *growth*, anxious to forget all that shady illegal activity before 1917, a sissy afraid to splash acid into his comrades' eyes, a *traitor* inclined to tolerance and democracy. And he left their *school* as their equal in their art of *daring* or perhaps even superior because he had had a much harder and tougher life than the two middle-class boychiks and after their training he could show *them* a thing or two.

31

It is true that great Lenin had taught his men the art of *daring* ever since 1891. Yet the real school of *daring* started on November 7 (October 25, by the pre-1918 Russian calendar), 1917.

Democratic institutions, like the Provisional Government seated in the Winter Palace, had by that time so few soldiers as against Trotsky's and Ulyanov-Lenin's armed forces that to defend the Provisional Government or any other democratic institution would have been as futile as, say, for the Czechs to defend Czechoslovakia against the *soviet* armed forces in 1968.

According to Trotsky, the Winter Palace contained several hundred people, but it is not clear how many of them were prepared for the suicidal defense. There were some youngsters (cadets) among the defenders. But according to Trotsky, some of the cadets had "left their weapons in the entrance" and were "going home, in obedience to orders received from the commandant of the Constantinovsky school." There was also a company of the Woman's Battalion, but it left too, or at least this is what the *greatest revolutionary poet* Mayakovsky claims in his poem which we all read at school. So how many defenders were there?

Sometime later there arrived unexpectedly forty of the Cavaliers of St. George under command of a staff captain who walked on a cork leg. Patriotic invalids acting as the last reserves of democracy.

Against these forty invalids (and perhaps as many boys and women who might have remained) Trotsky and Ulyanov-Lenin arrayed a good hunk of the *tsarist* army either as regular units which did not want to go to the front or as soldiers who had deserted privately, so to speak. As today's *textbook of history* modestly notes: "These forces numbered more than 200,000 armed men."

That was not enough, of course: more than 200,000 armed men against those forty invalids. And what if as many boys and women had still remained as defenders? The *revolutionary forces* must be reinforced!

Warships and a 5,000-strong force of Baltic seamen had arrived already by October 25.

Trotsky realized that more than 200,000 armed men and new forces, such as a 5,000-strong detachment, were painfully inadequate against those forty invalids. More, more, more *revolutionary forces!*

The Peter and Paul fortress frowned threateningly from the other side of the river. The *Aurora* looked in from the Neva with her six-inch guns. Destroyers steamed back and forth patrolling the river.

However, even with these destroyers, the *revolutionary armed forces* could not and would not defeat the forty invalids. A year or two later, this would have been simple. Those who would have refused to attack would have been shot by *special-purpose units* (always stationed behind their backs) or sent, if possible, to the network of physinfluence which was crudely called torture in those crude days. As a result, the more than 200,000-strong *revolutionary armed forces* would have rushed into attack against the forty invalids, and millions all around the globe would have *believed sincerely* in the *infinite heroism (heroic idealism, revolutionary enthusiasm)* of our cluster of good as opposed to *their* pole of evil. Yet at the time there were no *special-purpose units*, nor could the *bolsheviks* apply, at the time, large-scale physinfluence as several months later they began to do.

But what about the *proletarians*? Indeed, some low-skilled workers (*peasants* and *petit bourgeois* who had begun working at big plants during the war, and were practically unskilled labor) had been issued arms and been brought to the scene, to hang around in the background and symbolize the *revolutionary proletariat*, lest some skeptics might think that the *proletarian-socialist-revolutionary-democratic*, etc., army was the *tsarist* army, unwilling to go to, and having deserted from, the front. The *greatest revolutionary poet* Mayakovsky described how one of the *revolutionary workers* robbed a defender *after* they finally penetrated inside the Winter Palace.

> A certain
>   embarrassed
>   son of a bitch
> While the Putilov worker
>   stands
>   over him,
> More tender
>   than his father:
> "Out with your stolen watch,
>   dear boy,
> "Your watch
>   is
>   now ours."

That is, whatever the pariahs owned down to the wrist-watch was now proclaimed to have been stolen from the aryans, and the aryans only did justice as they looted them. If that was the behavior of the *class-conscious worker* of the Putilov plant which the *greatest rovlutionary poet* thought necessary to describe in his *epic poem*, what can be said of all irrelevant hoodlums, mobsters, or small-scale criminals who had gladly joined the *assault*? However, in order to rob the defenders, it was necessary to get *into* the Winter Palace. And the forty invalids? So the *revolutionary army* did not budge, aided though it was by all willing looters.

According to its commander-in-chief, Trotsky, "until the arrival of armored cars on the Square, the besiegers feared a sortie of cadets from the palace which might cut them off." Suppose, indeed, that the *revolutionary armed forces* would have launched an attack? Several youngsters, never to mention forty invalids, could have rushed out and cut off, say, that force of 5,000 seamen from the more than 200,000-strong main body. Why, that nearly happened even *after* the arrival of armored cars! More youngsters decided to stop the defense and surrender. Some of the forty invalids decided to join them. They went out. But the cordons of the more than 200,000-strong army with marines, warships, armored cars, and fortress cannon did not notice or would not believe that these youngsters and some of the forty invalids wanted to surrender. And here Trotsky achieves a Shakespearean touch: "The unexpected appearance" of several youngsters and invalids nearly put to rout his *heroic army*. Quite unintentionally, Trotsky writes a great tragic farce with himself and Ulyanov-Lenin as star clowns. When *bolsheviks* tried to be playwrights, philosophers or literary critics they produced nothing but hopeless old hat, but when they described themselves or each other, the unintentional tragic hilarity of their writings matched the greatest masterpieces in the study of human nature.

The unexpected appearance of these cadets on the square throws the cordons into confusion.

. It is all over with the *greatest of the revolutions*. Why—why did those youngsters and invalids appear so unexpectedly in order to surrender? What will all those Western diplomats, *communists* and just *friends* celebrate each year on November 7? Yet take heart, *all progressive mankind*.

But there is no end of joyful shouting when the besiegers discover that these are surrendering troops.

Thank God, the more than 200,000-strong army in all those armored cars, aboard the warships, and in the fortress realized in due time that these youngsters and invalids were "surrendering troops." What if they had continued to mistake them for *attacking* troops? What if they had thought that, say, the terrible invalid on a cork leg himself was attacking? Imagine that invalid hobbling ahead in hot pursuit of all the armored cars, machine-gun companies, land artillery, destroyers, and all the other former *tsartist* arms and services under the command of the greatest military genius of all time Trotsky?

True, as a good commander-in-chief, he kept far, far from the battlefield, not to expose himself to the danger of the forty invalids' breakthrough. On the other hand, great Lenin was not satisfied with such passive measures of safety. From the network of propaganda we learn that he wore a wig, and even on the next day *after* the news of the defeat of the forty invalids he was in hiding in a private apartment, and "all the pistols had been checked." If the invalid on a cork leg had risen from the dead and put to rout the more than 200,000-strong army with all those weapons, he would have been compelled to search all the city to find *that* apartment, and anyway all the pistols were ready to fire, fire, fire at the indestructible invalid on a cork leg.

Meanwhile, hours passed, but the *revolutionary armed forces* would not budge. True, there was one infinitely heroic attack which Trotsky describes in this way:

One of the armored cars approached the main entrance of the palace, disarmed the cadets guarding it, and withdrew unhindered.

Do you see the picture? From the armada of "steel monsters," as Trotsky calls armored cars quite poetically, one steel monster rolls forward and approaches a couple of youngsters. "Throw away your rifles, you brats, or we will let fly with our machine guns." Having thus routed the two boys, the steel monster rolls back. *Unhindered.* If all those boys and invalids could have been defeated as safely as that. But they were *inside.* And armored cars could not roll safely upstairs and through all those rooms and then roll back *unhindered.*

So the cruiser *Aurora* was ordered to start shelling the building. Allegedly with blanks, but as Trotsky writes (very poetically again):

Who can ascertain the truth about a cannon shot fired in the thick of night from a mutinous ship at a tsar's palace where the last government of the possessing classes is going out like an oilless lamp?

In other words, the cruiser was *allegedly* ordered to fire first with blanks, but no one can ascertain the truth. While the fortress was ordered to fire live shells right from the start, and it did.

Keep shelling the building in which that invalid on a cork leg lurked. Finally, he would be buried under the rubble. True, the building contained much of those art treasures for the sake of which tourists have since been flocking to former St. Petersburg. But it is better to own a country without art treasures than not to own it at all.

Anyway, the Provisional Government and its defenders—those invalids and youngsters—surrendered rather than let themselves be shot, that is, shelled quite safely for those who were shelling them from the fortress and the cruiser. But one episode during the shelling is noteworthy. The Duma, now elected without any franchise restrictions as before 1917, decided to go into the Winter Palace to share the destiny of the Provisional Government. To die for democracy? Trotsky described the episode as a farcical joke. When Trotsky wanted to be serious, his writing was a sardonic ridicule of himself and perhaps of all of us to a certain degree. But when he tried to be farcical, his intentional farce sounded as the only serious reading in his hilarious volumes:

> From the general confusion of ideas and speeches a practical plan is at last produced, and wins stormy applause from the whole meeting. The Duma must march in a body to the Winter Palace in order to die there, if necessary, with the government. The Social Revolutionaries, Mensheviks, and Cooperators are all alike seized with a willingness either to save the ministers or to fall by their sides. The Constitutional Democrats, not generally inclined to risky undertakings, this time decide to lay down their heads with the rest. Some provincials accidentally turning up in the hall, the Duma journalists, and one man from the general public request permission in more or less eloquent language to share the fate of the Duma. The permission is granted.

Some foreigners who have been more fortunate historically in the twentieth century than we have say that *russians* (as they call more than a hundred nations of former Russia) are not fit for democratic development, for Russia never knew any. I can only say that when and if *their* democracy is destroyed by forces called left wing, right wing, anticommunist, red, national, socialist, green, communist, liberating, peaceful, pragmatic, or any other name, I hope *their* representatives of the people will decide to share the destiny of *their* democracy. In Germany in 1933, for example, I do not notice the spirit.

Anyway, reading Trotsky's piece of satire above, one is supposed to double up with laughter. Evidently there was nothing funnier for a *communist* of that time than someone's decision to die for something other than his personal share of possession-power, wittily called *communism*. Judging by Trotsky's description of the *assault* of the Winter Palace, glorified ever since then as the culmination of infinite heroism, not a single *communist* wanted to endanger himself in the least of his own free will. And that there might be representatives of the people who decided to go unarmed under artillery fire seems to Trotsky sheer rollicking fun:

The members of the Duma are just on the point of setting out on their last journey when the telephone rings and news comes that the whole of the Executive Committee of the Peasants' Deputies is coming to join them. Unending applause. Now the picture is complete and clear: The representatives of one hundred million peasants, together with the representatives of all classes of the city population, are going out to die at the hands of a despicable gang of thugs. There is no lack of speeches and applause.

"But where is the school of *daring*?" the gentle reader may ask at this point. "Quite common self-adulating gangsters who happened to be grotesque cowards made an absolutely safe bandit raid and naturally laugh at their defenseless victims who wanted to die of their own free will while every smart guy knows that a smart guy must try to kill others, not die himself. Where is the school of *daring*?"

On the day before the raid *Pravda* had announced:

Soldiers! Workers! Citizens!
The enemies of the people have launched the offensive at night.

On October 26 and thereafter the *bolsheviks* could jeer at less than forty invalids opposing their more than 200,000 men and all those heavy weapons. But on October 25 the fewer than forty invalids were, in the same *Pravda*, countless hordes of mortally dangerous *enemies of the people* (the same who killed Kirov in 1934 or threatened from Czechoslovakia in 1968?), treacherously attacking the trusting, democratic, peace-loving *bolsheviks*, as well as all soldiers, workers, peasants and citizens in general.

The counterrevolution has raised its criminal head.
All the gains and hopes of soldiers, workers and peasants are in great danger.

Yes: fewer than forty invalids were about to seize the country. But that was not all because the invalids' seizure of the country would no doubt be accompanied by pogroms:

Simultaneously pogrom-makers may try to bring about in the streets of Petrograd general chaos and massacre.

Those invalids would also disperse the Constituent Assembly, according to *Pravda*. True, Ulyanov-Lenin and his men did disperse it a month later and promptly shot those demonstrating in its defense. But on October 25 it was useful to ascribe this megacrime to the same invalids.

In other words, not only did the *great october socialist revolution* never exist—except as the farcical shelling of fewer than forty invalids, and perhaps as many youngsters—but even this farce was an agent provocateur's trick: those army deserters and all the others were instigated to enact that farce by *Pravda*'s false announcement of a certain massive enemy offensive which had started at night and menaced them all.

That was a grand agent provocateur's universal method. The grand agent provocateur is always a heroic idealist, trusting, even somewhat naive, and almost defenseless, and he is all for peace, democracy, cooperation and all that. But suddenly he is attacked by numberless hordes armed to the teeth (such as fewer than forty invalids). Yet owing to his infinite heroism (he is a *heroic* idealist) he routs these numberless hordes, armed to the teeth. After this he may, rather inconsistently, jeer at the fact that the numberless hordes, armed to the teeth, reduced essentially to fewer than forty invalids, as against his forces of more than 200,000 men and all the rest.

The first lesson given to Stalin-Djugashvili in the school of *daring* would be incomplete without Trotsky's speech *before* October 25. At the Petrograd *soviet* he read aloud an article which had appeared in *The Day* about the "plan for the Bolshevik's forthcoming attack." Of course, the audience simply reeled with laughter on hearing such a canard.

The "plan" outlines in detail the routes by which the armed forces of the Bolsheviks are to proceed and indicates the strongholds to be captured. Mention is even made of the fact that in the districts of Novaya Derevnya the forces are to pick up "criminal elements."

The reading is accompanied by general laughter. Comrade Trotsky notes:

"I beg you to listen so that you should know exactly by which route each army is to proceed." (Laughter.)

The first step in an agent provocateur's trick is laughter. Your enemy or your victim suspects something, is uneasy, may resist.

So you laugh. Much depends on the boisterous, ebullient, effervescent sincerity of this laughter. Finally your enemy-victim begins to laugh too at his fear. Is not this what has been happening to many Western statesmen, diplomats, and scholars? In the midst of the enemy-victim's laughter the provocateur—with a sudden scream: "They are attacking us treacherously!"—splashes acid into the enemy-victim's eyes with quick, calm, self-assured *daring*.

Some twenty-two years later Trotsky might perhaps also become uneasy when he saw an alpine ax in the effects of someone who was *almost a member of the family*. How that man must have laughed! He, *almost a member of the family*, the best friend, the most devoted disciple, would suddenly approach the seated Trotsky from behind (laughter) and (unable to continue for laughter) plunge this ax ("I'll die laughing") into the skull ("Gee, that was a good one!").

In the first lesson in the school of *daring* Trotsky also made an apparently minor suggestion which was yet of great help later to his pupil Stalin.

Originally, some Cossacks were to defend the Provisional Government, but this is what they saw, according to Trotsky:

There was nobody but strangers around: cadets—among them a number of Jews—invalid officers—yes, and then these female shock troops.

Strangers around. Those Cossacks wanted to see someone of their own people. But they saw only *strangers*. Jews.

With angry frowning faces the Cossacks gathered up their saddle bags. No further arguments could move them. Who remained to defend Kerensky? "Kikes and wenches . . . but the Russian people has stayed over there with Lenin."

With Lenin and Trotsky. As against the kikes. And Trotsky was right. If the Georgian Djugashvili could later be the purest Russian on earth (and his *georgian* or *jewish* nose became with every year more and more *russian* on all portraits), why could Trotsky not be, along with the ethnically German and Kalmyk Lenin, the embodiment of the *russian people* as opposed to the kikes? What is important is to declare aryan that group of people whose support is currently useful for your possession-power, and to change the *ideology* accordingly. Those good, useful, obliging Cossacks (Trotsky notes that they "were in touch with the besiegers") said that the *russian people* supported the possession-power because they hated kikes, and there were kikes among the *enemies*, that is, the defenders of Russian democracy.

Five years later Trotsky explained in *Pravda*: the Russian tsar "barbarian Peter was more national than all the bearded and embroidered past that opposed him." More *national*? But is it good to be more *national*? Of course. "Bolshevism is more national than the monarchist and other emigration," continued the supernational (super-Russian?) Trotsky. But what about the previous class approach? Listen: "In dynamics, the national essence coincides with the class essence." That is, "in statics," the essence of a chauvinist Russian tsar-barbarian (of the early eighteenth century) and his wars of conquest against Sweden or Turkey may not coincide with the *interests of the world proletariat* (in the twentieth century). But in *dynamics*, that is, when Trotsky *is* the tsar, or pseudo-tsar, or at least a top-ranking retainer of the pseudo-tsar-god, oh boy, how the two coincide.

Djugashvili and his successors had only to apply the teacher's suggestion. Against the teacher himself, to begin with.

The second lesson in the school of *daring* was naturally devoted to the division of the loot. When, say, four ordinary small-scale criminals divide the loot, a bright idea may occur to one of them: to kill two pals in cahoots with the other pal, and then it will be easy to kill the other pal—just one remaining pal, see?

True, the proper beginning had been made right after the collapse of the monarchy, even before Ulyanov-Lenin arrived. Local councils had been formed. However, first of all, it was imagined that they were something brand new in the history of mankind (so new that the word, first translated as councils, was then transliterated as *soviets,* just like *vodka, tsar, samovar,* or other unique realities). Second, it was decided that only parties or *parties* who called themselves *revolutionary* and were elected by blue-collar workers, soldiers, and farmers could participate in the local councils. Constitutional Democrats, elected by historians, scientists, engineers, businessmen, and such, were thought to be unworthy of participation, presumably because they could not understand the coparticipative strings or clusters of images (such as *revolutionary-progressive-socialist-democratic*, etc.), while those who could not read and write knew the proper way of *revolutionary-progressive-socialist-democratic*, etc. *transformation of society* so well that they could certainly be represented in the local councils, if they voted for the proper parties and *parties*, of course.

So Ulyanov-Lenin and Trotsky were off to a good start. If there are *revolutionary* parties so privileged, why should not, say, two parties *within* the local councils (*bolsheviks* and *left-wing social revolutionaries*) declare that the other two parties within the local councils are not *revolutionary-progressive-socialist-democratic*, etc. at all, but only call themselves so?

Naturally, those Constitutional Democrats who had previously been merely barred from the local councils (*soviets*) had first to be removed altogether and forever, and within three days after his open seizure of possession-power, Ulyanov-Lenin dashed off the following *law* (or rule, decree, order, behest):

The members of the leading bodies of the Party of Constitutional Democrats as a party of enemies of the people are to be arrested and put on trial at the Revolutionary Tribunals.

This done, it was now time to turn on two old pals *within* the local councils: *right-wing social revolutionaries* and *social-democrats-mensheviks* who got together an absolute majority of votes, and in January 1918 *Pravda* already wrote the following about those whom Ulyanov-Lenin had so movingly called "Comrades!" just a few months before.

What can one call them? There are no such words. They have yet to be coined. For there is no greater vileness on earth, no greater betrayal of the entire future of mankind, than the jobbery of these hirelings and Black Guard pogrom bandits wearing the mask of Socialism. . . .

After a good countrywide pogrom (which I will describe somewhat later) to exterminate the Right-Wing Social Revolutionaries, they were later, in 1922, put on *trial,* for *they,* the victims, or rather those of the victims who had survived the pogrom, were "Black Guard pogrom bandits." First an all-out countrywide pogrom, and then a *trial* for the survivors as Black Guard pogrom bandits. In certain ways the *trial* in 1922 was even more farcical than the *trial* of Bukharin and others in 1938. At the *trial* of 1922 there were *councils for defense* who were to deliver and did deliver thunderous exposés of the endless heinous crimes of the Social Revolutionaries and then asked the *court* for condescension, considering their defendants' confession and repentance, and one of such *councils for defense* was—Bukharin! For how could the *trial* manage without *his* intellectual flowers?

Anyway, now it was necessary only to bump off that last pal— the *left-wing socialist revolutionaries*—in cahoots with whom the other two had been eliminated so nicely.

Naturally, *Pravda* announced that the comrades of yesterday, the Left-Wing Social Revolutionaries, had suddenly and treacherously attacked the kind, trusting, peaceful Ulyanov-Lenin, Trotsky, and all workers, soldiers, peasants, and citizens. What had Ulyanov-Lenin and Trotsky to do? Fortunately, the leaders or delegates of these *left-wing social revolutionaries* were with the *bolsheviks* at the *congress of the soviets* in the Bolshoi Theater. So Ulyanov-Lenin and Trotsky had them *arrested* in the Bolshoi Theater as hostages. It is not quite clear how and why the party of these *left-wing social revolutionaries* should have chosen for attack precisely the time when its leaders or delegates were sitting next to the *bolsheviks* in the Bolshoi Theater as co-sharers of possession-power. Anyway, on July 7, 1918, *Pravda* announced on behalf of the *soviet power* which now meant strictly Ulyanov-Lenin and his armed *party*:

> The Soviet Power has detained as hostages all the delegates of the Fifth Congress of the Soviets who are members of the Party of Left-Wing Social Revolutionaries, and has as well taken all measures for the immediate military suppression and liquidation of the mutiny of the new servants of the White Guard designs and the movement of Ghetman Skoropadsky.

Of course, later it would be not only White Guards and Skoropadsky, but also Hitler, Trotsky and all the Old Bolsheviks, the governments of all democracies, the *social fascists* (that is, Social Democrats), Tito, the *maoist regime* in China, and all the other *enemies,* all rolled into a single manichean coparticipative cluster of evil. But at the time of their evil attack, the Left-Wing

Social Revolutionaries coparticipated only in the White Guards and Skoropadsky (the ghetman of the Ukraine occupied by Germany). Fortunately, all these Left-Wing Social Revolutionaries were fleeing while attacking (the usual behavioral pattern of all enemies who have been pals just a second ago).

The Council of People's Commissars has sent the following telegram to all volost, village and uyez Soviets:

"The routed bands of Left-Wing Social Revolutionaries in rebellion against the Soviet power are fleeing into the areas beyond the city, the leaders of the venture are on the run. Take all measures to catch and arrest those who have dared to rise against the Soviet Power. Stop all cars. Set up roadblocks everywhere. . . .

Chairman of Council of
People's Commissars: Lenin"

And within three days Trotsky explained in *Pravda* that those Left-Wing Social Revolutionaries were not at all arrested in the Bolshoi Theater as hostages, but quite on the contrary

we took measures to surround the Bolshoi Theater because we thought that the rebellious force would like to surround the premises of the All-Russia Congress, and therefore we locked in the faction of Social Revolutionaries inside the theater and surrounded it with a wall of reliable protection.

So the Left-Wing Social Revolutionaries inside the Bolshoi Theater were protected against the rebellious force (Left-Wing Social Revolutionaries), and therefore *all* Left-Wing Social Revolutionaries must be eliminated. From which Djugashvili-Stalin could conclude that no intelligence is necessary for a grand agent provocateur—not even the mental effort of reading the issue of *Pravda* of three days before.

Was there really any "uprising of the Left-Wing Social Revolutionaries"? Did many *social-revolutionaries* sympathize with Blumkin's assassination of the German Ambassador? Is it true that the *bolshevik* Bukharin and other such anti-German *bolsheviks* sympathized with the assassination? How many *social revolutionaries* took to arms? Did they do it on their own in self-defense *after* their delegates had been *protected* in the Bolshoi Theater?

All that mattered no more than the real circumstances of the "assassination of Kirov" in 1934 or of the "Reichstag fire" a year earlier. As Trotsky graciously admitted in the same speech in *Pravda:*

Of course, all the party is not guilty, and many members of the party will denounce this outrage.

So even according to Trotsky, if there was an *uprising,* many Left-Wing Social Revolutionaries had nothing to do with it. Many? But how many? It did not matter. If certain members (or even one member) of a group do a certain *outrage* quite spontaneously, or under cultivation, or in self-defense, this enables the grand agent provocateur to accuse *all* the group and attack it as a whole.

As he attacks, some members of the victimized group will commit more *outrages,* and he must use every sign of the resistance of any member of the victimized group as fresh proof of the villainous attack of the entire group. As the torture-murder stations began their specialized activity in 1918, it was inevitable that some members of victimized groups would reciprocate in kind. Some victims who had lost their dear ones to torture would torture the torturers, if caught alive, or whomever they could wreak their vengeance on. "Aha! This is what *they* are doing to *us! All of them* are beasts! *They all* are at one! No mercy for *any one of them!*" The more cruel the torture-murder of a group, the more cruel the resistance of some of its members will be, and hence the more *material* will there be for stepping up the torture-murder of the whole group and shifting all the blame on the victims.

Much to Ulyanov-Lenin's and his *comrades'* surprise (and indignation) the population resisted their fervent desire to make it happy by their owning it completely and without reservation. Accordingly, every sign of resistance, down to some lonely desperate terrorist's potshot, was taken just as the killing of Kirov was in 1934: as a treacherous attack of numberless allied hordes of evil who must be foiled by striking back at all of them with might and main ten thousandfold.

Owing to unlimited torture and extermination, the torture-extermination stations quickly stamped out all the once world-famous heroic terrorism in Russia between 1861 and 1917. But some isolated revenge-seekers, acting on their own, managed to kill one torture-extermination chief and one irrelevant "head of a press department," and to wound Ulyanov-Lenin. And each isolated individual revenge of this kind was met as an over-all offensive of all numberless coparticipating forces of evil which must be all tortured and exterminated as hostages, potential enemies, or those guilty by association.

To wound great Lenin! He had only *liquidated* by torture and extermination all independent organizations of Russia, including those which had existed under the tsar. And to wound him for that! *Pravda* could not understand how a human being—a certain woman Kaplan—was able to conceive of doing such a thing to the kindest and gentlest of men.

To the question how she could dare to deprive the proletariat of its leader, she mutters that Lenin is a traitor of Socialism because he has dispersed the Constituent Assembly. The Bolsheviks are usurpers and traitors who have gained power through violence. They are enemies of the people. All Russia must rally around the Constituent Assembly in Samara.

Her political and mental development produces the impression of being below the average.

Not only that, but she must have been stark mad: to rally around the Constituent Assembly, instead of rallying around great Lenin (ousted and confined), Bukharin (tortured and exterminated), Trotsky (banished and assassinated), and other *great* political, social, juridical thinkers who met the same end.

At school we were taught that great Lenin had let that lady Kaplan go and she was still working at a library somewhere. Can anyone imagine that I believed it? I believed it because it was worthwhile for Ulyanov-Lenin to exterminate pests by the million and then let go that lady who wounded *him*. So many people all over the world would love it. He is as impersonal as a pure idea, see? "Neither do I condemn thee: go, and wound no more." The millions of pests would be forgotten in several years, but the gesture would be remembered for centuries.

However, even this delusion of mine did not survive when I began to unearth the sources. Not only was that lady, "developed politically and mentally below the average," tortured to death or at least *officially* butchered right in the cellar where she was caged, but barely mentioned and unmentioned, uncounted myriads of hostages or pariahs followed suit, as in a classical invaders' orgy of revenge.

Every sign of resistance was used to start not only a wave of torture-murder in the specialized network, but also what we may call *state* pogroms. After the autumn of 1917 the *state* was officially at the head of the pogroms: all the vast hierarchy of possession-power from top to bottom combined with the wanton saturnalia of drunken savage aryans out after the property and blood of the pariahs—the *enemies*. On the pretext of an entirely accidental killing of a certain Volodarsky, a minor figure in charge of the press, there was to be a magnificent countrywide pogrom, but in March 1918 great Lenin moved to Moscow from Petersburg and the local comrades restrained in their city the scheduled pogrom, or as great Lenin called it, the *action of mass terror against counterrevolutionaries*. How do you like that? As soon as you yourself are out of a city, there is no pogrom there! No pillage, no massacre—nothing! And this despite the fact that the pogrom was aimed above all against the pariahs whom *Pravda* called "counterrevolutionary Social Revolutionaries," without intending it as a pun, but simply assuming that any *enemy* of great Lenin and his comrades was *counterrevolutionary* by definition, and so death to *counterrevolutionary revolutionaries*.

To: Zinoviev, June 26, 1918
Also: to Lashevich and other members of the Central Committe
    Comrade Zinoviev, it is only today that we have heard in the Central Committee that the *workers* in Petrograd wanted to reply to the assassination of Volodarsky with mass terror and that you (not you personally, but the Petrograd Central Committee and the Petrograd Soviet members) restrained them.
    I protest emphatically!
    We compromise ourselves: in our resolutions at the Soviet we threaten with mass terror, but when it comes to real business, we are *impeding* the revolutionary initiative which was *perfectly* correct.
    This is im-pos-sible! The terrorists will consider us sissies. We must encourage the mass-scale-ness of terror against counterrevolutionaries, especially in Petrograd, whose example is decisive.

Greetings!
Lenin

    The editor's note to the letter says that "in all more or less significant inhabited areas," except Petrograd, the pogrom was quite a success. Of course, torture-murder at the stations of the specialized network is very good, but there is nothing like a really savage country-scale all-out *state* pogrom.

The third lesson in the school of daring—the *civil war*—was a variation exercise to memorize better the two previous lessons. Ever since childhood we have been told that it is not Ulyanov-Lenin and his men who launched a war of extermination to destroy every vestige of civic or intellectual freedom, but on the contrary the numberless hordes of monsters armed to the teeth, including fourteen (yes: fourteen) *imperialist powers* attacked treacherously the trusting, democratic, peace-loving idealists, hungry, unclad, and almost unarmed.

For example: Makhno, the *enemy* whose name has been known to every school-boy for half a century (the fact that Makhno, an Anarchist as he was, fought against *all* authorities of any kind is not mentioned, of course). How his numberless hordes armed to the teeth were routed by a handful of heroic idealists! In a *children's garden* we recited:

> We routed Deníkin, we routed Makhnó
> All will thus be flapped off!

"Makhnó" and "flapped off" rhyme so snappily in Russian. It is only when I began to study the sources on my own, I found that Makhno's main striking force was represented by five hundred peasant carts, and his total strength ebbed, unless his war luck was in, to four thousand men. And his enemy, a handful of heroic idealists, hungry, unclad, and almost unarmed?

To the Revolutionary-Military Council
6 February 1921
Comrade Sklyanky:

I enclose yet another Warning.

Our military command failed and Makhno slipped out (despite our gigantic preponderance of forces and strict order to catch), and now it is failing even more disgracefully, unable as it is to crush a handful of bandits.

Order for me a *brief* report of the commander in chief (with a simple sketch showing the dispositions of the bands and those of the troops) on what has been going on.

What use is made of perfectly reliable cavalry?

Of armored trains? (Are they located rationally? Do they not ply back and forth *needlessly* and consume bread for nothing?)

Of armored cars?

Of airplanes?

How many are there of them and how are they used?

Bread and fuel and everything are being lost because of these bands despite our one-million-strong army. We must pull up the commander in chief as much as we can.

Lenin

In 1918 *Pravda* published an article entitled "Where New Life Is Created." Where is it created?

Go to the military induction stations. Look at the happily excited faces of those mobilized, listen to their talk.

The faces were so happily excited because, the "overwhelming opinion is that all are fit for military service." Do you hear? All. "No exemptions for those who were exempted by the tsarist regime." Such was the opinion of those mobilized.

"War is made not only by, say, the people in the trenches," one of them explained. "Why cannot a lame person or a person having a hernia be useful as well? All are useful!"

Pravda became really ecstatic about the notion that *all* could be mobilized.

Everyone is fit, and each has his place.

If he is lame, put him into a military office, and if he is blind in the one eye, he is fit too.

Why, anyone with any defect is. Everyone will find his road.

After another exclamation that "all are fit, all!" *Pravda* concluded:

As one listens to all this, this thought fills one's heart with joy:
This is where new life is being created.

To put it a little less poetically, the new owners of Russia carried out, relying on the network of torture-murder stations, such a mobilization as no country in human history had even imagined possible. So that the forces of their enemies in the *civil war* were microscopic in comparison.

The latest American biographer of great Lenin gives the strength of Admiral Kolchak's army in the autumn of 1919 as 103,000 men and that of General Denikin's as 93,000 men.

What the biographer does not seem to know is that according to the network of propaganda, 155,000 senior and junior *tsarist officers* of the *tsarist army* were mobilized into the *red army* in 1918 (the figure is anything but overestimated since there is no pride for the network of propaganda in the fact that the *red army* was the *tsarist army*, only far, far more ruthlessly mobilized by the new owners of the country and far, far more ruthlessly compelled to go into any action, no matter how suicidal). So the number of *tsarist officers* alone in the *red army* far exceeded already in 1918 the total strength of Denikin's puny Volunteer Army or Kolchak's force in 1919.

As far as the foreign forces, such as those of Britain or the United States, Britain *and* the United States landed in the North a force which reached at its peak about one fifth of Denikin's strength. Microscopic as all these "anti-Bolshevik" forces were, they were uncoordinated in space and time, fought for different purposes, and often even fought each other (like Makhno Denikin).

The *civil war* was a good exercise for Djugashvili-Stalin: mobilize *everyone*, hurl a million-strong army with all the weapons against five hundred peasant carts, spare no lives in the process, and let your network of propaganda create a myth of your military genius and of the unheard-of heroism of your combat serfs, though in the summer of 1921 you were still unable to crush those five hundred peasant carts.

Finally, it is in the school of *daring* that Djugashvili-Stalin learned: a grand agent provocateur must always be able to find the scapegoat for his own megacrimes, and that scapegoat is better to be just the population group, inside or outside his territory, whose resistance he wants to break. The masterpiece was the *confiscation of church valuables*. Unprecedented famine? Let the churches give all their articles of value to aid those dying of hunger.

The churches tried to remonstrate. Suppose they would destroy all icons to donate all the gold, silver, gems, and other *valuables*? How could they be sure that these *valuables* would be used to aid those dying of hunger? Ulyanov-Lenin personally had been pouring "many, many millions" on his comrades abroad during the famine. How could the churches be sure that their donations would not go into these "many, many millions"? But since freedom of the press existed for the *bolsheviks* only, no such arguments could be heard. And the agents provocateur whipped up a pogrom hate in their network of propaganda. The churches do not want to save those millions of people dying of hunger! They want the death of millions of people! They are murdering millions of people!

The murderers of millions of people must be shot: those who would resist the confiscation of all church valuables by word or deed would be shot.

In the *civil war* (and hence its aftermath) it is those who resisted the conquest that proved to be guilty. So, too, it is the churches who proved to be guilty of the famine. Were they not causing all those millions of deaths by their resistance to the confiscation of all their valuables?

The confiscation of all church valuables. If an icon a thousand years old contains some gold, silver, or precious stones worth a couple of dollars, prize it out of the icon. Thereby you will get two dollars' worth *and* will destroy the icon and the church, which is also useful.

Besides, you will *provoke*. It is unthinkable that no one will resist. Some will. Make a show trial of them, shoot them officially with great solemnity (the murderers who are causing millions of deaths) and under the cover of all that righteous wrath, secretly grind them all to dust like so many pests. Some Christians! Now it is clear who are the *real*, indeed, *early* Christians! We, Communists, who are ready to feed the hungry people at any price (even at the price of looting all the churches). These priests and devout Christians are Christians only in name, but actually they are large-scale murderers, and shooting them is really a mild measure.

The Mongol nomads of the thirteenth century spared the churches, valuables or no valuables. The twentieth-century invasion from within proved to be more mercenary, bigoted, vandalic than the thirteenth-century conquest from outside. National minorities were preferably used to destroy Russian churches, ethnic Russians to destroy mosques or synagogues. An exemplary lesson in the school of *daring* all round.

And what about its pupil Djugashvili-Stalin?

Since great Stalin became in 1956 the villain of the post-1917 piece of Russian history, it was soon found east and west that the villain had not that sunny disposition which Sir Winston Churchill and many others described, but on the contrary that suitably bad (brooding, paranoiac) temper which villains usually have in vaudevilles.

A bad temper? The present author is not sure that *his* temper (or moral nature) is any better. True, he has done much less evil than great Stalin. But he has been able to do evil only within a tiny compass, and within that tiny compass he has been doing a lot of evil. True again, the present author did not join the *communist party*, while Djugashvili-Stalin did. But how many extraneous sensibilities beyond good or evil entered into the author's abstinence from this slippery step into the abyss? Privileged enough to spend his childhood in the last residual enclave or afterglow of Russian culture, the author found *bolsheviks* like Ulyanov-Lenin, Bukharin, Trotsky or Lunacharsky cheap vulgarians of the most unpleasant kind. It would be aesthetically unpleasant for the author even to aspire to become their colleague, or subordinate, or superior. But not so for a cobbler's son, young Djugashvili-Stalin. These humorless, pompous, intellectually illiterate megacriminals could well represent the acme of exquisite and prestigious life for a provincial Georgian at the turn of the century.

Megacrime starts as easily as small-scale crime, and once you have taken the first slippery step you roll into the abyss.

By 1922 a graduate of the school of daring named Djugashvili-Stalin knew that if he behaved like that Rojkov no one would even remember his name. Do you know, gentle reader, who and what is Rojkov? Yet in *party* pedigree or seniority he was once above Djugashvili-Stalin. *Compared* intellectually with any *bolshevik*, he *was* just a man of genius! His only credential for oblivion was his unwillingness to be a megacriminal. A minor point, isn't it? On the other hand, if that Rojkov or he, Djugashvili-Stalin, behaved like Ulyanov-Lenin and Trotsky with respect to those whom they called comrades, laughed at some *canard*, and screaming that the comrades were attacking them, killed them off like fleeing rabbits, then *all progressive mankind* would know him, fear him, and respect him. Some would seek part of his wealth in the form of trade profit and natural resources as the British Government did in 1921 in the midst of the Kronstadt uprising and the suppression of Georgia. Others would be anxious to show off to their electorate how chummy they were with him, and the electorate would rejoice in his gracious smile as the best guarantee of its security against his further conquest. Still others would be discontent with their own regime or their own life and would glorify him to spite it. Even his worst enemies would concede him his genius, greatness, grandeur, for the only yardstick is the scale of success measured in terms of wealth, especially if including human property, fame-notoriety (which is one word in Russian), plus military might. Does not the very word *great* in all languages still imply bigness first and foremost? Should he be the *greatest* criminal ever, he would seem to quite a few people even in the West the greatest scientist of all sciences, the handsomest, noblest, kindest man on earth, yes, almost a deity in human flesh.

Like everyone of his rank he had a residence in the Kremlin and a country house, for right after the final open grab of possession-power he became in comparative status what had been called before 1917 a "cabinet minister." Working at his ministry was a secretary, and as it happens to some seventeen-year-old secretaries in some ministries, she was pretty. It is silly to demand that pretty charming seventeen-year-old girls fall in love with men twenty-two years their senior only because these men have a handsome profile or a tall athletic figure, and not because these men are cabinet ministers with whatever befits the life of a cabinet minister—though, in the country at large, an average-size potato, not to mention a pair of stockings, is a treasure for perhaps 99 percent of the population.

What it would have been like if he had not been in compara-tive status a cabinet minister, but would have lived like some Rojkov exiled from Moscow to a corner rented in some local cottage in the suburbs of Pskov? Please imagine: a seventeen-year-old girl enters the ramshackle cottage (oh, my, that smell of poverty), and there in a dark corner she sees a shortish old-looking man, perhaps an electrician from somewhere in the Urals and perhaps recently out of prison. The old man has a dark Oriental face, pockmarked, sallow, with a low retreating forehead. What is he? Revolutionary criminals, criminal revolutionaries, or counterrevolutionary revolutionaries are all mixed up so that you can never tell which is which. Perhaps he is just a criminal? Anyway, he is a fugitive, exile, guilty of something. Was in prison before 1917 for his revolutionary activity? But these days all criminals say that: all the doors of all the prisons were appropriately swung open in 1917. A "shady type," as they say when nothing definitely bad is known. Besides, since she is a Russian and hence ex-Christian, the first feeling she has is the fear of Oriental men associated by Christians with lack of chivalry, cruelty, devious sexual ways, and such traits, unless and until the fear is overcome by successful courtship. But how can the old-looking Georgian court her? If in your own tongue you are not witty and smart with girls it is bad enough, but if you speak an alien tongue clumsily and with an accent, it is disastrous—your jokes will be insulting to the girl, confirming her fear of your Oriental lecherous crudeness, simply disgusting her, especially considering your age.

Your smile is so irresistible that it will charm Sir Winston Churchill, not to mention *all progressive mankind* of both sexes. The *best representatives of the western intelligentsia*, not to mention the local ballet primas and operatic divas, will love your smile so that your loving young wife will be just a nuisance for you to get rid of. But to the girl in that squalor your smile will seem the inane smirk of a vaguely dangerous ugly character who has the nerve to try a kind of courtship because she has walked into that house by mistake.

Or perhaps he should say to her, trying to control his Russian as best as he can:

"Please have some pity on me. Don't you find at least my smile beautiful? I was a big criminal. But I have decided to be honest and have given up an enormous loot. Enormous. The biggest in history. Does not this touch you? Is not this worth your love? If you saw this in a movie you would weep—all the ladies in the audience would weep, and some men too."

The oldish man in that squalor will be crying. Is he drunk? Or just sick? How can *she* help him? She is only a secretary, a lonely defenseless girl, and her life is hard enough without bothering about some wretched crazy or drunk oldsters in some godforsaken hole of Pskov. After all, there are proper authorities to take care, and the nursing homes of the new regime are said to be much better than in the old days.

But would Ulyanov-Lenin or Trotsky, and their pupils in the school of *daring,* Zinoviev or Bukharin, let him die in that corner somewhere in Pskov if one of them gained that *dictatorship* all for himself and became able to consign him easily where they all had consigned, say, those *social revolutionaries* whom they had called comrades before? And no one would be able to recall even his name. "Remember that Georgian freak we dispatched?" someone would say. And they would laugh at the thought that they were known, feared or admired by the entire world while no one could even remember his name. What was the purpose of all his horrible life? He got money for them by robbery while they frolicked all their lives in Europe. One of them would be elevated to the heaven of glory while no one would be able to recall his name. As the thieves sang in the Urals in my childhood:

> I will die, I will die,
> I'll be shoved into earth,
> And no one will know
> Where my grave will be,
>
> No one will know
> No one will come. . . .

Certainly not pretty seventeen-year-old secretaries. And there can be no other purpose in life but to outsmart, exterminate, and forget before one is outsmarted, exterminated, and forgotten.

32

But more later about the universe I was born into, and now if the gentle reader recalls, I am six, the former Odoyevo manor house is on a hill, we see it from afar.

But if the former manor house was a *house of rest*, how could I live there with my parents? Everyone knows that even today the family at a *house of rest* for, say, rank-and-file doctors, engineers and scientists of Moscow is divided: its children go to children's collectives elsewhere; the man goes to a men's common bedroom and the wife to a women's. It is cheaper to build two sleeping premises for two dozen human units than six bedrooms for six families of four. And this is true even today, while in 1918 the family was to be abolished altogether in favor of collectives. In the provinces the *revolutionaries* often went indeed the whole hog in the *socialization of women* (still mentioned by some Western experts on post-1917 Russia as the best example of wild lies to which ignorant anticommunism once led). The *soviet* of Vladimir (about a hundred miles from Moscow) issued the following order or *law*:

Every girl above the age of 18 is hereby declared to be state property.

Every unmarried girl who has reached the age of 18 is obliged, on pain of a severe penalty, to register with the Free Love Office of the Welfare Commissariat.

A woman registered with the Free Love Office has the right to choose a male aged 19–50 as a cohabiting partner. . . . Men also have the right to choose from women who have reached the age of 18.

Interested persons may choose a husband or wife once a month. The Free Love Office is autonomous. In the interests of the state, men aged 19–50 have the right to select women registered in the office even without the consent of such women.

The offspring of such cohabitation become the property of the Republic.

The *liberator of women* Kolontai, the only woman among the twelve apostles of the Apotheosis published in 1918 on the first anniversary of possession-power, struck in Moscow a more sober metropolitan note:

There is no need for the family any longer. The state has no need for it because household economies are no longer of advantage to the state; they needlessly divert female workers from more useful productive work.

True enough, *female workers* have been doing usefully all the lowest-paid, meanest, or hardest work. Nearly all rank-and-file doctors for male and female commoners are women, while nearly all doctors of the highest caste are men. And so on. Liberated women usefully fill the lowest stratum of serfdom and thus liberate men for higher-paid jobs where the outstanding ability to rule, or other masculine or allegedly masculine qualities are thought to be necessary for the possession-power. Nearly all chiefs, even at the lowest level, are men who can often be seen leisurely watching their *female workers* sledge-hammering railroad spikes or picking potatoes for fourteen hours on end.

However, if there is no family, the whole institution of hostages, the motivational groundwork of the regime, will collapse. So the family has, since the mid-thirties, been *strengthened* more and more. So much so that the provinces again overdid it, and in 1935 *Pravda* complained about the

school of Sidorenkovo where the care for the morality of children (an important and topical problem) led to an insane project: all school girls began to be examined "pursuant to the establishment of virginity."

The family has been *strengthened* more and more where it does not run counter to the interests of those in possession-power. At *houses of rest* it is still thought to be more expedient to treat the inmates not as many families but as two collectives (male and female adults) which may fuse during processes like eating into one collective.

And yet in 1935—how could I live with my parents at a *house of rest*?

Ha! It was not a *house of rest* at all. It was a *house of creativity*. Like every other group, writers, *writers*, and writers-*writers* had been fighting for the freedoms of individualized life for themselves.

True, the *proletarian writers*, of whom there were more than four thousand in 1928, said that just as smiths work with their hammers at their anvils, so, too, writers labor with their pens at their desks in collective workshops. How could they be answered? Well, the comrades who say that a writer is a proletarian using pens and desks as means of production and paper and ink as raw materials are quite right, of course. In fact, the former manor house in Odoyevo is not a house of rest at all, but a house of creativity, a specific kind of collective workshop. The writers' desks ought to be installed in this workshop, just like any other machine-tools would.

But here a good word was fished out of Karl Marx himself: *specifics*. Good old Marx noticed that every kind of labor is not only generic, but is also specific. A discovery stamped by his genius, and anyway at that time he could not be wrong as yet. *Specifics*! The *proletarian writers* are right, of course, but we should not forget about the *specifics* of every kind of labor either. The *specifics* of a writer's labor is that his machine-tool, that is, his desk, must be installed in a *separate* writing workshop of a collective plant.

In 1932 all those four thousand *proletarian writers* were *closed* (like a store) as *vulgarizers of marxism*. For workers were ceasing to be aryan: passport-Russians were becoming aryan, and the purest Russian was the pseudo-tsar-god, a Georgian.

Naturally, the word *specifics* now became an offensive weapon because those who objected could publicly be called *vulgarizers of marxism*. The specifics of a writer's work (or labor) is that you can never tell (unless you are a vulgarizer) the difference between work and rest, because a writer can work inwardly while outwardly he may seem to be holidaymaking. A writer's wife (whom you may also call his mistress or beloved, for the difference was not yet as distinct as later) and his child joined him in his individual writing workshop of the collective writing plant by tacit agreement of everyone concerned: specifics of a writer's work!

So we walked by a winding path toward the former Odoyevo manor house, and from afar we must have looked like those tiny human figures somewhere in the right bottom corner of an old hilly landscape.

Father halted and said: "Barbizon."

The word was the tuning fork, and a happiness called inexpressible in Russian filled me. Barbizon: a beautiful infinity was evoked by the word, mysteriously promising that I would *bathe in a river*.

We had glided over a river in a boat. But how could one imagine *bathing in a river*?

I close my eyes and try to imagine it thirty-four years later.

A few days ago my son and his friends went for a dip in a lake not far away, and I went with them because my wife and I would be worried if he bathed without adults nearby.

With what squeamish indifference I went into water—an adult's water, a forty-year-old man's water—the substance of some science, a kind of light and limpid vegetable oil.

Yet it was a lake fed by running forest water, a miracle.

Water, here you were, thirty-four years hence, resilient, yet ponderous, you may be plunged into, or scooped, or poured, or drunk. Your mysteries were the same, but I entered you slowly and away from the children and heard their shouts, no more meaningful to me than the twittering of birds, and one of them, a girl of fifteen, swam over to me and flung herself onto my neck, and on dry land it would have been impossible, but in water it was still childhood for all.

To *bathe in a river*. No, I cannot imagine it.

33

The *specifics* of a writer's work made the collective writing plant just like a manor house of old (say: a writer, not a *writer,* because at that time there were writers, and even *writers* still wanted to be writers, or at least writers-*writers*).

A writer would suddenly feel at midday or midnight like mixing his visions (are not his visions his work?) with an apple or whipped cream. The writer would approach Katyusha, a maid flippantly nicknamed Katyusha Maslova from Tolstoy's *Resurrection* for an easier reference.

I do not know whether she looked like Katyusha Maslova, but she had a fresh, pretty, modestly blushing face because the *specifics* of a writer's work demanded that he should see such faces around, especially while eating.

No, not eating (what a word), but partaking of what is in harmony with his visions—what may give them a new twist, intertwine with them, become those visions.

The writer would not, of course, say to Katyusha that his wife or he wanted an apple or whipped cream. That would imply that Katyusha was not the end unto herself but a means of serving food. The implication would be obtuse, caddish, philistine. A writer knows only human beings—he knows no classes, nations, professions. Between him and every human being arises a living and growing novel, so subtle that it will defy the crude craft of writing should he ever try to commit it to paper. All these evanescent sensibilities may be destroyed or damaged beyond regeneration by the remotest implication that Katyusha is just a maid bringing him a pair of apples on a plate with a dainty ivory-handled brass fruit knife.

The request for apples, or whatever visions, varied infinitely from writer to writer and from day to day, but I remembered for life one such request.

"Give me apples fresh and fragrant, it is from love I am wasting," a writer said to Katyusha. I did not know it was a translation in verse of the Song of Songs. Nor did Katyusha, I am sure. We both looked at him fascinated. What an extraordinary man. How life becomes extraordinary around him. How bold and beautiful and exciting what he says is.

Katyusha regarded her work as the rarest stroke of good fortune. It had saved her family and herself. She could not afford it to be ambushed by anything. She knew that these creative heaven dwellers enjoyed an incredible degree of freedom and happiness and were free and happy as though rapturously drunk yet somehow calm and decent.

Desperately anxious to keep her job (her friend when dismissed had wailed for several hours as though she had been at the funeral of a loved one), she played by unerring feminine ear the best response expected of her.

She had been registering what these heaven dwellers liked or disliked, and had been readjusting her speech and manner accordingly. She would never say more than one or two words at a time, and these were the words she had selected as their favorites. She found that they abhorred anything citified. She was to be immaculately clean and neat, of course, yet more rustic than she actually was, more naïve, modest, shy. Whenever she was sure they had said something funny she was to let her lips curl in a shy smile. They were never angry when she could not understand what they wanted as long as she was embarrassed. Embarrassment. Maidenhood. Nature. They took their time, life was all theirs, and they enjoyed everything including her flustered face.

Dinner was the time to gather and converse. To announce the occasion Katyusha would knock softly at every door saying the same pleasantly illiterate phrase which had been used on Russian estates for perhaps three centuries: "To eat has been offered" (when Tolstoy decided to become a simple peasant and do some plowing, his servant reportedly announced: "To plow has been offered").

Mother would begin brushing her hair indolently. That would frighten me. Growing up in collectives, high-caste and high-rank, yet still in collectives, a little scared monk-soldier, I could not understand how she could begin to brush her hair *after* that signal. *Dinner* was in my psyche a certain synchronized exercise. I begged her to be reasonable and not to abuse our fantastic freedom.

Actually, stragglers kept coming to dinner long after, and some would eat nothing, but just sit and make everyone laugh, while others changed the dishes they did not like, and when something spectacular was brought in, there was applause as though it were the entry of a favorite ballet dancer.

As for the diners themselves I have a memory of some general flame of splendor. And of my own moment of triumph. I was asked which of the two pictures on the wall I liked better: *Paris at Night* or the other one which I do not remember. *Paris at Night* was all rough inchoate daubs, and I don't know whether I really liked it or just thought it would be smart to say I did. There was a second's hush, because I was to settle the argument as an innocent referee, unspoiled by false wisdom. I answered barely audibly: "*Paris at Night*," and above the general laughter of approval a voice said: "Three hundred thousand rubles—your son has good taste."

34

It was as though the owner of the manor were entertaining his guests.

But the guests—who were they?

There is an opinion that the pre-1917 Russian intelligentsia was, owing to its apocalyptic nihilism, love of violence, and so on, the mainstay of Ulyanov-Lenin's *revolution*, and has since contaminated the whole world so that now such intelligentsia is rife everywhere, spelling the doom of democracy.

On December 22, 1917, *Pravda* reported the regular meeting of the Society of Novelists at the writers', artists', and actors' club of Moscow. Shortly before, a certain minor author named Serafimovich had agreed to work on the now *bolshevik* newspaper *Izvestia*, and one of those present took the floor:

"Among us, ladies and gentlemen, there is a writer who does not belong here. We all know him: Mr. Serafimovich. He has accepted the editorship of the Art and Literature Department in the *Izvestia* of Moscow. Thereby he has joined the usurpers of power, and there is no place for him among us."

Serafimovich wanted to know if there was a single writer, artist, or intellectual against the demand:

"Of course, if there is a single voice of protest, I will stay. I want to know if any one here does not share the opinion expressed by the group."

A deep silence followed.
Serafimovich left.

The Russian intelligentsia resisted *communism* more unanimously and suicidally than, say, the French intelligentsia the Nazi occupation. Just on the defeat of France, Mauriac dedicated his *La Pharisienne* to Lieutenant Heller of the Propagandastaffel. And what about Gide, Châteaubriant, Céline, and the rest? In the autumn of 1941, Van Dongen, Derain, Vlaminck, and other outstanding French artists were officially invited to visit Nazi Germany and accepted. Celebrities in other fields joined them, and the French movie star Harry Baur provided himself for the gala occasion with a document proving he was not a Jew. As the first trainload of foreign Jews arrested on French soil left for Auschwitz in the spring of 1942, a magnificent reception was organized for Maillol at the Nazi Embassy after he inaugurated Arno Breker's show, with Abel Bonnard as the main speaker and Jean Cocteau as a guest of honor.

In 1943 the war luck of the Third Reich turned bad, but what if it had continued as in 1941? How far and wide would this intellectual-artistic brilliance have spread all over the world, not to mention Germany proper? This despite the fact that the *national-socialist* aryanism of 1940 to 1943 was largely exclusive (a French, let alone French-Jewish, intellectual would not become automatically aryan, as a German did at birth, no matter how he might try to deserve this honor), while the *communist* aryanism of 1918 to 1921 was largely inclusive (any *bourgeois* or *bourgeois* intellectual was hailed as the purest aryan *if* he had shown his infinite devotion or servility to the orthodox faith).

As for the extent to which the French intelligentsia was forced to accept the *national-socialist* conquest from outside compared with the Russian intelligentsia forced to accept the *communist* conquest from within: during the occupation M. Sartre was released from a Nazi prison camp on account of his poor health! His books were published and his plays staged! Even during these comparatively lenient, opulent, and happy sixties in Moscow, the highest-caste exhibition for foreigners, the Muscovite playwright and historian Amalrik was not released even when he had meningitis; on the contrary, he will no doubt be *sentenced* to a *second term* right there (his crime evidently being his failure to die of meningitis), until he either dies or becomes an innocuous wreck, existing simply to show interested foreigners that he has not been put to death for his books. And it is even odd to complain against this Amalrik case. After all, they were merely putting him to death for a crime inconceivable under great Stalin: the publication of his works abroad of his own free will! An amazing oasis of freedom (or lenience), luxury, refinement, the foreign exhibition Moscow is in the sixties. M. Sartre can imagine what it was from 1918 to 1921 when every intellectual could be put to death by a simple refusal to issue him his *rations*. Surely M. Sartre had some rations in a Nazi camp before his release on account of illness? Yet one should not take his rations for granted. Not in 1918 to 1921! And after more than three years of harder than Nazi-camp conditions for the resistance of the Russian intelligentsia, *Pravda* ruefully made note of

that apparently striking fact that the West-European intelligentsia, actually connected with capital much more than our "people-loving salt of the earth," produces a far higher percent of sympathizers with Communism and the working class.

But what about *communists* like Trotsky, Ulyanov-Lenin, Bukharin, or Lunacharsky? As of October 1919 about 95 percent of *members of the executive committees of the soviets* had neither college, nor even high-school education. So they could not read or write as quickly as Ulyanov-Lenin, and cannot be called therefore intellectuals. But what about the remaining five percent?

Trite, intellectually illiterate, or downright stupid as their *ideas* can be said to have been, they can be claimed to have been motivated by these *ideas*. They are often assumed to have been intellectuals—the intelligentsia—because they were allegedly motivated by *ideas,* in contrast to, say, cleaning women motivated by their pay and other vulgarities.

But were they motivated by *ideas* more than, say, randomly sampled cleaning women?

In our century of mass education it is pointless to lower the name of intelligentsia, intellectuals, to embrace whomever "received education," with his middle-class parents' money, as did

Ulyanov-Lenin, Trotsky, Bukharin, or Lunacharsky. Today there are millions of Trotskys, Ulyanov-Lenins, Bukharins, or Lunacharskys all over the world because the middle class is much larger than it was in Russia.

A child of the "lower classes" in the old, traditional sense wanted to be a gentleman, a bourgeois, a middle-class man. If he made enough money to dress well, to buy a nice home, he would win prestige, love among his pals, his girls, his poor family, and in his poor neighborhood. If he could not get the wherewithal legally, he tried to get it illegally. A middle-class child wants attention, fame, glory, love full out. A Trotsky, an Ulyanov-Lenin, a Bukharin, or a Lunacharsky wants all these without that paltry vulgar intermediacy of filthy lucre, because he wants them on a mega scale. And if he wants money, some day in the future, he wants it on a mega scale too: he gambles for countries, not soiled ill-smelling banknotes; for continents, not disgusting middle-class wallets; for the globe, not the humiliating chicken feed in the cash register of the local bank. If he cannot get megattention, megaprestige, megalove legally, he is apt to become a megacriminal, out for the destruction of democracy or whatever the regime is, and not an ordinary small-scale comparatively innocuous criminal from among the poor.

Just as any child, a middle-class child wants to rise above his parents and his childhood milieu, but the trouble is they cannot be impressed or surpassed or challenged by a smart suit and some cash. To rise above them he has to rise much higher.

Ulyanov-Lenin and all the others could have done it legally *if*. If Ulyanov-Lenin could have become a *great* chess player. Or Trotsky a *great* mathematician. Or Bukharin a *great* painter. Or Lunacharsky a *great* playwright. But they could not.

A movement (whatever its name) of middle-class failures who are after what no money can buy (and as the highest prize, possession-power which gets *everything* no money can buy) involves large numbers, and hence statistical exceptions are inevitable. Any motive is a probability, never an absolute certainty. A plaintiff stood up in a court of justice and said: "Your Honor, if you decide the case in my favor no matter how unjust it may seem to anyone else except me, I will give you a bag of gold."

Though it has been assumed for several millennia that there

is a high probability that the ensuing decision of the judge in favor of the plaintiff has been motivated by the bag of gold, there is no absolute certainty: the judge can claim, for example, that owing to the rarest temporary aurical aberration he did not hear the promise, and such a possibility cannot be entirely excluded.

Recall again how Ulyanov-Lenin defined in 1906 and 1920 what he and his *comrades* had been after:

The scientific concept of dictatorship means nothing else but completely unlimited power, restrained by no laws or rules whatsoever, and relying directly on violence.

Except for the word *violence,* which connotes in Russian not only "violence" but also "coercion, outrage, rape, compulsion, use of brute force," and for the word "power," which connotes in Russian "possession, ownership, mastery," the definition, translated into all the main languages of the world, must have been known to every *communist* who could read any main language of the world.

But, of course, no one can rule out the statistical probability that Ulyanov-Lenin or any follower of his since 1906 anywhere in the world was in a state of temporary aphasia or insanity or other aberration whenever he said or read the above words. Nor did he know, perceive, notice, understand these words when they had been realized in Russia after 1917.

"Here are all the kingdoms of the world, and the glory of them," whispered the tempter in the Gospels. "All these things will I give thee."

Christ fought the temptation and won, according to the Gospels. But any *communist* can claim that he is so much not of this earth that he did not even hear. "You will first co-own Russia or whatever is your native country and then the earth. You will be one of the possessors of the earth. Completely unlimited power, restrained by no laws or rules whatsoever. You will possess mankind—all the kingdoms of the world, and the glory of them," shouted the tempter, his shout amplified by millions of loudspeakers, printing presses, and film projectors all over the world. The super-Christ did not even hear. "The heroic idealism of early Christianity," he says. "This is what motivated me. An untapped reservoir of infinite compassion for all those toiling, suffering, and downtrodden. A lifelong yearning for world perfection." Then the tempter spoke in an inaudible voice, or rather not a voice at all: "You call it world perfection? Do you remember Lunacharsky and his diva? What a he-goat he and what a beauty she. He had been married *before* world perfection. A plain frumpy prosaic wife. And alas, not young any more either. But in world perfection an operatic diva fell in love with him! And you are not a he-goat! Oh, come on—we are alone. Or rather you are alone, because I am only your inaudible voice, an imageless thought, a total vacuum which is yet your future behavior. Come on—even Ulyanov-Lenin was interested very, very much in foreign medicines for growing *his* hair. For the happiness of mankind *his* bald head is unimportant. On the contrary, a bald-headed revolutionary is more Socratic, self-sacrificial, not caring a rap about how he would look in the eyes of pretty women like Inessa Armand. But his bald head was all-important for *him*. And you are not even bald-headed! Or if you are, how handsome you are all the same! Listen: in world perfection, the world's most perfect (and luxurious!) car will take you to the good old Imperial Opera. . . . No matter what your status in a free society is, no free society can give you the fame, glory, importance that world perfection can bestow on you. A large city was named Gorky when Gorky was alive. What city in a free society was ever named after a living author, artist, intellectual? Nor are the fame, glory, importance of world perfection fickle, controversial, ambivalent, as they are in a free society: in world perfection they are eternal, absolute, immortal as long as you observe the *party discipline,* and surely you do? So the world's most perfect car will take you to the good old Imperial Opera. . . ."

The super-Christ did not even hear.

Arthur Koestler said to himself when he was in a death cell in Spain that should he go out alive, he would tell the world the whole truth about himself. I have read his two-volume auto-biography—his whole truth about himself. He is a remarkable writer (his description of his love affair during his stay in Russia in the early thirties has the Chekhovian ring of sterling literature). He is blunt about some sexual experiences of his, though in this respect he has long been surpassed: the vilest description of common lavatory or sexual physiology is often accepted today as searing self-cognition. But why did he become a *communist*? Not a word about the offer to Mr. Koestler to co-own Germany and then perhaps the world. According to Mr. Koestler, he was motivated solely by beautiful ideas like his yearning for world perfection. In sex, a twentieth-century super-Christ likes to explain how he is motivated by horrible, uncontrollable and even improbable lusts, but when it comes to the grab of status and wealth, all his motives become on the contrary so brazenly pure that the most puritanical Puritan would have gasped.

Of course, a motivation is a live kaleidoscope of myriads of visualizable images or verbalizable invisible fluids like love or respect or self-denial, as well as myriads of no-images and no-words. Say, the world-perfection yearning might have flashed or sparkled in any *communist's* motivational kaleidoscope, too. Statistically, there must be, say, one *communist* per 10,000 or 100,000 or 1,000,000 who is motivated largely by this yearning. But not to say a word about the offer to co-own first his country and then mankind? Not even to hear of the offer cried from the housetops? Not even to surmise the offer? Not even to see it realized in Russia? Not even to be motivated by the offer to any degree at all?

His own alleged absolute purity in status and wealth is ascribed by Mr. Koestler to the "dedicated millions" of *real communists,* that is, super-Christs like himself, who allegedly existed at some pristine time before wicked Stalin's corruption.

By the same token it can be claimed that no "dedicated millions" of gamblers have ever been motivated to any degree at all by their hope to win at cards, in a lottery, or to whatever they may dedicate all time, interest, energy, money. No artists, scientists, or intellectuals, have ever been motivated to any degree at all by their hope of popularity, prestige, status, or royalties. No military or civil officers, no employers or employees, have ever been motivated to any degree at all by promotion, wages, salaries, property, or profit. And no criminals have ever been motivated to any degree at all by the loot, and when criminal gangs fight each other to death they do it out of pure heroic idealism, for the sake of liberation of all mankind, or solely for the benefit of the poor.

But suppose a *revolution* or transformation or transfiguration had occurred in their country, or in all countries, and world perfection had set in. What would these millions of super-Christs be in this world perfection? The *greatest revolutionary poet* Mayakovsky said that he would like to be even a cleaner. Cleaning is a low-paid job done by women in some countries, and if poor men must be liberated, surely poor women must be liberated even more so? But did a single *communist* ever actually become a char in the world perfection?

The wife of Ulyanov-Lenin recalls in her memoirs that during the days immediately following the *great socialist proletarian revolution* (and surely this is the time of the most pristine springtide of heroic idealism among *communists*), Ilyich, that is great Lenin, saw a woman who had been cleaning his office and the staircase in the new world perfection.

Once during the days immediately following the revolution, Ilyich was coming down the stairs, which she was washing. She stood leaning on the banister, resting. Ilyich stopped and talked to her. She did not know who he was at the time. He said to her: "Well, Comrade, don't you find things better now under the Soviet power than under the old government?" And she answered: "Oh, I don't care, as long as I get paid for my work."

There were several hundred thousand *communists* in Russia, and soon super-Christs abounded in fifty countries. But not a single super-Christ volunteered, in the newly come world perfection, to be a char even at the office of great Lenin. The char in paradise-on-earth was an old-regime char who cleaned the office of great Lenin for filthy lucre, and in less than a year that filthy lucre dwindled to rations of a quarter of a pound of bread a day.

But what about the *greatest revolutionary poet* who wanted to be a cleaner in world perfection? He became instead what he called the *first poet*. He eliminated his critics and rivals by accusing their criticisms and poems of insufficiently *revolutionary* spirit and content. He also became the fastest money-making *poet* in human history because he turned into a machine-gun of versified propaganda. He was allowed to go abroad, and published documents contain his telegram to his beloved (the most fashionable lady of Moscow) about his buying in Paris of a "gray beauty," a beautiful gray car, a seclusive luxury even today, almost half a century later. Could he find in his life, crowded as it was with intrigues, pay rates, fashions, travels, restaurants and card games, even a second for being a cleaner?

Did Arthur Koestler volunteer as a cleaner during his stay in the world perfection of Russia? No. He was a rich foreigner, traveling on a deluxe train and having an affair with a passenger, a Russian girl to whom he was more than a nobleman would have been to a serf maid before 1861. To be a char for a while—and be photographed, filmed, described, while cleaning. Yes: this is what *communists* just love. But to become a char, *really*?

A *communist* who had, before world perfection, been a cleaning woman became, in world perfection, say, *assistant for education of the chairman of the gubernia committee.* But certainly not a cleaning woman! And *communists* who had been above cleaning women *before* world perfection, were as much higher during world perfection. For example, Lunacharsky had been not a char, but an unsuccessful or amateur playwright and poet, as his pen name Lunacharsky, Charm of Moonlight, indicates. If a cleaning woman became a gubernia official in world perfection, he became, respectively, a *great* playwright, and, of course, *great* philosopher, *great* critic, *great* scholar, and so forth. Like every college-trained chatterbox he became a Leonardo da Vinci of whatever field he chose. The megacrime, high above money, brought the super-Christ those megavalues which no money on earth could buy: some of the most out-standing playwrights, poets, and critics of pre-1917 Russia and hence of the world were ready to find even his pen name, Charm of Moonlight, the most striking manifestation of twentieth-century genius (presumably in poetry), for their *rations*, and hence life, depended on his kindness, and often only his kind intercession *at the top* could save them from the-worse-than-death of hunger.

Remember an aristocrat of old keeping a carriage waiting? Lunacharsky kept a train with all the passengers waiting for his new beloved (or his new wife, that operatic diva). To describe his fireplace of green semiprecious Urals stone is a sorry anti-climax: grand aristocrats and high ecclesiastics of old had had such. Yet no Charm of Moonlight of old had ever kept a train with all the passengers waiting for his mistress just as if it were his carriage filled with his lackeys.

But, of course, any motive is only a probability, never an absolute certainty. Therefore, what I will say about the motivation of Ulyanov-Lenin (or anyone else, except myself) may be all entirely wrong. Yet while the motivation I will describe may not apply to Ulyanov-Lenin at all, it applies to millions of Ulyanov-Lenins all over the world, in all countries at least as free as Russia was between 1861 and 1917. I take Ulyanov-Lenin as a random sample simply because there is no person in human history on whom so much biographic information has been published, and not much of it has perhaps been suppressed, for if what great Lenin said or did is anti*soviet,* or anti*communist,* then what is not?

A middle-class child considers himself infinitely far above his parents and their ridiculous careers. But at a certain point he may find that he cannot make even such a ridiculous career.

The motivational turning point in the life of great Lenin was evidently his inability to get the top mark in Logic at school. To an outsider this may seem a ridiculous trifle. But to the insiders —to the members of the family, and especially to Ulyanov-Lenin, the event was a trauma, a sobering setback, a fatal flaw in the hitherto perfect panorama of ambition and achievement. Once in the eight years of school Ulyanov-Lenin did not get the highest mark for conduct: he had teased the French teacher. Decades later his sister Anna could not forget this horrible disaster though it was certainly less crucial than the Logic catastrophe.

Since my brother was already in the seventh grade, that was no trifling matter. Father told me about it in the winter of 1885 when I came for my vacations and added that Volodya had given him his word of honor that this would never happen again.

Great Lenin's discomfiture in Logic has been a deep unhealing wound in the network of propaganda as well, and there is even a special study: "Why V. Ulyanov Got 'Four' in Logic."

The network has been brilliantly demonstrating that a pupil of a pre-1917 school, *gymnasium,* is a man of versatile genius *ipso facto.* For example, a *soviet college graduate* is supposed to understand somehow foreign scientific and technological magazines in English (or in German) in his field of weapons or *means of production*: that is all the knowledge of foreign languages required. A *gymnasium* (high-school) pupil studied Greek, Latin, and Old Slavic: hence the network can pass Ulyanov-Lenin for a classical humanist, a new Erasmus. A *gymnasium* pupil spoke, not just barely read, two or three modern foreign languages, and hence hosts of foreigners can be quoted as admiring a *gymnasium* pupil like Ulyanov-Lenin as a polyglot, linguist, and semantic philosopher. Thus, the pre-1917 school program can be extolled as proof of versatile genius, especially since Ulyanov-Lenin had top marks, and only Logic is a never-healing wound.

Naturally, the author of the probe into that wound demonstrated that the villain was the teacher of Logic (also the head master), named Kerensky, the father of the head of the Provisional Government who dared in 1917 to resist Ulyanov-Lenin's destruction of democracy. Unfortunately, all memoirs of relatives and classmates note that Kerensky Sr. "loved Volodya very much" (he officially attested his favorite as the most exemplary, diligent, and dutiful pupil of his school), "praised his work constantly and gave him the highest marks," often, indeed, the highest with special honors.

Ulyanov-Lenin's wife describes very movingly that he broke away from *religion* (that is, Orthodox Christianity) when he was fifteen: he "snatched off his cross which he still wore and threw it down." Ulyanov-Lenin answered the question: "From what age have you been an atheist?" in the *party* questionnaires: "Since sixteen." Nevertheless, at the age of seventeen he got the top marks in all three subjects of Religion: Catechism, Theology, and the Holy Writ. An atheist as he was, he crammed Catechism, Theology, and the Holy Writ to get the top marks, and he got them. But in Logic he was unable to get them, no matter how hard he tried.

All *bolsheviks*, including Ulyanov-Lenin's wife, tell us that the pre-1917 Russian *gymnasium* was nothing but *tsarist* stifling regimentation and inane cramming, and Ulyanov-Lenin hated it.

Himself a former pupil of a classical gymnasium, a typical old-regime secondary school, he hated this old-regime school with its inane cramming and stifling regimentation, with its isolation from real life.

He saw and knew the minds of pupils in this old-regime school burdened by masses of data, nine-tenths unnecessary and one-tenth distorted.

So for eight years Ulyanov-Lenin crammed more zealously than anyone else the masses of unnecessary or distorted data in order to be the *first* pupil in the school he hated. He memorized to perfection even the three subjects of Religion, this opiate of the people, which must have seemed to his dry pedant's mind just a pack of absurd lies. As for the *stifling regimentation* of the school he hated, that same Kerensky Sr. summed it up for a period of eight years as follows:

Neither in the gymnasium nor outside has a single case been noted when Ulyanov would cause by word or deed a less than commendable opinion of himself in the directing and teaching staff of the gymnasium.

True, there was one case. As one of the memoirists notes, almost tearfully, already in the first grade Ulyanov had developed a highly useful habit: he "sharpened his pencils with great skill." Another pupil kept breaking the tips of his pencils on the sly out of sheer mischief. Finally, the nine-year-old Volodya Ulyanov "caught the culprit in the act."

Promptly, Volodya collared him and gave him a good thrashing.

The headmaster must have been moved really: nine years old, and what a love for perfectly sharpened pencils.

His conduct for eight years: Excellent. His attendance: Highly precise. His preparation of homework: Highly accurate. His execution of written assignments: Excellently diligent. His attention in class: Highly attentive. His interest in studies: Studies all subjects with zeal.

But why? An odd question. Because he wanted to get on in the world—in *tsarist* Russia as the case was. To this end, he had to know Catechism, Theology, and the Holy Writ, and he knew them. Even though he regarded them as a pack of absurd lies. He had to become a machine for memorizing Orthodox Christianity and a paragon of *tsarist stifling regimentation*, and this is what he was for eight years, and could perhaps have been for another eighty if he had had the illusion that he was succeeding.

But the world was so callous. If his kind of pedantic conformity, zealous obedience, ritualistic precision, from his skillful sharpening of all his pencils in the first grade to the memorizing of Orthodox Christian texts in the last, had been duly rewarded he would have been a great success. But there are no really famous men of genius in, say, the sharpening of pencils, or even in the memorizing of Christian texts.

Behaviorally, he was bound to realize that while he had been thought of at school in his small native town as a great man, a prodigy, a versatile genius, the callous world at large took him on the contrary for a perfect all-round mediocrity having no gift for anything and failing even in school Logic, inasmuch as it transcended sheer memorization, pedantry, and diligence.

In fact, he did not know what he should be because he had no interest in anything, and he took a college degree in Law just as at school he had taken exams in Religion. Without a spark of interest and without a spark of talent, but with the same enormous drive to be the *first*. From memoirs we learn that he despised Law, as he despised Religion, and, again, he crammed the despised Law more zealously than anyone else in the whole enrollment. Again he was the *first* in all subjects. And naturally he was bound to fail as a lawyer, and he failed. He did not want to be a *bourgeois* lawyer? But why had he then crammed the *bourgeois* Law as no one else did? Becoming a *great* lawyer, as he would like to be, required perhaps just that unmemorizable ingredient of logic which he could not grasp. And much more besides, which he did not possess. And perhaps which even great (if still unknown) Bonosky does not have either.

Actually, fifteen years of *education* had made him a misfit. It has been often repeated since the time of Karl Marx that manual or *proletarian* labor "produces all values on earth." However, *education* ruled out all such low occupations for Ulyanov-Lenin: education in the humanities was in the time of Plato and is today a sign of nobility, and the bearer of this sign is *ipso facto* a thinker, a creator, a teacher-leader for whom *proletarian* or any other utilitarian labor is usually deeply humiliating: even when Ulyanov-Lenin was expelled from the first year of a university for a fight in which an inspector was hit with a chair, never for a second did he ever stir to do any *proletarian* work which "produces all values on earth." To sink so low would be the same as to do without a maid. But his *education* did not simply provide him with a degree certifying that he was a spiritual nobleman. His *education* kept repeating in black and white for fifteen years that he was the first, the best, the top highest. But in life it turned out that memorization was useless.

For about four years after his discomfiture in school Logic his life was dual, as is usually the case with such decisions: he already wanted to overthrow the regime which had been assuring him since childhood that he was the *first,* and then began dashing all his hopes to be the first, yet he still crammed frantically to be the *first* in the hated Law of the *tsarist regime* (to be overthrown) in order to succeed in that *tsarist regime* (not to be overthrown).

In that ambivalence he met—no, not Karl Marx, but Nikolay Dolgov. As for Karl Marx, we can assume that he never existed: nothing would have changed—at least in Russia—if he had not. But Nikolay Dolgov was important. He was a *secret combatant* of the *army (party?)* of Nechayev, an associate of Bakunin. Once Bakunin was considered to be an equal and a rival of Marx, and they insulted each other just as great Lenin (or great Stalin) and great Trotsky did. Bakunin conceived the *party* as a secret war force, a replica of the military-official pyramid of Nicholas I. Only his, Bakunin's, secret hierarchy was good, from the point of view of its secret members, because it consisted of these secret members, and surely no one would consider bad his own self? Since the secret hierarchy was good, it must have the *daring* to do anything for the sake of establishment of its possession-power.

We have been taught since childhood that Bakunin, Nechayev and other such megacriminals of the 1870s were indeed just megacriminals. The *Great Soviet Encyclopedia* defines Nechayev in this way:

In all his activity Nechayev was guided by personal ambition and vanity. For their sake he would not hesitate to use means like deception and crime. . . . Marx called him a "scoundrel," and Engels a "scallywag." "Nechayev is either a Russian agent provocateur, or at least he acted as such," Engels wrote in 1872 to Kuno.

Dostoyevsky was not published and was practically banned until 1956 because the above is just what he described in his novel *The Possessed*. For forty years the network of propaganda called his novel "malicious slander"—and printed this malicious slander in its encyclopedias as a historic fact.

From the network of propaganda we learn that Dolgov met Nechayev in 1869, and at the age of twenty

V. I. Lenin maintained his acquaintance with Dolgov in order to familiarize himself from a primary source with the principles of revolutionary organizations of the seventies.

It is said that Dostoyevsky was prophetic. Why, he and Ulyanov-Lenin simply came in touch with the same activity—he to describe it, Ulyanov-Lenin to use it. And that was all Ulyanov-Lenin needed to know as he made up his mind: he would be the first, the best, the top highest—not in the *tsarist regime* as he had hoped for fifteen years, but in his own hierarchy which would topple the existing hierarchy and take over. It was a gamble, of course, but it was worth his while, because the stakes were global or at least continental.

Meanwhile he would lead a much more varied, exciting and even prosperous life than that of an assistant lawyer in a provincial town of Russia, living as he now would on collections, donations, robberies, dues, or any other proceeds accruing to an organization of this kind promising a share of possession-power to its members, and *compassion* to everyone else.

The rest was a verbal exercise, a *teaching, ideas*. Those of Karl Marx, for example. But if Ulyanov-Lenin memorized, for all his atheism, Catechism, Theology and the Holy Writ, better than anyone else in the whole school, for the sake of *that* career, surely he could memorize the *new* teaching as well, for the sake of his new career?

It is as absurd to call, say, Ulyanov-Lenin a Marxist or Communist or Bolshevik in the sense that he was motivated by *marxist* or *communist* or *bolshevik ideas*, as it is absurd to call him, say, a Christian or Orthodox Church Christian just because he surpassed all his classmates in the memorization of Orthodox Christianity.

It is true that Ulyanov-Lenin applied certain ideas of *communism* to the populace he enserfed. But *private* serf owners before 1861, including his grandfather, also applied these ideas to their serfs, and also only to the extent they believed it to have been useful to them. To *himself* Ulyanov-Lenin never applied those *ideas,* and there is no evidence that he was ever motivated by them more than his grandfather or any other randomly sampled person. Many children are collective because they are bored unless they play together, and many young people are communal because communality gives a young person a chance to get acquainted with as many young people as possible, something he or she may not be able to do individually. But even as a child, Ulyanov-Lenin was unusually individualistic (he never had a single school friend throughout eight years), completely absorbed in his personal career of being the *first*, and even his sports, as part of his care for his health, were mostly strictly individual exercises rather than games in which even the most individualist bourgeois indulge in the most individualist societies. As a young man Ulyanov-Lenin was also a strictly individualistic, money-conscious, if not yet close-fisted, childless Oldster (his *party* name) who never had a single friend in his life, but only subordinates: any equal of his, like Trotsky between 1903 and 1917, was automatically a rival to be hated and insulted like the worst enemy until he became his subordinate. And Ulyanov-Lenin's way of life before 1917 is the strictly private way of life of a common petty bourgeois of that time, having a common, private, rather philistine "good time within reasonable prices." While after 1917 his life became that of a common *soviet* top-ranking pseudo-tsar-god making a top military secret out of his top-caste life because he is at the same time a hypocritical high priest of his own divine self.

Ulyanov-Lenin (as a randomly sampled person calling himself a *communist*) never applied or intended to apply his well-memorized collective-communal creed to himself. Barring inevitable statistical exceptions, *communists* have been no more motivated by their *ideas* than any other randomly sampled group. Nor should they be identified with the Russian pre-1917 intelligentsia that resisted suicidally their conquest, subjugation and enserfment from within.

35

Those who gathered at Odoyevo were still partly the intelligentsia of pre-1917 Russia, or rather they were its last vestige. In other fields the best of the intelligentsia emigrated, but in literature the language, the soil, and the absence of that literary milieu which lingered in Russia well into the thirties prevented some from emigration and made some others even return. As for those in possession-power, in view of the implacable and sometimes suicidal hostility of the intelligentsia, it was initially important for them that at least some writers ceased to be *political enemies* of the regime and attended strictly to their art, so to speak. In 1922 *Pravda* published Trotsky's critical essays (just as he had been a *great* military commander, so now he became a *great* literary critic), and in these essays he called such writers literary fellow-travelers.

To be just a writer. Not to be political, social, civic. Now this began to suit some of those who had survived and had not emigrated.

The fact is that the words *political, social, civic,* had been the most frequent words since 1861 among those groups (including later the *bolsheviks*) who wanted to sacrifice free culture for those political, social, civic values that these groups allegedly propounded for the benefit of mankind. Thus, these words came to be associated with creative sterility seeking a subterfuge in political, social, and civic sermonizing.

By the end of 1917 it turned out that all these lay priests who had been preaching the sacrifice of free culture for the sake of their social, civic, political sermons and activities proved to be ignorant precisely in the social, civic, political fields: most of them were exterminated or barely managed to flee abroad, while others became the exterminators (to be exterminated in turn within twenty years). The social, the civic, the political began to connote not only creative sterility (often intolerant and even militant), but also pompous ignorance. Anyway, the post-1917 era showed the complete bankruptcy of all Russian political, social, and civic thought of all trends and shades. The Chairman of the State Duma Rodzyanko, the "patriarch of Marxism" Plekhanov, or Ulyanov-Lenin and his "favorite disciples" (who all had been duped so easily and ousted by 1929) seemed to have been equally helpless flotsam, carried by the torrent of history.

Tsar Nicholas II and his advisers. In 1914 the mere thought that Russia might become a German colony was horrible for ethnic Russians. But after 1917 the Kaiser's Germany seemed in Russia to have been an idyllic, humane, civilized country. Nicholas II should have made any concessions to the Kaiser rather than plunge into the war which undercut the European civilization perhaps forever and ushered in something no European could even imagine in his most fanciful diatribes against the *existing regimes* before 1917.

Milyukov. The leader of Constitutional Democracy. The founder of the Provisional Government in the spring of 1917. On paper it sounded all right. But in reality he could not even imagine what strong countermotive was required to keep soldiers from deserting the war front and following anyone who preached *peace* the secret of which (no separate treaty with Germany!) he allegedly knew.

Kropotkin. The founder of Anarchism. Anarchy is a titillating intellectual pastime when the police of at least a semiconstitutional monarchy defend you from the consequences of your theory. But what is Anarchy otherwise? Any gang will seize possession-power, and all the Anarchists either will become *heroes of labor* and *heroes of battle* in the *new* regime or will be exterminated—at the very best, painlessly.

Or Tolstoy. Nonresistance to violent evil as a social, civic, political creed. Again very good in a regime with at least a semi-constitutional legal and penitentiary system. But how does this apply to post-1917 Russia? Do not resist violent evil, my dear Count Tolstoy, and at the best you will be kicked out like Gorky or Zamyatin, if your name has become too well known in the West (and if the West still exists!), and every dissident line of your works—and in particular the preaching of non-resistance, if necessary—will be tracked down and destroyed (few people of my generation have even vaguely heard of what Gorky wrote in 1918).

Besides, the political, the civic, the social was associated with the *rational,* and the *rational* had been thought, at least since the close of the nineteenth century, to be the opposite of spiritual depth, illumination, genius in art. The opposition had originated as a reaction to nineteenth-century *rational* (that is, mechanical) schemes, explaining life, man, society as machines consisting of machines. Today millions of schoolchildren believe they are great talents if what they write or paint or sculpt is sufficiently *irrational:* the *irrational* is now as much a sign of commonplace spiritual sterility as those schoolchildren's *perfect* poems about nightingales were a hundred years ago. But in the early twenties the irrational was still a sign of genius. That *irrational* naturally assumed various forms, such as the *core, viscera, people, folk, earth,* as opposed to the futile, ugly, and fatal cerebrations of the intelligentsia. Sometimes the creative *irrational* was mythically assumed to be exclusively "Russian," in contrast to mythical "Western" spiritual mechanization, philistinism, and effete soul-lessness. It should be recalled that Andrey Bely and others pre-ceded Joyce, as Evreinov and Vedensky preceded Beckett. It is simply that after the destruction of old Russia and her culture the Russian Joyces, Kafkas, or Becketts were forgotten, while Joyce, Kafka, and Beckett became, decades later, world-famous symbols of Western artistic sophistication. But in the early twen-ties a Russian writer had good reason to believe that "Russians" incarnated that *subconscious* in art which the "West" acclaimed decades later.

Nor had the years of the famine, cold, typhus, and intense torture-murder passed without effect. More than ever before did man seem to be of this poor earth, pathetically frail, and dependent on forces beyond his will or mind or soul.

> There is nothing I wouldn't give for life,
> How I need the tiniest spark of sympathy,
> A sole match could warm me like a hearth.

Writers had actually been beggars living on alms—*rations,* issued by *it,* the plague, the monster to be screened out of mind. Man was free from all civilized conventions, moral precepts, or abstract creeds. He was a lonely, naked, helpless supplicant. A savage in all earnest, a pagan of necessity, a pauper anxious to survive.

A writer was through with political, civic, and social thought. He was just a human being. On the first day of the creation, so to speak.

Except that some unpleasantness soon came up. A famous poet was shot in 1921.

He was shot because he was declared to be a *political enemy* of the regime. Those who had not tried to emigrate undertook thereby to be apolitical (acivic, asocial). But he was not, it was declared. So he was killed. By whom or what? Certainly not by the new serf owners, or by the new superautocracy, or by *revolutionary justice,* because all these are political names. Simply by plague—by something. In Russian one can say not only: "It is raining," but also, as in an immortal line of verse: "It is praying and it is believing and feeling so light, so light." Something like "methinks" in old English. Not *I* think, but it (something) thinks (in me—to me). "The government is killing me. *I* am being killed," says an English-speaking person, personalizing both source and object of his grievance. In Russian all the personalization can be avoided. At a great gain to poetry, sometimes, but at a great loss to legal clarity. It is killing. Mekills. It killed that poet yesterday. Himkilled. It killed (hard) yesterday. Just like: It rained yesterday. The others would not stop doing what they did—writing and publishing as before. Even thriving and enjoying life. Nothing can be done or said about that death. It plagued hard yesterday. It hit that poet. It may hit you if you are political.

There was one tiny flaw in this reasoning. Who had proved that he was a *political enemy* without due legal process? In this way anyone may become a *political enemy*, with some references to sinister conspiracies. It is quite possible that he was shot simply to show that those in possession-power have the *daring* and let everyone know that acid may be splashed into anyone's eyes no matter who and what he is. To be apolitical one could only say: It killed hard yesterday, and it killed (him).

An unpleasantness of a different kind arose almost simultaneously. In poetry it is possible perhaps to be asocial, acivic, apolitical. But what about prose? A writer wrote a novel which anticipated Orwell's *1984* by a good quarter of a century. Naturally: if the workers and sailors of Kronstadt had understood by 1921 what it was all about, how could Russian prose fail to? That novel was *political,* wasn't it? Especially if those in possession-power took it as referring to themselves, since there was no *fascism* as yet to refer it to.

Prose, as inevitably more political, was killed more quickly than poetry, but poetry did not want yet to die and still throbbed its way well into the thirties, through the cold, narrowing, calcinating veins.

> Petersburg: I do not want yet to die,
> Your telephone numbers are still on my roll,
> Your dead are sure to answer my call.

There were two birds in Slavic folklore: the bird of joy and the bird of sadness. There were two poets of genius, both of whom had matured before 1917. One published his poetry in 1912 as a genius of joy who seems to have no analogue in the history of poetry. If a little girl rushes in from the garden with a twig in her hand, a raindrop on the twig becomes a source of concentric ecstasies, and an instantaneous reflection of the twig in a cheval glass becomes another source, and the ecstasies interfere like the waves when a swish of raindrops from a twig hits the water.

Priests of sacrifice of free culture for the social, civic, political goals, which now meant possession-power, had been gaining in strength and number, but for a while they could find no serious fault with this joy.

According to their earthly religion, the time since the autumn of 1917 was the new era of joy, heaven on earth, festival of spring, youth, and beauty. And here was, quite appropriately, that poet with his joy. True, his joy had originated in 1912, and at that time he ought to have moaned in the old regime, but then that girl and the twig and the raindrop and the cheval glass can always be said to have been so joyful precisely because they anticipated the *proletarian revolution*, and cheval glasses love *proletarian revolutions*.

The other poet also began publishing long before 1917, but rather as a genius of sadness, and this was what he continued to be after 1917, of course. Already in the early twenties that made him an easy target: why was he so sad in the new era of joy? Why not emulate his colleague, that genius of joy? If his colleague, admittedly a poet of genius, is a genius of joy, why should *he* be a genius of sadness?

So it went on and on, worse and worse: the usual pattern. He was one of those who are born perhaps once in five hundred years in a country. But intellectual illiterates would not understand this: someone who could spell the words well in his poems gradually came to regard himself as his equal if he had the same rank (*a member of the union of writers*) and in duty bound to *criticize* him in the serf press for his sadness in the era of joy. True equality for intellectual illiterates was coming: everything was to depend on the rank granted by the pseudo-tsar-god, not on such unjust prejudices like genius versus creative sterility. But the genius of sadness had the prejudice instilled into his mind before 1917, and the still-lingering milieu of intelligentsia of the pre-1917 vintage kept assuring him privately that he was one of those who are born in a country once in five hundred years. He reacted to *criticism* with what appeared to intellectual illiterates to be offensive arrogance that had to be disciplined by more *criticism*, especially since it was the new *writers, critics,* and *editors* vying for the pseudo-tsar-god's favor and rank who were taking over all the presses. He reacted with even more violent arrogance, and finally he wrote a *political* poem (aha!) and read it to some people, whereupon *it hit him*, of course. It did not yet plague hard, but the poem was bound to attract the plague. His wife has survived miraculously, and now she says that his troubles began way back in the early twenties, while the other writers, including the genius of joy, continued to write and publish—to thrive and enjoy life. What are they—scoundrels?

Of course. He who chooses not to emigrate when there is a chance, but decides to survive inside a serf war machine—to write, publish, thrive, and enjoy life as an apolitical, acivic, asocial man—is a scoundrel or will be a scoundrel unless he manages to commit suicide in due time. How else? When the possession-power hits his colleague, friend, or next of kin, he is to assume that the pseudo-tsar-god is an apolitical *it*—like rain or plague.

It was quite encouraging to know that so far (the summer of 1935) the plague had been hitting writers only sporadically, not epidemically, while epidemics had been raging since 1918 among hundreds of other groups like *left-wing social revolutionaries* or engineers or waifs. The plague hits one because one is careless, or unlucky, or has sinned—is guilty of something. And spares another because he is careful, or lucky, or innocent. The healthy must just take care not to catch plague from the sick. That's all.

This was how the genius of sadness himself and his wife had behaved when that poet was shot in 1921. The genius of sadness continued to write and publish—to thrive and enjoy life (if there was a chance) until the sporadic plague hit *him*.

So, too, the genius of joy continued to live and create when the plague had hit the genius of sadness—in a humdrum sense, his friend he had corresponded with, seen more or less regularly, and valued as a unique poet. How else could it have been? To the genius of joy the disappearence of all political, legal and civic freedoms in Russia, the *civil war,* typhus, famine and enserfment, had been just a plague, or rather many interplaying (or interplaguing?) plagues—the *elements*. There had been no sense to ascribe them to human agency. Why should he stop living when the plague (one of the plagues?) had hit his friend?

At the peak of the *civil war* and the riot of all the other elements, he wrote: "Into the triptych mirrors a cup of cocoa is steaming." In Russian the words "verse," "the elements," "sudden mood" sound similarly. The elements had been raging outside, the elements had been playing in his poetry. He created the most egoistical world ever created in a human language, and at the same time, this riot of Slavic paganism, the Renaissance and the last dazzling flash of culture of Russian manorial estates was unique, beautiful, and seething with that joy of life which makes a child laugh "without any cause at all" except for the absurd, groundless, unreasonable joy of living.

He saw a drop of rain slithering down a leaf, and can there be a more excruciating joy? But suppose there are *many* raindrops? Who would not go mad with joy? When the garden has just been crying and now is all aglitter with a million sky-blue tears? Talking of raindrops! Everything in a rain promises and gives heaps of pleasure. Are the barrels and pails, put under the downspouts to store rainwater, overflowing? "What a drinking of thunderstorm at cornucopias of blisses." A spout of rain water tilts one of the pails? "That clanging thirst! That clinking greed! Is not the sky enough, for God's sake?" There is a saying: "Dull as ditchwater." Not for the genius of joy. The rainwater in the ditch flows with a vehement gurgle like frantically coursing blood: "A hundred hearts are beating in the ditch."

Children may know sometimes no regrets of the past and no anxieties for the future, no conscience and no compassion, no rules and no curbs. Only joy. Migraine, a severe headache of which some people suffer after a rain? *Dies ire*? Fate? These are only new sources of joy.

> Oh, please believe my play, believe
> Migraine, pursuing you with a roar,
> Please—fate decrees Dies ire to burn
> As a rain-drunk wilding on a cherry-tree.

The reader could see that all this cosmos of joy had been created out of the most ordinary, indeed, philistine habitat of an ordinary middle-class gentleman of pre-1917 Russia: a comfortable cottage on a property not far from Moscow or Petersburg, strolls in forests, a city apartment, country-city train commuting. And that was about all. The genius of joy needed no more because ordinary mud on ordinary roads in February 1912 burned with black spring, and roared and clicked with the cabby wheels flying (for sixty kopecks, as the poet noted with his innocent love for bourgeois detail) through the ringing of the church bells to where the wind was pitted and scarred with the cries of rocks, sweeping suddenly down, and verse came on like sobbing, the more unexpected the truer.

Then the pagan March (what matters of what year—the

poet once asked the children at play: "What millennium is it now?") stole into the austere chorale of the fir forest, and soaked the still snow-laden paths with the astringent bluishness of sinful thaw.

> Please close your eyes. In the mutest organ
> Of spaces in delirium for thirty miles around,
> Adrip and steaming are the snorts, the snarking,
> The laughter, babble, crying, ecstasy and trance.

No, the genius of joy needed nothing outside his cosmos of joy. Outside there were those plagues, and one of the plagues had hit his friend, that genius of sadness. That was just an interplay of the *elements*—of the verse-elements and plague-elements—and no one was to blame, because there was no guilt, as there was no conscience, regrets, anxieties, or compassion.

But can a twentieth-century poet of genius be a scoundrel? Perhaps, only as long as he can believe he is apolitical, acivic, asocial not because he is a scoundrel, but just because he lives on the first day of the creation—just because he is a child who does not know what is political, civic, social, and simply: a twig, a raindrop, a cheval glass—life, how insomniac is your sleep, how dreamlike your vigil.

When the sporadic plague hit the genius of sadness, pseudo-tsar-god II called up the genius of joy over the ordinary human telephone.

The novelist Bulgakov thought up a story he would tell to his friends about great Stalin deciding to phone the director of the Moscow Art Theatre. The director answered, but then there was silence. The man died. The story was originally thought up, but it circulated as a true episode, and few doubted its authenticity: how can a mortal hear great Stalin's voice addressed to him all of a sudden like that—and live?

And here great Stalin was *really* calling. But the genius of joy had been living since 1912 on the first day of the creation. He was a divine child. A blessed idiot. He was to live up to his image now that the pseudo-tsar-god was calling him. If he had not, he would perhaps have ceased to be a genius.

To any normal adult the purpose of the call was obvious. If

he, a poet of genius, renounced (or as the Gospels say: denied) another poet of genius he would be safe, yet he would not be a blessed child, a poet of genius at all, but just a clever versifying scoundrel. If he interceded for another poet of genius he would doom himself.

The pseudo-tsar-god is calling. The pseudo-tsar-god?

To a child, a lunatic, or a man of genius who has lived since 1912 on the first day of the creation, there are no pseudo-tsar-gods, chars, chiefs of the *organs of state security,* madmen, great poets, assassins, senior clerks. There are only human beings.

A human being calling him, a Stalin by name. The human being has no connection with the plague. No more than any other being. Simply the plague plagues. It is not plaguing very hard, but the genius of sadness has attracted the plague. It may hit him, the genius of joy. It may hit a street, a city, a country, like God's scourge. Or rather like a rain. A certain Stalin has nothing to do with it, for he is just a human being.

First the genius of joy said that it was awkward for him to speak from a communal apartment (in which he lived).

The sentence needs comment. When a Russian intellectual spoke, he wanted to give of his best no matter with whom he spoke, as long as the other speaker was a human being. Yet giving of his best requires complete ease, abandon, freedom. But the neighbors who keep fussing in the corridor (in our communal apartment the Marleviches had to pass by the telephone as they went to the kitchen) are indifferent strangers to the conversation and an indifferent stranger may break the subtle fabric of the conversation by his mere presence alone. So his only concern in speaking with the biggest serf owner in human history, who could destroy practically any man on earth in any way possible, was what was called in that day an *interesting conversation,* a kind of intellectual concerto which requires inspired concentration. And these neighbors might spoil it all.

Besides, the conversation was taking a wrong turn. About that poet who had been hit by the plague. What had he or the speaker at the other end of the line to do with the plague? They were only human beings, and the plague was God's scourge, or perhaps just something like a rain of water, gold, or blood in the awesome metamorphosis of nature.

"This is not what I would like to speak with you about," the genius of joy said, annoyed, like an infant prodigy asked to play the version of a concerto which did not fit his mood.

"What about then?"

"About life and death."

Trivia like somebody's life and death were of no interest to the divine child. His own life and death were of no interest to him either right now. Perhaps they might be, in some other context, some other time. You can never tell. But right now he wanted to speak of life and death in general. Please. Why should they engage in some nonsense like the conquest of the world, or the destiny of some plague victim, or even the exchange of a communal apartment room, while they could speak of life and death? O life, how insomniac is your sleep, how dreamlike your vigil.

So he was after all a sick village idiot or a child. Or a man of genius. He had lived up to his claim.

When pseudo-tsar-god II heard that the human, whom he could wipe out, along with his communal neighbors, or entire street, or entire city, by raising his eyebrow, wanted to speak with him about life and death (because it is a good theme for a really interesting conversation) he hung up in disgust, as though having touched the filthy rags of a sick village idiot, or so at least it was said in my childhood and reverberated apocryphally many times since.

Pseudo-tsar-god II could, of course, have that sick village idiot swept into nothingness—just as a matter of personal hygiene. But when a *world congress in defense of culture* was convened in Paris, and that sick village idiot entered, the audience, the crème de la crème of the world literati, stood up to greet him. His message to the congress was as apolitical and irrelevant as a child's babble: poetry lies under our feet and we have only to stoop to pick it up. But it didn't matter: the crème de la crème of the world literati and millions of their readers in all countries were expected to see how human and humane—how gifted, original, and exquisite—*communists*, or *russians*, or *soviet people*, are. To many foreigners, all those whom the pseudo-tsar-gods own on their territories, hold as hostages, or keep as prisoners, including a genius who made his debut in

1912 by an esoteric poem about early spring, are *communists*, or *russians*, or *soviet people*, and all of these names are often essentially the same in their minds. Owing to this sick village idiot, the crème de la crème of the world literati and millions of their admirers would aid the pseudo-tsar-god's *fight for peace*, that is, for his possession-power on earth. This is why the pseudo-tsar-god himself had stooped to calling up that microbe who managed to be disgusting despite his vanishing size: great Stalin wanted to check personally that the filthy microbe would continue to *function* for his benefit after the plague had struck his fellow microbe.

Scoundrels gathered at that feast in Odoyevo. To what extent each scoundrel was a genius, a child, a blessed madman, and to what extent he only claimed to be such and was really just a scoundrel, is only for God to judge.

But apart from the claimants to genius, there were many avowed scoundrels: *writers*, and since every social process is ambivalent, there were also writers-*writers*, of course.

The last printing presses had been taken from writers and given over to *writers* shortly before. Henceforth there were to be only serfs of different ranks attached to the department of *literature*.

A writer was asked by some *state magazine editor* why he never wrote an essay for them. The writer made a frightened conspiratorial face.

"I'll bring you my essay—"

There was a hush: both writers and *writers* knew that a genius was speaking, and no matter what serf ranks had recently been established at the printing presses, here, in conversation, *he* still was a genius.

"I'll bring you my essay—," he said again, gesturing to show how he apprehensively brings the manuscript, to repeat for the benefit of those who had not heard, and to establish rapport as perfect as the music of silence itself.

"You'll all gather around it . . ."

He acted the *editors,* crowding around, clawing fiercely at the manuscript.

". . . and will start plucking out its eyes."

The audience listened in reverence. Who knew: perhaps

writers, not *writers*, would be needed again? *Writers* still wanted to become writers—even those of them who attacked writers in the serf press were still anxious to listen, to learn, to emulate. At the printing presses they were the chiefs, but in conversation they were still disciples, worshipers, apprentices. The plague that struck writers as an epidemic was still ahead, and so they still *conversed*. Deprived of the last printing presses, writers or rather conversants poured their genius or whatever claim to genius into conversation.

These scoundrels, these claimants to genius, these fellow travelers, made up the last enclave of Russian culture. They had grown out of the great free culture of old Russia, and after the Odoyevo time some of them survived the next two years' plague, but only as lone has-beens, useless eccentrics, or simply wretched drunkards. Or sometimes as high rankers of the department who could even remember with difficulty what it was like in that different era of mankind,' before the plague. I saw the last ambiguous enclave of Russian intellectual peers in an environment still congenial and attuned for perception. Conversation, a concerto created as it is performed, an invisible fabric of sudden harmonies elevating to tragic poetry an apparently hopeless truism, reducing to humor what has been accepted as a revelation, intoning, juxtaposing, alluding.

I know: Russian culture may yet revive, but it will not be the culture of Russia, a country that once existed; it will never be what it was in its last innocent, insane, riotous flowering—its last throbbings in the last oxygen of spiritual freedom, in its last feast before the plague, almost during the plague, that summer in Odoyevo.

36

I revisited. Some three decades later. Though not the Odoyevo *house of creativity*, which had been disposed of, but another *house of creativity*, once even more manorlike than the Odoyevo.

At the train station I discovered that I had not arrived alone. I recalled the speech of the *party secretary* of the Tula *region*: "Once in our region there was only one writer." He meant Tolstoy. "Today there are dozens of writers in our region."

We were dozens of writers: it would be stupid to handle lone individuals. We were to be transported by a bus. Collectively. I said I would go on my own. I walked and then a truckman gave me a lift. I was young enough to cling desperately to an illusion —to create it as far as possible. The truckman invited me into the cab, but I climbed onto the open platform. I wanted to be at least a tramp, if no other variety of lone individual. It was a fine trip, through swishing, space-cleaving solitude.

Only when I arrived did I see the full scope of the disaster.

There was a line of new arrivals queuing to a man in white overalls to have their identities checked. I tried to stir up some rebellion or at least sarcasm on the part of the lined-up writers.

I recalled a poetess visiting her son in a prison camp before 1953. Her son bore the name of another poet, her husband, that same poet who had been shot in 1921. The crowd was waiting before a loudspeaker, and the names of visitors and prisoners were called forth: "Ivanov to see Petrov!" "Sidorov to see Nikolayev!" Then: her and his names.

Something like: "Emily Dickinson to see T. S. Eliot!"

Not a single facial muscle twitched in the waiting crowd. A human being may concede fame or money or privilege to another in freedom and wealth, but the more the collective coercively persuades its unit to be a self-sacrificing altruist, the more the unit is likely to become an egotistic absolute, unwilling to concede anything to anyone. Just let your muscle twitch in recognition of that Dickinson, and she will be issued her rations —a meeting with T. S. Eliot in the present case—ahead of you and hence at your expense, for nothing good in the rations is ever sufficient to go around. Your gain is somebody else's loss, your neighbor's grief is your happiness, his death is your life. Do all harm you can to any man, for any man will do all harm he can to you. Though at a split second's notice a collective egoistic absolute may enact a self-effacing hero-saint as part of self-defense trained from the cradle.

I intoned several variations like "Sappho to see Dante!" to my alleged peers in that line because certainly they would appreciate the humor of a line of writers waiting to be identified. I expected a response because that prison camp story was well known, and between 1956 and 1968 my dig at the past was even fashionable in such circles: no one would be afraid, certainly.

They all stared at me—the eyes of a woman expressed the fear of light glassy bulging eyes, while another girl's dark eyes seemed just to whisk inward in panic: there were recesses in her eyes, of course, all sorts of turns and corners, and there her eyes still lurked, but as I talked more, all these people in the line were sure that I was drunk and anyway menacing, and the woman's eyes became lighter, glassier, and more bulging, while the girl's whisked still deeper inward where no one could see them at all.

There were no high rankers in the line, of course. A high ranker arrived later and behaved like a bureaucrat in a novel exposing *class inequality in soviet society*. I could well understand him though.

There are no unique individuals and unique values in culture anymore on the territory in the sense that genius of joy had been unique. Except for certain scientists engaged in the production of weapons, everyone is replaceable. A *writer* often knows that practically anyone able to read and write can write and say what he writes and says. He must, therefore, emphasize, cherish, keep up his rank, or he may be taken for a medium ranker, or even for the small fry, and I felt how the blood of shame, humiliation, and frustration suffused the high ranker's face at the very thought that this might ever happen. Strictly speaking, he was to go to, say, a *tseka sanatorium*, but since he had degraded his rank by coming to a *house of creativity*, he appeared to us at a distance, when he could not help it, wearing that special ever-hurt expression, savage rather than vicious: the skin on his face was rough, pinky, scalded as it were, much like inflamed pigskin, and I recalled his nickname: "The enraged boar."

The enraged boar?

Hardly anyone knew or remembered (did he remember himself?) that once he had published a book of poetry, unique, amazing, stamped by genius. He came from a peasant family, just a peasant fellow. But in the twenties he got into the lingering afterglow of Russian culture, into the milieu of those who knew that literature is always something that is not literature, for it is unique, and therefore it alone is literature, while everything else is something that has *gone into* (the words *gone into* meaning in Russian *trite, vulgar, conventional* and everything else *gone into* any circulation, habit, or use). This is what they taught the peasant fellow. For God's sake, don't try to write like anyone. Forget about the fashions in art, whether ancient or modern or supermodern. You are a peasant fellow: be a peasant fellow. Don't be afraid in art to be anyone. You are a peasant fellow, except that you are unique; everyone is. Be your own unique self. This is what we will publish at those printing presses which we still influence, and this is what we will value at least in our own milieu.

He is just a peasant fellow, it is a peasant hut, the hungry children watch their mother cutting a loaf of bread, hot from the oven, and gradually the loaf cutting turns to a horrible, pathetic, joyous rite, a bacchanalia of hunger to the tattoo of raw, cutting rhymes. A Rembrandt in mad crescendo, a Van Gogh dancing, and how will it all end? Here I have to do what I always do when explaining Russian poetry to foreigners, because there is no other way: here I have to explain that in Russian the words *cut, smash,* and (you) have some (bread) *too* make up a unique triple-rhyme orchestration.

> Ma,
>> *cut!*

the children holler at the acme of the orgy,

> Ma,
>> *smash!*

they yell, the gloomy *smash* of all-out destruction rhyming with the fierce *cut* of ruthless brigandage, and there seems to be nothing to add, while the poet ends with the third rhyme:

> Ma,
>> you have some *too.*

When I explain the poem to foreigners, I recite it also in Russian to them to give the sound of it, and they understand even when they do not know a word of Russian, by God—they understand it in Russian, and I recite it all in Russian except the last line because I know I will burst into tears, probably because at my age I already anticipate my own death, but anyway, it would be awkward, a certain half-crazy native, otherwise pleasant, crying, and so I skip the line discreetly in Russian.

The unique peasant fellow had published at least one book of poetry when an event happened (in the summer of 1934) known as the *first congress of soviet writers.* The event was to attach all writers, *writers,* or writers-*writers* to a single department of *literature* as part of a larger department of religion-propaganda-culture as part of a single hierarchy of possession-power.

The founding patriarch, Gorky, decided to improve the occasion by criticizing the poetry of the unique peasant fellow.

"So what?" a citizen of a democracy would say. When the generalissimo of literature *criticizes* you, it is not he who speaks: it is the whole million-headed network of propaganda who speaks via millions of presses, screens and loudspeakers, while you cannot answer even in two typewritten copies. The generalissimo laughs at your poem, and all his army-hierarchy laughs, and all the country, or perhaps, all the universe laughs.

Why did Gorky do this? Gorky had once been a common, provincial, barely literate fellow himself. He also owed everything to a more refined milieu of old Russia. As this milieu began to disappear, the generalissimo of literature began to slip back into his provincial barbarity, and in particular to imagine that he was a great judge of poetry. Besides, he believed that the source of all evil is *the* peasant: all his life, Gorky had been working up a hatred for *the* peasant, and now it was a good occasion to pour it forth safely and usefully on that unique peasant fellow.

Gorky demonstrated in his speech that the peasant fellow's poetry was ridiculous, raw, disgusting, and he was right. The peasant fellow had expressed his unique self—his soul—and is anything more ridiculous, raw, disgusting to an unkind outsider's eye than a human soul? But this is what those cultivated intellectuals had taught him: forget about the garbs of art, whether ancient or modern or supermodern—it is only your unique self, your soul, that is interesting.

From the rostrum of the *first congress of soviet writers*, Gorky jeered at the ridiculous, raw, disgusting soul of a nascent genius, and the audience, the collective, the *first congress of soviet writers*, laughed, and trampled, and kicked the soul, so helpless (what is more helpless than the soul?), so hateful (what is more hateful?), so shameless (what is more shameless?).

But what about those intellectuals who had cultivated the peasant fellow's genius of self-expression? They had provoked him into expressing his unique soul, and now the collective was mobbing it, with shrieks of laughter. Yet what could they do? Everyone was to be apolitical, acivic, asocial, wasn't he? That soul was out of luck, that's all, and so the *writers* beat it collectively to a pulp as departmental exercise. It was ridiculous to contradict Gorky. Gorky had been made the generalissimo of *literature*, and when a captain or even a major contradicts a generalissimo, he can never be sure of the consequences. Not in a serf society. They were glad they had been invited, which meant they were permitted at least to live and write, if not publish and thrive. Besides, a pogrom of *kulaks* had been on since 1929, every peasant may be a *kulak*, and every poet who expressed himself as a peasant may be one too. When there is a pogrom of some *jews* you can save no one as a *jew*—you can only claim he is not a *jew*: "Comrades, this is a mistake: he is not a *jew*, I can prove it, and yet you treat him as a *jew*." But in this particular case it was impossible to argue that the victim was not a *kulak*, because he had been writing that poetry as a unique peasant fellow—he had exposed himself, see?

Why didn't he commit suicide after the *congress*? Perhaps because that cultivation of his genius of self-expression now seemed to him just the gentry's evanescent whim. As a child I saw a film about a pre-1861 serf owner who wanted a serf of his to become a violin player, but when the serf showed promise, the owner changed his mind. Similarly, the owners of the peasant fellow decided that literature did more harm than good, and *literature* was what was really needed. For that unique peasant fellow, serfdom was reality, while art was an evanescent whim, once cultivated by a certain part of the gentry and now to be forgotten as quickly as possible for the sake of becoming a high-ranking serf of the department of *literature*.

The unique soul of the nascent genius died, mercifully, long before it became a pulp. Perhaps it died at the first shriek of collective laughter, and a boar was borne from the pulp. The boar became a high-ranking versifier of a particularly vulgar kind. I wanted to approach him and say something—to lay a wreath at the dear tomb, so to speak. But how could I? He assumed that everyone except some high rankers of various departments hated him as a vicious sterile strangler of every trace of creative freedom, and this is what he was, by and large. He was a boar, he had nothing but a boar's rank, and there was nothing for him to do but to defend it like an enraged boar fighting against wolves or dogs. The attempt of myself, so low, to approach him, so high, would be an insult in his eyes, for it would diminish the only value he had: his rank. As for that dead nascent genius of self-expression, was it really his self? Did he remember it? Could—would his new self understand his former soul trampled to death?

There were few medium rankers in that line of new arrivals. In fact, most arrivals were not *writers* of any rank at all, but *auxiliary personnel* of the huge department of *literature*. It was with them that the low rankers as well as the relatives of the medium rankers were to mix at the *house of creativity*, and in a way it was fair according to the anecdote about a poetess bringing her handwritten manuscript to a *state publishing house.* "Could you type it?" they ask annoyed. "If I could type," she answers, "why would I write verse?"

As we stood in that line beginning outside and extending into the vestibule I took a look around: there was *furniture* one could meet in a district hospital, or a barber's shop, and each piece proudly displayed an oval disk stating its inventory number. State property. General issue. Imitation oak.

But it didn't matter. Nothing did matter in fact. The man in overalls who checked the documents was a *doctor,* a human zootechnician, a thickset man who looked like a cheap vaudeville butcher, owing to his smug, glossy, crude face and hair arms displayed in vivo below rolled-up sleeves. Manpower of the department of *literature* had to improve its health under his supervision—to increase its weight on the hoof, so to speak.

The issue of food now resembled Strumilin's *norm of consumption* which I will describe later in my narrative. Potatoes were rare (far from potato fields), and the brewing of tea, once the Russian intellectual's awesome ritual, had been supplanted by the boiling of it into a strange dark odorless medicine. I knew why a high ranker of *literature* was so hurt by his very presence in the *house of creativity.* Even the food told him that he was a low-ranking serf: he felt stripped of his status, surrounded by humiliation, as a citizen of a democracy might in a particularly bad prison.

Except for the few high rankers, *writers* were now cheap serf manpower, easily replaceable and reproducible on any desirable scale. In the late fifties pseudo-tsar-god III suddenly wanted a study and report on the average income in cash of *members of the union of writers*: it was found, rather to his surprise, that the average was close to the lowest pay in Moscow. Since within the number there was a steeply tapering high pyramid of ranks, the income in cash of the majority had to be below the lowest pay in Moscow.

Seated at a table with me was a couple, he a theater critic, she a playwright, belonging to this submerged majority. The *house of creativity* was a kind of almshouse to them.

"But how do they live at home?" an American correspondent recently asked me with the smile of one stepping into irreality as I described the situation.

"They live on the mushroom."

"What mushroom?"

"Well, I don't know if it's a mushroom really. It is called a mushroom in Russia. It is some vegetable or animal, something inchoate and vaguely monstrous. You keep it in a jar of water, and you put some sugar in. The mushroom eats or absorbs the sugar, makes the water yellow, and it is drunk."

All the friends and relatives of the couple would bring sugar to feed the mushroom as they might any other pet. "Don't forget the sugar for our mushroom," I heard her saying in a dead vivacious voice: a rich gentlewoman crazy about her pet.

Of course, it would have been better for the couple simply to eat up the sugar their visitors brought without the mushroom's intermediacy, but then what would they be—beggars?

Theirs was a special kind of genteel starvation.

The lowest-paid charwoman in Moscow at least always gets her monthly pay. In her leisure time she can also wash floors privately, and the private pay is at least ten times higher (in Moscow) than the possession-power pay for the same job. Unlike shoemaking, and other such occupations known as *forbidden trades,* floor washing for profit in leisure time has never been a crime, though the *means of production* in the form of a pail of water and a rag are obviously involved.

The playwright and the critic would not wash floors because they were pseudo-noblemen, and the mushroom instead of a pedigree dog was simply a caprice of rich sophisticates.

Millions of serfs want to become *writers* precisely in order to escape from their otherwise inescapable squalor. They hope for success solely because what they write is no worse (if no better) than what is published by the highest rankers of *literature.* They are often quite right, but fail to understand that all soldiers cannot be made marshals or even lieutenants.

The playwright and the art critic had been struggling toward a higher rank in *literature* with the obsession of those who live on the sugar fed to the mushroom.

But it was not that simple. The couple would write a play

about how a young painter became an abstractionist and then inevitably ruined a very good girl and then inevitably became (almost) a spy. But as they *pushed* the play it was too late— many had written such plays, and besides, they were all out of date: they ought to have written a play about how a painter assured everyone that he was serving the people but actually he merely wanted to succeed and therefore labeled as abstractionists all rivals of his who painted better and really served the people. But by the time they had written such a play, many low rankers and one medium ranker had written such plays, and of course, the medium ranker's was accepted for production, and the low rankers' were all rejected: "Look, we have already a play dealing with the theme."

Only by a rare stroke of good fortune could a low ranker move aloft. Once a low ranker who had been in Yugoslavia during the Second World War was writing a huge epic about how the Yugoslavian people had gained freedom and were now creating a paradise on earth under the leadership of great heroes, altruists, and intellectuals. When he was well past the middle of his huge war and peace epic, *Pravda* explained without any previous allusion or warning that the paradise on earth was a fascist concentration camp. But the low ranker had already written all the landscapes, the characters of common people, and battle scenes. So he had only to cut out the leadership as great heroes, altruists, and intellectuals and substitute vaudeville villains called fascists in order to convert an epic battle for freedom into a sinister fascist plot to turn the country into a fascist concentration camp. Thus he was far ahead of thousands of those who had just started off! He became a high ranker with a secretary, maid, cook, watchman at his country house, and everything else befitting his new wealth and station.

True, the problem of disposal arises. How can all the millions of copies of his book be disposed of? Before 1953, say, a *member of the party* was supposed to buy certain books unless he wanted to get the reputation of a bad *member of the party* and face the hazards of the reputation. In the sixties other methods of disposal prevailed. Hundreds of thousands of copies of a high or medium ranker's book will sediment at the *state libraries* as they have for decades. Thus these *libraries* are essentially repositories of waste paper, with two or three books, mostly translations or detectives, in demand.

A book or a set of works may also be processed directly into paper pulp, with much profit to the *people's economy*. But if the agencies utilizing waste paper are not efficient enough, the excess may always be sent into the hinterland, where it will be bought up because there is no paper for smoking or wrapping, or because there is a local belief that every family should buy a thick book for the children to learn to read more quickly.

A young man who did some repairs in my country house once asked me to let him choose a book for himself from the former owner's *library,* which I had dumped out wholesale to burn in the open air. He browsed in the huge heap for a very long time. I was moved because he looked like a neanderthal man in school text-books, and I thought how deceptive appearances are. I was also ashamed, and told him that all the books were worthless. "Never mind," he said with a kind of calm superiority that put me in my place, "I'll find." With a happy neanderthal smile he finally emerged carrying a dark red volume on which I read: I. V. Sta'in, *Selected Works.* I discovered that he had never heard of the author, nor did he suspect that the book has what may be called content. A good book was to him a book with a good cover. He said in triumph: "Look!" and moved his hand over the cover, which was indeed very good because the book had been published in Leipzig.

The playwright-critic couple felt that fortunes were made overnight, and yet their chance would not come.

He used to be a gambler, so he must have been inured to the situation. He had a cane and some clothes from better days, and he stepped out like a gentleman of old, throwing back his Roman-nosed face, twirling his cane, and speaking in such a way that you wanted to punctuate his sentences, as in a classic writer's text used for a school punctuation exercise: "When one becomes old (dash) and evidently (comma) I am becoming old (dash) one sees no longer. . . ."

Why was he such a bore that even quite ordinary people could not stand him? The first principle of the progaganda-religion-culture in which he was steeped is its complete disregard for the other, perceiving side. Its aim is the *uplift* of people of all ages.

No real response of those being *lifted up* is expected or noticed. The art critic had carried the principle into everyday life. As a resu.t everyone with whom he came in touch hated him and did just the opposite of what he wanted if only to spite him. Therefore, the playwright had miscalculated if she had married him to help her to get on. Secretaries mislaid her plays just because her husband bored them to hatred.

What he said was always almost unreally decrepit like everything in their living space, in their room of a communal apartment, which I had the privilege to see, with the mushroom in a glass jar as the only source or symbol of renewing life. He was childless, and though this was stupid and cruel, I could not get rid of one childhood image: when we pinned beetles to the bottom of a box (that was called a collection) they finally became empty within, and only the decrepit surface parts remained. It was the carefully preserved decrepitude of his clothes that suggested the image. He adopted a child who was now a young man with whom his wife lived, if only to spite him for his sermons to improve her upbringing. She wanted to seduce me too by a design as simple as the thinking of a butterfly, and it was quite some trouble for me to pretend that I was even more naïve than a butterfly to understand her: to hurt her by implying that I relished a love affair with her much less than even drinking the yellow water that mushroom produced out of charitable sugar seemed to me as mean as to hurt an innocuous moth. She did look like a moth when on gala occasions she wore on top of her ancient dress a *pelerine* of large-holed lace made perhaps at the turn of the century out of something looking now like old cotton. The ho'es in the lace seemed to have been eaten out, perhaps by other moths of a different size, and one should have seen the *ewigweibliche* gesture with which she put it on.

Sometimes there would even be a certain moth kindness about her. Barring a mushroom love affair, I rather liked her by contrast with her husband, who did not seem animate at all, certainly much less so than their mushroom. Compared with her husband, she was very much alive, even if that aliveness of hers was often a rather frightening cold fluorescence. As we sat at that table over the issues of feed, there was a picture straight ahead on the wall. Such pictures are sold at shops called cult-goods, that is cultural goods, namely stationery for various departments, posters, and so on, and also such pictures. I wanted to invoke in my table companions a ghost of another life, and told them that when I was a child of six, *Paris at Night*, yes, an original—it cost three hundred thousand rubles, I remember because—

"How could a picture costing three hundred thousand rubles hang on the wall here?" she suddenly burst out, with a strange cold excitement as her face glowed white. "You are a strange man living in clouds," she fluoresced as though my living in clouds explained all their failures. "And you said, too, that Afanasyev might help us. No one helps anyone. You live in clouds. Who will help you? No one. A picture costing three hundred thousand rubles hanging on the wall. No one will help anyone."

The critic wanted to stop her outburst or rather indiscreet cold feverish glow. Whenever he wanted to speak he would press his cane to his chest in a very gentlemanly manner, but at table he could only press his caneless hand to his chest, saying: "Valya! Valya!" He wanted to give some *uplift* of his to both of us, and we both knew equally well what he would say in order to extinguish that cold glow of life in her.

37

At Odoyevo there was a river bathhouse exactly as at the beginning of the century: all of boards, and inside was a heaving
slab of water with its walls and floor also of boards, only deep
golden, dark green, and silvery black. According to some rules,
descending from the good old times of river bathhouses, children
were allowed to remain in that slab for one minute .at first and
then each time a little longer, and finally for a full eight minutes.

That was what *bathing in a river* meant. It was getting *into*
that heaving slab, two or three steps down. Off the last rung one
could plunge into that slab, and do anything—oh, whatever
cannot one do with water, alive, substance and nothing, all yours
and elusive, laughter, tenderness, and oblivion. But perhaps
infinite happiness is not boisterous because it has no strength left;
it is perhaps inane, clumsy, and helpless. We did not plunge into
that slab, we slid into it as into an instant recognition, into the
envelopment in blissful laughter, into the breathtaking wrappers
of oblivion.

When I met her when walking with my mother, in my mind
I called her Alexandra Pavlovna, though she was actually a
writer's divorcee, and I even remember the writer's name. I will
call her Alexandra Pavlovna because I mixed her in my memory
with Alexandra Pavlovna and other kindred or complementary
sensations and cannot really tell now who is who.

This Alexandra Pavlovna was not distant like the sun. I was

no longer one of the midges dancing: sun, sun. I had the unbearable responsibility of facing her and speaking to her as though I were also a human being in my own right.

I remember that she was trying to reduce: she was always talking about how much she had walked that day and how useful it was.

Whenever we saw her in the Barbizon distance I begged mother to turn off her path. I thought that everything was so fine that I could only spoil it all. That was my prayer for a long time in later life: let everything be as it is. I was afraid to move to ruin what had sprung up by itself—like flowers. I might displease her. After all, what was I? A little agitated nothing within me, and I had heard her say to my mother: "I am simply in love with your son" (unless it was not she, but the *real* Alexandra Pavlovna who had said this to my mother, and I just mixed it up).

At that time it was already considered smart for an educated woman to say: "I am in love with your son" instead of "I adore your little boy."

But naturally I understood this literally. I also understood that it was sheer luck, that there was nothing intrinsically good in me to deserve this, that it was all a kind of coincidence that might all collapse anyway, and was sure to collapse if I moved. It was like toy structures we made out of bricks and whatever came in handy. It would hold together precariously, and then an adult would add just another fragment to improve, and we would all shout in horror "Oh, don't touch it," but he would, and everything would collapse, and how we would scold the guiltily smiling adult for his reckless self-confidence.

38

To sustain or intensify or vary the Odoyevo harmony (whether sexual, asexual, or multisexual), Alexandra Pavlovna was an artist.

In Russian, painting is called so exquisitely: live writing. Apart from *Paris at Night* and other such treasures of live writing, I cherished a postcard I had at home in Moscow, representing a lake and boats. Ladies and gentlemen sat in the boats, and you could see even an umbrella one of them held sedately—or a leaf in the forest on the bank. But that was not all. The postcard was glossy, it was a magic vision of life over which your fingers could blissfully glide if not for the fear of spoiling it, and all that certainly made it the greatest object of art in its own way.

Whenever we looked through the postcards we never just opened this one like all the others. We knew that the next postcard would be that greatest masterpiece, and we prepared ourselves and exchanged triumphant and mysterious glances. We would linger, and then—open it! And after taking in with a gasp the miracle as a whole, we would fall to admiring the detail. Once we even thought we saw the ferrule of an umbrella.

Hard as it is to imagine this, Alexandra Pavlovna could live-write better than that postcard, and what more can a human being attain than her gift of immortalizing life, of mirroring a real river with real water—look, here are some rapids, and it's at sunset, and through my eyes at that time it was life immortalized.

"Just a river—water, I mean, life immortal, do you understand me?" I asked, thirty years later, an American painter, a young girl whose parents had sent her on a world art tour, including Moscow, to help her to quit hashish. She was a sophisticated professional to whom Braque was perhaps as old-fashioned as Rembrandt was to me. She was sure to take me for a provincial uncle, admiring pretty postcards. But I wanted to break through to her: "Please forget Braque, and everything post-Braque, and please forget everything. It is just a river—water, I mean, life immortal, do you understand me?" I would repeat desperately.

I had spoken with very few English native speakers before. It was like speaking in a code to a dweller of a distant star. And suddenly she said in such a sterling clear voice—calmly as though I had said something perfectly obvious: "Of course," she said, "there is nothing else—I mean what else is there?"

39

My Barbizon harmony glided timelessly on (with ecstasy splashing like water or laughter) until there came a vague but ominous threat from an entirely unexpected quarter. As part of her program to reduce, Alexandra Pavlovna decided to do morning exercises, and since she thought she would be bored if she did them alone, she was to act as instructor and we children as trainees.

A proper time next morning was fixed. It horrified me to go, and it horrified me not to go.

It horrified me not to go because I thought she would be deeply hurt. Like all people I tended to exaggerate my importance.

I did not go.

To have wronged her so for all her love of me. I had ruined everything myself. What if I met her? I was prepared never to meet her again, of course. "I must be happy with what I have had. One cannot have everything forever."

I know now that as she saw us she simply asked my mother: "Why didn't your son come?" But even now I have difficulty imagining that it was just like that.

Terrified, I saw her approaching. Her smile was like the sun's glint before a thunderstorm, which is too cheap as a figure of speech because it is not meant to be—it was a literal sensation: I saw the yellow blaze behind her face, the disarray of nature in a violent wind, and the glint was yellow because she was annoyed, jealous, vengeful.

"Why didn't your son come?"

Once we had guests at home, and my mother said: "You'll stain your collar" because I was wearing my beautiful white *silken* shirt and bent very low over the plate. It is true that nothing can be more expensive than a *silken shirt*, and yet her remark seemed to me so rude, cynical, materialistic, that the gala occasion was ruined completely because I could not stop crying. Here it was all different. I was in the wrong. It was like with those food rations. The Marleviches' domworker Tasya ran after me as we walked with Polya in the Lermontov Garden. Then she found that she had lost the food rations, and not unnaturally she supposed that she had lost them just as she ran after me. So the Marleviches could well regard me as a criminal who nearly doomed them to death from hunger. Now, too, I felt I could not defend myself coherently. I was in a thunderstorm, the dust and leaves and everything were up in a mad vortex, and all I knew was that I must weather it somehow.

I did not turn up the next morning either.

"What am I doing? What will happen to me now?" But I could not go, I really could not.

I recalled that in the kindergarten we sang under the guidance of a thin nervous lady with big deep-sunken eyes who played the piano. I loved the beginning.

> Astern each ship the water's churning,
> The horizon's still unseen,
> Full steam ahead the ships are forging,
> The red fleet's all at sea.

The first line was long, and one felt how those ships emerged and were approaching, because the music emerged from nothing into a two-beat water-churning crescendo, a kind of lullaby reversed into a naval procession.

> Astern ta-ra ta-ra ta-ra.

The next line was a short observation one wanted to sing in a mysterious voice, because it was still night if the horizon was still unseen, and one wanted to let his voice fall gently on the word *unseen,* a kind of delicate finality—the word did not dissolve, it was simply the last to sound as though the question as to whether there was anything beyond was to be left answered-unanswered, resolved-unresolved.

The horizon's still *unseen.*

The third line resumed the crescendo of the first, the ships were in full view, approaching in a louder two-beat rhythm, and the fourth line repeated the pattern of the second, but now it was the morning news about the red fleet which was called red, in my opinion, because ships are painted, just like the roofs seen from the balcony of our home, a russet or purple red, since ships are also made of iron (unlike boats, made of wood).

But then followed something revolting.

> A-h-h-e-ey, seamen all,
> Our country has called,
> May its strength be tasted
> By our foes.

Even now this "a-h-h-e-ey" seems to me ridiculously phony, perhaps because I know that is the High German version of "ahoy" implanted in the Russian eighteenth-century navy to keep the naval serfs in good cheer. But at that time it seemed to me not merely phony but struck me as an outrage. A-h-h-e-ey.

The lady at the piano was so thin, nervous, miserable (perhaps she had been once a promising conservatoire graduate and had been reduced to banging at a piano which was all shattered and badly reverberating?). Anyway, when she brayed forth in her emaciated gentlewoman's voice: "A-h-h-e-ey, seamen all. . . ."

The morning exercises in which Alexandra Pavlovna wanted me to participate somehow belonged to this "a-h-h-e-ey, seamen all." Quite scientifically, they were called morning charging, physical charging, or physcharging, and even now I don't know which of these words is more revolting.

How could I participate? I couldn't, I just couldn't.

40

It was perhaps my first insight into the society I was born into.

Physical charging. Still, a kind of compulsory measure for nearly all collectives. The more general term is *sport*. The serfs using this English word in Russian rarely know it is English. Still less do they suspect that it connotes in English pleasant or amusing pastimes. In *science, sport* is above all a medical act—something like an act of personal hygiene, but it is carried out in public because certainly shame is an atavistic redundancy.

Physcharging haunted me all my life. Quite recently I happened to see young girls, fully developed women in fact, young ladies, engaged in this compulsory act of private hygiene in public, and I looked away because decent men did not look at, say, women undressing *against their will*, and I just had time to notice that one of them cast her eyes in appreciation.

Physcharging. What an edifying pantomime for serfs. A paradigm of obedience and conformity. An enactment of torture. A symbol of work or fight, mechanical, empty, useless, for the sake of those in possession-power. A costless and miraculous rite of their concern for collective health and collective cheer. Finally, a weaponless and hence costless military exercise, in the old Prussian sense when precise collective uniformity was regarded as the most essential element of military efficiency. Combined with health, strength, and cheer, of course.

Physcharging. Isn't it a parody of life in *science*? Life as functioning. As mechanism. As model.

I have never been able to overcome my aversion for *soviet sport*. Perhaps this dislike was bad for my health, but then there is no such thing as *my* health, for my health is *theirs*. Mine has only been my own self deep within, invisible, undetectable.

At the age of six, my revulsion was one of those illuminations that often save people whose minds cannot grasp the danger. If I had had to explain at that time this revulsion of mine I would have used the word *obscene* had I known it.

At this age children are often very shy—they may be ashamed of something in which adults find nothing shameful. Those psychiatrists who feel infinitely superior because they do not know what shyness (or shame) is may as well be proud of their skin, so insensitive compared with a child's, or their usual inability to learn in fifty years a foreign language as well as a child usually does in a year, or that coarseness that can be traced even in some angelic adult faces, while in many adult faces it is monstrous. Many psychiatrists who treat children for shyness or shame would not have been shy or ashamed of the physcharging in my place, but are they ashamed of *anything* at all? "I am ashamed" is one of the pet everyday clichés of adults: shame, shameful, ashamed. But have they been really ashamed of anything in the twentieth century *when* they had to be ashamed?

Shame was one of my main emotions before seven, and again after fourteen, and as my face is getting coarse, I still pray that some shame be left in me.

Shame has been one of the most vital emotions of Russian literature and philosophy, with frequent desperate antiurbanite, antiprogressive, antiscientific, and anti-Western reactions. Some intellectuals even said that 1917 was the suicide of Russia, to be followed, it was hoped, by the general reduction of the entire world to primordial chaos, to savagery, to the beginning, but anything would be better than the brave new world of several billion Freuds.

A young girl arrives in Moscow now or at the turn of the century from some area of the old tradition. She will not take off her kerchief in the presence of strangers because she is ashamed—this is a sacrilege, an obscenity, a violation of something holy. Of course, her urban relatives will explain to her with infinite superiority that she is a village fool or a psychopath (since "neuroses" are regarded as a kind of malingering one who is not *normal* is a psychopath). They will destroy her sense of shame, sometimes by sheer coercion—they will force her to believe that there is nothing obscene about the exposure of her head and nothing holy about her braids of hair, and there will be nothing obscene or holy for her about *anything*.

At the age of six there may be something like this traditional, natural, or *wild* sensitivity that may later vanish.

I remember my father and myself watching the physcharging from a safe distance—my flush of humiliation and resentment when I imagined that I would have to sit down on my haunches and stand up and then sit down again, and so on. I looked up at my father and smiled the smile of a man who has just been insulted in public and wants to show that he is above this. I did not want my father to see my humiliation and resentment. Partly because I did not want anything to spoil the Odoyevo harmony. And partly because I wanted my father to see that I was happy because he might think that I did not appreciate his taking me to Odoyevo and keeping me company. Also, because to show my emotions would be against my father's Russian, or I should say Muscovite, ethics of ironic understatement.

I smiled, but my eyes smarted.

In Odoyevo I was an individual, a separate human being, a gentleman. As I had always been in my own family. Here it was our family attitudes extended onto society. My relations with Alexandra Pavlovna were as personal, as individual, as *intime* as with my father and mother.

The *intime* implied grace, chivalry, uniqueness. What would either of us say should the other one smile ten times in exactly the same way? That would be *clowning*, something some children do, to which adults respond with well-deserved anger: "Now, stop clowning." The physcharging was worse, because *clowning* was at least a lame attempt at being funny, while here each gesture seemed to me just a humorless contortion, violating the intimate grace of a human being and becoming ever deadlier with each repetition.

I never participated, and my mother would say apologetically to Alexandra Pavlovna: "But he is so shy, you know. He is simply a psychopath, a real psychopath."

41

On his fiftieth birthday in 1929 pseudo-tsar-god II named Stalin was perhaps almost as happy as I was on my sixth birthday. All mankind—that is, whoever came to visit us—congratulated me on my birth: life had been created so as to enable everyone to love me and be happy that I was born.

Pseudo-tsar-god II resisted the love of mankind, and his modesty out-Lenined even great Lenin. When the *party*, that is, its *delegates*, had gathered to celebrate great Lenin's birthday in 1920, he even expressed his disapproval during his brief appearance at the ceremony (he had to—it was not yet 1922!). Pseudo-tsar-god II did a cut better: no *party meeting* of this kind at all! But he could not overcome the love of mankind.

The *Pravda* is actually the main part of the one and only *newspaper* in the country because all the other *newspapers* are just its local branches. On the occasion every line of the first six (out of the eight) pages of the main part of the one and only *newspaper* was devoted to the birthday of the most modest of men, great Stalin. That was all the news in the country. Perhaps the only disappointment in this respect was tucked away on the last page: one spot the size of a hand in the left corner was concerned with "Housing Construction in 1929–1930" (a 96-word item). That anyone could think of housing construction on such a day! Waste a 96-word item on such nonsense! To insult great Stalin in such a callous, brutal way! It was the same as if some

guest who had come to us on my sixth birthday had said that
no, he did *not* congratulate me on my birthday. Which shows that
for a fifty-year-old man owning one-sixth of the inhabited globe
it is difficult to attain that happiness which comes so naturally at
the age of six to one who has loving parents occupying, on very
ambiguous terms, a former drawing room in superslums.

There was another unpleasantness that clouded the happiness
of great Stalin's birthday, though he had already begun to remove it.

The unpleasantness was the *partial admission of capitalism*
which finally had to be ushered in in 1921, to avoid the *(socialist?)* death of *(socialist?)* hunger of even the aryan caste.

But what is unpleasant about *capitalism?*

What source available to me in former Russia can answer that
better than *Britannica?* The trouble is that the secret, closed,
special repository at the office for which I free-lance is usually
locked because the staffers are not interested. When I come, the
chief of the *special repository* is annoyed, since, according to
instructions, he should be present. He cannot leave me alone, but
neither can he refuse to let me in. Suppose I am translating Dostoyevsky into English. Who can tell what information I need? He
does not know what I need, nor does he know a word of English.
So he stands over me, plainly showing that I alone am keeping
him busy, that is, standing over me, while he could do something
else with much greater benefit to himself—eating, for example,
or strolling in the corridor and chatting.

Anyway, I find that the *Britannica* of 1964 defines *capitalism*
as the economic system in which "laborers do not possess the
means of production" and "must, of economic necessity, offer
their services on some terms to employers who do control the
means of production." Of course, one could ask: Why: *of
economic necessity?* Suppose a laborer finds it more profitable
to labor with somebody else's, and not his own, identical
means of production, because this somebody else is a gifted
organizer, and/or financier, and/or salesman, and knows how to
make much more money with exactly the same means of production? An even more impertinent question is: Suppose there is
no employers' *means of production?* A repairman of electric
household appliances, a brick layer, a precision tool maker, may

not need more *means of production* than a screwdriver that anyone can buy even here. Does he offer his services to "employers who control the means of production" out of economic necessity? What means of production do they control—screwdrivers? And if a repairman or a brick layer may offer his services to an employer not out of economic necessity, but for a higher pay, why does not a steelmaker or a miner ever do the same?

In the services, farming, or building of democracies there are millions of modern efficient enterprises run by a family or partners who do not employ anyone. Are they not Capitalism, according to the *Britannica*?

A government as in Britain today may *nationalize* the big means of production, but it cannot *nationalize* screwdrivers— it can only *ban*, say, under pain of imprisonment, all government-independent employment of a repairman's or a brick layer's services themselves, that is, ban the freedom to employ for all except the government, something that even Hobbes thought impermissible in his Absolutism. The *soviet* regime has been unable in forty years to suppress free enterprise equipped with screwdrivers and other such means of production. How can a government as in the United States or even Britain today do that unless it has become even more pre-Hobbesian than great Stalin's regime?

For more than forty years the *soviet* regime has been ruthlessly persecuting all but *nationalized* medicine. The result? There is a definite *private*, illegal pay for every service from the most brilliant Moscow surgeon's pioneer operation to a rural hospital nurse's bringing you a cup of water. You are a commoner yet want quality, attention, kindness? Pay the private, illegal, market price. Will not pay? Croak free of charge. Even the *soviet* regime cannot detect and punish the illegal desire of a certain individual to live and pay illegally for medicine on the basis of free-market prices, no matter how illegal. How can a democratic government do it?

But let us suppose for the sake of argument that there may be a combination of pre-Hobbesian, super-Stalinist, perfect serfdom and twentieth-century civic democracy.

Certainly the nationalized means of production will be *controlled* by economists like those esteemed contributors to the

Britannica of 1964: certainly repairmen, bricklayers or tool makers cannot be trusted with a problem of such specialized economic sophistication. So what will the resulting system of nationalized means of production be? Superbig capitalism? Supermonopoly capitalism? Superbig business?

The esteemed economists controlling the *nationalized means of production* will receive salaries, but these salaries will be not, I am sorry to say, a gift from David Ricardo, Karl Marx or Beatrice Webb, but part of very, very vulgar profit. And the only difference between their profit and free-enterprise profit may be that their profit will be fixed, constant, independent of the efficiency, creativity, success or progress of production—much to their satisfaction and as much to the detriment of production.

The esteemed contributors to the *Britannica* article *Capitalism* as of 1964 are not supposed to answer questions like: "What if no expensive means of production and/or no employees are involved in free enterprise?" because they are to satisfy man's need for faith, not for thinking. And just like a special type of mentality, called upon to repeat rather than think, was much in demand a century or two ago in some heavenly faiths, so, too, it is now much in demand in earthly faiths.

The very word *capitalism* with its *capital,* that is, *means of production,* allegedly crucial in exploitation and thus distinguishing evil *capitalism* from something very, very good (supermonopoly capitalism?) is an eighteenth-century misnomer, converted into a credal symbol of these earthly faiths. What has always existed and will always exist, inasmuch as there is freedom in society, is free enterprise, which can be *nationalized* anywhere except in perfect serfdom no more than literature, thinking, or humor can be *nationalized.*

But why did pseudo-tsar-god II find free enterprise unpleasant? Partly because he shared the age-old prejudice that every employer except the *state,* that is, every *private* employer, or *the* Capitalist, is the same as what *the* Jew was thought to be a century or two ago. Or not so recently in Germany, the most formally educated country of Western Europe. Not a particular Jew. But the *Jew.* Not necessarily a thief, embezzler, swindler in the direct sense. But a machinator who gets rich somehow at the expense of the *state* (that is, great Stalin) and the *people.*

The Capitalist is vaguely dangerous because everything *private* seems all the more dangerous to a certain social group the longer and the more recently the group stayed in various states of servility whether called serfdom, Absolutism or *religion* in which independent activities were banned either altogether as too sinful, or allowed only to a chieftain's ranked and salaried subordinates as too profitable and/or sinful to be allowed to someone unranked and unsalaried.

In 1928 *Pravda* carried an item entitled: "Privateer Battens." The *privateer* is an indispensable word for the contributors to that *Britannica* article. Sometimes it is awkward to call *the* Capitalist by his name because he has no *means of production* but simply employs Laborers, say, to collect rags or litter and they find it profitable to offer their services to him rather than work each on his own or in a cooperative. Some scholars may find this impossible, absurd and unnatural, but isn't this because they never collected rags or litter for a living? The *privateer* is anyone, whether with big or small or zero means of production, who has the unholy impertinence to employ someone or be employed by a *private* person or even merely work as a *private* person without the sacred attachment to the *state* or the State.

Last year those odds and ends were carried as litter to the dump. The privateers of Leningrad, Tula, and Nijny got wind of it and suggested buying this litter. The price was first 2 rubles for 32 pounds, and then went up to 5 rubles. Dozens of thousands of pounds have already been sold.

See what the Capitalist or the Privateer does. Buys up litter! But the worst is to come:

The litter has proved to be quite valuable. It is now being processed into various ornaments for musical instruments and into small haberdashery: cuff links, cigarette holders, knife handles, etc. All this is being manufactured by the privateer selling its products to the Muspred and other agencies.

Some cynical agnostic may say: "So what? First, they collect litter, second, they pay money no one would have paid, and third, they produce something other people value and will pay money for. They enrich society in three ways. What is the harm?" What is the harm! But the privateer battens! This is how the article is titled. This is as vaguely ominous as when *the* Jew battened. To let the poor (or the *state*) loot him is to enrich and thus befriend the poor or enrich the *state*, to punish the evildoer, and to attain equality, purity, and well-being.

However, a much stronger motive was impelling great Stalin to suppress the *officially* readmitted free enterprise.

That strong motive of great Stalin was his fear of losing three infinities, three infinite values, or three stages of infinite bliss: his possession-power, an infinite value which turned him into a deity on earth; his life, which was another infinite value (for him); and death without torture, for such death may be an infinite value (or stage of infinite bliss) compared with torture.

Free enterprise, as every freedom, endangered the three infinite values, in his perception of history and in particular Russian history. I will present in three passages Russian history as he saw it, as practically every inhabitant of Russia, wishing to draw after 1917 a motivational lesson from history, saw it (and sees it today), and as I saw it before the age of nineteen. In parentheses after each passage I will mention what we all failed to see.

Early in the eighteenth century under Peter I there were no noblemen as independent individuals: a high ranker was the tsar's serf. It was not until after his death that these high-ranking serfs were allowed in 1736 to serve *only* forty-five years, a great mercy and relief. He founded the Inquisition, which was called not the Holy Office but the Holiest Synod, to deal with the heretics not in a holy but in the holiest way. He died in glory. Milyukov, a historian of Russia, the leader of the Constitutional Democratic party, foreign minister of the Provisional Government in 1917, would have been deeply hurt even in the 1940s if someone had encroached on the sacred glory of Peter the *great*. Since Peter's military training of his serfs in metalmaking, artillery, navigation, and so on required the absorption of what was militarily valuable in the West, it is still glorified as *westernization* in English-language encyclopedias (well, the Inquisition, the Prussian serf war machine, and later the Gestapo were all geographically in the West, of course, not in the Golden Horde). Thus, in glory, Peter the *great* lived, in glory he died, and in glory he abides today.

(The goal of Peter I was military might, yet his wars were

disastrously inefficient, though the pious imagination of many historians duly turned them into glorious victories. Not unsimilarly, great Stalin's war of 1941 to 1945, disastrous in terms of military efficiency, was turned even by some Western scholars into a series of superb examples of military cunning at the outset of the war and dazzling flashes of military genius at the end of it.)

In 1762, the high-ranking serfs began to receive *noblemen's freedoms*. They could now be just *private persons*. In 1783 they were allowed to have *free presses*. Whereupon, a nobleman Radishchev published two works, *Freedom* and *A Journey from St. Petersburg to Moscow*, regarded as the first Russian major work of *revolutionary propaganda*. The free presses were banned, and again quiet and peace reigned in the realm. Private presses were allowed again in 1801, along with the import of foreign books and unlimited residence abroad (for noblemen, of course, like Gogol, not for serfs). The author of the *Journey*, once regarded as a dangerous mutineer, exiled and forgotten, was called back and awarded the tsar's order. The result? An uprising of noblemen in 1825, regarded as the beginning of Russian *revolutionary activity* (as a result of *revolutionary propaganda*). Then Nicholas I, nicknamed the Gauntlet Chaser, withdrew some *noblemen's freedoms*. And he walked freely all his life unguarded, and in perfect tranquillity he ruled his vast country! Alexander II the Liberator began in the 1860s to grant civic freedoms to all the population, and not just to the noblemen. And properly liberated men hunted him all his life until they assassinated him, since which date they have been glorified as saints, heroes, and martyrs, and he as a nincompoop.

(When freedoms are introduced, a whole spectrum of new behavioral attitudes originates: at the one end of the spectrum are the people who begin to support the regime behaviorally, and not just verbally, and at the other end are the people who use the freedoms for overthrowing the freer regime by any means and establishing a superautocracy of two hundred or two thousand years ago under beautiful and often supermodern names. The latter part of the spectrum inevitably exists in any large country, such as the United States today, and the only moral is that Alexander II ought to have developed better personal security measures.)

Finally, Nicholas II put on the final touch: *Pravda* began to appear legally in 1912. And its publisher began to propagate freely *ideas* hostile to the regime, overthrew it, and destroyed, to the thunderous jubilation of *all progressive mankind,* not only Nicholas II (a supernincompoop), his wife and children, but the whole civilization called Russia, including all freedoms, developing since 1762. For which, the megadestroyer will perhaps be revered even in the West until the end of the century as a supergenius who founded a *new* civilization.

(If civic development had been in Russia as early and intense as in the United States, then, far from conniving at Ulyanov-Lenin's destruction of democracy in 1917 or at least being rather indifferent to the process until the Kronstadt uprising of 1921, when it was too late, the *proletariat* would, on the contrary, have been the mainstay of democracy in 1917, even if the Kaiser had passed enough money to publish a special *Pravda* for each *proletarian.*)

The lesson of Russian history was clear to pseudo-tsar-god II: it is in the ruthless suppression of everything free, *private, state*-independent that there is safety and glory (even according to English-language encyclopedias of today), whereas any free, *private, state*-independent activity finally destroys the regime, and the freedom-granter is killed with his family and scorned henceforth by mankind as a nincompoop, while his killer and the destroyer of all freedoms is glorified as a supergenius, a deity on earth.

42

In West European (and Russian) Absolutism at its worst the *great* owners of countries dreamed of establishing their monopolies in all fields. But they never quite realized their *great* dreams. Great Stalin could only pity them. Any free activity is dangerous to the *state,* and for a whole year great Lenin resisted those *bolsheviks* who wanted to readmit for a while small-scale enterprise, and it was only the growing famine and the Kronstadt uprising of workers and sailors that finally forced his hand. Similarly, great Lenin fought (and this time defeated) those *bolsheviks* (including Djugashvili-Stalin) who expressed the dangerous notion that *privateers* (how horrible!), and not only the *state* (that is Ulyanov-Lenin and his overseers), could trade with foreign firms.

This fear of free enterprise coincides with the hostility toward it of a nineteenth-century German named Karl Marx. Here I can be suspected of the manichean coparticipative approach—of looking for guilt by association. Am I not trying to blame good old Marx for the fact that long after his death a certain war serf caste society into which I was born is said to have been founded on his *teaching?*

It is not commonly remembered that by 1953 Engels had been chastised publicly by great Stalin and practically thrown out of *propaganda.* Chastisement of a subordinate usually heralded his superior's arrest: the subordinate was chastised and arrested while his superior was barely mentioned. Marx was barely mentioned. His good luck was that he was dead.

Great Stalin finally did openly what had occurred to his teacher Trotsky right on the day of the open grab of the country in November 1917 when a friendly Cossack told him that only kikes defended democracy in Russia, while the Russian people were all on the right side: great Stalin repeated almost textually what Trotsky had said in *Pravda* in 1922.

Ivan the Terrible, Peter I, and Suvorov, the Generalissimo of Catherine II, were now at the heart of the cluster of the manichean good of *propaganda* as opposed to the cluster of evil into which Engels had *officially* moved. Certain discrepancies originated. Thus, Emelyan the Terrifier was still glorified as the *leader of the popular revolutionary uprising of the poor* against Catherine II, but her brave Generalissimo Suvorov who duly brought him to Catherine II in an iron cage was glorified much more. Who cared? Discrepancies originated in 1918, 1921, 1934 or 1941, but soon everyone was used to them, took for granted and never questioned. As the rumor had it, after the hanging of the "Jewish doctors" on Red Square, to resurrect a good Russian medieval custom (Red Square had once contained a Place of Execution), and a good wholesome country-wide Jewish pogrom, great Stalin wanted to crown (this time, with a literal imperial crown directly on his head). And again everyone would have become used to the word "emperor" or "tsar," as earlier to the words "directors," "officers," "generals," "marshals," "ministers," or "generalissimo," all of which had belonged to the cluster of evil until they were transferred to *our* cluster of good. The coparticipative cluster *progressive-holy-russian-tsarist-revolutionary-imperial-democratic-scientific-proletarian-christian*, etc., would have seemed to the respective intellectual savages all over the world to be an *ideology* as integral, self-consistent and *scientific* as the coparticipative cluster *democratic-proletarian-socialist-progressive-revolutionary-marxist-scientific-heroic-soviet*, etc. once seemed or seems today to many of those who hear or repeat such combinations often enough as *our* or as *their* cluster.

Pravda began to publish articles suggesting that *our ideology* is *practical* Christianity, in contrast to Western Christians only in name, pseudo-Christians, not at all Christians. This resembled the conversion in 1918 of all Western Social Democrats into the *worst enemies* headed by the heinous ogre Kautsky, whom Ulyanov-Lenin had called the Marx of today shortly before (Kautsky indeed co-authored the last part of *Capital*). Anyway, some *practical* Orthodox Church Archbishop, with whom great Stalin had become as chummy as with his newly named marshals or ministers, was to anoint the new Emperor by the grace of *practical* Christianity. Great Stalin was to be the Orthodox Church God, having come as the Father Himself at long last to create a *practical* paradise, a paradise on earth.

Marx was to play a very modest role if any in the rumored new turn of the propaganda-religion-culture, though his role in it had been steadily diminishing ever since 1930 when *russian* aryanism, instead of *proletarian* aryanism, began to take over. In the conquest of the world it is necessary to choose the most currently advantageous aryanism: by proclaiming all the poor of the other countries aryans, the chieftain expects them to help him to establish his satrapies from within their countries, and by proclaiming passport-Russians aryans he relies more on the passport-Russians for the conquest of these countries from outside, with occasional reliance on the Orthodox Church Christians abroad, Moslems, South Americans, or whoever may be stirred against Jews or the Jewnited States of America (to use Dr. Goebbels' witticism, showing his intellectual charm at its best).

What is the place of Karl Marx in *propaganda* at this writing? A characteristic incident has happened recently: a magazine, appropriately entitled *Young Guard*, began to preach Konstantin Leontieff (the "Russian Nietzsche," a nineteenth-century preacher of a caste society, whom we never called at school simply a reactionary, but only the "archreactionary of archreactionaries") and attacked the magazine *New World*, a remnant of the freer or more lenient early sixties. How did the freer magazine defend itself against the attack? By an appeal to Karl Marx. If an inhabitant of Russia is *criticized* in the late 1960s in the name of a nineteenth-century Russian preacher of a caste society, the only way is to appeal to a nineteenth-century German named Karl Marx who has not been chucked *officially* out of *propaganda* and who at least did not say openly that society must consist of different castes or estates of the Russian medieval type in order to "achieve efflorescence."

In fact I am also going to pay a tribute to good old Marx. Those who have never read a single line of poetry will perhaps do well to read the poems of Karl Marx with which the Russian edition of his works solemnly begins. Those who do not know, say, the Austrian school of economics of the nineteenth century may do well to read some economic studies in the last volumes of *Das Kapital*. Those who have never read, say, Jeremy Bentham and think that man is motivated mainly by his love of God, and/or his love of Science, Peace, Mankind or other no less beautiful ideas (and many *marxists* of various hues do think that way—in application to themselves) will perhaps do well to read in good old Marx that mankind consists of groups motivated by *material interests*. This is a statement so crude as to be false, but the reader may improve it by adding mentally that Karl Marx's love of influence or prestige, or his father-in-law's love of promotion to the rank of Minister of the Interior in Prussia, are as much *material* interests as, say, a private employer's love of money (all of which, incidentally, he may spend to gain a much lesser influence, prestige or promotion than Marx or his father-in-law achieved). In other words, it is perhaps better to read good old Marx than to know nothing at all except the belief (unfortunately, harbored in particular by Marx himself) in *our* Goodness in motivation and behavior as opposed to the Evil of the Enemy.

However, mankind would not be aware today of that poetry of Karl Marx, or his studies in economics in the last volumes of *Das Kapital*, or even his statement about the *material interests* of different groups, and indeed hardly anyone would know the very name of good old Karl Marx if he had not made, long before he started even on the first volume of *Das Kapital*, the following *greatest discovery* in one definite field:

The remuneration of *the* private employer (*the* Capitalist) is actually created-earned by his employees, but he *expropriates* it—he *exploits* them, loots them, by some complex process of Capitalism, that is, swindle or robbery or extortion, intrinsic to *the* Capital (*das* Kapital) itself, since he owns *the* Capital (*the* Means of Production) and they do not, and are compelled therefore to offer their services (their labor) to *the* Capitalist.

Several years earlier good old Marx had made another *greatest discovery* which may be given as a straight quotation:

What is the lay cult of the Jew? *Commercialism.*

This is merely the gist of the discovery (the italics belong to Marx), while actually there are also endless variations:

What is the lay god of the Jew? *Money.*

The Russian edition gives an interesting linguistic footnote. Some Germans (no doubt the most *revolutionary-progressive-socialist*, etc.), including good old Marx, used the word Jewishness (Judendum) in the sense "swindle and usury," and Marx (who considered himself a *pure* German, naturally, since he was a Christian born) bases his discovery on that meaning of the word, amazingly profound, *revolutionary-progressive-socialist,* etc., and showing his aryan wit at its sparkling best. Anyway, the closer translation above is not *commercialism*, but swindle-usury. "What is the lay cult of the Jew? Jewishness" (that is, Swindle-Usury).

The Jew, the Swindler-Usurer, actually ruled the world more than a century ago. He had succeeded in

attaining world domination and converting alienated man, alienated nature, into *alienable* objects, into objects of gross trade, depending like slaves on egoistic needs, or swindle-usury (Judendum).

In conclusion good old Marx calls for the "liberation of mankind from Judendum."

It can readily be seen that the later-day *greatest discovery* of Marx (the one about *the* Capitalist) can be obtained from its Jew-variant by substituting *"the* Capitalist" for *"the* Jew," "Capitalism" for "Judendum," "Means of Production" for the "Lay Cult of the Jew," and so on. It is only essential that not some Jews or some Capitalists be meant in some circumstances, but *the* Jew—all Jews, Jews in general, Judendum, with its Lay Cult; just as *the* Capitalist, all Capitalists, Capitalists in general, Capitalism, with its Means of Production. It can also be readily seen that such *greatest discoveries* can be made at a rate of ten *greatest discoveries* per minute, each time with a new Enemy. The problem is simply to write up each *greatest discovery* into huge volumes, which takes time, of course, especially if it is done by hand, as it was in the nineteenth century. But why did good old Marx take as *the* Enemy first *the* Jew and then *the* Capitalist? And why these two, and not, say, *the* Medical Doctor, *the* Christian, or *the* Chinese?

Both *the* Jew and *the* Capitalist are the most common lootable minorities available in many countries where the populace can be roused against them. Jews came to the then barbarous gang-war societies from a more sophisticated civilization. Naturally, many Jews were richer than the local common barbarians who did not understand banking, commerce, many crafts, and believed that these were so much swindle. Too well known to need elaboration is the hostility, since the fall of Rome to our day, of *christian*, military, and bureaucratic *heroic idealism* toward *commercialism*: why make values for sale (how filthy!), trade them for profit (how dishonest!), or save them at an interest (how criminal!) if a priest-knight-official (propagandist-party-functionary-official) can get these values by propaganda and/or force? Many *socialisms* I know (there are more than two hundred of them) are not interested in how saleable values are made, traded or saved: *heroic idealism* is naturally interested only in their *just distribution*, whereas their creation, trading or saving are too low, filthy, or indeed, criminal to notice.

The barbaric group hatred for *the* Jew did not yet subside in Germany (as Marx exemplifies) when a similar group hatred for *the* Capitalist began to gain momentum and was to surpass the hatred for *the* Jew because *the* Capitalist constitutes a much more ubiquitous, large, wealthy lootable or fleeceable minority than *the* Jew (in many areas of Asia, Africa or South America *the* Jew is virtually absent). The multi-volume *demonstration* of Karl Marx that *the* Capitalist is a swindler has no more to do with economics or sociology than the *demonstration* of *the* Jew's ritual use of infant blood with ethnography or genetics. In fact, when good old Marx made his second *greatest discovery* (the one about *the* Capitalist) he had not yet studied economics: he simply *knew* that *the* Capitalist is a swindler just as he *knew* that *the* Jew is a jew.

Naturally, some of those human beings who can be labelled *the* Jew have often been engaged in anti-Capitalism, while those who can be labelled *the* Capitalist have often been engaged in anti-Semitism. This is a rule of manichean coparticipation: a sufficiently acivic human being tends to seek another Enemy in order to divert group hatred from *us*. Accordingly, an anti-Semite is prone to be hurt when *Merchant of Venice* is found to be one of the cheapest displays of anti-Semitism ("Do you deny the genius of *our* Shakespeare?"), whereas an anti-Capitalist is apt to be annoyed when *Das Kapital* is found to be a semantic transcript of the *Protocols of the Learned Elders of Zion*. Especially since *genetically* Marx "was a Jew," and to debunk this anti-Semite is to hurt *us*. It is just like the debunking of great Stalin which still evokes fury among many Georgians though great Stalin considered himself the purest Russian and did more harm to Georgians than any foreigner or alien has ever done.

When I read (at the age of sixteen) good old *Capital* I had the inevitable sensation that either I was mentally sick, and very badly too, or a good half of mankind was mentally sick or so mentally retarded that it was practically the same. Later I found that neither alternative need to be true: it was simply that to me, these volumes were just books. I had never seen a single Capitalist to love or to hate, nor had I ever had any Capital to defend or part with. I knew that everything of value in the country belonged to great Stalin and his men, a single super-monopoly, but the *greatest thinker in the history of human intellect* did not even mention such supermonopoly capitalism though it had existed for millennia before he was born and would perhaps exist for millennia after that sheltered, safe, cozy world in which he lived and which he called *capitalism* had been engulfed by megagangs with their war supermonopolies.

To many citizens of twentieth-century democracies or countries at least as free as Russia was between 1861 to 1917, good old Marx has been something entirely different.

In a civic democracy there have always been and will always be some who are richer, and some who are poorer (or less rich), for as long as civic democracy is civic democracy (and not, say, pre-Hobbesian Asolutism) it is impossible to prevent those who are more gifted in a certain field from making more money compared with those who are less gifted. Nor is it possible to conceal the fact. Since self-expression cannot be forbidden in democracy either, some of those who are less rich (or more poor) will always express through their spokesmen their (sincere) belief that *the* rich (in particular, *the* Capitalist—or *the* Jew, if the less rich are *not* Jews) can only be richer than they because *the* rich are swindlers (looters, extortionists, usurers) and hence must be looted and killed or at least fleeced for the benefit of those who are more poor (less rich).

Predictably, the persecution of *the* Jew, *the* Capitalist (or *the* Enemy under any other name and image such as *the* Doctor allegedly spreading cholera) correlates territorially. For example, the population of Russia has been prone to massacre *the* Enemy (whether *the* Doctor, *the* Jew, or *the* Capitalist), while England, which began to tolerate *the* Jew very early, provided he was sufficiently scorned and shorn, tolerates *the* Capitalist now in the same way: To a good half of the population he is barely tolerable. The Labor Party (note its righteous purity in the very name—Labor, as opposed to Capital) tolerates the Swindler-Looter in medium and small-scale production if he is properly shorn. Strictly speaking, the Capitalist mulcts the poor by his Means of Production, but the trouble is that without the filthy Swindler-Looter Britain would starve her population out of existence back to the level of the righteous Dark Ages.

If even in Britain the symbol *karlmarx* verbalizes for a good half of the population the possibility of getting more wealth and higher status by fleecing the other half of the population, what else can be expected of civically more backward democracies, let alone semidemocracies? Yes: the symbol *karlmarx* is on everyone's lips, for the symbol means more wealth and higher status for some, so much less of both for others, and often an economic collapse for all, in any country at least as free as Russia was between 1861 and 1917.

But why is *his* name used all over the world as the symbol of fleecing or looting *the* Capitalist? Surely anyone could *discover* that *the* Enemy is a swindler-looter and hence must be fleeced or looted for the benefit of the righteous.

In the nineteenth century, another German *discovered* and *demonstrated* that laughter exists in man for the regular clearing of his lungs (how the lungs of animals are cleared was not inquired into). Nor was his study dismissed with some clearing of the lungs: William James criticized it in all earnest. An Englishman would have presented such a discovery in a tract, a Frenchman in an essay, a Russian in a leaflet, while the German *demonstrated* it in a huge study. It was the much derided habit of many Germans of that day to demonstrate any clearing of their lungs in stupendous tomes that singled out the group-hate slogan of Marx from the same of other group haters. The group-hate slogan was coded by Marx, as was the custom of his time and country, into thousands of pages of pseudo-Hegelian (and very crude) exercises. *Socialists, communists,* or *marxists* need not even understand the code. I read Hegel before I read Marx because I enjoyed Hegel's semantic play as long as it was concerned with heavenly problems like *being.* I enjoyed it as a kind of metaphysical poetry in prose. But perhaps no *communist* of my generation ever opened Hegel. Or Marx—except when and where required by office. However, *communists* have been able to refer any opponent of theirs to the endless volumes in which he is sure to be quagmired unless he has a preliminary grounding in Hegel. "Ah, you haven't read all those volumes of Marx? Then how on earth can you argue that *the* Capitalist does not Exploit his Laborers owing to his Means of Production?" The poor opponent would open Marx—and perish in the verbal quagmire.

In 1917 the symbol *karlmarx* (the greatest scientist with a suitably big beard) verbalized for the Russian *bolsheviks-communists* a chance to grab the country with the aid of some *proletarians* who were promised fabulous wealth at the expense of *the* Capitalist and encouraged to *loot the looter* (an official slogan). Then the symbol *karlmarx* lost all meaning for the population and began to verbalize for its owners the harm and even danger to their possession-power of *private* (that is, not their own) economic activity.

Private enterprise! Free enterprise! Surely thousands of dangers to possession-power lurk everywhere. Was not the *bolshevik party* under the tsar financed by private people who had made their money privately: the privately published writer Gorky or the private factory owner Morozov? Did not Parvus and Ganetsky, who passed on the Kaiser's money, both pose as private businessmen? It was private tradesmen who sold the *bolsheviks* printing presses, weapons, and whatever was sold privately for money (and a lot was!).

Was it not free enterprise that after 1917 gave such opportunities to agents of the possession-power abroad? An agent would usually be a businessman of a kind, dealing with other businessmen, who are ready sometimes to sell anything to anyone who will buy. Pseudo-tsar-god II wanted some weapons in 1936, and his agent Krivitsky procured them quite simply:

We made large purchases from the Skoda works in Czechoslovakia, from several firms in France, from others in Poland and Holland. Such is the nature of the munitions trade that we even bought arms in Nazi Germany.

So even Hitler's regime could not keep a private firm from selling arms to the enemy.

As for businessmen in democracies—why, quite a few of them have been vying with each other ever since 1921 to sell any pseudo-tsar-god a better and cheaper rope to hang them with, as great Lenin put it. Even if all businessmen knew that the rockets they will be building, say, in Siberia are trained on the cities in which their families live, enough of them would rush to the site to build these rockets in the hope that they would manage to evacuate their families before the firing. Not that businessmen are more treacherous or greedy or ignorant than any other randomly sampled group. Up to three-quarters of the population of a democracy may be willing (as in Germay in 1933) to sell democracy for any personal gain in status or wealth. But there is no way they can do it at a high profit (the pseudo-tsar-god pays notoriously little to rank-and-file spies because there are very many of them and hard currency is too valuable). Now, businessmen handle unique equipment, patents, weapons and what not. They can lobby their statesmen amid the complete indifference of the rest of the population.

Why should a pseudo-tsar-god have a rich, numerous, powerful subversive or treacherous group like that in *his* country?

True, free enterprise would create in his country "high living standards for the entire population." But does a pseudo-tsar-god need that? No. To each serf according to his rank. That is, according to his value to the pseudo-tsar-god and his devotion to him. Serfs who will enrich themselves on their own as *privateers* or will be enriched by such *privateers* will be so much less devoted to him. They will also be freer, for independent property means so much more latitude. And freedom for them means danger to him. He must be the only source of all values of all serfs of all ranks and castes. From a *writer*'s world fame to a death-slave's extra day of life.

43

Man's intelligence or psychology can often be usefully divided into verbal and behavioral.

A great Russian tragic actress who survived into the thirties played a nineteenth-century merchant's religious wife who committed suicide, tormented by her conscience. The play was filmed, and during the filming the actress ran to the bank of a river to throw herself in. However, as she reached the water's edge the camera was switched off and she stopped, to be replaced by a supernumerary. She thereupon had a serious fit of hysteria because she had been intending to throw herself in. It was only her behavioral intelligence that had stopped her right before the water's edge.

This does not mean to say that her experience in that play was untrue, ugly, or valueless. Quite the contrary. But the scale of values and that of motives do not coincide. In the delusion stemming from the time of magic thinking, they do. If someone could hold a piece of red-hot iron, his words were thought to be true. Value was measured by one's ability to walk on air by means of fervent faith, think of the highest values, and even sing of them, during torture, be motivated by them all around the clock. Inversely, it was only magic—the ability to live without food owing to the exertion of will, to rise from the dead if sprinkled by water of life, or to defeat the hordes of enemies by brandishing a sword for seven days without a second's rest—that was thought to be the highest value.

The Inquisition tried in particular to prove by torture that a heretic's values had no value. Giordano Bruno or Galileo or at least their biographers tried to show that they triumphed over all torture (which is a pure magic statement, like walking on air by means of fervent faith) and thus proved the highest value of their values.

We have to state today that perhaps the highest value created by man is music (or so it seems to me because I hear my son playing Beethoven records in his room), and music is also perhaps the closest approximation to the mystery of life (as is truly noticed by almost all heavenly religions). But a uniquely great musician composing the most heavenly piece may stop composing it, motivated as he may be by the concern that the eggs brought this morning are not fresh (one of Beethoven's concerns).

Unfortunately, most people are not great tragic actors, nor are they unique musicians. The verbal activity they use in life—in order to conceal their behavioral motives, for example—is often just "bad theater or bad art in life," as is the case with *communists* for whom the need to conceal behavioral motives and present instead theatricalizations as *real motives* has become a way of life perhaps to a greater degree than for any large group in the history of mankind. Predictably enough: for if many adepts of the enforced belief in heaven were hyprocrites, what an unprecedented power of creedal dissimulation must be possessed by those who want to force mankind to believe that the *earth* is heaven as soon as it becomes their property.

That great tragic actress had a fit of hysteria, so far had her verbal intelligence penetrated her behavioral intelligence. Most people, however, would have no conflict hysteria in such cases. In their behavior they would trot merrily, if sufficiently strongly motivated, to the water's edge, and would *think* that they were going to throw themselves in, then stop merrily at the water's edge, and *think* that they were not going to throw themselves in.

Many people all over the world *thought*, when sufficiently strongly motivated, that they would not be able to live without great Stalin, but when one fine day in 1956 their behavioral intelligence told them that it was safe to *spit on* great Stalin, every high school pupil (as I stood watching) thought himself duty bound to spit on the bust of the deity on a school staircase landing as they scampered by down the steps. No one had suggested or instigated this: it was purely spontaneous. Why not spit if it is safe?

A *soviet* writer said in the West that the "whole country wept when Stalin died." Perhaps 0.01 or 0.001 or 0.0001 of 1 percent of the population wept, but statistically small numbers can display any behavior on any occasion. Fortunately, there is a contemporary newsreel depicting the *sorrow of the soviet people* on the day the deity was announced to be dead. The faces of the crowd in the newsreel provide documentary evidence: their *sorrow* corresponds to the *sorrow* expected, and since not a tear was expected to be part of the sorrow, not a tear is shed in the newsreel, and since a certain indifference seemed to be tolerated, most faces do not show even the required *sorrow*.

The infinite devotion to our beloved *father, teacher, and friend for the sake of whom each of us is ready to sacrifice man's most precious treasure, his life* (and so on), proved to have belonged to the verbal intelligence of more than one billion people all over the world. It was a theatricalization motivated by altogether different motivations, and when those motivations stopped supporting the theatricalization of about 300 million people (in Russia, except Georgia, and in Eastern Europe, except Albania), no school pupil I witnessed could resist the tiny pleasure of gratuitously doing something nasty to great Stalin, and no adult would take the tiny trouble of admonishing them or any other iconoclasts, demolishing, desecrating, insulting the holy relics all over Moscow with much gratuitous gusto, jeering, and laughter.

So many people in Europe and America *thought, sincerely believed*, were *firmly convinced*, that a paradise on earth (the name taken from Heine's poem and applied to the regime) was in the making in former Russia under great Stalin, while they lived in hell.

I heard by American radio, in English, how the American *communist* leaders during the time of McCarthy were offered the choice of going to the paradise on earth instead of an American prison and how they all heroically preferred to perish (no doubt, under torture) in any McCarthyite *fascist dungeon* rather than go to the paradise on earth. How fantastic, monstrous, insane their verbal intelligence has always been with respect to *others* in the paradise on earth or elsewhere. How wise their behavioral intelligence has always been with respect to *themselves.*

For one's behavioral intelligence is concerned with oneself. That is why, in simple, direct, short-range decisions concerned with his own self, an ordinary person often proves to be wiser than the greatest scholars, philosophers, and intellectuals when they are concerned with others and hence may exercise their verbal intelligence only.

But, of course, there were statistical exceptions, and one American lady, named Anna Louise Strong, *lived* practically all her life in the paradise on earth ever since 1921 of her own free will and wrote book after book about how she was enjoying the *new world* and was *remaking* herself to become worthy of it.

I can find no better example than this lady, the daughter of a Congregationalist minister, the youngest student ever to have won a Ph.D. degree (*magna cum laude*) from the University of Chicago. In her opinion, she inherited from her father "his indomitable will which served without wavering whatever he found good and true." Except that what was God to her father became to her the Great Unknowable, that is a Common or Combined Consciousness or Will, that is Socialism. She hadn't wasted her time at that University! In 1921 Miss Strong crossed the border into Russia and found that she had no American passport. But who needs a passport to hell while going to the nascent paradise on earth? She says that if at the border she had to "choose either to turn back and never see the Soviet Land or to go forward and know I could never return—I would not risk even an hour to say farewell."

The serf owners of former Russia valued her highly, as they did all the other *world-known friends of the soviet union*, because these friends were lying in an amazingly brazen and often childish and self-exposing way, but were expected to be believed since they were, as the *Pravda* cliché ran, the "best representatives of progressive intelligentsia of the West, often spiritually quite remote from Communism, yet impelled by their conscience to tell the great truth about our country." It is funny to ask: "But why did they do it?" The grossest lie seemed to be perfectly safe since the muzzled serfs could not answer back, and if something—say, plucking other people's eyes—would be safe, a certain number of people would do it, just as they, say, collect stamps because this is safe, their other motives being so weak as to be often untraceable. Besides, if one is absolutely sure that what he sees will never involve *him*, he may very well *think*, be *firmly convinced, sincerely believe* that the people whose eyes he is plucking are shouting with joy, not with pain. A bit naïve? Innocence, trust, and gullibility have no limit in verbal intelligence, that is, when *others* are involved.

Miss Strong engaged in some squabbles in the English-language newspaper *Moscow News* (still published today) and wrote a letter of complaint to great Stalin. This is routine: our neighbor's maid once a month sends a long letter to all the *politburo*, asking it to sell her some roofing for her house. Her grounds: as a railroad signalwoman she saved a *state* tractor but lost her leg. A very long letter. Her letter is duly received and dispatched down the levels until it reaches the local warehouse, against which she complains in her letter as failing to sell her that roofing *despite* many such previous letters sent by the *politburo* to the warehouse. Similarly, every inhabitant spoke only via great Stalin about the loss of shirt buttons in a laundry (this despite its owner's being a Hero of the Civil War) or the squabbles on a newspaper, as was the case with Miss Strong.

In response to her complaint she was taken to very official quarters, and there appeared before her great Stalin and two *members of the politburo*. Try to make the American President alone (even without the Secretary of State and the Secretary of Defense) appear before you when you have such personal troubles as buying some roofing, lost shirt buttons, or an office squabble! In half an hour great Stalin, assisted by the other two men, unraveled Miss Strong's office squabble. And how! I cannot describe it because I am like a sober, cynical, coarse cleaning woman having no Ph.D. degree, while it would take pages to quote Miss Strong. A few random lines at the beginning:

Here was a man to whom you could say anything; he knew almost before you spoke; he wished to know more clearly and to help. Never had I found anyone so utterly easy to talk to.

And a random passage from the end, after the office squabble was smoothed in half an hour (by allowing Miss Strong to rule the roost on the newspaper):

How swiftly everything had happened! How suddenly it had all come clear! So swiftly and suddenly that I could hardly catch it. That night and all next day and for many nights thereafter, the memory of that half hour began to grow. Day after day I understood more of it. It began to explain my work; then it began to explain the Soviet Union. It solved new problems as they arose; it gave me a method. Other hours in my life that were marked by great emotion—when I have adored great men—have all died out; I cannot recapture their feeling. But that half hour grows with years. Even today I can feel the atmosphere of that meeting—its sympathetic but unemotional analysis, seeking fundamental lines and relations and acting to set them right.

After ten pages of these Ph.D. raptures, a man appears who wants to marry Miss Strong. He explains his pleasantly unexpected yet blunt intention in this way: "You always attracted me. But in former years I never felt sure that we were on the same side of the barricades."

Of course! Now he could be sure. Great Stalin would not lavish so much time, love, and care on someone on the other side of the barricades. The callous cleaning woman in me prompts me to say that the wealth of great Stalin consisted of both natural and human property, and stupendous as the bribes, rewards or prizes in trade profit, natural resources, lavish fetes, and such could be, the bribes in human property could be even more valuable and effective.

Miss Strong was, it will be recalled, a pure spirit of Combined Will. As such, she can be imagined to have been thin and flat-chested, while quite incongruously, nature had conceived her as a kind of huge Venus of some tiny minority having no alphabet of its own, but silly men, east or west, had studiously avoided marrying her, perhaps for fear of being dwarfed, swamped, dissolved.

Miss Strong accepted her suitor's rather matter-of-fact proposal in this way:

I told him my impression of Stalin, and ended enthusiastically: "I'd like to take orders from those men anywhere in the world. I feel they wouldn't give an order until I knew myself it was the thing I must do."

The Bride mused, according to her own record:

I should like Stalin for a boss, but they wouldn't give me Stalin.

So the Bridegroom was really great Stalin, while that suitor

Shubin was only a fair substitute, the Golden Rain sent by Jupiter, so to speak.

I do not know what exactly happened in 1949. A rumor had it that the Bridegroom Stalin did not like his Bride's adulation of Mao: you cannot have two Bridegrooms, you know. So he said: "Throw her out!" Which has in Russian, just as in English, two meanings: to pick up (a piece of junk), carry it, and throw it out, or to "turn out" (somebody). To be on the safe side, they lifted her bodily and *carried* her. Like a piece of junk. Surely a piece of junk must not *walk*! She said she was afraid she would be tortured. Never before had she mentioned the word "torture" in her endless bulky volumes. For they constituted the verbal knowledge for *others*, while she knew behaviorally what she needed to know. No, they did not torture her. The Bridegroom said: "Throw her out!" So they carried the piece of junk into a car, and when the car was across the border, they threw the piece of junk out, and if the piece of junk walked *after* it had been thrown out, such miracles were none of their business. But why was the piece of junk only thrown out? She was rather well known abroad, in particular by Mao, but was that enough for her safety? During the search they had found—yes, her passport to hell, her American passport! But she had said, "I have no passport," as she had crossed the border in 1921, and "I would not risk even an hour to say farewell," not to mention a second's thought about some passport to hell.

Verbally, as a philosopher (Ph.D. *magna cum laude*), poet, writer, intellectual, scholar, preacher, truth-seeker, prophet, hero, saint, social worker, revolutionary, she had no American passport and never thought for a second about it—was sure perhaps that had she seen it again she would spit on it, and tear it to pieces, and spurn the pieces (as Ulyanov-Lenin that *raise* to his *salary*). Behaviorally, she had treasured it for twenty-eight years (as much as Ulyanov-Lenin that nest egg of his during the Epoch of World Wars and Revolutions) and duly registered it and reregistered it (as a cleaning woman her *number* in a line for our daily bread this day in the provinces). They say there are from twelve to fourteen billion cells in the human brain, and in the case of Anna Louise Strong, it was fourteen billion no doubt. But out of these fourteen billion cells, thirteen billion nine-hundred-and-ninety-nine million nine-hundred-and-ninety-nine thousand were perhaps filled chockful with philosophy and with whatever has been producing even in the freer countries so much social literature, social philosophy, peace statesmanship and what not, and only one cell out of the fourteen billion, or perhaps not even a cell, but some cleaning woman's neuron ("Torture: keep-your-American-passport-above-all!") that was the mind and life of Mrs. Anna Louise Shubin, née Strong.

Verbally, pseudo-tsar-god II (or any other *bolshevik-communist*) would perhaps never imagine that what he called, say, *communism* is his ownership of as many treasures and human beings as possible. He was perhaps always perfectly *sincere*: not a single cell of his brain perhaps ever suggested anything like the expression or image: "my ownership."

Without interfering in any way with his behavior and its goals, *sincerity* on the contrary gave him additional strength, courage, determination to pursue these goals.

Behaviorally, it was enough for one neuron to imply without any image that *communism* was *his* ownership. And that one neuron would only be of interest to us, and it is the behavior caused by that one neuron of great Stalin which I proceed to describe.

44

Just a century or two before 1929, having suppressed the partial admission of free enterprise and thus restored the social *status quo ante* March 1921, pseudo-tsar-god II could have lived happily ever after. The social *status quo ante* March 1921 took into account all the *mistakes* the monarchy had perpetrated after Peter I and even earlier by way of allowing *private* independence (called personal freedom by some *bourgeois*) to various groups of the population and finally the population as a whole. All these *mistakes* had been eliminated in 1918 to 1921, and pseudo-tsar-god II had only to carry on in the same vein. Indeed, perhaps he would not even have eliminated the partial admission of free enterprise: had he not come out against Ulyanov-Lenin's *state monopoly of foreign trade*?

If only it had been 1829, and not 1929! He would have lived according to his will and at his pleasure. He could have attacked a neighboring country such as Turkey. Or he could have been peaceful, and then no murderous *industrialization-westernization* of his serfs as under Peter I would have been necessary. The situation would have been just as many Western statesmen (and their electorates) have been imagining it to be ever since 1918. Thinking in conventional diplomatic terms of a century (or a millennium) ago, they have been assuming that the pseudo-tsar-god's motivational situation and decision-making is the same as of any potentate of a century (or a millennium) ago: if the potentate wants, there will be peace, and if he gets angry, there will be war. Therefore, all that is important is to humor him by all means possible and to remove whatever may frighten, displease, or inconvenience him. To be a good neighbor, in short, as one would be in his native town in a democracy with respect to some irascible neighbor just beyond the backyard fence. Finding no outside cause for displeasure, the potentate will turn his attention inward to the well-being of his subjects (the last phrase having been in use for several thousand years).

In contrast to those Western statesmen who are merely anxious to show to their electorates how capitally they can get on with their irascible neighbors (and *build a structure of peace*), pseudo-tsar-god II realized behaviorally that he lived in a new world. Something mortally dangerous was there that had been quite inconspicuous just a century before, when Nicholas the Gauntlet Chaser had just begun his long rule of happy tranquillity. *The world outside was developing!* Even if a country— say, Germany—had not invested as of 1928 a single pfennig in weapons, it was, just the same, much stronger with respect to Russia than it was in 1913, because she had been *developing*. For example, better, cheaper, and more numerous field tractors meant better, cheaper, and more numerous tanks even if no one even thought of tanks—even if everyone in Germany was as pacifist or defeatist as *Pravda* wanted him to be.

The most peaceful economic, scientific and technological development of the outside world threatened great Stalin from outside, because it meant latent superior military strength, and that also meant a threat from within, a threat from his human property, from the serfs great Stalin owned.

A serf wants above all to know, or rather not even to know, but just to *feel*—to register inwardly for his behavior: "Will the regime last to the end of my lifespan?" The higher the chance that it will, the more he is willing to commit himself to it. The lower the chance, the more he is willing not to commit himself more than he can help, to be able to say, just in case: "I haven't done more than the majority has done: please check it." This is why the supreme goal of the network of propaganda since 1918 has been to assure every serf that the outside world gets ever weaker while the regime ever stronger. Since 1918 the network has used every sign of the outside world's nobility, restraint, kindness (as well as servility, flippancy, ignorance) to inculcate into every serf's mind the outside world's soft-brained anarchy, spineless idiocy, fat-dripping cowardice as against the approaching omnipotence of the perfectly organized, single-willed, all-heroic war regime. Millions of words like *doomed, decay,* or *agony,* have been describing the outside world ever since 1918 as against millions of words like *might, growth,* or *victorious* (describing the serf war machine), so that against this psychic background of coercive persuasion from the cradle to the grave even the stiffest diplomatic courtesy of a foreign statesman suggests automatically yet another proof of *our final victory.* Of course, a serf's will secretly struggles against the coercive persuasion, which must, therefore, find ever more persuasive evidence of the approaching omnipotence. But none such is possible without actual growing military might compared to that of the outside world.

The stronger a serf's secret realization that the ownership is weak in comparison to the outside world, the stronger is his will for invisible and visible resistance and rebellion. No system of surveillance and torture will help: a serf will only simulate better his infinite devotion to his owners, but deep down he will note with glee: "Aha! So you will not last to the end of my lifespan? You are just an episode in human history? I will yet see that D-day of reckoning, and I must live and enjoy life, have children and try to make more money, drink aerated water and avoid trouble—but all that with an eye to D-day."

Once there was God, who was to punish the High and Mighty for their sin of serf ownership. Today a serf knows that there is another world—only not above, but outside: there is another, higher court of justice, another, higher scale of values. The more he is forced to vilify this world the more he will take it into account in the treacherous secrecy of his will. And there can be no way to prove to the serf that his hope is illusory except by proving that his owners' military might will smite the Other World as it smites every individual serf or a whole satrapy that is not infinitely devoted to them.

The weaker his owners are compared to the outside world, the more boldly the outside world will sympathize with a serf's sympathy for the outside world, his resistance to serf ownership, his struggle for freedom at least in the privacy of his will if not his mind. Inversely, the greater his owners' military might compared to the outside world, the more eagerly the more countries will even return to them their runaway serfs for exemplary punishment, and the more fearfully the fewer others will refrain from anything that the owners might construe as *violation of friendship* with them.

The conquest of the rest of the world will eliminate the serfs' hope of freedom forever, and at the same time it will elevate, say, all serfs who are passport-Russians (before 1930, *proletarians of all countries*) to a rich aryan caste living at the expense of the rest of the world. Today those attached to Moscow constitute an inborn superior caste with respect to those areas which foreigners are not allowed to visit. The goal is just to make the world a wider similar structure: passport-Russians will constitute a new big Moscow, so to speak, a new top caste, living at the expense of the world's lower castes.

Everyone can notice how important the urge to acquire property and/or status is in a democracy. This is not because citizens of democracies are greedy, corrupt or vain, but because the freer a society is, the better the real nature of man is revealed, whereas in an infinitely unfree society it is infinitely concealed behind infinite hypocrisies. Actually, serfs such as passport-Russians want property and/or status at least as much as democratic citizens. A pseudo-tsar-god can satisfy their urge—only not in the way it is done in a democracy, but by acquiring the rest of the world and thus enriching them and elevating them in status. A pseudo-tsar-god's urge to acquire the world is something at least as well expectable as a democratic citizen's urge to buy a set of furniture and/or become a professor. It is simply that in a democracy like the United States a majority wants to *make* values, rather than obtain them by fleecing a certain group inside or outside the country. While the way of a war caste society is to acquire values by conquest and thus give wealth and status to, say, passport-Russians who the pseudo-tsar-god expects to be infinitely devoted to him as a result. The urge to acquire wealth and status simply takes a different route compared with a democracy.

To gauge the urge of a war caste society like post-1917 Russia or post-1949 China to own them and their property, citizens of a democracy need only to summate all the urges of all of them like the urge to acquire a set of furniture or to become a professor.

But a pseudo-tsar-god must act cautiously, very cautiously. As the tiny Muscovy acquired outside areas until they exceeded her fifteenth-century size. Six times? No, rather *sixty* times! And now the territory of former Russia has only to exceed its area sixfold. In terms of inhabited land. While the oceans, air and space are no one's and hence will belong to those who will fill them with their arms. And that will be all. The end of all worries, troubles and dangers, the beginning of glory unprecedented since the origin of life.

Considering the speeds of locomotion and communication today and several centuries ago, it is clear that the entire world has shrunk compared with, say, Germany or Russia when they were just patchwork quilts of independent lands. Owing to radio or aviation even the biggest country is surrounded, penetrated, made part of the whole more than some tiny German principality a century or two ago. It is clear that the world is to be one unified country, and the only question is: "What pseudo-tsar-god will unify it?"

Two types of societies face a pseudo-tsar-god's conquest. Societies similar to his. Will they devour him and his serf property some day? They may. Just as Trotsky, Zinoviev or Ulyanov-Lenin might have destroyed great Stalin. This is part of the game. The moral simply is that it is even more necessary to increase military might daily—not only against the democracies, but also against these possible independent societies similar to great Stalin's. As for the democracies, they stand no chance against big serf war machines. Of that every pseudo-tsar-god is sure behaviorally, and not only verbally. In a serf war machine its owner and operator gives away the lives (and earnings) of his serfs (perfectly obedient, replaceable, expendable cogs) in order to acquire more territory, wealth, and hence more military strength (and global glory) for himself. Whereas in a democracy citizens themselves have to decide to give *their* lives (and *their* money) to resist acquisition. How can fatiguable, vulnerable, varying, self-centered, conflicting human wills match for a long time a war machine, always at war, secret or open, extensive or intensive, in *battle* or in *labor*? At some point most human wills of each democracy will *believe in peace,* no matter what evidence to the contrary, and then it will be its turn to be acquired.

The democracies will be the food of serf war societies. So it is still more important to acquire and reclaim at their expense as many natural and human resources as possible, before the rival serf war societies do so. A pseudo-tsar-god's growing military might is his only ultimate value, for it is the only ultimate guarantee of his possession-power and its survival-victory. And meanwhile it will bring him global fame, friendship, respect, compliance, obedience, servility, trade.

The whole advantage of the global game is that nothing is ever lost in the middle of it: while democracies will disapprove of a direct open attack on them, no one will be able to blame great Stalin for all-out war preparations he will start in 1929. Even the United States occupies less than 1/50 of the global surface. But on the other 49/50 of the global surface, and especially in no one's oceans and in no one's air, these war preparations, including guerilla war, wars by proxy, and spy infiltration, may grow without even displeasing the United States. Indeed, great Stalin will be able even to grab from time to time a country or a slice of it no less safely: should democracies raise more stink than he expected, he can always move back (as in the good old game of chess), and the bigger will be his military might, the more grateful to him those democracies will be for his *love of peace.*

In other words, the daily all-out growth of military might offers to him no harm or danger: it is an unmixed good. This all-out growth will be valuable as such every day, and with every next day its value will only increase. And its ultimate value will be the ultimate ownership of all treasures and humans on earth.

So on his birthday in 1929, great Stalin's concern was: tanks! This is how a German general later named his book: "Tanks!" And even a Luftwaffe officer mentioned tanks as he recalled later in 1943 that touching if secret trade, friendship, and co-operation between the statesmen, officers and industrialists of a democracy (Germany between 1918 and 1933) and a war caste society, entrenched today in Berlin as a due reward for the brilliant German sample of the brilliant *foreign policy* of democracies since 1917.

The German army had been in close contact with Soviet Russia ever since the Polish war of 1920/21 and had even built up the Luftwaffe partly on Russian soil. A German air base was established somewhere in Turkestan. A factory for the manufacture of poison gas was built there also, and experiments with poison gases and with tanks were conducted.

In 1925 *Pravda* published a big article about a book by Colonel Fuller of the British General Staff:

> In his book *The Transformation of War* (1923) Fuller develops his concept that the tank will revolutionize war.
> "Thus," he says, "we can predict that the tank will rapidly transform the existing methods of warfare."

Somewhat anticipating, let me say that with the aid of democratic Germany before 1933 and the United States after 1933, great Stalin fulfilled the British colonel's concept of 1923 quite brilliantly: in 1941 he had 24,000 tanks, a force that dwarfed Hitler's, not to mention all the unarmed or half-armed or quarter-armed democracies of Europe. It is known even in the West from runaway serfs (*defectors*) like General Alexey Markoff that in the autumn of 1941 great Stalin's tanks were to burst into Nazi Germany and crush its puny tank force. The trouble was that for the first time in his life great Stalin did not deal with someone whom you can make smile and even laugh (friendship, peace, cooperation) before you suddenly splash acid into his eyes. Oh, Hitler smiled and even laughed all right (friendship, peace, cooperation). Just like Nicholas II, or Miluykov, or Bukharin, or Sir Winston Churchill. The only difference was that before great Stalin splashed acid into his eyes, *he* splashed acid into great Stalin's eyes. *His* 2,400 tanks suddenly burst in, and within three months knocked out 17,500 of great Stalin's 24,000 tanks at the expense of only 550 German units.

But that was later. And in the twenties it was: tanks!

To build many tank-making plants it was necessary to have, say, cement (Germany would not give gratis *everything!*).

In 1913 Russia (usually visualized in the West, with the aid of *propaganda*, as an exotic village of the time of Ivan the Terrible) produced more cement than France, whereas in 1928 she produced only 44 percent as much. Electric energy was thought to be a general index of economic development indispensable for military might, and in particular for tank-building plants. In 1913 the exotic village Russia (in operatic bast shoes and with picturesque wooden plows) produced 10 percent more electricity than France, whereas in 1928 she produced 66 percent less of it than France.

In other words, Russia before 1917 was developing economically, scientifically and technologically in the same all-round way as France or Germany or the United States. She had started later, but she was catching up quite briskly. On the other hand, in the ten years since 1917 she had been slipping back, with respect to the outside world, precisely in those fields which are readily associated with military might. The reason was that forced by famine to readmit free enterprise in 1921, Ulyanov-Lenin had readmitted it partially—mainly in the less militarily important branches like the making of cigarettes or the selling of nails and window glass rather than branches like the generation of electric power, the large-scale production of cement, heavy machine building or coal mining.

But since the Swindler-Looter, that is, *the* Capitalist was more efficient or productive or creative or roguish (remember how those *privateers* bought litter, made it into goods and battened on that?) he paid employees more than *state* enterprises, paid more for raw materials, semi-finished products and equipment, and sold goods more cheaply, or met demand more quickly. The thirteenth *conference of the party* in 1924 complained that easy unskilled work (cigarette packing) at *private* tobacco factories was better paid than coal picking or high-grade metalwork at *state* enterprises.

True, at first the *communists* still believed that they would oust the *privateer* in free and fair competition, so to speak. After all, some *communists* were even economists with diplomas from real bourgeois universities. Surely they can beat some vulgar seller of nails and window glass at his game, with the aid of, say, urban and rural *trade cooperatives*. Alas! Said the great *communist* scientist, thinker and planner Krjijanovsky to the thirteenth *congress of the party* in 1924:

The situation is even worse with our rural cooperatives. Suffice it to take at random some data from the Central Control Commission account. Here is the rural branch in the village Ulyanovskoye, Rjev Uyezd: nails cost 11.40 rubles for a pound at the cooperative, 8 rubles in private trade, or window glass 1.20 and 0.75. Even when . . .

In other words, the *privateer* sold similar or better goods more cheaply, and stupidly, customers bought them, even if they knew the whole of *karlmarx* practically by heart. The *privateer* kept expanding, sucking in the resources, including the vulgar manpower seeking a higher pay and ignoring *karlmarx*. Of the 48 million people who were registered in 1927 as gainfully employed, 41 million were in the *private sector*, and only 7 million in the *state* and cooperative *sectors*, despite the ruthlessly growing taxation since 1924 in favor of the last two sectors. And just try to pay less to any one of these 7 million people or save on working conditions or drive him or her harder: he or she would slip into the sea of 41 million like a carelessly held fish into water. "You are exploiting me," he or or she would say or think or just feel behaviorally, a filthy vulgarian unwilling to be motivated by the *greatest discovery* that it is *the* private employer only who exploits his employees.

So the aim was: to prevent him or her from slipping into the *private sector*. To eliminate it, see? Then socialism, equality, and justice themselves (that is, pseudo-tsar-god II) would set at will all the payments or rewards in cash and kind, all the working conditions, and all the prices of all goods and services. As it had been before 1921. Except that now this opened unprecedented vistas for the growth of military might.

The article "Capitalism" of the 1964 edition of *Britannica* distinguishes between human wants which the author of the article approves, such as educational institutions (in the *soviet union*, of course), and human wants of which the author does not approve, such as (predictably, American) cars, and which therefore "are not very urgent in any fundamental sense" and are "superficial private wants artificially generated."

Great Stalin had only to determine (with the aid of *science,* of course) which wants are *not* superficial private wants artificially generated, but are urgent in the fundamental sense. All the payments would be fixed accordingly, and the difference between the payments as they were in 1927 and the new payments would be used for the growth of military might.

But how big could this difference be as of 1929?

45

In 1922, the high ranker Andreyev said to the 11th *congress of the party*:

If we compare the present-day wages of the worker with the prewar level, the result of the comparison will be catastrophic. For Russia on the average, the wages of the worker who now earns 4.50 rubles equalled 22.83 rubles, while for Petrograd the wages were higher and equalled 30-odd rubles.

In 1927, the *founder of socialist planning* Strumilin said in *Pravda* that in September the real wages of our worker reached 33.60 prewar rubles a month. A sheer glance at what Andreyev had said in 1922 shows how much the worker in 1913 and 1927 spent on superficial private wants artificially generated. He earned 33.60 prewar rubles in 1927 and "30-odd rubles" in Petersburg-Petrograd in 1913! Whereas in 1922 he lived on 4.50 rubles, and 1922 was so much better than 1919 to 1921! Yet those aryan workers *lived* even in 1919, 1920 and 1921, and looked happy, as *heroic idealists* should, and those who did not were enemies to be dealt with as such.

In the sixties an American family which lived on 1,000 dollars of 1913 a year was officially classed as the *poor* (and 9 million families or about one-fifth of 47 million families were the *poor*). About 3 dollars a day instead of 2.25 dollars a month. How far can superficial private wants be artificially generated! So far that the American *poor* cannot perhaps even imagine (let alone live) a life on 2.25 dollars of 1913 a month.

Yet the *founder of the socialist planning* Strumilin *demonstrated* in his numerous volumes that such a life is not only possible, but is, indeed, the *scientific ideal*, and thus he laid the *scientific basis of socialism* that will perhaps inherit the world.

Obviously, any amenity, amusement or adornment created by mankind in the last six millennia is a superficial, indeed bourgeois (or philistine) private want artificially generated. As of September 1965, the United States: "Man's two-piece suit, new wool, hard finished worsted, good grade: $85.75, average retail price." All right, an American crane operator (perhaps a philistine, and also a reactionary) bought it in September 1965 for about one day's wages. In several years or even months the suit did not look so brand new or he did not like it any longer, so he stopped wearing it, or even threw it out. My friend's grandfather, a Ukrainian peasant, bought a green woolen suit before 1917. (I don't know when such suits were fashionable: in the nineteenth century?) He was a thrifty man, wore the suit with great care, and in the 1930s his son, a scriptwriter in Moscow, had this suit turned and wore it himself. The cloth was amazingly strong. In the 1950s my friend had this suit turned for himself because the previous side was very good, and vivid suit colors like greens or blues were just all the craze abroad (a return to some Victorian fashions?), and so my friend struck it rich.

One suit may serve for a century if the owner knows its almost infinite value and takes almost infinite care. The same applies to practically everything except food and water. Indeed, some young *communists* had proved well before 1928 that practically everything except food and water constitutes superficial and, indeed, bourgeois or philistine wants. For example: furniture, like beds and everything. Certainly only a philistine may care to sleep on a bed! True, so proud of their hypersensitive compassion, these healthy young people forgot that a healthy young man can certainly enjoy (as I did) sleeping on cement prison floors, a heap of dry sharply sticking branches, or the roof of a freight car, but the trouble is that not everyone is always a healthy young man (picnicking with a healthy young girl). Anyway, those healthy young *communists* had demonstrated that to enjoy life (especially in good summer weather out in the country) a healthy young man (and a healthy young woman) need practically nothing except food and water.

So the *founder of socialist planning* Strumilin had only to develop the *norm of consumption* of food and water, and that would practically be the cost of human upkeep (the rest being locally improvised barracks, suits left over from the pre-1917 regime, and other fairly cheap inessentials).

In the process of work, up to 2,000 calories are expended on the idling of the man-machine, but as this input increases we can, according to the calculation of professor Slovtsov, obtain, for each new 500 calories added, up to 42,000 kilogram-meters of useful work, an equivalent of 100 calories of thermal energy.

A *scientific basis* was thus laid as early as 1921 for keeping the human machine (or serf machine) running at optimum, that is, producing maximum output at minimum input.

The frontline rations of the Red Army man amounts in terms of nutrition to 2900 calories (see table 4).

These 2900 calories constitute a "close approximation" to the "scientifically developed norm of consumption." Though this *scientific norm of consumption* was developed in 1921, Strumilin's five-volume study, published in 1963 to 1965, repeats it without a change: the *scientific norm* is as eternal as *science* is, and, indeed, except for the period of 1922 to 1928, all serf commoners, outside of territories visited by foreigners, have subsisted on this *scientific norm* (unless they were *labor-camp slaves*).

This *ideal norm* of about 3000 calories is the peak intended for the rank-and-file male at the front, whereupon all the less important commoners get less of the *ideal norm*.

Thus, for workers of the lowest rating (i.e., the least heavy work), in which women account for 64 percent, the average norm will, if we proceed from 3,000 calories for men, amount to about 2,600 calories.

Woman needs only 80 percent of man's 3,000 calories, and hence the corresponding saving is obtained. Male *students* must eat 2,600 calories—like women—because "they are free from physical work." For hospitals, *houses of rest*, and so on, the *ideal norm* is "no more than 2,400 calories per diem."

For unemployed, invalids, and children of pre-school or school age at orphanages, colonies, and boarding schools of the People's Commissariat of Education it is sufficient to establish the same norm as for other dependents, that is, 1,800 calories per diem.

Finally, the *ideal norm* slopes down to 1,250 calories for children under three. But what is the peak of the *ideal norm* (male at the front), according to table 4?

Man's wants, not superficially private and artificially generated, are, at this peak, essentially two: 1.54 pounds of rye flour and 0.25 pound of groats a day, which together yield 1210 calories.

The price of 36 pounds of rye in 1913 was 0.80 rubles, that is a little less than 40 cents of 1913. Since coarse rye flour, in contrast to shelled rice in China, is something man can live on without getting sick, 2.5 pounds of it a day will ensure 3,000 calories a day, and so the *ideal norm* of a male at the front will cost $1.74 of 1913 a month, that of a female $1.39, and that of an invalid, an orphan, or unemployed, $1.00.

However, the *founder of the socialist economic planning* evidently has no scientific courage to say that there is only *one* human want, not artificially generated: 2.5 pounds of rye or less a day plus water without restriction if available in a river, lake or on tap. He adds to the *ideal* norm seven more wants as an obvious concession to bourgeois superfi,cial artificiality. Pepper: 0.002 pound. During my two periods in the army in the mid-fifties I never saw pepper. Salt? Yes: they put some into groats as they cooked them. The third want is: "Potatoes or other vegetables: 0.63 pound." This alternative of "other vegetables" did not exist in the non-Ideal reality as I experienced it in the mid-fifties. As for potatoes, they are considered in the *ideal norm* a coveted delicacy which only those who live near potato fields (or in the cities visited by foreigners) ought to eat. The *founder of socialist planning* explains how absurd it is to indulge otherwise in this luxury:

Even if it is possible to store so many potatoes without freezing and without rotting three-quarters of it, the procurement would be extremely irrational from the point of view of our transportation facilities.

The fourth want in the *ideal norm* sounds almost bourgeois: *Meat, fish*—0.25 pound. As I found in the fifties, the war stocks indeed contained stockfish (dried cod), and when it began to go bad it was issued or sold; since a quarter of a pound of this meat-fish included bones, the actual food constituted leathery inclusions that could be sucked for a purely gastronomic delight. The fifth want sounds even more bourgeois: *Fats*—0.05 pound, and indeed *fats*, known as *combifat*, that is "combined fat," produced out of unspecified waste products, tasted like soap to my palate, and a pound of it for three weeks, dissolved into the groats, is about as much soap as one can eat. Finally, the sixth and seventh wants are, strictly, not food, but drink. Man need not drink only water. Strumilin's Science has prepared an astonishing surprise: 0.003 pound of tea and 0.06 pound of sugar. Without sugar from fruit or some other source, man is said to die or get sick in the brain. In order to make a pound of tea last for about a year, it could not be brewed as in tsarist Russia, but had to be boiled until it tasted like pure hot water, colored a medicinal brown. Not only in the army, but also at every *house of creativity* for writers of Moscow. All of which ends the *ideal norm of human consumption,* adding almost nothing to its cost in terms of rye flour, but varying it amazingly.

Naturally, like any property, the man-machine must be kept in good repair—in good health, we may say, by analogy with other livestock. A strict officer named Arakcheyev who founded serf-soldier settlements in pre-1861 Russia knew how to do it with hardly any expenses at all. Cleanliness the serfs themselves must always take care of. Bathhouses, steam, boiling water, lime for sanitation. Any infection to be tracked down and liquidated at the expense of the sick but for the benefit of all. And good cheer: the best medicine. Besides, new and even cheaper means of disease prevention, and in particular of disinfection and vaccination, have appeared since Dr. Arakcheyev, a great pioneer of cheap, efficient large-scale war serfdom. Since the *medical* (or any other) *personnel* for commoners also thrives on the *ideal norm,* the cost again dwindles to negligible minimum.

As for the *founder of socialist planning* himself, he has been receiving top secret *kremlin rations* which contain, say, caviar rather than any component of the *ideal norm*. The trouble is that though caviar costs *officially* about 2,000 times as much as *rye bread* (or whatever is sold to commoners under the name), some insolent low rankers might go and buy caviar if it were sold *on open sale*. True, if the price of caviar were made 20,000 times as high as that of *rye bread*, and the salary of Strumilin were made 20,000 times as high as the wages of a commoner, then the *founder of socialist planning* could buy caviar freely, while the lower ranks even in Moscow could not. But suppose a lower ranker, or even a commoner, will *see* Strumilin buying caviar at such a price? Stupidly enough, that commoner might doubt the universality of the *ideal norm* or even of *science* itself! To ride about since 1918 in a luxurious car is simply to be efficient. But to be seen *buying* caviar? Therefore, at this writing there is no caviar *on open sale*: it is being passed to Strumilin as a top secret diplomatic pouch. Similarly, *free* medicine for *him* requires the most expensive equipment and medicines imported from abroad as soon as they appear there, regardless of the costs (how else, if it is a matter of life and death sometimes?).

The *planning* is simplified enormously (as all serf owners have known since times immemorial) if the *planners* have for themselves all the best goods and services produced anywhere in the world, and their serfs the *ideal norm*.

In 1961, the specialized economic magazine explained to the *soviet economists* what computers are and how they apply to economic planning—that is, how real planning is possible at least for eighty-four economic variables (while an economy may contain billions of them). The editors of the magazine footnoted the article: "By way of statement of the problem." To show that the problem of planning of eighty-four variables can at least be stated, the author noted:

It is known that in the U.S.A. more than 10,000 electronic computers are used today for economic computation and steering of production.

Ai-ya-yai, *unplanned capitalism* is being planned while *planned socialism* is not yet, after a good thirty years of *planning*.

Such major firms in the U.S.A. as Sylvania Electric, General Motors, Chrysler, Bell and many others have systems of planning and steering of production and trade on the basis of electronic computers. In some cases, using different communication channels, they steer the activity of hundreds of different enterprises, scattered all over the country, as a result of which a highly effective use of resources and a quicker turnover of the funds are attained.

Strumilin and all those who had been *planning* whole economies or admiring this *planning* (at a safe behavioral distance) did not know that without electronic computers even the planning of shipments of one grade of cement in one region was practically impossible.

What did Strumilin do on hearing the news? Naturally, the *founder of socialist planning* attacked viciously the first attempts at planning partly because he did not even understand it. But no luck this time! Planning had to be borrowed from *capitalism* for the production of weapons and *means of production* just as many other *bourgeois, capitalist* and *reactionary* sciences had to be borrowed ever since 1918 for the same purpose.

But outside weapons and *means of production*, the *ideal norm* holds good, and what Strumilin resents is the unscientific propensity of the population to eat, far from potato fields, that extravagant delicacy—potatoes—rather than cheaply stored and carried rye flour and groats. This indulgence in potatoes is the only deviation of the real diet of 1920/21 from the *ideal norm*. That real diet in which potatoes constituted "17 percent of the calorie content was quite far from the ideal," he notes. The desire of the population to make up for having less meat and sugar than in 1913 by eating potatoes rather than rye flour and groats is the only danger to the *ideal norm*:

But since we do not consider it expedient to make up for less meat and sugar by potatoes and vegetables, we have had to increase above all the proportion of bread in the total diet budget. Our increase in the proportion of bread and groats from 68.2 to 70 percent, that is by 2.6 percent compared with the consumption of 1913, makes up precisely for the decrease in the proportion of sugar from 5.6 to 3 percent.

Before 1917 the *greatest revolutionary humanist* Gorky wrote after his visit to the United States that he knew the horrible face of hunger well enough, but such hunger as existed in the United States he had never seen. Ulyanov-Lenin pointed out that the Russian worker's wages were only one-quarter of his American counterpart, and so how much more terribly the Russian worker was starved! After 1917 Strumilin naturally discovered that according to the *ideal norm*, the Russian worker before 1917 was a horrible glutton:

In our diet we have made the greatest decrease with respect to meat. Even including fish, which can substitute for meat. We have decreased the meat nutrition to almost one-third compared with 1913.

The Russian worker of 1913 overate—he gorged, he devoured almost three times more meat than the amount of dried cod (*meat-fish*) in the *ideal norm*. He ate 4.6 times more fish than he should, and the "proportion of sugar in his calorie content before 1917 was 3.5 times higher." "Before 1917" evidently means 1916, for the sight of the prodigious quantities of candies, honey, or jam the Russian worker gobbled up in 1913 are perhaps too painful for the scientist to contemplate.

Similarly, right *after* 1917, *Pravda* discovered that the *peasants* in Russia had also been gluttons, wallowed in money and wealth, and indulged their most artificially generated superficial private wants.

There is a lot of money in the countryside. We hear quite often from the peasants themselves that one has so many pounds of Kerensky banknotes, and another that many. It is significant that in the countryside they measure paper money, even light Kerensky banknotes, just by the bulk.

Are these the oppressed, robbed, ruined paupers in the abjectly poor Russia in the fourth year of the all-out war? Yes: a peasant who had only 11 to 14 acres had been considered to be below the level of subsistence: the *bolsheviks* and *left-wing-social revolutionaries* had kept assuring him that he would perish unless he took land by force from the richer landowners. But in 1918 *Pravda* readily explained the wealth of tillers of 11 to 14 acres (4 to 5 dessyatinas).

A bit of reasoning will explain this. An average tiller with one horse can easily till 4 to 5 dessyatinas, and more, if the family joins in. The average yield of rye is 60 to 70 poods per dessyatina, hence he gets 240 to 350 poods of rye, that is, about 7,000 rubles at the fixed prices, but actually many times over. The same applies to vegetables, milk, eggs, and other natural wealth.

In short, it was clear that the *world's first state of workers and peasants* must not ruin their bodies and their souls by artificially generated wants, including gluttony, as the tsarist government had done, and as the *partial admission of capitalism* brought back. What was the average worker's wages as of 1927—33.60 rubles? Very good. The *ideal norm* for the male at the front? Close to 3.48 rubles a month? All right, make it 3.60 rubles for a round figure: 33.60 minus 3.60 would yield the pseudo-tsar-god exactly 30 rubles in net profit per average worker a month. Or 360 rubles a year, right? The pseudo-tsar-god knew his arithmetic! The "total civilian employment" in 1928 was 50.7 million. The number could later be doubled, in particular by forcing all women (and many children age twelve or over) into *productive activity,* for women had become equal to men, and indeed much more equal than men as regards unrewarding arduous or harmful work. But never mind! Let us work from the current figure of 50.7 million in 1928. Assuming that each gainfully employed person received the worker's average wages, the pseudo-tsar-god would gain, by putting them on the *ideal norm,* more than 18 billion rubles, or about 9 billion dollars of 1913, or some 20 billion dollars of 1950 (by the wholesale price index). This is the sum that business in the United States invested in 1950 in all new plant and equipment of all industries, mining, transport, and such. In other words, with the money, the pseudo-tsar-god could have bought every year since 1928 as much plant and equipment, or means of production, as was produced in the United States in 1950. A sophisticated economy matching that of the United States could have been created with this money decades ago should great Stalin have wished so.

Actually, outside of weapons and *means of production,* the money thus extracted from the serfs has since been largely dissipated every year because *communists* have, naturally, as much talent for economic activity as for chess playing, art criticism, or cybernetics, and the serf *economy,* created instead of free enterprise, has been paralyzing anyone who happens by odd chance to have some knack, intelligence, or initiative in this respect.

The *founder of the socialist heavy industry* Ordjonikidze describes how they handled the "best machine tools" bought from American or other businessmen:

We now have the best tractor-building machine tools; but how can we make a tractor? We walked around those machine tools for a long time: probably many of you read about this in the newspapers and can recall how much trouble we had before we mastered this new equipment. I remember that when we opened this plant we made one tractor—that was in summer—but then four or five months passed and we still couldn't put out a single tractor. We could neither manufacture parts nor assemble them.

It rarely occurs to a *communist* that he is not fit for some job. Or rather, it should be put the other way round. *Communists* must be and are mostly those who are not fit for the job to which they are appointed. If a *communist* happens to be fit for it, he will not be infinitely devoted to the regime and may indeed even flee to a democracy. His all-round creative sterility is the best guarantee of his infinite devotion to the regime. A *communist* must have at his disposal specialists who understand: at the councils of his *tsarist* military specialists Trotsky would sit reading a French novel. What was *his* role? To be infinitely devoted and supervise their devotion. Trotsky and other *commissars* interfered whenever they thought that infinite devotion required their interference, and thus often botched a professional job and brought about huge war losses, but this is absolutely inevitable. Such is the structure of every unit of the war caste society down to a ballet company in which *infinite devotion* is in inverse ratio to talent and joins therefore the *communist party* to be above talent and supervise its devotion. As the wife of great Lenin recalls:

Elino Rahja relates that when the list of first People's Commissars was being discussed at a meeting of the Bolshevik group, he had been sitting in a corner listening. One of the nominees had protested that he had no experience in that kind of work. Vladimir Ilyich had burst out laughing and said: "Do you think any of us has had such experience?" None had any experience, of course.

See? None had any experience (of course!). But History itself has chosen them to inflict themselves by force on any field of human endeavor, from machine-building to literary criticism, and Nature has endowed them with such enormous and versatile genius (growing with rank) that the fact that one has had no experience in some such field can only evoke an outburst of laughter at his lack of belief in himself.

The inevitably resulting waste did not worry great Stalin too much. Naturally, his serf supermonopoly would never even resemble a creative and productive economy, as, say, in the United States, in anything except the output of weapons and *means of production*. But as the gentle reader may recall, great Stalin saw infinite dangers to his possession-power in the indiscriminate self-enrichment of his serfs. Now, suppose even that the economy of the United States could stay where it is and pass all its goods and services to the pseudo-tsar-god who would distribute them as rewards according to the degree of infinite devotion and/or usefulness to him of each serf, that is, his rank. This is realized partly in *foreign trade*, that is, trade between the pseudo-tsar-god (with his *monopoly of foreign trade*) and outside countries. This will be realized fully if the United States becomes a satrapy like, say, Czechoslovakia is today.

So each serf would be rewarded by the pseudo-tsar-god according to his rank, the only difference being that all the rewards would be proportionately much, much higher since the economy of the United States would be the source. But here is the question: Does not wealth as such, even if bestowed by the pseudo-tsar-god according to rank, lead to private leisure and unspent energy? Recently the *organs of state security* held a *closed* exhibition for *propaganda workers* who were to see for themselves a whole arsenal or museum of confiscated equipment and products made or bought or rented by groups and individuals in their struggle for freedom and/or against the regime and/or for the future possession-power of some new Ulyanov-Lenin. The exhibits ought to have included the two revolvers and police uniform of Ilyin who was *officially* declared *insane*. Having donned a police uniform, Ilyin calmly and safely approached the *government car* and fired, reportedly, both pistols at once, but the cars in the motorcade had changed order accidentally, and he killed someone else.

All these exhibits resulted partly from the comparative wealth, money, and unspent energy of some privileged serfs, mostly belonging to the richest one percent of the populace. What if wealth increases proportionately for all castes? If a prosperous citizen of a democracy or his leisured children are so often bored, how much more will a prosperous serf and his leisured children be bored? It is a fierce struggle for physical survival that prevents that boredom, and is not the *ideal norm* the best way to keep up the struggle among the lower castes?

So a bit of waste was not important for great Stalin. What really mattered was that he could now pour the annual loot of some 20 billion dollars (by the wholesale price index of 1950) into what he called the *means of production*. The *means of production* are not plant and equipment—means of production in general—but only those means of production which produce either weapons or new *means of production*, the latter producing in turn, either weapons or new *means of production*.

The democracies were *developing* economically, scientifically, and technologically. But they were putting a tiny portion of their income into the means of production in general, and still less into the *means of production*, while the rest was wasted on those billions of artificially generated wants that the free imagination of millions of free people can devise. The pseudo-tsar-god would finally *overdevelop* the outside world in military might because all natural and human resources above the *ideal norm* of the lower castes would henceforth be channeled over and over again into arms and *means of production*. And as for the natural resources, I recall that I heard a *closed* lecture in the late fifties: the lecturer would utter a kind of bubbling guttural breathless scream as he mentioned the figure of proven or supposed natural resources of *our country* in comparison with the United States. All these natural resources would be made into a single war machine based on a countrywide power grid and supply networks—into a single weapon the size of the country and extending out all over the globe and into space.

The dilemma which pseudo-tsar-god II faced in 1928 was not unlike that of Alexander II in 1855. Alexander II decided, following the unsuccessful Crimean War, not to enserf the free section of the population but, on the contrary, to emancipate the serfs, to admit *private* activity and free enterprise everywhere, and in short to move along the road which, say, the Danish monarchy had traversed quite safely. Pseudo-tsar-god II decided to abolish free enterprise—return to the state as before 1921, that is, to unrelieved uniform *state* serfdom.

One reason for the diametrically opposite choice in the dilemma was the realization after the First World War that the nineteenth century was over in 1914. Before 1914, and especially in the mid-nineteenth century, it was thought that military might and freedom went together: the freest countries, Britain and France, landed troops in Russia in 1854 and forced her huge serf army to admit defeat in about a year. In 1914 it became clear that the less free Germany was stronger than the freer Britain and France put together.

Another reason was that some advisers of Alexander II and Nicholas II were intellectually superior in the sphere of social knowledge to any *communists* I have been privileged to read or meet. Most Russian *communists* of 1918 to 1935 were like Ulyanov-Lenin. Just as some priests in the Dark Ages, they were interested only in their credal books, explaining that *they* should enserf and possess mankind because *they* are Mankind (or at least its only future-oriented, paradise-bringing, selfless part), the Consciousness of Matter and hence of Life, the Custodians of Science and hence of all knowledge, experience, and wisdom, the Creators of New Man, and so forth. True, there were fewer *communists* (like Bukharin or Lunacharsky) who still preserved a certain lay polish from the pre-1917 times; up to the mid-thirties they still read lay magazines and books published abroad to which they had access. However, the resulting scraps of lay sociology, anthropology, or psychology produced in their heads a barbarous mishmash and were used only as "flowers of intellect" in their sermons, basically as ignorant as the sermons untainted by lay knowledge.

They did not seem to want anything but to conquer, enserf, and possess. But they could do nothing else even if they wanted to, because the creation of a freer society takes more intelligence than conquest, enserfment, possession. Murder, torture, and destruction are so much easier to accomplish than the civic evolution of society.

46

But the serfs—how did they like the return from 1927 back to March 1921? From the average worker's wages of 1927, that is roughly of 1913, to the *ideal norm*?

A very annoying incident did, indeed, happen in 1921. The workers were the aryans, encouraged by the *party* superaryans to loot and kill the pariahs. Many journalists, statesmen, or scholars of today's democracies, not to mention Russian *bolsheviks* or *communists*, understand democracy not as a set of civic guarantees of personal freedom which began to evolve with trial by jury (and later Magna Charta) in England about a thousand years ago, but as *democracy* in the literal sense, that is, the *cratos* (power) of the *demos* (of the people). If a certain party or *party* in Spain, South America, Asia, or elsewhere receives more votes than any other party or *party*, surely those voters are the *demos* who now have the *cratos* even to eat up the rest of the population. When another party or *party* overthrows the *cratos* of the *demos*, sometimes with a great deal of massacre, many journalists, statesmen, and intellectuals are quite indignant: to overthrow *democracy*—the *cratos* of the *demos* who ensured for its *party* the electoral majority, one-*third* of the votes in a free election! When it is noted that Hitler got almost *half* the votes in a free election, and so he, by their reckoning, represented superdemocracy, even greater indignation follows, usually because these journalists, statesmen, and intellectuals want to associate themselves with the *demos* whose *cratos* loots and kills *others*, and not *us*, as that wicked superdemos of the super-democrat Hitler did.

Though *communists* never got nearly as many votes as Hitler did, it was still pleasant for Ulyanov-Lenin and his comrades to know in 1917 that they still had some *demos*—low-skilled workers, soldiers, and sailors—behind them. They were still *democratic*, ensuring the *cratos* of the *demos*. In March 1921 their *demos*, their *people*, the only segment of the population that had not been against them, seized the Kronstadt fortress, Baltic ships, and warehouses of weapons and ammunition.

First Zinoviev announced in *Pravda* that "spies sent by French counterintelligence have been behind the seamen of the Petro-palovsk." Then *Pravda* reported that the "mutiny has no doubt been led by the old officers who concealed themselves skillfully behind the Red Army men and sailors of 'the Revolutionary Committee', some of whom are no doubt traitors and have sold themselves for money." After the proper extermination of their *demos*, the *people*, the *workers and peasants*, who had turned into as many French spies and/or tsarist officers and their paid agents, *Pravda* could afford a different description of their motives and goals in the uprising.

On March 2 they adopted at a general meeting in Anchor Square a resolution the main points of which reduce to the following: reelect the Soviets by secret ballot, give the freedom of speech to all parties, convene a nonparty conference of the Petrograd Gubernia not later than March 10. Abolish all Political Departments, make the rations equal for all working people, and abolish the Communist Combat Detachments.

It was, no doubt, to protect the nerves of their readers against such brazen claims and hopes that *Pravda* rather ignored the following passage of this resolution, published in the Kronstadt *Izvestia* on March 3 and 4:

The worker, instead of becoming the master of the factory, has be-come a slave. He can neither work where he would like to nor reject work that is beyond his physical strength. Those who dare to say the truth are put into the torture chambers of Cheka. . . .

Ai-ya-yai, what a brazen filthy low word: torture chambers. The 1970 *Britannica* article "Torture" does not even mention post-1917 Russia and in fact concentrates on Western Europe, with a proper reference to the article "Third Degree," which describes the United States today, of course. And here—such words in 1921! Obviously, those workers had no education like these contributors to *Britannica*. To repay Ulyanov-Lenin in that fashion for having made them the *demos*, the aryans with respect to all those pariahs down to doctors, lawyers, and writers!

The *demos*, the *poor*, the *people*, the *workers and peasants*, who dared to imagine that Ulyanov-Lenin expressed their will worse than they did themselves in their Kronstadt *Izvestia* were exterminated (not as *fascists* though, because the word *fascist* became widely known only a year later). But Ulyanov-Lenin got frightened: to the 10th *congress of the party* which was held during the uprising he said the opposite of what *Pravda* was saying:

... we have run into a big—I suppose the biggest—internal political crisis of Soviet Russia, which has led to the discontent of not only a considerable section of the peasantry but also of workers.

So the French spies and tsarist officers were—workers. The *demos*. The aryans. However, even to the *congress of the party* Ulyanov-Lenin did not say how the Resolution in the Kronstadt *Izvestia* started:

We joined the Communist Party to work for the good of the people. . . .

So the French spies and tsarist officers were Russian Communists. Now, the *communists* accounted for a fraction of one percent of the populace, and if they were up in arms, then who supported great Lenin? Just as in Hungary in 1956—only the personnel of the torture-murder network, including that remarkable *tsarist secret police agent* whom its chief Dzerjinsky found a bit showy and hot-tempered though.

Ulyanov-Lenin announced to the *congress* then and there the *partial admission of capitalism*. A *temporary retreat*, as he called it.

However, in 1928 the network of torture-murder stations was much bigger and better than in 1921. No time is wasted during a retreat. When a pseudo-tsar-god retreats in some area of the globe or does not advance at least, a statesman, diplomat, or expert of a democracy often imagines that he has outsmarted, stopped, neutralized the pseudo-tsar-god. An extremely shrewd smile, with an occasional smart wink, appears on the face of some foreign minister Jan Masaryk of Czechoslovakia, and as he smiles and winks to the delight of his electorate, the pseudo-tsar-god's activity is going on full blast in secret preparations for a new offensive, should it be the pseudo-tsar-god's pleasure to launch such, until some strangers come up from behind the smiling and winking foreign minister of a democracy and throw him out the window of his office. His former electorate below scatters in dismay, and while the statesman is falling, his mind works perhaps behaviorally, not just verbally, but it is too late for him and his electorate.

During the *retreat*, the network of torture-murder stations had been developed enough to make *heroic idealism* everyone's behavior. The expression *heroic idealism* is applied to the time of 1918 to 1921 by Professor Carr, the author of *A History of Soviet Russia*, which will consist of some fifty volumes, considering his average rate of production to date. All the workers and peasants would now be again *heroic idealists* without the danger of Kronstadt uprisings, properly taken care of by a much bigger and better torture-murder network.

As pseudo-tsar-god II could well conclude, man is, or at least looks the more discontent, the better off he is, provided he has not only wealth, good health, and youth, but also freedom, and in particular the freedom to express discontent.

In the summer of 1917 *Pravda* (and great Stalin was then its co-editor) carried a protest sent by a fitter of the Donbas fields. He, a fitter, makes only 5.50 rubles a day, while meat at the local shop costs 0.37 a pound! His daily pay buys only 15 pounds of meat. Great Stalin gave much prominent space to the indignant protest and published it in big type: it was very good that the worker was discontented. But behaviorally, great Stalin must have made this mental note: "The country is in her fourth year of an all-out war against a militarily superior enemy, and that cretin has the cretinic nerve to bemoan his poverty, cry for sympathy, and vehemently protest in *Pravda* that his daily pay buys only fifteen pounds of meat. Will the workers of the United States ever be able to get fifteen pounds of meat on their daily pay without any rations or anything in the fourth year of an all-out war against a militarily superior country?"

After 1917, namely, in 1922, that prosperous year compared with 1919 to 1921, *Pravda* did not bemoan a worker of the Donbas fields whose daily pay bought only fifteen pounds of meat. The reporter met a girl of fifteen at the end of her workday: not only women but indeed even girls of fifteen had become equal to, and usually more equal than, men.

> The girl faltered. But another girl prompted her:
> "Come on. It can't be worse. Do tell."
> And without waiting, she spoke up herself.
> "We receive no money. Perhaps once in three months. And they do not issue bread every day. They issued a pound and a half yesterday, but nothing today."
> "How do you mean—nothing?"
> "Just like that—nothing."
> "What have you eaten?"
> "We have eaten nothing. We have been working hungry."

Was this girl the daughter of that fitter who protested vehemently that his pay bought only 15 pounds of meat a day in the summer of 1917? Were they all happy now?

> I had to go seven miles by cart. It was a hot day. The miners—men, women, and children—"were having a rest" all along the way, by each fence, at each wall, or just in the field.
> Saturated by coal dust, they seemed to be hunks of coal scattered all along.
> Women were clad somehow, but men and children were in scanty rags.
> I have never seen such rags. The most tattered beggars in Moscow seemed bourgeois and dapper in comparison.
> Some were having a snack. I did not see anyone eating anything except bread and water. The children picked up watermelon and melon rinds and gnawed them greedily.

Were they happy now? The author ends the article by showing the local love for great Lenin.

Man's unhappiness or misery often depends on the alternative he perceives to his present state. When that fitter with his daily pay could buy 15 pounds of meat in 1917, he was miserable (indignant, rebellious)—at least verbally—because the alternative was, as it seemed to him, to get still more by taking the profit and/or property of the shopkeeper, the meat-packer, the rich cattleman, the owner of the mine, the banker, and all those who were just looting him. In 1922 he was happy—at least verbally—and loudly thanked great Lenin for what he had done for him in these five years, because the alternative was what those Kronstadt workers called unpolitely the torture chamber, and compared with *that*, his state in 1922 was rare, unique, priceless happiness. Read the above description: to be whole and healthy, to bask in a fine generous sun (so nice it is—in that scanty, almost beach dress), to feast on bread (a rare feast, and hence sumptuous), washing it down with good fresh sweet water. Holy (anthracite) smokes! What imagination could fancy or wish more?

The more inevitable and terrifying the torture expected by everyone suspected of unhappiness, the more happy all will be at least verbally, that is, as long as *it* threatens. Happiness, called good cheer, was officially an obligatory part of behavior of Russian pre-1861 serf soldiers who had conquered territories exceeding sixty-odd times the size of Muscovy. A Russian pre-1861 soldier knew behaviorally under Nicholas I the Gauntlet-Chaser that the worst that could happen in battle was death, while if his officer thought his good cheer insufficient his officer could—no, not kill him. Capital punishment? How cruel, horrible, and European! Simply, an insufficiently happy soldier would be dragged between two rows of sufficiently happy soldiers, working like a living torture machine. The sufficiently happy soldiers constituting this collective torture machine to the strains of heroic and, indeed, idealistic music would now remember very well that death from an enemy weapon was comparatively nothing and they would *show*, accepting it suicidally, as much cheer as they could and perhaps would *feel* as much cheer even as they died. This is how they routed with *unprecedented heroism* (or *heroic idealism?*) all enemies throughout the centuries.

Of course it is better for a serf not even to know of any better alternative: it is important to inculcate into his mind that his is the happiest life, while in comparison the rest of mankind can live only in misery. On May 1, 1932, *Pravda* gave a whole page to descriptions various serfs offered as to how happy they were compared with their life before 1917 and the life of the *working people* outside. Take for example the *working people* of Germany which a smith named Osipov *visited as a tourist.*

There is no daylight in their apartments, ever. In the daytime the electric lights are always on. They subsist on greenery—they never see meat. If they can earn 80 rubles (in our money) they pay 20 rubles as rent. They pay all kinds of taxes, and live in poverty though they are clean people.

In Italy the situation is even worse.

But whether a serf knows anything of a better alternative, being unhappy must be a criminal offense, carefully tracked down. Technically, being unhappy had been named in Trotsky's army "demoralization and depression." That was now to be applied to the whole population, and as the world knows from the Smolensky Archives, the *organs of state security* were to watch and report secretly signs of "demoralization and depression" in the "mood of either the country as a whole, or of a locality, enterprise," and so on, down to "individual negative political or moral attitudes."

But suppose there should be a leak in a secret report about a group's or an individual's unhappiness? The instructions demanded: wrap the report in nontransparent paper before putting it into an envelope, sew the flaps of the envelope and seal it, and use only the personnel of the *organs of state security*, for typing, copying, and sending it through a special courier.

Some apprehension was caused by such trained serfs as engineers, doctors, and scientists. For them the fall from their salaries in 1927 or 1913 to the *ideal norm* was simply gigantic. The engineer Berezovsky testified at the Shakhty *trial* that his salary before 1917 was initially 400 rubles a month (plus free apartment with all services, car or buggy, paid leaves, bonuses, and so on) with a prospect of 750 rubles and still higher free benefits. Not that the pseudo-tsar-god wanted an engineer, doctor, or scientist to earn as little as a cleaning woman. No. Today in Moscow a rank-and-file engineer, doctor, or scientist earns about twice as much as a cleaning woman: that motivates him in his training from the age of seven to twenty-two. For any other opportunity of making this differential has been reliably cut off. But all the same his fall from the level of 1927 was to be much greater than that of the average worker, whose pay was to fall to about one-tenth, while the engineer's to about one-hundredth.

At the 13th *party conference* in 1924 Mikoyan complained: the Kuban factory offered an engineer the maximum legal monthly pay in cash, bonuses, a free four-room apartment with a bath. . . . The audience laughed with the speaker at each new item as though he described the whims of an Oriental potentate. True, the wife of Ulyanov-Lenin notes in her memoirs that their lovely summer retreat in Hills had a bath. How else? But for an engineer, doctor, or scientist who is not even a *member of the party*, that is, who is just a commoner, to demand a "four-room apartment with a bath"! The *members of the party* just roared.

Rank-and-file engineers, doctors, scientists, and all such specialists were to be reduced to commoners. Then the pseudo-tsar-god would be able to afford, say, sixty times as many of them as in the United States.

It is to wake them to the new reality that the Shakhty *trial* was arranged in 1928. Does the gentle reader still remember the *defendant* Skorutto whose wife suddenly shouted from the audience: "This is not true! Kolya, why are you saying this? Don't believe him, this is a lie!" and who indeed renounced his *confession*, and then *confessed* again (after an intermission) that his *confession* was true?

"I always thought," said the defendant Skorutto in his last speech before the sentence, "that if I do my duty formally honestly, what else does the Soviet power need?"

He realized that *formal* honesty was a heinous crime for which at this *open trial* he could well expect to be *officially sentenced* to be *officially* shot.

"Citizens of the Court," Skorutto said in conclusion, "if you believe that a transformation has occurred in me, that my old psychology has been eradicated, you will perhaps give me a chance to work. You will see that in the future I will be able to work only consciously honestly, and not formally honestly."

He had been working formally honestly for an adequate salary of 1913 or 1927. There would be none such. Conscious of his heinous crime in the past, he (and all engineers, as well as doctors, scientists, and so on, who would benefit from his example) was to work *consciously* honestly, irrespective of any pay. "You will perhaps give me a chance to work." "And to live without pain," he might have added. Exactly. He was to be happy to work with *conscious* honesty, without sparing himself, and doing his utmost, not for any filthy money, but for the highly privileged opportunity to work (and live without pain).

The name of the aircraft designer Tupolev is world famous, or at least the first syllable of his name, TU, is, because it is part of the name of various TU planes flying all over the world as airliners, easily convertible to heavy bombers. Soon after Skorutto made his confession, he was *arrested*, a word which I always italicize if only because the husband of my mother's colleague was *arrested* in the fifties, since he made an important discovery in rocketry. The best way to keep a discovery secret is secretly to *arrest* the discoverer right in the street (who will know what for?) and transfer him with all his laboratory into a secret *prison*, sealed reliably from the outside world. There is no such person. He has disappeared no one knows where and how. The fact that he is alive and thriving may later be told as a top military secret to the family, who will correspond with the discoverer through a mailbox number.

The *arrested* Tupolev's *special designing office* had the following incentives to motivate the best *state*-slave scientists, inventors and designers—the incentives they valued as greatest treasures because they had been kept preliminarily for a while in a death-by-labor camp: an iron cage on the roof of the building (in Moscow) into which the scientist, inventors, designers could go and thus *have fresh air whenever they liked*! Breakfast: *plain yogurt, sweet tea, butter*, apart from porridge and *bread that could be eaten without restriction*! *Dinner*: two courses plus *stewed* fruit as a dessert! *Supper*: a *hot* meal, plain *yogurt* again, *sweet tea* and *butter*, not to mention bread again! A *shower three times a month*! Sleep in a kind of Gorky's doss house (*Lower Depths*) with *sheets*, a *pillow*, and a *blanket*! *Soap, cigarettes, candies* on sale! And a motivational reward which was even higher than any of these!

Strictly speaking, these scientists and technologists were

slaves, not serfs: they were not allowed to have families at the *special* designing office. However, they were enslaved while they were still serfs and had families. Therefore, the strongest motivation of a slave scientist was the *meeting with his wife for ten minutes in the presence of the leading comrades* (a cynical person may call them overseers) as a bonus for 1,019,800 minutes of diligent, productive, and indeed, creative work on heavy bombers, rocketry or whatever it may be.

Indeed, what happened in Russia in 1918 to 1921 and was reaffirmed again in 1928 was the eradication of the old motivational psychology, to which the *defendant* Skorutto referred, and a motivational transformation (or shall we say, revolution?) which we will fail to grasp unless we realize how much our mentality is still the mentality of the pre-1917 world in which most citizens of most democracies are still cozily wrapped.

47

How have, indeed, the democracies been reacting to the re-emergence in 1917 and re-affirmation in 1928 of a militarily daily growing, globally expanding, all-infiltrating serf caste war society which the recorded social history of Europe had never yet seen and which was bound to bring forth similar societies either by way of self-defense or through imitation or both, and finally perhaps submerge the entire world back into the night of ruthless gang war—only now global, scientific and technological?

Naturally, there are more sophisticated students of mankind in the West than in Russia today: creative freedom, even as it existed in pre-1861 Russia for the nobility, is a stimulating ambience. Besides, vast-scale education in the United States (for the first time in the history of free societies) is a powerful quantitative and hence qualitative factor in the development of intellect—not in the sense that every Nobel Prize winner is more intelligent outside his field than a randomly sampled crane operator or a cleaning woman (so far it has often proved to be just the other way round), but in the sense that vast-scale education brings forth more intellect and talent than in, say, pre-1861 Russia where education was confined mostly to the nobility.

But at the same time a sheltered, free, wealthy island that a twentieth-century democracy is (an island as transient perhaps as Periclean Athens amidst the millennia of gang war) creates—as any other sheltered, free, wealthy milieu does—adult babies, innocent, trusting, devoid of underworld defense mechanisms.

Dostoyevsky once wondered why a convict at hard labor who was considered the most dangerous man in the prison camp seemed to like him. The criminal told him: "You are so simple that one cannot help feeling sorry for you . . ." To this man of the underworld, Dostoyevsky, the product of a safe, prosperous, humane milieu, was so "simple" that even when he robbed Dostoyevsky he genuinely liked and pitied his victim as one might a little cherub-like child.

The European and Russian nobilities created their sheltered, wealthy, gentle life largely at the expense of their hereditary lands (and serfs), while the democratic citizenries did so due to ingenuity, industry and enterprise in freedom. But some psychological consequences of this life are strikingly similar. For example, an early nineteenth-century nobleman often believed that there is only one fatal threat to man: the destruction of *nature* by *civilization*. By the stifling, unbearable, fatal destruction of nature he meant the fact that some houses were built of artificial stone, and not of natural wood. He also *stifled* because he could not live like Gipsies, savages, and such others. Horrified, the most famous Russian poet of the first third of the nineteenth century (incidentally a serf owner) wrote:

> The people there behind walls of stone
> Cannot breathe the cool of early morn,
> Ashamed of love they are.

A democracy tends to convert into a secluded, parochial, cozy island of frolicking innocence, wrapped, to the exclusion of all outside realities, in harrowing dramas like last year's liaison of a cabinet minister with a call girl, or last week's two-percent rise of gasoline prices.

I will never forget the American film made from Steinbeck's *Grapes of Wrath*. The author and the film-makers wanted to show the *life of the poor* in the thirties. The poor rode about in trucks. The Russian audience stared. Even a small dingy car thirty years old is a status symbol here perhaps as high as a yacht in the United States. But the ownership of a truck is something as would, in the United States, be the ownership of, say, a fleet of dirigibles. The audience perceived Steinbeck's wrathful message of *poverty* as a futuristic fantasy about terrestrials riding about in their fleets of dirigibles.

Certainly, one might permit oneself to hope, intellect can rise above sheer empirical experience. A gentle, kind, polite criminologist can know the criminal world (the common, *private*, small-scale underworld) better than its shrewdest denizen. Dostoyevsky, the childlike, understood and predicted the destiny of all those treacherous, tough, ruthless "greats" in Russia of 1917 to 1938. A mild, sensitive, compassionate man like George Orwell understood the psychology of certain societies in which he never lived better than the "creators" of those societies. But the Englishman George Orwell was not an adviser to the President of the United States, as he ought to have been: he was an author who had difficulties even in publishing his books after 1937. Instead, the President of the world's strongest democracy between 1933 and 1945 had Joseph Davies as his adviser. As ambassador in Moscow Davies discovered one fine day in 1937 that his life was watched all round the clock by the *organs of state security*. At an antique store he bought a painting which was a fake. What could the *organs* do? Let it pass? Suppose Davies would find that the picture was a fake and the story would get into the newspapers abroad? Great Stalin himself would know! "How did you let it happen?" Those who shadowed Davies came into the open and forced the manager of the store to give the money back. Since 1918 every embassy staffer has been monitored all round the clock: to know everything about a man is often as good as to own him. A French Ambassador revealed a common banal weakness (girls) several years ago, and if not for a runaway serf (*soviet defector*), he would, perhaps, still be a *soviet* agent as Ambassador or as, say, Prime Minister of France. On the other hand, ambassadors or experts or heads of government like Joseph Davies must be safeguarded against any accident because they are, in a sense, even more valuable than agents.

So the discovery of Mr. Davies was not new. But in his book of confidential reports to the President and excerpts from his diary he decided to express his delight with the *organs of state security*. They were watching him all round the clock. How these fine people cared for his safety and well-being. He described himself trying to recognize them and smile his appreciation.

If brought into a torture chamber, the American ambassador and expert on Russia would have probably playfully wiggled his hands and legs since certainly these kind people wanted to tickle him.

A free, sheltered, prosperous society enables Orwells to develop to their full intellectual stature: herein lies its viability —its strength. But it also reduces the less endowed to a kind of babyhood in everything outside their professional occupation (Joseph Davies was a lawyer). Unfortunately it is mostly the Davieses rather than the Orwells who have been appointed by democratic electorates to shape the behavior of their countries toward the mega underworld. Since Lloyd George in 1921 all these people, including statesmen, official experts and even perhaps intelligence and counterintelligence men of democracies have been mostly the Davieses, and democracy has so far survived perhaps owing to fortuitous circumstances like the Atlantic Ocean. In a sense it can be said that since 1917 there has been as yet no diplomacy, foreign policy, or even intelligence work of democracies equal to the challenge: what have been called by these names are simply vestiges of the nineteenth century, misapplied to the entirely different post-1917 world.

In the nineteenth century, electorates could afford the luxury of not knowing societies different from their own and of electing statesmen who hardly knew anything about them either. A statesman was to be creative and useful inside the democracy, not globally. He was often a lawyer: law helped him to be persuasive when promising the satisfaction of needs or wants of his electorate, to avoid legal pitfalls, to fight his opponents, and to act in office. And those shaping today the behavior of democracies toward the unknown mega underworld are still lawyers who often imagine that war serf societies inside which not a single law has ever been observed (and indeed, there are no laws in the Western sense, but only orders called *laws*) will behave like parties to a legal dispute. Let us sign more agreements. True, the owners of post-1917 Russia have broken more than a thousand of such agreements. But why not sign another thousand? The electorate will be duly impressed. The electorate for its part wants to believe that war caste societies reclaiming oceans and space all around them and infiltrating them up to their government levels do not exist as realities, that it is still 1855 when the freer and hence more scientifically and technologically developed Britain and France defeated Russia. And hence the electorate keeps electing lawyers who will remove that last week's horrible two-percent rise of gasoline prices on their cozy little island, and never, never will live with call girls, while remaining as innocent of the outside world as their electorate is or as their predecessors have been.

Therefore, the gentle reader will not perhaps regard it as a sheer waste of time if I pay such attention to Joseph Davies. For there is Mr. Davies in all of us, including myself, because I have been living, after all, on the outmost fringes of the mega under-world into which I was born. And it is only by our intellect that we can grasp and match its inbred psychology.

From Moscow, Ambassador Davies wrote confidential expert reports to the President of the United States, and there was one problem especially important. A *constitution* was soon to be accepted, much more *liberal* than the American Constitution. But in the local power elite there were, naturally, diehards afraid of super-American constitutional liberalism. Fortunately, Stalin was on the side of the liberals, though it was *his* stay in power that the Constitution might discontinue (he would not be voted for?).

Stalin, it was reported, insisted upon liberalism of the Constitution even though it hazarded his power and party control.

So liberal (up to the point of self-sacrifice) Uncle Joe was, and yet he and Addy (Hitler) were not good neighbors (as Mr. Davies and his neighbor across the backyard fence back home). The two countries were reported to get angry at each other in 1934 and hence were arming. Why quarrel? Why not live in peace? As a good lawyer Mr. Davies knew that a quarrel is only bad for both parties: even if a sum at issue is big, the legal expenses may consume even more money, time, energy. While both parties could live amicably, trade, and help each other in difficulties like good neighbors should, should they not? President Roosevelt instructed Ambassador Davies to suggest to *both* the liberal constitutionalist Stalin and his neighbor Hitler "limitation of armament to defensive weapons only such as a man could carry on his shoulder." In other words, rifles. Unless scythes, yataghans, and pickaxes were also meant. To Berlin and back to Moscow Ambassador Davies flew (these were two countries on which he was an expert: Russia *and* Germany).

The President
. . . Schacht literally jumped at the idea. He said: "That is absolutely the solution!" He said that in its simplicity it had the earmarks of great genius. His enthusiasm was extraordinary.

It is perfectly clear why. If all the soldiers of both countries carried on their shoulders only rifles or scythes, they would not need to be afraid of each other, and a stable durable peace on earth would prevail, along with trade, friendship, and even love. No wonder the German *statesman* almost jumped out of his seat with enthusiasm.

When I outlined the President's suggestion of limitation of armament to defensive weapons only, such as man could carry on his shoulder, he almost jumped out of his seat with enthusiasm.

Before outlining the preconceived image of history, and of Russia after 1917 in particular, as it existed in the mind of Mr. Davies, and exists to some degree in the minds of many citizens of democracies, it is necessary to stipulate that there are no motives which would in any way bar their understanding. A citizen who expects to benefit from the pseudo-tsar-god, as some British and American oil firms did in 1921, may well believe verbally anything to suit his behavioral self-interest. A statesman of a democracy is not its owner, but its agent (representative, executive), and as such he easily becomes a double agent: the pseudo-tsar-god gives him concessions which are good only to show off to his electorate, whereas he makes in exchange (not necessarily officially and triumphantly, as Chamberlain did in Munich, but tacitly or by implication in all kinds of secret or *quiet* diplomacy) such concessions as would bring the democracies a step nearer to their end.

In short, Russia after 1917 has been an unprecedented reservoir of one-man wealth, including human property, plus unprecedented one-man military might (including an army of secret agents) and so the pseudo-tsar-god may lavish natural and human wealth as well as temporary safety under thousands of forms and disguises. He may buy, bribe—or rob, as well as menace, browbeat—or protect. He can afford more than thousands of Standard Oil Companies and as many Al Capones put together once could, and the beneficiaries may be well motivated to bar, resist, screen out all knowledge of war caste societies.

In every democracy a certain segment of the population prefers to overthrow whatever regime there is and to become the upper caste in a serf caste society rather than to be low-status freemen in a democracy. A writer who goes out of fashion in a free society, as Maxim Gorky did in the West by 1928, may prefer to become as famous as no writer had ever been in a free society, and to enserf himself for the sake of this—to become a top-caste serf in a serf caste society.

To overthrow democracy in their countries and to grab them, local potential megacriminals expect aid from big war caste societies like post-1917 Russia, Nazi Germany, or post-1949 China, and different groups of megacriminals may fight each other as the worst gang-war enemies depending on whether they receive or expect aid from, say, post-1917 Russia or post-1949 China. Naturally, it would be funny to expect a potential or actual top caste, receiving or expecting aid for establishing or maintaining a caste society in *their* country, to feign anything but perfect innocence and infinite enthusiasm with respect to the donor caste society.

But there is another series of motives barring a democratic citizen's knowledge of war caste societies.

Many citizens of democracies do not want to believe behaviorally that a war caste society may conquer them and make them one of its lower castes (with subcastes within the caste). For a citizen of France to believe it behaviorally in 1933 to 1939 meant to give away *his* money for defense, and who, pray, wants to give away *his* own money of *his* own free will? But apart from money, the belief meant a lot of other troubles, including that mental strain which is involved in contemplating a danger and racking the brains to find the ways to avert it. Not that a citizen of France was necessarily against defense. No. But let *others* pay and worry. This is the difference between cancer and conquest.

In case of cancer, a citizen cannot shift all the anxieties, expenses, and sacrifices onto *others*, while in case of conquest he can. And naturally it might happen that so many citizens do so that there are no *others* to speak of.

In my comparative analysis of democracies, each democracy (or indeed, each sociohistoric group) has a certain "average civic index." Thus, Russia between February and October of 1917 had all the democratic freedoms the United States has today, but the average civic index of the former was low, while that of the latter was high and is still higher today; other societies can be grouped between these two points on the civic-index scale. In other words, I realize that democracies are different. Yet the differences are rather quantitative degrees of roughly the same social processes: the civic unwillingness of France to survive in the thirties is in evidence in the United States today—it is only perhaps a matter of lesser degree. Inversely, what I say of the United States applies to, say, Continental European democracies to an even greater extent: these democracies today are, perhaps, not much more viable, when confronted with war caste societies, than they were in the thirties.

If there is no civic behavioral belief in the danger of being subjugated by war caste societies, why know these societies? A democracy's knowledge of them then turns into verbalization, make-believe, and among manicheans—into coparticipative symbolism.

A certain expert on Russia named Joseph Davies suddenly imagines that the owner of a caste society is a *liberal* who is fighting against the *conservatives* in his cabinet for a super-American Constitution. Curiously, the expertise of Joseph Davies need not even correspond to the creed of *propaganda*. The word *liberal* has belonged in the creed ever since 1891 to the pole of evil, not the pole of good. It is *tsarist-liberal-bourgeois-fascist,* etc., and not at all *revolutionary-liberal-socialist-democratic,* etc. But even that does not matter. The war serf society on the territory of former Russia is only a make-believe symbol, whereas the behavioral reality is the *fight* of Mr. Davies, who calls himself *also* a liberal, against the local *enemy*. Since the owner of a caste serf war society Stalin and Mr. Davies are both called *liberals,* they coparticipate, they are both *we* in the make-believe—at least to some extent. As against *them*, the real behavioral *enemy*. With gusto Mr. Davies describes how he told, while in Britain, the "truth about Russia" straight to the face of Winston Churchill and how he thus crushed the hated *conservative*. That was *our* real, behaviorally all-important, and intoxicating victory over *them*, the *enemy*.

After 1956 Professor Carr of Cambridge, Britain, could collect even more documentary evidence for his amply documented, supposedly fifty-volume *History of Soviet Russia*. After 1956, a new neighbor in our Moscow apartment, a waiter at a circus refreshment stand, thus evaluated once great Stalin: "Our Hitler, only much worse." In 1958, Professor Carr, quite on the contrary, believes that "our Hitler, only much worse," is still every bit great Stalin, who

carried out, in the face of any obstacle and opposition, the industrialization of his country through intensive planning and thus not only paid tribute to the validity of Marxist theory, but ranged the Soviet Union as an equal partner among the great powers of the Western world. In virtue of this achievement he takes his undisputed place both as one of the great executors of the Marxist testament and of the great Westernizers in Russian history.

But this is not enough!

Stalin laid the foundation of the proletarian revolution. . . .

Stop! Here the esteemed professor has mixed up two pre-1953 clichés: "Lenin was the leader of the proletarian revolution" and "Stalin laid the foundation of socialism." The professor of Cambridge outdoes *after* 1956 the pre-1953 *propaganda*: he ascribes to great Stalin all the glory of great Lenin.

Do not assume that Professor Carr, who studied Russia all his life with all the documents and libraries at his disposal, could not understand even after 1956 what a Russian waiter at a circus refreshment stand could.

But why should he? The real population of real Russia has been safely muzzled since 1918. So in this respect there will be no unpleasant reaction to any myths about it. Nor do the humanities entail the responsibility of the exact sciences: a myth instead of a bridge may give the bridge designer a lot of trouble, while a 50-volume myth instead of a history of Russia may, on the contrary, be a piece of new brave scholarship. On the other hand, there are so many motives making it worth while to create a 50-volume manichean myth in order to accomplish something really behaviorally important! To crush some local *enemy* on the scale of the town, university, or department, for example. Political elections in the country, struggle for academic status, popularity among students, fight against the opponents of children's grounds in the neighborhood. What vital, charged, far-reaching issues in which the faraway abstract silent Russia may conveniently act as a manichean symbol of *us* as against *them*.

Suppose you call yourself a *socialist* in a democracy. Classified today are about two hundred different (and sometimes mutually excluding) Socialisms, and many of them are sets of measures having no more to do with each other than the measures of any randomly sampled election program of any party. Some *socialisms* are coparticipative clusters in which entirely heterogeneous phenomena are fused partly either as a result of intellectual or literal illiteracy, or mostly deliberately: for example, public philanthropy, insurance and working-class prosperity (all of which were pioneered and achieved in the United States without any of two hundred *socialisms*) are fused with the abolition of free enterprise (which is possible only in a *perfect* serf owner-ship) and/or the institution of hierarchies of saintly govern-mental officials who will (of course!) create more values more cheaply than evil free enterprise and will distribute them with saintly justice except that for any better value bought hitherto for a legal higher price some of them will (fortunately) take an illegal bribe-price many times as high. Obviously, many *socialists* of many *socialisms* may draw manichean myths from post-1917 Russia to support their local struggles. Take the speed of building of some railroad in Russia after 1917—and imply or suggest to your electorate that *your* Socialism out of about two hundred other Socialisms will build railroads at the same speed, because here is *socialism* in post-1917 Russia and you also represent *socialism*. See how quickly railroads are built over there in Russia under Socialism, by Socialism, and due to Socialism? Socialist Industrialization, you know. State Planning. Government Takes Over. And hence, by coparticipative association, there originates the abundance of all goods and services, the justest distribution of them, the most efficient generous medicine and all social services, as well as concern, kindness, and humanism above all. Socialism, in short. "But what about the two underground *human*ways which ensured the speedy building of that *rail*way? What about that remarkable technological rule: 'Two (human) heads for one (railroad) tie'?" Ah, that. These heads in the humanways are *not* Socialism, of course, and so why drag them in, if they are *not* Socialism? Can't a fellow see the good (Socialism) in Russia after 1917 (that *rail*way), and not only the bad (those *human*ways)? One must form an objective, unbiased, many-sided view, you know. Here is the good of Socialism (that *rail*way). Let us not minimize the tremendous achievements of Socialism, its unprecedented triumphs, its breath-taking victories. The speed at which that *rail*way was built is a fact that only rabid anticommunists will deny.

The manichean opposite of the *socialist* is the *capitalist*. This is quite funny because public philanthropy has existed in every humane society and if a program of public philanthropy—in a democracy, of course—is a breakthrough of genius, who, except manicheans, will object if it is called *socialism, communism* or *supercommunism*? (For all his vitriolic sarcasm Dickens admired *socialism* in the United States about a hundred years ago though he or most Americans hardly knew the word, or else thought that it denoted assassinations and promiscuity). Yet an effective, humane, and useful program of public philanthropy does not exclude but, on the contrary, requires a versatile, sensitive, and abundant creation of values and valuables. Free enterprise is to produce what philanthropy is to consume. Anyway, free enterprise will, by definition, exist as long as man is free to think or create, provided his activity does no harm to others according to a legal decision, obtained in a due civic process of law. But in a manichean mentality there are only polar dualities: God and Devil, doves and hawks, peace and war, *communism* and *fascism*. So there must be the opposite of the *socialist,* and this is the *capitalist,* an adept of *capitalism,* who wants to starve all those orphans, the blind, and other unfortunates.

However, if you are a *capitalist* in the style of nineteenth-century tycoons, you may draw from post-1917 Russia as many symbols to support *your* local struggle. After all, the owners of post-1917 Russia are a supermonopoly—initially it was *officially* called *state capitalism,* and only great Stalin had *state capitalism* called *socialism.* Anyway, look at the results: the speed at which that *railway* was constructed is simply phenomenal. This is what *real* capitalism does. Good hard efficient boys run business in Russia, and it is a pleasure to trade with them in computers for their rockets, or whatever.

Many scholars, journalists, statesmen of democracies see post-1917 Russia largely through the eyes of its owners and in terms of its owners' religion even though they may think it totally unacceptable in their own countries. The fact is that ignorant of the post-1917 war societies, most citizens of most democracies have been hoping again and again every few years since 1921 that their *diplomats* will "negotiate," "sign agreements," "build a lasting peace," and so on, with the *russians,* the *soviet people,* the *soviet union* (as they call the pseudo-tsar-god). Needless to say, this kind of *diplomacy* of democracies has been, since 1921, like *medicine* without knowledge of anatomy—quack medicine. And though every few years this becomes clear, most citizens of most democracies forget it, and the same building of a lasting peace is repeated by new demagogues, eager enough to act as quack peace-builders, much to the delight of the largely innocent electorate of their country. The bulk of scholarship, journalism, or perhaps even intelligence work of democracies, has been since 1921 a manichean adjunct of this *diplomacy.* As soon as the pseudo-tsar-god graciously smiled upon yet another Lloyd George to get something out of him and his democracy, thousands of Professor Carrs and expert Davieses would preempt whatever little demand there is in the mass media and whatever space is available in encyclopedias or academic studies in the smiled-upon democracy.

For Professor Carr's *History* no humans exist in Russia except the pseudo-tsar-god and his retainers. With them the *diplomats* will consort, dine and wine, and build a lasting peace. So why should Professor Carr know of anyone else in Russia? *They* are called in most Western newspapers, studies, reports, the "Russians," "the Soviet people," "the Soviet Union." So why should Professor Carr be interested in some hypothetical, invisible mutes?

But why do some verbal manicheans choose for verbal coparticipation, say, Hitler's Germany, while others Stalin's Russia, and still others Mao's China?

In the absence of the motivation to know, any motive may become decisive in a verbal manichean's choice of a war caste society to mythologize it in his struggle against his local *enemy*, such as the *establishment*, that is, all people who have succeeded while he has not, or that lady in the neighborhood who is against the children's grounds. In other words, individual motives become as untraceable as in the case of a fan's choice of a sports team or a hobby. However, certain statistical regularities can be observed.

Though a verbal manichean may be engaged in a purely verbal pastime glorifying death camps or torture chambers in the firm belief that *he* will never get into them, he usually projects himself mentally into the society with which he associates himself verbally. Would *he* be an aryan in that caste society or a pariah? Verbally, he may be horrified by the very word: caste. Behaviorally, he knows that there *are* castes in his chosen society, and though he may not want ever to live in any caste society, he mentally determines even in his purely verbal make-believe to what caste he would belong in the society which he mythologizes.

The ethnically Russian middle class was exterminated in Russia between 1917 and 1921. The ethnically *pure* Anglo-Saxon, *pure* French, or *pure* German middle class mostly cursed Russia as hell on earth, whereas many manicheans who were Jews hailed the holocaust as paradise on earth because *they* were to perish in it, while *we* were aryans. In today's democracy many intellectuals, artists, or scholars are at a rather low income and hence status level, compared with even skilled blue-collar workers, on whom so many tears were once shed by some of these same intellectuals, artists, and scholars. In the caste Russia of the early thirties some serf scientists, crucial for the growth of war capacity, writer-*writers* like Gorky, or ballet primas, were given a caste status next only to the *government* itself. At last the *intelligentsia* took its rightful place, well above all those vulgar dentists, greedy bankers and insolent crane operators. The manichean vision produced an explosion of verbal allegiance which has since lasted, though those manicheans who were Jews began to opt out as Jews began to be turned into pariahs in Russia. Today, the war caste society of China, a much less lenient and more closed serf ownership than that of Russia in the sixties, is the make-believe of some of these manicheans, for there are few Jews in China to reduce to pariahs and exterminate by gas or *heroic labor.*

On the other hand, when it was the turn of passport-Jews to become pariahs, many manicheans from among the Gentile middle class of democracies were displeased by "Jewish hysteria" merely spoiling the *trade with the russians.* The 1970 edition of Britannica says not a word in its article on post-1917 Russia about the *disappearance* of Jews (500, 5,000, 50,000 a day?) between 1948 and 1953, not to mention their ouster since then from all higher-status education or work. The "arrest of nine doctors" is still remembered in the West, and the article (signed by a professor of Oxford and the editorial board of the encyclopedia) falsifies the still lingering memory with superb skill:

Although much was made at the time of the fact that seven of the nine doctors were Jewish and though the revelations about the "plot" were accompanied by vigorous anti-Zionist propaganda, later events made it seem probable that the whole affair was part of an obscure internal struggle for power.

Not a word more. It was, you see, just anti-Zionist propaganda. Cannot a newspaper *criticize* those Zionists? My mother and all her Jewish colleagues were summarily fired. As Zionists, I suppose. Zionists were attacked in the streets with impunity. And concentration camps were quite ready for more than two million Zionists. Yet some hysterical Jews made much *at the time* of some doctors being Jewish. *At the time.* While *now* everyone can see that they were mistaken: "the whole affair" was simply "part of an obscure internal struggle for power." "Later events," you see, made this "seem probable." Not "made it probable," mind you, because the reader may then inquire *what* later events are meant (and none such exist). But "made it seem probable." It seems that it seems. The sentence (just as the whole article, and libraries of similar manichean stuff) is as mendacious (and/or ignorant) as great Stalin's *Pravda,* but what a scholarly subtlety, masterly pseudo-detachment, academic not-of-this-earthness.

It always seemed to me amusing to scan the list of world-famous philosophers, poets and scholars who were *friends* of Hitler's Germany. Not a single Jew! But why? Surely world perfection remains world perfection if a certain microscopic segment (one percent) of the population has been liquidated. You cannot make an omelette without breaking eggs, eh? Alas, world perfection is not world perfection, but its opposite, if *you* are a pariah—even if purely verbally.

But let us assume that Mr. Davies had no motives barring his knowledge of war caste societies. And here comes the preconceived image of history inherited from the nineteenth century and naturally permeating the twentieth-century democracies because they are an extension, success and triumph of nineteenth-century humanism. Many citizens of democracies will retort that I am simply unable to see the howling monstrous drawbacks of their societies. "Our erstwhile proletarians are now rich like noblemen or bourgeois of old, but what about the conservation of wild fowl life?" Or: "We have just landed man on the moon, while some people still stifle under bad housing conditions!" Exactly! This is the triumph of overall progress: it is the bitterest criticism that usually implies that the society has been making and/or is bound to make and/or ought to make overall progress. A very useful approach *inside* a democracy. The only trouble is that citizens of democracies tend to assume that overall progress is not a social program they have been realizing in their societies, but a certain universal natural law working for the best throughout history everywhere, including societies whose social realities have, behaviorally, nothing to do with the overall progress of nineteenth-century Europe, the Enlightenment, or even the Renaissance.

It is easy to trace the origin of the creed of spontaneous overall progress. The state "celestial religion" of "medieval societies" like pre-1861 Russia was hostile to sciences if only because life on earth was postulated to be a transient ordeal before life in heaven. Therefore, sciences and technologies flourished in freer countries such as Britain or France, and as a result the latter defeated Russia in 1855. Hence it came to be assumed that freedom, "progress in all fields," including military might, civilization, education, humaneness, refinement, intelligence all closely correlate. They all occur, advance, or do neither—always together.

It has been forgotten that the "state religion" of societies like post-1917 Russia is no longer celestial, but military-scientific-technological. Without any freedom at all, such societies can make stupendous progress in military-scientific-technological fields and no less stupendous regress in others, and their notion of civilization, education, intelligence may be entirely different, while humaneness or refinement may be considered harmful or criminal.

The creedal assumptions of overall progress have been built into the very languages of the West (and hence the modern world), so that it is sufficient just to express in conventional language any reality beyond democracies in order to turn it into a creedal myth.

The creed of global overall progress starts with the words *slave* and *slavery*. A slave wears a loincloth, and is always with that pickax of his. Why not a space suit, and not always with that slide rule of his? Overall progress: there is not much progress in dress (loincloth), and hence there is not much progress in social or civic relations (slavery), and hence there is not much progress in technology (pickax). Needless to say, those naked men in loincloths are *private* slaves. The word *private* is built into the words *slave* and *slavery*. Large-scale slavery cannot exist semantically because on reaching a sufficiently large scale the slave owner becomes semantically a *state*, and his slaves citizens.

The less humane a society is the less as a rule we know about it. Hence there is a chance for those who wish to do so to declare that the most closed and the least known societies like the China of the 1960s (anno domini) are the most perfect, a little less closed and hence a little better known societies like the Russia of the 1960s are a little less perfect, whereas open societies like the United States are clusters of horrors. "What about Sacco and Vanzetti?" an American on an exchange program here screamed in fury when I praised uncautiously the United States. Sacco and Vanzetti are remembered very well all over the world, half a century after the verdict of the jury in their case. Millions of times more information is available on the execution of the two Anarchists (and every phase of the seven-year struggle to reverse the verdict and the sentence) than on the torture and/or extermination of *all* Anarchists in Russia, and besides (shall I add such an obscure, barely remembered and perhaps apocryphal detail?) of ten, or twenty, or eighty million irrelevant civilians (not even the number is known accurately to within a million or ten million).

Similarly, we know in great detail how, about twenty-four centuries ago, Socrates might have easily evaded the death sentence, but would not, and how he might have fled, but would not hear of it, preferring to drink the hemlock—in front of his admirers, a month after being sentenced, and hence with a lot of publicity, to use a modern word. Meanwhile in China four-hundred-thousand anonymous humans who did not want to be heroes or stoics or saints or suicides were anyway beheaded without any ado, in an obscure little mishap (which the 1970 *Britannica* and some American histories do not even mention in their description of the wonderful achievements of the age of great Ch'in—no doubt in order not to revive the cold war). And perhaps those four-hundred-thousand people thought themselves lucky to have died so pleasantly, without any torture to speak of. And perhaps one is entitled not to mention the little obscure unpleasantness under great Ch'in, that is, Shih Huang Ti, because there is no *hard evidence* for it, and the number is not even known for sure.

Accordingly, at the word *slave* or *slavery*, Athens (or Rome) spring up in the minds of Joseph Davieses, and *slavery* there was *private*. Slaves were, say, prisoners of wars with barbarous tribes. As for Ch'in's China, certainly the enslaved native population were not *slaves* at all, but *subjects* or *citizens*, four hundred thousand of whom were simply inconvenienced by some Internal State Affair. The *league of nations* or the *united nations* or other institutionalized collective Joseph Davieses would goggle their collective kind eyes if asked to sympathize at least privately with four hundred thousand slaves so inconvenienced. Slaves? Slaves were in ancient Athens! No evil slave owner has ever killed four hundred thousand men! Only a Great State, a Superpower, a Leagued or United Nation has been equal to such a great, glorious, almost divine if secret Internal State Affair.

After *slavery* there was *serfdom* (*feudalism*), something that extended up to 1861 in Russia. Why *after* and not before or concurrently? There must be overall progress, and here it was.

Serfdom came about *after* that wicked *slavery* because it was more useful economically *and* more humane. Usefulness and humaneness just cannot go apart. But why was it more useful? Here Homer is quoted for perhaps the ten-thousandth time in the last one hundred years: "The lazy slave, unless compelled by his master's strict order . . ." See? Already Homer knew that the slave is lazy! He did. But he said unless. A free man may also be lazy. And how! Unless well paid. It is a moot point whose laziness is done away better: of a free man expecting to be well paid or of a slave afraid to be robbed of what he has, including his life or his painless death.

Naturally, just as the *slave* is a loin-clothed ancient, the *serf* is a medieval rustic with that wood-engraved face against the background of a harvested field. The latter symbol suggests that *serfdom* was *before* the *industrialization* in England, that is, *capitalism* (the name in which free enterprise is fused coparticipatively with a certain arbitrary level of technological progress). Actually, all the means of production or weapons that eighteenth-century *capitalism* produced in England were produced by special Industrial Possession Serfs in Russia, a process that might have safely continued uninterrupted up to this day. Modern war plants could be run as efficiently with, say, Negro slaves as cotton plantations once were. Slave cotton-growing in the southern states of America was *more* efficient than even comparative free farming. The Nazis attained within a year or two quite high efficiency with *foreign labor* despite all the war difficulties.

Also, was *serfdom* in the nineteenth century more *humane* than *slavery* in ancient Athens? It did not pay to grow *slaves* in ancient Athens, so they were mostly acquired from barbarian tribes. Or perhaps the process of human cattle-raising also disgusted free Athenians. In Russia, with its abundance of fertile land and natural resources, the *attached* were ordered to *have families*, and then *members of a family* could be sold, before 1838, separately, head by head, though they were native White Christians, just like the sellers and buyers. Is this more humane?

There was one difference, though. Nicholas I expressed his deep indignation at the fate of Negroes in the south of America. "But what about *his* country?" Serfs? What serfs? There had never been any serfs in Russia (nor capital punishment). There were *souls* (the name of serfs) or the *attached*. What had, indeed, been definitely achieved in twenty-three centuries since the Periclean Age in Athens was verbalism, the belief in names: if slaves are named souls, the country becomes paradise by definition.

But never mind: *after* serfdom there came, as more efficient *and* more humane, *and* more everything else, Capitalism and later Socialism, so that now they coexist. In both, overall progress reaches its peak, and one should really write *capitalism-socialism*, because the difference between the two is that "in the Soviet Union" (states the article "Capitalism" of the 1964 *Britannica*, assuming that post-1917 Russia incarnates *socialism,* of course) "teachers are plentiful, but automobiles are scarce, whereas the opposite condition prevails in the United States" (representing *capitalism*, no doubt). Since cars belong to "superficial private wants, artificially generated," it is clear that *socialism* is something like *capitalism,* only with more correct emphasis on the more fundamental needs of overall progress as against superficial private wants.

Automobiles have never been scarce in Russia since 1917, nor will they ever be. In 1918 Ulyanov-Lenin and all the people who *ought* to have cars had the world's best, most powerful, and most luxurious cars. In half a century, in 1968, the population was said *officially* to have bought 86,300 cars. The output of cars in 1968 could have been three times (or thirty times, or three hundred times) as big, but this is none of the *private* population's business: 111,700 cars were in fact exported in 1968 because such was the will and pleasure of those in possession-power. Given their will and pleasure, not a single car will ever be sold to the population (as Khrushchev threatened publicly).

But why were 86,300 cars sold graciously in 1968? Why not 8,630 or 863? As the authors of the *Britannica* articles will kindly notice, the figure constitutes about 1 percent of the annual sales of cars in the United States. Because about 1 percent of the population of Russia after 1917 has constituted (barring the irregularity of 1921 to 1928) a caste for which it is proper, moral, and necessary to buy new cars, just as it was proper, moral, and necessary for a very small percentage of the population under Russian eighteenth-century Absolutism to have horse-driven cars known as carriages. Within this percentage, the luxury of the carriage had to correspond to the rank. A low nobleman would not be able to drive in a seven-in-tandem even if he had all the money in the world to buy one.

Much more so, the upper 1 percent of Russia after 1917 divides into rigid subcastes. A low nobleman of the upper 1 percent cannot buy a 90-horsepower Chaika, let alone a 220-horsepower 3IL-111, no matter what money he has: when the film director Eisenstein, admired in the West, returned from the United States in the thirties, *commissar of foreign trade* Rozengolts took away the car he had bought abroad on grounds of its being *too* luxurious for him, but proper for the Old Bolshevik Rozengolts, and gave him instead a lower-class car. Quite noble, because all *private* cars were *requisitioned* in 1941 without any compensation ever and cozily found new owners. A still lower nobleman can buy a 27-horsepower four-cylinder air-cooled-engine Zaporozhets, which is rather at the level of the dawn of car building.

Like a suit, a car will last indefinitely, but when it becomes twenty or thirty or forty years old, it is not allowed to turn up in Moscow and other cities which foreigners visit (just as poorly dressed passers-by will be immediately apprehended): it goes to lower-caste localities and there thrives on, owing to which another 3 or 4 percent of still lower castes own cast-offs, these 3 or 4 percent being mostly the aura of the upper castes: what was called in the Russia of the Middle Ages *shlyakhta*—neither rankers nor entirely common serfs.

As for the latter, they fared worse after 1917 in this respect as well than at any time throughout the Russian or West European Middle Ages: after 1928 they were forbidden to have a horse and a cart—for the first time in Russian or West European history. A certain inconvenience (quite superficial no doubt!) that all common serfs have been experiencing as a result for forty-odd years since then was described by *Pravda* in 1935 in this way:

Ivanova lagged behind in her work because she was pregnant and sick with malaria. Ignoring this, the teamleader Efremov displayed her name on the blackboard. Upset, the collective farmer mustered her last strength, fulfilled the quota, but fell sick with overstrain. In the morning Ivanova requested that she be given a horse to go to the hospital. The chairman of the collective farm Karandayev turned down her request. Ivanova walked on foot. Her overstrained organism could not take the new strain, and Ivanova died.

It can be argued that only 86,300 cars were sold to the population in 1968 because when the Weimar Republic in Germany in 1929 was weak, divided, defenseless, the pseudo-tsar-god of serf caste Russia had to set himself the aim of producing in twelve years at least ten times as many tanks as Germany; and when it became clear in 1943 that it all was over with Germany, the pseudo-tsar-god naturally wanted to produce in a while ten times as many tanks as all Western Europe, the United States and Japan combined; and there was also the due turn of producing ten times as many rockets, submarines, aircraft carriers and all that. Given such fundamental needs, the superficial wants like cars have not yet been taken care of as of 1968, considering the relative youth of the automotive industry. But surely the horse (and cart) did not originate as a mass transport in the 1920s? The point is that except for the upper 1 percent caste and its aura, the population should have no cars, horses, helicopters, camels, ships, and so forth because, first, their remuneration since 1928 has been so low that they might use these means of transportation to carry goods and passengers and make thus many times more money than they get from the *state*; second, they will become too mobile for attachment; and third, they will rise in general above their proper station in life.

The imagery of spontaneous, universal, overall progress is so deeply ingrained that if my narrative reaches still extant democracies in, say, 1996, some scholars there will no doubt note above all that *more* cars are sold by the owners of caste Russia to the population in 1996 than in 1968, should more cars be indeed sold or at least *reported* to be sold. See? Overall progress. As though the well-being of the serfs since 1918 had depended not on the current pseudo-tsar-god's ego, but on a certain providential, universal, natural law of overall progress. As though most serfs had not been better off in 1926 than in 1953. As though they could not be worse off in 1996 than in 1968 *and* 1953, not to mention 1926 or 1913.

As for teachers, allegedly as scarce in the United States as cars are here, it is perhaps relevant that as the *Britannica* edition of 1964 went to press, there were 494,514 teachers in higher education in the United States, while the *country of socialism* even *plans* for 1974 fewer "teachers in higher education" than the United States already had in 1964. But this arithmetic license of *Britannica,* evidently quite all right in new brave scholarship, is not the point. The point is: what is *taught* by *teachers*?

In the United States, 334,000 students are studying engineering at this writing. The number in the *country of socialism* is almost seven times as large, and they have never been intended for the production of too many cars, to be sure. Probably less than one-tenth of these American engineers will work in military fields, whereas at least nine-tenths of these *socialist* engineers will work in arms and *means of production*, and thus the ratio is 1:60 at least. Since the overall number of students in the United States is larger than in the *country of socialism,* this ratio means that in the fields which the owners of serf caste Russia consider to be useless for war (building and maintenance of cars, training of lawyers for *private* cases, growing of flowers, asparagus or anything beyond the seven edibles of the *ideal norm*) the number of students, apprentices or trainees is infinitesimal compared with that of the United States. Besides, the *socialist* pay in the *socialist* production of *socialist* arms and *means of production* is much higher than in the fields satisfying superficial private wants (such as a commoner's insane whim to ride in a car or a cart), and so only rejects or statistical small numbers are left over for the latter fields.

In other words, from early childhood the entire program of *teaching* since 1928 has been intended to train all human property (with rare exceptions like those suitable to be musicians and other performers to tour foreign countries) into human arms and human *means of production*, with due reliance on serf medicine (care for the bodies of the serfs) and *propaganda* (care for their souls). No time to be lost. Though a few *higher schools* are still called "universities," *higher education* is not at all university education in the Western or old Russian sense: if a *student* is to be an engineer in a *means of production* called tractors, he will not be allowed to waste an hour on anything but what he should know to make tractors, plus the study of tanks to make him a human weapon simultaneously, plus a subject which is the religion of possession-power.

The *teaching* of this religion is to inculcate into every *student's* mind a view of the universe, mankind, and history as uniform, closed, and ruthless as, say, the faith of the Inquisition at its worst, except that the latter guarded the cannons of heaven: Giordano Bruno and Galileo were not persecuted for the as-sertion that one way of farming is better than another, while *socialism* or scientism or whatever one calls it is a religion of earth, and hence all the heresies to be eradicated are concerned with earth, down to its last petty trivia at which the gloomiest bigot of a heavenly creed at any time in history would just laugh.

We can now return to the good, honest, capable American lawyer, expert on Russia, Ambassador Joseph Davies, strolling with his charming wife in Moscow when? In 1921, 1957, or 1996—what does it matter?

Moscow February 18, 1937
The city of Moscow looks much like any other European city, with red and green traffic lights, large motor buses. . . .

If he saw at least some loincloths. Or at least noticed some rustics with wood-engraved faces being dragged into museumlike buildings full of those medieval machines showing through the lancet windows. Then he might have given some credence to those nightmarish rumors he had heard. But look—red and green traffic lights! For God's sake, he is way, way *after* Serfdom, he is well into Capitalism-Socialism, that is, the Socialist, more modern part of Capitalism-Socialism which differs from the other by plentiful teachers and scarce cars, and some savants say that both differences are only for the better.

Besides, Mr. Davies knows that in every twentieth-century democracy millions of people have been screaming about the dungeons they have been thrown into for their convictions, third degree, torture, genocide, slavery, the Dark Ages, massacre, slaughter, serfdom, insanity, cannibalism, concentration camps, and whatever they can think of. But certainly these are just figures of speech. Figuratively speaking, Ulyanov-Lenin was thrown into a dungeon in which molten metal was poured down his throat, yet he shouted his symbol of faith. But in our modern prosaic civilized reality, in our time, in our Capitalism-Socialism, or just Capitalism, even in *tsarist* Russia, it was not molten metal, but *his* brand of mineral water which he ordered and sipped with pleasure.

The other day I read an American lady's statement that "women are slaves" in the United States and "every woman is raped every day." For example, this American lady was raped by her father (this means that her father pampered her and did not treat her like a boy), and she was raped by her college (this means that her education was inadequate, in her opinion). The American lady, to make her statements more forceful, or colorful, or memorable, says that she is raped every day to mean that her fine sensibilities are affected every day—for example, by poignant memories of inadequacy of her education. In this way, the lady believes, she fights in particular against rapists (though if anything she helps them by devaluating the notion of rape to zero). Why cannot all citizens of every democracy use the same method with respect to everything? Why not call anything that seems to you unpleasant or wrong the death of all enslaved mankind—or still better, of all life in the universe —under torture? Deafened from childhood by millions of such lusty screams, multiplied millionfold by all the techniques of mass media, Mr. Davies cannot perhaps even grasp words like "torture." They have no meaning for him since childhood, they are no more true or real than "hell" in the phrase "What the hell," and at the best, they are phony and stupid affectations.

And as Mr. Davies strolls around Moscow, a prosaic civilized twentieth-century Capitalist-Socialist telegram is being sent all over the country. It is coded, but some telegrams are coded everywhere, aren't they? Besides, even if decoded, it would be found to contain nothing ajar with our good modern civilized Socialism-Capitalism with traffic lights and all. It would be found to contain an odd term, "physical influence." But surely Mr. Davies has heard of "physical therapy" in his American bourgeois medicine back home? This is also a medical term: "physical influence."

The Central Committee of the All-Union Communist Party (of Bolsheviks) makes it clear that the application of the methods of physical influence in the practice of the People's Commissariat of Internal Affairs is permissible in accordance with a decision of the Central Committee of the All-Union Communist Party (of Bolsheviks).

So Mr. Davies strolls with his charming wife about Moscow with traffic lights and all, and even makes a special note of one very handsome building. The fourth floor has neat curtained windows, but behind them? Nothing unusual again. A medical department. Only—what is medicine?

Medicine is what its clients want it to be. In the country of Mr. Davies, he, paying his fee as a patient, is the client. But here those in possession-power are the clients. Not only the clients, but also the owners of medicine, including all the medical personnel. So they will have such medical fields, medical arts and sciences, as *they* want, and these fields will all make stupendous progress in the direction they like. What fields do they want?

One field will be just like the medicine to which Mr. Davies is accustomed, except that it will be lavished free on the upper caste in which the individual patient's life, health, welfare, and happiness are all-important.

Quite another medicine will be concerned with low common serfs. Here the principle is to produce the greatest possible number of the most productive serfs as human *means of production* at the cheapest price. The individual's aversion, horror, pain, and death are of no importance: from the early thirties and at least up to the mid-fifties not a single cost-involving attempt was made to alleviate the birth pain of more than 99 percent of women in confinement: it was declared that *soviet* women gave birth without pain because they had been properly lectured on there being no birth pain. Teeth were treated and pulled without pain too (and without lecturing!), and the news that a sufficiently prosperous common Muscovite could go to a newly opened *cost-accounting outpatient clinic*, pay the full price of his treatment, and have his tooth pulled *really* without pain was a sensation even in Moscow in the fifties.

But these are all more or less open fields, some of them similar to medicine and others to veterinary sciences in democracies— at least as veterinary sciences were practiced before the prevention of cruelty to animals became part of overall progress in democracies. But the owning clients naturally wish other, closed, *special* arts and sciences to make no less stupendous progress, and these branches of *special* medicine may be totally nonexistent in democracies.

For example, why should not the owning clients want a branch of *special* medicine like *physical influence* to make stupendous progress compared with the Middle Ages when there existed only a pitiful rudimentary unscientific effort at physical influence called, naïvely enough, torture? The study subject of physinfluence—the production of maximum vast-scale inquisitional, motivational, and obliterative results of physinfluence per unit cost—is as challenging to a scientific mind and lends itself as well to stupendous progress as, say, ordinary, bourgeois dentistry in the country of Mr. Davies.

Speaking of dentistry, *special* dentistry may also flourish and develop as part of physinfluence, and this is what was behind those neat curtains of the fourth floor .of the building that Ambassador Davies especially admired. Most human beings like their health, right? Improvement of their health fills them with hope, joy, pride. Therefore, the opposite process—*medical* destruction of their teeth, for example—must fill them with as much *special* horror (quite apart from a *special* pain). If medical improvement of health is a motive, then medical destruction of health is also a motive, only negative. People can be motivated by the (top secret) horror of *special* medical destruction of their teeth perhaps much more than by the hope of *bourgeois* improvement of their teeth.

Of course, a *special* patient may not like *special* treatment. But he is not the client, you know. It is not for him to judge. Next he will judge whether he is mentally sick or sane, and how his sick mind should be treated! It is for the *specialist* to judge, and the *specialist* is owned by his client. Should the owning client want it, all medical personnel, except for small or small small numbers, will be made *special* medical personnel in some *special* medicine. To make stupendous progress, a breakthrough, a revolution in the field.

There has been stupendous progress all right *under socialism*, but it is not the overall progress of democracies, and how could it be? It is stupendous progress in an entirely different direction —in entirely different fields sometimes, and it is perhaps unpleasant for Mr. Davies even to surmise that such fields exist, must exist, are bound to exist outside the good, kind, safe world of Mr. Davies, and no one of his world can really know what is behind those neat civilized twentieth-century curtains right in Moscow. Not to mention millions of square miles which a foreigner's foot has never trod since 1921.

Serfdom and slavery (the only difference being the absence of progeny in the latter case) have proved to combine magnificently with all the sciences, technologies, and industries which were thought to be the privilege of a certain allegedly universal post-feudal, civilized, humane society, stage, or era. Having borrowed these sciences, technologies, and industries, serfdom-slavery has moreover patronized as client the stupendous progress of such *special* branches and scions of these sciences, technologies, and industries, or indeed of such new sciences, technologies, and industries, as have been lying dormant or unknown in the democracies because there has been no client even to surmise their possibility.

Mr. Davies still assumes that since sciences and technologies originated in the comparative freedom, safety and humaneness of Western Europe, their principal evolution is bound to be forever the creation of new ways of making man's life more secure, wealthy, and enjoyable. Though the issue was clearly foreseen in the trite expression "the Hun with an engineer's brain" which was applied to Germany in 1915, Mr. Davies does not want to understand that once these sciences and technologies have been assimilated by a serf caste society their principal evolution will be the creation of new ways of increasing the pseudo-tsar-god's military might intensively (within the *border*) and extensively (beyond it), of owing his human and other property to his best military and other advantages, and of acquiring new serfs or satraps from among freemen or his enemy's serfs for the survival-victory-glory of his own royal-divine ego and his upper caste according to rank.

Suffice it to *visualize the radiant vistas* of *special* physiology or *special* psychiatry for serf- and slave-ownership. Before the twentieth century slaves or serfs fought for their external freedom. Now the owners have penetrated inside their organisms and in particular inside their brains. They can interfere in their pre-natal state, regulate secretly their hormones (by, say, adding certain substances to the *bread* on which the owners have the absolute monopoly of production and sale), and *treat* them secretly and openly as part of general *preventive medicine* for all commoners, or *special* medicine for individual cases. General and *special* physiologists, psychiatrists, chemists, electronics specialists and so on can develop techniques of owning serfs and slaves much more efficiently, safely and cheaply than ever before, yet with all *hard evidence* obliterated much more reliably and cheaply again.

Does serfdom-slavery look like a twentieth-century democracy, with traffic lights, large motor buses, neat curtains, and all? Of course. For presenting that appearance is also one of the *special* sciences, technologies, or industries that have been making stupendous progress in that society.

48

Having neutralized to some extent the nineteenth-century imagery of overall progress in the mind of Mr. Davies, who personifies to a certain degree each of us and even whole institutions of democracies, we can contemplate more soberly the enserfment and enslavement of Russia after 1917 not as a certain romantic or sentimental figure of speech, or a certain temporary misunderstanding, or a fleeting nightmare in the overall progress of mankind, but as a civilization as socially real (rooted as it is socially, in the millennia of history all over the globe, and perhaps even ultimately for millennia to come) as the society of Mr. Davies, which is a bold pioneer effort, a humane thrilling and precarious experiment, with very frail, ambiguous, and uncertain antecedents anywhere before the eighteenth century.

In his infinite omniscience, pseudo-tsar-god II was pleased to decide that slaves in his caste society must constitute about one-tenth of the population, and serfs the other nine-tenths. This proportion he thought to be the most useful for the production of arms and *means of production* and hence for military might. "But this is not useful because this is immoral and godless: already Homer said . . ." Sh-sh-sh, dear Mr. Davies. What is immoral and godless may and can be useful. On the scale of the seizure of a bank and on the scale of the seizure of the globe. Perhaps it would be even more useful to have nine-tenths slaves and one-tenth serfs. But pseudo-tsar-god II was himself a person of pre-1917 Russia: he had heard about the uprisings of slaves in Rome, and he feared them, though slavery in Rome was essentially *private*, and that is why it got into nineteenth-century histories in the first place. With a *state*—that is, country-scale—system of slave ownership, equipped by *special* sciences and techniques making stupendous progress, no such private mishaps would be possible. Great Stalin was also something of a Mr. Davies, compared with, say, his Chinese followers perhaps.

The one-tenth, the slaves, was not to have progeny (the progeny that they might have had in their previous lives as serfs were taken care of as any other human property or were converted to slavery on reaching the age of twelve). The food of this one-tenth was (except for the few unique mental slaves) below the *ideal norm*, or rather the *ideal norm* was to be the highest motivational reward a manual slave could reach (in its motivational intensity it was something like becoming a millionaire in a twentieth-century democracy). All the less sturdy, persevering, or lucky were to die out more quickly, the average lifespan after the conversion into slavery being about eight years.

Why only eight years? Why not use a slave for a longer time? At the beginning of the nineteenth century, even a nobleman on the shady side of thirty was called an "old man." A village serf woman past thirty in post-1928 Russia often looks like a woman past sixty in a democracy. For slavery the *average* life of eight years after the conversion into slavery, usually not earlier than in the late teens, is not a short lifespan at all! Perhaps it is the optimum in terms of costs, considering that it is average, that is, that those who are old, sick, or weak, may die within a month, and the strongest, healthiest, and toughest will live much longer than eight years, while the few unique mental slaves may have, quite cheaply, an even longer life-span than in a twentieth-century democracy, since they will be safely guarded against suicide, accidents, illnesses, or disorders in their health.

Naturally, as punishment a slave may be sent one infernal tier lower—to a shorter-life span enclosure. And so on, down the spiral of the secret hell on earth, until its lowest tiers of physinfluence where the chance to commit suicide is the paradisal bliss.

In other words, the motivation is negative: first everything is taken away from a slave down to the remotest chance of painless death, and then the loot is returned to him as motivational rewards. First he is infinitely happy to be able to die painlessly or commit suicide, which is absolutely denied by a branch of *special* medicine called physical influence (and this alone shows how progressive and indeed revolutionary it is compared with its crude, pathetic, obsolete predecessor called torture—like a TU jet airliner-bomber compared with horse and cart). Then the next infinite reward to him is his life. The motivational rewards of mental slaves include even some delicacies over and above the *ideal norm* (as I have described earlier, using the world-known aircraft designer Tupolev and his slave, or *special*, designing office as an example) because the brain needs more delicate food than the brawn, or perhaps this is also the influence of just another nineteenth-century prejudice.

Slaves can often be used more effectively than serfs: for example, the new Moscow *state university*, a delight of foreigners, was built by slaves because huge masses of manpower had to be moved into a small space. If common serfs had been employed, they would have required more space and would have crawled all over Moscow, and their horrible aspect would have frightened higher-born Muscovites—not to mention foreigners. Slaves, however, could be moved very neatly in enclosures, concealed from everyone and yielding maximum manpower per unit space.

There has never been since 1918 a hard and fast line between slaves and serfs. Practically anyone could always be *mobilized into the army* and kept there indefinitely without a single leave. In the forties experiments were made to desexualize the *soldiers* by pills or injections—to have as many sexless *heroes of battle* as long as the pseudo-tsar-god would need (another challenging yet useful and promising field of *special* medicine). Slaves are enclosed (and hence their official name: the *enclosed*), whereas serfs are attached (the attached). But if a serf is attached to a remote unisexual territory (say, all women, because men have all managed to escape elsewhere or were all *mobilized* and thence disappeared) the line of demarcation is blurred. "You live very well," those attached to some villages are reported to have said as they were turned into slaves, to slave in *labor camps* for the rest of their lives. "You eat bread every day."

How were serfs to be converted into slaves, in great Stalin's design? In many twentieth-century sciences and technologies there are processes called sifting, separation, selection, and so on. The processes are statistical, not individual. Similarly, serfs were to be sifted, separated, selected all the time, to isolate a certain percentage of less infinitely devoted or valuable or desirable than the remainder. What percentage? The slaves die out in eight years, right? So to replenish them the serfs must yield for slavery about one-tenth of their numbers in eight years or slightly more than 1 percent annually. If it is desirable to have, besides, say, the annual 1 percent serf population growth. The birth rate of serfs can easily be boosted by rewards for birth to allow for the serf depletion owing to the desired serf-into-slave conversion.

The overall conversion target was to be conveyed over the network of physical influence, extermination, and serf-into-slave conversion so that each station could meet its local target.

It would be very silly for some serf, whether in 1918, 1937, or 1996, to exclaim: "What for? I am more infinitely devoted than anyone else!" It would be the same as for a molecule in a scientist's chemical separation, or a microbe in his biological selection, or a grain in his sifting, to exclaim that the process is all wrong. Of course, it may be wrong individually, but the owners are naturally interested in their human property as a whole, and not in some human molecules, microbes, or grains. That particular serf may well be individually more infinitely devoted than anyone else. But statistically, there is a higher probability of his being less devoted than the other 99 percent: it was by accident that he fell into the 1 percent group expected to be less infinitely devoted than the other 99 percent. Individual desirable molecules, innocuous microbes, or sufficiently good grains inevitably occur in such processes among undesirable molecules, harmful microbes, or chaff. The same with tiny, usually invisible beings called serfs. But on the whole the serf property gets better and purer, and there is a higher chance that the right serfs are consigned to slavery and extinction than if that annual 1 percent were selected at random.

When a citizen of a democracy buys or owns something, he wants quality in that which he owns. Similarly, the pseudo-tsar-god wanted quality in that which he owned. He was to press the button, and his one-sixth of the inhabited globe was to obey with perfect sensitivity. He sustained a certain loss in the process of purification, but surely the *quality* of his property was worth it.

Naturally, the process was to be carried out through a pyramid of chiefs down to the local overseers, and these would inevitably settle their personal scores with the local serfs and not only fulfill the purest scientific principles of the process in the interest of the pseudo tsar-god. But this is inevitable. There are five thousand *districts* in the country. Not only the chiefs of each district, but even the smaller overseers inside each district, like the *chairman of the collective farm* (the overseer of serfs on a latifundium), naturally tend to convert each tiny bailiwick into their own tiny satrapy to be used for their own benefit.

In the late forties the *chairmen of collective farms* were ordered to select a certain percentage of their *collective farmers* to be turned into slaves. The order was to select less infinitely heroic and/or less infinitely devoted (looking unhappy, and all that) *toilers of socialist agriculture.* Now what did the female chairman do on the *collective farm* where I later lived? Men were very scarce at that time, and she would turn into slaves (immediately sent away into some mines thousands of miles away and practically forever) those who refused to become her lovers.

But then an order or *law* or instruction from the Metropolis is often distorted locally beyond recognition, and *Pravda* reported in 1935 with metropolitan indignation an even more bizarre distortion. The order-slogan was: "Develop the Shock Workers' Movement in Pig Breeding." And in a *district* near Sverdlovsk they rushed to fulfill the order:

The chairman of the collective farm Lebedev and the manager of the pigsty Chernykh encouraged the feeding of pigs by the breast of the collective farmer Votinova. They passed the feeding of pigs by a woman's breast for a manifestation of the shock workers' movement. They bragged about this at a Plenary Meeting of the Verkhosluinsk Rural Soviet and at a District Rally of Collective Farmers chaired by the head of the District Land Department, member of the Party, Uglov.

The five thousand bailiwicks (*districts*) have been wrapped since 1918 in their own real nightmares, mostly unknown, inconceivable and unimaginable in the *central* cities or foreign-exhibition areas. But all local abuses, perversions, or blunders aside, the conversion into slavery was to follow certain rules established by the *center*, similar to the rules of extermination or separation of harmful molecules, microbes, organic particles, plants, insects, domestic animals, and such. And serfs could take into account these rules, too, to keep out of slavery just as in a democracy one follows certain rules of hygiene not to catch a disease in an epidemic, though no one can, of course, guarantee anyone's immunity. If *your* group is pronounced to be pariahs, you are at the epicenter of the epidemic. Commit suicide while there is time. Or they will *arrest* you before you do.

The life of even a common serf was, in great Stalin's design, to be protected, though caste was to be important, of course. At one time a commoner who killed a commoner was *sentenced* to a term of slavery from which he emerged in three or four years sometimes, owing to his *shock work*. While a commoner who had killed even the lowest chief was *officially* shot. On the other hand, the life of a slave was, in great Stalin's design, to be entirely unprotected: a slave was to be just like any (usually *private*) slave that a citizen of a democracy knows from history, yet he was also a sexual or any other chattel of not just one person, but of the whole hierarchy of slave overseers in a network of slave areas spread over one-sixth of the inhabited globe, as well as of other slaves—stronger, younger, healthier, or united into supercriminal gangs. If Europe and America has its underworld, the underworld of Russia after 1918 has, accordingly, its underunderworld. Two Russian supercriminals persuade a pal of theirs to run away with them in order to cannibalize him during the escape.

In *state*, that is, mega-scale, slavery, the individual slaves cease to be even individual dogs or pigs or draft horses as they are likely to be in *private* (small-scale) slavery. It is only the maximum output of the whole machine of millions of slaves per minimum input (mainly of food below the *ideal norm*) that is important, while not only individual human animals, but thousands of them, become microscopic, invisible, and meaningless as they are mutilated, raped, or worked to death. The procedure of slave ownership becomes a huge transcontinental "machine of natural torture" chewing up humans, millions of whom are perhaps already too mad or too subhuman to throw themselves on the high-voltage wire or pretend to attempt to escape and be shot or torn up by dogs.

However, unless a serf is a low commoner used to famines, fuel shortages, and work for sheer physical survival, he must be *transformed* psychically for the conversion into slavery. And so in addition to the inquisitional, motivational, and obliterative uses of physical influence, here was to come its fourth use: transformatory. A serf may have had a high rank. He has lived outwardly like a citizen of a democracy, and though he has taken orders from his owner with infinite devotion like any other serf, his way of life has made him believe, with Ambassador Davies, that he lives in a certain era of overall progress, definitely proved by his own high rank. "And this is in the twentieth century!" he is likely to say as though there can be no ruthless slavery in the twentieth century, what with traffic lights, his high rank, and all. Not that any serious part of the program of *physical influence* should be used on him. But during his *confession* he must also realize that he is a filthy, guilty, pitiful microbe who should be happy to live henceforth as a slave. There must be what the engineer Skorutto called a *transformation.*

As for the serfs, four-fifths of the population were, in great Stalin's design, common low serfs hovering around the *ideal norm* (by the data as of the mid-fifties, suddenly revealed owing to the struggle of pseudo-tsar-god III against the more direct heirs to pseudo-tsar-god II). The higher one-fifth of the population, was to receive motivational rewards above the *ideal norm* to stimulate its outstanding manual or mental contribution to arms or *means of production* and/or its infinite devotion to its owner. The monthly pay of the lower end of this upper one-fifth bought in the sixties one Italian $1.40 raincoat, and the monthly pay of the upper end of this upper one-fifth minus the very highest superaryan 1 percent bought from one to three $1.40 raincoats.

At the three-$1.40-raincoats-for-a-monthly-pay point there began the very highest superaryan 1 percent with its income curve rising precipitously and then, somewhere within 1 percent of 1 percent, zooming into infinity when approaching the pseudo-tsar-god himself, owning the natural and human wealth of former Russia and her satrapies.

Common doctors, engineers, scientists and so on were to be at the upper end of the upper one-fifth, without yet entering the very highest 1 percent. In the sixties their monthly pay bought two $1.40 raincoats at the beginning of their career, and three at the end of it (to stimulate them throughout their career) unless they became high-ranking doctors—say, doctors treating the highest 1 percent—and then their pay swept upward with this 1 percent.

When I say: "In the sixties their monthly pay bought two $1.40 raincoats" I mean a certain average price of the fabulous "bologna raincoat" for the sixties. Actually, in the early sixties the monthly pay of a *common* doctor or engineer bought only *one* such raincoat, which is, basically, a kind of big shopping bag of some transparent plastic, cut as a coat. But as the sixties roared on, the owners of former Russia kept decreasing the price since this item of exquisite luxury has been intended for the higher castes, those above the *ideal norm*, and these have finally been saturated by bologna raincoats. Therefore, in the seventies the role of bologna raincoats will evidently be taken over by $1.90 "automatic foldable umbrellas," and as these saturate the higher castes, another item of exquisite luxury for the higher castes will come to the fore in the eighties.

A foreigner who visited Moscow and other foreign-visiting cities in 1968 said abroad that the young girls of Moscow were dressed better than those in America. He did not know then that thirty-four years before *Pravda* announced that according to the London *Times* the population of Moscow looked better than the "population of any other European capital as of the end of the summer of 1934." *Pravda* announced the same in 1922, and in 1996, the news will be as fresh no doubt.

True enough, since the daughter of a Moscow rank-and-file doctor buys that $1.40 raincoat for half of her father's monthly salary, she cherishes it as the daughter of an American doctor would cherish something a thousand times more expensive. As for a $1.40 raincoat, this American lady would, in the sixties, rather don a picturesque (and perhaps quite expensive) bleached and patched pauper's attire, to distinguish herself from what she preceives as (vulgar) middle-class, or for some other reasons (the children of the rich landlords in Russia at the beginning of the nineteenth century wanted to be Gypsies, African Corsairs, or Spanish guerrilleros because they were "stifling in the conventions of civilization, and especially the high society of St. Petersburg").

Sheer trained or even untrained muscular strength and stamina may get its possessor within the highest 1 percent. In some fields as in *sports* or in mining it is worthwhile to institute higher-than-three-$1.40-raincoats-a-month prizes, to attract all the outstanding muscular strength and stamina in the country. Thus, since the early thirties manual (and often mental) work has been a contest of stamina and strength for survival, the breaking of records for life, the chasing after quotas the owners keep increasing for the same pay. Those who can do it become champions, record-breakers, prizefighters in their work, and those who cannot are eliminated from the contest of life much as aspirants are eliminated from sports in a democracy.

Fabulous wealth, that is, incomes comparable to the American worker's wages, starts within fractions of 1 percent of 1 percent of the population. All *members of the union of writers of the ussr* constitute about one-quarter of 1 percent of 1 percent of the population, but only perhaps 1 percent of this one-quarter of 1 percent of 1 percent of the population have incomes comparable to the American worker's wages, though compared to the sea of low serfdom below they are nobles, aryans, humans of a different race.

Several thousand such prizes also exist for world-unique scientists, inventors, designers, and others indispensable for weapons and *means of production*. Unique performers (such as musicians) who can successfully tour foreign countries get similar prizes. In pre-1861 Russia skilled musicians, artists, craftsmen and other gifted serfs were permitted to go off to make more money and pay a higher *métayage* tribute in cash to the owner; so, too, in the sixties serf musicians and other gifted serfs began to go abroad more often, and up to nine-tenths of the money they earn is taken away from them, of course, but even the one-tenth that remains or whatever they manage to conceal is enough to put them very high within the richest one per cent: at a par with world-unique scientists or designers indispensable for weapons and *means of production.*

In other words, the income curve in a democracy or even in a semiconstitutional monarchy like Russia before 1917 tends to be egg-shaped: its middle part tends to pouch. After 1917 and again 1928 the income or rather upkeep-and-prize curve was to be shaped like a precipitously tapering water-spout rising from a sea of general serf destitution undulating near the *ideal norm*, with sea deeps of slavery down below, invisible and impenetrable. The spout-shaped curve may motivate serfs or slaves much more strongly than the egg-shaped curve may motivate citizens, with an enormous saving of money. Just as in a lottery it does not matter if very few high prizes are awarded as long as the few offered are high enough. Such a lottery may exert a stronger attraction than a lottery in which a far larger sum is distributed in more numerous but more moderate prizes—certainly so in a country where there are no statistics, and the serf populace relies on pure visions of some serfs much richer than they are, without knowing how small their numbers are and how low their own chance is.

For example, all common *medical personnel*, that is, the *medical personnel* taking care of common serfs attached to common *district medical institutions*, was divided in 1935 into 26 main *categories of pay*. *Pravda* did not report the lowest, 26th, pay (in the table the place is a blank; the figure must have been removed right before press). The next lowest, 25th, pay was 60 rubles. Strictly speaking, each *category of pay* was divided into subcategories, and each subcategory into subsubcategories. Thus, 60 rubles constituted the pay of the 3d subsubcategory of the 2d subcategory of the 25th category of common *medical personnel*. The pay of the 1st subcategory of the 1st category of *medical personnel* for commoners was 750 rubles, that is, 12.5 times as high.

Thus, the pay range is essentially not smaller than in the United States between, say, the pay of a young nurse at the start of her career and that of an average doctor for median-income people. But what an enormous saving of money!

To begin with, the whole pay scale of these 26 pay categories is shifted downward compared with its "counterpart" in the United States by a factor of one thousand or so.

From another no less triumphant *Pravda* article of about the same time we learn that two pounds and a half of potatoes were henceforth to cost only 0.4 rubles at *state* prices in some areas privileged enough to be supplied with this luxury. Since everything—even the rye bread of the *ideal norm*—was priced out of the pay of this *medical worker* of the 25th category (perhaps because her owners did not yet know how to make *bread* out of starch and other non-grain synthetic or cheaper-than-grain products), she was to subsist on potatoes only. If she spent all her pay on potatoes and nothing else, her pay would not be sufficient to buy enough potatoes for herself and one dependent, even according to Strumilin's *ideal norm*. But did not Strumilin warn against overindulgence in potatoes?

As for all the other needs except potatoes, what are these? She can live in hospital barracks free of charge, and if she falls sick, another such nurse will take care, so that it will cost next to nothing unless she falls seriously ill, and then, of course, only nature is to blame.

Quite a few economists of the cozy sheltered wealthy islands called democracies have been doing the following calculation. At a corner store, where an economist's wife buys their food, a pound of potatoes (say, Select California Baking Potatoes in a dainty nylon bag) is quite expensive (almost twice as expensive as canned asparagus weight for weight). So the economist takes this price and calculates in dollars the value of potatoes which that *medical worker* of the 25th pay category consumes. To his satisfaction, he finds that this value in dollars, indeed, exceeds the value of his diet, never to mention the fact that he has also to pay his rent or his doctor's bills, while she receives all this free.

A slave of antiquity in Egypt or China can be proved exactly in the same way to have been better off than an American professor of economics today. The only disadvantage of the slave was that he had to eat either figs (in Egypt) *or* rice (in China) every day, while an American professor of economics can choose at any point of the globe from millions of ways of satisfying his superficial (artificially generated?) wants, *including* Egyptian figs *and* Chinese rice *and* Select California Baking Potatoes in a dainty nylon bag *and* asparagus at 60¢ a can *and* an apartment wherever he stays *and* a doctor he likes *and* a dirigible *and* a horse—*and* sturgeon with horseradish (the latter phrase denoting in Russian the extreme end of conceivable human whims).

Insipid monotony, which is so nice in social or economic studies for *others*, is a slave's and serf's disadvantage. There was a Chinese torture: drops of water falling on the victim's shaven head. He would go mad from sheer monotony. The value of the dripping water in dollars may be found to exceed the value of the running water an American professor of economics consumes when he takes a shower, and the professor's only advantage is that *he* chooses that water to flow just as *he* wishes and when *he* cares to satisfy precisely this superficial want or whim or fad of his.

What I mean to say is simply that it is about a thousand times cheaper to sustain a *medical worker* on potatoes, often wet or half-rotten and coming from nearby fields, than to pay her the initial pay of a medical nurse in the United States and provide her with all the variety the pay implies. Yet the motivational interval for common *medical personnel* will be roughly the same as for the medical personnel of ordinary medical institutions for ordinary people in the United States.

But it is not only the shift downward of the whole scale of pay that yields an enormous saving.

A large number of doctors can become in the United States "average doctors," while to get the same differential compared with the *medical worker* of the 25th pay category a serf doctor in the serf supermonopoly must become, say, the *director of a hospital* with more than 500 beds in a city or an *industrial settlement*, and obviously there can be much fewer such directors than "average doctors" in the United States. The hierarchy is, structurally, an eighteenth-century serf army, with such *directors* corresponding approximately to colonels. And the same hierarchy as in *medical personnel* is in every department, with the only difference that the range of, say, *special medical personnel* will be all raised somewhat as a whole. The pyramid of possession-power is a set of such open and secret serf-army hierarchies all converging at the apex and each relying on its local network chiefs at the bottom.

The *director of a hospital* for 500 beds, the equivalent of a colonel, belongs to the 1st out of the 26 pay categories dealing with commoners. But above him there begin, more secretly, the higher ranks up to the marshals and chief marshals of medicine, so to speak, and though their remuneration may be hundreds of times higher than the pay of that *medical worker* of the 25th category, the overall cost will not be too large because there are many fewer chief marshals or even marshals than soldiers in the army—at least in the eighteenth-century serf army.

A single serf supermonopoly may vary incomes (that is, up-keeps and prizes) in cash and in kind, depending on the military importance of weapons and *means of production*, so that all the human talent, intelligence, and skill as well as the best natural resources will go into the militarily most important activity, then the militarily second most important activity, and so on. Finally, what is of no earthly military use may go into, say, the production of civilian buttons, which are necessary in a way because humans find it difficult to do without buttons, nor can they indefinitely use the buttons sewn on before 1928 or before 1917. Many such productions have been allowed to employ only chronically ill people, too sick to be trusted with any more important work. If a mental patient is violent, he is a *first-group* invalid, but if he is still able to make buttons, he is a *second-* or *third-group* invalid who can and must work in such *easier* productions. In the mid-fifties buttons on sale even in Moscow were produced out of a material dimly resembling asphalt, and they swelled in the sun, bulging and warping. But must one go into the sun? Is not going into the sun a superficial private want again, artificially generated? Evidently, the asphaltlike material was a waste product that could not be used by any production of weapons and *means of production*.

Besides, the *means of production* cannot produce weapons and *means of production* every day all around the clock. There is inevitable idle time. For example, it was decided that trans-atlantic bombers were not necessary any longer in such quantities, but more global rocketry should be built instead. The *means of production* could not switch over to global rocketry overnight. And a lot of sheet aluminum was left over. To keep the *means of production* busy, a real abundance of aluminum saucepans was made, at least for Moscow. The highest estate territory, Moscow, has been so spoiled in this respect that the Muscovites now want not aluminum but *enamel* saucepans! Do they expect that nuclear submarines will be made out of enamel and then scrapped? To enliven its program, the Moscow television studio announced in summer that those who would put on winter coats and come first to the studio would get a prize of enamel saucepans. The studio barely survived as coated crowds converged as in a city uprising, but the real disaster was that foreign correspondents got wind of the event and reported it under titles like: "Forty Thousand Muscovites to Get a Saucepan." They rather missed the point: an *enamel* saucepan.

Aluminum saucepans or whatever the common serfs have accumulated since 1928 have been made as an evitable by-product of the production of weapons and *means of production*: inevitable idle time, idle equipment, idle personnel, rejects, waste, and such. The only exceptions perhaps are the Newspaper, Radio Set, and Television Set, which are not mere superficial wants like *enamel* saucepans, but the means by which the one and only *propaganda* is inculcated into every mind.

By setting all the prices of all goods and services and introducing special moneys and passes for secret or known *closed stores* and *supply networks* of different ranks, the serf supermonopoly may force the serfs of any estate to accept any consumption pattern. The serfs are attached and cannot move to live elsewhere. If some food, no matter how obnoxious it tastes, can be produced even more cheaply than rye on which *private* serfdom once thrived, all the other foods, including rye bread, can be priced out of the reach of the estate. Rye bread, which was the cheapest food at the time Strumilin drew his *ideal norm*, is evidently not such any longer. Bread is a certain porous structure, and obviously it is possible to produce such a structure with the aid of chemistry out of starch made out of wood waste products, or God knows what else. If vodka is produced for commoners entirely out of sawdust, certainly starch is no problem. Each caste gets *bread* of a different top-secret content and has to eat it, because a local serf can, theoretically, visit Moscow in the daytime (provided he is properly dressed and will only stay for 72 hours), but how can he travel there for his daily bread if the journey from his caste may cost a fortune and last many days? And since it may be as difficult for a foreigner to penetrate into this caste and take a sample of bread for analysis as to get a certain part of a nuclear rocket, the *bread* for this caste may well be all so cheap to produce that a pre-1861 serf owner would have wept out of envy and anger and Strumilin would have revolutionized his *ideal norm* way back in 1921 (and here is yet another *special* science, technology, and industry: the growth of human livestock by forcing it to eat the cheapest synthetics made out of military waste products).

49

Pseudo-tsar-god II could not very well announce in 1928 that he wanted to have ten times as many tanks as Germany so that he could acquire Germany in the autumn of 1941. Even the word "acquire" is dangerous for a pseudo-tsar-god to use. Did anyone acquire the Baltic countries in 1940, or the same again in 1945 plus Eastern Europe, or Czechoslovakia once again in 1968? Simply, the people of Germany would have established in the autumn of 1941 the regime they wanted. Just as more than one hundred nations of Russia did from 1917 to 1922. Pseudo-tsar-god II had been fighting for peace ever since 1918 when he was a modest disciple of great Lenin. I remember the utter surprise of even ordinary Russians when Hitler declared war on the United States. Did the man go mad and imagine himself a medieval knight? Declare not war, but peace, when you attack a democracy. Throw on them more tons of peace propaganda than of explosives. Even when the one last fighting citizen of a democracy remains, surrounded by numberless tank divisions, shower him with (Picasso) paper doves, and continue to fight for peace even more vigorously when subjugating the conquered population by extermination, torture, and conversion into slavery.

International *peace*, also called *detente*, also called *friendship*, has been the natural export version of domestic *soviet democracy*, *genuine humanism*, *real equality*. It is when more serfs

began in 1937 to disappear each month into the infernal unknown than throughout the sway of the Inquisition of all time
in all countries that the serfs' play at *unprecedented freedom*, the
world's most democratic elections, the *most extensive human
rights granted by the most democratic constitution* reached its
all-time peak. Naturally, the more sudden, perfidious, and sweeping military attack has been prepared or realized ever since the
military attack on Russian democracy in the autumn of 1917,
the more it has been dissimulated into a fervent *fight for peace*
as part of spontaneous overall dissimulation, often done quite
automatically, even before any use or need of dissimulation becomes clear.

The World's First Standard-Bearer of Peace (an official appellation of great Stalin) was so eager to beat all swords into
plowshares, and all tanks into tractors! And the great pacifist
Henry Ford could well help him to construct *tractor*-building
plants almost with good kind tears in his good kind eyes. Good
kind Uncle Joe! He wanted tractors, and the Industrialization
in general (just like the Industrialization in such democracies
as the United States) in order to provide, in his Industrial and
then post-Industrial society, all that healthy, varied, inspiring
food like 60¢ cans of asparagus instead of the average Russian's
monotonous diet of 1913 and 1927.

There were some tiny suspicious signs. To produce bourgeois
asparagus (or proletarian cabbage, or peasant cucumbers) one
needed garden tractors. But great Stalin was always interested
in large standard field tractors only. Because they produced
grain, the main element of the *ideal norm*, prior to the discovery
of synthetic starch. And because one could not *extend fraternal
help to* Czechoslovakia even in 1968 with these puny fanciful
garden tractors. Besides, one *enemy of peace (reactionary, fascist)* calculated that as of 1934 the number of horses in the
country had decreased by 18,900,000 since 1919. And the
tractors in 1935 had only a total of 6,500,000 horsepower. So
the big tractor-instead-of-horse frenzy could not be caused by
the pseudo-tsar-god's sudden yearning to make his serfs' diets
more nutritious, varied, and sophisticated, than they were in
1927 and 1913.

In fact the *means of production* making large standard field tractors are twice *means of production*: they make standard field tractors producing grain as the main element of the *ideal norm*, and they produce—tanks!

Like all undertakings of 1929, the production of double *means of production* had originated in 1918 to 1922 and had been simply lying dormant for a while. In 1922 *Pravda* carried an article "Big Air Fleet":

In contrast to the old weapons, the air fleet is a commercially expedient, profitable undertaking in peace, and serves the cause of culture, while in war it fulfills its combat mission.

In other words, bombers and such have since been built, and some of them have been transporting people and cargo because some people and some cargo have to be transported as human and mechanical weapons and *means of production* anyway, at least by horses, which are also quite expensive to keep. This temporary use of bombers "serves the cause of culture," rejoices the eyes of many citizens abroad who see for themselves pursuits so peaceful, and keeps the human and mechanical weapons well in training.

So aircraft- or tractor/tank-building plants are double *means of production*. Specialized garden tractors for the production of asparagus are no *means of production* at all because asparagus, an exquisite companion of Roman villas, belongs to those billions of various and varying superficial private wants, artificially generated, and commoners should have no such wants. Meanwhile, for the highest aryan 1 percent, or 1 percent of 1 percent, it can be imported in cans, and for 1 percent of 1 percent (including statesmen, intellectuals, and clergymen of democracies as its guests) it can be grown by hand on *special farms*. For the 23rd *party congress* in 1966, canned asparagus and other such goods were bought abroad to satisfy the superficial private wants, artificially generated, of the representatives of *communist, workers', national-democratic, and left-wing-socialist parties of eighty-six countries of all continents of the globe*, but they did not eat all of the asparagus, perhaps because most of them *live under capitalism* and are quite choosy, and so the leftovers were sold to common Muscovites *on open sale* for *soviet* money. I bought a can with delight and gratitude, because before 1953 such leftovers would have been destroyed in top secrecy rather than used to indulge and spoil even Muscovites. A *congress* of all benefactors of mankind like that may not occur too soon again. Once it did not occur for twenty-three years, and it is by no means certain that such leftovers will be sold *on open sale* even in Moscow in another twenty-three years.

Special ponds were dug up to breed some world-unique species of fish for the cuisine of pseudo-tsar-god II. His was a *special* personal or private economy, stinting no effort or cost to meet the most superficial personal wants, artificially generated by the richest throughout the millennia, and aided by agents who procured all over the world whatever could not be created in that *special* economy. Nevertheless he was even more modest than pseudo-tsar-god I, and *all progressive mankind* described his self-sacrificial asceticism.

Barring these caste rewards, the cheapest best *means of production*, human or otherwise, must produce the cheapest best weapons (human or otherwise) and/or *means of production* (human or otherwise).

Medical personnel is a *means of production* as long as it is used to ensure the cheapest growth of manpower used as a *means of production* or as human weapons (military manpower). *Teaching-training personnel* is a *means of production* as long as it is used to train human *means of production* or human weapons (military manpower). Part of teaching-training is, of course, the *upbringing of our people in the spirit of infinite devotion to our,* etc. For human *means of production* and human weapons must be as infinitely devoted to the pseudo-divine operator of the war machine-universe as all the other *means of production* and weapons are in their infinite monolithic reinforced-concrete devotion.

But it was not all at once that great Stalin *created* a social formation, a civilization, a world, so self-consistent and self-contained. I italicize the word *created* because if all progress in, say, engineering for six thousand years were destroyed in any country today, haulage of heavy loads over runners greased by fat (or *combifat?*) would be *created*, since a sufficient residue of knowledge would remain in some minds to reinvent the technique used six thousand years ago. Similarly, the destruction of all social progress (which may be accompanied very well with stupendous progress in sciences, for example) leads to the *creation* of what existed socially long ago. Anyway, it was not all at once, in 1929, that all the social prewheel runners were *created* and greased by social combifat. There were difficulties.

As I have said, more than 40 million were privately employed or self-employed in 1927/1928, while only 7 million were employed by those in possession-power. As soon as the possession-power paid less or displeased their employees in any other way, they would drift away to join those 40 million.

It was necessary first of all to deprive the farmers of their land as a source of employment and self-employment. Accordingly, it was announced that land was the Means of Production whereby farmhands were exploited. But what about those farmers who hired no farmhands but worked themselves on this Means of Production? No answer was given, but I suppose it can be said that they exploited themselves via this Means of Production: if a *marxist* usually knows better than the employees themselves that they are exploited by their employers, clearly similar care should be exercised with respect to those who are exploited by themselves unbeknown to themselves. Liberate them all from the pernicious privately controlled Means of Production.

In the summer of 1917 *Pravda* called the *bolsheviks'* intention to *nationalize* or *socialize* land the "biggest lie slandering socialism":

> This is the biggest lie slandering socialism. No socialist ever proposed to take the property (that is, "insist on the renouncement of all proprietary rights") of "dozens of millions," i.e., petty and middle farmers.
> Nothing of the kind!
> All socialists have always spurned such nonsense.

Once in possession-power, *Pravda* resumed the "biggest lie slandering socialism" and "such nonsense," and carried in 1918 an article entitled: "Again About Kulaks." The *kulak* is the same with respect to farmers as the bourjuy (or bourjuin) with respect to urban owners of any kind, or the kike (or kikin) with respect to Jews. It implies that *the* (successful private) farmer is a criminal, a looter, swindler, usurer—and a scoundrel (greedy, coarse, treacherous), and when one says: the "liquidation of kulakdom as a class" it is as vague as the "liberation of mankind from Judendum" which Marx proclaims in the conclusion of his (first) *greatest discovery*: anything can be meant, from a moral appeal to *the* Enemy to stop being evil down to death of *physical influence*. Anyway, *Pravda* reprinted the following letter from a local scene:

In the village Nikolskoye there are more than 10,000 inhabitants. There was an intention to organize the Committee of the Poor, and then? There were only eight or ten poor people in the whole village, and the kulaks took advantage of the fact in order to avoid control by the organization of the poor. "Here we do not have many poor, and as to these men we will give them a just share of land, grain, and cattle, and establish their equality." I do not know how the Extraordinary Commission of Samara has managed to make short work of these 9,990 kulaks wishing to avoid the control.

Pravda criticized the letter: should the *organs of state security* make short work of the 99.9 percent of the farmers, who would feed the country? *Pravda* explained that (some) of those Kulaks were not real Kulaks but had only been made by real Kulaks to look like real Kulaks by letting them be as rich as real Kulaks.

To act as benefactor, the kulak usurer lets his victim keep a horse and a cow on purpose, in order to make the victim work more and suck more out of him.

Only the real Kulak, the real Enemy, *the* Enemy, must be liquidated, and not those farmers who had been made by the Enemy to look like the Enemy.

Yet even this restricted extirpation of the Enemy was not to be realized, because the famine, caused partly or largely by this struggle against the evil in *the* farmer, had assumed such scope that soon only the population of the Kremlin, including Bukharin's numberless pets, could survive owing to the stores of infinite love they had accumulated inside (at the worst Bukharin's pets could subsist on caviar). And so in 1921 the criminals and scoundrels transformed, by aryan-pariah conversion magic, into *productive farmers*. For seven years the *propaganda* was proud of these productive farmers some of whom did better than the best farmers of Iowa, in the United States, and published their photographs and biographies. Then in 1928, the record-breaking productive farmers transformed back into criminals and scoundrels after seven years of their record-breaking productive activity.

Besides, land, cattle and everything had to be anyway taken from all farmers because their plots were so *tiny* (as great Stalin said) that the tractor had no room to turn in, and certainly we must use tractors and not those backward humiliating horses (which would make no tanks, besides). At school we were to imagine the picture: a *tiny* plot, the size of a tractor or less, and the poor tractor cannot even budge. No chance for the progress of farming as in America or Japan!

Even today a "typical corn-belt farm" in the United States is 200 acres, according to the 1970 edition of the *Britannica*. In Japan, where 80 percent of the working population was engaged in farming early in the century, the average farm holding even today is about 2½ acres, and more than half of the farmers cultivate units even smaller. Whereas the land allotment (for a family of ten) in Russia in 1921 was 86 acres, according to *Pravda*.

No, great Stalin could not conceive of economic progress as in America or Japan with *tiny* 86-acre plots. He had to *collectivize* them. Into his own single country-scale superlatifundium.

In 1928, *Pravda* carried great Stalin's interview, containing a table which indicated that in 1913 the landlords sold 47 percent of their grain, while the smallest landowners only 14.7 percent. Great Stalin would become the one and only superlandlord and would have more grain to sell. Why and how? Either by making the production of grain more efficient, as it was more efficient among the landlords in 1913, or by taking more from his farmhands working on his superlatifundium. The former alternative was out of the question, of course, as was clear from a specialist's article *Pravda* published in 1928 when the decision to loot all the farmers of all they had been acquiring since 1861 was still in mid-balance. The article, titled "Concerning Cavalry Attacks on the Economy," stated that even the 5 percent of farms that were collective farms in 1928 would be efficient only in ten to twenty years. That was a very benign estimate because they have not become efficient in forty years. The estimate was so benign perhaps because the specialist was already risking his head, for this is how he started his article:

In our article we will be perfectly truthful and impartial. To shout: "Happy to do my best, sir!" and be anything but happy at the prospect is perhaps either folly or crime.

The honest specialist did not understand that the owner of the vast serf superlatifundium can always get a lot out of his serfs if he wants to, even if the productivity falls back to the Middle Ages. Ivan the Terrible, Peter I, Catherine II, and all those landlords of their day—where did they get whole new cities like St. Petersburg, all the money for wars, the world's best picture galleries, unique treasures, huge palaces, lavish fetes, vast parks, and all that?

And why not be the superlandlord? Way back, in 1918, *Pravda* wrote:

What about hired labor, exploitation?
And again a socialist will ask: But just who hires, who exploits? It will turn out again that the Soviet power hires, the Soviet power exploits.

No cause for worry. Of course, in a democracy this might lead to trouble: a certain party *nationalizes* some enterprises because they belonged to *privateers*. The productivity decreases, the wages go down, and the employees of the enterprises begin to shout that they are underpaid and exploited. "For God's sake," the party pleads, "*we* cannot exploit you, only *they*, the wicked, can." But the employees do not listen, and the party is kicked out by an armed force or in an election until its next chance or round.

Here there was no cause for worry: the *soviet power* exploits. That is, great Stalin, now the latifundium superlandlord (and not only the supermonopoly capitalist and the housing superlandlord), exploits. Not some Catherine II, or some Labor Party in Britain, or some *kulak*.

Pravda began a *campaign* demonstrating that the *kulak*'s exploitation may be invisible, but this is only because it is demonically skillful and thus imperceptible.

Though it looks as if there is no exploitation in this case, Citizen Lapshin can exploit so skillfully and imperceptibly that this exploitation is invisible. I will give examples.

The examples are terrifying, such as:

For one bag of potatoes which Lapshin offers to the poor in the spring, they reap for him one day or two. Potatoes here cost 0.8 to 1 ruble a bag, and two days of work pay 2 rubles. So this means 100 percent of profit.

Pravda was right: the *kulak's* exploitation *was* invisible. To begin with, the pay of that kulak-exploited farmhand bought from that kulak in spring in 1929 at least 10 times more potatoes than did the pay of the *medical worker* of the 25th category at great Stalin's state store in 1935. But this is irrelevant because the *soviet power* does exploit, according to *Pravda*, and the more it exploits the better this is, perhaps, for the exploited. Something else is interesting about the kulak's exploitation. A farmhand may reap for that kulak one day and get for his work a bag of potatoes in the spring, says *Pravda*. So according to *Pravda* (and first-grade arithmetic), the kulak does not make a single kopeck when he gives a bag of potatoes for one day of work.

Nor was this demoniacal exploitation *the* Kulak's only crime. The Kulak also hated bitterly *the* Jew. "From where could the anti-Semitic mood come into the working class?" asked *Pravda* in 1929. Answered *Pravda*: from *the* Kulak. Among the five highest top rankers as of 1918, including Ulyanov-Lenin, only Bukharin's parents and grandparents were Russian. And he was for *the* Kulak. And here he was going down. Savvy? For the last time Jews were elevated to the highest aryan peak to use up as many of them as possible for the extermination of the new pariahs—kulaks—and then to parade them as propaganda against Nazi Germany, and *then* to bring *them* down to the caste of pariahs.

The *state* pogrom of Russian farmers by the *organs of state security*, armed forces, and all who would or had to give a hand was under way. The same agent provocateur's technique as in the school of *daring* of 1917 to 1922 was used. When farmers began to be robbed of their property, including land, they began to resist. (Incidentally, those economists all over the globe who hail the welfare of one group gained by looting another would behave in the same way if *their* salaries, savings, homes, cars and everything else began to be taken away from them.)

Aha! Those kulaks are attacking perfidiously, in countless

ruthless numbers armed to the teeth, *us*, peaceful heroic idealists who want to do them good by liberating them of all those means of production by which they exploit themselves and each other. Look what is happening at a sugar refinery in Kiev, according to *Pravda*!

Anti-Semitism became especially acute when kulaks ceased to be hired. Things went to such lengths that the hoodlums locked a Jewish worker inside a cabin filled with sulfuric gas.

Obviously, those hoodlums are *kulaks*. Even more obviously, these *kulaks* took revenge on a Jew. Most obviously, these *kulaks* are *the* Kulak. *The* Kulak is killing *us* by gas! Set his villages on fire! Crush, rob, ruin, shoot *the* Kulak!

The agent provocateur's game is quite exciting. No social group is homogeneous: even if six million say: "Let us surrender," six out of six million will resist. "Aha, *they* are attacking *us*!" More of them are killed as hostages. This evokes more resistance, and finally there is an all-out massacre. More than half of the country's population or 99.9 percent of farmers could well be exterminated or turned into slaves, but great Stalin wrote his article "Dizziness from Success" and stopped the dizzying success at a reasonable percentage that could be compensated by a higher birth rate within a reasonable time. There were lots of loose ends, such as millions of waifs who flew way out like fledglings from destroyed nests, but all that could be cleaned up in time. And the remaining serfs?

As an example of serfdom, that is *private* serfdom, in Eastern Europe, the 1970 Britannica edition indicates that a serf peasant in fifteenth-century Poland was to labor four days a week for his master (*corvée*). As of the mid-twentieth century, a serf on the superlatifundium on the territory of Russia had to work seven days a week as *corvée* for his superlandlord. The superlatifundium was divided into local units called, quite wittily, *collective farms*. Whatever a serf produced on the *collective farm* by dint of seven-days-a-week work was either *procured* free or *purchased* at an arbitrary price.

In *private* serfdom there was a bonus for *corvée*. The landlord would not pay for a serf's work on his land, but would give him some present or token pay. The superlandlord Stalin would not lag behind his *private* colleagues. The *chairman of the collective farm* "Twelfth Year of the October Revolution," Smolensk Region, reminisced in 1963, at the peak of lenience:

I came in August when the results of the year were obvious. They were: the average yield of cereals about 5 centners per hectare; 10 kopecks, that is, one kopeck of today, per work-day. Having done the obligatory 200 work-days, the collective farmer could earn 2 rubles, in today's money.

So it would have taken him only 30 years to buy one $1.40 raincoat of that transparent bologna plastic. How the superlandlord spoiled his beloved serfs. What a generous *corvée* bonus. Only 30 years of diligent *corvée*—and here you get a present. A mere 30 years of hardest work for $1.40.

Work-days? It sounds like a day's work, right? Actually, it is a *quota* you are *supposed* to fulfill within a day, and if you have to work for 14 hours, from dawn to dawn, to cope with that *quota*, who except God (or Dialectical Matter) is to blame for your inadequacy? According to Strumilin's *ideal norm*, only a mature healthy male is entitled to its maximum. While the *quotas* know of no sexist or other such discriminatory distinctions: total equality. Do your *obligatory* 200 work-days each year, and in some 30 years, here you are: $1.40. Not that the rascal received $1.40. Instead, he received *state*-loan *bonds* which would then be *cancelled*. Nothing like *state* serfdom!

Also, in private serf ownership it was usually either *corvée* or *métayage*, a serf's cultivation of a plot of land for a share of its yield. At school we read *Eugene Onegin*: that Eugene Onegin, about a hundred years before our birth,

> Light *métayage* he introduced
> Instead of the *corvée* of old,
> And blessed his destiny the slave.

Instead. The superlandlord wanted both: *corvée* for seven days a week *and* largest *métayage* possible: if a serf had the last hen, keeping it near the cottage, let him sell the last hen. According to Khrushchev's *secret report* of 1956:

Moreover, during our work on the project Stalin suggested raising by 40 billion rubles the tax which the collective farms and collective farmers paid; in his opinion, the peasants were prosperous and a collective farmer had merely to sell an extra hen to pay the entire tax.

But where exactly could a serf keep that hen to sell it and contribute to 40 billion rubles in *métayage*?

Would you believe that in his infinite kindness the superlandlord permitted the *happy collective farmer* to fence off a spot of land at his hut? Just a spot, known as *personal plot,* to plant potatoes (which need not be transported in this case) because without this infinite kindness all the *happy collective farmers* would have died of hunger some forty years ago, and who would then do *corvée* and *métayage*?

However, the size of the *personal plot* has since been an agonizing problem. If it is too small the rascal will die, and hence will be unable to do either *corvée* or *métayage*, and if it is too large the rascal will snatch more hours from *corvée* in order to put these hours into his *personal plot*. How big then must that *personal plot* be?

Before 1917, and indeed, as early as the close of the nineteenth century, great Lenin discovered that while about half of the Russian peasants had much land, about half of them were real paupers in this respect: they had only 13.23 acres per household, on the average.

Today's Great *Soviet Encyclopaedia* says about those paupers of old:

This pauper's plot of land . . . doomed the millions of the peasantry to hunger.

However, among these paupers, great Lenin discovered superpaupers: about three million poorest households who owned only 8.37 acres of land apiece.

Today the personal plot is no bigger than one-eighth of the superpauper's plot. Yet for forty years this one-eighth of the superpauper's plot of *tsarist Russia* has been a source of agony to the superlandlords: the serf would pay too much attention to it at the expense of *corvée*, and it is very difficult to make sure that a *métayage* levy on his *personal plot* stripped him down to the *ideal norm*. The hens could not be hidden, of course, and here the sharp vision of pseudo-tsar-god II and his hosts of overseers pinpointed the last hen to be sold for *métayage*. But what about carrots, for example? The scalawag would tell the overseer that he had potatoes sown only, while actually he had also sown carrots which he would sell at a high price to the rich city dwellers who would rent his cottage for the summer.

It would be a good thing to take away those *personal plots* at last. But according to a specialized economic magazine, as of 1964 these one-eighths of the superpauper's plot yielded, for example, 60 percent of potatoes produced in the country and 73 percent of all eggs. For four decades before 1917, all the revolutionaries, including great Lenin, of course, kept assuring the Russian farmers that they could not live off the pauper's, not to mention the superpauper's, plot of land, and must take land by force from those who owned more of it, or they would starve to death. And for four decades since the early thirties, not only all the farmers, but many city dwellers as well, have been living off the one-eighths of the superpauper's plot of *tsarist* Russia.

As of the mid-twentieth century the solution was to leave this fraction of the superpauper's plot to the villain and even permit him to sell the produce off his plot, at city markets, capitalist and bourgeois as the very word "market" is. But if he did not do 200 work-days of *corvée,* send him as a slave down the spiral of the secret hell on earth.

Now, if the pseudo-tsar-god was to become the one and only superlandlord in farming, surely he was to become the one and only supercapitalist in all urban activities. To begin with, all those urban capitalists who had kindly been allowed to save the country from famine and increase the real wages and salaries of urban dwellers tenfold, up to the level of 1913, had made some money in the process, eh? And surely that money had been obtained by swindle-robbery, for what else is capitalism? Therefore, they should all be arrested, and here is where the inquisitional use of physinfluence came in: they all would tell where all the savings and valuables were hidden. They all would now cough up whatever they had saved since 1921, or perhaps before too, for full measure.

Then all who hired no one (but exploited themselves) went the way of all (*soviet*) flesh, and then a curious problem originated that would interest any *economist,* really interested in the subtlest aspects of his earthly religion.

The gentle reader is sure to remember my friend's father who turned his father's suit, wore it, and gave it to his son, who turned it again and became quite fashionable owing to its still quite vivid green color? He has been a *member of the moviemakers' union* since the thirties. So you will not send him away as a *parasite* to work as a farmhand: he has been attached, he has been *working*. And yet suppose—oh, I know this is horrible, but strange criminal designs do come into some heads. Suppose that while working officially as scriptwriter merely for safety, he makes shoes and—sells them! But how can he—without machines, assistants, skill, talent, experience? The point is that since the prices set for nearly all goods are usually many times higher, with respect to the pay of about 99 percent of the population, than they were in the Middle Ages, it will pay to make any of these goods at a level of productivity even below that of the Middle Ages and sell them below the set prices.

But why should *he* do it, a scriptwriter? As everywhere, in the *moviemakers' union* there is one generalissimo of moviemaking, several marshals, and so on, while its soldiers like my friend's father are often below the level of prosperity of a cleaning woman in Moscow. Yet they are usually more inclined, perhaps, than cleaning women to have visions of, and even pretensions to, being as rich, elegant, and free with money as their few fabulously rich colleagues, a common case in the artistic world in general. Besides, in the mid-fifties an illicit brothel, a free, not closed brothel, a brothel, so to speak, for *every* Muscovite of any rank who had money, was rumored to have opened in Moscow as an illegal, secret, yet a large, sound, luxurious institution, and the scriptwriters excited each other with tales about that apocryphal brothel (in truth, the tales were drawn from the sexlore of the beginning of the century). Typically, the scriptwriters would say with pathetic professional briskness that a patron who could *make a whole flower* (the girls lying in a circle with their bodies petallike, as every professional knows) had all his money refunded and received a share of the losing bets against him. My friend's father, a thin-faced, nervous, badly stammering wisp of humanity, could hardly be expected to prove equal to such a chivalrous venture. But sometimes he would inadvertently let his golden tooth gleam as he contemplated the exploit. That tooth was different: it belonged to a successful Moscow scriptwriter of the thirties (his movie theme was the Victory of the Soviet

Power in the Ukraine)—a well-groomed, pampered-ladies' man. The tooth clamored for the money to accomplish that insanely chivalrous flower exploit. Such was the genesis of the crime: he began making shoes.

At this writing, if a suspect's premises are searched and the searching party finds several self-made shoes or, still worse, what the *Britannica* article "Capitalism" calls the *means of production* (as signs of exploitation), this is as sufficient to sentence the suspect as would be so many corpses, with the blood spattered all over the murderer.

Unless severely checked, about 99 percent of the population would abandon itself to primitive medieval shoemaking and other such medieval crimes and vices. To fight ubiquitous myriads of crimes and vices, a special countrywide network of secret *economic* police (OBHSS) has been created, in addition to the countrywide network of *organs of state security,* the *militia* (rather like ordinary police as applied to caste society), and other countrywide networks of overseers.

At the height of his heinous crime of self-exploitation the scriptwriter's second wife, with whom he had quarreled, perhaps in anticipation of his insanely chivalrous exploits, told someone about the crime, and that someone allegedly denounced him or threatened to denounce him as a revenge for something.

An amateur criminal as he was, he tried in panic to dismember the corpses—especially those shoes which were only half-made— and to disperse them all over Moscow, among his distant relatives mostly: he hoped that the alarm was false and he would get them all back and resume his heinous but irresistibly lucrative crime.

50

Pseudo-tsar-god II destroyed that subtle tissue of millions of interdependent and intertwining neurons of industries and services that have been developing in each European country, including Russia, since the Middle Ages owing to a certain twilight of freedom that lingered in every European society even under the worst European Absolutism. He deindustrialized, decooperated, and asocialized Russia for the sake of all-out serf militarization under euphonic European names like Industrialization, Collectivization, Fight for Peace on Earth, and so on. A farmer growing a certain fancy variety of asparagus, a writer engaged in subtle probing of human nature, a fishmonger hurrying to deliver this night's cod for dinner tables, a banker extending a loan, a greengrocer buying that particular variety of asparagus from a farmer, an independent scholar studying history, and all such others exchanging the results of their skill, art, knowledge, and experience at every inhabited point of Europe, once including Russia, were henceforth all criminals or criminal gangs to be tracked down by the OBHSS, the *organs of state security*, the ordinary police, and other networks of overseers.

Great Lenin and great Stalin destroyed not only the European legal, civic, political framework of Russia, but also her European socioeconomic fabric much more thoroughly than the invasion of the Mongol nomads did in the thirteenth century. When Professor Carr in his multivolume *History* still glorifies great Stalin for his Westernization, and not only Industrialization of Russia (or Fight for Peace on Earth?), the esteemed professor is seeing the neatly reversed multivolume mirage of what has happened.

Not that the human (Oriental? Jewish?) criminality of the *westernized* population of Russia has ever stopped its incessant secret war against this *westernization.* More new curbs were imposed, more new secret loopholes opened, and more new curbs were imposed to close these loopholes. The serfs, though attached for life to a territorial caste, would change *state* jobs frantically within the caste. Why on earth? Can any *state* job be bad in any respect?

I remember that our *domworker* Polya would take me across the square, along the Sadovaya Ring past the high stone fence of Yusupov's palace (Prince Yusupov who assassinated Rasputin). At the end of the high fence there were basement windows which shot out an invisible acrid chemical cloud. Some passers-by knew of it and gave it a wide berth, while others walked into its midst and darted out as though scalded by steam.

"Polya," I would say. "Just wait." I felt that I could not involve the women, especially the ever despairing Polya. Holding my breath I would run and dive like a diver wishing to see the life of underwater creatures. Quavering in the hot vapors was an ocher-walled basement with a round aperture in the floor and creatures mixing some concoction with wooden spades. They must have been as different from me as fish are to have survived.

Every passer-by understood that no human being could exist for long in that basement. But the creatures in that basement were not the local chief's property. He was only an overseer. So *he* didn't care. They came, perished, and came again, with somewhat different names and faces. Should the chief care, he was only a low-ranking serf himself, doing the bidding of someone above him, and so on. To get a fan which had not, perhaps, even been *planned for production,* they would have to apply way up, almost to the pseudo-tsar-god! In his infinite kindness the pseudo-tsar-god personally approved the paradise-on-earth designs of all candy wrappers. Yet the contemplation of such candy wrappers was pleasant—that was the bright, nice, cheerful side of his possession-power—while some ugly ventilator might spoil his mood, causing all the supplicants, all the way down to the local chief, to suffer.

In 1928 *Pravda* carried a speech of Tomsky, the *chairman of the all-union council of trade unions*. Yes: *trade unions*. A big serf ownership can afford the luxury of mass serf theatricalizations, simulating any institutions of any democracy, from the *world's most democratic general election* to *street demonstrations, meetings* or *press of (all) working people*. So the *leader* of all *trade unions* in the country said, according to *Pravda*:

It is no secret that there are cases when the labor protection agencies and the trade union call for the installation of ingenious ventilators in factory premises with smashed windows that allow a wind to blow in everywhere.

Not enough ventilation for them from smashed windows! But while smashed windows sometimes produce a strong and indeed violent draft (quite wholesome for sweating workers), it is also true that sometimes there is no draft at all, while the industrial vapors and gases continue to be produced. But can the *leader of the trade unions* be so finicky? What in hell do those hoity-toity workers want? A strong draft: they catch pneumonia! No draft: they get poisoned!

In this field we have the least of science and the most of philanthropy. We must, in our labor protection work, put an end to this philanthropy and Manilov's daydreaming.

Manilov was a *private* serf owner in Gogol's *Dead Souls,* and Gogol ridiculed him in particular for his spineless lenience toward his serfs.

Surely the ban of women's work on night shifts is conducive to their ouster from production? Adolescents are also being ousted out of production owing to obscure age restrictions.

To oust not only women (helpless widows) but also children (defenseless orphans) from factories ventilated only too well by wind. To prevent them from working at such factories for wages established by great Stalin, his comrade Tomsky, and all the others. How Tomsky's *trade-union* heart must have ached (until he was kindly suicided).

Anyway, a man, a woman, or an adolescent may not like a

state job in that chemical cellar ventilated by wind and may go away, though that chemical concoction may be quite important for the future happiness of mankind, or more specifically, for tanks.

In 1932 the *trade unions* (everything as in the best of democracies!) *approved* (see how it is all *genuinely* democratic!) the *law* (not the pseudo-tsar-god's will or whim!) according to which an *employee* who skipped one day of work without a properly certified disablement was to be deprived of food rations and to be evicted. Only a network of *medical labor expertise commissions* could certify whether he was disabled enough to be freed from his particular work and for how long.

Yet there were some wicked serfs who would leave one *enterprise* and go to work at another of their own free will: there they would spin some yarn and would be taken on—how can one check all the dismissals throughout the country? Besides, the local chief could evict the scoundrel only if the scoundrel lived nearby. How could the local chief evict him if he lived elsewhere? So every *employee* got a *labor book*. No one could take him on unless his *labor book* indicated that he had been fired, and had not just left of his own will. The *director of the enterprise* also stamped his seal in the serf's passport. So he was attached for life to the *enterprise*. If he was late more than twenty minutes for the first time in his life he would be fined for a quarter of his *pay* for six months. This extraordinary lenience had an explanation: collective transport was so bad that being twenty minutes late once in a lifetime was inevitable. But for being twenty minutes or more late for the second time in his life, the criminal was sent to a prison camp for one year automatically, without the chief's consent: on the contrary, the chief was to be *put on trial* if he had failed to report the crime to the *court*. If a mild, almost friendly admonition—one year in a prison camp—did not change his or her criminal ways, and the male, female, or adolescent serf misbehaved inside the friendly one-year admonition, one tier down the secret infernal spiral he or she was to fall.

However, human ingratitude, egoism, and cunning sought and found ever new loopholes, and one of these was: secret and open prostitution. If all means of production and sources of income have been taken away, there is still the serf's body, right? Of course, a good number of serfs can be desexualized (male slaves are desexualized by hunger, cold, fear, and so on), but it was only in the forties that this branch of *special* medicine got well under way.

In 1928 *Pravda* wrote ruefully:

Take Tsvetnoy Boulevard. Hosts of prostitutes walk here by day and night, drinking vodka and starting fights.

However, the article was entitled "Enough of Complacency." By sentimentalizing, complacency, and mollycoddling *Pravda* has meant, since 1918, letting serfs be, without, say, turning them to slaves. And when it is enough of *complacency*, it is enough of *complacency*, though the secret struggle against the common serfs selling their bodies to other common serfs has been going on like an underground fire ever since then.

Another loophole is stealing from the pseudo-tsar-god. The pseudo-tsar-god owns everything while his low-caste serfs have only the *ideal norm*. But these low-caste serfs produce, store and handle his wealth, and they may absorb it, suck it in, seep it up as parched desert sand a stream of water.

In 1932 *Pravda* published a *decision* (the same as *law, rule, instruction*) according to which those who stole from the *state* were to be not merely turned to slavery, but exterminated immediately (shot, according to *Pravda*). The property of the *collective farms*, and in particular all animals or plants, was "equated in significance" with *state* property. To touch the pseudo-tsar-god's grain of rye was to be killed as by a bolt of lightning for touching a sacred talisman belonging to a jealous vigilant wrathful deity. No mere conversion into slavery would suffice. Curiously, the *collective farms* and whatever they produce have been proclaimed to be owned not by the *state*, but by the *collective farmers* themselves (like a cooperative in Sweden or Canada), and it is only the infinite altruism of great Stalin that can explain such a passionate lightning-bolt solicitude of his for someone else's property down to the last grain of rye.

All the land and whatever was in it or on it, all the waters and their fish, all the forests and their fur, all the skies and their fowl were the pseudo-tsar-god's. At one time a common serf killing another common serf incurred the same penalty as for the felling of a tree. A common serf's life was no more valuable than a tree even when another common serf took it. Man, that is, a common serf, was born into the pseudo-tsar-god's universe in which he could touch nothing or do nothing on his own. He could not build a shelter, garner plants, hunt animals, net fish, or ply even a Stone Age trade: the meaning of his life was to give to the pseudo-tsar-god the maximum amount of work his body and mind could give at a minimum price and disappear, neatly, cheaply, and without a trace from his owner's property. It was sufficient for the pseudo-tsar-god to say to his serf: "I do not love you, wicked serf: go and live on your own," and that was the death sentence, for the serf would not be able to live on his own, since nothing was to be his. He and his family were to perish from cold, hunger, thirst, or heat. In this benign case of mere alienation from the pseudo-tsar-god's paradisical care, only the serfs' own bodies were to be theirs—though certainly not for sale to other common serfs.

51

Obviously, the pseudo-tsar-god's property was to be the most expedient not only in the production of human and other weapons and *means of production,* but also in the use of them, so as to acquire the rest of the world for their owner.

Some of the pseudo-tsar-god's enemies were, naturally, democracies. There was democracy in Russia, too, after February 1917. But what happened?

In the summer of 1917, capital punishment, that is almost painless death, for desertion from the front was believed to be again in force. The situation was, of course, not at all as in the times of Russia's greatest military victories between the fifteenth and nineteenth centuries when a serf soldier suspected of less than infinite heroism would run the gauntlet. But still, there lingered some belief that capital punishment for desertion was not altogether improbable, and, therefore, there was no wholesale desertion.

By the autumn of 1917 the population knew that there was no longer any authority to enforce any penalty for desertion, and hence in the choice: to fight or not to fight (and in particular, to desert or not to desert) the fighting was stimulated by motives which may be called civic: if no one defends the country, the Kaiser will seize it, or will hit the allies first and thus prolong the war.

Actually, what happened after the total desertion was that the Kaiser captured as much territory as he wanted and then hurled the east-front troops against the Allies. Anyway, all the deserters were remobilized in 1918 and fought *heroically* (that is, with unknown, arbitrary, suicidal losses) for three years longer than any country in the world (and this time the family of a soldier, and not only he himself, would be exterminated with any degree of cruelty on sheer suspicion of insufficient *heroism*).

The desertion of 1917 was inspired largely by motives which may be called acivic, such as immediate personal safety.

Civic and acivic motives have nothing to do with any dichotomy of altruism versus selfishness. The difference is simply that the civic behavioral intelligence behaves in longer-range terms for its own benefit (such as safety, wealth, freedom), whereas an acivic Russian deserted because his behavioral intelligence could grasp only the shortest-range personal gains: with no notion of the longer-range benefits or disasters, he fought or deserted only to preserve his life right now.

For centuries Russian soldiers had been motivated to theatricalize, as their true and only motives, symbols like as Our Mother Russia, Our Father Tsar, Our Orthodox Faith. So in 1917 they said they were deserting because they had realized that the war was against their Conscience. A motive as good, noble, or beautiful as Our Mother Russia. Never would the Russian soldier go against his Conscience. And Conscience awakened in all minds simultaneously just when it had become clear that no penalty for desertion could be enforced.

Statistically, the following conscience curve can be charted: only about one million conscience cases between the summer of 1914 to the spring of 1917 when at least some penalty for desertion was probable. An outburst of conscience in the spring of 1917 when desertion became perfectly safe: a million people deserted every month, conscience being limited evidently by the haulage capacity of the railroads. A drop of conscience cases in summer back to the old pre-1917 level when capital punishment for desertion was proclaimed by the Provisional Government. The desertion of all the armed forces when it became clear by the autumn of 1917 that the Provisional Government had no power to enforce any penalty. A drop in the number of conscience cases between 1918 and 1953 to the pre-1861 statistical zero level (what is known as small, and small small numbers), no matter how monstrously treacherous, ruthless, and militarily

wasteful the conquests of the pseudo-tsar-gods were. True, initially after 1918 there were a few conscientious objectors who
did not yet understand the new world they had helped to create.
But they were shot even without being offered the alternative of
joining the *penalty battalions* at the front: they were shot so that
no one would ever dare to whisper that he was a conscientious
objector even when fighting just like everyone else, and it would
have been still better to make these conscientious objectors run
the gauntlet, but torture was not advertised publicly: only shooting was.

As I have said earlier, the "average civic index" of my comparative analysis of democracies is the lowest for Russia in the
summer of 1917 and the highest for the United States at this
writing, with other democracies arranged between these two
reference points. Democracies with a low average civic index have
no chance if pitted against serf war machines of a comparable
size. The higher the index the more strengths the democracy has
to compensate for its intrinsic war weaknesses (whereas a serf
war machine has its own weaknesses too). However, the owners
of post-1917 Russia and their experts cannot go into the subtleties of comparative civic analysis. They have been assuming
since 1918 that all democracies will collapse for the same reason
the Russian democracy did in the autumn of 1917 or the French
democracy in the summer of 1940. Who is right? History will
show. Meanwhile let us see democracies through their, not my,
eyes.

While a democracy may easily become defenseless since Conscience and/or conscience may awaken in most minds, the serfs
and slaves of a pseudo-tsar-god's war machine are motivated
by alternatives compared with which even the inevitable death
from enemy weapons is a better—sometimes infinitely better—
behavioral choice. All the slaves and serfs of a serf war machine
are thus *boundless heroes of labor and of battle, infinitely devoted* to their owners. Their combat arrangement follows a
definite pattern though.

In an ant hill the queen is hidden in a safe secret place: one
may destroy all the ant hill down to the last ant (with poison, for
example), but the queen will be alive and well somewhere.
Similarly, one may wage a one-hundred-year war and destroy all

the population of a serf war machine: its pseudo-tsar-god or his successor will be as fresh as a daisy in his secret recesses deep underground which no weapon can hit and which will be, if he so wishes, an Arabian Nights' palace, with an artificial neon-lighted sky over hydroponic gardens. When pseudo-tsar-god II (of former Russia) called for eternal peace on earth, it was fair in the sense that no matter what war raged over the globe, eternal peace on earth would reign in his microworld deep, deep under the Kremlin or under the Urals. If the enemy finally gets at the pseudo-tsar-god's underground world over the dead corpses of all his serfs and slaves, the pseudo-tsar-god will always have the time to commit suicide. Painless death. His readiness for this end of the world game should not be overdramatized: in case of failure, loss, or defeat, many gamblers, suitors, students, military officers, highjackers, businessmen, statesmen, and murderers commit suicide. This is a trifling risk considering the stake: the possession of the world.

But what about the others—the serfs and slaves? They are to be exposed to military danger in inverse ratio to the height of their rank. Slaves are either to be sent as *penalty battalions* on suicidal combat missions or to engage in militarily important, suicidally hard or dangerous labor in the hinterland. Then come, without any distinct line of demarcation, the lowest serfs, super-vised by the lowest overseers. Even under battle conditions, all suspected of less than *boundless heroism* can be sent to a local physinfluence station just as all wounded are sent to a local first-aid station. After all, physinfluence is a branch of *special* medicine, and *special* first aid must be administered as quickly, cheaply, and efficiently as in the case of a wound from an enemy weapon.

As for the castes intermediate between the pseudo-tsar-god and the commoners, military safety is distributed like everything else according to rank. Several years ago the *minister* of a certain industry complained to me that they, the *ministers*, were not admitted to the highest-rank nuclear shelter (just as they may fail to be admitted to some highest-rank doctors, medical equipment, medicines). He may be afraid or weary of war be-cause he is less safe; but still lesser is his influence on when, where, and how a secret or open war will be started, conducted, or stopped; and besides, he is also to be a *boundless hero* no matter how many years or centuries the war has been on because he shares the same risk of physinfluence on suspicion as does the last commoner: actually, he is much more under surveillance. He must be grateful for the second or the nth best shelter, the second or the nth best wartime supply of food, and so forth.

Therefore, there is no war fear or war weariness or war scruples for a serf war machine: the war danger, losses, and deprivations precipitously increase as the rank decreases, but the possibility of influencing the pseudo-tsar-god's decisions decreases even more precipitously.

Now, a citizen of a democracy is just a human, assailed by doubt, weariness, pity, conscience—or by the fear of being maimed or killed, or losing money in defense taxes or property, and this fear he may verbalize as conscience, heroism, altruism, or anything else. Gandhi the Great Souled, a preacher of non-violence or *truth force*, was against the war against Nazi Germany becaue he was against all war, and against any country's, including independent India's, maintenance of her own armed forces. What would the Great Souled have said and done if a fairly advanced Nazi institution of physinfluence had threatened *his* family? Since Gandhi is dead, and I do not want to take a cheap shot at someone who cannot answer me, I will assume what I believe would have been his noblest pattern of behavior in this situation: he would have defended his family with whatever he could lay his hands on until the last flicker of consciousness in his brain. So what is the wisdom of Christian, Moslem, Hindu, or whatever ethics in the interpretation of the Great Souled as applied to the case? It is this: "I am unable to let *my* family face physinfluence because no man can, whether enlightened by truth force or any other wisdom, magic, or exercises. However, if *others* fight Nazi Germany, they will save *my* family from physinfluence as well."

The ultimate goal of a serf war machine's *fight for peace* is to convert every citizen of a democracy into one of the innumerable varieties of Gandhi: no matter what he thinks or says verbally, let him behaviorally leave defense to *others,* and then there will be no others.

Facing this frail human flesh, so fond of imagining itself the Great Soul and what not, is the inhuman functioning of a serf war machine knowing, by virtue of its construction, of no human frailty.

A *hero of labor* will take along with him his habits, customs, and attitudes as he becomes a *hero of battle*. A serf who subsists on the ideal norm as a happy civilian will be a happy combatant on the same. If there is no *ideal* norm, he will eat nothing for days or even weeks. Anyway, he will cost next to nothing: in the mid-fifties, when I served twice for three weeks as part of officer training, he wore a patched-up cotton tunic, cotton cap, and cotton trousers, all worn by several generations before him, and subsisted on Strumilin's ideal norm of 1920/1921 minus pepper. And while costing next to nothing and looking happy, he worked even on Sundays: serf armed forces yield profit rather than call for outlays.

A rank-and-file combatant of a rich democracy may cost hundreds or thousands of times as much, while doing no work, but simply serving in the army in peacetime, and yet feeling unhappy by contrast with the freedom, variety, and abundance of his civilian life.

The military of all serf war machines have a good laugh when they study the wartime military orders of democracies. One of these orders mentions—well, *blankets!* Soldiers sleep under *blankets*. Ha-ha-ha! Like hoity-toity ladies of old. When it gets so cold that a serf soldier may freeze to death in his cotton tunic, he is ordered to put on his greatcoat, which he otherwise carries, rolled into a kind of huge doughnut, around himself and across his shoulder. When unrolled, this greatcoat is not only all of his warm dress, but also his blanket—and mattress, and pillow, and home: in fact everything, because he is to carry on foot his home and everything he needs to live and fight. Unlike cotton tunics and cotton trousers, which can, because they have to be worn, last only for decades, no matter how patched, greatcoats can last for centuries because most of the time soldiers simply *carry* them.

Or here is another big joke: already in the first world war the British soldiers wanted to be transported—in *passenger* cars! While everyone knows that as a great stroke of good luck soldiers are loaded into freight cars, the more the warmer, and how happy they are not to go on foot, with all they need to live and fight, seventy kilometers a day, with those who drop shot as deserters, for everyone who leaves the march column is a deserter, isn't he?

There was only one danger lurking in a democracy that pseudo-tsar-god II was more and more afraid of, and therefore his life was an ever mounting *fight for peace*, carried on even more intensely after his disappearance. From 1922 on, there were more and more examples of democracies which would be impelled by the danger of conquest from outside and within not into surrender, but into the conversion to war machines similar to the serf war machine which was preparing to acquire these democracies. Though there was no such irreversible conversion of the United States in the early forties, once Nazi Germany had declared war on this country, and Japan attacked her navy, the United States proved to be quite hard with respect to Germany and Japan. In war, a democracy hardens, and therefore there should never be war with a democracy, and there has never been any war since 1918 (while Georgia, the Ukraine, Estonia, Hungary, or Czechoslovakia has simply joined and rejoined the selfless heroic peace fighters in the Kremlin for the love of peace too). Hitler could have withdrawn from Poland on Britain's demand in 1939, and there would have been no war. He should have. He might have grabbed that silly Poland easily on another occasion without any war: Poland simply would have joined him, and no one would have minded, except some warmongers whom the democratic electorates would not even notice. If there is any danger of war, take back your move, smile, hug, kiss—make even some insignificant concessions to show your *fight for peace*. Sign as many of the most peaceful peace utopias as there is paper to write them on. Join or set up all kinds of peace phonies like *league of nations* or *united nations* or *world peace council*. Do anything not to give a big democracy the slightest *casus belli*. Keep it always in its loosest, most complaisant, indulgent state, help it to elect the most dovish Joseph Davieses and call all the others the most hawkish warmongers, play up to all peace fighters—preserve them in power, do not compromise them, enable them to show off to their largely innocent electorate what geniuses of diplomacy, international statesmanship, and global strategy they are. Help them to *build a world structure of peace* they have been *building* since 1918. Remember that they are only temporary officials, and in tacit cooperation with them you can very well dupe their electorate for the time of their stay in office, and as for what happens later, they may happen not to care a hang.

Declare peace, not war, make peace, not war, wage peace, not war, and there are many kinds of *peace*fare such as *peaceful liberation* or *fight for peace*.

Every civilization develops its own kind of warfare corresponding to its own social structure. When a Western journalist, statesman, scholar uses the word "war" he usually means "war" in the sense of his civilization, his notion of "war." But for serf caste war societies this is the *bourgeois* kind of war, the kind of war at which their advantages may often be indecisive. Why should they wage it? They must impose on each democracy *their* kinds of war by which they can gradually acquire all democracies without any risk to themselves. *Their* wars are *peaceful liberation* and *fight for peace*, as great Stalin named them.

In *peaceful liberation* a pseudo-tsar-god's serfs are sent into enemy territory while their families remain on the pseudo-tsar-god's territory and can be physinfluenced at his will. On the enemy territory a *base* is set up with a physinfluence station: any local inhabitant refusing to be an infinitely heroic peaceful liberator or helper is kidnapped and taken to the station. The *liberated areas* thus spread, the network of physinfluence stations grows accordingly in quality and quantity, and the number of peaceful liberators increases in the same proportion. Would this work even inside the United States? Before answering, it is useful to recall that Al Capone *liberated* part of Chicago, although he had only about 700 *liberators* and acted at an amateurish level, usually killing only those who resisted his liberation.

Before the forties, *peaceful liberation* (or *partisan war*) had not figured in the military textbooks even of Nazi Germany, much less democracies. Yet owing to this peace waged by originally quite small serf war machines, the strongest democracy lost mainland China and seems to be losing Southeast Asia. Quite naturally, democracies have been unable to wage this kind of war, because this is the war of an entirely different civilization: serf caste war society. And obviously, the latter civilization prefers to wage *its* kind of war, which democracies cannot wage. But they can be helped to believe that no war is raging on earth. What war raged between 1945 and 1949, for example? Ah, only a quarter of mankind was conquered. What a trifle. No war at all. Just peaceful liberation.

Another kind of aggressive warfare—of continuous military offensive that a serf war machine can wage on an unlimited scale, and democracies cannot—may be called *fight for peace*, or peace war. This is an appropriate name because when an agent of a serf war machine recruits a citizen of a democracy he does not offer him to be a spy, a thief, or terrorist, or anything so vulgar, illegal and old-fashioned: he asks whether the recruit wants to *fight for peace*—to be a *peace fighter*. As a *peace fighter*, the Britisher Harold Philby, who was privy to every secret of Western intelligence, had a certain officer rank, which is quite in the spirit of *heroic idealism*, for surely the *peace army* must have officer ranks, just like any other? In his book he published in 1968 Philby says that he was a "fully-fledged officer of the Soviet service" already in the thirties, and a "fully-fledged officer" is entitled, is he not, to a full-fledged salary, bonuses, promotion and even pension all of which may simply dwarf the same rewards (quite pitiful!) of a British intelligence officer (in 1941, "£600 per annum"!). However, hypocritical verbalism is still so strong even in the freest democracies that all the relevant Western journalists, biographers, officials I have read have been referring to the *mad* (or some other) *idealism* of Philby, without even try- ing to imagine what ranks, bonuses, promotions the "fully-fledged officer" Philby has been receiving since the thirties, and what wealth and status are due to "fully-fledged officers" of the *organs of state security*, as compared with the ridiculous "£600 per annum." Since many officials, scholars, or journalists the world over anyway believe, as salaried employees often tend to do, that they are heroic idealists, it is only natural that Philby, who has betrayed democracy in complete safety and become a "fully- fledged officer" of the upper caste of a superempire extending from Cuba to Viet-Nam, is also an *idealist* if *mad* or *misguided* rather than just *heroic*. In other words, the verbalization: *fight for peace* is perfect—a British intelligence officer spurns his ridiculous "£600 per annum" and becomes a really high-salaried high-caste mercenary of an army of conquest, and yet is considered a (*mad*) *idealist*, out above all to establish peace on earth no matter what his personal sacrifices are.

In 1963, Philby moved, in complete safety, to live in Moscow, where he became my pseudo-colleague: since exposed spies must have a certain pastime, to divert them from drinking, brawling or spending the *peace* money in some other objectionable way, and since they "know English" (amazing that Philby knew at least that), they "work with the English language," and so I have been watching them under alias for about twenty years.

Three journalists of *The Sunday Times*, London, who published a biography of Philby in 1968, after five years of research, note that since Philby is an idealist, he "should not find it hard to adjust to such unavoidable austerities as Moscow imposes." The *Sunday Times* journalists do not seem to understand the world they live in: they cannot evidently imagine either the squalor in which the invisible lower castes of post-1917 Russia live, or the equally top secret wealth of the highest ranks of the upper caste.

Sir Winston Churchill was not a pauper in England. But when the British Prime Minister was ensconced at State Villa Number Seven near Moscow in 1942, he began to admire, among other never-seen-before luxuries, an automatic bath water mixer which gave "exactly the temperature one desired" and which he had never seen in England and had certainly never had at his English home. With the satisfaction of a low-middle-class provincial who learned something in the supermodern capital, he says in his memoirs: "In a modest way I have adopted the system at home."

Nor did great Stalin want to daze the British Prime Minister: on the contrary, the order was: "Simply, modestly, but comfortably and in good taste"—from the British Prime Minister's point of view. To daze the British Prime Minister! What man on earth except Mao after 1949 is not a pauper compared with the pseudo-tsar-god? Does a Rockefeller own hundreds of millions of serfs and satraps? Did the Sun King have one sixth of the inhabited land? Was he reclaiming the globe and space? Could the upper caste of ancient India make use of modern science, modern technology, world trade? Great Stalin could create for anyone a mode of life in which the most spoiled monarch or owner in human history would feel like Sir Winston at that simple modest State Villa Number Seven. And while Sir Winston, the direct descendant of the 1st Duke of Marlborough, examined, fascinated, its modest simplicity, the conveniences that had been created in Moscow before 1917 like electricity or running water were all switched off in our superslums: we had to sit in darkness—all commoners lived or starved almost as in caves because electricity and water were considered to be too valuable to be spent on commoners even in Moscow.

A *peace fighter* named Krivitsky (who bolted from his owner in 1937 and was duly *suicided* in 1941 for his disobedience) described in his memoirs what a *heroic idealist* he had been, and with usual inconsistency, mentioned a tiny detail of his life (between his *fights for peace* abroad) in serf caste Russia during the famine of the early thirties:

I was then taking my annual month's rest at the Marino Sanatorium in the province of Kursk, Central Russia. Marino was once the palace of Prince Buryatin, the conqueror of the Caucasus. The palace was in the resplendent style of Versailles, surrounded by beautiful English parks and artificial lakes. The sanatorium had an excellent staff of physicians, athletic instructors, nurses and servants.

Could the British officer Philby re-create this mode of life— say, in the United States—with his "£600 per annum"? Krivitsky was in perfectly good health. Yet just in case, he was surrounded by the country's best physicians cherishing his perfectly good health. Try to surround yourself on £600 per annum with the best American physicians to dote on your perfectly good health: how many hours or minutes will your £600 last? And what is the cost of all the rest of that Versailles resplendence with servants and English parks? And Philby will also have all this *free* after the age when an English official retires on his ridiculous pension. Till his death will he be a revered and pampered pseudo-aristocrat-ecclesiastic in a serf caste society, a superaryan surrounded *free of charge* by servants of all ranks and kinds, and— if he wishes so—by girls, boys, friends, sponges, animals, birds, artists or whoever he chooses to have in his bed, at his side, or before his eyes.

Or perhaps His Excellency Philby, Lieutenant General of great Stalin's Torture-Chamber Force, wants to spurn some 300 rubles in cash or pass some caviar on to orphans as great Lenin in 1918 to 1922 did? Or perhaps he wants to out-Lenin great Lenin so far as to wear a shirt of hair next to his skin and scourge himself every Friday, as was done (allegedly) by Thomas More whom the Catholic Church reveres as a Catholic saint and the network of propaganda extols as a pioneer of Communism, while reprinting with gusto historical evidence exposing those saintly Catholics of old as devilishly secretive, fat-dripping, lecherous hypocrites and/or ruthless power-crazy bigots. A bit of contradiction? But who cares about contradictions if he is rich enough rather than reduced to living on £600 per annum? Wealth is desirable precisely because you may do what *you* want—to be a saint, or a hypocrite-bigot, or both, because *you* want it that way, or choose this in the morning and that at noon, and both in the evening. And wealth, as we know, is often only a status symbol. What would Philby have been without his *fight for peace*? A penny-a-liner on a tiny impoverished island? An official on "£600 per annum"? And then an old man in a nursing home run on the free benefits of English socialism. That ridiculous "£600 per annum" was a fit symbol of his status in English life. To belong instead to the highest superaryans of the world superempire extending its tentacles all over the globe, high into the skies, and deep into every democracy. That secret Versailles resplendence which he will enjoy to his death, with the country's best physicians treasuring a *heroic idealist*'s perfectly good health even during the worst famine, is a fit symbol of his caste status. And there are many, many *heroic idealists* in democracies who will abandon their microscopic careers and ridiculous salaries in democracies and join the *peace army* in a suitable rank.

Very elaborately, Philby demonstrates in his book that it is perfectly safe in a democracy to become and be an agent of the owners of a serf caste society, a cog of their secret war machine-network inside all the vital nodes of democracy to be conquered.

Judith Coplon, a young American lady, "was caught in the act of passing documents to a contact." But according to Philby, all that an agent of a serf caste society has to have in such an emergency is a bit of *heroism* that a *heroic idealist* has by definition.

Coplon, though caught red-handed, was resolved to fight to the end.

Predictably, Ms. (or Comrade?) Coplon put to rout what Philby defines as "Hoover's totalitarian empire." It will be recalled that the Enemy always attacks in numberless hordes (or even in whole totalitarian empires) and is *infinitely* ruthless. Yet the Enemy has always a streak of cowardice, while even a lonely heroic idealist is *infinitely* heroic. So quite safely, Ms. Coplon, "caught red-handed," not only went free, and all the charges against her were dropped, but she became another personification of heroic fight against the *totalitarian empire*, and once again she *exposed* that *totalitarian empire* which even had to fire its official Harvey Flemming as a scapegoat, according to Philby.

How could an unarmed lady rout single-handed a totalitarian empire? To begin with, the *totalitarian empire* could arrest a spy of great Stalin only "in imminent flight" unless the relevant warrant had been taken out in advance. And Ms. Coplon was picked up walking *away* from a station of the subway from which she had just emerged. It is not quite clear why "imminent flight" assumes the subway, and not, say, a taxi, but it was clear that Hoover's *totalitarian empire* had perpetrated yet another of its heinous *totalitarian crimes*, and the case went smash into Hoover's *totalitarian empire* which scattered in panic, like a bunch of juvenile delinquents at the sight of a huge police force.

Never, not in any McCarthy era, has an agent run any risk in a democracy, according to Philby, except through his own spineless idiocy or glaring neglect of elementary rules of *peace fight*. The failure of chains like Klaus Fuchs-Harry Gold-David Greenglass-the Rosenbergs, Philby attributes to the lack, in at least some of the links, of that infinite heroism (that is, of that infinite insolence of a criminal, absolutely sure of his impunity unless he messes it up himself) which Judith Coplon or Harold Philby displayed with such persuasive brilliance.

Indeed, Philby was found out in 1951. He moved to Moscow in 1963. Between 1951 and 1963, that is for twelve years, the found-out spy lived at his pleasure wherever he wanted: there was no hard evidence of his *peace fight* since 1932. What hard evidence could there be? A murder inside a democracy entails a corpse or its traces, a robbery a loot, a rape a victim. Whereas all the secrets of Western intelligence that Philby had been passing to great Stalin were in the top secret repositories, say, somewhere under the Urals.

Democracies tried to help some runaway inhabitants of serf caste societies to liberate their countries, as it was attempted in the Bay of Pigs, Cuba, or to smuggle in literature forbidden there as heretical. Philby would inform promptly the *organs of state security*, the commandoes would be seized and sent to great Stalin's torture-murder stations (I happened to be in the midst of one such operation in Moldavia). And the Western press would write that evidently some Albanian or Georgian or whatever people had not yet matured for the struggle for freedom (in contrast to the French, for example, who since 1934 defended one and all their freedom against the Nazis like enraged lions). However, the torture-mutilated corpses that Philby thus produced as agent provocateur or murderer (in Albania in 1949 he thus producd 300 such corpses) were again safely out of reach of any democracy.

Similarly, a Russian named Volkov who worked in the *organs of state security* decided to defect with his wife and pass to the West the addresses and layouts of all the buildings of the *organs*, including the alarm systems, key impressions and guard schedules, the names of agents operating in England, and what not. No intelligence of any democracy has made a single penetration into any vital center of either post-1917 Russia or post-1949 China, as serious American intelligence analysts admit, no high-grade codes have been cracked, and practically nothing is known even today about the inner worlds of China above the local chiefs' level, and only what the Russian runaways have described is known about the inner worlds of post-1917 Russia. Therefore, Volkov's contribution was the windfall of the century. Even Penkovsky, who survived longer than Volkov simply owing to his pull at the top, was of less value. Philby duly informed the *organs of state security*, Volkov was preliminarily physinfluenced at the *soviet embassy* in Turkey, then a *soviet* military aircraft calmly invaded the airspace of Turkey, calmly landed at Istanbul airport as though Turkey had long been a *soviet republic* and Istanbul great Stalin's private resort with an airstrip, and a heavily bandaged figure on a stretcher was lifted into the aircraft which calmly took off: the final touches to the unprecedented, uniquely heinous criminal could only be applied in Moscow, perhaps even great Stalin himself was interested, and anyway the corpse Philby had produced was again safely out of reach of any democracy. Alternatively, the *embassy personnel* would have burned the corpse in a special crematorium at the *embassy*, and surely embassies are extraterritorial and so no analysis of the chemical traces is possible.

But suppose an accident, perhaps no more probable than a traffic accident, has happened. A spy is, finally, in *prison*. Certainly no more than that, unless he is a sissy like Klaus Fuchs, because by the laws of the United States, for example, the burden of the proof that a spy's transfer of information has damaged the United States lies with the prosecution, and how can the damage be proved if all the information is safely under the Urals? George Blake, a British intelligence officer who had been a *soviet* spy for nearly ten years, was, indeed, put into *prison* from which he duly disappeared in 1966, and here is another "worker with the English language," my pseudo-colleague, under an alias. When the warden of the American *prison* in which Abel *served his term* (Abel's daughter was once my pseudo-colleague under the alias Fisher) learned that his *prisoner* decided to go to Moscow (in exchange), he said: "Are you *seriously* going?" It was, indeed, so good in his *prison*: Abel was addressed as a colonel and was a lecturer at some *prison* courses. A *soviet citizen* would take the *prison* for a *house of rest* of a pretty high caste. Still, the poor warden did not know that the mode of life of *some* castes in caste Russia is much, much more comfortable than even that of his *prison*.

Philbys may indeed veer their careers in complete safety. In 1937 Philby's life in serf caste Russia would have been unsafe, and he stayed heroically abroad. If his owners had demanded his going to Russia, he could have made a clean breast of it in England, and England would have forgiven him, of course, and have even honored him as a heroic idealist who finally became a *real* heroic idealist since he saw the light at last. His owners, who knew he could have done this, would have never risked losing him. He was not some native serf Krivitsky replaceable overnight. In 1963 Moscow looked perfectly safe, and he moved to Moscow to join physically his caste of the superempire.

If to become and be an agent of the owners of a serf caste society is so safe in a democracy, then those who will claim that the motivation of some particular Philby, in contrast to millions of Philbys, is not common, but very rare or unique, cannot and need not be contested. To ask why one of the Philbys does something quite safe for him is the same as to ask why Harold Philby drinks so heavily, keeps canaries, or makes home jam. For example, it can be claimed that Philby's canary-keeping or jam-making is motivated by exalted visions of Communism. In his book Philby tries to convince the reader that it is exalted visions of Communism and nothing else whatsoever that have been motivating him in his espionage since 1932. How odd that any relation, connection, or association between *communist beliefs* and espionage has been repudiated as a Nazi-Trotskyite-McCarthyist-White-Guard smear, while nothing the spy Philby would like to prove more in 1968 than that it is his *communist beliefs* and nothing else that motivated his espionage for great Stalin since 1932. A particular Philby can indeed be motivated in the safety of a democracy by exalted visions of Communism or by anything on earth. But for millions of Philbys those exalted visions of Communism will behaviorally verbalize a status and wealth (or a "socioeconomic position") they could never acquire except by becoming secret or open officers of the upper caste of a superempire.

A war serf caste society is impenetrable. The post-1953 *secret reports* and *letters* were read either to millions of *members of the party* or to dozens of millions of *working people*. The Western intelligence services have not secured a single text except the "Krushchev report"—about six months after its delivery, in Eastern Europe, and as an incomplete version, evidently planted there specially for the West. So the Western intelligence still does not know today what millions and dozens of millions of inhabitants knew in the fifties.

On the other hand, a democracy has not even a *border*: it is as penetrable as a sieve, or a piece of jelly, or a solvent into which molecules can freely diffuse, provided the democracy is kept by a war serf caste society in a sufficiently intense *peace*. The more *peaceful* that *peace* is, the easier the penetration. In peace war, the mounting penetration must be accompanied by mounting *peace propaganda*. While the intelligence of democracies has been unable to "penetrate" even into what millions or dozens of millions of inhabitants of former Russia knew in the fifties from the *secret reports* and *letters* which were read to them, the *soviet peace army* intercepted between 1952 and 1964 all the top secret messages dispatched via the code room of the American embassy in Moscow. Two American officers of the National Security Agency, the most secret department of the CIA, surfaced safely in Moscow in 1960, as *Pravda* gladly announced. Lieutenant Colonel Whalen who had access to almost all of the American national intelligence estimates was found in 1966 to have been—well, a *peace fighter*. Much of the American top secret cryptographic machinery was seized intact aboard the *Pueblo* in 1968, not to mention all those damaging *soviet* penetrations into British, French, German intelligence, or those delightful pranks of an American vigilant NATO guard, Sergeant Johnson, who kept passing piles of top secret documents to a *soviet peace fighter* for ridiculously paltry sums, and would perhaps continue to do so up to this day if the *soviet peace army* had been more generous.

To subject a democracy to *peace,* the pseudo-tsar-god presses, say, the button: "Love the Americans!," and the entire population of his serf society begins to theatricalize their *love* for the Americans. Many citizens of the democracy rejoice: who has ever loved them all so much? Ignorant of societies entirely different from their own, most of them do not even understand (though George Orwell described this in 1949) that in the middle of some love-the-Americans sentence, the pseudo-tsar-god can and may press the button "Kill the Americans!" and all the population will theatricalize their infinite desire to kill the Americans. In 1941 great Stalin pressed the button: "Love the Americans!" He received the lendlease goods he urgently needed. The penetration into the United States was ridiculously easy: there was hardly a single official or vital agency without *peace fighters* of great Stalin. The secret information was carried from the United States to Moscow *by the ton.* President Roosevelt, his Vice-President Wallace or his Ambassador Davies were not agents of great Stalin in the sense some of their subordinates, advisers or intelligence experts were, but they were perhaps better than that: they adored great Stalin—almost in good earnest, and approved of his regime—for others to live in. President Roosevelt made two presents to great Stalin: half of Europe and several million serfs (the exact figure is still concealed) who had escaped from their owner to democracies owing to the crackup of the *border* during the war.

But here great Stalin made a mistake similar to the one Hitler had done as he declared war on the United States. He proclaimed the United States an area of predominantly pariahs, while South America, Asia and Europe areas of predominantly aryans: he hoped to raise the aryan rabble globally and converge it all on the pariah United States, the same technique as in the pogroms of *kulaks* or *cosmopolitans* (Jews)—only on the global scale. After several years of great Stalin's threats, insults and instigations, the United States finally hardened.

Great Stalin did make a mistake: he ought to have, on the contrary, pressed harder and harder the button: "Love the Americans!"

How more and more penetrable the United States would have been and how more and more *peace fighters* could have been planted in the key positions, in addition to those planted between 1933 and 1947!

Peace fighters can be trained on the territory of the serf caste superempire or its satrapies just like the other, conventional army: as much or even more human and other property may be lavished on it. One officer of the *peace army* like Philby is worth more for conquest than, perhaps, one million serfs of all ranks of the conventional army.

Naturally, the cost curve of the hierarchy of *peace fighters* is shaped as that of any hierarchy in the serf caste society; there are very few like Krivitsky or Philby whose rank and cost are high, and then the cost curve goes steeply down as it reaches the level of numberless rank-and-file *peace fighters*. It is noteworthy that some Americans are recruited as spies at the price of welfare.

The sojourn of a *peace fighter* of a pleasantly high rank is quite pleasant in the *country of socialism*. But to be sent into, say, the United States as a *native canadian*, a *polish trade representative*, or a *scientist under an exchange program* is an even more pleasurable diversion, promising a lot of foreign luxuries, amusements and excitements which will make him the most fashionable, aristocratic, distinguished man in his own eyes, quite apart from being a heroic idealist too. The migration of *peace fighters* from a serf caste society into a democracy is a natural, almost spontaneous and self-paying proposition: the serfs need only be trained quickly and cheaply enough on a mass-industrial scale in special sham new yorks, tokyos, or munichs.

Peace war may be waged inside a democracy on the cost scale of conventional war, and it may lead to the victory of a serf caste society without any risk to its owners. *Peace fighters*, whether legals (that is, agents sent legally into a democracy as *united nations officials*, for example) or illegals (that is, agents operating in the United States as phoney Europeans, Asians or South Americans) are not just old-fashioned spies interested in military secrets only. To begin with, the owners of a serf caste society must know everything inside each democracy. If they monitor inside a democracy every person of any importance to the resistance of the democracy like they watch every embassy official in Moscow to know everything about him, they will be able some day to manipulate him or even perhaps recruit him. The owners of the serf caste society must be present by proxy everywhere inside a democracy just as they are on their own territory. "We are in our country everywhere," said the *chief of state security* of the post-1917 Russia almost forty years ago. The problem was to steal something from someone's home in France. The chief rang and the subordinate brought in the lay-out of the house: "We are at home in the home of everyone who matters under the sun." Perlustration of letters or telephone bugging: Hoover's *totalitarian empire* will be afraid to do it for fear of public scandal. But Philby's *genuine democracy* is not afraid —being at home in any country. In 1941 to 1945 every private letter of a German killed or taken prisoner in the war was carefully filed so that all the personal information about any citizen of both future Germanies could be known. After all, every citizen of every democracy must also have a *passport,* so far invisible to him and kept in the *proper quarters,* with the rest of his dossier, pending the day he receives his *passport* as the citizens of the Baltic countries once did. Citizens of any democracy are only human. Some of their actual or potential representatives may want to be elected or reelected even at the expense of any damage to democracy. Some employers may want trade, business, profit above anything else. Some officials may want promotion above anything else. Many in all walks of life want more money, fame, status above anything else, are favorably manichean, are anxious to hide something, or are carried away easily by a certain passion. A free open society consists of rivalries, clashing interests, struggles. Some citizens of a democracy, for example, may be ready to betray other democracies for the sake of transient safety or other benefits to their own country. The more his serfs and recruits mingle, eavesdrop, ferret, the better the pseudo-tsar-god will be able to live, expand, participate in a democracy via his *peace army* saturating a democracy as with molecules of a gas, invisible yet all pervading.

From time to time there may be a minor battle lost in his *fight for peace*, and a democracy will discover *peace fighters*, not in singles, as old-fashioned spies, but in whole platoons, swarming in every crucial area of resistance. Here the pseudo-tsar-god must step up his love, peace, trade or whatever, with a hint at his military might and all the unpleasantness in case of his displeasure (*cold war*). Anything, but not to jolt a democracy into hardening. Like putting to death, conquest has many forms, and it is up to *special* sciences to know which form to use for each social group or country, and certainly the best way to conquer a democracy is by peace war.

But what about the counterintelligence of democracies? A proper question, for Harold Philby was precisely the head of counterintelligence of Britain and its link-man with the intelligence of the United States. Practically, the counterintelligence and intelligence of the democracies was (at least as long as he was at the top) a kind of involuntary branch or institutionalized agent provocateur of the *soviet organs of state security*. That one fact alone is enough for the pseudo-tsar-god and their upper caste (including recruits like Philby) to be confident that they will conquer the democracies without any risk for themselves. And the ownership of democracies, these global Joseph Davieses, these babyish yet fat moneybags, these *bourgeois countries* represented in the *propaganda cartoons* as lazy, stupid, helpless penguins, is certainly worth the cost.

But let us suppose that Philby was *not* an agent of the owners of post-1917 Russia. What is the intelligence/counterintelligence of democracies like in the description of Philby in 1968 and of those writing about Philby in 1968? Neither Philby nor those who write about him suspect that compared with its "counterpart" in post-1917 Russia, the intelligence/counterintelligence of democracies, as they describe it, is a thirteenth-century cartwright's shop compared with General Motors. The preconception of overall progress in the spirit of the Crimean War is still so alive in democracies that it may be difficult for many citizens to understand that whereas a pregnant woman may die so easily in former Russia in 1935, 1968, or 1996, because a ride in a thirteenth-century cart is too much of a luxury for her, though her "counterpart" in the United States throws out an "old car" like an old suit (or an old yacht?), just the opposite may very well prevail in intelligence/counterintelligence.

So Philby and his colleagues are, according to our conjecture, honest specialists in the counter-*soviet* intelligence of democracies. And here we discover in Philby's book of 1968 that he is innocent of the first rudiments of life different from his little cozy worlds in democracies, *fascist countries* like Spain, and the upper caste worlds in former Russia. He starts his book with his *heroic exploits* in fascist Spain: in a serf caste society it is as much fun to read this as the *heroic exploits* of *bolsheviks* like Ulyanov-Lenin in *tsarist* Russia. Without suggesting in any way that Nazi Germany is any less evil than post-1917 Russia, it has to be remembered that the mode of life for most inhabitants even in Nazi Germany was entirely different: von Neurath told Hitler over the telephone that he, von Neurath, was too tired to see him, Hitler, tonight—a situation as absurd in Russia after 1921 as a debate in parliament or a newspaper calling for the overthrow of the regime. Whole *ministries* stayed up all night in case one of great Stalin's secretaries *might* call and ask something. In *fascist* Spain Philby was arrested during the war—and released for lack of incriminating evidence. In the Russia of the same time, the baby master spy Philby would be put to physinfluence, and after he had told his baby master spy story, he would be put into a block of liquid cement and carried out next morning inside a new, good, solid construction element to be disposed of as a defective building part. And that would have been the end of all the *heroic exploits* of the *master spy of the century*, Harold Philby.

From his own book it is clear that the *master spy of the century* is an ignorant sucker, the criminal variant of Joseph Davies, with honest Joseph Davieses as his colleagues. The Russian Volkov proposed to them the biggest top secrets of the *organs of state security* they ever had during the time of great Stalin and perhaps ever thereafter. They could not decide on their own (certainly not, since the decision involved money): they had to ask their superiors in London (surely officials are not supposed to spend *their* money without a 100 percent certainty of reimbursement). The question as to which bureaucracies may be less efficient, more useless or more harmful—democratic bureaucracies or serf caste bureaucracies—is too complex to go into here. However, serf caste bureaucracies may be motivated by fear, while, say, governmental agencies or universities in democracies may be motivated by nothing and simply luxuriate in their salaried belief in the salaried (heroic) idealism of salaried men. If great Stalin's relevant department had missed some American Volkov, great Stalin would have only kindly shot (considering that it was their first mistake) *all* guilty of omission, indifference or slowness, and next time their successors would have decided on their own what to do *in the interest of the state*, and, indeed, would have *collected* the needed money instantly among themselves even without any hope of reimbursement.

(One of the reasons why Philby and the other two *peace fighters* went in complete safety to Moscow was the fact that one interrogation was interrupted by a weekend. Surely, an official or officer of a democracy must not spoil his weekend because of a trifle like that? As Dostoyevsky's character says: "Which is more important: the universe or my missing my tea?" Which is more important: the freedom of mankind or an official's weekend?)

While waiting for their superiors' approval, Philby and his colleagues tried to phone Volkov at the *soviet embassy*. That would have destroyed Volkov even if Philby had never been great Stalin's agent and had never reported Volkov to great Stalin several days earlier. To phone Volkov, as Philby describes it in 1968 with the modest pride of the *master spy of the century*, was as illiterate as it would be for an expert on the United States to assume that in the United States all goods and services are bartered for pebbles which inhabitants find at sea resorts. Philby phoned Volkov just to pretend that he, Philby, was an honest, hard-working British intelligence officer. But surely he, the chief, would not have displayed such ignorance of his to his sub-ordinates, nor they their ignorance to him, had they not been all equally ignorant. And how could they not be ignorant?

In the *soviet organs of state security*, the General Motors of espionage in the new, overall, twentieth-century sense, a serf who monitors the life of a girl secretary at the French Embassy studied for 23 years (for 12 years he studied French) to be en-trusted with such a responsible, high-paid, top-caste job: he is still quite young, but makes even in cash several times as much as a surgeon with 20 years' experience at a *district hospital* in Moscow. The French girl is in good hands, he is actually her god-behind-the-scenes, her invisible live stage producer, her *alter ego*, and at her *alter ego's* disposal are bevies of young men speaking enough French to be exotically irresistible. Actually, all the country and its population is at his disposal, for all the population (and many satraps) is the recruitment and training material for *peace fighters*, and all the country with its satrapies is the stage, base, training ground for *peace fight*.

The British counterintelligence chief and *master spy of the century* Philby had not studied a second before entering the thirteenth-century cartwright's shop of British intelligence, and in their book of 1968 the journalists of the London *Sunday Times* do not imagine that the profession requires education or knowledge or talent. Surely Philby and his colleagues were not to build cars at General Motors or make operations on the heart or dance in a ballet? Someone who had failed to do good in tobacco making became Philby's colleague. Of course. To make tobacco is a devilishly responsible, specialized, and sophisticated profession. The ambitious man had wanted to make more than 600 pounds a year in tobacco. Many are called, but few are chosen. He *had to* work instead as a specialist in counter-*soviet* intelligence. With delight, it is noted in the introduction to the book that at one blessed time the "dons, artists and intel-lectuals had swollen the ranks of SIS and engineered its greatest triumphs." They could not engineer the greatest triumphs in to-bacco making, not to mention car building or heart surgery. To start ballet dancing they were, perhaps, too old and heavy. So they *had to* "engineer the greatest triumphs" in intelligence/

counterintelligence. Needless to say, the chief of British counter-intelligence against post-1917 Russia did not know a single word of Russian or of any language of more than a hundred nations of post-1917 Russia, and it is not clear why he should have, ever, if all master spies of all countries speak English in Hollywood movies? In the latest Hollywood spy movie, Muscovites also drink tea from samovars, which they indeed did a hundred years ago. And if even the moviemakers, who spent millions on this trash (extolling *soviet* spies and exposing Hoover's *totalitarian empire*, of course) did not care to check (for who knows anything about post-1917 Russia or post-1949 China?), why should some rejected tobacconist care to know anything for his 600 pounds a year?

In the allocation of human and other resources in a war serf caste society, the weapons and *means of production* take priority, and in these, the *peace army* takes the priority of priorities, for it wields the weapon of weapons to conquer democracies without any risk. The intelligence/counterintelligence of democracies is not in evolutionary line with General Motors, heart surgery, or perhaps even tobacco making. At any rate, as of 1951, at the peak of great Stalin's open war threats (*cold war*), it was a serene, loose, carefree, thirteenth-century cartwright's workshop, and though it had no idea of security or secrecy, hosts of those who can write or type have been *exposing* it for what the three journalists of the *Sunday Times* call in dead earnest "obsession with security" and "mania for secrecy." They have also been divulging or leaking whatever they have been able to know, and in general trying to do the pitiful cartwright's workshop all the harm they possibly can, and in a democracy again, a lot of harm can be done that way quite safely.

It was incomparably easier for Philby and his colleagues to go to work in British intelligence than for a *soviet citizen* to go to work at, say, a tobacco factory or on a tobacco-growing plantation. To begin with, the *soviet* citizen carries on himself his dossier, his *passport*, which gives all the data about him since his birth. To go to *any* work, to reside, to live without a passport is absurd.

Philby's *master espionage* for the owners of serf caste Russia was as follows. Lying about in that famous British *intelligence service*—more openly, freely, or negligently than any documents in the office of a *soviet* tobacco-making factory—were the source-books which contained the names of all agents in all countries. So Philby copied the names (here his Cambridge education in the Humanities was indispensable) and passed them to a contact. At a *soviet* tobacco factory with its secrecy and security, the whole heroic exploit would be inconceivable even for a day. Whereas Philby, Burgess, McLean and hosts of other baby master spies frolicked like that practically all their lives, and simultaneously many of them drank, whored, changed girls and/or boys, kicked up rows and brawls, refused to take any *soviet* money (heroic idealism), squandered *soviet* money openly in chic restaurants, said everywhere "I am a Soviet agent," played at aristocrats and/or artists and/or democrats. A pre-1861 Russian serf soldier often assumed that freedom is the freedom to secure money in any way possible, to get drunk and then to rush about brawling, whoring, chest-beating and squandering the money. Thus I found that some Britons had no more British or Western or democratic about them than randomly sampled Russian serf soldiers or thieves in the Urals. And no wonder: how many people are there in democracies who are serfs, free simply by accident of birth? If Philby had not opened his mouth I would have taken him for a Russian peasant who has made a big career in the *organs of state security*: a big, fleshy, crude, yet hard, smug, cocksure face, "Russian" bushy eyebrows, a hard slit of a smile several years ago, and a tipsy village granddad's pancake of a face now: great Stalin's torture chamber operative Ivan Ivanovich enjoying his serene Kremlin old age.

According to a published *law* currently on display at every *district military induction station*, any inhabitant between eighteen and thirty can be *mobilized* (for the peace war is on!), and having thus become a *military man*, he may be ordered to any part of the globe in any role, function, or capacity, under any conditions, and *officially* be *executed*, should he *betray his motherland* anywhere in the world. Or rather, in a democracy, it will be known that he, say, has committed suicide, while to his colleagues an official order will be read to the effect that he has been *executed*.

I do not remember such a *law* ever before. Not even during the last World War were the military allowed to mobilize so freely just *anyone* they wanted to, age 18 to 30. Are our owners less lenient today than great Stalin? True, a serf's written expression of a dissident opinion today still entails no more than 15 years of slavery, while before 1953 any dissidence entailed 25 years, and the *sentence* could be based on denunciations only. But the correlation between the owners' lenience and the scale of peace war may not be so close. The owners may be still more lenient than great Stalin, while their peace war may be more intense than great Stalin's. And the peace war has called for this mobilization *law*.

Besides, our owners' lenience has been diminishing, as it did between 1923 and 1937, with the imperceptible yet steady precision of the hour hand of a clock. At this rate we may soon have a *more* repressive society than great Stalin's. After all, I have had what I regard as a happy life because I managed to avoid the *mobilization* under great Stalin, owing to his *laws* which ensured exemption as long as I studied, and took other such precautions. Now I would not be able to repeat the trick. Yet owing to the hour-hand gradualness of this "tightening-up of the screws," democracies are wrapped in the ever more peaceful peace and the most-favored-nations *trade,* as they call their aid to expand the war potential of war caste serf societies. And in the peace war, a new global offensive is starting with this new *mobilization law* that has, perhaps, no precedent since 1919.

Quite likely, the intelligence services of the democracies have never even heard of this *law.* How could they? And how would it help them even if they had? The CIA of the United States has about 6,000 men as "authorized manpower for counterespionage, espionage, and covert action." When we read such figures, we laugh: the whole number is not enough even for watching *legals* in the United States alone, that is, those who are *known* to be spies, but cannot even be asked to leave the country because they are *united nations officials* or other *legals.* And as for "covert action," that is, defense against the *soviet peace army,* for which anyone between 18 and 30 can now be mobilized even *officially* and which is on the offensive all over the globe, including the most secret intelligence departments of the United States, that puny American "authorized manpower" with its ridiculous "authorized budget" had better stick it out at home, for lone individuals should not, except in movies, fight properly mobilized armies on which all national resources of a huge country are lavished first and foremost.

However, those adult babies of democracies who divulge or leak these ridiculously puny figures do not laugh: they either brag of the great strength of Western intelligence or *expose* (quite safely) this obsessively secretive, heinously criminal, supergiant *totalitarian empire*, with a frolicsome spontaneity unwilling to know that anything outside the nursery really exists.

"So what?" a citizen of a democracy may tell me. "Granted that with few individual exceptions, we have no intelligence, journalism, or scholarship adequate to the twentieth-century challenge of war serf caste societies, and hence we can have nothing but quack foreign policy. But the United States did not have even the conventional, *bourgeois* armed forces either—in 1913 or 1938. But comes a war—" That's it: comes a *war*. Here a *war* will perhaps never come. But Philby has not entitled his book: *My War*. He has entitled it: *My Silent War*. The silent war, or peace war, or the *fight for peace* is expanding globally with every day: human and other weapons and *means of production* are *developing* on an ever greater scale, infiltrating and saturating the continents, oceans, space—and the intelligence services or whatever may resist in any democracy.

Great Stalin knew what he had been doing since 1928, for it is better to be acquiring the world without any risk at all, than not to be acquiring it and risk the possession of even one-sixth of the inhabited globe.

52

Can one be happier—at least if one is myself at the age of six—than when coming back home, even after the happiest Odoyevo summer? Home is home, nothing is more beautiful than home, no home is more beautiful than Bloom's former drawing room.

Polya has waxed the floor, and how beautiful everything is, how neat and clean, how homelike and dear.

Both window and balcony door are open because it is still warm, and I run onto the balcony to see the wide, wide world, so large, so varied, so detailed that you can study every compass point endlessly. Why, even the balcony itself is a whole world. On the cement floor and barrier I know every dent, every tiny trifle that escapes an adult's attention. I examine everything: nothing has changed. Polya must have hung out some washing, my socks or something, a row of little pools of water are drying, they are all infinitely varied, these pools, and they are all drying quite differently, and I have such a sense of freedom, of space (with that breeze stirring the creepers in pots on the windowsill), of future.

Then I run in to drink milk. I am so happy that I cannot be happier no matter what I would do, but since I cannot be less happy either, I may as well move swiftly through happiness without impairing it in the least. I know now that many children, and not only little Dickens, cannot drink milk, and milk still imparts a tearful quality to my happiness.

But life seems to be determined to pamper me, and very mysteriously Mother plays the heavenly arpeggio of opening the mirror door of the Alexandrine wardrobe and produces a *chocolate* candy, very expensive because the candy is enormous, almost the size of my finger, at least the little finger for sure, and is all encased in chocolate, with a chocolatelike stuffing, for it cannot be *all* chocolate, you know. First I nibble at it very cautiously, then I slice it as one might a birthday cake. There are waffles inside too (oh, human ingenuity) because it crunches under the knife, and I eat each slice separately. The open windows, the breeze stirring the creepers, the waxed floor, the milk, the candy—I go back to the balcony, and I feel that as I move, happiness becomes almost as tangible as the water of the Odoyevo river bathhouse.

Beyond the other door, *in the corridor*, there is a nomadic camp, and this is how it should be: a born nomad finds the camp outside his tent the only natural way of life.

Each family *in our apartment* led its own life, but since we lived so closely together—here some of us were born, and here all of us could well expect to die—we were one monstrous artificial family—or perhaps tribe?

I never knew Nikolay Nikolayevich, but later I often imagined him, driven into the corner room by our invasion, and playing his Chopin prelude, and the music hovering over the nomads' chores, hatreds, deaths, for I hope that in his eyes we were nomads, and not just criminals.

The Grekhovs rolled into the room rather late, on the crest of their own great proletarian revolution, and no outsider can understand what this acquisition, the only one in the life of the smith and his wife, really meant to them.

When my Aunt Vera had received a living space, not the one where they live now, but their first living space in Moscow, I was not yet five, and we all went to call on them in order to congratulate and share the unbearable burden of joy. When we came Aunt Vera repeated for our benefit the story of getting the living space, and whenever anyone else came she would repeat it once again so that I remembered the story for life. The culmination of the story was Aunt Vera's injunction addressed to her husband Grishka (that same straw-haired teacher who later nearly perished, like a knight errant, because of his chivalrous

devotion to the American actress Deanna Durbin): " 'Grishka,'
I said, 'run straight to the place with two chairs and put them
in as our furniture.' "

In the living space battles in Moscow, with its foreigners, it
is still very important, apart from everything else, to put in some
furniture ahead of the other contestants so that you can defend
the living space as your own. Babies, sick people, and pregnant
women are even more valuable as contributors to the pathos of
an eviction scene. When some Grishka *disappeared*, it was all
right because such *disappearances* are not *capitalism*. But a
harrowing eviction scene is, and suppose a foreigner will see it?

Today the technique and countertechnique have been worked
out to perfection, and furniture is put in through the windows of
any story before the door is open, along with some invalids or
other beings having a high street-scene value, but at that time
Aunt Vera's device of carrying two chairs to the living space was
still a highly imaginative move.

" 'Grishka,' I said, 'run straight to the place with two chairs
and put them in as our furniture,' " Aunt Vera would repeat
as one repeats the story of winning the first prize in a country-
wide lottery, and no matter how often one repeats it, there are
eager listeners to ah and oh again, ask for more detail, comment,
and analysis, and beg to tell the whole story right from the
beginning to enjoy it all as an integral piece.

" 'Grishka,' I said, 'run straight to the place with two chairs
and put them in as our furniture.' "

There was only one defect in Aunt Vera's living space. No,
not the leaking (and occasionally bursting) pipeline to a local
factory running through the room. Not the aircraft wind tunnel
in the yard which the windows face. Not even the leaking roof
as in our room, though this is hardly a defect.

The defect was that the living space was too *large*. Was it
Trotsky who had promised that working people would live in
palaces of marble? The living space Aunt Vera got *was* a sooted,
smutty palace hall of marble. Yet Trotsky or whoever did not
know that a palace hall of marble cannot be partitioned: when
we looked up we could not see the ceiling; there was just darkness, like the starless sky on a bleak night.

Do you remember Rembrandt's *Rest during the Flight to*

Egypt? It was in our *Treasures of Art*, of course. Huge, dark, brooding masses of the night, and a tiny oasis of light below: the Holy Family. That was it: the usual electric bulb Aunt Vera could afford made a tiny oasis of light in their starless living space, and one walked toward the oasis as toward a lonely camp-fire in the forest, and as one raised one's hand, some huge shadows stirred in the nocturnal depths of the former palace hall.

Aunt Vera was a graduate of two universities, to begin with. She knew all great Russian poets and writers because she was one of those devotees who have never written a line in their lives not because they cannot, but because they do not understand how they can aspire to something so high. They have a flair for recognizing talent, they have a fine taste, and they know everything in or near literature. Now she was overjoyed at the prospect of living in a kind of sooted cave.

Bloom's former library, which the Grekhovs got, was free from this defect of superhuman vastness. Nor did the roof leak, because there was another floor over each corner room (pseudo-Moresque), and it was over *that* story that the roof leaked. The Grekhovs got the best prize imaginable as a result of their own proletarian revolution. And the windows in the living space were so beautiful that they could very well pray to them as to icons.

Yet Grekhov was extremely gloomy, and there was a kind of riotous gloom even about the revelry of the Grekhovs.

Their son Volodka was said to have stolen some roofing, went to prison, and could never live in Moscow as a result (they would not sign him in), but on holidays he would come with his wife Dunya. The Grekhovs observed only Russian Orthodox Church holidays; they wanted to live in the old regime, and completely ignored the new paradise on earth. That was quite common: those who before 1917 had been called "persons of the Orthodox denomination" and were now called *russians by nationality* commonly regarded the possession-power as Jewish, Lettish, Polish, or whatever.

The thirties were a transitional period for the Grekhovs. As ethnic Russians, they were no longer pariahs as in the twenties, but not yet aryans as in the fifties. In the thirties, they still behaved as a persecuted minority group, and the Smolensk Archives confirm that at that time common Russians put into their Orthodox Church festivals the same bitter zest that young Jews in Moscow put into their observance of Jewish holidays today.

On Orthodox Church gala occasions Dunya wore a cheap cotton kerchief—vengefully red, yellow, green flowers—and even now such a kerchief somehow reminds me of the apocalyptic sects like "the self-grave-diggers," who dug themselves large graves where they lay as in crypts until they died of suffocation. Thus they buried themselves, and since they were buried and yet had not killed themselves (which would have been a mortal sin) they were to go from Russia to heaven.

The Grekhovs would first stay inside their room. We did not know what was happening, except for mad thumps which might be dancing, or fighting, or the falling of corpses, or wild thrashing about. From time to time the door would burst open at the end of the corridor and some figures would rush from around the corner shouting and screaming. To an outsider it sounded meaningless, but to the Grekhovs it evidently expressed something, because they would plead with each other, explain, coax, appeal to conscience, declare love, threaten, laugh, or suddenly become insulted. Just as though human relations of a lifetime were compressed into seconds within which everyone should fall in love, begin to hate, swear, be seized with remorse, accuse, laugh it all away, and then return to hate.

Then they would cluster on and around their huge coffer in the corridor, and Dunya would lead solo in a mad voice:

> If gold I had in sky-high mounts

That was one of the songs all common Russians had been singing everywhere: it belonged to the old regime.

"That Dunya is a thief," my mother would say. "She stole our iron. Volodka, her husband, was in prison. They are all thieves."

My father would laugh: "But this is the Russian soul. Why do you love Dostoyevsky then?"

Dunya wore village earrings. Her canary blouse stuck to her dry back, arched inwards.

> If gold I had in sky-high mounts
> And rivers flowing with wine . . .

What followed was an avalanche of shrieks and tears, raw, discordant and terrible as though the Grekhovs really had gold in sky-high mounts (and rivers flowing with wine), and not just the coffer on which they were sitting:

> I'd give it all for your caresses,
> That I be yours eternal-e-e.

Then the Grekhovs would sing songs about Siberia, about prisons and fetters, and I thought they sang them about themselves, the songs evoked those desolate expanses into which the Grekhovs' sons would disappear forever after stealing something, and I was sorry for Volodka and all of them, especially when they sang a long song about how a former convict wanders home from Siberia and meets his mother as he crosses Lake Baikal. He asks her about the family, and something has happened to each of them. The Grekhovs would sing the last question he asks about his brother in the plaintive, almost howling voices of the last hope and the last despair, one voice trembling discordantly longer than the others, and then they would answer in a loud sobbing roar:

> Your brother's been long in Siberia,
> His fetters he carries again.

Then they would take in more breath and roar it even more desperately, especially "Your brother's":

> Your brother's been long in Siberia,
> His fetters he carries again.

None of the Grekhovs' sons would adjust in the new regime. The Grekhovs were too broad-souled, too emotionally riotous, too "Russian," to stand the ordered emptiness, bleak squalor, drilling *toská* of the new paradise on earth. One son after another would disappear, to turn up again on a holiday as an outcast forever, tall, with a close-cropped knobby head, gloomy, like their father, but with a kind of embarrassed smirk. And when the Grekhovs sang "We Were Rowing," an old song, so corny and cheap, it must have been a breath to them of that old life which now seemed so precious.

> We were rowing in a boat
> In a boat all of gold,

Dunya would begin (shaking her earrings) so coyly that it was clear that something bad would follow.

We were not rowing, we were kissing,

she would sob but recover her coyness:

It's too late to shake your head.

Suddenly she gave out a yell either of danger or of joy:

In woods—

and the Grekhovs roared as though crowding her to the brink of a precipice:

They say!

She:

There grows—

The Grekhovs:

They say!

She:

A very lithe and slender pine.

Now she was loose and flying off that precipice, and screaming so that one could make out no words unless one knew them:

A-boy-once-liked-a-boy-once-liked
A-very-lithe-and-slender-girl.

53

Even as the Grekhovs' music belonged to the night, the
Marleviches' music belonged to the morning, usually a very early
morning on days off.

Four Marleviches lived in their room: Professor Marlevich,
his wife, his daughter (one year my junior), his sister, and a
domworker, of course. The first bar of the Marlevich morning
music which invaded our sleep was usually lisped loudly and out
of tune by the daughter, waking up on a day off ahead of anyone
else:

> The Central Park's mignonettes are so lovely
> In the morning, and this is why . . .

That paradisal Central Park had existed long before 1917,
and only an extension, in imitation of quite common foreign
amusement parks or carnival sideshows, had been added, but it
was this addition that was hailed by *all progressive mankind* as
an unprecedented triumph of the new era of mankind. President
Beneš of Czechoslovakia who was busy *building a lasting peace*
to the delight of his electorate called the carnival sideshows a
"really new understanding of life," while Romain Rolland burst,
on behalf of all honest representatives of western intelligentsia,
into a long eulogy which ended in this jubilant finale, worthy no
doubt of any amusement park in any provincial town:

I would like the West, vainly draping in its "humanism" intended
to swell the pride and dissipate the ennui of the hollow pseudo-elect,

to come here in order to learn genuine and noble humanism which is warming and fertilizing all mankind, rejuvenating its body and spirit.

To cool the wild enthusiam of *all progressive mankind* apropos some carnival sideshows in a hungry drab miserable serfdom, with a generous admixture of slavery, a young man approached a group of English-speaking tourists and began, deathly pale, to explain to them in English that the park was just eyewash. The young man was afraid that on seeing this paradise on earth, and especially the *alleys strewn with ground red brick*, not to mention the sale of ice cream and a kind of seltzer water (called aerated water), the foreigners would imagine that the whole country was like that. He wanted to open their eyes. But a lady in the group (was it Beatrice Webb?) suddenly gripped him and screamed: "Help! A spy! A spy!" The group could overpower the young man (did the group include Theodore Dreiser? The Reverend Hewlett Johnson? Bernard Shaw?). But the young man struggled like an animal out of a trap, and the lady in her agitation could not recall the Russian word for "spy" and kept screaming: "A spy! A spy!" which sounds in Russian like the distorted: "Sleep! Sleep!"

Like a broad straight alley strewn with ground red brick lay the life of Marlevich, with vistas as enjoyable as carnival shows.

When Comrade Madame Radek railed that the Trotskys had a better residence in the Kremlin, young Marlevich still lived in some obscure town in the Ukraine beyond the Pale and wanted to go to Switzerland to study medicine. He wanted to be a doctor and nothing else. Then word came that a Jew could go to Moscow, be enrolled practically without exams and ahead of others as a *national minority* to study medicine *free*, and get some hot meals every day and a bed in a hostel.

He was a furrier's son, and as such he should have known that nothing is *free*. When something is *free* in a democracy, a citizen knows exactly how much has been *paid* in taxes. But when it is just *free*, then someone wants to buy you, and you will pay with your flesh, and the flesh of your children, and that of your children's children. This is what everyone knows. But when something *free* is offered to *you*, you begin to believe that the offer is made owing to *your* amazing aryan traits, which must have moved the buyer to selfless extravagance.

Marlevich had little schooling, and he did not speak Russian. Within the next fifteen years he became a professor of medicine, practically blind from poor food and too much reading in Russian, English, German, and French.

There was a kind of frenzy in his face, he looked a bit like a bridled bespectacled faun, and when he spoke he seemed to roll the bit in his mouth to get rid of it—there was even a hint of foam around his distempered lips. His success whipped up his frenzy even more, and he would *fly* up the five flights of stairs, through the corridor, and into the kitchen, where he would rush about and tell the neighbors how nobody could diagnose an ulcer, until finally he said: "Know what it is? An ulcer!" He would myopically brush off one of the salt shakers or butter dishes, and then *fly* into the bathroom, where he washed, jerking his hands up and down his face like a tightly wound-up toy with a broken regulator, snorting, gurgling, warbling, blowing into the water, and still suffering from excess of energy.

Then he would phone all his colleagues, repeating all the medical peripeteia of the drama of diagnosis, which always ended happily on the same jubilant note: "Know what it is? An ulcer!"

Just like other kinds of free enterprise, *private* medical practice did not exist, but existed. In particular, it existed as visits after hours, because one such visit brought a physician more money than days of his *service*. And that was very bad for us, because having paid their own money, the clientele of Marlevich would expect his full attention and phone him in the small hours—if his patient died, for example—and he had to console them, usually by recalling all the good side of life of the bereaved.

"Please listen to me closely: your daughter might have been run over by a car—yes or no? Tell me: yes or no? Yes. Now, she has not been run over by a car, has she?"

He would also make the bereaved recall everything in the life of the deceased that was good by comparison with what might have been. It was the dead of the night. I would go back to sleep and then wake up again. "You know what? He might not have been born at all. Do you know how many miscarriages our maternity ward has?" It was hard to tell when Marlevich was serious. "But he lived, yes, he lived, and he lived very well, let me tell you—I wish I had such a life. Do you believe me? *I wish I had such a life.*"

As he repeated the last sentence with ever greater emotion he seemed to be moved more and more by his generous if somewhat hypothetical wish. Finally he would always make the same conclusion: "You know what? Everything might be *seventeen* times worse. Do you hear? *Seventeen* times."

The freer (and richer) human beings are, the more they can concentrate on the tragic in human life, and murmur, lament, or complain that they will die, that they will be old, that they may fall ill, that they are poor, that they are not free, that they are victims to a host of unpredictable accidents. Tragedies on the stage were devised and enjoyed by a people freer than their predecessors, descendants, or neighbors for millennia.

A free and rich citizen of a wealthy democracy can *think* (and declare publicly) that he lives in, say, a Nazi gas chamber just after its doors have been bolted. Especially if he is also young and in good health. *Thinking* this does not detract from his freedom, youthful health, or even wealth, and the better off a human being is the more he can afford the luxury of depressing himself as much as possible—of *thinking* that he is in the worst predicament humanly imaginable. Inversely, the worse the reality was throughout Marlevich's life—the unfreer, poorer, and more endangered Marlevich became—the more frenziedly he had to *think* that he was in the best, the most youthful, and the most beautiful land, and his own position in that land was the best possible.

As youth and health and strength under the strain of his life and work in the most youthful and beautiful land ebbed away, Marlevich had to whip up his good cheer even more. Everything might have been *seventeen* times worse, yes: *seventeen*. To have the energy to live and work (and he worked like a horse or at least a bridled faun) he had to see everything *seventeen*, yes, *seventeen* times better than it really was—he had to see, outside of his work, only what was as cheerful as the *alleys of the central park strewn with ground brick.*

> The Central Park's mignonettes are so lovely
> In the morning, and this is why . . .

The professor's sister, nervous, unmarried, no less myopic, yet having risen only to the school teaching of literature, would pick up in a self-trained impetuous contralto invading our sleep in force:

> A heroic past master of labor
> Sports a Young Pioneer's red tie.

Marlevich would take over in a humorous gutty baritone:

> How's that: mignonette—and why a red tie?

He was skillfully playing utter amazement, and then pouring forth quite humorously into a tremulous tenor:

> This I cannot at all understand.

And the family minus domworker Tasya triumphed in chorus:

> 'Cause one is so young, 'cause one is so young
> In our youthful and beautiful land.

54

When I was asked later in life why I would never go to the theater, I answered that, for God's sake, I had been living on the stage, with five rooms—five plays running on simultaneously—and each play getting entangled in another.

The Grekhovs were very populous. Since they had no property and had even taken their coffer out, there was a lot of floor space for children, because Bloom's library was very large. Of course, there was no wheat flour as under the tsar, but the Grekhovs baked shrovetide pancakes out of rye flour which they managed to procure somehow—and for several days they feasted, drank, and screamed "Mounts of Gold" and all the other songs.

When Grekhov was still alive (he died in summer, and when we returned, the pale, almost white Anastasia was all in black), we would suddenly hear a different scream above a screamed song. This meant that Grekhov had become jealous of his wife. That is, he had seized a knife, and was darting after his wife, who was fleeing and shrieking: "Oi, Lord merciful, he'll kill me." She would run to us or other neighbors, to hide. "Oi, Lord merciful, he'll kill me," she would repeat in a kind of trance, her face pale, unseeing. "Oi, Lord merciful, he'll kill me."

"The last of the Russians," my father would say, with his usual mixture of sadness and irony.

"She is a grave hysteric. Dunya is a typical grave hysteric, too," my mother would reply with the expression of a physician seeing a disgusting but common disease.

The first name of Grekhov's wife was Anastasia, like that of the tsarevna shot with the tsar's family. However, her patronymic was Kuzminishna, which evoked the image of a plain, poor, hefty village wench. A smith's wife, quite likely. As always, the first name and the patronymic described the dichotomy of the person. Her features were chiseled quite delicately, perhaps she was a priest's daughter, and they were so finely in keeping with the name: Anastasia. Anastasia—the penultimate syllable is stressed —isn't it something of Byzantine icons, the flickering of icon lamps, and those mosaic arcs? Yet there was a village wench's vulgarity about her face, a kind of gaping stupidity and froglike laughing boisterousness in agreement with the patronymic: Kuzminishna. The family name *Grekhov* fitted her because *grekh* is sin in Russia, and since the word "sin" is not used in the propaganda-religion-culture at all (those who sin against the pseudo-tsar-god are accused of "monstrous moral depravity," "profound moral degradation," "abominable moral degeneracy," and so forth), I did not know the word for a long time except in the name Grekhov. Therefore, sin in my mind is still associated with the poverty of the Grekhovs, compared with our family, the sour smell of diapers and sauerkraut, the threadbare black dress of Anastasia in mourning, and everything else. Even more ir-relevantly, I associated sin with walnuts because the two words begin quite similarly in Russian, and the way walnuts taste—that must be sin, I thought, partly because walnuts were terribly expensive, and certainly the sinners Grekhovs had never tasted them after 1928: of that walnut sin they were innocent.

As Anastasia grew older she began also to repent more, espe-cially after her husband, the victorious proletarian, died in 1935, the very year for which Ulyanov-Lenin had set the deadline for his paradise on earth. Finally she would wear only threadbare black, was a zealous churchgoer, and was pale, quiet, and serious like the holy mother of a sect.

She had given birth to many children as part of the general holy riot of life, but her sons could not live in Moscow, and as for her daughters, well, she vehemently hated her daughters.

She vehemently hated her daughters, but wanted, as vehe-mently, to *love* us, her neighbors. Love thy neighbor as thyself. Thy neighbor, not thy daughters. During their riotous holidays (and all their life seemed to be the preparations for holidays or after-holiday hangovers) Anastasia's unconfined mirth would also change suddenly to sorrow, and she needed to pity someone outside her family circle—her neighbor, not her next of kin. Once she wanted me to eat a pancake of rye flour. That was absurd because our families belonged to one residential caste, but to entirely different classes. We never ate *rye* pancakes, and those pancakes were awful. Yet when she saw me she imagined that I was neglected by my parents, that I was unloved and denied rye pancakes, and she suddenly began to struggle to give me a rye pancake.

"Lemme go," she shouted, as a mother wishing to see her son for the last time. "No one will bake him a pancake, no one." Dunya shouted something too in utter despair, though no one thought of not letting Anastasia go to give me a rye pancake. She poked the pancake near my face, and I had to take it and eat it, like a pursued spy eats a secret letter, perhaps because I knew that my father would have eaten it out of an innate feeling according to which it is bad to show anyone that you are above him.

Before the Pushkins moved in, their predecessor had once brought a woman of ill repute—right from the train terminals, as my mother later claimed, while his wife was visiting with her parents in the provinces. As I have said, the possession-power fought a war of extermination on common serfs selling their bodies to other common serfs (which was thought to be more evil than even private shoemaking because it was even more lucrative), and the professionals of the trade took to the terminals, where they could pretend they were meeting relatives.

However, in the morning that lady would not go away and began to claim her share of living space. Perhaps she was not a professional at all! Perhaps she had just enacted that trick of commercialized vice in order to grab some living space. There was no distinct legal difference between lovers and spouses at that time: the *family* had not yet been *strengthened* that much.

Anastasia entered the triangle, her love for the lady from the terminals stemming from the lady's being socially downtrodden, and then, what do the Gospels say in a similar case, remember? Anastasia's love was decisive in the issue, and the object of her love got her share of living space. But later it seemed to

Anastasia that she had been all wrong—that she had interfered to reward vice and punish virtue. Perhaps the Gospels did not apply at all because the lady from the terminals was a hypocrite who pretended that she was a sinner to grab that living space.

So Anastasia now fought to the death with her former love. No less naturally did she then switch her love to the man, and then back to the lady from the terminals. It was a tragedy, with Anastasia cast as the ancient gods, and the trio realized that they would all perish of Anastasia's thirst for love. They united to deceive Anastasia, and they did deceive her by exchanging the whole space for a larger space in Ufa, a step of rare despair, while the Pushkins moved in, a stroke of rare good luck, which was still permitted as *exchange* at that time.

Another object of Anastasia's love-hate was a Lett in the corner room at the opposite end of *our apartment*, a Lettish rifleman, one of those who had shot at those demonstrating in support of the Constituent Assembly, dispersed, as the gentle reader may recall, because the *bolsheviks* could not garner more than one-quarter of the votes, though after their grab of possession-power the *bolsheviks* repeated again and again that the population could recall all those wicked members already elected and elect them instead. Letts were entrusted with jobs like the shooting of those demonstrating in support of the Constituent Assembly of Russia. Very important jobs. Letts ranked first in the *organs of the state security*, well above Poles, Jews, and Georgians. This extraordinary trust was natural. They were more foreigners than Poles or Jews or Georgians: most of them could speak no Russian. Yet at the same time, they were highly civilized, even spoke German sometimes, and hence were good at all kinds of official work (such as the calculation of the cost of bullets in mass shootings, and so on). The *bolsheviks* had promised them the ownership of their Baltic countries, and they did a lot of official work there, but failed. However, countries such as Latvia are not like big countries: if someone has murdered someone else in a small country, the whole country will know the criminal by sight, and will remember him for generations (which partly accounts for a low crime rate in small countries). Those Letts could not now get out of Russia because revenge awaited them everywhere, often as vicious if not as professional as their own torture-murder in their Latvia. They were total foreigners in Russia, yet nevertheless obliged to remain in Russia: the best manpower for the genocide of the highest cultural stratum of ethnic Russians, along with the crushing of all civic resistance. So pending the *democratic-socialist-proletarian,* etc., *revolution* in Latvia, our Lettish rifleman received one of the bedrooms in Bloom's apartment and lived in that bedroom quite alone, amid a strange nomadic camp of a strange country whose freedom he had helped to destroy down to the last trace.

He looked like a West European worker, and I recalled him whenever I read T. S. Eliot's lines about going at dusk through narrow streets and watching the smoke rising from the pipes of lonely men in shirtsleeves, leaning out of windows. Apart from leaning out of windows or rather one window of his bedroom, he blacked his shoes every morning: that must have linked him in spirit with Western civilization. He had once intended to raze it to the ground, but now he was evidently determined to salvage out of it at least a gentlemanly shoeshine.

Anastasia wanted the Lettish rifleman to black his shoes in his room, whereas he wanted to black them in the corridor. I wonder what his expression was when he shot at those demonstrating in support of the Constituent Assembly, but here he seemed to be a mild, polite man, smiling to us, perhaps partly out of fear. However, he decided to fight for his shoe blacking in the corridor. She was more than his match, of course, since he was now without his *rifle,* and she made his life miserable until. . . .

One morning I realized that something important had happened overnight. Our neighbors, if the members of our artificial family could be called that, had already exchanged all the news there was to exchange, but still, there was an air of overwhelming mystery about them as I entered the kitchen to brush my teeth (children brushed their teeth in the kitchen, since the bathroom was thought to be too ceremonial for them). *They had taken him away at night.*

The *real* plague was to start the next year, but no one thought this early disappearance unusual: he was involved somehow, he was almost a foreigner, and all foreigners were shady men, bound to come to a bad end.

Everyone expected Anastasia to gloat, yet she was the only

person who would not understand that his disappearance was not a disaster but a natural process—like rain. Tears—limpid, abundant, rainlike—were streaming down Anastasia's face, pale, almost calm, open-eyed. "Dina Vladimirovna," she repeated to my mother, "I feel I will soon die too."

For all her neurological knowledge of hysteria, my mother could easily be moved. "I said to her: Buy a candle for him—in church. What else could I say?" My mother shrugged.

On the other hand, her daughters Anastasia suddenly began to hate, and henceforth never exchanged a word with them. One of her daughters made Anastasia give her a share of living space and partitioned it off, while the other had to marry without a partition. It was one of the innumerable living-space *King Lear* versions. As there were living-space *Othellos*, *Macbeths*, *Hamlets*, and all the other tragedies, ancient or modern. Except that all the dramatis personae lived and died on the same living-stage all together no matter what tragedy.

The partitionless Regan had many children—yet not as part of Russian riotous abandon, but on the strength of a dreary calculation: it paid to have as many children as possible to live on sheer *benefits of socialism*, since the pseudo-tsar-god wanted to make up for the depletion of his human property. Both sisters lost the Russianness of their mother: they were superslum drudges, most likely not different from slum drudges elsewhere, only quite prosperous compared with many wage earners on the territory. They had none of their mother's physical exuberance. Goneril was abandoned by her husband, despite the partition, right at the outset of the lucrative process of childbearing, and she was scrawny and sallow-faced. Regan seemed to have been bled white by the process: she was asthmatic, watery, obese.

They did not celebrate any Orthodox Church holidays because it would be an insane extravagance for them to begin with. On a *soviet* holiday, the sister with a large family bought *one* sausage for all the children, and they sat watching it as a source of health, strength, and longevity. Having eaten the magic viand (the rest of the repast consisting of everyday potatoes), they sat mutely staring. They had screwed out the everyday dim bulb and screwed in a brighter one, and they just sat there, blinking— luxuriating in this luminous festive magnificence (though vaguely apprehensive that the neighbors would now claim that they should pay a larger share of the electricity bill because a more powerful bulb was on; Anastasia would, of course, testify against them).

The brighter electric light meant festival extravagance, reckless abandon, and uneasy conscience. But they enjoyed it in complete immobility. They had no strength or interest or ability for anything else. Russian history ended at them: they were *soviet*. Except perhaps for their noses: these were still exactly like those of the shrews cartooned in the old Russian magazine *Satirikon*— protruding, with a hollow in the middle of the tip.

But their most memorable feature was their dead fish eyes. Except that Goneril, the scrawny one, who was abandoned by her husband, had something the matter with her eyes, she squinted or winked nervously, and so one eye gave off a sudden gleam of the color of a fly's wing on a dull day.

55

As for the Pushkins in Bloom's dining room straight down the corridor, the Pushkins scraped and saved and, in general, showed how dangerous it is to refer to a certain *national character* (or *national mind*, or *national psyche*).

My Jewish aunts and uncles had all clung to Russian culture, and when Russian culture still lingered in the twenties and they were still young, they were more Russian than many *russians by nationality*, that is, *by passport*. Their children, and especially one of my cousins, brought up in a literary family, are over-Russian or super-Russian because they have brought themselves up on the sublime Russians of Russian (mostly aristocratic) literature, and where the best living *russians by passport* would be generous, they are sweepingly so, and where the best living *russians by passport* would be hospitable, they are lavishly so— and all the Russian sensitivities are oversensitized in them because they know they are *not russian*, according to their passports and all the other documents, and so they must be very good, very Russian, to be worthy of those sublime Russians of Russian (mostly aristocratic) literature.

The Pushkins were Russian, according to their passports and all the documents, that is, their parents were Orthodox Church believers, and as to their grandparents, it didn't matter, because the documents relating to that generation (not to mention its predecessors) were mostly lost in Russia, and as for the earlier ancestors, these were never known unless they were aristocrats recorded in the Velvet Book.

The Pushkins did not need to try to be Russian because they were *pure* Russians, according to their passports and all the documents. Even Tsar Nicholas II was only 1/128 Russian, which was known because his ancestors were in the Velvet Book for at least three centuries. A namesake of our neighbors was the Russian nineteenth-century poet Pushkin (a circumstance that gave Marlevich a chance for a joke when answering the phone: "Do you want Pushkin? But he was killed in a duel a hundred years ago"). Unlike our neighbor Pushkin, *that* Pushkin was in the Velvet Book, and one of his ancestors was known therefore to have been an African Negro. Or another poet—the genius of joy—I have mentioned, or still another—the genius of sadness. They were creators of the Russian language in the twentieth century, of the Russian spirit, and hence the creators of Russianness, for any Russianness in any other sense is just another manichean creed of one gang proclaimed aryan to fight their chieftain's enemies proclaimed pariahs. Yet those two unique creators of Russianness, two poets by whose names perhaps the very word—Russia—will be remembered, were both *pure* Jews, according to their passports, because their parents or grandparents were known to have been "persons of the Judaic denomination." Perhaps their awareness of the fact stimulated them? A *pure* Russian may believe that everything that flows from his pen or out of his larynx is remarkable because it is *pure* Russianness, since his brains and hands and larynx are all *purely* Russian. And then this *pure* Russianness proves to be musty clichés one hundred years old.

Anyway, our neighbors, the Pushkins from Ufa, were pure 128/128 Russians. This is what twentieth-century *nationalisms* do as soon as they are switched into aryan-pariah motivation: they turn anyone in any country into an aristocrat so thoroughbred, so pure, so aryan, that its tsar or its poet is only a mongrel, bastard, and foreigner in comparison. *Pure* Russians, the Pushkins did not need to try to be Russian, and therefore they were just the way Russian writers described Western philistines in contrast to soulful Russians—as calculating hoarders and misers, scraping and saving for generations to buy something.

The trouble was that the Pushkins could buy nothing because hardly anything worth buying was on sale. From Ufa they had brought chairs called Viennese. Perhaps such chairs had been fashionable in Vienna when Freud quarreled with his bride about the buying of furniture? They had brought all the other furniture, including beds with framed-metal backs adorned at each corner with a pile of nickel-plated knobs of various sizes. In the fifties a friend of mine saw such a bed in the bedroom—of Strumilin! I understood why the Founder of Socialist Planning never imagined that anything could go out of fashion: the paradise on earth was to be built once and for all, the nickel-plated knobs were to shine through the millennia, and only the food—rye flour or caviar depending on the rank—would have to be supplied.

As for objects of beauty and luxury, the Pushkins had no need to buy them either, because Nina's Uncle Victor worked at a famous china factory which had been founded in the eighteenth century and was now making porcelain for export. Whenever a porcelain pepperbox fashioned as a shepherdess was no good because it had no holes to pour the pepper through, he would present it to the family, to be used as a sheer object of art, and art must not be utilitarian by definition.

So the Pushkins scraped and saved. But how could they do it if only Nina's father worked, and mother did not (he was jealous even when she just walked in the street). Although the class status of the Pushkins was above the Grekhovs', it was below us and the Marleviches, a circumstance which we tactfully concealed and ignored. The Pushkins had to live on the usual diet of such families: rye bread, potatoes, and sauerkraut used to make cabbage soup. How could one save on that?

Yet they had made an invention: for three or four decades they bought somewhere (where?) a strange sauerkraut, cheaper than the usual *state price*. That strange sauerkraut had only one defect: as it cooked it stank, and that strong, rotten odor finally clung to the Pushkins and everything that was theirs, but the worst was when the cabbage soup cooked. "They are asphyxiating us again," my mother screamed. "The door! The door!" She would go and shut the door of the kitchen too, and the Pushkins suffered this in silence. They were humbly aware of their sauerkraut imperfection, but I found my mother's conduct tactless and tried to show my sympathy to Nina, porcelain white from anger.

In the most conspicuous corner of their room, where once the icon would have been, hung a bicycle which belonged not to the Pushkins, of course, but to Nina's Uncle Kolya. Whenever Nina mentioned Uncle Kolya we would look to the bicycle as to Uncle Kolya's image or icon.

Uncle Kolya worked in something called the geepeeu, the word evoking in my mind short stout men in khaki breeches—not unlike the father of my cousin Tulya.

Later in school I learned that uncle Kolya's geepeeu means GPU, *state political administration*. The *extraordinary commissions* were abolished in 1922. What a jubilation followed! The era of law and order had started for good. Except that there appeared exactly at the same time some inconspicuous, irrelevant, innocuous *state political administration*, but really only a paranoiac could associate this obscure institution with the *extraordinary commissions*. In the thirties the *organs of state security* in their reincarnation disappeared again, much to everyone's triumph. Except that there emerged exactly at the same time a *people's commissariat of internal affairs*. Very good for *international peace, cooperation and friendship*: do not interfere in a people's (a nation's, a state's) *internal affairs*. The new abbreviation was the NKVD, and Nina was hurt when I said, as Father did, that Uncle Kolya worked in the geepeeu. The NKVD certainly sounded like Uncle Kolya's bicycle, brand new, glittering—not at all like the stodgy geepeeu in broad riding trousers.

Uncle Kolya was always busy somewhere in top secrecy, and the Pushkins never expected that such an important man would come to, say, Nina's birthday party. He would lend his phonograph for the occasion, with a note that said "Look inside," and indeed inside there would be a bar of *solid* chocolate some three inches long. He visited the Pushkins once or twice a year, hardly more often, whenever it was convenient for him, and he did it perhaps to show that he was not riding such a high horse as to forget his insignificant brother altogether.

That was a great occasion. Uncle Kolya would phone them and tell them he was coming, and after that the Pushkins were all jittery, and we, the neighbor children, were present and shared the mood.

We all roamed from room to room, but the Pushkins' room was a sort of club because the Pushkins had two children, and I was an only child, and the Marleviches also had only Lyalechka. We never went to the Grekhovs, the sinners, because they were too much below our class, the smell of their sinful diapers being unbearable. They were rough, uneducated paupers in our class view. And the Lettish rifleman never invited us because he had no family and perhaps secretly despised all of us as unworthy of his heroic past.

Uncle Kolya was punctual. Nina's father would sit down to dinner, and here you are—three rings at the door, that was for the Pushkins, and Uncle Kolya passed through the corridor, swiftly, noiselessly, and precisely like a bicycle.

The dinner essentially consisted of cabbage soup which did not stink at all when on the table, or at least Nina's father sat down to it with such pleasure that this was how we felt about it. The rye bread (the same as under the tsar, except for some top-secret quantities of who knows what added to the rye flour) lay in puffy hunks on a wooden tray: the Pushkins could afford it, for it was procured from a lower serf caste ("Procured: Total") and was *given* to them more cheaply, in relation to world prices, than anything else, except for potatoes. The plate brimming with cabbage soup was followed by a plate moderately full of cabbage soup, and here the dinner ended, but the highlight of the dinner was something else: a jigger of vodka.

In the Russian tradition, vodka is not drunk like whiskey or pernod. Rather it is a kind of medicine taken for its effect, not for its taste, and only a foreigner can relish the taste of the medicine as something sensuous and exotic. A real vodka drinker turns up his face, opens his mouth, and pours the dosage into his throat, the trick being to prevent its spasmodic contraction. He does not swallow it: he *pours* it through his throat. But that jigger of vodka was so expensive that Nina's father sipped it as foreigners do. He became a gourmet savoring every costly sip between spoonfuls of steaming cabbage soup, because he wanted it to last throughout the repast: under no circumstances would he get another jigger. He was to have a nap and then sit down to writing "Procured: Total." And so he worked until midnight to make money because he would not let Nina's mother work, and had to work for two, procuring that grain in his tiny neat letters.

Uncle Kolya would decline the cabbage soup, and have only a jigger of vodka which he didn't touch until the end of the visit, then tumbled it into his throat, sat on for a while, and said: "Well, Sergey, I must be going." He stood up, brand new, swift, and glittering (on his uniform collar were the bars showing his rank, very low no doubt), and moved noiselessly out, almost like a film of himself played backwards.

Throughout the visit Uncle Kolya would not say a word, except that I remember two sentences he had said once before. "You know," he said, "I have begun to work with politicals. You say: 'Have a smoke,' and he says: 'Thank you.' "

Before he must have been dealing with toughs of the under-underworld, and they could eat him up, or be eaten—they had ways different from humans. And suddenly he heard: "Thank you." He wanted to convey to his brother how refined his new appointment was—with what refined society he now mingled. "Have a smoke." "Thank you." But Uncle Seryozha neglected the news from another department. Uncle Kolya never spoke again, and Uncle Seryozha provided all the entertainment. Having sipped off most of the jigger, he would lift it and say: "Life has become better."

We would reel with laughter because Uncle Seryozha's political wit struck us as really uncanny. Great Stalin had just said: "Life has become better, life has become merrier." By coincidence the price of half a liter of vodka was raised from 3.15 to 5.00 rubles, and since the word "rubles" rhymes with "merrier" in Russian, the saying was: "Life has become better, life has become *merrier*, it was three fifteen, and now it's five *rubles*." It was enough to say a certain part of this ditty, which everyone knew, to ridicule something that was very dangerous to ridicule and yet be perfectly safe. What delighted us was Uncle Seryozha's allusion to the new price of vodka (of which so little remained in his jigger). Then he would tell his favorite story about a clerk having a magic pen which wrote for him any clever memo or report he wanted. In great detail Uncle Seryozha described a dizzy rise of the clerk to prestige and power.

That was perhaps a dig at Uncle Kolya, because Uncle Seryozha would say to my father: "Andrey, I'm a sm-a-all man, right?" He would drawl the word *small* plaintively to show how small he was. "But there is a good proverb: "The higher you fly. . . ." He peered into a high, high distance and added as though in a tipsy sleep: "The lower you fall."

So that clerk with his magic pen finally arrived at some super-conference very high up. "Now, his pen. . . ."

Though we knew the end (the clerk had lost his pen), we enjoyed the story each time again. "His pen. . . ." Uncle Seryozha protruded his jaw in a very humorous way and made his eyes very tipsy. "His pen. . . . He had lost his pen!"

The last word would be drowned in our laughter. The walls of Bloom's dining room were darkly paneled, and the room was in darkness like the pit of the theater, with the table in spotlight.

When Uncle Kolya was about to say: "Well, Sergey, I must be going," he said instead: "Well, Sergey, what about another one?"

It was as though the bicycle had suddenly spoken up.

The Pushkins did not want to know anything about Kolya's high-up work or to have any closer relations with him. They believed in staying low and saving money by eating that special sauerkraut. They were neat, precise, reserved. His rare bicycle-like visits had suited them, and here he was suddenly speaking like some wretch in a beerhouse: "What about another one?"

His voice was strange too. It was a strange piece of unpleasant humanity that suddenly emerged to their disgust and dismay out of the neat bicycle.

His face had changed. I remember very well that he always looked above our heads, like a statue looking straight out from its pedestal, except that the statue moved very briskly about. Now something about his face was similar to the smirk of guilt or despair of one of the Grekhovs' sons, Mitya.

As he very awkwardly put his elbows on the table, he brushed off the plate that had been set for his bread as for a high-society guest. He said: "Apologizing, of course" (which was thought to be the educated way of saying "I am sorry"), but he did not understand what a broken plate meant to the neat, precise, money-scraping Pushkins. Was he drunk? Or ill? Or tired? The Pushkins did not know and did not want to know.

"Nikolay Timofeyevich," Nina's mother (whom we called Aunt Nyura) said in a high-society voice. "Perhaps you will spend the night at our place?"

She did not add: "Rather than going to. . . ," because no one knew where he lived.

Aunt Nyura had been the first beauty of Ufa or at least some street of Ufa, and married Uncle Seryozha "on the rebound." Like Nina she looked very much like a pepper shepherdess. The same porcelain whiteness touched with a china painter's red. From Ufa she had brought their own notion of high-society talk, and she spoke with his brother-in-law as though she were eighteen and he fourteen and wearing a suit for the first time and looking quite a grown-up man, so that a bit of quizzical flirtation might be quite proper.

Of course, Uncle Kolya was supposed to pull himself together back into a bicycle, say something like "Thanking you, of course" (instead of "Thank you"), and roll out the way he rolled in. Instead he continued to unravel into a drunken beerhouse wretch. "I cannot sleep at your place," he said, "because I try not to sleep at all." He said this as though expecting them to exclaim: "Not sleep at all? Oh, how very horrible!"

Instead Uncle Seryozha wanted to be as funnily in his cups as he had been before when telling the story about the magic pen.

"How's that?" he asked, protruding his jaw.

"Just as one tries not to get drowned. That's how. I sleep for a second, and . . ."

"But why?" Uncle Seryozha asked as though he still were very much in his cups.

"Because as soon as I fall asleep, that thing is there."

Uncle Seryozha was silent, his eyes radiating sober green aloofness. But Uncle Kolya continued to rave:

"How do I know, eh? Nothing. But it is there. I know."

"Ye-a-a-h," Uncle Seryozha drawled vaguely as though winding up the discussion about elliptical integrals by admitting the awesome abstruseness of the subject and his own utter inadequacy.

"It is there," Uncle Kolya repeated. "There is nothing, but it is there. And I yell. Hell, how I yell."

Aunt Nyura froze into a porcelain pepper shepherdess. Now Uncle Seryozha was not in his cups at all. His eyes were light, cold, greenish, somewhat bulging, and there was now a light greenish coldness even in his voice.

"I want the world to crack," Uncle Kolya raved on. "I'll yell so that the world will crack. Maybe I want it to get scared. Or I want it to take pity on me."

The word *pity* was outrageous. Mitya Grekhov could speak that way. Uncle Kolya—brand new, machinelike, glittering like his bicycle—had descended before our eyes to Mitya Grekhov! He was making a scene. It was clear he could do now anything —smash all the plates, for example. Instead he said, rather quietly: "Hell, how I yell."

"Well," said Uncle Seryozha greenishly, coldly, determined to stop the scene—in front of the neighbor children too.

"I yell also because I do not want to hear it. And the world cracks. But it's my noodle that cracks," he said with a tinge of self-irony. "But this is really all right. It's bad when there's nothing, but it is there. Nothing—but growing. Because time is slow maybe. It passes through me, and when my top's cracked I sleep for a second."

"Is that all?" Uncle Seryozha asked, very rudely, to show that the spree was over.

"No. Then it differs. I may laugh."

About thirty years later a slow-death camp inmate told me a story when I described to him my childhood memory.

A Lett escaped from their camp, and when the men in pursuit almost overtook him they fired point-blank. Dumdum bullets were used for fear that a wounded fugitive might escape and *tell*. The Lett spun, the men saw that the bullet had torn out his whole stomach, and they began to laugh and could not stop.

There was no pain on the victim's face, the former inmate told me, but surprise—disbelief as he looked at himself and perhaps still heard that laughter. "This could not have happened to me," his face said. "I remember the socks my mother put on my feet, I dangled my feet, *this could not have happened to me.*"

Uncle Seryozha was now really angry, but Uncle Kolya would not notice.

"Because it makes you laugh," said Uncle Kolya. "The way he is looking. Then I laugh because if I laugh this means it is not me."

"What next?"

"But I cannot stop, see? I am asleep, but cannot stop it. I feel foam—on my lips. Help me, I want to yell, my stomach will burst with laughter, here it bursts in my stomach, and then I think I wake up into him."

"Clear," Uncle Seryozha said with businesslike sobriety and put his jigger upside down to show that the spree was over now beyond any doubt.

Uncle Kolya got up, moving more like a sack than a bicycle, and when the door we called the *main door* banged after him, Aunt Nyura came to life and said: "You could at least see him off."

To which Uncle Seryozha wheezed (now one could see he was asthmatic): "He'll manage on his own."

56

Since every communal apartment had once been intended for one family, there was only one electric meter (and gas meter), and so each apartment received one bill though it consisted of many families, and some rooms had split into separate families.

They were to divide the bill among themselves, but even today there are still as many methods of division as there are communal-apartment families, and each family tended to defend its own method as the best and argued for it in the sphere where it felt itself at the strongest. Those kindred to the humanities argued in terms such as "imminent justice" and tried to crush their opponents by academic erudition, brilliance, cogency. The formally uneducated people retaliated by plain common sense, physical vigor, and rudeness. A bookkeeper would make havoc of the enemy ranks by esoteric invocations like "*pro-rata*" or "carryover," while scientists and engineers used the arguments derived from their respective fields.

Should the gas bill be divided per capita? But if it were, the populous families like the Grekhovs would bear the brunt, and they naturally fought like lions against this egalitarian sophistry. Could any sane person assert that their tiny tot consumed as much gas as the Lettish rifleman (still unarrested at that time) who drank a huge pot of (artificial, barley) coffee each morning? Anastasia was temperamentally an artist rather than a scientist. Therefore, she put in more and more color as she varied the theme, and finally the picture of social injustice was overwhelming: a helpless tiny tot who hardly consumes anything at all is made to pay as much as the mammoth Lett *devouring* whole vats of coffee, and Anastasia showed by artistic gesticulation how prodigious those vats were, how they were brought to a sumptuous boil on the raging sky-high gas fires and *devoured* by the monster of social depravity, wishing also, in his anarchic Western individualism, to black *his* private shoes in the communal corridor belonging to *all*.

The decisive dispute would take place on a *day off*, and at the hottest point of the debate Anastasia (who had not yet quarreled with her daughters at that time) brushed our pan of potatoes off the stove, and the potatoes rolled all over the floor, much to my delight because they all rolled simultaneously and my eyes ran away with me as I watched so many fanciful rollings. Repeating my delight, my mother shoved off *their* pan of potatoes, and though the pan belonged to one of Anastasia's daughters it was all right because at that time she was at one with them.

Communal apartment existence like ours has been a highly privileged mode of life compared with life in barracks or even newly built barracklike housing developments. Yet this highly privileged mode of life was marred by endless feuds, quite apart from the living-space tragedies, and the struggle for living space, the chief wealth of urban serfs. Inside a communal apartment it is very difficult to enforce even those crude laws or rules which exist to deter commoners from killing other commoners, because it is often impossible to prove who killed whom in self-defense or as a revenge, deliberately or unintentionally, while breaking into a neighbor's room or while defending his own. At the dawn of communal apartment life, in the early twenties, *Pravda* reported that a *worker of the organs of state security* murdered his communal neighbor. The neighbor happened to be a fairly high ranker, and so *Pravda* interceded, as was its custom in those days of not yet monolithic unity. But then the case bogged down, and according to one rumor the neighbor had been attacking the *worker*, while according to another, the *worker* had provoked his neighbor into attack in order to kill him and get hold of his living space.

A magazine writer friend of my father specialized in communal-apartment humor. His vignettes showed the readers how petty, vulgar, and imperfect they were if they engaged in communal-apartment feuds. As luck had it, the aristocratic humorist himself had to live for a while in a communal apartment where the electric-bill debate took a bad turn. Insisting on his own method of computation, one of the debaters cut off the electric wires leading to the room of his opponent, the aristocratic humorist. As the aristocratic humorist sat in the thickening evening dusk of his room, the debater rushed in to continue his argument. The aristocratic humorist picked up an ordinary table knife and thrust it into the debater. He was acquitted by the court, owing to his money, pull, and the fact that all members of the victim's family testified against the victim: locked in with him in one room, they had been engaged in bitter strife for years.

Whenever enemies lived in one room, their strife would go on day and night, and there were unlimited opportunities for harming the other side without leaving any provable evidence. The mildest harm was to find and regularly eat up the enemy's food or the choicest bits of it, and a more serious damage was to set the enemy on fire, sounding the alarm and loudly cursing the enemy's culpable negligence, before the fire had spread over the friendly section of the room.

Later in life, I would look out from my eternal abode and see the same windows on the house opposite, and more windows down the street. As the windows began to warm up with light like icon lamps, each window became a family, and sometimes two families, locked in eternal abodes, and sometimes a dweller had to return for the night to his eternal abode, especially in winter, in order to kill his enemy with a table knife, or to be set on fire, or to be poisoned.

Our neighbors were, indeed, very good by comparison, and finally the Pushkins suggested a method of gas pay division no one could defeat in a debate.

Henceforth every payer—a single neighbor or a family—was to hang up his own slip of paper over the gas stove, and each time write down for how long he had used it. Then all the figures on the slip would be added to yield the sum total in hours for the respective payer. All the totals would be added to get the grand total in hours. The bill in rubles would be divided by the grand total in hours, to get the cost of one hour, to be multiplied by each payer's sum total in hours.

The method depended on conscience.

Thus, if you had made the fire lower, you would consume less gas within the same time than you would over a high fire, and it would be only fair to write down less time. But how much less? An entirely introspective conflict of conscience ensued: the user had to listen to his innermost—no, not even a voice, but a diffuse orchestra, a troubled sea of violins and yearnings, as Rilke said.

Now, take Anastasia. She had a Christian or, more exactly, Orthodox Church conscience. Very good. But the Lettish rifleman had only a class (*party*, and so on) conscience, according to which one had to have conscience only with respect to his class (*party*, and so on). And Anastasia's daughters had no conscience at all.

The strife soon resurged in mutual exposures, recriminations and appeals to conscience. There was nothing else to appeal to, since a *very* low fire could well consume just a tiny fraction of gas consumed by a *very* high fire, and actually it amounted to each neighbor's declaration as to what portion of the bill he wanted to pay according to his conscience.

The Marleviches and we had to pay almost the whole bill, for our consciences were less pressed by poverty and what Keynes calls the propensity to save. Besides, even Anastasia, who hated all whom she once loved, never hated Marlevich's wife because she was an angel. As an angel, she found any method of gas pay division full of justice, elegance, and wisdom. As for Marlevich himself, he shunned the debate as something likely to undermine his energy, while my father just laughed. "Essenes!" he would shout. "Cenobites!"

57

Professor Marlevich enjoyed the regime as he enjoyed washing himself: he enjoyed it frenziedly, if only because this frenzied enjoyment was good for his health and energy, every ounce of which he needed to move on in his professorship, to become some day perhaps a general or a marshal, if not the generalissimo of medicine, taking care of the health of great Stalin himself, becoming internationally known among his colleagues, and even living, yes, in a whole apartment as big as Bloom's apartment all for himself and his family. Suppose great Stalin fell ill? "Marlevich! Call Marlevich! No one but Marlevich!" And Marlevich would turn up. "Do you know what it is? An ulcer!"

When some fifteen years later Marlevich lost, as a *jew by passport*, his professorship, a major achievement of his insanely hard single-minded frenzied life, he could not believe it. Jews pariahs? Anyone can be a pariah, but not a Jew, certainly. He a pariah because his passport says: Jew? But this simply could not be. Why, what about those huge luxuriously bound volumes, published since 1935, in which children from all over the country castigated in verse and prose the persecution of Jews in Germany?

He clutched desperately at what he had been creating all his life with as much frenzy, but the possession-power which he had been enjoying with such frenzy was kicking his desperately clutching hands and his utterly surprised rather than horrified face. He still washed every morning frenziedly, but now it was like drowning. He was a drowning man kicked but refusing to drown. He *flew* up the five flights of stairs as before in fresh outbursts of frenzy, and one day, once on the last, the fifth, landing, he fell dead because his heart had failed.

Today some *russians by nationality* recall this frenzied love for the regime of some *jews by nationality* and explain it as a special perversity of the *jewish mind*, in contrast to the *russian mind*, for example. That perverse *jewish mind* absorbs *marxism*, *communism*, or at least *socialism*, and no matter how reality contradicts it, this mind casuistically blocks out anything but its perverse belief.

Unfortunately, *russians by nationality* who present such an explanation display exactly the same perverse casuistry. As we know, in the *propaganda*, the symbolism: proletarians-of-all-countries-unite-and-help-those-in-possession-power-to-acquire-the-rest-of-the-world began to change in 1930 (though the change can be traced to Trotsky's stance in 1917) into the symbolism: all-Russians-here-and-abroad-and-all-who-hate-the-Jewnited-States-of-America-in-South-America-Africa-Asia-and-Europe-unite-and (the rest as before). When a *jew by nationality* defended *marxism* or whatever up to 1949 to any lengths of absurdity, he defended his aryanism, which the symbolism still suggested, signified, promised. When a *russian by nationality* today condemns the *jewish mind* as incurably prone to casuistry like *marxism*, and defends his *love for our holy russia* to any lengths of absurdity, he defends *his* aryanism, which the new symbolism has been indicating more and more clearly.

"So I cannot sincerely, selflessly, fervently, love my sacred motherland Russia?" a *russian by nationality* may say in indignation.

Similarly, a *jew by nationality* once exclaimed in indignation: "So I cannot sincerely, selflessly, fervently, love the world brotherhood of proletarians of all countries?"

When the loud expression of one's love of something or someone begins to be in consonance with his aryanism, promised or already received, in almost every situation his love begins to express merely one motivation: promised or granted aryanism. Only the symbols will be different, depending on the aryan group with which the sincere, selfless, fervent admirers identify or associate themselves. Some *russians by nationality* will be surprised to know that the expression of their *russian* faces when they now exclaim: "Russia!" is exactly the same as was on those *jewish* faces when the exclamation was: "Proletariat!" It is simply that one notices how phony, blind, and dangerous somebody else's aryanism is, but his own aryanism seems to him the truth itself or sublime poetry or innocent frolics at the very worst.

Professor Marlevich's love of the regime expressed itself mainly in frenzied cheerfulness, and there was every reason to be frenziedly cheerful.

To begin with, any living space in Moscow was a sign of the highest caste, nobility, achievement, just because it was in Moscow. But do you grasp the class distinctions inside the caste between different communal-apartment rooms in Moscow? Not some has-been like my father's friends, but really successful people like stage director Kedrov, who took over from Stanislavsky, said when he came to us: "What a magnificent room you have!"

To be sure. True, the roof leaked, but it would not always leak when the guests came. In fact when it was in order it leaked only in spring, and why should the guests come in spring? If it did leak in summer, autumn, or winter, then it was indeed out of order. True, the guests would ask as they saw the dark blotches on the ceiling: "Does the roof leak?" "Yes," we would answer. "But only in spring." They would nod their full understanding: nothing is perfect, there must be a certain tiny disadvantage to a magnificent room like that, and if spring is *one* bad season for our room, there are *three* good seasons! As for the Marlevich room, it always leaked less because the corner of the roof was over our room, and the water of the Marleviches would roll toward our roof corner.

But what about Switzerland, where Marlevich had once intended to go to study medicine? Or Russia before 1917 in which he had lived? Neither Switzerland nor pre-1917 Russia existed except as abstractions like, say, the star Alpha Centauri. On that star there are perhaps even better modes of life than the Marlevich room with its barely leaking roof. But one is hardly interested in life on stars when one is encumbered by a family and is fighting frenziedly for survival. Besides, a more leisured family man could find it a pleasant hobby to meditate about stars. But for Marlevich to meditate about more-remote-than-stars regions like Switzerland was infernally dangerous. A danger so infernal may arrest thinking. Perhaps Marlevich would not have been able to think of life in Switzerland no matter how hard he might have tried, just as an agitated man cannot produce saliva because the functioning of his salivary glands is arrested.

In the thirties, the word *border* began to occur in all manifestations of *propaganda*, from exhibitions of children's drawings to cigarette packages and German-language textbooks, perhaps as frequently as pretty girls, tourist scenery, or fashions in a free country's advertisements. The song "Katyusha," later sung all over the world, and indeed danced to by Americans, Canadians, and even Britons at diplomatic and international festivities, rendered the vocal equivalent of a vernal scene on a candy box. A candy-box girl, Katyusha, is longing for her candy-box boy, a *border* guard: let him *guard* our dear mother country, and their love Katyusha will *guard*! Band and all dancers once more in chorus:

> Let him guard our dear mother country!
> And their love—Katyusha will guard!

As the gentle reader may recall, the *border* was created in 1918. But by the thirties it had become a magic line, a sacred area, a holy wall: if a child had a dog, for example, that meant he should give the dog away to Katyusha's boy, the *border* guard. Or to help in every other possible way to catch the satanic *violators of the border*.

A medieval man died and his soul went to heaven—that is, paradise—or to hell. A twentieth-century *state* serf is *born* into paradise. His soul *is* in paradise. Now, suppose a paradise-dweller is suddenly thinking: "What if I scram, eh?" Should a thought so unnatural, impossible, and satanic (very much so already in former Russia in 1918) occur to him, will he not realize himself that his cursed soul must be sent to hell, that is physinfluence as the realization of hell on earth with the aid of *special* sciences making stupendous progress? Sciences have made possible the realization of much of what was thought to be magic or religious miracles, and certainly they can also bring about an infinite and eternal hell, once thought to be possible only through the intermediacy of God. They can ensure the infinity and eternity of superinfernal suffering within a human lifespan, at minimum cost, and with maximum obliteration. Hells for the infernal network can be invented, designed, and produced like X-ray machines, heavy bombers, or maternity wards.

Marlevich had better look not aside at some hell-threatening phantoms like Switzerland, or upward at some Alpha Centauri or the heavens of heavenly religions, but downward: at those who were worse off than he, descending lower and lower in hazy vistas down to the inferno, and then descending into the infinity and eternity of its spirals. No matter how low a serf is, he can almost always be happy and proud of a certain peak he occupies, compared with those descending below. And Marlevich could contemplate with pride the majestic descending panorama at his feet.

58

The key of the whole structure is attachment. A serf is born in a *maternity ward* of a certain caste (by territory) and rank (by department) to which his parents are attached by their caste and rank. This determines the cost of his birth. He is registered in the passport of one of his parents as belonging to the caste territory. From infancy he is attached to the *children's institutions* of his caste by territory, or if one of his parents is not a commoner by department, then by that parent's rank. This determines the cost of his upbringing. The family can move of its own will only in their own caste territory or down the castes. On the other hand, anyone can be moved up and down and anywhere by the pseudo-tsar-god's will.

At the close of the thirties every *collective farm chairman* was to count up his male and female *collective farmers* between the ages of fourteen and fifty-five, divide the sum by 100, and multiply by 2. The figure he derived was the number of males aged fourteen to seventeen he was to earmark for *labor mobilization*. The word *mobilization* has in general been used so commonly since 1918, whether in *peace* or *war*, that a boy of fourteen and his family would have found it strange to think that a boy of fourteen could not be *mobilized* in *peace*, just as in war. Anyone can be *mobilized* always: that *mobilization* of their boy of fourteen was a plague, an elemental calamity, a sudden enemy raid against which it was futile or dangerous to murmur. All they could do was forever lose their boy to the mines, relinquish him to some other such attachment practically for life, or hide him, which was much more hopeless than hiding a Jew in Nazi Germany.

On reaching the age of sixteen the urban inhabitant is issued his own passport, a highly elaborate 14-page pocket dossier (printed on special paper with ingenious secret precautions, filled out with special pens, which are kept in safes, and stamped with seals of every kind). The passport is a portable replica of those dossiers which the *proper quarters* keep, so that every passport can be checked within minutes. The passport indicates the serf's caste by territory to which he is attached by birth or *mobilization* (*exile*, or other transfers not of his will), the work to which he is attached (unless he is still attached to a *school* of his caste), and the *nationality* (*russian*, or *jew*, or *armenian*, or whatever) in which he was born, according to the *nationality* in the passport of one of his parents. Coded information is said to indicate secretly the bearer's secret caste: for example, he may be thus destined never to be permitted to migrate beyond a certain territorial caste even if he marries into a higher caste or gets into it by other such means allowed for the other serfs of his caste.

However, the passport openly indicates its bearer's *social position*: *peasant*, *worker*, or *serving man*, an old Russian word meaning a bureaucrat, serviceman, officer, official, office employee, scribe, clerk. Those who are not *peasants* or *workers* are *serving men* of all fields from literature to *special* medicine. This rough open triple-caste division of all passport-bearing serfs is also useful. If the bearer is a *peasant*, this means he may not be entitled to be in Moscow even if he is properly dressed and it is daytime. His passport has been issued for a short trip to the nearest *district center*, while the rascal has dressed well and sneaked right to Moscow. If he is a *worker,* he may be entitled to be in Moscow in the daytime, but he is a nobody and will be handled accordingly. Only a luxuriously dressed *serving man* can turn out to be somebody who may have pull at the top and make some trouble for those who mishandle him.

Throughout his life the serf will be attached to the *medical institutions* of the corresponding caste by territory or one of his parents' rank by department, and if he reaches a higher rank by department, his attachment will move up to the *medical* (and all other) *institutions* of his own rank, and when he dies, he will be buried according to his born caste by territory or his own rank by department, if it is sufficiently high above his born estate.

The role of *ordinary* (common) *money* in a serf caste society is naturally limited. Apart from common money, that is money for lower castes, there are different high-caste monies (thus, stripeless rubles of one caste buy what neither yellow-striped, nor green-striped certificate rubles of the somewhat lower castes can buy). Besides, there have been, since 1918, high-caste rations, *closed distributions* and all kinds of high-caste benefits, issues, or rewards free of charge or at different high-caste low prices for different high castes. As for *ordinary money*, it merely creates different classes (a class society) within each caste: an exceptionally strong and capable miner, a champion of mining, so to speak, may make several times more money than a local doctor, but neither will transcend his territorial caste to which they are both attached, with its own range, quality, and prices of all goods and services, with its own cost per capita of all *free benefits of socialism*, and so forth.

If in a twentieth-century democracy like the United States wages are higher, or prices and rents lower, or any aspects of life more attractive in California than in New York, the population of New York may migrate some 3,000 miles to California. In a country of territorial-departmental attachment, entirely different civilizations can be ordered for adjacent territories, and no migration is possible. The map of the country once called Russia is actually that of thousands of entirely different countries (or civilizations), some of them completely closed or top secret.

As mountains are shown by color gradations on a conventional geographic map, the mountains of departmental ranks can be shown on this map inside each country of attachment. The *collective farm chairman* will be the absolute peak of a certain tiny country (called *collective farm*) in one of the lowest castes, with several hundred or thousand commoners attached as eternal inhabitants of this country in which they are to live and die unless snatched away all of a sudden by a force more inexorable than death. But the absolute peak of this country is below the caste status of a janitor's wife in a local *district center*: the *collec-*

tive farm chairman has reached the very top of his tiny country, exhausted the civilization into which he was born, and now he may die in the greatest glory he can achieve, barring the interference of that force which can snatch anyone all of a sudden and turn him into nothing or make him a high superaryan—even in Moscow. And in a *special zone* he may be attached to, say, the training for *foreign work* in a sham new york or a sham los angeles, from where he will go to New York—or California if you like, because a secret agent who visited his village decided that he looked like somebody who was needed.

Not that a serf must remain ever passive, waiting all his life until someone from above comes, appreciates some value of his for his owners (like the facial resemblance to someone in a democracy), and takes him up to a higher caste. He is allowed to do his utmost locally to show his value for his owners, and perhaps the most important common means to do so is *education*. A member of any caste may show his value locally in this way and finally get up as high as Moscow to study at an *institute*. If he shows himself at the *institute* in Moscow to be a genius in mathematics, or any other field indispensable for weapons or *means of production*, he may be allowed to stay in Moscow (or in some open or secret *science township*, equivalent by estate to the *central districts* of Moscow) and climb the central mountain of ranks, dominating all the local mountains of ranks in former Russia, former Hungary, and so on. If he is not recognized during his *education* as valuable for his owners, he will be sent back to his born caste—or lower.

Unless the *chairman of the collective farm* or his *farmer* has shown extraordinary ability as human *means of production* or has married into a higher caste, they are destined to live and die in their tiny country, even the peak of which lies below perhaps the lowest of the *district center*. The mountain of ranks of chiefs of the *district center* is, in turn, below the entire civilization, which is called a *regional or republican center*.

Kazan is the center—the *capital*—of the Tatar *republic*, which is called *autonomous*, meaning that it is a lesser *republic* than the Ukraine. The *minister of social security* of this *republic* belongs to a level not far from the top of the mountain of ranks in the *republic* on our map of *soviet* civilizations.

In the fifties my mother was once told that the *minister of social security* of the Tatar *republic* would come to see her at home. We were rather embarrassed. A *minister*, a *member of the cabinet*, so to speak, in our communal apartment! We opened the door to five rings (four is to the Marleviches and six to the Grekhovs) and saw—well, only Muscovites who were definitely down and out, who "let go," as mother used to say (she despised the weak-willed, no matter in what regime), were dressed and shod like that. The woman minister was tongue-tied, frightened, awkward. She said that her children had never seen oranges, and here in Moscow she had bought them an orange apiece. "When a vacation pleasure ship arrives from Moscow, there are oranges aboard, and some people manage to coax the passengers into buying some for them," she said shyly. There is a shyness about Tatar women that makes them even more Russian than Russians sometimes. "We have money," she added, to show that she belonged to the respectable monied people. "But it is awkward for me, you know."

She meant it was awkward for a *minister of social security* to hang around (like a Pacific native near a western cruise liner) in order to get some oranges. In the fifties the near-peak of the mountain of ranks in the *autonomous republic* was below the lowest level of the whole highest-estate plateau: Moscow.

59

Attachment was partly stimulated by the need to conceal from the outside world the lower-caste serfs (not to mention the slaves) used as human *means of production* and human weapons.

It was naturally assumed that foreigners should see at close quarters only the most aryan 1 percent caste, and at a distance (as figures in a landscape or cityscape, for example) the richest one-tenth of the population, dressed (or costumed?) more or less decently, especially if viewed at a distance.

The privileged few, whose income starts at three Italian $1.40 raincoats a month and zooms to infinity, numbered about 2 million by the mid-fifties, and even if 2 million are attached to the *central districts* of foreign-exhibition cities, they will fill up almost all of them, with their aryan privileges like telephones, foreign dress, and even cars sometimes.

The concentration of the richest 1 percent of the population at the *centers*, and especially at the center of centers, Moscow, is anyway inevitable in every society centrally ordered, stimulated, and inspected. The highest ranks by department must naturally concentrate in the highest territorial castes.

Pseudo-tsar-god II remembered the lesson of St. Petersburg in 1917: he wanted to be surrounded territorially by the checked, chosen, attached, highest estate—let a janitor in Moscow be more prosperous, aryan, and hence devoted than the *minister of social security of an autonomous republic*. Keep the *center* in safety, and the periphery can always be reconquered. The nearer to the pseudo-tsar-god territorially, the higher and richer must be the caste by territory and department. His Winter Palace, his Versailles, his court, must be at the same time the highest mountain of ranks in the highest-caste territory, with several second-highest mountains of ranks in the second-highest-caste territory, linked up by special routes along which he can *travel* with his foreign guests.

Territorially adjacent to each estate or rank must be the nearest estate or rank: there must be a gradual, not abrupt, transition of castes. Each caste should see only its adjacent higher or lower caste. It is bad for both castes when they are too socially disparate yet are not completely isolated.

At Moscow *district hospitals* there are special wards for those who are not low enough by rank to share wards with common Muscovites, yet not high enough to be attached to special hospitals above Moscow *district hospitals*. Hardly anything causes more outbursts of social indignation among common Muscovites. They rarely notice, however, that nearly all equipment at these Moscow *district hospitals* has been bought abroad, while at a *hospital* elsewhere there may be no equipment at all—the *hospital* may be essentially a barracks called a *hospital*. They are indifferent to the thousands of castes below them, but as soon as they come in touch with just an adjacent higher estate, they are indignant. Therefore, even adjacent castes, territorially quite near, must be isolated. However, when possible, castes should be separated territorially as well.

Separated territorially, one caste may know nothing about the mode of life of another caste: even if a writer, official or underground, describes—without any statistics, photography, or any other modern methods, but on the basis of his own naked-eye observations, as in the day of Herodotus—the life of a too low or too high caste, compared with the castes of the exhibition areas, his writing will be *antisoviet* by definition and will entail, if distributed in any form, up to fifteen years of slavery for himself and up to five years of slavery for his readers, though our owners' lenience has been steadily diminishing.

A citizen of a democracy may imagine that a member of one caste can, say, speak at least over the telephone to a member of a higher caste. This is part of the nineteenth-century dream that "civilization," "technology," "science" will "diffuse class distinctions in all countries," "make all countries converge." "unite mankind." Actually, the highest caste has a separate, secret, untappable telephone system of its own. No member of the lower caste can phone to a member of the highest caste over this system. Every high caste has its secret *dialing code* which disconnects any telephone conversation of any lower caste. The number of telephones decreases precipitously as the territorial castes get lower, and more than 9/10 of the populace have, practically, no telephones at all.

This is the universal principle of information and communication in caste society: the higher the caste the more (closed) information and intercommunication it enjoys, while the lower castes, muted and disconnected, receive only one-way *propaganda* from above in the form of a single *newspaper, film, radio and television program* under different titles, presenting *statistics, literature*, and other varieties of *propaganda*.

All the important books or periodicals published all over the world are secretly translated and secretly published in an edition of several dozen or hundred or thousand copies for the respective highest castes. There are real newspapers in the country (like *Blue Tass*) which have nothing to do with *Pravda* and which differ in secrecy and hence quality from caste to caste and from rank to rank. So that the very highest caste may receive much more detailed, objective, and comprehensive news than, say, the readers of the New York *Times*, while 99 percent of the population did not know that Nazi Germany had been invading the country.

The serfs of the higher castes shown to foreigners must engage in exemplary-demonstrational activity: they must be live exhibits and not only rich aryans or superaryans, although special live exhibits can be created, too, of course, to personify *prison inmates* and such.

Exemplary-demonstrational activity originated at least as early as 1919. Does the gentle reader remember the *socialist*, the heroic idealist, nay, the saint Angelica Balabanoff? She describes her role in the reception of the British Workers' Delegation, accompanied by Bertrand Russell:

When I arrived I found Radek already on hand. The food question was being discussed, and Radek had just proved the "absolute necessity" of placing our guests under extraordinary privileged conditions and of providing them as well with the wines and liquors which were forbidden in Russia at the time.

The time was the *civil war*, the *breakdown of everything*, the famine of many years, with 25 million expected to die of hunger in the Volga region alone, according to *Pravda*.

The receptions, parades, demonstrations, theatrical performances etc., staged for the English delegation as long as they were in Russia . . .

When we arrived in Moscow I found that an entire hotel had been renovated for our English guests and that their visit in Moscow was to be initiated by an impressive banquet.

According to Miss Balabanoff, she alone ("my attitude was unique") "protested vehemently":

Why should we make exceptions for our English comrades? Can't they live a few weeks as our people have lived for years? What have we to conceal?

So even then, during the time which many Western scholars recall as the pristine springtide of heroic idealism, social revolution and great experiment, untainted as yet by subsequent ulterior motives, even then—during the *civil war*, breakdown of everything, and unprecedented famine—foreigners were to enjoy themselves, like those inspectors general that Gogol had satirized a century before, in a certain closed, cozy, artfully staged world of revelry, abundance and entertainment, a happy country of deception, make-believe and bribe. The owners of Russia correctly decided that to make the foreigners look through the eyes of the serf owners, and not through those of the serfs, to induce the foreigners to identify the "Russian people" with the pseudo-tsar-god, and to prompt the foreigners to help the pseudo-tsar-god to destroy world democracy, it is useful to bribe, in Gogol's way, all those fastidious humanists, hypersensitive prophets, or tireless specialists of selective compassion for the poor, the down-trodden, the miserable. In their democracy, they show their selective compassion—and get elected. Why should all these statesmen of democracies, champions of the underprivileged, show their compassion for the serfs dying of hunger who cannot elect them or carry to power or high status? Bribe all the pious, the righteous, the saintly—bribe them as boldly as provincial officials bribed inspectors general in pre-1861 Russia. There might be failures (and there were some), but there is no risk in trying, and so try it boldly on whoever you want to buy, and on the whole it will work. "We do not need to bribe these people; they are not coming here for a good time," the socialist Balabanoff protested vehemently, all alone, against the bribing of the British Laborites, and straight on, next paragraph, she writes:

I left for Petrograd immediately, and with the help of some women comrades prepared an apartment in the Naryshkin Palace, formerly owned by a Russian princess.

The palace of a Russian princess, prepared by some women comrades (not chambermaids?) is assumed by the Western *socialist* to present a fair average of how "our people" had been living "for years." The lowest depths correspond no doubt to the palace of only a countess or a duchess.

Like many other aspects of the *great experiment*, the creation of the imaginary country not only by means of "dead propaganda," such as *statistics*, *documentary films*, and *literature*, but also by means of "live propaganda," that is serf theatricalizations for the benefit of foreign visitors, developed as a result of many accidental rediscoveries, transformations, and coincidences.

Originally, it was suggested that since, say, all printshops could not be made good all at once, it would be worthwhile to make *one* printshop *exemplary-demonstrational* so that all the other printshops could study, emulate, be inspired, and all mankind could see what a bright future awaited it. It was to be a futuristic exhibition which was to have no bearing on the average cost for enterprises or projects or services of the same name. A live exhibition, with ordinary printshop employees as exhibits. A large good modern printshop had, indeed, been created and run before 1917 by a *capitalist* named Sytin. The new owners of Russia began to show it to all visitors as an advanced sample of unprecedented progress of their regime. Sytin's Printshop was duly renamed the First Exemplary Printshop. The name implied that not all printshops had as yet been brought to the same unprecedented level of post-1917 progress. However, it was soon found that many foreign visitors were so spontaneously or deliberately gullible that adjectives like *exemplary* or *demonstrational* could also be safely dropped, and it became clear that the possibilities for such exemplary-demonstrational activity were infinite because everyone was attached to his *place of work*, and hence every unit or area in the country could have a certain positive (to show!) or negative (to hide!) value without any risk of movement of the attached toward better conditions.

One of the boldest exemplary-demonstrational projects of the thirties was prompted by one of the famines. When the propaganda-religion-culture had proved beyond doubt that the once pauperized Russian peasants now lived in plenty, the starving began to gather, just as birds flock before going south, and the south of the hunger flock was Moscow. The fascists, pro-fascists, or quasi-fascists could call it a huge hunger march (or, perhaps, hunger flight?) on Moscow. Before Moscow the hunger flock was surrounded and seized, to disappear somewhere in top secrecy, and the event was mute, irreal, evanescent like a ghost pantomime, yet a whisper crept on.

To dispel the whisper, pseudo-tsar-god II decided to stage a bucolic play just as at the Russian court a couple of centuries before, but on a huge scale. The play represented a kind of *agricultural exhibition*. Again, the idea had originated as early as 1921 when the *congress of the soviets* decided to hold an all-Russia *agricultural exhibition*. To exhibit what—in 1921? Those 25 million in the Volga region who were expected to die of hunger? Or their skeletons? No. According to *Pravda*, the project was to be a "demonstration in front of the capitalist world refusing to recognize us," a "state project of vast historic importance," a "systematically selected expressive panorama of our farming and its mapped-out development." Pravda referred to "some Gubernia Land Boards which keep in secret their proposals on the character and number of exhibits in order to 'stun' the Center and the neighbors with surprises." Out with their stunning surprises! Take the last food from those dying of hunger or fed by the United States and bring it to the all-Russia *agricultural exhibition* which will stun mankind. So even in his exhibitions great Stalin was only a modest disciple of 1918 to 1921. He demonstrated! He proved! He stunned!

The foreign visitors could now see for themselves that the country was bursting with choice food, and at the same time, the *communists*, that is, the actual and potential superaryans of all countries, as well as all the other important guests, could enjoy the event as a fete at the new world court, as a bucolic play, enacted by charming rustics, shepherds and shepherdesses, in numerous agricultural palaces combining pretty-pretty Versailles coyness with honky-tonk garishness. The problem was the foodstuffs which were not just props, but *real* foodstuffs, and had to be renovated all the time, and it was not easy to get them even as props for the play.

There was only one drawback. Why was it called an *exhibition*? Why not set up such exhibitions just as real life which foreigners can see for themselves and thus dispel all the slander spread by enemies abroad?

A foreigner was not only to be put up at special residences, feasted, entertained, and so forth, according to his usefulness for the possession-power, but looking out the window of some former Princess Naryshkin's palace, he was to see the equally pleasant scenery of the imaginary country—an eternal exhibition-festival, showing the big-hearted, pleasantly exotic, if somewhat naïve happiness of the natives.

If necessary, properly costumed serfs may theatricalize an exact replica of any society on earth. Of the United States? Here you are.

In addition to *taxation, trade unions, independent courts,* and such, there will be a *congress*, an *opposition party*, an *election* with many *parties*, and in short there will be absolutely everything, down to the dress, that is, the costumes. Indeed, in the thirties a superdemocracy was theatricalized, with a super-American Constitution. The only problem is to costume the serfs properly. That's the snag: there is never enough currency to buy enough costumes, props, and other items to enact the imaginary country on too large a scale, and therefore the United States or the super-United States can be theatricalized only just enough to provide a suitable landscape as seen from the Naryshkin palace or wherever foreigners are entertained.

The theatricalized imaginary country, the exhibition-fete-park for foreigners, is actually the imaginary paradise on earth. It is made to look like the United States simply because the serf owners secretly believe that this is the closest approximation: this is what the paradise on earth should be. Serf culture is always provincially imitative because it is not creative in the individualized, *bourgeois,* Western sense.

Except that some purely paradisal features are imagined in addition. In the imaginary country there are no accidents of any kind, let alone any natural calamities, crimes, or social misadjustments like unemployment. The Tashkent earthquake, the Odessa cholera, or the latest crash of a huge airliner a couple of miles from our house simply did not happen: there were no foreigners aboard the airliner, and so by morning the bulldozers had buried the airliner with all the corpses.

A *district prosecutor* is perhaps the only person who knows something about *crime,* that is, the crime perpetrated by commoners against other commoners of his *district,* in contrast to what may be inflicted on them by a superhuman force from above, called the *state.* For it is at these lowest levels that secret data on *private* crime or anything else begin to be adulterated in top secrecy: each *district,* then *region,* then *republic,* wants to look better than the other, in their secret data submitted upward, and certainly not much worse. "We have very little crime," a *district prosecutor* told me in 1956. Relatively speaking, he is right. His *district* is near Moscow, and the protection of serfs against the crime of other serfs varies, like everything, with the estate, rank, and/or the exemplary-demonstrational value of the territory: in a *district* at the *center* of Moscow the number of policemen may exceed many, many times the same in a district which foreigners do not even visit and to which quite common serfs are attached, so that a bit of self-destruction may be cheaper than police protection.

"We have very little crime, practically none. One murder a week, on the average. Can you imagine? Several factories, saloons with brawls every weekend, a highway, and just one murder a week. Often rather silly, too. A guy goes across that field to the station and meets another guy, hatless. 'Give me your hat,' the hatless guy suddenly orders. The guy in the hat won't. So the hatless guy knifes the guy with the hat and puts it on, then goes home and hides it, but we find him out by this hat. That guy couldn't even understand that he would get capital punishment. With people like that, only one murder a week. I don't understand it myself—touch wood."

Only one murder a week per district, which is so safe, good, and law-abiding, that is, has almost no crime at all, means a quarter of a million cases of murder a year per country (which is, incidentally, 25 times as many as the number of cases of murder and nonnegligent manslaughter in the United States for the same year).

From one-third to one-half of the population of the country has been seasonally unemployed for about forty years because in winter there is no work like farming or building but they cannot leave the villages or *settlements* to which they are attached. Those towns and cities which do not fit a *plan* for foreign exhibition, weapons, and *means of production* are simply left without a *state* kopeck for employment, repairs, supply, trade, or anything, while *state*-independent activity is a crime. Yet the population cannot move out.

When the British Prime Minister said in Parliament a few years ago that *some* unemployment is inevitable in *any* country, a Laborite shouted: "And what about the Soviet Union?" That Laborite levelled those Conservatives all right. Except that in 1964 the head of the Laboratory of Economic-Mathematical Studies in Novosibirsk, Abel Aganbegyan by name, said unguardedly in his lecture at a Moscow University seminar that from 25 to 30 percent of the population of small and medium cities of the *country of socialism* could find no employment. Nor could they move out: they were attached. Nor did they ever receive any relief, and even their very unemployment had been top secret: when Aganbegyan's lecture leaked to the West, and was published in *Bandiera Rossa*, a *communist* organ of Italy, the foreign correspondents were eager to see him, but he merely mumbled, at an interview, that "small and medium towns presented an employment problem," as the New York *Times* put it, and gave no figure as though arithmetic (not to mention statistics) had never existed in the history of mankind. And no figure will be leaked until the next lenient time in, say, half a century.

However, all this trifling static seasonal and permanent unemployment, measured by thirds or halves of the population and intrinsic in *state* serfdom, is diversified by unemployment explosions of all sizes as military orders (*plans*) of all sizes are changed, replaced, scrapped (like the studying of Spanish almost on a countrywide scale), and all those involved prove to be redundant yet often unable to go elsewhere because of attachment. Serfdom in Russia after 1917 has been not only static but cataclysmic as well: the serfs have been suffering not only because they cannot move, but also because they have been moved by the million against their will according to urgent *plans*, which clash with other *plans*, no less urgent, or which prove all wrong as suddenly, and are supplanted by other no less urgent *plans*.

But a single case of unemployment has been as inconceivable in the imaginary country since the early thirties as the latest crash of that airliner a couple of miles from our house. The turbulent chaos of cataclysmic serfdom involved in the global war game becomes in the imaginary paradise on earth a perfect harmony, a cosmic tranquillity, a *planned order*. A yesterday's teacher of Spanish (should Spanish become unecessary today since the capture of South America is rescheduled) transforms magically into a nuclear submarine mechanic or whoever fits today's *plan*. No means of transportation ever collide, sink, fall or get derailed, no structures burn or collapse, no infections spread, and no natural calamities occur. A kettle of boiling hot tea, should it ever fall, contrary to the *plan*, falls in a trajectory of perfect harmony, and if it scalds anyone, this only happens as a happy-end parable of *soviet medical care,* that is, of perfect harmony again.

As it is said in Revelation 21:4: "Death will be no more, neither will mourning nor outcry nor pain be anymore." This final touch is still lacking: the dead should be buried also secretly, or still better, they should be carried secretly outside the foreign exhibition areas and dumped there. And should any foreigners in the foreign exhibition areas inquire about someone missing, they should be told that he or she is on an important mission in accordance with the *plan*.

60

Naturally, live propaganda—the enactment by costumed serfs of the imaginary country—may be studied, described, and filmed, and thus be a source of dead propaganda, such as *statistics, literature,* or *documentary films.*

Thus, *statistics* invents *data* that look credible for the view from the Naryshkin palace and extrapolates these *data* for the total number of serfs and slaves (the *population of the country*), though until 1956 the nonexistence of about 20 million serfs and slaves had been successfully concealed: the *population of the country* in *statistics* had included some 20 million serfs (or *souls?*) which did not exist except as *numbers,* and only Khrushchev let the nonexistence of such a trifle in his property be revealed in his struggle against the direct successors to great Stalin.

It would have been absurd to expect that some *league of nations* or *united nations* or some other institutionalized collective Joseph Davies expressed any concern at this existence-nonexistence of some 20 million lives. Thousand of officials, national or international, experts, and scholars all over the world copy, quote, and process these *data,* and then thousands of others copy, quote, and process their *data,* and so the mirage spreads, reflected again and again, its source long lost. Those who have the will (and talent) to know, and not merely copy, try to catch discrepancies and leaks, and succeed sometimes, for no work of imagination is entirely imaginary and perfectly self-consistent. But these triumphs of detection are possible only until the skill of *special* sciences like *statistics*, is not sufficiently advanced, and with time the *data* will give fewer and fewer clues to reality while the imaginary country in its live and dead propaganda will become more and more hermetic, self-consistent, lifelike.

Some problems of *statistics* are quite interesting. Every democracy has a gross national product, doesn't it? Say it and we have it in our imaginary country too. Let it be about half of the gross national product of the United States. Why about half?

Since 1918 the imaginary country has been intended to seem almost, indeed, unarmed. As a result the democracies will be unarmed, too, refusing even to produce toy weapons for children. From this point of view it is worthwhile to indicate in *statistics* that the *military expenditures* are zero and the tanks that are reported slanderously in the Western press to appear in Europe from time to time are actually powerful (say, 500 horsepower) tractors, and this is what they essentially are. If the *military expenditures* are zero, a *gross national product* of about half that of the United States is not credible even for the exhibition as seen from the Naryshkin palace. An exhibit of Moscow, such as a rank-and-file doctor, engineer or scientist attached to Moscow, buys a $1.40 raincoat with his two-weeks' pay. A foreigner can read the prices at the exhibition at which he is allowed to stroll. And from the exhibits he may learn confidentially their wages and salaries. He may also conclude that the serfs outside the exhibition are even worse off than at the exhibition at which he is allowed to enjoy himself and benefit the possession-power in whatever big or small way he can.

But while the pseudo-tsar-god must seem almost pathetically unarmed, he must also seem omnipotent. More and more citizens of the democracies must feel behaviorally his growing omnipotence and compel their elected representatives to try their best to keep him in good humor, to reassure him in every way possible as to his sacred right of serf ownership, to—oh, no, not quite surrender like Finland, but half-surrender, quarter-surrender, or just a tiny bit surrender like the countries which have reportedly joined the secret club of those democracies that secretly undertake to give runaway serfs back to their great (or big) owners (some American officials have tried this too again, as in 1945, but were officially reprimanded). From this point of view, the *military expenditures* of the imaginary country must in *statistics* be 10, 100, 1,000 times larger than those of the United States, with the *gross national product* of the imaginary country raised accordingly. The democracies will then all surrender. Alas, not all yet. At least the United States still has the will and margin to increase its military expenditures. Therefore, to instill in the democracies both the inclination to *fight for peace* in order to be as peaceful as the pseudo-tsar-god is, and the inclination to surrender in face of his overwhelming and growing military might, the imaginary *military expenditures* must about match the real figure for the United States. In other words, when the American military experts take the *military expenditures* in rubles in the *soviet budget* and convert the sum into dollars by quite a complicated procedure allowing for all kinds of discrepancies, the imaginary military expenditures of the imaginary country they will present to Congress will just match the real military expenditures of the United States.

Accordingly, the *gross national product* of the imaginary country must be about half of the real figure for the United States. The *data* will be plausible as viewed from the Naryshkin palace: the shepherds and shepherdesses of the imaginary country are about half as prosperous as the citizens of the United States, but the *defense* of the paradise on earth consumes a larger portion of its imaginary *gross national product*: there have always been enemies all around since 1918, and the peaceful if heroic idealists have been compelled to defend the paradise on earth ever since then, for who would not be envious of the paradise on earth or greedy for its wealth or afraid of its shining example?

While *statistics* and other such *special* sciences are publishing *scientific data, literature* must re-create, in terms of literature, the *new life* of shepherds and shepherdesses on the basis of their live exemplary-demonstrational activity. *Literature* must show that the serf exhibits do not merely act, but really live that way, and the serfs outside the exhibition also live that way. A trend in the arts familiar to us from the arts of France under Absolutism at its European worst, and from the arts of Russia before the nineteenth century. To many people of the highest aryan caste today, any dissonant note in the imaginary country of shepherds and shepherdesses seems to be an impudent, coarse, perverse outrage of a ruffian, a drunk, a madman, a criminal.

All the *special* sciences and arts creating the imaginary country in live and dead propaganda are unified by a single world view of *propaganda*. This world view is a mixture of scientism and fragments of traditional (heavenly) religions.

There were several sciences in the nineteenth century, and there are many more now. Each science has its own field of application, and its imagery may lose all scientific validity beyond this field. Inevitably there must be people who would hodgepodge all misapplied imageries of sciences they know into *science*. What science? Oh, *science*. Several centuries ago any rigmarole was called theology, then it was called philosophy, and now it is called *science*. Ignorance, intolerance, and possession-power are usually clad today in scientism.

In a democracy, a *scientist* who believes that man and life are a machine (as many *scientists* did, including great scientists in their respective fields, up to the close of the nineteenth century) is perhaps no more likely to scrap his fellow machine than a believer in the divinity of man to ruin a divine miracle called man. For both may even be executed as a result, and a believer in machinelike life may try to avoid its destruction as carefully as a believer in miraclelike life, since the behavioral intelligence of each may hinge on the undesirability of *his* own life being destroyed—be it mechanical or miraculous.

But in a serf ownership, it is not unimportant what imagery fills the minds of the serf owners and their overseers down to the local chiefs.

Science may thus easily be the most benighted religion ever known to mankind because it suggests the utter worthlessness of any life (except the destroyer's, of course), the necessity, nobleness, and beauty of its destruction (the destroyer is a *scientist*), and *scientific* ways of destroying it with the greatest *scientific* benefit for the destroyer as part of his *great experiment* on mankind.

In all the religions of large civilizations that have predominated in the last two or three millennia, heaven and earth have been differentiated. Finally, the Holy Office or the Holiest Synod left even the physical heaven to astronomers, and retained only the proper abode of God: the metaphysical heaven, the domain lying beyond the fields of application of any sciences as we know them today and having in the physical heaven only a metaphor.

The Holy Office or the Holiest Synod did not assure anyone that he dwelled in paradise. No. He dwelled in the valley of tears, and paradise was in heaven. A *scientist* puts his victim into a machine constructed according to his mechanical-bestial-cadaverous fantasies (for most sciences have dealt largely with "models" analogized to machines, animals analogized to man, or corpses analogized to life, and this is the usual hodgepodge of misapplied imageries). But this is not the valley of tears. This is a heaven on earth (for others) in which he exalts and for the sake of which he is as ready to—well, say, subject some unscientific people who disagree with him to proper *treatment*: they are just not quite healthy and need *treatment*, or perhaps even *special treatment*, you know. Let us see what is in their brains. Of course, there are special clamps to keep the patient motionless so that he does not interfere with the *scientist*, and will you check if the windows are properly curtained? Some snoopy foreigners may be passing by.

It is one of the dear nineteenth-century preconceptions that training in sciences and technologies makes a trainee more humane or socially minded or educated in the general sense. A Nobel Prize-winning scientist or technologist may have no general culture beyond the ability to read English sufficiently well to get the gist of articles in the American magazines in his particular field and write Russian at the elementary-school level, both requirements being necessary while he has not yet risen in rank and has no secretaries and translators to perform for him this general cultural activity. If he switches over to *special* sciences or is trained in them, he may derive no less satisfaction from them than from *bourgeois* sciences.

Many (*bourgeois*) sciences studying man abstract themselves from the unique in each man in order to obtain results that can be applied to another man, or a specified group of men, or all men. The practical and cognitive value (in a democracy) of such sciences within their fields of application is obvious. But a *scientist* easily infers from his religion—scientism—that the unique does not exist at all: men are expendable and replaceable because the only reality is the *genus man,* and that *man* will always remain until there is at least one man, the *scientist,* the superman, the new man, the Chinese man.

Science in a serf war machine suggests to every chief that those below him can be physinfluenced and liquidated with great *scientific* satisfaction because man is a machine cog that can be scrapped and replaced by another machine cog, man is an animal that can be raised, selected, and slaughtered as domestic animals are, or exterminated like pests, or drilled like dogs or apes, or experimented upon like guinea pigs, and man is a functioning corpse, a medical model, a biological mechanism, and can be dealt with accordingly.

Man has evolved from the ape: this is what great Stalin read at the age of fourteen.

About three thousand years ago it was believed that man had come from clay, dust, earth. Indeed, earth transforms into grain, the grain transforms into a child's flesh, and so on: thus earth transforms (or evolves?) into man. Man dies, and reduces to earth again. Why has it been drilled into my head that man came from the ape, and not from earth, as the Bible says?

The trick is in the word: evolution. The translations of the Bible do not say: man *evolved* from earth. They say: man *came* from earth. When one says that man came from clay, dust, earth, one must admit that something essential happened during the transformation. Say, something airlike, breathlike, butterflylike (in contrast to woodlike or *material* earth) got in during the process. When one says man *evolved* from inorganic matter, unicellular organisms, or the ape, one slurs over the airlike incident because the word *evolve* implies a *gradual* transformation.

If a hare suddenly appears from a hat, this is a deception or a miracle. But if a hare *gradually* appears from a hat—if it *evolves* (slowly, gradually, imperceptibly) from the hat, or from earth, or whatever it might be—this is a truth, a fact, an axiom of *science.* Darwin's observation, valid in a certain field of application, has thus been transformed into scientism, a crude cult of magic metamorphosis, intellectually below the cognitive level of three thousand years ago.

The hare *evolves* from the hat, and man from the ape, and

therefore the difference between hare and hat or man and ape is negligible, as is clear from those smart references to man, such as the naked or crazy (or some other) *ape,* the most predatory, voracious (or some other) *animal,* and so on, which millions of *scientists* use daily whenever they philosophize. It would be even smarter for them to call the hare the jumping hat or man the hairy clay, but I suppose this is unscientific.

The *propaganda* has been inculcating into my mind that man *evolved* from the ape, and not just came from earth, because the former proposition suggests more insidiously, less abruptly, more *scientifically,* via more unusual, opaque, *scientific* words, that man *is* the ape, an animal, *matter,* and must tremble lest he be exterminated by the *scientists* and be grateful that they allow him to live for the benefit of his owners and be experimented upon. And above all, he must physinfluence and liquidate all enemies with zest, for they are all (naked) apes, animals, *matter,* and this is all a scientific experiment.

But what about those above me, including the pseudo-tsar-god?

In the fifties the propaganda-religion-culture issued a painting-photograph-poster depicting a young man kissing the "banner, the holy of holies of the regiment." The holy of holies? But you have been inculcating into my mind from babyhood that "life is a form of existence of protein," that man is an evolved laboring ape, a tool-producing animal, a modification of *matter,* and that there is no truth but *science!* What is the banner from the point of view of *science?* A set of dead organic molecules. *My-russia-my-sacred-motherland?* But there is nothing sacred from the point of view of *science,* nor has there ever been, nor can there be. Why must I, an evolved laboring ape, regard as holy or sacred a set of dead organic molecules, or a group of evolved laboring apes, called a motherland? *Science* knows nothing sacred, and nothing has been sacred for you—as you destroyed shame or thousand-year-old Russian icons, unique relics of Russian culture or Russian poets of genius, nature or good manners, the family or friendship. Yet now you want me to kiss the "holy of holies, the banner of the regiment, hallowed in the military glory of my Russia, my sacred motherland."

There is no truth but *science* when anybody or anything should be physinfluenced or liquidated for the sake of the pseudo-tsar-god. But as soon as the possession-power is concerned, everyone and everything becomes *holy* and *sacred,* the process of deification growing with rank and attaining its greatest divine apotheosis at the pseudo-tsar-god currently in possession-power.

Scientification downward, and deification upward: the rest in the *propaganda* of possession-power has consisted of freely changeable arbitrary verbalizations, suiting the possessive need of the hour.

61

The imaginary country—the fete-park-exhibition—was to be housed mainly in the several larger cities and southern resorts of former Russia, and in 1931 great Stalin was able to set to the task in all earnest.

Before 1928 there had been no money for that because the working people had been gluttons, bibbers, and spendthrifts as in 1913. Besides, when it had been decided to build a Paris-like subway in Moscow and call it the Metro just as in Paris (which was considered the cultural capital of *that* world), the brazen working people said right in *Pravda* (Bukharin's handiwork?) that there had been no housing construction to speak of since 1913 and they were overcrowded.

To be or not to be for the Metro? Should it be built immediately or postponed until better times?

"We are cramped, seven to eight people living in one room," said Comrade Barantseva.

This article was titled "Too Early," another "Not Until the State Becomes Rich," and still another "Advice of the Provinces."

There is a danger that the estimated sum of 55 million rubles contemplated as outlays for the building of the Metro will come up to a round 100 million; there are many such cases in our construction.

Because of a paltry 55 or 100 million rubles great Stalin had had to listen to the whine of some paupers of the Yava factory,

Moscow. So many of them lived in one room. They had spoiled his birthday, too, with their whine. Now he counted his money by billions. Those whining paupers had only to be squeezed, and he could spend billions every year. True, these billions were to be hurled into weapons and *means of production*. But the *metro* was the best propaganda imaginable, that is, a weapon.

The Webbs' monumental study of the imaginary country called the *soviet union* appeared in 1935: "It is bound to open a new epoch in the Western understanding of the life-goals of mankind," wrote *Manchester Guardian* according to *Pravda*. And even the London *Times*, much to *Pravda's* pleasant surprise, reviewed the Webbs' two-volume fantasy rather favorably.

Great Stalin wanted to have a *metro* that would give a further powerful impetus to the imagination of *all progressive mankind*, and as the Metro opened, when the Webbs' masterpiece was still in print, all foreign visitors just gasped: nothing like it had been built since Absolutism was finished in the major countries. The Metro linked those carnival sideshows, which President Beneš and Romain Rolland considered a new era of mankind, and another park of pre-1917 Moscow, not far from us. A foreigner could get from park to park, a pleasure ride of several miles, rather useless for a common Muscovite going not from park to park, but from work to work (many *happy working people* had to have *two jobs* or *a job and a half*). Now did those serfs imagine the billion-ruble *metro* had been built for *them*? They were to be live exhibits: the happy shepherds and shepherdesses of the new era going to work in *that* Metro.

In *that* Metro! The pleasure ride between the two parks was divided into eight sections, and ten underground palaces were built as *stations*, all of marble. One palace was of red marble, another of gray, and there were all signs of palatial luxury as in pre-1917 bath houses for middle-class sybarites, usually cited as the lowest mark of architectural vulgarity. There was no architecture in the *bourgeois* sense, of course, but who cared? There was enough architecture in France and in the United States. *All progressive mankind* went wild with joy at seeing this billion-ruble bath-house luxury. Palaces—real palaces all of marble—real marble. Slaves had quarried it, serfs carried it over thousands of miles, and both serfs and slaves dressed it, polished it, and installed it. *All progressive mankind* went wild with joy, and *Pravda* published their raptures: an unprecedented civilization was in the making: why, the workers and peasants were even carried to work through palaces of marble so that some once exploited cleaning woman or once downtrodden swineherd could feast her or his eyes on mosaics or candelabra, a pleasure that few millionaires can afford while going to their offices in their dull cars.

During and after its building, that *metro* was something that no one will understand except those who lived inside a single propaganda-religion-culture. The closest metaphor is that you live inside a deranged brain, and its obsession is the *metro* (in the thirties) or the *patriotic war* (in the forties) or the *first industrial atomic power plant* (in the fifties) or the *space exploration* (in the sixties) or whatever the current obsession is. The deranged brain inside which you exist wants to make you believe by compulsive ubiquitous inculcation, repetition or suggestion, using all arts, sciences, advertisement, philosophy, candy wrappers, school text-books, New Year's toys, or excerpts from foreign media, that, say, a pleasure ride between the Central Park at the one point of Moscow's former Boulevard Ring (destroyed for some reason) and an old park a little off the former Boulevard Ring solves all problems of mankind forever, has always been the goal of world history, and is the only subject that can be really always interesting to everyone. In the late fifties it was decided to show all citizens of the democracies as well as all serfs on the territory that if a rocket can accurately hit the Moon or Mars it can certainly hit even more accurately any city of the United States: military exercise, thinly veiled as collection of scientific data. But apart from the inculcation into the minds of the serfs of their owners' military might, it was just another *metro* except that the goal of mankind had always been not the pleasure ride between two parks of Moscow, but the geophysical data on some planets.

A foreigner's sojourn in the imaginary country has since consisted (with proper variations according to his reliability and usefulness) of his residence at some simple Naryshkin palace in the midst of sumptuous streets with splendid shopping, his participation in festivities and pleasure trips with stops at parks, former imperial ballet theaters and art galleries, his exemplary-demonstrational play with shepherds and shepherdesses at their *progressive-soviet-socialist-democratic*, etc. *life and work* in the new era, and finally his recreation in former tsarist palaces in the South where a high-ranking *communist*, a banker, an autocrat, a *left-wing revolutionary*, a statesman of a democracy, a great humanist, an admirer of Hitler, a high ecclesiastic, or whoever can be expected to be useful, can rest after his or her *tour of the country*. Whatever could rejoice the eye or gratify the palate of a useful foreigner or contribute to his general sense of happiness, revelry and excitement in the *country* which he is *touring, seeing* or *studying* could, after 1928, originate immediately in the imaginary country like scenery in a theater production on which the stage producer can lavish as many billions of rubles or dollars as he pleases. In 1935 *Pravda* announced: "Exemplary Fish Store." It was exemplary all right: the serfs outside the foreign exhibition and/or high caste areas and far from fishing localities have never seen fresh fish on sale these forty years since 1929 and will never see it in their life, most likely. And here there opened in 1935, a year perhaps as bad as 1922, a *state fish store* having an aquarium with all kinds of *live* fish on sale. Two hundred high-quality fish products, "down to live *sterlyad* brought in special cars from Astrakhan." Marble, of course. Statues sculpted specially for the store. A pleasure ride via the marble palaces of the *metro* took right to the *live fish store* the once exploited cleaning woman or the once downtrodden swineherd, tired of just *fresh fish* and wanting *live fish*, to be chosen from the aquarium and slaughtered on marble right in their presence or carried home to be slaughtered right before dinner to have that fish really *fresh*.

Some foreign economists have since been compiling tables of comparative prices, wages, and cost of living in Moscow, New York, London and Paris, and demonstrating thereby their ever fresh innocence of a society different from their own. The *price* of that *live fish* (or whatever has been *sold* in foreign exhibition areas) has no relation to its cost or to its value or to the life outside the exhibition area. Those in possession-power can take that fish free (or at any price) and *sell* it in Moscow also free (or at any price). Or they can not only just *sell* that fish free, but also give a prize in cash to every *buyer* of that fish to throw into a more salient relief the difference between the paradise on earth and a twentieth-century democracy. They can increase the wages of all cleaning women in Moscow with respect to the price of that fish 10, 100, 1,000 times, without any relevance to the population at large, securely attached to its territories. What then determines the price of that fish? The exhibition must function. Though the serfs are attached, Moscow is not sealed watertight: serfs of castes higher than the *peasants* or *soldiers* can come to Moscow on their own without spending a night (or three nights in these lenient times) provided they are suitably dressed (or costumed). They can grab quite a few $1.40 raincoats and hence the price must be high enough to forbid the impudence. As for fresh fish, whether alive or not, there is not much point of grabbing it because even if a serf lives near a railway and can spare enough time and money in order to bring this fresh fish home, it will not be *fresh* by the time he arrives. Besides, at harder times, all outgoing trains are searched and those who carry too much food are dispossessed. So the *price* must be high enough to forbid too many Muscovites to converge on the commodity as they did on those *enamel* saucepans in a kind of movie city uprising, but low enough to enable the exhibits to display a calm yet brisk trade. A foreigner should see that live fish is bought well, but not too eagerly: there is neither rush, nor emptiness—the exhibition must function in the most picturesque way. If representatives of foreign mass media come to film or interview the *buyers,* more live fish should be *thrown* (the words: "sell" and "buy" were dropped forty years ago, and they *throw* or *give* or *issue* while you *grab* or *catch* or *get*). The wages of cleaning women in an exhibition area and the prices of live fish at its *store* must then be such as to enable a real cleaning woman to appear before a foreign camera's eye with some *real* live fish, brought in special cars from Astrakhan, and explain simply, clearly, naturally to the audiences all over the world that she is a cleaning woman, who was exploited and downtrodden 22, 55, or 83 years ago, in 1913. Everything depends on the cost of current exemplary-demonstrational activity versus its current usefulness for the owners of the country.

Outlays, quite insignificant, if spread over the whole country, can give a tremendous effect for live and hence dead propaganda if concentrated within a sufficiently small number of exhibits. In 1935 *Pravda* announced the building of a hospital, compared with which the best medical institutions of democracies would look like shabby amateurish hostels. Every patient would have not only a separate apartment in this hospital, but also a separate balcony for his personal use only. The *palace of soviet medicine* would have its own medical research facilities which would use 140,000 experimental animals annually, and every experimental dog would have three square meters of *living space* (more than most Muscovites, which was unfair because a human is often bigger than a dog used in medical research). The dogs and other animals would also have "immaculate operating rooms, exemplary medical aid facilities, and courteous medical person-nel." Per 600 patients of the *palace of soviet medicine* there would be 10,000 rooms for all purposes, 1,200 kilometers of cable, 300 to 350 kilometers of various piping, 6,000 employees (that is, ten doctors and other specialists per patient), a mu-seum of history of medicine, a hall for medical congresses, a medical filming studio, a library of 600,000 medical volumes, and whatever else the most forward-looking medical imagination could devise. About the same time *Pravda* published excerpts from a doctor's letters: the young, energetic, advanced doctor was busy improving a hospital, thus setting a bright example for all local doctors all over the country.

I found the hospital in a horrible state: for the second day the patients have no hot water because our dear Alyosha (executive man-ager) is too lazy to send someone to a forest to fetch the wood. I went to K. to get bread and meat.

But if there is not even hot water, why is it a *hospital* or even a *hostel*, and not just neglected barracks? It does not matter: in *statistics*, the overall *number of hospital beds* would go to the *league of nations, united nations,* or universities all over the world. And if they want to see what this *number* is like, let the *metro* take them via those palaces of marble to *that* hospital with an individual balcony, ten specialists per patient, and everything else. Not that *statistics* cannot just invent any numbers. But it is pleasant if the *number of hospital beds* is scrupulously correct.

Yesterday I came from the city. I cannot call my trip successful, but I got something. I got neither mattresses, nor blankets, nor linen, nor bed pans.

Then the exemplary doctor says with pride that he *got* fabric to make bed linen from, some sugar, soap and window glass (no glass in the windows, for good ventilation?) and also "finagled a few medicines and instruments." But what if the new doctor had not been so exemplary? What if he had failed to get any mattresses or window glass, to finagle any medicines or instruments, or to start the *executive manager* Alyosha into the heating of some water? How had the *hospital* fared before the exemplary doctor came?

In three days after its description of the *palace of soviet science, Pravda* surveyed less fortunate hospitals to shame the doctors into dedication, energy and advance:

In the room for the reception of patients there is a table covered by a dirty tablecloth, one chair, a rusty washstand and a dirty bowl below.

In the adjacent room they have a "pharmacy": in a decrepit wall chest there are a pair of empty wine bottles in lieu of pharmaceutical containers, a dozen bandages wrapped in a white kerchief, and several pill boxes.

"Surely you ought to get the medicines?"

"Of course, but—I have ordered medicines from a department of the All-Ukraine Board of Pharmacies. The parcel has arrived, but there is no money to pay. The Rural Soviet gives no money."

Comrade Prilutsky, the medical assistant in charge of the outpatient clinic, waved his hand with an air of hopeless finality.

"The parcel will go back. We won't be able to pay for it."

The client is not the patient but the *state*—his owners. The owners do not want their common serfs to die off for nothing: the owners want very cheap but effective veterinary science for their common serfs, with maximum effect and minimum cost. But those who execute their will locally do not see it that way because the serfs are not theirs, and so why should they care? This is why *Pravda* chastised them until it was decided that this reflected badly on the regime. Between the mid-fifties and the mid-sixties a specialized medical newspaper chastised the *medical personnel,* and then it was decided that even this was detrimental. As for the death rate, in 1935 *Pravda* published the data of *Michigan Public Health* N7, 1932. According to these data, the postnatal death rate in the United States, the world's highest, exceeded seven times our country's, the world's lowest. The absence of hot water, mattresses, blankets (and so on) must have wrought that *miracle of socialism* in former Russia.

More than thirty years later, a delegation of American psychiatrists, officials, lawyers, mental health activists, and so on, *toured, inspected, studied,* and has just published a voluminous *special report,* which is, in the authors' modest appraisal, a "thoughtful and accurate picture of mental health services of the Soviet Union."

There is no national statistics on the prevalence of mental disorder in the Soviet Union and local statistics are likely to be inadequate. However, the delegation was of the opinion that the system was effective, particularly in the urban areas.

No statistics, but they *feel* that the system is effective. Thus, the system "could respond to a psychiatric emergency within less than ten minutes."

It's an enviable aspect of their program.

To be sure. If the *doctors* (continue the enthusiastic Americans) are "unsuccessful in persuading a psychiatric patient to accompany them, the police are called." The fact is (as we learn from the Report) that the effective system can do so since 1961 "without the consent of the patient himself and his relations or guardians" (not to mention some absurd institutions like courts). Ten minutes—and you have disappeared. Without all that dawdling in Chekhov's *Ward Six.* Why do you need any statistics, for God's sake?

True, the authors of the Report stipulate that the *system* is very good for the "Russians" only, not for the authors of the Report: Dr. Visotsky (a common Russian name, and the doctor looks Slavic-Russian) or Dr. Sirotkin (a common Russian name, meaning "Orphan's"). And if the effective system without statistics is good only for Russians, why should Dr. Visotsky, Dr. Sirotkin, and other pure Americans worry?

The cover of the book displays an old Russian church. Rather irrelevant, but entertaining. Exotic. The book has been published by the American Government.

Decisively, there was no point of extending the scale of exemplary-demonstrational activity if everything went so well. For example, great Stalin believed that even the exhibition Moscow should be held strictly in the streets or inside exhibition structures: no foreigner was to peep inside any ordinary building. Therefore, up to the late fifties even in Moscow nearly all hospitals, restaurants, theaters, movies, stores, living quarters, or railway terminals, had been built in the forty years before 1917, and not in the forty years after. In the forty years after, they had been nearly all converted inside into derelict superslums the like of which history had never known because there had never been such a turn from a comparatively civically free, socially modern, and culturally European country like post-1861 Russia to a superautocracy as in ancient China. Great Stalin thought it quite sufficient to keep painting the façades of these superslums and asphalting the streets in front of them (a foreigner was not to see a single blemish on a façade or a single crack in the asphalt). Since the labor cost next to nothing, the asphalt was a by-product of production of aircraft and tank fuels, and only those paints which were also by-products could be used, the façades of superslums were painted until the coating fell off, and as soon as there was any imperfection in the asphalt, dozens of male and female serfs would crawl on their knees to cut out the imperfection and spread the hot asphalt.

No foreigner was to peep inside the teeming superslums, but a terrible giveaway nearly ruined the whole fete-park-exhibition. Since the first generation of even the highest and richest 1 percent of the population mostly lurked behind the urban scenery inside their cubicles getting partitioned into still smaller cubicles, in the evenings all windows would be alight, and an observant foreigner would remember that in his democracy a large family often kept only one room in its twelve-room house or six-room apartment lighted.

In the thirties lampshades on sale in Moscow were produced by *cooperatives of invalids* in two colors: the pink was to hint to a foreigner at the voluptuous atmosphere within, while the blue was to impress him with comfortable home serenity. Actually, some large window would instead be sectioned: a section of somber tremulous gold (unshaded bulb!), a section of voluptuous or nervous pink, and a section of serene or gloomy blue. The foreigner would not know that all his questions had been asked by his predecessors: for many decades, millions of foreign spectators pass through, mostly as ignorant or innocent as the previous wave, and they ask the same questions, and are given the same answers which they carry away home, to be succeeded by new waves of ambassadors, intellectuals, scholars, and others who ask the same questions here, or in former China, in former Cuba, or some other former country. The answer in this particular case was that electricity is very cheap in our country and every family likes to keep on all the lights—the delightful gold, the voluptuous pink, and the serene blue all together—in all their six or twelve rooms all at once.

So that aspect of the fete-park-exhibition was all right, but the real pain in the neck was the costumes. The live exhibits cannot just lurk inside the scenery all the time, glimmering gold, pink, and blue through the windows and hinting at their electrically lavish family lives. They must walk in the streets. One can buy costumes abroad in exchange for grain, raw materials, or whatever, but no matter how diligently death slaves were processed and no matter how carefully rural and urban serfs were looted of every clandestinely grown carrot or criminally made shoe, the weapons and *means of production* consumed so much that too little could be spared for the costumes. It was only the apparel industries (*fresh from capitalism!*) of despoiled Eastern Europe that made it possible to costume properly so many live exhibits.

The problem of establishing closed, picturesque, all-pleasure touring routes initially gave a lot of trouble. Versailles was a relatively small area. But in the super-Versailles the aim was to *travel* by certain routes from show to show. The Metro with its underground palaces of marble was the best solution: the guards will not admit anyone suspected to be drunk, for example, the exhibits can thus be screened, and there are no decrepit serf habitations even in a hazy distance. But the purpose was to make a *tour all over the country*, from the eighteenth-century tsarist treasures in St. Petersburg to the tsarist palaces in the south where the *tourists, guests, visitors* can rest if they are currently useful enough. Originally, important foreigners like André Gide traveled in special closed cars, but in the mid-fifties some representatives of *all progressive mankind* said they wanted to get off at stations just like passengers! My mother went on a mission somewhere as a medical expert and was put into a car with some American ladies (Mrs. Roosevelt?) who wished to see Russia as Russia really is—to share the ordinary life of ordinary Russians. No tourist shows for them! Mother had been checked and found suitable: a doctor of medicine, senior research worker, head of a medical ward. Jewish? Still better! So mother was trusted with impersonating an *ordinary soviet passenger*. Everything was as in real life. Except that a *special* railway train moving half an hour ahead carried all the props from heavy Oriental carpets to chicken soup. The propsmen jumped off and transformed each station into their vision of the future paradise on earth, with heavy Oriental carpets that signified middle-class prosperity at the turn of the century and were thought therefore to be still the highest chic in the West, and with chicken soup at a railroad station as the most fastidious whim the modern Western consumer may conceive of.

The Americans alighted, asked for some brand of cognac no one ever heard of (when there is chicken soup, they want cognac!), and neglected the chicken soup. Both passengers and representatives of ordinary passengers were stirred: chicken soup. But that famous "chicken in every house" for the benefit of visitors in pre-1861 Russia, so that the Western intellectuals ever since Voltaire could appreciate Russian bucolic abundance, was the same: it was simply carried in the backyards from house to house while the visitors moved in front of the houses. And similarly, the same chicken soup was to be carried all along the route of Mrs. Roosevelt or whoever it was. Yet here Mother stepped across, ordered a plate of chicken soup, and *drank* it. The propsmen perhaps thought: "Scurvy Jews, always spoiling everything." On the other hand, did not my mother's gesture emphasize the spontaneity of the whole scene of ordinary life of ordinary Russians?

Of course, extensive *cleaning* had to be done by great Stalin to make the exhibition-fete-park really enjoyable and unmarred by all kinds of numberless beggars, paupers, waifs, cripples, and other pieces of humanity that would be intensely unpleasant to a visiting humanist, moralist, *left-wing revolutionary*, statesman of a democracy, and so on. As in every relatively free country, Moscow and other larger cities of pre-1917 Russia had collected the so-called lower depths from everywhere—alcoholics, prostitutes, natives from remote areas, including China, nervous wrecks, bohemians, unconvicted criminals, tramps, idlers, gamblers, and such. One of the most famous works among *all progressive mankind* in Russia and elsewhere before 1917 was Gorky's play *Lower Depths,* which had a run of more than 500 performances between 1902 and 1906 in Berlin alone. You are happy and prosperous: but here next to you in your huge city are the lower depths—your brothers and sisters perishing from alcohol, cocaine, lack of energy, unemployment, crime, degradation, idleness, incapacity, asocialization.

The relevant *laws* of the thirties started with these words: *On the cleaning of . . .*

The Chinese laundryman did not exactly belong to the lower depths, but *some* Chinese did, and *some* Chinese were drug addicts or drug pushers, and surely a *modern-progressive-socialist,* etc, city like Moscow was therefore well advised to be *cleaned* of *all* Chinese?

The children of the *kulaks* were often not enclosed along with their parents, to die off with them far from a foreigner's view. They became waifs, and flocked for survival to the larger cities to join the lower depths. They ought to have been inscribed in their parents' passports if they were to live in the larger cities, but their parents had been *liquidated,* and anyway had no passports in their own possession as the lowest serf caste: *peasants.*

In 1935, *Izvestia* published an inconspicuous tiny item, entitled "Measures to Combat Crime Among Minors": it was an inconspicuous tiny *law* which extended death penalty to children "starting from the age of twelve" for everything from larceny to treason. Now *cleaning* could really start apace of all these passportless orphans. Since they had no passports, every brat would assure all concerned that he was under twelve, but all concerned could assure themselves that he was *above* twelve.

However, as always there was the pseudo-tsar-god's order (*law, decree, decision*) executed at the *center,* and there were local distortions, violations, or exaggerations. The local *organs of state security* in Leninsk-Kuznetsk roped in 160 children above the age of ten, not twelve. The fools had not understood the order: it was the waifs—orphans—of whom the cities were to be cleaned, and they tortured the good healthy children of good healthy parents (who would perhaps even adorn the scenery as viewed from the Naryshkin palace) into confessing "counter-revolutionary, fascist, terrorist activity." The fools were sentenced with great *éclat* to prison terms of five to ten years, though no one knows what really happened to them.

So all the lower depths were cleaned out, and all the *social problems of cities* as posed by *all progressive mankind* were cleaned out with them, and Gorky, the author of the *Lower Depths* which had made so many hearts bleed all over the world, was cleaned out with all the lower depths (after he had been used up and had not known what else he should do to placate his owner). And *all progressive mankind* have since been admiring the social cleanliness of exhibition areas (the hygienic admiration shifted in the sixties to the imaginary country inside mainland China), and especially the *virtual elimination* of crime, drug addiction, prostitution, and such. The expression *virtual elimination* meaning the pleasant invisibility in exhibition areas of all such evils.

Still, what about those audiences of Gorky's *Lower Depths*?

The 1970 edition of *Britannica* introduces André Gide as a moralist and humanist, a champion of social outcasts, whose integrity and nobility of thought give him a permanent place among the great masters of European literature. The moralist and humanist saw children hunted by *plainclothes policemen.*

I saw a very small one—certainly not more than eight—being carried off by two plainclothes policemen. Two were needed, for the child was struggling like a wildcat—sobbing, howling, stamping, trying to bite. . . .

Is it this scene that made the champion of social outcasts at least cool off towards what he called "more than the chosen land"?

He did cool off in 1935 compared with the early thirties. But why? What had since changed in his "more than chosen land"?

In the early thirties homosexual couples could still openly appear everywhere, while later they were punished practically by hard labor to death, and Gide wrote:

With the restoration of the family (in its functions of "social cell"), of inheritance, and of legacies, the love of lucre, of private ownership, is beginning to dominate the need for comradeship, for free sharing, and for life in common.

It is from the family that the love of lucre and private owner-ship stems. Spinsters, bachelors or homosexual couples cannot love lucre and private property. "But from a Marxist point of view, what can one think of that other, older law against homo-sexuals?" Gide asks. All other *laws* since 1918 had been in keeping with a "Marxist point of view." But certainly not the *law* against homosexuals. Physinfluence to death or liquidate all the population in a country: it will still be a "more than chosen land," quite moral, humane, and in keeping with a "Marxist point of view." But to persecute homosexuals too? Everything that had been quite moral, human, in keeping with a Marxist point of view, or just inessential between 1918 and 1933 (such as the persecution of authors) became immoral, inhuman, out of keeping with a Marxist point of view, and quite essential.

Yet what happened to that child, certainly not more than eight years old, whom Gide saw struggling so that it took two *plain-clothes policemen* to carry him off?

Nearly an hour later, happening to pass near the same place, I saw the same child again. He had now calmed down and was sitting on the pavement. There was only one of the two policemen standing be-side him. The child was no longer trying to run away. He was smiling at the policeman.

The *plainclothes policeman* could have told the child that the *law* applied only to the age of twelve, and surely he was younger, certainly no more than eight to look at him, wasn't he now? There was a good little boy! He *looked* no more than eight, and here he got frightened that some wicked people would claim that *really* he was twelve! Was that kind *plainclothes policeman* the Uncle Kolya of the Pushkins?

A large truck drew up, and the policeman helped the child to get in. Where was he taking him? I do not know.

You will think that this is what happened. The great moralist, humanist, and champion of social outcasts rushed after the van, shouting: "Stop! Tell me where you are taking him! I must know!" The passers-by saw a foreigner running after the van (his hat blown off, rolling over the perfect if dusty asphalt) until he had no strength left in him, and then collapsing, and perhaps seeing the light of new morality while lying prone on the perfect if dusty asphalt. Nothing like that happened. Instead, the great moralist began to recall the face of the *plainclothes policeman*. How kind it really was. To be able to persuade a child that nothing threatened him. To be able to coax, to lull, to soothe a child into a state of almost happiness while lifting him and carrying him into that van.

And I only relate this little incident because few things in the Soviet Union moved me as much as the attitude of this man toward the child; the persuasive gentleness of his voice (ah, if I could only have understood what he was saying!), the kindness of his smile, and his caressing tenderness as he lifted him in his arms.

I thought of Dostoievski's *Moujik Marei*—and that it was worthwhile coming to the U.S.S.R. in order to see such a thing.

62

The gentle reader will now see that Professor Marlevich and all of us had every reason to be in good cheer: we were to be the merriest exhibits because we happened to be attached to former Moscow, the central area of the exhibition-fete-park with its pleasure routes stretching to former St. Petersburg and the palaces of the south.

All the time ever new entertainments—pleasure trips over a canal dug by the *enclosed*, aircraft shows, military parades—were invented for foreigners and Muscovites: the carnival never ended, the new Versailles was ever more spectacular, and we were its shepherds and shepherdesses.

But was Marlevich or other Muscovites ashamed?

Ashamed? Did Tolstoy, called the conscience of Russia, a man of sensitive, versatile, humanist European culture, let go of his serfs, that is, chattel family slaves, until they were taken away from him by force and freed in 1861?

Tolstoy wrote after 1861 about serfdom, in connection with *War and Peace*:

I know what is thought to have constituted the character of the time and is not found in my novel: the horrors of serfdom . . . But I do not regard this picture of the time which persists in our imagination as true, and I did not wish to convey it. . . .

Yet Tolstoy called on the tsar to pardon, for the sake of Christian love, someone who tried to kill the tsar. He, Tolstoy, had owned his Christian brothers and sisters as chattel slaves, yet he did not regard "this picture of the time which persists in our imagination as true." But someone who tried to kill must be pardoned by his potential victim (the tsar, in the present case) for the sake of Christian love.

Millions of citizens of democracies may insist that all criminals should be pardoned or at least kept in co-ed *prisons* combining a health resort and a university. And many of these same citizens have been flocking to former Russia since 1919 to enjoy, praise, or use the labor of low serfs, slaves, and death slaves, and if asked at any time since 1919 how they can hug the serf owners and share their loot, they would answer, as Tolstoy did, that they do not regard this picture of the time which persists in our imagination as true.

How could some Marlevich who had worked his way up from illiteracy in a tiny town to expertise in the alimentary tract be expected to have been seized by social remorse? Marlevich treated all of us, his neighbors, free of charge, if something was wrong with the alimentary tract of any one of us. That was the sphere in which he felt he could help. As for social remorse, each caste has been receiving since 1918 whatever it can, without a thought as to how these rewards, splendors, or entertainments are obtained in the lower castes all the way down to death slavery. To show interest, to think, to mope would, to begin with, be bad for the alimentary canal: "Do you know what it is? An ulcer!" One is ever young in our youthful and beautiful land, and in the best possible cheer.

In 1917 it was suggested to the poor that the paradise on earth would set in as soon as they had robbed all the rich of everything down to wrist watches and thus become sufficiently prosperous to live happily ever after. In 1929 it was announced that the paradise had yet to be *built*. So the serfs and slaves were to live self-sacrificially for a while in purgatory or on the construction site of the future paradise on earth (that is, the plants building tanks and other weapons). However, pseudo-tsar-god-II thought that this was somehow depressing. Let all these self-sacrificial serfs and slaves make merry (if not eat and drink) as though the paradise on earth had already come. Let both death slaves who quarry the marble for the *metro* and show serfs who ride via the *metro*

532

palaces to the *central park* or the *live fish store* dance and sing and go wild with joy.

And an avalanche of frenziedly good cheer burst upon the country from all the movie screens, printed pages, and loud-speakers of a wired network called *radio* which was cheaper than wireless radio and safely blared forth only frenziedly good cheer.

The good cheer was produced by hacks in all arts and sciences, with a ready response from those like Marlevich who feared or suffered from a loss of energy, illness, old age, depressions and other weaknesses, lethal in the ruthless scramble for survival, and wanted to believe frenziedly that they were and would always be healthy, young, vigorous, if they were cheerful just for the sake of good cheer, and there was nothing except health, youth, vigor, as science had proved, plus a sufficiently high territorial caste, if not a high departmental rank.

The era of frenzied good cheer of serfs, slaves, and death slaves was ushered in by a song of Shostakovich, who was once a cynical wit, admiring the sarcasm of early Ehrenburg, and then a nervous wreck who loved the *party* as only a man insane from fear can. It was proper that a cynical wit, insane from fear, should have composed the paradisical song of joy for serfs, slaves, and death slaves, and that the song was reportedly accepted as the hymn of the *united nations*, the word *nations* denoting both democracies and the biggest serf owners in human history, all *united* in the mind of Franklin D. Roosevelt, especially after his secret gift of several million runaway serfs to their owner for exemplary punishment:

> Don't sleep, get up, you curly-head,
> At plants, at plants,
> The country's rising merrily
> To the glory of its day.

Since then and forever, on the territory of the possession-power there always was to be a candy-box spring and an operetta morning, and always everything in corny-song blossom or in propaganda-cliché creation, and always poster girls marching, their filmland breasts firmly pointing forward.

I remember the change very well. The printed photographs of the early thirties were still photographs. But after the mid-thirties there were no printed photographs any longer: the *photographs,* such as those reproduced by the 1970 *Britannica* in its article on post-1917 Russia, have since been candy-box pictures hooked up photographically. All the information about life in the country has since been the imaginary world of the *special* arts and *special* sciences.

There is nothing unusual about hack culture, of course. In every country I can imagine a teenage girl reciting with feeling her doggerels on every occasion and shrilling every day in a way which seems a sickening affectation to everyone except perhaps her mother.

Imagine the girl getting for her affectations a salary several times larger than her father's, holding a high rank on account of them, encouraged to make her affectations more and more sickening, and able to inflict them on all the population by force or threat of force. Her girlish slush will be used on two occasions: she is to utter unbearable screams of pain (like a woman—a daughter, wife, mother) over whatever can be ascribed to her owners' enemies (especially the sufferings of children—in antiquity, in old Russia, in the beleaguered Leningrad, in Yugoslavia, in Spain, in Southeast Asia) and go into inconceivable raptures over whatever emanates from her owners. "I feel like singing, laughing, dancing," she is to exclaim, in that starry-eyed, spontaneous, irresistible way, at seeing, say, her owners' weapons which are to bring peace, abundance, and happiness at last to all those suffering children.

Imagine dozens of thousands of such girls (and boys), with their sickening affectations, constituting a ranked supermonopoly.

It was also from the lower-type provincial or amateur theatricals and recitals that another affectation burst onto Moscow: *pathos.* "Oh, die, ye perfidious wretch!" a boy servant exclaimed in Chekhov's story to amuse the guests in a provincial town. But now it was not an amusement which Chekhov found vulgar even as amusement. *Pathos* was to be the masculine element of the propaganda-religion-culture, in contrast to its tearful or rapturous femininity, both merging in consummate jubilation, anticipating the final triumph of what is good, noble, beautiful, and, indeed, holy or sacred, over creatures reduced by *science* to humanlike ogres, human pests, or harmful molecules of protein.

The good cheer blared forth from all the *radios* every day, but on two days the merrymaking reached its most frenzied peaks. One was the anniversary of Ulyanov-Lenin's and Trotsky's agent-provocateur stunt: the deliberately false and later never reproduced announcement on November 7 that they had been attacked and must therefore attack and smash all democratic institutions (which practically no one thought possible to defend against such odds). The other was May Day, a festival of solidarity of all blue-collar workers, though most of them in, say, the United States are stauncher defenders of democracy and hence more hostile to big serf ownership than those of the biggest bankers, businessmen, and corporate lawyers who have been successfully bought and manipulated since 1918: the May Day of solidarity of these businessmen of all countries helping the serf war machines to destroy democracy (and these businessmen too) ought to be really celebrated.

After the morning family chorus, Marlevich would wash, singing an aria from *Eugene Onegin*.

Just as my grandfather in the photographs, he raised his eyebrows like a harlequin whenever he joked, though his humor also depended heavily on a frenzied stimulation of energy. He would rush into the kitchen and blurt out to someone peeling potatoes: "Do you know what I found when I married? My wife turned out to be a virgin." That was a statement in the form of a joke, which he would bleat and bray in slightly different keys, quickening his hand-rubbing about the kitchen, until he hand-rubbed himself into the corridor, bleating-braying: "She-e-e-turned-out-to-be-a-vi-i-i-r-gin."

Marlevich developed, quite unexpectedly, an occult creed of his own. Preoccupied with survival, he discovered that if one drinks the water from a bathtub after somebody has taken a bath (without soap, though) he will be cured of many diseases and will attain youthful energy (to work even more frenziedly!) as well as longevity (to become at least a marshal of medicine!).

The application of this scientific magic was thwarted by the fact that no one took a bath. In our communal apartment, for example, we just washed out of pans, because the bathtub was one for all.

Every people deserves its regime (has the right to choose it).

A saying as true as the saying that every patient deserves his health or illness (has the right to choose between the two). When I look at a photograph of some Chinese after 1949 I catch myself thinking that these are only Chinese—they must be fit for that sort of life. Similarly, a Czech or an Englishman (before the conversion of *their* countries to serfdom) would say that we, *russians*, must be fit for the communal superslums and our regime in general. Actually, the Russian language has a special verb meaning: "it disgusts me to touch (to taste, or whatever) something after someone else has touched it." There is also a corresponding adjective in this special sense, and foreigners tell me that this kind of squeamishness is more developed in the population here than in their countries. The same applies to many other sensitivities, and sometimes it seems to me no one would have suffered more from the regime than those who speak Russian.

Anyway, none of us would take a bath to provide Marlevich with his cure-all elixir, not to mention drinking it.

Jerking his wound-up hand over his face, Marlevich would sing into the holiday morning water:

O-ne-gin!

Then he would rise to the surface and sing quite operatically (he had a good ear):

Let me tell you frankly.

Again diving into the water, with an operatic surfacing:

Ta-tya-na—I adore her madly!

Here there was a special point: his myopic sister's name was Tatyana. Marlevich found the coincidence extremely funny. That was the point of *Eugene Onegin.*

Ta-tya-na—I adore her madly!

Then he would put his daughter astride his neck, to stimulate as much more energy as possible, and dance goatlike around their magnificent room to an exuberantly cheerful holiday tune. He liked to combine good cheer with a bit of clowning, to make it funny and, therefore, even more enjoyable. With his Lyalechka now walking with him in the *column*, now astride his neck, he would *march* to Red Square, quite a walk, which took a whole day sometimes. In Red Square he would put Lyalechka astride his neck, and as he passed by the mausoleum he would wave with the free hand to the pseudo-tsar-god (or his double) on the balcony-platform. With his Lyalechka astride his neck, he was one of the apparently genuine if somewhat pathetic figures of spontaneous infinite love for the regime, and when I tried later to recall someone who really liked the regime I recalled Marlevich.

63

But did he really like the regime? Just a tiny bit?

What a strange question. Did Sir Winston Churchill like the regime of great Stalin?

Before 1941 Sir Winston knew that pseudo-tsar-god II or Joe Steely differed from Al Capone only in scale: Joe was to Al just what Al was to a fellow who tried (unsuccessfully) to force several nightwatchmen to pay him a couple of bucks a week. Accordingly, Joe had thousands of times more men than Al and was willing, for reasons of his own, to send them into suicidal fight against another megagangster who threatened Britain directly.

So Sir Winston was riding from State Villa Number Seven near Moscow to meet the so far biggest gangster in human history in order to supply him with arms against a smaller but currently more dangerous gangster, at least currently more dangerous to Britain since only the Channel separated them. Hence the reader is sure to find in Sir Winston's memoirs the following passage:

I reached the Kremlin and met for the first time the vast-scale danger-ous gangster and cunning Georgian criminal and scoundrel with whom for the next three years I had to be in disgusting, painful, but highly necessary, and at times even indispensable, contact.

That would be in accord with the truth as Sir Winston had seen it as early as 1918. And here the passage is:

I reached the Kremlin and met for the first time the great revolutionary chief and profound Russian statesman and warrior with whom for the next three years I was to be in intimate, rigorous, but always exciting, and at times even genial, association.

The volume was published in 1950. In *Triumph and Tragedy*, which was published in 1953, Sir Winston still adores great Stalin. "There is no doubt that in our narrow circle" (note this touch of cozy intimacy) "we talked with an ease, freedom and cordiality never before attained between our two countries" (this is what distinguished great Stalin: ease, freedom and cordiality, and what a great statesman Sir Winston was to have been able to bring forth these virtues). "Stalin made several expressions of personal regard which I feel sure were sincere" (who can doubt it?). "But I became even more convinced that he was by no means alone" (this particular piece of wisdom Sir Winston borrowed from Joseph Davies: way back in 1937 that wise diplomat had realized that the conservatives fought against the liberalism of great Stalin).

A little *soviet man* throve inside Sir Winston. He was still alive even in his memoirs, on sound, sober, cold, second thought, carefully pondered and shaped in writing. But how was he born?

Sir Winston was riding from State Villa Number Seven, and this is where begins the psychology of man—or of a citizen of a twentieth-century democracy like Sir Winston.

He was going to meet a megagangster. He had to. But why not smile to him? All good old nineteenth-century diplomats smiled to each other: this is what any good old textbook on diplomacy says. Those good old diplomats were very shrewd: they got a lot of concessions from each other by their smiles. Anyway, not to smile would be not only boorish but also positively unpleasant. Good cheer was what Sir Winston himself needed.

If he had to deal with a gangster anyway, why not smile to make their contact more pleasant? What would he gain by moping? State Villa Number Seven, prepared for Sir Winston, had proved to be magnificent, especially the bathroom with that automatic water mixer. And the goldfish too! How did they know exactly what Sir Winston liked? He had slept well and felt rested. A gorgeous day. Why not enjoy life and be cheerful and smile? He needed every ounce of his health and energy for his work ahead.

And why should he call, even mentally, *that man* a gangster? Names are purely conventional, you know. Unpleasant names would only spoil his own mood—it would be so depressing to dine and wine with a gangster: It would be humiliating too—to rise to the top of life in order to depend on the good favors of a criminal.

A *soviet man* was born inside Sir Winston. This *soviet man* already *believed* that the megacriminal was a great revolutionary chief, profound statesman and warrior, and that collectivization, one of the three megapogroms, was not as bad as it had seemed before. For it was to the advantage of Sir Winston to *believe* so: it improved his mood, made his life more pleasant, raised *him* in his own eyes.

Exactly in the same way the *soviet man* in Marlevich told him that the pseudo-tsar-god was a great revolutionary chief and profound statesman and warrior, or something like that. Why could Sir Winston *think* this as long as it was of behavioral advantage to him, and Marlevich could not? Isn't it odd? So many citizens of the democracies that can arm themselves are ready to humiliate themselves through their representatives or personally in front of any big serf owner for the sake of his favors or promises or simply smiles, and even *believe* that he and his regime are not so bad after all, contrary to what they believed before. And yet the democracies hope that some helpless, isolated, lonely Marlevich, kept in ignorance, exposed to the *propaganda* since 1918, barely surviving and ever threatened by hell on earth, will resist that same force before which they themselves are ready to grovel often for no handout at all, but out of a general feeling that servility is never amiss.

Sir Winston needed his inside *soviet man* for three or four years. But surely Marlevich needed him so much more all his life after 1918. Nor could Marlevich go back to Britain like Sir Winston: his *soviet man* had to stay with him and indeed be put into the coffin with him. For even if he fled in, say, 1945 to Britain or the United States, these countries, too, gave the serfs back to their owner. And what if *he*, Sir Winston, could not go to Britain either?

64

What if *he*, Sir Winston, could not go to Britain either and had to wake up in, say, that corner room (where the Lett lived) of our communal apartment to the strains of very cheerful music on a fine May Day morning? Quite a few proud Britons got into the territory, never to get out, and I witnessed the lives of those of them who had not *disappeared*. Besides, there is nothing about, say, Cambridge, England, or University of Chicago, essentially different from Prague University. When Jan Masaryk, Foreign Minister of Czechoslovakia, was "building a lasting peace with the great Soviet people," it would seem quite surreal to him that he would be duly thrown out a window and his country become a satrapy of the *great soviet people* very soon and perhaps forever, that is, until Prague University became a historic memory and only its name remained if it pleased the conquerors. Even I, born into a serf war machine, getting old, and having never seen anything else, will not believe in my bad luck and feel sometimes that this is all a sheer misunderstanding which must end somehow because *I* am involved. Count Alexey Tolstoy (a relative of Lev, also an author) emigrated after 1917, could gain no recognition in the West, returned and became a marshal of *literature*, rich and famous, but as the joke had it, one morning he strolled in Red Square and suddenly saw Nicholas II prancing on a white steed. "Good morning, Count," said Nicholas II. Alexey Tolstoy clung to the stirrup, then looked up and said: "Your Majesty: if you only knew what a horrible dream I have had!"

In short, Sir Winston wakes up, and since this is no dream, why not wake up with pleasure? Once he woke up with a dull pain in those nerves which are called the heart. The pain would start as soon as he realized that it was no dream, but now he wills himself to wake up with pleasure. A damn good tune. Shostakovich.

> Don't sleep, get up, you curly-head,
> At plants, at plants. . . .

Sir Winston will *march* today, or as they say, *go for a demonstration*, just as one goes for a walk. There is an unprecedented freedom of assembly (marches and all that) in our country. In democracies such freedoms are purely *formal* rights. But in our country all democratic rights are also guaranteed *materially*. Suppose the working people of Britain or the United States want to demonstrate their infinite devotion to a certain great revolutionary chief, profound statesman, and warrior. *Formally* they can do it, of course. But who will pay for all those streamers, portraits, and everything else? Here the right is also guaranteed *materially*: the cost of the demonstration will be paid for, and the working people have nothing to worry about on that score either.

Once or twice Sir Winston may skip the *demonstration* on the plea of sickness or something. But if he starts avoiding it conspicuously he will attract attention and will disappear.

How can it be otherwise? If he does not even try to conceal that he is *not* infinitely devoted, what a desperate enemy he must secretly be! Now, even one enemy *inside* the country can do a lot of damage, especially in wartime—he can in fact decide the outcome of a war by some unexpected desperately bold act of subversion or espionage.

Once he has decided he will *go for a demonstration*, he had better do it with pleasure. Nothing would be gained by his brooding, irritation, low spirits, and all that. A gorgeous day. He slept very well and feels rested. His room is simply magnificent. Not like State Villa Number Seven, of course. But what is the point of comparing his actual life with some has-been or would-be or might-be lives? He has a magnificent room. Would you believe that the roof does not leak even in spring? There is a towerlike story above his room (pseudo-Moresque), and *their* roof leaks! Ha-ha-ha! Good Lord above: *their* roof leaks! A magnificent room he has. Some Lett lived here. Was arrested, of course. Letts are being arrested nowadays. Shady people. Not like the British, second only to Russians themselves. So he *got* the room. What a subtle intrigue he had hatched to get it. That reference did the trick. "Hereby we request to give the room in question to Comrade Churchill. During his work in our organization Comrade Churchill has shown himself as . . ." A magnificent room. Magnificent. A gorgeous day, too. The month of May, the loveliest of months. Awakening nature. Life. Spring.

> Don't sleep, get up, you curly-head,
> At plants, at plants. . . .

Get up, Sir Winston. Those who have never waked up to this Shostakovich tune (now the hymn of the *united nations*?) played by a band on a morning like this simply do not know what happiness is. The brass fairly screams with pleasure, and your diaphragm thumps in response to the drum.

Here is Sir Winston in a column of marchers. This is just like a march in Britain except that the marchers make a holiday stroll out of it because they have no other purpose of their own. Splashes of red glint in the sun, and red is a very pleasant color if you have set yourself the proper mood. The color of roses and rubies. The symbol of blood and hence of health, vigor, and sex. Ice cream, seltzer, and balloons are sold all along the way. A city of wealth and luxury: Moscow. Some marchers or strollers carry twigs, just bursting into leaf, which they have snapped off the trees on the way. Continuous eddies of laughter as some columns straggle or enmesh. There is confusion and commotion as on a huge promenade—the best opportunity for a man to get to know the girl he glimpsed a couple of days ago in the office or shop. What a scraping of feet, scrape, scrape, scrape, and one column strikes up: "Don't sleep, get up, you curly-head," another: "Up the hill and down the valley" (how strange it sounds in a narrow street, girls' voices mostly), while a band somewhere thumps away at: "Still higher, and higher, and higher."

Of course, behavior differs. The *educated* mostly talk, flirt, laugh, the *uneducated* sing, even dance at times, and many of their men who know the nice little secret of being hilariously happy disappear discreetly from time to time and swill some more. For God's sake: this is a holiday, a unique free-of-charge chance for joy. The next chance, the anniversary of that agent-provocateur stunt, is half a year away. Will you miss the chance, Sir Winston? How are you going to survive then? Especially at your age when depression sets in so easily. And then: you know what it is? An ulcer.

Finally Sir Winston passes by the mausoleum stand, and the behavioral pattern he has set himself is realized even more easily than in his *other* life in Moscow in 1942. Then his mood was entirely his own—it was individual. Now he may laugh or smile simply because all the others laugh or smile.

The column in which Sir Winston marches or strolls actually laughs because a man who has been shouting slogans through a microphone ends each slogan with a *hurray*, and the passing columns cheer. Either the microphone or the loudspeaker or both are no good, and so some educated people laugh because they have been shouting hurrays without understanding a word of the speaker's, and some shout hurrays more loudly on purpose, while the others laugh because the loudspeaker's gutturals are so funny, and if one has swilled properly, oh boy, this is the funniest thing on earth, and all laugh because they want to make the most of the holiday and use every pretext for mirth and because they have been excited by walking, crowds, colors, sunshine, music, noise.

There are the diplomatic corps and all foreigners on the stands along the Kremlin wall looking at Sir Winston, his face tired yet happy, his big mouth shouting and laughing.

"What possessed that decent-looking, stout oldster to walk several miles and laugh with happiness at seeing the biggest gangster in human history?" a Westerner on the stands may wonder. As he wonders in former Moscow or former Peking or former Hanoi, and will perhaps never stop wondering. Religious fanaticism? Indoctrination? Mass psychosis? Induced insanity?

National soul? Pavlovian reflex drilling? Freudian libido trans-ference? Spiritual perversion?

But Sir Winston will now know. A lonely, sad, terrified man, struggling for his survival, he will look at the foreigners on the stands, his face belonging to the happy, shouting, laughing *soviet man*, while the *other man*—alert, tired, aging—lurking in his eyes so cautiously that even great Stalin would not detect him.

My generation was happy enough at least to be born into this society rather than get into it at a later stage of life. Therefore, my *soviet man* is like a suit: I can put it on, and even great Stalin would have been reassured, and I can take it off, and even great Stalin would have been frightened (not that he did not scare or panic quite easily). But many people like Sir Winston or our neighbor Marlevich, especially those who grew up in different societies, cannot develop an analytic defense hypocrisy: the *soviet man,* their defense hypocrisy, is inside them, along with the *other man*, and they themselves do not know who is who.

65

The Pushkins had their Uncle Kolya, and the gentle reader should not assume that *we* were without high connections entirely. We were no worse than some Pushkins!

We called one of my aunts, my mother's sister, Tusya, though Tusya is actually Natasha. Russian names can be changed so nicely in many ways. For example, if the name is Natasha you can naturally change it for fun or endearment into Natusya or Natulya. Then the initial *na* can be dropped, of course. We called my aunt Tusya, and her daughter of my age, my cousin, Tulya, because she was also Natasha. And the husband of Aunt Tusya was a *responsible worker* (the official name of a high ranker: all are workers by hand or by brain, but some are *responsible*). The gentle reader will understand presently how important or *responsible* he and his post were.

If a restaurant customer in a relatively free society with relatively free enterprise does not like a meal and/or its price, he goes to another restaurant. Suppose those in charge of the supermonopoly want an inhabitant of a certain caste and rank to have a certain meal at a certain price, but those appointed or attached to make the meal steal part of the food, or cannot cook it, or are careless, and the consumer gets a much worse meal than was intended by those above. If the finicky customer does not go to the restaurant next time the *director* of the restaurant will just laugh: the less these finicky customers pester the restaurant the less work and trouble for him and his personnel. Their pay is a tiny fraction of the value of food they can steal. Their pay is so low that the personnel is not expected to live on it and is supposed to steal in moderation, so to speak. Since they steal expensive food in the raw, the art of cooking is entirely of no interest to them: an artificial process by which the good food that can be stolen in the raw is simply made inedible, and naturally they try to make inedible as little good food as possible. I remember that in a restaurant, very expensive, but open for all, that is, for rich natives (not foreigners, that is) of any rank, in a resort city of the Crimea in the late fifties—only one item was served: semolina porridge (normally used to feed little children), although the deluxe menu included names to excite the most sophisticated gourmets. Evidently, no dishwasher wanted to steal semolina anymore because all the little children of the personnel were amply provided for by way of semolina for several years.

However, since 1929 there has been an even worse enemy than mere stealing from the *state: left* activity.

In a relatively free country with relatively free enterprise one private person extracts or mines *his* raw materials, another private person produces *his* goods or services out of these raw materials, and still another sells them. In a supermonopoly one overseer or *state official* is in charge of the *state* extraction or mining of *state* materials, another is in charge of *state* production, and still another of *state* trade. Suppose some *state official* in the chain gets chummy with those he is in charge of and says: "Look, boys and girls. Some of the goods you make you will make for *me. I* will pay you twice as much for the same work." The expression is that both overseer and his charges work *left*, and the goods they make, perhaps out of *left* raw materials, are called *left* goods. The *left* official passes his *left* goods to a similar *left* official in trade who sells the *left* goods at the *state* prices, but the *state* prices are so high that both officials get a high profit, and their charges also get much more for their *left* work and keep mum, of course, unless they feel they have been done out of their just and fair share (here is where the *real* labor movement comes in!) and inform on the *leftists* out of spite, whereupon the whole network of *left* enterprise is put on trial as a criminal gang.

Everything that can be done *right,* can also be done *left.* There are *left* prices for all those goods and services which cannot be obtained at the *right* prices at all, or they can be, but not quickly enough, or they are not of a desired quality. *State* enterprises are also engaged in *left* activity not only to enrich those in charge personally but also to *fulfill the plan.*

Left enterprise is a hideously trammeled and distorted free enterprise inside the framework of the supermonopoly, and it is easy to guess that the supermonopoly may thus readily become just a fiction, façade, skeleton for *left* enterprise to flourish inside. All the profit of the supermonopoly will thus end, because all the profit will be consumed by the *left* officials and *left* employees. In fact, *left* entrepreneurs have vast advantages compared with free entrepreneurs. They need not compete for quality to fetch high prices: the *state* fixes exorbitant prices for them. They need not haggle with the employees for wages or salaries: the *state* fixes them so low that every *left* raise is a blessing. They need not struggle for efficiency, creativity, ingenuity, and so forth: the supermonopoly is an easy competitor in this respect too. As for the competition among themselves, the market has been so starved of supply, and hence demand is so vast that *leftists* need not compete with each other.

The only means of combating *left* enterprise is inspection. An inspector, a salaried official, is to ferret out all salaried officials who are engaged in *left* enterprise and have them sentenced as criminals. Similarly, an inspector is to track stealing, low quality, negligence, and everything else. For that purpose he has to evaluate all values. For example he must *taste* a disputed meal and decide whether it is the meal that was intended at the price, or whether the local personnel have been stealing the food, failing professionally, or showing negligence.

The same applies to all fields where anything is made by man or found in nature and is of value to someone else. Alas! To begin with, in many cases there are no methods of objective evaluation. Someone who has to buy or use for his own money a certain value like a meal in a restaurant, a course of medical treatment, or a jet plane may say that the value is the worst for its price or its cost, while someone else who does not have to use the value for his own practical needs, but has only to study it scientifically, to philosophize about it, or inspect it, may declare that the value is the best for its cost or its price, and that the practical client or customer is simply a psychopath, an ignoramus, or a scoundrel.

Another unpleasant aspect of the principle of overall inspection was discovered and indeed described by Gogol in the first half of the nineteenth century. Since inspectors must be very numerous in order to be able to inspect whatever is created or discovered or found, or whatever is sold or issued or exchanged, their salaries cannot be very high. If their salaries are very high, the whole national output to be inspected for consumption will go instead into the inspectors' salaries. And since their salaries cannot be very high, all kinds of better goods, like choice food, unspoiled by the low art of cooking, are quite valuable to them.

Bribes! Of course Gogol, who published his *Inspector General* in 1836, would be baited nowadays as a monster of cynical perversity, even a Jew (wasn't Gogol's face, and especially nose, *jewish*?), a vicious criminal slandering the paradise on earth— as well as the (pure) Russian people and entire Russian history, too, including the era of Nicholas I. Yet the problem of bribes is there. The solution is to appoint some higher-ranking inspectors to inspect the more numerous lower-paid inspectors, and if higher-ranking inspectors are also swayed in their evaluation of a certain meal in a certain restaurant by accepting, say, the food in the raw, still higher-ranking inspectors inspect them, until the whole pyramid of inspection ends in inspectors general, and it was one of such inspectors general that Uncle Anas was.

Talking of some Uncle Kolya of the Pushkins!

66

The newly built huge *house of the government*, intended for those whose rank was not high enough to live in the Kremlin or in a mansion, was the color of asphalt. In the yard, even the air was strangely dark, perhaps because the asphalt on the ground, also naturally of the color of asphalt, was always black with moisture owing to the janitor's zeal, and the pools caught the sky in snatches of a hysterical dark blue. In the cellars of the building there were dogs which seemed to me as big as tigers. Whenever one approached the barred casement windows they would rush up and rage behind barred storm windows, so anxious they were to tear to pieces whoever encroached on the safety of my uncle and other *members of the government,* though he was nearly always out (*in the kremlin,* as the family often whispered in awe, and indeed once the Inspector General *was* in the Kremlin with the secret mission of having the paradisical pictures on candy wrappers shown to, and approved by, great Stalin).

I don't know why my aunt had invited me and Polya to live with them for a while. They were very kind to me. I seemed to them, no doubt, savage, dirty, smelling of superslums, as any child of the people.

My aunt had married Anas because he was a very good, successful, and, therefore, gifted man, just as Al Capone must have seemed to Mae Capone, while those who said that her Al Capone was a gangster seemed to her evil slanderers.

Like many of his new pals, my uncle combined the two first principles of man's love for women, one of which we may call European and the other Oriental. According to the European principle, Anas married my aunt because she was a pretty girl who would make a devoted wife, and at home, which he visited rather rarely (a couple of hours every several days), he founded a European, monogamous love, deemed by Europeans to be stronger than death and as unique as the soul. At home he realized man's urge to love and be loved by one and only one woman all his life, while in the mysterious outside which was said in an awesome whisper to be his work and was often associated with the *kremlin*, he realized, as far as his rank permitted, man's urge to possess *all* women on earth who seemed to him beautiful and therefore worthy of his love.

Since each local chief of the *organs of state security* could *arrest* anyone in his area, the population of the area was practically his harem provided he was so inclined: if he could not *arrest* a woman or a man who appealed to him sexually, he could always watch and *arrest* someone near and dear and use the victim as a hostage. The pyramid of harems culminated in the all-country-level harem activity of the chief of the *organs of state security*, who had permanent concubines kept in his top-secret harems, but who also procured teenage girls for just one occasion: the whole country was his harem except for the families of rankers sufficiently high to complain to pseudo-tsar-god II personally and win his support.

This kind of harem activity was quite inaccessible for high rankers like Uncle Anas. Somewhere in the outlying provinces a ranker could often coerce practically any commoner to live with him or with her, because all local rankers are often in collusion, and it may be impossible to complain over their heads. But not in Moscow, where there were quite a few high rankers like my Anas himself, and it was perhaps only the all-country-level *chief of state security* (and pseudo-tsar-god II, of course) who could use Moscow so freely as his harem. In Moscow, the Oriental visions of chiefs below the illustrious top of *state security* were realized differently: from 1929, even the crudest necessities of life were poured into the apex of the pyramid, while its base, representing the country at large, was left to the *ideal norm* or worse. Young girls who had discovered that they were pretty would struggle to the highest territorial castes, where the sharers in possession-power elevated them from dreary starvation to glamorous concubinage. The high rankers especially devoted to this activity were called life lovers. That meant they loved life in contrast to Christian life haters, money-crazy philistines, and women-enslaving reactionaries who instituted marriage, the family, monogamy, and all the rest.

On the hungry girls from the provinces they could lavish innumerable rewards that could not be had for any money, and above all, *living space* in Moscow. Like all the choice food, none of which could be had for money (it was only sold to the common populace of the highest territorial estates for gold and jewelry), the country's choice sexual beauty had to be purveyed for something much more valuable than money.

Some life lovers were accidental rapists as well: that is, they could not simply *arrest* any teenager in the streets of Moscow as the *chief of state security* did, but when the circumstances were favorable they could indulge in rape with impunity; the very notion of the crime became vague if the criminal had sufficient possession-power. The notion would glimmer only if his rank was not high enough and the victim was able to complain and was fearless enough to do so.

Recently I chanced to talk with a young man for whom everything in pre-1917 Russia was perfect, and the longer time ago the more perfect. I said to him that serf communities in pre-1861 Russia were at the same time harems, and since the serfs were of the same ethnic origin as their owners, even the ideal of beauty was largely the same. Fantastically enough, the thought had never occurred to him, though he said that the horrors of the *right of attachment* were still mentioned at school. "But are you sure this was not against the law?" he asked, completely lost. "It was," I said. "A victim would take a helicopter, fly to the capital, and have an audience with some high rankers, whereupon the local lawbreakers would no doubt be punished."

As Polya and I entered the brand-new apartment in the *house of the government*, I sensed a familiar smell: oil paint. The walls had been freshly painted with *oil* paint. Oils were used for pictures. Or for the walls in the *children's garden*. But here? I did not say anything because I realized that I should not show any surprise even if the walls had been of gold like those mountains which the Grekhovs would give away in their song.

Yet if someone had told me that these relatives of ours lived better than our family this would have seemed to me ridiculous. Better? Of course we lived better—that is, better for me, and this was what mattered. They lived simply differently—perhaps better for my cousin, but certainly not for me.

In one room two men were still planing the floor to get off the oil paint. As soon as I overcame my shyness I asked my cousin Tulya if we could be permitted to try to plane just a little.

Tulya was delighted because her life consisted of the invention of wishes. The more resistance her wishes were likely to meet among her subjects, that is, her parents, German governess, and so on, the more she enjoyed their final unconditional surrender.

"My father," she would say, an ecstatic infinity on her slightly upturned pretty face, "can get us—thousands of huge hats." She spread her swaying arms to embrace the infinity of thousands of huge swaying hats.

This infinite wish fulfillment was much reinforced by one circumstance that must have seemed to Tulya quite magical indeed.

Uncle Anas received no salary to speak of. Just as pseudo-tsar-god II received hardly any *salary* at all, much to the delight of *all progressive mankind*. The wishes of pseudo-tsar-god II were realized without money. He could wish all within one-sixth of the inhabited globe, and a great deal beyond, and if he had wished a tripe made out of some Western intellectual's bowels, the wish would have been realized, and the corresponding democratic government would have probably stopped grumbling after some good trade agreement. My uncle's wishes were realized within his share of possession-power. Apart from the usual *rations* of his rank, including a chauffeur-driven car and everything else, he had tremendous pull because his pals in charge of other privileges could do him favors in exchange.

But the magic of wish fulfillment that so fascinated Tulya lay elsewhere: it was connected with my uncle's activity: *inspection*. To be able to inspect something, the inspector must taste or test it, right? There is a word in Russian meaning both a taste and a test: a taste-test.

So there would be a ring at the door and Aunt Tusya would say: "Pay no attention, it's for a taste-test, Anya will take it."

The *directors* and others in charge sent the taste-test all way up the pyramid of inspection, but the higher the level of inspection the more carefully they had to produce the taste-test. An enterprise produces rotten vodka out of sawdust at a price several times higher, in relation to the lowest wages, than in 1913. But it is possible to distill several *perfect* bottles of vodka if you put into them as much work as into, say, several million bottles. The same with everything. Out of millions of peaches which are no good you may pick several boxes of *perfect* peaches. Peaches to taste-test for the highest inspector general.

Bribes? Oh, no. What a word—bribes!

In a nineteenth-century play an ignorant merchant's wife persuades her daughter to make her honest husband take bribes: "What a word those louts have thought up: bribes! Not bribes, my dear, but gratitude!" As I said before, I grew up on stories of how carloads of food were sent *at the personal disposal* of great Lenin during the great famine. Great Lenin played at an official getting a salary. Then surely in his play these tributes were bribes. "Bribes? Not bribes, my dear, but gratitude!"

An enormous exhibition of *gifts* to pseudo-tsar-god II, served up with the crudest sycophantic dressings, evoked delight from a good quarter of the population of continental Western Europe: "Not bribes, my dear, but gratitude," reiterated dozens of millions of Western Europeans in the mid-twentieth century, "Infinite gratitude, and also infinite love and infinite devotion."

Bribes! "Not bribes, my dear, but taste-test."

The distribution of gratitude or taste-test has been a highly sophisticated, almost symphonic activity of those in charge. Who should be bribed, when and how? The wrong pitch, rhythm or timbre of a bribe, and those in charge will be put on trial—for bribery, for example.

Correct symphonic bribery is connected with correct symphonic stealing (and correct symphonic *left* activity). To be able to bribe correctly, all over the symphonic area involved, one must steal and/or act *left* correctly, and to be able to steal and/or act *left* correctly one must bribe correctly.

The trouble was that no matter how much cost the supervised enterprises put into the taste-test for my uncle they could not make clothes and many other things as well as they were made abroad. However, my uncle's sister sent them whatever foreign goods they needed from abroad. She had married an Austrian and learned to speak German enough to pose as an Austrian lady in any country except Austria. The family whispered about her admiringly: "A spy—a real spy" because she looked like one of those elegant foreign lady spies in foreign films. I remember that the grownups stood examining as a treasure of art a pair of shoes she had sent from Spain. Of course my cousin Tulya demanded that the admiration session be stopped immediately because we wanted to see the shoes (she always included me in the spirit of true friendship). I was somehow sorry for the twin treasures of art when Tulya put her small feet into them and dragged them for several steps to the stifled cries of agony of the adults around.

Against the background of all that power to have our wishes fulfilled, our wish to plane the floor was not very great, but Tulya led me to the planers.

One of them had a calm, tired, resigned face, and very quietly he gave his plane to me. I took up the plane and tried to plane with all my strength, but the plane would not budge.

He took it back and said: "You haven't eaten enough porridge." Which means: You are too small and weak. But I took it literally and asked: "What porridge—buckwheat?"

Buckwheat porridge was once a very folksy meal: Savva Morozov was said to have it issued with milk to his employees free before 1917, and until 1928 it was very cheap. At the same time we ate it in our family too. I am glad I mentioned something that was not above that planer, something that was in common between him and us, rich, well-fed, romping children. He thought for a while. "Buckwheat, too," he said.

67

My uncle wore exactly the same quasi-military khaki tunic and riding breeches as were worn by the public image of great Stalin and the *state* shoemaker Vasya (who wanted our Polya to marry him, but Polya was afraid of him, or perhaps just of that quasi-military air of his). Since the three of them were also rather short, they fused somehow in my memory. They all wore that khaki tunic and breeches to show that they belonged to a certain superhuman order whose members had been engaged since perhaps the time of Spartacus in extraordinary missions, always urgent, secret, and heroic.

Aunt Tusya was not supposed even to think where her husband had been: he had been fighting against unprecedented odds in awesome secrecy, and he would be so tired that at home he could only immerse himself in tender monogamous tranquillity.

I remember that one night, when we must have been long asleep, my uncle came in. We heard my aunt's voice. Tulya, in her nightie, jumped up and rushed out of the bedroom, and a few moments later I heard her yelling.

She had left the door wide open, and in the doorway my uncle appeared with Tulya on his back, like a snow leopard clawing a bear.

"But I didn't know," he repeated in guilty dismay, addressing me as the only possible intercessor and trying to avert his face because his hands were busy behind his back supporting Tulya. "But I didn't know."

What had happened was this. When he had arrived, my aunt was asleep in a chair, waiting for him. He was terribly thirsty, perhaps because the *fight against unprecedented odds in awesome secrecy* provokes terrible thirst. First he tiptoed into the kitchen and saw a melon to taste-test. The choicest of the choicest taste-test samples were set aside by Tulya as her sacred property. The taste-test melons had come in the morning, and my uncle did not, indeed, know that she had decided that one of the taste-test melons was the world's best melon and henceforth no one was even to look at it with a covetous eye. He cut up the sacred melon and was about to plunge his burning mouth into its depths when my aunt came in. She stifled her scream as any devoted wife would, anxious to conceal her husband's unwitted crime. My uncle dallied vaguely with the corpus delicti as though trying foolishly to put it all back together, when Tulya ran in and saw what was going on. She jumped onto a chair, then onto the table, and from there pounced on him as from a tree. Obeying some deep instinct, the quarry rushed with his tormentor on his back toward our bedroom, and indeed I saved him. I explained to her that he did not know about the melon, and Tulya finally accepted the plea. She asked me what she should do to the unwitting transgressor, and granted him mercy on the condition that the new blue electric record player would henceforth be hers. The record player was *foreign,* of course: no one outside the highest caste could imagine that good old Gramophones could be *electric.* And so cozily small. As though they were *children's.* We carried the ransom to the *nursery* and went to sleep.

68

Aunt Tusya's husband Anas, which is a kind of Caucasian name, had been famous before 1917 because his brother assassinated a tsarist governor and had to emigrate. I am sorry to say that I do not even know to which faction of *social revolutionaries* Uncle Anas belonged. Since 1922 the term *social revolutionary* was such a frightening name of a criminal that to ask in my childhood whether Uncle Anas had once been *left-wing* or *right-wing social revolutionary* would have been something like asking in a democracy whether your relative robbed his victims, too, or merely cut them to pieces.

By profession, Uncle Anas was a physician, a Sorbonne graduate (not to be confused with my mother's brother, the psychiatrist), but this is how he was identified before 1917: "That man whose brother killed a governor." It was the remote association with a perfectly senseless murder, not with the Sorbonne, that made him distinguished. Still, for all his glory, my uncle's brother *had to* emigrate. Later, in my teens, I would jibe: "So he killed a governor and *had to* emigrate: how monstrous the tsarist regime was." My uncle emigrated, too, to keep his brother company, so to speak.

They did not have to stay abroad long, though, because the Russian monarchy suddenly ceased to exist. There was nothing new or strange about the disappearance, because many similar hierarchies had disappeared in a similar way, and yet no *revolu-*

tionary of any kind had even anticipated the *revolution* on its very eve. Those *revolutionaries* who happened to be on the streets of St. Petersburg by sheer chance, simply because they lived in St. Petersburg and were eager enough to run out (good weather—spring!) did not know that the crowds they were in were *revolutionary* and that what was happening could be called a *revolution* until the monarchy proclaimed officially its cessation, to the utter surprise and disbelief of every *revolutionary* in the country or abroad, including Ulyanov-Lenin or my uncle and his brother.

Even three days *after* the actual demise of the tsarist administrative branch, that is, *after* the *revolution*, on March 26, Kerensky, a *social revolutionary*, invited to his home, unofficially, all kinds of *revolutionaries*, including the *bolshevik* Yurenev, who declared:

There is no revolution, nor will there be: the movement in the troops is petering out, and we must prepare ourselves for a long period of reaction.

There was no instruction as yet as to what to name what had actually happened (irrespective of the will of any *revolutionaries*). So how could Yurenev know that a *revolution* had happened? If even Ulyanov-Lenin did not yet know. Asking some Yurenev!

The Russian monarchy. I saw a French newsreel which was shot during the coronation of Nicholas II. Those candles against the shimmering blackness, and every woman is Anna Karenina, and every man is Vronsky, and the tsar wants to flick a midge or something off his temple, and twitches his facial muscle several times, while his face remains perfect as that of a statue, and then he raises his hand and touches his temple in a precise clear-cut gesture.

It was to a society such as in Denmark, Sweden, or Britain, to constitutional monarchy (or constitutional democracy), that the Russian monarchy had been heading (with regressions and detours). Yet civic society means civic psychology, and not just civic institutions. While civic psychology develops, the monarchy still has to rule as an administrative or executive pyramid. The society is still only a semiconstitutional monarchy. It is this stage that is critical, and few monarchies pulled through World War I. The royal administrative pyramid may simply cease to exist one fine day.

Every member of such an administrative pyramid is ordered, inspected, motivated to act in a certain way largely by his senior, who is in turn activated by his senior, until the pyramid ends at its apex. No part of the administrative pyramid moves unless activation from the apex reaches it.

Communist, that is—serf, pyramids of overseers naturally collapse even more easily: the elements of the pre-1917 regime resisted for at least three years, up to 1921, and were at times not far from victory despite fantastic odds against them, whereas in Hungary no one even thought in 1956 of defending the *communist* pyramid that had dissolved one fine day: to reinvade one city, Budapest, the owners of serf caste Russia had to use about as many tanks as Hitler had used in 1941 over a front more than a thousand miles wide which he penetrated up to 200 miles deep within five days.

Early in 1917, several dozen people would mill here and there without any apparent purpose in the streets of the capital of the country. There was no order to, say, fine whoever had just come out of doors on a good sunny day in early spring without any apparent purpose.

Later great Stalin took this into account: his *militiaman* (after 1917 there was to be no stupid and brutal anachronism of suppression such as *police*) who saw anyone in the street without an obvious purpose was to approach him and ask him to produce his passport. If the suspect produced his passport willingly, and explained, as the *militiaman* studied his passport, the purpose of his presence out of doors quite plausibly, the ceremony ended, provided the *militiaman* had made sure that the suspect belonged to the proper territorial caste and had all the other credentials. Otherwise the *militiaman* would pocket the passport and make for the *militia* station, with the suspect following, of course, because without his passport he could not exist. No people could gather even if their purpose was obvious like gaping at something. If they did gather inadvertently and saw an approaching *militiaman,* someone would anticipate his remark by saying: "No crowd!" (or facetiously: "No crowd of more than one person!") and the group would disperse even before he approached.

Thus great Stalin, who had witnessed the dissolution of the semiautocracy in 1917, wanted to safeguard his post-1917 superautocracy. Though there are many other ways for its sudden cessation. Great Stalin was like a man who once saw the recrystallization of a solution after a crystal had been thrown into the solution and who is always on guard to prevent the throwing in of a crystal, never suspecting that the same reaction may come about if not a crystal but any bit or speck gets in, or without any apparent agent at all.

Anyway, early in 1917 several dozen people would mill here and there without any apparent purpose in the streets of the capital. What happened then is described in thousands of memoirs, scattered in libraries all over the world or sealed off in top secret repositories here. Many of these memoirs have been unavailable to me—or to anyone else. But are they so indispensable? Bridges of a certain type collapse because the type is a poor design. The collapse of the social bridge known as the pre-1917 regime brought down with it hundreds of millions of human destinies, and therefore thousands of participants and witnesses began to reminisce and describe *that* particular bridge as though its collapse had been unprecedented: it is in the same way that those who stood on a bridge when it collapsed may believe if they have survived that nothing like that has ever happened and they must describe how the ironwork under the banisters looked to them on that unique occasion, where they were bound for while crossing the bridge, and what they thought when they felt that the bridge floor was going under. I must confess that I am not too much interested in history in that sense, nor do I find it reliable. As evidence I rather prefer sources like *Pravda* which began to appear on March 5, 1917, because there is no better evidence on the pre-1917 regime in Russia than the testimony of its sworn enemies, and because that testimony was recorded right after the event. The *Pravda* issue describes the street gatherings on February 14, that is, still under the *brutal tsarist autocracy:*

Thus, soon after two, at the corner of Shpalernaya Street and Voskresensky Avenue there grew a crowd of 150 to 200 people. They were ousted onto Zakharyevskaya Street, where four or five mounted gendarmes came prancing. They rode onto the sidewalk and began to press the crowd off. One of the workers made a speech addressed to the gendarmes in which he indicated that King Hunger had impelled them to come here, and that gendarmes are also workers, only dressed in gray coats. "This is all true, of course," the gendarmes replied. "But disperse anyway."

However, the crowd kept growing. There were shouts: "Down with the War!" and the people went to Nevsky Prospect and marched several times from the Kazan Cathedral to Sadovaya and back, singing "La Marseillaise" and "You Have Fallen as Heroes in Deadly Fight."

The newsletter *Social Democrat* which had been published by the *bolsheviks* since *Pravda* was banned described a no less colorful and safe turnout over a year earlier:

On January 10, in the evening, a huge column of workers and soldiers marched along Bolshoy Samsoniyevsky Avenue.

So in the *brutal tsarist autocracy* (as the pre-1917 semi-democracy of Russia has been described in many Western studies, histories and reference books) soldiers took part with total impunity in antiwar demonstrations during a world war. An important fact since what is called abroad "Russian revolution" is essentially the mutiny of soldiers who did not want to go to the front in the spring of 1917 and the second mutiny of soldiers (and deserters) for the same reason in the autumn of 1917.

They sang revolutionary songs, made speeches, and shouted "Down with the War." The police kept at a distance and tried to convince the marchers to go home. The presence in the more-than-one-thousand-strong crowd of 300 to 400 soldiers had a tranquilizing effect on the police: far from trying to "disperse," it did not even threaten. The demonstration lasted more than an hour and ended because of the late hour (11 o'clock).

The late hour: of course! Time for supper and bed, not for the Deadly Fight Against the Bloodthirsty Tyrant. The population of the capital, including the soldiers in the barracks, was more sure with every passing day that antiwar marches and all the out-of-doors Deadly Fight Against the Bloodthirsty Tyrant were safe. Of course, nothing is perfectly safe, and a city dweller who, say, crosses the road runs a certain risk of being killed by a vehicle. But the population was more and more sure that this out-of-doors Deadly Fight Against the Bloodthirsty Tyrant certainly offered no higher risk than, say, city traffic. February 23 was a Sunday, and naturally there was no better Sunday pastime for many than the Deadly Fight. So many stayed out of doors that it would have been impossible to arrest them even if there had been an order to do so. A week or two earlier these people had just stayed out, sang songs, and shouted, but the more of them there were, the more safely they could also loot bakeries and other stores (a sufficient motive for many), stop streetcars, and threaten the members of the administrative pyramid who could not even reply, waiting for the activation from the apex.

It all started on Bolshoi Avenue, it seems, outside the Filipov bakery, where, having stood in a line for a long time, the women ransacked the store and moved en masse toward the Pekar bakery on Kamenostroyevsky Avenue. When it was announced there that there was no bread the crowd became agitated. Only the iron curtains saved the bakery. The policeman would not interfere, saying: "For us our lives cost more."

Then *Pravda* makes again the same characteristic observation:

It was only by ten o'clock that everything became quiet, the streets grew empty.

Now it was decided that eleven o'clock was too late to carry on the Deadly Fight Against the Bloodthirsty Tyrant: ten o'clock was thought to be a more reasonable time to have supper and go beddy-bye. The desire of the population to challenge the administrative pyramid (in the hope of not going to the front, for example) did not exceed its readiness to have supper later than ten. Thus, the overall motivation to challenge the regime was insignificant. But the overall desire (and ability) to defend it was even more insignificant. Those who did not belong to the administrative pyramid considered the regime to be the concern of this pyramid. And those who belonged to it (and constituted by definition a tiny minority) would not act on their own in defense of the regime because by February 23 this would already have been dangerous ("For us our lives cost more"), and then because they were to wait for an order from the apex of the pyramid anyway, and because finally each of them tended to consider the situation to be the concern of his senior, and he *his* senior, and so on—up to the apex.

The administrative pyramid—and hence the regime—did not actually exist any more, though in appearance it was perfectly intact, exactly as a week or a month or a year before. The non-existence of the regime on the next day, Monday, February 24, is clear from *Pravda*:

Nevsky Prospect was flooded by thousands of people. Those who moved from Vyborg Avenue were met on Liteyny Bridge by a line of Cossacks, and the colonel made a threatening gesture with his saber.

The gentle reader will now see at last how bloodthirsty the tsar was and how brutal his regime turned out to be: to make a threatening gesture with a saber!

The saber was snatched from the colonel and tossed over the bridge railing into the Nieva. And the Cossacks said: "Press a bit harder, and we will let you through."

Suppose Nevsky Prospect were flooded by thousands of people *after* 1917. What would those in possession-power have done? Later even a "crowd of more than one person" gaping at something was impossible. But in 1918 there was no such perfect order. When the Constituent Assembly, that is, the heart of Russian democracy, was destroyed, there were demonstrations. A proper measure? Quite simple: surround each demonstration and shoot them like partridges, as great Trotsky said. Next day the others would stay home. Well said, well done! Yet sinister rumors spread. Then *Pravda* decided to counter them: it described the shooting of each group of marchers in defense of the Constituent Assembly in one short passage, but at the end of each passage it gave a ridiculously small figure of victims, and said in conclusion:

By evening the situation was somewhat more calm. The most monstrous rumors about the numbers of victims of today's demonstration are circulating in the city.

Not that the number of victims were "most monstrous." No. Only rumors were. And *Pravda* came out to give the *real* numbers of victims. While in two days it turned out that there had been no victims because there had been no shooting:

Enemies of the people, counter revolutionaries and subversives are spreading rumors that revolutionary workers and soldiers were firing on peaceful demonstrations of workers on January 5.

So the *Pravda* of two days before had been an enemy of the people, a counterrevolutionary and a subversive. Never since has the content of this issue of *Pravda* been mentioned on the territory of former Russia. The shooting has never been, and the issue of *Pravda* never existed. Nor is it usually mentioned in Western histories, studies, or reference sources.

Two Americans closely watched the event, and one of them witnessed it: Colonel William Boyce Thompson, a copper magnate, later a Bethlehem Steel co-owner, a Conservative, and Raymond Robins, a social economist, an ecologist, a Progressive. The Conservative and the Progressive did not notice the little accident: they evidently went temporarily blind, for their Friendship with the owners of Russia, and hence Trade, and hence Peace seemed to them far too important to notice the shooting of a pleasantly unknown number of defenders of democracy in the streets. I often think: in what way have all these Conservative Thompsons and Progressive Robinses deserved democracy except by their luck of birth, and who will they have to blame or to curse if they find *themselves* one day ducking bullets of exactly the same caliber?

On the advice of Colonel Thompson, *The New Republic* removed the article of its Moscow correspondent about the nonevent. In 1967 the Viking Press, New York, published an anniversary collection of American press reports from Russia, cheerfully entitled "Revolution in Russia!" Three vague, insipid, wan lines about the nonevent were:

From Moscow it is reported that many persons were wounded and others killed as a result of the Red Guard firing on demonstrations there in favor of the Constituent Assembly.

Vaguely, vaguely, if at all, do the Thompsons and Robinses recall the nonevent. But once, in 1905, a crowd of 140,000 was moving on the Winter Palace. Imagine a crowd of 140,000 which presses on to enter the White House and have it out with the President and his staff. Except that weapons are banned in Washington, D.C., but they were not in St. Petersburg or anywhere in Russia. And so thousands in that 140,000-strong crowd in 1905 carried perfectly legal revolvers and rather illegal bombs. Once the crowd gained momentum it could not stop because, as the network of propaganda piously explains, the "back rows kept pressing the front rows." For the back rows felt safe behind the backs of those ahead and pressed on. What would those protecting the White House have done under the circumstances? They would have opened fire. Even today when there are helicopters, loudspeakers and tear gas. In the most democratic of democracies. Throughout the twentieth-century history of the United States troops opened fire on much lesser occasions. No government troops anywhere would have let a 140,000-strong crowd break into the seat of the government and trample to death, shoot and bomb everyone and everything.

After all futile attempts to stop the crowd, the troops fired above the heads and hit the observers who were watching the spectacle from the trees or other vantage points.

Even if a Western scholar knows nothing about Russia, he knows, with all the clichés of *propaganda,* about the unprecedented heinous massacre which Nicholas the Bloodthirsty had, with his stupid brutality, engineered to quench his insatiable thirst for blood. Half a century later, Western histories of Russia between 1861 and 1917 usually present this Bloody Sunday as the key event of pre-1917 life of the "Russian people," unfit for sensible democracy and forever immersed in heinous massacres.

The Viking Press book of 1967 which devoted three vague lines to the shooting of the demonstrators in support of Russian democracy—how many lines did it devote to the firing on the 140,000-strong crowd marching on the Winter Palace? Lines? Pages! The Viking Press collection of contemporary press reports devoted at least five pages to this really central epoch-making event, not to mention all the ensuing riots, which were, of course, infinitely more important than the Constituent Assembly or Russian democracy in general.

If the tsar had dared to open fire on February 14, 1917!

Hyperbolized cosmically, the *stupid brutality* of Nicholas the *bloodthirsty* would have been dinned into our heads since childhood, and from the network of propaganda it would have spread all over the globe down to most specialized studies or popular reference sources of all countries. And all those whom Pravda calls *all progressive mankind, including the best representatives of the Western intelligentsia,* who did not even notice the shooting of Russian democracy and have never recalled it, would have pounced one and all in their media on the *bloodthirsty tyrant.*

The manichean tide was against the tsar, he could not work upstream, the new bigotries, creeds and pieties wanted to see only *their* manichean side.

Nicholas did nothing in order not to be all in the wrong (and was shot with his family all the same and cursed as a *bloodthirsty tyrant, overthrown by the revolutionary heroes in the deadly fight*). And it is clear what had happened motivationally already on the 23rd. A member of the administrative pyramid had been motivated to defend the pyramid and the regime. From his senior he expected promotion at the very best in case of defense, and imprisonment at the worst in case of non-defense. It is true that his spiritual attachment to the Russian monarchy could well be greater than, say, a *communist's* spiritual attachment to his *communism* or whatever, but it must be borne in mind that the overall strength of such motives for the country as a whole had always been microscopic and had just seemed to be millions of times bigger than it really was simply because such motives had been considered good, noble or beautiful. These motives could not compete, except for individual exceptions, with the danger of being butchered by the mob, perhaps along with the family. "For us our lives cost more." Outwardly, a member of the pyramid looked the same: he carried his uniform, documents, and arms, but motivationally he was not a member of the pyramid anymore: he was now just an actor, a statistic, an outsider. There was also a good pretext for him: he was waiting for orders from the apex via his senior—certainly his senior was responsible.

But what about the apex?

There is only one apex to a pyramid, and one apex cannot be everywhere—at the war-front General Headquarters, in the capital, and elsewhere—at once. Members of the pyramid who were on the spot had to report the local situation to the apex, which had to mull over the information and send out orders. On the 25th, two days after the regime had actually ceased to exist in the capital and hence everywhere, because the capital *is*, normally, the apex, a telegram from the War Minister, General Belyayev, who was in the capital, to the apex at the General Headquarters, said that there had been some *agitation* in the capital, but there was nothing serious, and proper measures had been taken. What the War Minister meant was that the members of the administrative pyramid looked just the way they did a week or a month or a year before. Their uniforms, documents, and arms, were exactly the same. He could not understand that the regime no longer existed motivationally for he had no idea of motivational analysis. And who had—in 1917?

On the other hand, the War Minister was also a member of the administrative pyramid, and if the pyramid still existed, why should he present himself to the apex as incompetent to handle the situation? If, on the other hand, the pyramid did not exist, the apex could do no harm to him. The tsar could not take him to prison personally, could he? There would be a new regime in which he might even get into a new cabinet. The new cabinet of the new regime had, indeed, shaped up, unofficially. Perhaps the fall of the old pyramid was for the better and he should not scare the old apex before due time? He and Rodzyanko, the Chairman of the Duma (Parliament), met on the 25th.

Viewing the matter in terms of full-fledged (and not semi-constitutional) democracy, Rodzyanko was, as Chairman of the State Duma, to be Prime Minister. Actually, his Deputy at the State Duma had been appointed to the Cabinet and he had not. It is bad enough to miss promotion. But to be humiliated like that. Besides, in strictly legal, constitutional, democratic terms, Rodzyanko was quite right. Yet there are times in history when those who are quite right in terms of pure law, or pure constitution, or pure democracy, prove to be as wrong as those who want to settle their personal scores, redress their private wrongs, or attain their individual goals at the expense of some *agitation,* which may be also called the *beginning of a real revolution.*

Anyway Rodzyanko describes his meeting with Belyayev in this way:

Having outlined the situation, I noted that this was not just some agitation but the beginning of a real revolution, and that proper vigorous measures should be taken without delay.

And here Belyayev sent that telegram to the apex to the effect that on the contrary this was just some *agitation*, nothing serious, and anyway proper measures had been taken. What proper vigorous measures did Rodzyanko mean?

My arguments convinced the War Minister, and he immediately went to the Chairman of the Council of Ministers, Prince Golitsyn, and from there telephoned me that the conference we desired would be convened on the same day, the 25th, at the Mariinsky Palace, and I was entitled to invite the representatives of public organizations I would find necessary.

So the proper and vigorous measures at the *beginning of a real revolution* were: *we* must be the new cabinet. And the next day, one telegram to the apex from the War Minister said that proper measures had been taken (quite true), and another one, from Rodzyanko, stated that the situation was on the contrary hopeless, and the only proper measure to save the regime was to *change* the Cabinet. And who would be the Chairman of the *new* Cabinet? The author of the telegram, of course. For he was to be appointed to the post, legally, constitutionally, democratically.

An ironist of the twenties said: "We thought that there was only one idiot in the country: the tsar. Now we see that everyone was an idiot except the tsar." However, this was not a matter of intellect. True, in retrospect we can see that he was intellectually superior to Rodzyanko and many others, but that was not the point. It was simply that Nicholas II defended the status quo while many others wanted change, and at that particular time (until the war was over in a year), an intelligent man, endowed with at least some social intuition, if not knowledge, was to defend either the status quo or the signing of a separate treaty with Germany. But who would dare to suggest a separate treaty? Thus, Ulyanov-Lenin feared more than anything else that the very expression "separate peace" might be associated with his name even in the summer of 1917, after the monarchy had collapsed:

Concerning the separate peace I have already said that there can be no separate peace for us, and according to the resolution of our party thare is not a shadow of doubt that we denounce it as every agreement with the capitalists.

Even later, already in possession-power, Ulyanov-Lenin still had the separate peace he concluded called not a separate peace, but an "obscene bond imposed on us by force."

The demagogue who would be bold enough to promise a separate peace with Germany yet who would be cowardly enough to call it not a separate peace but something else (*world revolution,* for example, which would magically occur in Russia and Germany simultaneously and hence there would be peace, not a separate peace) was bound to carry the day, while all those decent, honest, well-meaning statesmen who did not want to promise a separate peace yet wanted constitutional, civic, or social changes in the last year of the war, were bound to perish.

Anyway, as the apex still tried to grasp the situation, his subordinates around him and in the capital pressed him to change the Cabinet (or change himself for his brother) or carry out some other no less brilliant changes, because they were actually not his subordinates anymore, and/or because they now hoped to rise to the status to which their rivals had been promoted, and/or because their understanding of human behavior was at the symbolic stage and so they thought that the *people* were displeased with the allegation (false) that Rasputin lived not only with Vyrubova, the tsar's wife's friend, but also with the tsar's wife herself. It was not clear even in purely verbal terms, why the *people* should have cared. Rasputin was a peasant, a man of the *people,* and certainly the allegation might flatter the *people* rather than displease them. Rodzyanko and many others were sure that this is why the *people* did not want to go to war (to be maimed or killed), because this is what many formally educated and formally semieducated people discussed for hours every day for many years. As often happens in a comparatively free society, an itch was taken for a gangrene because many people touched it, nursed it, and scratched it every day for several years until the itch became a gangrene—in their brains, cured very well as soon as the whole body politic collapsed, along with the itch and along with their brains, mostly blown out with bullets.

If only there were a new Cabinet. Or a new tsar. Or a new regime. Oh, how gladly the *people* would go to war (to get maimed or killed)!

On the 25th, a couple of days after the administrative pyramid and hence the regime actually ceased to exist, the first shot rang out in the capital at 3 P.M. Millions of people in Russia and elsewhere, like my uncle Anas, said afterward, quite seriously, that this was the *bloodthirsty tyrant's first armed offensive against the heroes of the revolution.* However, it turned out that the shot came from a Cossack: he thought it safer to be against the regime, and therefore killed the chief of the police detachment, who was still waiting for the order from above. So the shot was renamed, also quite seriously, the *first armed offensive of the heroic revolution against the bloodthirsty tyrant.* As *Pravda* described the event:

At that moment something happened which evoked great enthusiasm in the crowds. The Cossacks fired on the mounted police so that the latter galloped to Goncharnaya Street and stopped there, far away. The police officer lay dead, his head gashed with a saber. Loud hurrahs shook the square as kerchiefs and hats were waved to hail the Cossacks. The crowds were jubilant.

A fellow-in-arms of my uncle Anas, also a *social revolutionary*, who managed, however, to emigrate, described from abroad in more detail this *first armed offensive of the revolutionary heroes against the bloodthirsty tyrant*:

Only later did I learn that the first shot had been fired by one of the Cossacks and killed the police officer Krylov at the head of the mounted police.

Only later. But at that time who knew? Perhaps that shot was fired on the crowds—on the thousands of *revolutionary heroes*—and one of them could be wounded, maimed, or even killed!

I ran with the crowd—and lost one of my galoshes. As I looked back on the snow I saw canes, hats, galoshes—but there were no people on the square: the square had been quickly cleared, and the crowd had run into the adjacent streets, which suddenly seemed very narrow.

This demonstration on Znamenskaya Square during which the police officer was killed—the first casualty of the government in the revolution—occurred at about 3 P.M. As later was established by memoirists and historians, this shot from a Cossacks's rifle at the police officer was evidently the first offensive operation of the street revolution.

In a few days the offensive operations could continue without the need of dropping canes, hats, and galoshes in the process. As soon as the mobs identified a policeman, he would be pounced upon and trampled to death. The police had not been concerned with, say, my uncle's brother's assassination of a governor. Since the time of Nicholas I there had been an investigative branch for that, while the police had simply been handling drunks, thieves, and such. A week or two before it had been proclaimed that "gendarmes are also workers, only dressed in gray coats." Now not only gendarmes but ordinary policemen were hunted down and killed. Some of them opened fire (at last): realizing that they would be butchered by former criminals released from prisons, they fought for their lives.

As *Pravda* described the *revolutionary heroism* on the 27th, the fourth day of nonexistence of the regime:

Inmates of the Detainment, Kresty, and other prisons were released.

The destruction of police stations, Civil Courts, and Protection Department then began. The files were thrown out of windows and set on fire. Some police stations were in blazes too. The District Court was set on fire as well.

However, there was one difficulty. A month later *Pravda* announced in a bold headline: "During the Revolution 1,382 Persons Suffered in Petrograd." Very clever: *suffered*. Quite likely even more judges, jurymen, and policemen were massacred—by common criminals, for example. But who of the *bolsheviks* or their sympathizers *suffered*, and in what way? Would you believe it? One fallen hero was found! A certain student Osennikov.

Just about how the hero fell *Pravda* said not a word, but the gentle reader should not assume that the *revolution* was entirely devoid of that tempestuous element with which the word is often romantically associated. An outstanding event of this kind was prominently announced by *Pravda*. When the prisons were opened, some evildoers pretended that they were revolutionaries, and volunteered to carry an inmate's property. In *tsarist prisons*, inmates could have so much property that in case of a *revolution* they were in a very bad position because porters were not readily available owing to the ensuing chaos. So these impostors, who volunteered as porters, walked away with the inmate's property, including her pillow and pillow case (one hopes that this lady, presumably a *bolshevik*, who had perhaps splashed acid on Ulyanov-Lenin's instructions, spent later at least one day in a real, post-1917 prison), her linen, wickerwork basket, and lilac cardigan (all the craze of the day).

After this central tragedy, the gentle reader will be less painfully shocked by an even graver source of danger in the Deadly Fight. An announcement in *Pravda* warned:

Citizens!
You are requested most earnestly to stop climbing stacks of firewood on Martian Square, to avoid grave accidents in case a stack collapses.

Perhaps the fallen hero Osennikov *fell* with a collapsing stack of firewood? Anyway, the *bolsheviks* concentrated on the grandiose Wagnerian funeral of the fallen hero, with a repeat *Pravda* announcement of the event. Perhaps it would have been still better to bleed the fallen student Osennikov and smear with his blood all the revolutionary heroes in order to show how the bloodthirsty tyrant had shed oceans of blood, yet Ulyanov-Lenin, and/or my Uncle Anas, and/or all the others, overthrew the brutal autocracy in the deadly fight.

The mobs destroyed the courts in exactly the same way they destroyed the police stations, and if Mr. Milyukov or others, later residing abroad, could say that the police force was justly mobbed because it was *tsarist*, were the courts with the jury trial experience of several decades also *tsarist*?

If democracy is civic psychology and not mere buildings bearing civic names, it is not clear why the civic psychology of the population so greatly advanced as a result of, say, the destruction of the courts with their jury trial experience or even as a result of the ransacking of bakeries and other stores. However,

Rodzyanko, Milyukov, and many others decided that once *that thing* had happened anyhow, there was no alternative but pretending that it had happened as part of history's best design. They should preferably call it "revolution," as in the textbooks of history Milyukov read and wrote himself, give their leadership to *that thing*, and try to create full-fledged democracy. It was as though the tenants of a house on fire had said that since the fire was past extinguishing anyway, all they could do was to make believe that the fire was a good, purposeful, scientific process— of their own making, indeed—which was producing, under their leadership, a new bright edifice that could, already, indeed, be glimpsed shining ever so brightly between the still-raging flames.

During both world wars even the democracy of Britain and the United States was restricted quite severely—more severely than under the tsar in many ways. How could an entirely unrestricted democracy, with a wrecked professional police, court, executive branch, and so on, begin to work in Russia, with her much more meager civic experience, and hence much weaker civic psychology, when Russia was in her third year of the severest war? (The number of German divisions she faced about equaled that with which Hitler invaded the country on June 22, 1941). How could such a super-British and super-American super-democracy emerge in Russia because of a *revolution,* that is, a few days of destruction, mobbing, and incendiarism? Plus shouting, singing, cheap oratory, and other such activities, quite festive, colorful, and enjoyable, perhaps, for some of those who felt themselves in safety.

The historical role of my uncle Anas and all the *revolutionaries* who joined this play at *revolution* and at *democracy* (once *that thing* had happened anyway, and there was no choice) was to provide after the social fire a pretty screen behind which the charred building could be reduced to rubble—or dust.

But who is to blame that it was not democracy but just a pretty screen? If the Russian government had moved more boldly between 1861 and 1917 from serfdom to democracy there would have been a democracy in 1917, and quite likely the monarch would have stayed on as he stayed on in Denmark, Sweden, and Japan.

The tsarist governments had been achieving between 1861

and 1917 the only social revolution mankind knows: the revolution from serfdom to democracy. The road had been traversed by the monarchies of Denmark or Sweden over a much longer period. Today as we view this advance from serfdom to democracy between 1861 and 1917, we can see many elementary mistakes, and in particular regressive, backward, and conservative steps as a result of the fear that is inevitable in the treading of a new dangerous path. But will not a schoolboy of today see many elementary mistakes in, say, the development of air navigation between 1861 and 1917?

Anyway, in 1917, under the world-war conditions, there could be no democracy following the cessation of the monarchy, but only a pretty screen of democracy, and the role of the pretty screen proved to be dual.

The outside democracies believed, as they contemplated the pretty screen, that everything was at last all right in Russia, and now she could wage the war quite well.

At home the pretty screen also created the delusion that everything was going according to history's best design, and hence there ensued a certain reassuring lethargy, a pleasant paralysis of will, a blissful going to sleep to the lullaby of opportunistic, self-deceptive, cheerfully infantile *revolutionary* twaddle.

Those groups of the population who were actually or manicheistically hostile to the *bolsheviks* were not in fact represented in the pretty screen of democracy—in the Provisional Government, for example. How could *monarchists* be represented at all if Mr. Milyukov had called what had happened a *revolution*?

The manichean attitude immediately rebounded right on Milyukov himself: *he* was found to be not *revolutionary* enough to be the head of the Provisional Government and had to console himself with the Foreign Ministry. But to the local councils he and his Constitutional Democratic party were not admitted at all, and hence the term "local council" began to be translated as *soviet*, as though it were some newest invention of democracy, while it was a pretext for *social revolutionaries, mensheviks, bolsheviks*, and all other such manicheans to ward off their rivals: to divide the power of the local councils among themselves. Thus they themselves set a machine for their own destruction: each of them would be thrown out successively as insufficiently *revolutionary* exactly as they barred Milyukov and his party and exactly as Milyukov barred the *monarchists* (as though the majority of the population of Britain, Denmark, or Japan could not be called *monarchist* too).

Their own machine of their own successive destruction had now only to be energized motivationally, and the energy—the motivation—was lying there for anyone to pick up. Quite simply —in huge letters on top of *Pravda* all along the page: WORK-ING WOMEN, WIVES OF SOLDIERS, and then:

Your Husbands, Brothers, and Fathers Are Dying at the Front, Sent into the Offensive by All Bourgeois and Petit-Bourgeois Parties: Constitutional Democrats, Social Revolutionaries, and Mensheviks. If They Disobey They Are Executed.

Finally, the motive to destroy democracy and follow Ulyanov-Lenin's *party*:

Only One Party, SOCIAL DEMOCRATS BOLSHEVIKS, comes out against the PREDATORY WAR, AGAINST CAPITAL PUNISHMENT FOR SOLDIERS. Only This Party Is Fighting for Peace, Bread, and Freedom.

In a few months *Pravda* was overjoyed that lame people, people blind in one eye, or people with hernias, who had never been mobilized in human history, were mobilized as fit for military service.

Similar fantastic, unprecedented, breathtaking revolutions, spiralling down into the abyss of history, happened to capital punishment, bread and freedom. And when the four years of *civil war* were over, *Pravda* announced:

On the Fourth Anniversary of Universal Military Training
The military training of the next growing generation is of great importance. Attention to military training before the mobilization age.

For, as soon as the country had emerged from the seven years of continuous war, great Lenin said in *Pravda*:

Our policy in the Middle East is for us a matter of the most real and direct interest of Russia and the constituent states federated with her.

But that was later. While in the summer of 1917 it was necessary to convince, by turning out an avalanche of propaganda with the Kaiser's generous bounties, every man fit for service (in the tsarist sense) that he was committing suicide for the sake of some Middle East, and persuade every woman that she was killing her husband, brother, father as long as she did not persuade him to desert and rush after Ulyanov-Lenin and his subordinates.

But what did they propose: a separate peace? Good heavens! Whoever could invent such a horrible lie slandering great Lenin? But what else then?

The prize goes in such cases to whoever has the *daring* to shout "Fire exit!" in a burning building and rush towards a plainly visible, blank, solid wall. It does not matter that there is no fire exit in a blank wall. Many endangered people, at least in a civically backward country, will rush after the *leader* and will trample underfoot all the others.

Never, never would great Lenin conclude a separate peace. Simply, he would grab the country and then would conclude a separate peace, after surrendering to Germany a third of the country (in terms of population). He had the *daring* to shout: "Peace!" and rush ahead though he saw a plainly visible, solid, unrelieved war of German conquest. "Peace Without a Separate Treaty or any Concessions to Germany!" "No food shortages!" "Workers Will Control Enterprises and Fix Themselves Their Own Wages!" "Loot the Rich!"

Do you want all this? Then rush after great Lenin and trample underfoot all those so-called parties, the Constituent Assembly, bourgeois courts and everything else that had taken England a millennium to develop (not to mention the antecedents in Athens and Rome) and had been developing in Russia since 1861 or earlier.

Millions of deserters had brought along their arms from the front and were very good for the mad rush. In all cities there were so-called Reserve Battalions, that is training units from which trainees were to be sent to the front, a prospect they did not like, and they rushed after Ulyanov-Lenin along with deserters. Low-skilled workers had also been militarized some-how because they were concentrated at huge munitions plants where they could gather, receive arms, and be sent out as im-provised detachments to join the rush. There was no organized force to oppose the rush which trampled underfoot all those who resisted or seemed to resist the great rush into the blank wall.

Naturally, most rushers believed that Ulyanov-Lenin and Trotsky were *their men* who would always bide their will. Members of the Constituent Assembly tried to reason with the armed deserters (respectfully called soldiers) on January 5, 1918, and as one of them noted:

Some members try to convince the soldiers that the Constituent Assembly is correct and the Bolsheviks are criminals. An overall reverberating response: "If Lenin deceives us, there is a bullet for him too."

Most rushers had no idea of the civic, public, and democratic controls that had taken England a millennium to develop. Few of them suspected that there might be a *state* different from a single administrative-executive pyramid: the purpose could only be simply to put *their men* into the pyramid, and of course, shoot them if the sonsofbitches failed to do what they were told to do. True, before 1917 there were, for example, those courts with a jury trial in which some of them had participated. But surely those courts were tsarist, and were smashed as such, and besides, they were bourgeois, invented by the rich educated swindler-looter-usurer, the bourgeois, bourjuy, bourjuin, as were all the civic, public, democratic controls it had taken England a millennium to develop.

None of those tsarist-bourgeois tricks! Let it be just a *new state* in which they would shoot Ulyanov-Lenin or any other sonofabitch the moment the sonofabitch defied their will. What did they want? Have no penalty for desertion? Their friend, pal, comrade, Lenin, was sure that nothing was more noble, heroic, indeed, conscientious than desertion! To loot those who were or looked richer? Their comrade Lenin was ready to stimulate, encourage, extol their looting in every way possible! They wanted to run enterprises themselves and fix themselves any wages they thought fair, good, and proper? What a noble, just, sound idea! Their comrade Lenin would have the printing presses print as much money as they needed to pay themselves any wages they wanted.

That sonofabitch Lenin and that sonofabitch Trotsky were *our men* for sure, and they'd better be such forever! Of course, everything else except *our power*, the *council power*, must be smashed to hell.

A political party is essentially a network of locals, each local collecting dues and such. A *political party* is exactly the same except that every *local* right after the collapse of the monarchy began to collect arms. What for? Nicholas the Bloodthirsty, who had shed *oceans of blood* (contained mainly in the body of that fallen student Osennikov), might yet recapture his throne and shed *oceans of blood* again. So the *party* must be armed, and the *locals* of the *party* must be war bases, and at every war base there must, naturally, be a room where prisoners are kept, for what war can there be without prisoners? When the network of *locals* is sufficiently ramified and well armed, the country has been conquered by the *party*.

By the time the rushers had come up in the rush after great Lenin against a blank wall instead of a fire exit ("Mobilized? But you said there would be peace! And I have only one eye, am lame, and have a hernia!") the network was all ready to *receive* any rusher who did not like a blank wall instead of a fire exit. "You do not like to go to war to be maimed or killed, you one-eyed, one-legged, herniated coward, or to live on one quarter of a pound of bread a day, or to be henceforth a *state* serf? In that room of our *party local* you will feel something that you will understand, something you have forgotten since the good old early eighteenth century of Russia."

The rush was over. It did not matter anymore whether the rushers had found a fire exit or a blank wall. Their owners willing, the serfs would now bash their heads against the blank wall and shout: "A fire exit! We are all going through a fire exit ten feet wide! Thank you, our teacher, leader, and friend!"

It was just the time for that bullet stored for the sonofabitch in every rusher's rifle? But the sonofabitch was now inside a fortress-city, the Kremlin. His appearances before his beloved common comrades were over. None of their pitiful bullets would penetrate the fortress-city with its old all-round wall, plus modern warning system, guards, plainclothes men, and all the rest. *He* could do any harm imaginable to any of them, they no harm to *him*. And even that old Kremlin was just a makeshift, for some day the shelters were to be somewhere under the Urals which no rocket could penetrate.

But that pretty screen of democracy—what had Mr. Milyukov been doing? The pretty screen of democracy had been keeping the *monarchists*, and above all the officers, the only organized force in the country capable of coping with the *party*, from getting at the *party* until the *party* had conquered the country under the pretty screen of democracy. And then the officers and all the others could easily be tossed away, along with the screen itself, of course. As the worms ate the apple they needed the pretty surface of the apple to be intact in order to conceal what was going on within. The conquest of the country takes time, and the pretty screen of democracy was to provide that time.

Mr. Milyukov was the prototype of Mr. Davies and many others. The whole megacrime in Russia was perhaps the prototype of the same on the scale of the globe since then. Just as the *party* conquered, or let us say, *networked* one-sixth of the inhabited globe under the pretty screen of actually impotent democracy, the *party* has been networking the rest of the globe (and space and water are especially good since they are nobody's) under the pretty screen of "international democracy" of the *league of nations* or *united nations*, "peace-building" statesmen, the manichean sections of democracies, and so forth. And the question as to who will triumph, the *party* in former Russia or the *party* in former China or the *party* of former Indo-China, will be perhaps as inconsequential for democracy as who triumphed in former Russia: great Lenin, great Stalin, or great Trotsky.

Mr. Milyukov accepted a middle-class college-educated megascale criminal as part of democracy because no such criminal could exist even in his imagination. Like many people in Russia and even more in democracies today, Mr. Milyukov was sure that criminals cannot be middle class and college educated. A middle-class college-educated person is a gentleman, gentle man. How can a gentle man be a criminal, with a gruff voice, rough speech, and even horrible, vulgar, subhuman acts like splashing acid into somebody's eyes?

Gentlemen like Mr. Milyukov believe that if murderers, rapists, and robbers are not sent to houses of rest (*prisons*), but instead educated into gentlemen, after their very first inadvertent mishap, there will be no further criminal behavior. The fact that *all* political parties of Russia had voted *unanimously* for the abolition of capital punishment (at the beginning of the century!)

indicates how strong the trend was among complaisant, well-to-do, well-meaning statesmen of Russia of all colors and shades. By the same token it can be argued that if all gamblers are approached in a really kind way and promised three meals a day or a university post or a good salary (or life in some nice socialist, monastic, or other collective, a quiet bourgeois community, or a fine university campus), they will stop their silly, unhappy, harmful vice of gambling. Similarly, all drunkards will stop their wild drinking bouts, all drug addicts their drug addiction, all creative people of sudden inspirations and irregular lives their sudden inspirations and irregular lives.

If Milyukov and Kerensky and Tsereteli and others had approached Vladimir Ilyich Lenin, or if Franklin Roosevelt and Joseph Davies and Harry Hopkins and others had approached Uncle Joe with that sort of kindness, you know (and had given him more substantial presents than just half of Europe or several million Russian souls), then these people would have discontinued their unkind, uneven, harmful passions and perhaps have started collecting stamps instead, like Franklin Roosevelt, if they *had to* occupy themselves with something outside office hours.

Surely Ulyanov-Lenin was a gentleman—educated into a gentleman. A good neat educated half-German family. A prosperous childhood. Kind, intelligent, liberal middle-class parents. Father who is not a drunkard, and mother who is not a hysteric. Good education. Life in Switzerland. Love of sports. Neat, precise, pedantic habits. He was against the tsarist regime. Of course: a decent man! He is just like Mr. Milyukov or Mr. Davies. Only a paranoiac psychopath like Dostoyevsky (an epileptic, too, you know, and a gambler!) can imagine that such a neat gentleman who, indeed, loves Switzerland (not to live there forever, though) is—a megacriminal! Alleged to be after country-wide glory, European attention, global love for himself, and not after a paltry local bank with its chicken feed. Alleged to operate not as a wretched stray tramp in a tiny neat moderate Swiss community but as millions of worst criminals at once, acting in perfect cooperation, kidnapping, torturing to death, raping, murdering, looting, destroying, terrorizing—and obliterating all the traces of the megacrime to dupe successfully Ambassador Davies and millions of his likes even half a century later.

No wonder that Dostoyevsky was a man of such strong—indeed, violent and morbid—passions. What a paranoiac fantasy!

Ulyanov-Lenin accepted, via his men, money from the Kaiser: if he and his men involved had been put into a house of rest (*prison*) at least for a year, the democracy of Russia might have dragged on somehow until the end of the war and thus survived. Hence there would have been neither Hitler's Germany nor Mao's China, and democracy would have taken root globally perhaps. But if the babies of the American and British intelligence services let Harold Philby go to Moscow after his lifetime of espionage (in particular, because a weekend interrupted an interrogation), why should the babies of the Provisional Government be expected to have shown more maturity? To keep such a neat, decent, educated gentleman at a house of rest (*prison*)! The babies have no will, energy, canniness to do it: like the baby Jan Masaryk, they prefer to wait with complaisant if not placating smiles until an adult of the underworld throws their rosy soft-boned innocent selves out a window provided he wants only to *suicide* them without much ado.

69

My uncle's brother survived the countrywide pogrom in 1918 of *social revolutionaries* of all trends or factions, but he soon realized that now it would be not at all like before 1917: now his life would cost no more than that of a microbe of an undesirable strain, and to be erased like an anonymous microbe might turn out to be the best lot yet. The accepted form of penitence was to hand in his resignation, stating that he regarded all his former political activity as a grave mistake and so on. It was a sheer formality of penitence, since soon there was no party to resign from, but he came through the procedure not quite insincerely because his past and the assassination of a governor now did seem to him the play of children—no, the frolics of babies. Of course, there were terrorists in Russia between 1861 and 1917, and there are terrorists everywhere under such benign conditions. A terrorist would be famous, and the entire risk would be that if caught he could always snatch out and put into his mouth, say, a cigarette with a poisoned tip. And what for? To avoid hanging or electrocution or something like that, because it is unpleasant to be killed rather than commit suicide. That was what all the fuss was about. Like the fuss in well-sheltered families about taking an unpleasant medicine or the crying of a baby from too little sleep. Baby terrorists made their baby pranks. Baby lawyers wrung their hands. Baby scholars wrote thick baby books about the cruelty *and* uselessness of the death penalty. Babies asked each other: could they do such a cruelty to our baby? Such a cruelty, my God! Of course: that had been (and still was outside) cruelty for babies. Now they first of all pounced on your wrists like well-trained dogs and opened your mouth like skilled veterinarians. To prevent cruelty to babies. After the *arrest* a thorough medical examination followed, with the same purpose. Your life cost no more than the life of a microbe of an undesirable strain, and you would perish with about as much publicity as a microbe in a test tube, but your death of torture might be of inestimable value to *them*, and they knew how to *arrest* you alive and prevent suicide with absolute certainty first and foremost. That was simply a new era, and what had been before or was outside simply did not relate.

Considering his repentance, he was sent to prison for an indeterminate term. That was certainly a generous reward for his repentance: the prison conditions there were said to be not much worse than in the prisons of the *tsarist regime*, and that seemed quite miraculous. Those people who had once been indignant about his having had to emigrate after the assassination of a governor now whispered how lucky he was. "He was a *social revolutionary*," they would whisper, as though wondering that such heinous criminals (whose heinous crime had been the absolute majority of votes received in the general election to the Constituent Assembly of 1918) were allowed to exist. The lenience was not accidental though. Some *social revolutionaries* knew the Western capitals better than Moscow and were considered to be trigger-happy daredevils, of some potential value.

As for my uncle, he was tearing his hair out (as my mother put it) at the thought that he had ever let himself be associated with his brother in his silly play at revolution, and he fled to an obscure resort in the Caucasus to work there as a doctor. He suddenly realized that instead of becoming a bad social thinker, politician, or statesman, he could be a good doctor—and he could live almost as in 1913 (now the top notch of happy life), owing to the partial admission of free enterprise which had almost revived the resort to its pre-1914 splendor.

But then he had a shock. A man he vaguely knew accosted him. He was someone called *one of the leaders of the bolshevik movement* in the Caucasus who had come to a local *sanatorium*.

It is not certain that the healthy patient knew that my (future) uncle Anas was there and pretended he had met him by accident. Anyway, to complete my uncle's shock, the man invited him to be his assistant. To be in charge of some high-level inspection of *consumer production*. The fact that my uncle was a doctor of medicine, not of economics, did not matter, of course, but how could the man think of proposing such a high rank to *him*, practically a criminal, vegetating in some godforsaken hole, and a brother of a heinous criminal, leniently imprisoned?

To all mutterings of my uncle, the visitor would reply that my uncle was just the man for him, considering his revolutionary past and organizational experience.

So far his *revolutionary past* had been considered counter-revolutionary and his organizational experience criminal. But Uncle Anas did not understand the eternal aryan-pariah rotation. Since 1922 it was the superaryan *bolsheviks* of the pre-1918 vintage that had to be crushed. Inversely, all those social revolutionaries, mensheviks, constitutional democrats, monarchists, and all the other heinous criminals could now make much better serf underlings—that is, those of them who had realized that they were isolated, defenseless, despised, heinous criminals and were elevated to the peaks of glory and power owing to the infinite mercy of the pseudo-tsar-god. A good serf underling must feel that he owes everything to his master, that he has no merits of his own; on the contrary, he is a heinous criminal, a leper, an outcast *undeservedly* promoted to a sky-high post, and as soon as he displeases his master in deed or in thought he will naturally find himself again where he was and would have been if not for his master's infinite kindness.

This has been a general principle of the possession-power ever since the pogroms of 1918. Any group, political, social, cultural, which is declared pariahs is smashed beyond all resistance by another group that is made aryan for as long as this is useful. Then the remaining individual backbroken pariahs of the smashed group can be promoted and used for smashing the aryans, now declared to be pariahs because now they may have become a group capable of resistance. For example, in the thirties the *communists* became a group thought to be more capable of resistance than any other. Hence they were declared pariahs and exterminated by new aryans, also called *communists* (why not?).

My uncle did not know that his brother lived not in a tsarist and now privileged prison, but in a mansion in Moscow. He had been offered the choice: to remain a heinous criminal (with all the consequences following from his stubbornness) or to become the pseudo-tsar-god's agent abroad. Since he had once fought against the pre-1917 Russian police, he could fight against the police of a foreign country as well. Many techniques were, indeed, the same. Before 1917 a *traitor to the revolutionary cause* would be suicided: the Russian police were to take the murder for suicide. Now all undesirables abroad had to be suicided as skillfully.

Today, this *special* science has made stupendous progress, but at its primitive level of development my uncle's brother's pre-1917 experience in Russia was still quite useful for *foreign work*. The only difference was that before 1917 he had fought *against* the relatively free and progressing regime of Russia for some imaginary superfreedom, and now he fought for serfdom and slavery as a serf—as a piece of the pseudo-tsar-god's property.

But what was the alternative? Who would need his suicidal devotion—to what? To democracy? Democratic countries had been seeking trade ever since 1921 with the ruthless exterminators of democracy. Was he to be more dedicated to democracy than democratic countries were? They were rich, but they wanted trade with the ruthless exterminators of democracy in order to be richer still. He was all alone, a convict-slave in his owners' possession, and they could always transfer him to a quicker-death unit. They could arrange for his death in any form or fashion if he displeased them in any way. And he was to perish for the sake of exterminated democracy in Russia, which democratic countries did not even wish to recall so as not to worsen their trade with its exterminators.

He was henceforth a piece of the pseudo-tsar-god's property, and he remained such everywhere, for no democracy would have wished to protect him as much as the pseudo-tsar-god would have wished to physinfluence him as a penalty in case of his disobedience.

I saw him at my uncle's, a sick childless old man, and his

heavy plain wife, both silent, as though crushed by some grief no one would even care to know. He was very pale, like someone who has just heard bad news, turned pale, and stayed that way forever. He no longer had the strength for anything except to do mechanically what he was told to do. Their first job was to kidnap a Russian general in Paris. The general was at the head of an organization of Russian émigrés who thought that the population of Russia and those who owned it were *not* the same, though many citizens of democratic countries asserted that they were exactly the same. Pseudo-tsar-god II had decided not to suicide or car-accident the Russian general, but to kidnap him in order to investigate how such a monstrous criminal-heretical thought could have originated in his mind and the minds of his accomplices.

The kidnapping proved to be as easy as the buying of a carpet for home delivery, but the whole operation was represented to the pseudo-tsar-god as a great detective venture from the latest Hollywood movie, since the pseudo-tsar-god had never stayed abroad for a long time and could not understand that his agents felt much safer there, assassinating and kidnapping, than in their beloved motherland, living in luxury and merrymaking. Those democratic countries were indeed even better than the regime of Russia before 1917. Their prisons were even better too. But my uncle's brother was never exposed: in his tired, spent, middle-age way, always pale with exhaustion, and barely shuffling his feet, he kidnapped, suicided, car-accidented, and so on, with mechanical indifference and complete safety, for about a quarter of a century until he perished in 1954, along with his chief, in their own *organs of state security*.

So there was no need for Uncle Anas to worry about his brother: his brother's revolutionary past and organizational experience were being used to the hilt.

Verbally, my uncle thought that his revolutionary past and organizational ability had been noticed, recognized, and appreciated as indispensable for the *building of socialism*, while his behavioral intelligence did not perhaps think at all, but just glowed hotly, just lured darkly, just swayed as though suspended from hooks.

Besides, they showed that they knew who he was and where he was. If he refused flatly, vague, sickening dangers loomed.

They had invited him to share the biggest loot in the history of crime—one sixth of the inhabited globe—with all the wealth therein, created by centuries of Russian culture, and all the people therein.

All the *women* therein. Russian women, Jewish, Armenian, schoolgirlish virgins and sophisticated ladies and irreproachably chiseled provincial beauties. One-sixth of the globe, with some remote prospect of the rest (Polish aristocrats? Nothing will ever beat the Parisienne. And Spain, Andalusia, Tahiti?).

And many of these women would love him, for such is life.

Not that my uncle had been any special womanizer. But here was a dizzying prospect. An entirely new life. Why not imagine it?

Why not accept it? Surely that socialism could not be built without his social-revolutionary past and organizational experience.

70

I often thought that if my uncle Anas had remained a bachelor, after his dazzling climb to general inspectorship, he might have survived somehow. But it was an innocent foible of his devoted wife that doomed him. Like all my mother's sisters and brothers, my aunt had brought from Vitebsk some iridescent visions of the Russian arts in both capitals, and perhaps she married Anas partly because she imagined how famous writers would shine in her salon.

The *greatest revolutionary poet* Mayakovsky, who believed that *he* was a saint-hero-martyr, but had a sarcastic eye for everyone else, described in this way a medium-ranking *communist* and his wife right after the *great socialist revolution*:

To his wife,
                learning
                        to play the piano:
"Comrade Nadya,
By the next holiday
                I'll get a raise,
                        and with our special rations,
Giddy-up, troika!
                I'll get a pair
                        of Pacific-wide riding breeches,
And
        will jut out of them
                        like a coral reef."

To which his wife, Comrade Nadya, replies:

"As for me
          I simply must have a dress
                    with emblems.
Hammer and sickle,
            why, that's the rage
                  in society now!
What will I *chichi* in
           at the ball
              in the Revolutionary Military Soviet?"

This was published under the characteristic title "On Rubbish" as a fiery revolutionary idealist's satire on those who imagined themselves new aristocrats. The fiery revolutionary idealist himself and his most fashionable lady had the most fashionable dress and everything else straight from Paris. They were *the* high society, and naturally assumed that their way of life was not an aristocratic pretense, but something natural, human, spontaneous. If one wears the most fashionable (and expensive) dress in the world (which may be astonishingly simple, natural, human), one simply shows one's perfect taste: one reveals nature at its best, while those down the social ladder are ridiculous vulgarians, like that Comrade Nadya, just a former cleaning woman no doubt, now learning to play the piano (ha-ha-ha!), or her even cruder husband, a former smith perhaps.

He was that same greatest revolutionary poet who said that molten metal has been poured into *our* mouths, but only three words had come from *our* burning throats: "Long Live Communism." Which shows once again that chars stand no chance against people of education: all his life the greatest revolutionary poet behaved as though molten metal were poured into his mouth, and all his life he fought without scruples for his highest book sales, exclusive fame, and big money, and was mortally afraid of infections, diseases, bad press, and ridiculed aristocratically some Comrade Nadya.

Artists and intellectuals would visit a sufficiently high-society salon because they needed high-ranking patrons, since a patron who was high enough could do anything from providing them with free-of-charge accommodations at the best resorts to saving them from a shooting. In the latter respect the best salon was that of the chief of the *organs of state security*, but the trouble was that he could also fall, thus costing several outstanding men their lives because if a patron like that fell, his protégé was not likely to survive under his successors.

Originally, some high rankers (Trotsky, Bukharin, Lunacharsky) came from the more sophisticated cities like St. Petersburg, Moscow, and Odessa, and they could not conceive of their success without aesthetic refinement. They wanted to be Russian high aristocrats of the pre-1917 Petersburg. Trotsky, once a hypersensitive Jewish pacifist, kept pedigreed hunting dogs and struck a note of *our great russian military glory* perhaps earlier than anyone else. On the other hand, thousands of high rankers who came from the remote provinces, like Ulyanov-Lenin, patterned their image of high life on the life of some grubby, remote provincial serf owners of yore, perhaps a retired major general, whom his serfs were forced to worship as they would an Orthodox saint. As the more sophisticated high rankers fell out of favor in the twenties, so the more sophisticated salons also declined. However, as new rankers like my uncle Anas began to appear in their stead, their wives wanted to emulate the high-society brilliance of their recent, more refined predecessors, and their husbands became accustomed to listening to comments beyond their comprehension and learned to keep quiet, thus not making fools of themselves.

I am afraid that my aunt Tusya and her husband Anas did not belong to *the* high society, but only to high society, and even in his "Death of Ivan Ilyich," Tolstoy leaves no doubt that Ivan Ilyich belonged not to *the* high society, but merely to high society, which was no better than a vulgar, middle-class pretension.

There is no doubt that the Spy, my uncle's sister, was the highlight of Aunt Tusya's salon, whenever she was not abroad of course, because she was always just arrived, giving all the latest tittle-tattle from everywhere, but above all from Paris. Later in life, the Spy personified in my mind the acme of elegance, the elusive Paris as it was imagined in Moscow in the thirties, the Paris in which men and women moved in the trembling mother-of-pearl visions of Monet and French belles-lettres.

Receptions at my aunt's salon coincided sometimes with the

Spy's visits home. Perhaps my aunt wanted to show her sister-in-law that Moscow was not some backward province. The Spy had become a foreigner—almost, and a sweet tremor must have seized my aunt whenever the Spy came from abroad.

I remember M. Sartre's visit here in 1954. The Spy's daughter, who was then in her late twenties, was also invited to meet him, but she had no dress worthy of the occasion. With great difficulty a dress "straight from Fifth Avenue, New York" (the "Paris" of the moment) was secured for her, and when she put it on, everyone gasped at the sight of something so exquisite. The style was flat in front ("The West, the West!"), but had waves on the back ("The West, the West!"), until someone spoiled it all by saying: "You've put it on backwards."

71

The Spy was quite indispensable for my aunt's salon. She was wearing a dress from Spain, dark blue, yet not just dark blue, but also all bossy—tiny soft bosses, and therefore it was all like soft darkness, and it was cut as though the Spy had simply picked up a piece of that soft darkness and draped it around herself, and to keep it on, she fastened it with a huge red leaflike buckle on her—right or left shoulder? Let me see: it was opposite my left side, and so it was on her right shoulder. That soft darkness must be Spanish, and that buckle Paris. The Spy had brought phonograph records from Paris. Some records I did not like, no matter how Tulya admired them. One of the records was called "Three Jolly Penguins" and another "La Cucaracha," and I identified them together by their crude frivolous clowning, and assumed that La Cucaracha was also a penguin, singing or rather squawking through its fat trembling throat. Vaguely I conjectured that those penguins represented the doomed bourgeois, and why should they be so disgustingly clownish about their doom? But the song "Il pleut" was a source of life for many, never running dry, always tremulous and nostalgic long after the record was forgotten even in Paris.

Tulya first declared that we would take no part in the entertainments of the grown-ups and that she would have a separate salon, as aristocratic as her mother's. Then she announced that on the contrary we would take part in the grown-up reception at least on an equal footing with the grown-ups.

Pending her final decision I slipped into a brightly lit room, and in that room there was a gorgeous carpet, foreign. In the language of my aunt's family *foreign* meant magic. The Spy lolled in the chair, and she was also ravishingly foreign. She had cobalt blue eyes. One of her arms was bare to the shoulder and thrown aside with a cigarette in her hand poised over an ashtray.

Tulya meanwhile was settling the problem of our participation and investigating who, specifically, had dared open *her* phonograph without her permission. While I lingered unobtrusively in the carpeted room. The red soft floor was amazing: you could lie down on it, wallow about, even press your cheek to the floor.

But since "Il pleut" was playing, I felt it improper to frolic too much. I was in an exquisite—*foreign*—world, and that singing was *foreign* too.

"Do you know what he is singing about?" she asked, perhaps amused by my expression. Il pleut sur la route.

She took me for a fool, of course. Le coeur en déroute.

"About Paris," I barely whispered. Dans la nuit j'écoute les bruits de tes pas.

She laughed: "Do you know where Paris is?" A chaque bruit mon coeur bat.

"In France." Tu ne viendras pas!

Don't I know that Paris is in France? Why, my father took me to the show called the Exhibition of Modern French Paintings. There were two Russian merchants: Shchukin and Morozov: they bought French paintings when everyone laughed at them. Then they had to give up all the paintings because these became treasures. "Take him along with you," my mother said to my father. "He is never a nuisance—it is really pleasant to go about with him." My mother loves my father perhaps more than he loves her. She wants to be worthy of a real Russian, one of those she read about in Dostoyevsky when she was in Vitebsk, a man of soul-infinities, so unlike the ordinary townsfolk of Vitebsk. She wants to show that she has borne him a child worthy of him, that she has even contributed something, for who knows: would his son be a pleasant child to take to an exhibition of modern French paintings if he had married an ethnic Russian? "Take him along with you, really," my mother said, feigning indifference, but glowing with pride. "He knows all the artists—it's so pleasant to go about with him. Really." My mother wants to interest my father in the family. Like most men he strives into infinities outside the family, and with my father these infinities always lie in vodka.

To ask me where Paris is. I know where Fontainebleau is. Autumn in the Forests of Fontainebleau. To think that the cobalt-eyed Spy may *walk* in the forests of Fontainebleau in autumn. Oh, but just listen to these words: autumn in the forests of Fontainebleau.

Il pleut sur la route. It's autumn in the forests of Fontainebleau, and il pleut sur la route. The French tenor is hooting out the word "route"—"rou-ou-oute" in sweet androgynous despair.

What are you thinking about, cobalt-eyed Spy? Il pleut sur la rou-ou-oute. You will come back one day to Moscow—Le coeur en dérou-ou-oute. Yes, and what? Your chief himself will disappear: they will dissolve him in acid, perhaps to conceal the murder even from great Stalin himself. A chaque bruit mon coeur bat. You will open your veins: some spy you are, poor, poor, cobalt-eyed Spy, frail like that *real* Chinese bowl you gave us, you don't even know that veins are opened in a bath. The blood will not flow out otherwise. Tu ne viendras pas!

Another pride of the salon was the man about whom we wrote in school essays in which we compared his *literary mastership* (that was the phrase) with that of Tolstoy and concluded that the new Tolstoy wrote exactly like his old-regime predecessor. So he was an imitator? All distinctions between imitation and originality had been lost by that time: to write *like* Tolstoy meant *both* to imitate him and be as unique as he had been in his time.

Like many high rankers of the department of literature, he had shown promise in the twenties (he was one of the few *proletarian* writers who showed promise in the real, *bourgeois* sense), and then degraded with every decade, so that by the fifties no one could tell how the man could ever have been an intellectual at all. Yet at that time the process was not complete. He was still regarded as gifted in the real, bourgeois sense, and at the same time he soon became the *secretary general of the union of writers*, the generalissimo of literature. To replace Gorky.

Although my aunt and her guests must have valued his top rank, they never said so: it was assumed that *real* values were values outside the department, and it was chic to remark that he was a *really* gifted writer (neglecting his top rank completely).

As it happened the new Tolstoy drank very heavily, and one of the reasons he came was the test-taste vodka made with greater care than the choicest wine.

Whenever the new Tolstoy came, my father was invited too, to keep the wheels of literary conversation running. "That would be very good for your Andrey," my Aunt Tusya whispered kindly to my mother, hinting that the new Tolstoy was not only a *really* gifted writer but also my father's top chief. But my father's demonic pride mixed with self-effacing shyness, his improvidence, and his exuberance made him unlikely to benefit from these invitations.

Besides, my father was a periodical drunk. He would not drink anything for weeks, but could not stop as soon as he drank anything at all, and what the salon would accept from the new Tolstoy, it would not accept from my father. Before the visit, my father swears to my mother that he will not touch any alcohol, for that would be a disaster for our family, a manifold disaster, an uncanny combination of a terrible disease, insanity, chaos, a loss of everything and, dearest to us, of my father's intelligence.

I know how it will be. Father will say "No" and then add something that will make everyone laugh because Father sober seems intelligent to others, while Father drunk seems intelligent only to himself. Then the others will ask him to drink just a little. In the salon one is aristocratic. Aristocratically, a wife cannot boorishly protect her husband. Therefore, Mother will laugh— she will expect Father to refuse of his own will—and when she laughs there will be horror in her eyes which only I will see because I understand it all and nobody else will. Father will begin to drink, and then it will be all over, and there will be no need to care anymore, because once he has started it's all the same.

Cousin Tulya rushes in because more guests arrive. Since Tulya has decided to participate she now wants the Spy to join the other guests immediately instead of wasting herself alone. The Spy complies reluctantly. Perhaps she looks down on her sister-in-law's salon with that new Tolstoy, and she is following Tulya like a grown-up, made to join the playing children. Tulya is leading her by clasping her hand and shouldering it, and the diamond on the Spy's hand gives off a piercing flash just before my eyes.

The table in the dining room is very long, and from my end

I can hardly see the other, especially because of the bluish haze of the fragrant—foreign—cigarettes. There is a row of different bottles of wine all along the middle of the table. I know that when people drink they gather around a bottle of vodka or wine. But here the table-long stockade of bottles is several bottles deep because one may want some particular wine, and not some other! I am afraid to do anything wrong, and I want to just sit quietly, but the Spy hears that I have put aside a candy wrapper and said reverently: "Foreign!" So she begins to unwrap different candies, throw them into the ashtray (to discard candies like that!), and pass the wrappers to me, each time saying: "Foreign!" The game attracts general attention, and then there is a roar of laughter, because accepting busily all the wrappers I say: "This is my monopoly of foreign trade."

"He will be a new Radek," someone says, and all laugh again.

Somebody tells two of Radek's jokes, heard allegedly straight from him, and this is important, because it is still in to know Radek personally despite his decline. There is a good harvest of apples this year—at least around Moscow but otherwise nothing is on sale, least of all clothes, and so Radek's joke is: "Surely it is a paradise on earth that we have built: we have no clothes and eat apples." The joke is a huge success, and encouraged, the guest launches on another, about someone he calls *our himself*. *Our himself* convenes the politburo: since there was a terrifying famine and the rumors have seeped abroad, he wants a quick, cheap solution which will cause a sensation abroad *and* will make the population happy. There is a silence, and only one politburo member whispers something to another. "What's that?" *himself* asks. "Well, there is a sure measure, but you won't like it, Comrade Stalin." "Now, what is it?" "Oh, no, you won't like it, Comrade Stalin." "Now, if it's a sure measure, I want to hear it!" "All right: if you hanged yourself in Red Square, Comrade Stalin. That would be quick, cheap, would cause a sensation abroad, *and* would make the population happy."

There is an uneasy silence. Uncle Anas is smiling vaguely, his smile running out like ink on blotting paper. He does not want to show himself a philistine, a prig, a boor. Naturally, there can be no aristocratic wit without trespassing on what is regarded by philistines as a taboo. But Uncle Anas also knows that he is a *criminal*, a *social revolutionary*, who is still only *allowed* to exist by great Stalin's will. It is all very well for Radek, an old friend of Ulyanov-Lenin. But not for a former *social revolutionary*, you know. What if the joke is known *there*, and everything is known *there*, as Radek himself said long ago.

72

There was a party for my seventh birthday. It ought to have been even happier than its predecessor, but how different it actually was.

It ought to have been happier because for the first time I wore a suit. Before I had worn a sweater which was not exactly mine: it was my grandmother's or somebody like that, and it was rather long, so that I wore a belt, and that sweater became a jacket. The suit was intended, of course, for festive occasions, while for several years I would go to school in that sweater-jacket, with ever new holes that had to be darned all the time, a damn good sweater, deep brown, nice wool, soft as silk, all iridescent if you carefully studied the separate hairs. But on my birthday I wore a suit—and what a suit! One could not *get* a suit for a boy, but mother *got* velvet (yes, Moscow was becoming a wonder-city) and a suit à la Spanish grandee was sewn for me at a *state dress-making atelier* which had just opened in the wonder-city. A la Spanish grandee meant that a large cut was made in front showing my white silken shirt. Naturally, Mother wanted my photograph taken in this Spanish grandee suit at a newly opened *state photography atelier*, and as I look at my face on the photograph I wonder if my personality has essentially changed. The photographer said that if I smiled a bird would fly out of his sleeve.

On my father's shelf I had already read the title: Buckle: *A History of Civilization in England*. Good old Buckle, an

English nineteenth-century scholar who was soon forgotten in England but was read by every educated Russian. The book attracted my attention because Father was fond of amusing his guests by mentioning the most incongruous books which I had allegedly read. If a guest mentioned a children's book his or her son or daughter had recently read, Father would say: "And my son has just read *Poor Heinrich*." General laughter would erupt, because *Poor Heinrich* was an impressionistic novel about a millionaire's son and his mistress in Germany. It was true: I had read the novel and thought that the author was one of the most brilliant men imaginable. Father would seem to be thinking what else I had read. "Then—*Sexual Upbringing of Children in the Family*." A louder outburst of laughter. That was also true, and in fact I recited passages from the book, while the guests almost fell to the floor with laughter. I did not understand many words and sentences and worked by sheer memory, stimulated by the obvious tremendous comic value of the text.

Father's listeners would barely stop laughing at this announcement that I had read *Sexual Upbringing* when he would finish: "And *A History of Civilization in England*." It was simply not true that I had read Buckle's *History*, yet I did not want to spoil Father's joke either, and I interjected the apologetic, deprecatory half-truth: "I am going to," which only added to the general mirth. In other words, I was committed.

I leafed through Buckle, I could not understand anything, but I knew that even a book that thick was not beyond me, and I looked at the number of pages and tried to calculate how many days it would take me to read it. And here that photographer wanted me to see a bird flying out of his sleeve. I smiled, but my smile said: "I understand that this is a convention, but I will smile to please you because you seem to be a good, kind, hardworking old man, but isn't it a bit sad and funny that in your professional activity you confuse me with a two-year-old who might be amused by your promise? Don't you understand that I am seven and *am going* to read Buckle's *History of Civilization in England*?"

During the birthday celebration I could not recapture the oblivion that is necessary for perfect happiness. How could I believe that the world was just made to love me and congratulate me on my birth? After all, the birthday was just a convention, you know.

Getting older is getting orphaned, and *toská*, the acute boredom, the desire of desires, which had haunted me only in collectives, now struck me at our dear home, our nest, which had seemed to me part of myself so shortly before. I walked about our room and repeated: "Boredom. *Toská*." I suddenly did not know what I had been born for, and what had exactly been celebrated on my birthday, though I did not phrase it like this, of course, but just paced the room and scanned as a kind of two-word poem or prayer: "Boredom. *Toská*."

Father had his drinking bouts. Later in life I also lived in bouts, not of drinking, but of something else. The trouble was that at that time I did not yet know how to find *my* bout.

Finally, it was decided that our family would spend the coming summer together—a full summer together for the first and last time in my life. A full summer: that meant *more* than one month, that is, more than eternity.

A writer who lived permanently in a village and had married a peasant girl rented us a hut in his village very cheaply, but I was worried that something might intervene, and I calmed down only on the train which we took instead of a truck because it was cheaper (or there were no trucks at all at that time to be used even by Muscovites for such trivial private purposes).

Anyway, we got off the train with our baggage, and found out that the village was still far away, and no one knew how to get there. That was why the rent was so cheap. Whatever Father did, it was always like that, Mother raved. I sat on a pile of baggage at the station in a June midday sun. I asked Father how many days we would be able to subsist here on the basket of tomatoes we were carrying. I was happy. We were traveling. All together. Even the ground outside the station building, right under me, was alive and pleasing—dusty, hot, littered with sunflower husks and cigarette butts.

For there could be only one disaster in life.

Not my death, no.

My parents' death before mine.

The fear that they would die before me had been gnawing at me ever since I began to count, shortly after learning to read.

In bed I would lie awake, counting. I did not know my parents'
age, and I am still afraid to know my mother's age, though
almost every mother's visit to these Vnukovo forests ends in a
quarrel.

So the most agonizing yet promising uncertainty was: How
old could my parents be? To say that they are twenty would be
too good to be true. Twenty. Come on. Now suppose they are
forty? This is frightening, but then this is reliably true. With a
good margin. What I lose in absence of fear I gain in reliability.
For a while I relax, enjoying the conservative soundness of my
initial datum. Forty. Ha! That's quite safe against error. Then
I begin to count as I sense the disastrous result lurking at the
end. I am seven now. I am not six anymore. I am seven, and in
twenty years I will be twenty-seven, which is too early to die,
while my parents will be sixty, and will die. But I soar above
despair, since the whole calculation is, as I remember throughout,
based on a very conservative initial assumption. Now I begin
to revise it. What was it? Forty. I ridicule it. Forty. My parents
forty. It kills me! But twenty? Am I not deceiving myself?

Our neighbor, Aunt Nyura as we called her, Nina's mother,
would ask me how old my mother was. I always answered:
"Twenty-two." And she would switch on the light in her face.
This is not merely an inept metaphor indicating that she laughed.
I *heard* the switching of the light in her face and then the
rhythmic chirping noise of the machine that evidently supplied
the electricity, and then the light would go out and the machine
would stop, of course.

She liked my answer so much that she would ask the question
whenever she saw me, and I would say brightly: "Twenty-two,"
starting each time the chirping machine that lit up her face.

But surely that chirping light on her face did not mean that
she laughed at my answer. It was a pleasant chirping light, she
liked my answer, and if I took twenty-two as the age of my
parents (I assumed that both were roughly the same age), it
worked very well into our simultaneous death, at which result
I would doze happily off.

As long as I was with my parents (and there was that calculation at the back of my mind that we would die all together happily ever after), our being stranded on a dusty piece of land under

a midday sun, with no prospect of getting further, was a beginning as exhilarating as any sequence of the venture would no doubt be, and indeed was, because the place we finally reached was a world in which God's design was obvious.

According to that design (traceable in thousands of Russian villages), at one end of the world was a graveyard, with tall generous shaggy pines, their branches swaying like kind shadows or protective wings. But despite their protection, not only was the church decrossed and vandalized as everywhere, but the tombstones were lifted and thrown about the sunlit glen before the churchyard, in order to spite the Christian rite of burial. Or to spite the dead. Or to spite the old, who are more attached to the dead than the young.

What had the church been like before? I recalled later one of Father's favorite poems:

> A girl in white in the church choir
> Was singing of travelers in strange lands,
> Of ships on high seas, weary and lonely,
> Of all forgotten, unloved, and sad.

I can imagine the young people laughing, shouting, swearing as they lugged the tombstones and jeered at those who were weeping.

> This is how her voice soared to the dome,
> And sunshine gleamed on the white of her dress,
> And each in the darkness gazed and listened
> To the beam of sunshine singing above.

And the vandalization of the church—it is difficult to imagine what it was to the villagers. An educated urban dweller has libraries, music, enlightened friends. They had nothing but the church. But perhaps the shaggy protective pine branches did not care overmuch. "This is not really so important," they would sigh. "What is important is the dark eternal tranquillity in which we sway up here."

> And each believed the ships are in haven,
> And joy will come to all who are sad,
> And lonely travelers back at home
> Are leading a light and happy life.

In the tall grass of the glen the gray tombstones scattered about looked like flitting moths, some of them drenched in the sun.

> And the voice was sweet and the beam light and golden,
> And only near Our Lord's Gate,
> A child wouldn't hush up and kept crying
> That no one ever will come back.

We could climb to the belfry and watch swallows at the level of their flight and see God's entire wondrous design, down to the other end of His world, the stone quarries on the riverbank flattening into nowhere, and in front—what was right in front?

The village was on a high, high bank, and the opposite bank was sown out of gussets of forests, one gusset a blue, another a golden violet, and still another a green: "It is seven leagues to the skies," I would recall Polya's saying, "and all the seven are forests," and between the seven leagues of forests of the yonder bank and the merry light green slope of ours God had devised a large river, so pure that not a grain of sand would whirl without showing all its sides, including a flat golden facet, a large river which you could ford at the age of seven with infinite variations of immersion down to chest-deepness near the other bank. This was a children's river, a toy river in the sense that we could not be drowned except on purpose and were finally allowed to play with it as much as we liked, and yet it was a *real river*, only given to us as a gift, our own real river, a vast lifelike toy, a play with nature in flux, a divine game of water.

Muscovites come to villages for summer much as foreign tourists come to Moscow. They come to enjoy themselves, and the sordid life of the natives is of no interest to them, and indeed does not seem to them very real. "How nice it is here," a Muscovite's wife would say, looking at the seven leagues of forests to the sky. I have since heard only one answer. The native woman would look in the same direction, a smile of sympathy on her leathery, yellowish, old-at-thirty face. What can she say, visited by these people who seem to her so rich, free, and happy, in her village to which she is attached for life and which is just as it was several centuries ago, but without the church? The urban serf owners bleeding them white have done one great service to them in exchange—they have had the church kindly vandalized by the hoodlums. "Yes," she answers with that smile of good will. "It is nice here—in summer." This "in summer" is a tactful hint. To be cooped up inside a hut for winter—the whole family inside practically one medieval box of logs, isolated from all the world, unable to leave because of attachment, left without the meaning of life the religion supplied. No wonder almost everyone drinks illicit homemade brew from the age of five or six, and while a drunkard makes himself artificially happy for a while, he adds to the violence, brutality, and filth of everyone else's life cooped up with him. "Yes, it is nice here—in summer." That is, if you just come here to frolic in summer on the bosom of nature. But the visitors neglect the hint.

As we arrived there was a rain, a glittering, green-blue, white rain that made the window panes look as though they were subtly stained glass. But I kept persuading my parents that there was no rain to speak of, that it had stopped, and that it was not wet any longer, until one of them said something like: "Go, for God's sake, go anywhere, go to hell," and as I slipped out I heard them exchanging uncomplimentary reflections on my character. "A Jewish monomaniac," Father said good-naturedly. "A devilish character," Mother raved (her eyes, of course, like butterflies with wings dark on one side and white on the other). "When he wants something he is like the devil. A real devil. A real devil."

My Jewish monomania or Russian bout or devilish obsession was a box of *oil* paints. No child of my age could possibly have a box of *oil* paints. Unlike watercolors, oil paints do not wash away if you have smudged your clothes. Suppose I would smudge my beautiful brown (but if you look at the hairs on a sunny day, quite iridescent) sweater which had actually been my grandmother's and had to be darned quite often? Say, a yellow smudge somewhere on the sleeve and *one cannot wash it off*! How would I go to school next autumn? I realized how dangerous it was to possess *oil* paints, and of course, they were terrifically expensive, too, but to allay my boredom, even if only for a time, my parents had bought me oil paints on the condition that I would use them only in the country where the danger could be somehow dissipated in open spaces, and besides, I could wear only trunks, and certainly there was no harm about smearing my body indelibly. True, since there had been a rain, I had my canvas suit on, but my parents could no longer resist the pressure of my newly found bout, and Mother's exclamation that I would get my canvas suit smudged by an *oil* paint was rather a plaintive prophecy or desperate appeal than direct interdiction. Besides, she was sure that I would get the new canvas trousers wet in the grass, much to their detriment, and since the situation was disastrous anyway, yet another peril did not matter somehow: when a flood is imminent a fire alarm is less frightening.

On our valises there were railroad tags of plywood, and a true maniac that I was, I immediately understood that these tags were very good to paint on with oils.

I was walking through the after-rain serenity under patchy skies toward the enormous pines of the graveyard. I was no longer just a soul looking from within and seeing the world as its receptacle. I was a body, a fairly small body in space. I looked at myself as I moved through space—shoes, socks, knees, trousers (the cuffs of which the rain-heavy grass had quickly wetted, fulfilling half of my mother's prophecy). I was a passer-by, a walker, a small moving thing in the universe.

Two girls of my own age saw me and asked me where I was going and whether they could come along. I said yes because I thought it would be rude to say no. "No character," my mother would say in such cases, quite forgetting that she called me a real devil. "A real milksop. A real milksop."

"Rude. Awkward. Somehow wrong," she would mock me, opening her mouth helplessly in imitation of complete lack of backbone. "Like your father. Wretched Hamlet. I cannot. I could not. To-be-e-eya or-not-to-be-e-eya."

Anyway, here we were all going, the three of us. I looked at myself (how wet the cuffs of my new canvas trousers were). I felt the touch of loneliness a small separate living being is bound to feel, but it was all right: this is what life is.

We sat on a tombstone in the shade of the pines. The girls fussed with the paints, made many irrelevant remarks, and finally one of them asked me to give her the picture that emerged on the railroad tag. Of course, I could not say no, and I explained to her how she should carry it while the paint was fresh.

Mother would again be shocked by my lack of backbone, yet

606

it was partly to our family that I owed this inability to say no in such cases. In our family no one would say to me: "No, I will not give this to you because I need it myself." Therefore, I developed a curious misconception, perhaps quite common for children in such families. When we had lived in the Urals, a certain Uncle Kolya, a charming thief, being reeducated according to that day's fashion, presented me with a huge box of wooden bricks of all possible forms and sizes which he had made himself at a sawmill where he worked. Several children began to ask me to give them a brick apiece. But others wanted one also. "Line! Line!" someone shouted, and they formed a line. I gave a brick to each applicant, and those who got one brick joined the line again to get a second, which seemed to me perfectly fair provided everyone had already got one brick, and so I dispensed the whole huge box. "Why did you do it?" Mother asked, horrified at my low chance of survival in the survival of the fittest. "But they *asked* me," I explained. I thought that asking expressed not someone's wish to get something, a wish that can be rejected, but a part of a certain preordained harmony, a fact that could not be denied any more than my or someone else's existence. If any claim of mine to my mother's or father's or Polya's property had to be fulfilled, so, too, any wish of anyone was as inexorable. Once it existed it had to be fulfiled, or it would never have originated in the first place.

Usually in the evening we would crawl though a hole in a fence to a meadow where we played, and, therefore, that meadow seemed to be the other world, so to speak.

Evening is in the air, and it is nice to be left all day to your own freedom, and yet it is nice to feel, especially as evening comes, the presence of your parents. Up there stands the hut which the writer has rented for us, and there they are, or perhaps at the cottage of that writer himself, who has married a peasant beauty and is so poor that he plays cards, and when he wins, his partners pay, and when they win, they pretend they do not notice.

Up there my parents and that writer are playing cards. These are diminutive cards, very glossy and beautiful, and one by one we are being called home.

"Z-z-z-i-i-na!" comes trembling in the evening air.

The meadow is not as green and sweet as in the daytime, but we lap up whatever joy there remains. And tomorrow. . . .

Two of us are the gatekeepers. They lock both hands raised aloft, and we pass under them as through a double-arched gate:

> Go once and go twice,
> To granny's barn or paradise.

And tomorrow—oh, tomorrow: vast and splendid. We will wade across the river: first there will be whirling sand underfoot (a grain of sand will rise, showing all its sides, including a flat gold facet), then velvety weeds, then deep sand or shallow sand again, some pebbles or roots, and only near the other shore will the water be chest-deep.

"Z-z-z-i-i-n-n-a-a-a!" How softly it rings in the evening—as though a very thin golden hoop is being trundled.

> Once, you are forgiven.
> Twice, you are forbidden.

This means that we can still get through.

"Z-z-z-i-i-n-n-a-a-a," the evening is ringing softly.

> And now comes the fate
> To shut up the gate.

At which the gatekeepers lower their locked hands and one of us turns out to be within a clasping, tickling, laughing lock and becomes a gatekeeper—not today, but tomorrow.

True, the next evening after the painting session with the two girls, there was a surprise for me as I crawled through that hole in the fence. At a broken cart which served as a rallying point, like a monument in a city square, three girls stood and sang a ditty from which I remember only these two lines: "Your love is very ardent because it's very recent but let me tell you, Lyova, it's utterly indecent." They had put my name into this song which had probably existed for generations. Most names can be made into a two-syllable version, and so practically any name can be put into the song as the occasion requires. The trio was led by a pretty-pretty girl, and faltered as I came nearer, while the pretty-pretty girl hummed the song without words, as though the rest was so indiscreet that one could only hum it.

The third in the trio did not sing at all, and had evidently been recruited to provide numerical support. She was a village girl, or rather not a girl, but a tiny village woman, with a village woman hairdo combed with a huge comb. She looked at us, Muscovites, and life in general through her deep sunken village woman's eyes. She clung to us because we didn't fight and hurt her, but she didn't play—she was satisfied by simply being with us, and as she would stand with us, she would peer somewhere off, at the bridge, for example, and predict in a low calm reasoning voice some disaster in her village: "Here Kolka's going for vodka. He'll get drunk and fall off the bridge."

The song about my allegedly ardent love was quite groundless, and it unpleasantly surprised me that the pretty-pretty girl already knew everything and no one could say how. But as I recall it now, I think: Can it be that somebody's lips moved to mention my name? So I existed. Someone noticed, cared.

At some time of my life several people are going somewhere, and someone in the group wonders why I am not going. I hear my name said. "Why won't Lev Andreivich go with us?" someone says, and at first I am so puzzled that I cannot understand. There is only a glow inside me. So I exist? Someone is even saying my name?

Before it melts away like that trembling in the evening air: "Z-z-z-z-i-i-i-n-a!"

Source Notes

NOTE: *No quotation in the book starts with a new paragraph unless it does so in the original. No emphasis is added in any quotations. If a quotation has been shortened, ellipsis points have been added, the circumstance being mentioned as such in the Source Notes. When English translations from the Russians are quoted, the text has been checked against the original.*

Page

4   What the government had done was to transform "every man not merely into an inquisitor": Henry Thomas Buckle, *A History of Civilization in England* (New York: Hearst's International Library Co., 1913), p. 354.

5   "If you are caught committing any of these crimes": *The Republic of Plato*, trans. by Francis Macdonald Cornford (London: Oxford University Press, 1941), p. 26. (Ellipsis points added.)

"[T]he liberty to buy, and sell, and otherwise contract with one another": Thomas Hobbes, *Leviathan* (Oxford: Basil Blackwell, 1960), p. 139

42   Jews could not migrate from Vitebsk to Petersburg or Moscow *unless*: *Entsiklopedichesky slovar Brokgauza i Efrona*, s.v. Evrei.

49   The worker's wages increased ten times: Strumilin, p. 257.

54   "A good collection of this new species": *Pravda*, 19 May 1928.

54–56   "I have just said that I handed in he statement" and the subsequent quotations: *Pravda*, 26 June 1928.

64   "The walls are covered by huge posters": *Pravda*, 7 December 1934.
The result of the investigation: *Pravda*, 22 December 1934.
"The death of Kirov will cost the enemies dearly!": *Pravda*, 4 December 1934.

65   "But it is noteworthy" and the subsequent quotation: *Pravda*, 5 January 1935.

67   The Ryutin apocryph: cf. Krivitsky, p. 203.

68 A medical orderly in the Urals: *Pravda*, 16 November 1928.

68–69 Elsewhere, in the city of Shatsk: *Pravda*, 22 November 1928.

72 The decision on legality: *Pravda*, 27 June 1932. (Ellipsis points added.)

The *secret instruction*: Fainsod, insert following p. 186.

A "good communist is at the same time an agent of the Cheka": *Protokoly*, Devyaty syezd RKP/b/, p. 377.

72–73 At 4:30 P.M. on December 1: *Pravda*, 4 December 1934.

Great Lenin never parted with his revolver: Krupskaya, p. 434.

75 All people who have an income of 500 rubles: Lenin, *Soch.*, 26:336.

The Trotskys got a better Kremlin residence than the Radeks: some echoes of the quarrel reached even the *friend of the soviet union* Arthur Ransome in his "Six Weeks in Russia in 1919."

76 Ulyanov-Lenin's Kremlin residence: Krupskaya, p. 452. His country residence: ibid., p. 484. "Hills afterward became": ibid., p. 485.

78 The "rent of a worker or office employee": *Pravda*, 17 May, 1928.

86–87 "Those not admitted to institutions of higher learning": *Pravda*, 13 September 1928.

88–89 The supercrown and the tsarist eagles: *Pravda*, 11 and 12 October 1935.

107 All *social benefits* cost about 30 rubles a month: *Izvestia*, 4 October 1964. They increase the *average wages* by 35 percent: *Pravda*, 30 November 1966. The average cost of one day's stay in hospital: *Izvestia*, 4 October 1964. "However once I heard": ibid.

109 "[A]t a conservative estimate 80 percent of the population of Moscow were seriously tuberculous": Wicksteed, *Ten Years in Soviet Moscow* (London: John Land and Bodley Head Ltd., 1933), p. 37.

114 The apotheosis poster was reproduced in the West in *A Picture History of Russia*, ed. John Stuart Martin (New York: Crown Publishers, 1945), p. 225.

115 "The scientific concept of dictatorship": Lenin, *Soch.*, 31:326.

117 "[O]rganizations which were not afraid": *Pravda*, 3 February 1922 ("Kak Lenin otnosilsya k chistke partii").

"Crawling into the Party for the sake of career": *Pravda*, 10 September 1921.

"Stuck to us somewhere": *Pravda*, 3 February 1929.

"[P]redominant fact in most local checkup commissions": *Pravda*, 3 February 1929.

118 "The leader of the globe": *Pravda*, 8 October 1922.

Strictly reprimanded by great Lenin: Lenin, *Soch.*, 35:272.

Biographers of great Lenin marveling at this miracle of self-sacrifice: see, for example, Fischer, p. 368.

119 "Zinoviev received us": Balabanoff, *My Life*, p. 289.

120 The "State Bank was ordered" and the quotation from Gorbunov: Krupskaya, p. 418.

121 "Several gubernias of Russia are hit by famine": *Pravda*, 6 August 1921.

The book mentions only 964,627 famine-stricken persons in 1891: Ivansky, p. 640.

While in 1921 *Pravda* mentions the figure of twenty-five million people in the Volga region: *Pravda*, 26 June 1921.

122 "The food assessment killed": *Pravda*, 3 April 1922.

123 "[N]ational disaster about which much has already been said": *Pravda*, 5 August 1921.

124 At least twenty-eight documentaries: *Pravda*, 28 January 1928.

"I am one of the very few": Balabanoff, *Impressions*, p. 6.

"There is another trait of his": *Pravda*, 22 April 1928.

125 "Another time, on one of my visits": Balabanoff, *Impressions*, p. 5.

American relief: H. H. Fisher, *The Famine in Soviet Russia: 1919–1923* (New York: Macmillan, 1927) pp. 292, 555, 124.

127 The average wages at the Putilov works: *Pravda* (*Rabochy put*), 23(10) October 1917.

Supply of meat and butter to Petersburg: *Pravda* (*Rabochy put*), 12 October (29 September) 1917.

The highest caste of commoners received a quarter of a pound of bread a day: *Pravda*, 10 October 1918.

128 "People of the professions": *Pravda*, 3 December 1918.

"The People's Commissariat of Social Security": *Pravda*, 27 September 1918.

129 Each caste was attached to its own food caste stores already in 1918: *Pravda*, 24 November 1918.

The *closed distributor* of the *organs of state security*: *Pravda*, 27 September 1918.

Allocated "are one million rubles of gold and academic rations": *Pravda*, 15 August 1922.

Even this tiny superelite was divided into six castes: *Pravda*, 15 August 1922.

130 A closed restaurant at Smolny: Krupskaya, pp. 413, 414.

"Saint!": Balabanoff, *Impressions*, pp. 3, 4.

The pince-nez scene: Balabanoff, *Impressions*, p. 45.

"When I thought": Balabanoff, *My Life*, p. 223. (Ellipsis points added.)

131 "[N]o one has ever doubted": Balabanoff, *Impressions*, p. 2. "For there was unanimity": ibid., p. 141.

"But I beg you, don't economize": ibid., p. 29.

"With one of those contributions": Balabanoff, *My Life*, p. 196.

"Everyone knew": idem.

132 "I remember he was not easily persuaded": Balabanoff, *Impressions*, p. 13.

"They have brought me": Balabanoff, *Impressions*, p. 13. (Ellipsis points added.)

133 The note on caviar: *Leninsky sbornik*, p. 141.

135 "Applause. Stormy, joyous applause": *Pravda*, 14 November 1922.

137 "If the Germans do not lie": Lenin, *Poln. sobr. soch.*, 49:399.

The circular to store acid: Lenin, *Soch.*, 9:390.

138 "The autocracy of ex-Nicholas": *Pravda*, 13 July (30 June) 1917. (Ellipsis points added.)

"[P]repared *The Development of Capitalism in Russia*": Krupskaya, p. 27.

"My mother told me": Krupskaya, p. 29.

"I have here everything": Lenin, *Poln. sobr. soch.*, 55:18.

139   "Life was surprisingly cheap": Krupskaya, pp. 36, 37.
139–141   Ulyanov-Lenin's life abroad, quotations: Krupskaya, pp. 236, 192, 270, 75, 265.
143   "Dear Al. M.!": Lenin, *Soch.*, 35:40.
"My esteemed M.N.!": ibid., 35:211.
143–144   Ulyanov-Lenin had pleaded with Pokrovsky: Lenin, *Poln. sobr. soch,*. 49:256, 274, 284.
He inflicted on Gorky his wife's piece: ibid., 49:182.
145   "There is no money": ibid., 49:138.
"He wrote to *Granat*": Krupskaya, p. 333.
146–147   Parvus, alias Helphand, does figure as a paid agent, Parvus did receive directly from the German Treasury little nothings: Futrell, p. 171. The Berlin Hauptarchiv does contain an agreement: ibid., p. 190. The quotations from the German archive documents: Z. A. B. Zeman (ed.), *Germany and the Revolution in Russia, 1915–1918* (London and New York: Oxford University Press, 1958), pp. 9, 14.
147   "Ganetsky was employed": Lenin, *Poln. sobr. soch.*, 34:31.
"Ganetsky earned his daily bread as an *employee*": Leninsky Sbornik (Moscow, 1959), 36:19.
148   "No money whatsoever": *Pravda*, 19 (6) July 1917.
Kozlovsky was, indeed, appointed to the top of Ulyanov-Lenin's secret police: Lenin, *Poln. sobr. soch.*, 32:562.
149   "Dear friends!": Lenin, *Poln. sobr. soch.*, 49:437.
"Dear comrade": Lenin, *Poln. sobr. soch.*, 49:438.
"Detail two or better three thousand": Lenin, *Poln. sobr. soch.*, 49:425.
Great Lenin had collected the money for the same trip: Lenin, *Poln. sobr. soch.*, 49:426.
"Attached hereto are the receipts": Lenin, *Poln. sobr. soch.*, 49:435.
"We lived mainly on this money": Krupskaya, p. 282.
149–150   "As for myself personally, I need a source of income": V. I. Lenin, *Sochineniya*, 3rd ed. (Moscow: Gos. Sots. Econ. Izd., 1931), 19:276.
150   "Let me repeat again": Lenin, *Soch.*, 43:302.
157   "When I finished reading": *Vospominaniya rodnykh o Lenine*, 1955, p. 36.
158   "The so-called society sounded the alarm": Ivansky, *Molodoy Lenin*, p. 642. (Ellipsis points added.)
"Lenin did not believe in the success of such propaganda": ibid., p. 641.
"By destroying farm households, the famine destroys the belief": ibid., p. 645.
159   "With the arrival of Vladimir Ilyich": ibid., p. 644.
"Yet Vladimir Ilyich" and the subsequent quotation: ibid., p. 647.
160   "Animation set in": ibid., p. 648.
160–161   "That was the first big evening party" and the subsequent quotation: ibid., p. 666.
164   "[A]ll your impressions are totally sick": Lenin, *Soch.*, 35:347. (Ellipsis points added.)
165   "M. Gorky is, as we all know, compassionate": *Pravda*, 4 September 1922.

166 "Whoever struggles": *Pravda*, 11 November (29 October) 1917.
General Statute of the Press: *Pravda*, 11 November (29 October) 1917.

167 Decision on the Revolutionary Tribunal of the Press: *Pravda*, 1 January (19 December) 1918.
"For the last several days": *Pravda*, 8 February (26 January) 1918.
"Retribution to an Enemy of the People": *Pravda*, 7 July (24 June) 1918.
The Kokuyev case: *Pravda*, 24 September 1918.

168 "For the permission of such a damage to Soviet property": *Leninsky Sbornik*, 35:132.

169 The *new court*: *Pravda*, 6 December (23 November) 1917.
"[F]or the public demonstration of Menshevism our courts must shoot": *Pravda*, 29 March 1922.

170–171 In May 1922 great Lenin penned an *article of the criminal code*: Lenin, *Soch.* 33:321, 322.

172 "And surprisingly, the constant expression": *Pravda*, 2 April 1922.
"All persons going abroad": *Pravda*, 7 December (24 November) 1917.

173 The Pavlov case: Lenin, *Poln. Sobr. Soch.*, 51:222.

173–174 "To: Central Committee of the Russian Communist Party" and the other facts of the Blok case: *Literaturnoye Nasledstvo* (Moscow: Nauka), 80:292–294.

175 Gorky's letter to Rolland: *Literaturnoye Nasledstvo* (Moscow: Nauka), 80:293.

176 "I have received from Dr. Pelletier" and the other facts of the case: *Literaturnoye Nasledstvo* (Moscow:Nauka), 80:284.

184 "P. Berezin is found guilty": *Pravda*, 27 December 1918.
"The opinion of Comrade Dzerjinsky": *Pravda*, 26 December 1918.

185 "Berezin became an employee": idem.
"Comrade Dzerjinsky, being aware of committing an illegal act": idem.

186 "An imposing figure": *Pravda*, 11 December 1918.

187 In 1906 Russian scholars "proved statistically": *Protiv smertnoy kazni*, ed. Gernet (Petersburg, 1907).

189 "The Graveyard of the Living": *Izvestia*, 4 December 1918.

190 "Anyway, apart from the telegrams and their possible interpretation": Futrell, p. 163.

192–193 "[T]he Cheka-men got a denunciation: *Cheka: Materials on the Activity of Extraordinary Commissions* (Berlin: Novaya Rossiya, 1922), p. 231. (Ellipsis points added.)

196 "The Proletariat-Run Furnace of Fire": *Pravda*, 11 September 1918.

196–197 "Those registered will be divided": *Pravda*, 8 September 1918.

197 "Look for no evidence": *Pravda*, 25 December 1918.
"I can imagine Karl Marx": *Pravda*, 25 December 1918.

198 "Can It Be a Medieval Torture Chamber?": *Izvestia*, 26 January 1919.

199 An article which called great Lenin a "principled demagogue": *Pravda*, 26 January 1921.

200 "A gigantic job": *Pravda*, 30 March 1922.
202 The "*least* evil would be now and immediately—the *defeat* of Tsarism": Lenin, *Soch.*, 18:55–56.
203 Great Lenin "might have become," in particular, a "chess champion": Fischer, p. 1.
204 Even when Hardin gave him a knight before the game: Ivansky, p. 628.
204–205 His schedule for the week: *Voprosy istorii KPSS* 2(1963):75–77.
205–206 "Comrade Zinoviev: I do not suspect you": Lenin, *Poln. sobr. soch.*, 54:319, 320.
206 "He was very pleased": *Voprosy istorii KPSS* 2(1963):77.
207 "Lev Borisovich, Because of a short letter": *The Anatomy of Terror*, p. 22.
208 "[T]he soviet socialist democracy": V. I. Lenin, *Sochineniya*, 1st ed. (1925) 17:89. (Ellipsis points added.)
  "Poor Shlyapnikov!": *Pravda*, 29 March 1922. (Ellipsis points added.)
208–209 "[I]t is necessary to mete out": idem.
209 A "professional exploiter of every kind of backwardness": *Za leninizm*, a collection of essays (Moscow and Leningrad, 1925), pp. 103, 104.
210–211 His lips trembled: *Voprosy istorii KPSS*, 2 (1963), p. 84.
  "Well," said the doctor: idem.
  "Besides, apparently Vladimir Ilyich has formed the impression": idem.
211 "On January 24 Vladimir Ilyich said": *Voprosy istorii KPSS* 2 (1963):80.
213 "[O]ur leader, teacher, and friend": *Pravda*, 22 July 1922.
215 "Our Party is not a religious sect": S. Shaumyan, *Sochineniya*, 1:267. I. Dubinsky-Mukhadze, *Ordjonikidze* (Moscow, 1964), pp. 92–93.
  "On April 3, word spread": *Pravda*, 5 April 1917.
  Pravda makes deletions in a "Letter From Afar": *Voprosy istorii* 4 (1956):49.
216 Stalin at the head of the committee negotiating with the Mensheviks: *Voprosy istorii KPSS* 5 (1962): 106–107, 112, and 6 (1962): 139–140.
  "I hear there is a unification tendency in Russia": Lenin, *Poln. sobr. soch.*, 31:112.
216–217 Trotsky later described with gusto: Trotsky, *Stalinskaya shkola*, p. 30.
217 Zinoviev's reply to Lenin: *Pravda* (*Rabochy put*), 2 November (20 October) 1917.
  "If the majority is yours": Trotsky, *Stalinskaya shkola*, p. 29.
219–220 "[S]ince then, there has been no better Bolshevik": Trotsky, *Stalinskaya shkola*, idem.
221 The Winter Palace contained several hundred people: Trotsky, *The History of the Russian Revolution*, p. 260.
  The cadets "left their weapons": idem.
  "Sometime later there arrived": ibid., p. 254.
  "These forces numbered more than 200,000 armed men": *Istoriya SSSR*, p. 56.

"Warships and a 5,000-strong force": ibid., p. 57.

"The Peter and Paul fortress frowned threateningly": Trotsky, *The History of the Russian Revolution*, p. 256.

223 "A certain embarrassed son of a bitch": Mayakovsky, 8:260.

"[U]ntil the arrival of armored cars": ibid., p. 258.

224 "The unexpected appearance of these cadets on the square throws the cordons into confusion": ibid., p. 264.

225 "One of the armored cars approached the main entrance": ibid., p. 256

"Who can ascertain the truth": ibid., p. 266.

226 "From the general confusion of ideas": ibid., p. 272.

227 "The members of the Duma are just on the point of setting out": ibid., p. 273.

"Soldiers! Workers! Citizens!": *Pravda*, 7 November (25 October) 1917.

228 "The 'plan' outlines in detail the routes": *Pravda* (*Rabochy put*), 2 November (20 October) 1917.

229 "There was nobody but strangers around": Trotsky, *The History of the Russian Revolution*, p. 261.

230 "[B]arbarian Peter was more national" and the other quotations: *Pravda*, 5 October 1922.

231 "The members of the leading bodies": Lenin, *Soch.*, 26:315.

Ulyanov-Lenin had addressed so movingly "Comrades!" just a few months before: see, for example, *Pravda*, 28 June (15 June) 1917.

"What can one call them?" *Pravda*, 18 January (5 January) 1918. (Ellipsis points added.)

232 The trial of 1922 was even more farcical: *Pravda*, 22 March to 9 August 1922.

"The Soviet Power has detained as hostages": *Pravda*, 7 July (24 June) 1918.

233 "The Council of People's Commissars has sent the following telegram": *Pravda*, 8 July (25 June) 1918. (Ellipsis points added.)

"[W]e took measures to surround the Bolshoi Theater": *Pravda*, 10 July 1918.

234 "Of course, all the party is not guilty": *Pravda*, 10 July 1918.

235 "To the question how she could dare": *Pravda*, 1 September 1918.

236 "To: Zinoviev, June 26, 1918": Lenin, *Soch.*, 35:275.

237–238 "To the Revolutionary-Military Council": Lenin, *Poln. sobr. soch.*, 52:67.

238 "Where New Life is Created": *Pravda*, 19 July 1918.

The strength of Admiral Kolchak's and General Denikin's armies as given by the latest American biographer of Lenin: Fischer, p. 371.

245–246 "Every girl above the age of 18": Khartsev, *Brak i semya v SSSR* (Moscow, 1964), p. 139. (Ellipsis points added.)

246 "There is no need for the family": Kolontai, *Semya i kommunisticheskoye gosudarstvo* (Moscow, 1920), p. 20.

"[S]chool of Sidorenkovo": *Pravda*, 27 May 1935.

254 "[T]hat apparently striking fact": *Pravda*, 16 January 1921.

About 95 percent had neither college, nor even high-school education: *Pravda*, 6 November 1919.

259   "Once during the days immediately following the revolution": Krupskaya, p. 413.

261   "Since my brother was already in the seventh grade": Ivansky, p. 215.
"Why V. Ulyanov Got 'Four' in Logic": *Proletarsky put*, 22 April 1940 (see: Ivansky, p. 246).

262   Kerensky Sr. "loved Volodya very much": Ivansky, pp. 263, 264, 314, and elsewhere.
He "snatched off his cross," an atheist "[s]ince sixteen": ibid., pp. 220–221.

262–263 "Himself a former pupil of a classical gymnasium": ibid., p. 247.

263   "Neither in the gymnasium nor outside has a single case been noted": ibid., p. 325.
His conduct for eight years, etc.: ibid., p. 307.

264   From memoirs we learn that he despised Law: ibid., p. 350.
He crammed the despised Law more zealously than anyone else in the whole enrollment: Ivansky, p. 597.

265   "In all his activity Nechayev": Bolshaya Sovetskaya Entsiklopediya s.v. "Nechayev."

266   "V. I. Lenin maintained his acquaintance with Dolgov": Ivansky, p. 521.

276   The Bulgakov story: Paustovsky, *Povest o zhizni* (Moscow: Sovietskaya Rossiya, 1966), 2 : 561.

307   "Privateeer Battens": *Pravda*, 11 February 1928.

315   "What is the lay cult of the Jew" and the subsequent quotations: K. Marx and F. Engels, *Sochineniya*, 2nd ed. (Moscow: Gosudarstvennoye izdatelstvo politicheskoi iiteratury, 1955), pp. 408, 112, 413.

320   "We made large purchases from the Skoda": Krivitsky, p. 105.

325–329 Anna Louise Strong in Russia: Anna Louise Strong, *I Change Worlds: The Remaking of an American* (New York: Henry Holt and Co.), pp. 32, 6, 96, 337, 341, 353.

336   "The German army had been in close contact with Soviet Russia": Hauptmann Hermann, *The Luftwaffe: Its Rise and Fall* (New York: G. P. Putnam's Sons, 1943), pp. 82–83.
"In his book *The Transformation of War*": *Pravda*, 2 April 1929.
In the autumn of 1941 great Stalin's tanks were to burst into Nazi Germany: Alexey Markoff "How Russia Almost Lost the War," *The Saturday Evening Post*, 13 May 1950.

337   The output of cement and electricity: *Narodnoye khozyaistvo SSSR v 1970 g* (Moscow: Statistika, 1971), pp. 102, 104.

338   "The situation is even worse with our rural cooperatives": *Protokoly, Trinadtsaty Syezd RKP/b*, p. 421. (Ellipsis points added.)
Of the 48 million people who were registered in 1927 as gainfully employed: Strumilin, p. 316.

340   "If we compare the present-day wages": *Protokoly, Odinnadtsaty Syezd RKP/b*, p. 323.
Strumilin said: *Pravda*, 30 November 1927.

342–347 "In the process of work" and the subsequent quotations from Strumilin, and his economic data: Strumilin, pp. 25–27, 30–35.

343   The price of rye in 1913: *Pravda*, 16 November 1921.

345–346 "It is known that" and the subsequent quotation: *Voprosy ekonomiki*, November 1961, p. 125.

347 "There is a lot of money in the countryside" and the subsequent quotation: *Pravda*, 5 December 1918.

349 "We now have the best tractor-building machine tools": *Istoriya SSSR*, p. 325.

"Elino Rahja relates": Krupskaya, p. 27.

354 Zinoviev announced: *Pravda*, 6 March 1921.

"[M]utiny has no doubt been led": *Pravda*, 20 March, 1921.

"On March 2 they adopted at a general meeting"; *Pravda*, 5 April 1921.

355 ". . . we have run into a big—I suppose the biggest—internal political crisis": Lenin, *Soch.*, 33:383. (Ellipsis points added.)

356 The protest sent by a fitter of the Donbas fields: *Pravda*, 13 July (30 June) 1917.

357 "The girl faltered" and the subsequent quotation: *Pravda*, 15 September 1922.

359 To watch and report secretly signs of "demoralization and depression": Merle Fainsod, *Smolensk Under Soviet Rule* (Cambridge, Mass.: Harvard University Press, 1958), pp. 163, 165.

The engineer Berezovsky testified at the Shakhty *trial*: *Pravda*, 8 May 1928.

360 " 'I always thought,' said the defendant Skorutto": *Pravda*, 4 July 1928.

361 Tupolev's *special designing office*: A. Sharagin (G. A. Ozerov), *Tupolevskaya sharaga*, a *samizdat* ms.

367–385 "Stalin it was reported, insisted upon liberalism of the Constitution" and the other quotations from, and references to, Ambassador Davies: Joseph E. Davies, *Mission to Moscow* (New York: Simon and Schuster, 1941), pp. 106, 105, 150, 74, 154. (Ellipsis points in the quotation on p. 385 added.)

371 "[C]arried out, in the face of any obstacle and opposition" and the subsequent quotation: E. H. Carr, *Socialism in One Country 1924–1926*, vol. 1 (New York: Macmillan, 1958), p. 185. (Ellipsis points added.)

381 Cars: *Narodnoye khozyaistvo SSSR v 1968 g* (Moscow: Statistika, 1969), p. 623.

382 "Ivanova lagged behind in her work": *Pravda*, 27 May 1935.

387 "The Central Committee of the All-Union Communist Party": *The Anatomy of Terror*, p. 42. The words "from 1937" are deleted since they do not appear in the Russian text.

395 "The chairman of the collective farm Lebedev": *Pravda*, 15 April 1935.

398 [T]he population of Moscow looked better than the "population of any other European capital": *Pravda*, 3 January 1935. *Pravda* announced the same in 1922: *Pravda*, 12 November 1922.

400 *Twenty-six categories of pay* of common *medical personnel*: *Pravda*, 5 March 1935.

401 From another no less triumphant *Pravda* article: *Pravda*, 26 September 1935.

408 "In contrast to the old weapons": *Pravda*, 15 August 1922.

410 "This is the biggest lie slandering socialism": *Pravda*, 1 June (19 May) 1917.

411   "In the village Nikolskoye": *Pravda*, 6 December 1918.
412   "[T]he land allotment (for a family of ten) in Russia": *Pravda*, 23 April 1921.
       The interview on agriculture: *Pravda*, 2 June 1928.
412–413 "Concerning Cavalry attacks on the Economy": *Pravda*, 24 November 1928.
413   "What about hired labor?": *Pravda*, 9 July (26 June) 1918.
413–414 "Though it looks as if there is no exploitation": *Pravda*, 16 November 1928.
414   "From where could the anti-Semitic mood come into the working class?": *Pravda*, 19 January 1929.
415   "Anti-Semitism became especially acute": *Pravda*, 8 March 1929.
416   "I came in August": *Novyi Mir*, 7 (1963), p. 200.
417   "This pauper's plot of land": Lenin, *Soch.*, 15:59 and *Bolshaya Sovetskaya Entsiklopediya*, s.v. "Nadelnoye zemlevladeniye."
418   The yield of the *personal plots*: Voprosy ekonomiki, No. 6, 1966, p. 81.
423   "It is no secret that there are cases" and the two subsequent quotations: *Pravda*, 11 February 1928.
425   "Take Tsvetnoy Boulevard": *Pravda*, 27 June 1928.
       Those who stole from the *state* were to be shot: *Pravda*, 9 August 1932.
435–453 Philby: a "fully-fledged officer of the Soviet service" and all the other quotations and references: Kim Philby, *My Silent War* (New York: Grove Press, 1968), pp. xvii, 11, 203–209, 159, 75; and Bruce Page, David Leitch, and Phillip Knightly, *The Philby Conspiracy* (New York: Doubleday, 1968) pp. 297, 197, 175, 176, 288, 8, 115, 118, 215, 155.
436   Churchill admires the automatic bath water mixer: Winston S. Churchill, *The Hinge of Fate* (Boston: Houghton Mifflin, 1950), p. 477.
437   "I was then taking my annual month's rest": Krivitsky, p. 9.
461–462 "I would like the West, vainly draping in its 'humanism' ": *Pravda*, 14 July 1935.
499–500 "When I arrived I found Radek already on hand" and the subsequent quotations: Balabanoff, *My Life*, pp. 283, 285–286, 284. (Ellipsis points added.)
500   The First Exemplary Printshop: *Pravda*, 1 April 1922.
502   The "all-Russia *agricultural exhibition*": *Pravda*, 11 November 1922.
505   "[S]mall and medium towns presented an employment problem": *The New York Times*, 21 November 1965.
515   "To be or not to be for the Metro?" and the subsequent quotation: *Pravda*, 24 November 1928.
516   The Webbs' book: *Pravda*, 26 November 1935.
518   "Exemplary Fish Store": *Pravda*, 3 November 1935.
519–520 The *palace of soviet medicine*: *Pravda*, 7 April 1935.
520–521 Excerpts from a doctor's letters: *Pravda*, 15 January 1934.
521   "In the room for the reception of patients": *Pravda*, 10 April 1935.
       The postnatal death rate: *Pravda*, 8 March 1935.
522   "There is no national statistics" and the subsequent quotations: *Special Report: The First U.S. Mission on Mental Health to the*

U.S.S.R. (Washington, D.C.: U.S. Government Printing Office, 1969) pp. 9, 24, 151.

526 The *law* which extended the death penalty to children: *Izvestia*, 8 April 1935.

527–529 "I saw a very small one" and the subsequent quotations: André Gide, *Return From the USSR* (New York: McGraw-Hill, 1964, paperback edition), pp. 93–94, xiv, 39, 38.

530 "I know what is thought to have constituted the character of the time": L. N. Tolstoy, *Polnoye Sobraniye Sochineniy*, 90 vols. (Moscow: GIKhL), 16:8. (Ellipsis points added.)

537–538 "I reached the Kremlin": Winston S. Churchill, *The Hinge of Fate* (Boston: Houghton Mifflin, 1950), p. 477.

538 "There is no doubt that in our narrow circle": Winston S. Churchill, *Triumph and Tragedy* (Boston: Houghton Mifflin, 1953) p. 238.

558 "There is no revolution, nor will there be": S. P. Melgunov, *Martovskiye Dni 1917 Goda* (Paris: Les editeurs reunis, 1961), p. 20. Melgunov indicates that the statement is confirmed independently by the memoirs of Kerensky (*Experiences*) and Stankevich.

559–560 "Thus, soon after two, at the corner of Shpalernaya" and the subsequent *Pravda* quotations, *Pravda*, 5, 8, March 1917.

560 "On January 10, in the evening, a huge column of workers and soldiers" and the subsequent quotation: *Sotsial-democrat* (Tsentralny organ RSDRP, Vilna-Paris-Geneva), 13 April 1916.

563 "By evening the situation was somewhat more calm": *Pravda*, 19 (6) January 1918.

564 "Enemies of the people, counterrevolutionaries and subversives are spreading rumors": *Pravda*, 21(8) January 1918.

568 "Having outlined the situation, I noted" and the subsequent quotation: M. V. Rodzyanko, *Krusheniye imperii* (Berlin: Gessen, 1924), "Gosudarstvennaya Duma i Fevralskaya Revolutsia 1917," p. 56.

 The telegrams of Belyayev and Rodzyanko to the Tsar: A. S. Lukomsky, *Vospominaniya generala A. S. Lukomskogo*, 2 vols. (Berlin: Otto Kirchner, 1922), vol. 1, pp. 123–125.

569 "Concerning the separate treaty I have already said": *Pravda*, 13 July (30 June) 1917.

570–571 "Only later did I learn" and the subsequent quotation: V. Zenzinov, Fevralskiye dni," *Novyi zhurnal* (New York) 34–35 (1953).

571 "During the Revolution 1382 persons suffered": *Pravda*, 23 March 1917.

 One fallen hero was found: *Pravda*, 7 March 1917.

572 A released prison inmate's loss of her pillow and other effects: *Pravda*, 12 March 1917.

 "Citizens! You are requested": *Pravda*, 23 March 1917.

575 "WORKING WOMEN": *Pravda*, 2 September (20 August) 1917.

 "On the 4th Anniversary of Universal Military Training": *Pravda*, 21 May 1922.

 "Our policy in the Middle East": *Pravda*, 10 November 1922.

577 "Some members try to convince the soldiers": D. Anin, *Revolutsiya 1917 goda glazami eyo rukovoditeley* (Rome: edizioni Aurora, 1971), p. 468.

Bibliography

The Anatomy of Terror: Khrushchev's Revelations About Stalin's Regime.
Washington: Public Affairs Press, 1956.

Balabanoff, Angelica. *Impressions of Lenin*, trans Isotta Cesari. Ann Arbor:
University of Michigan Press, 1964.

———— *My Life as a Rebel.* London: Hamish Hamilton, 1938.

Fainsod, Merle. *Smolensk Under Soviet Rule.* Cambridge, Mass.: Harvard
University Press, 1958.

Futrell, Michael. *Northern Underground.* New York: Praeger, 1963.

Istoriya SSSR: Epokha sotsializma, ed. Kim et al. Moscow: Izdatelstvo
politicheskoy literatury, 1964.

Ivansky, Anatoly. *Molodoy Lenin.* Moscow: Izdatelstvo politicheskoy literatury, 1964.

Fischer, Louis. *The Life of Lenin.* New York: Harper & Row, 1964.

Krivitsky, W. G. *I Was Stalin's Agent.* London: Right Book Club, 1940.

Krupskaya, N. K. *Reminiscences of Lenin.* London: Lawrence & Wishart,
1960.

Lenin, V. I. *Polnoye sobraniye sochineny*, 5th ed. Moscow: Gosudarstvennoye izdatelstvo politicheskoy literatury, 1960–70.

———— *Sochineniya*, 4th ed. Moscow: Gosudarstvennoye izdatelstvo politicheskoy literatury, 1951–67.

*Protokoly i stenograficheskiye otchyoty syezdov i konferentsy Kommu-
nisticheskoy partii Sovetskogo Soyuza: devyaty syezd RKP/b/.* Moscow: Gosudarstvennoye izdatelstvo politicheskoy literatury, 1960.

Strumilin, *Izbranniye proizvedeniya v pyati tomakh*, 5 vols. Moscow: Izdatelstvo akademii nauk SSSR, 1963–65, volume 2.

Trotsky, Leon. *Stalinskaya shkola falsifikatsiy.* Berlin: Granit, 1932.

———— *The History of the Russian Revolution.* New York: Simon & Schuster,
1936.

Index